Early Childhood Experiences in Language Arts

Early Childhood Experiences in Language Arts

EMERGING LITERACY

6TH EDITION

Jeanne M. Machado, Emerita
San Jose City College

Delmar Publishers

an International Thomson Publishing company I**T**P

Albany • Bonn • Boston • Cincinnati • Detroit • London • Madrid
Melbourne • Mexico City • New York • Pacific Grove • Paris • San Francisco
Singapore • Tokyo • Toronto • Washington

NOTICE TO THE READER

To my ever-encouraging husband, and Danielle, Romana, Claire, Scott, Patrick, and Brianna. Each is a uniquely special gift in my life.
And to my father who always looked for the best in me.

Cover Design: Charles Cummings Advertising/Art Inc.

Delmar Staff

Acquisitions Editor: Jay Whitney
Associate Editor: Erin O'Connor Traylor
Project Editor: Marah Bellegarde and Patricia Gillivan

Production Coordinator: Sandra Woods
Art & Design Coordinator: Carol Keohane and Jay Purcell

COPYRIGHT © 1999
By Delmar Publishers
an International Thomson Publishing Company

I(T)P™ The ITP logo is a trademark under license.

Printed in the United States of America

For more information, contact:
Delmar Publishers
3 Columbia Circle, Box 15015
Albany, New York 12212-5015

International Thomson Publishing
Berkshire House
168-173 High Holborn
London, WC1V7AA
England

Thomas Nelson Australia
102 Dodds Street
South Melbourne 3205
Victoria, Australia

Nelson Canada
1120 Birchmont Road
Scarborough, Ontario
Canada, M1K 5G4

International Thomson Editores
Campos Eliseos 385, Piso 7
Col Polanco
11560 Mexico D F Mexico

International Thomson Publishing GmbH
Konigswinterer Str. 418
53227 Bonn
Germany

International Thomson Publishing Asia
60 Albert Street, #15-01 Albert Complex
Singapore 189969

International Thomson Publishing Japan
Kyowa Building, 3F
2-2-1 Hirakawa-cho
Chiyoda-ku, Tokyo 102
Japan

2 3 4 5 6 7 8 9 10 XXX 03 02 01 00 99 98

Library of Congress Cataloging-in-Publication Data

Machado, Jeanne M.
  Early childhood experiences in language arts: emerging literacy /
Jeanne M. Machado.—6th ed.
    p.   cm.
  Includes bibliographical references (p.   ) and index.
  ISBN 0-8273-8361-4
  1. Language arts (Early childhood) 2. Language acquisition—
Parent participation. 3. Literacy. I. Title.
LB1139.5.L35M335 1999
372.6—dc21

98–11429
CIP

Contents

SECTION ONE: LANGUAGE DEVELOPMENT— EMERGING LITERACY IN THE YOUNG CHILD

SECTION TWO: DEVELOPING LANGUAGE ARTS PROGRAMS

SECTION THREE: LISTENING—LITERATE BEGINNINGS

SECTION FOUR: INTRODUCING LITERATURE

SECTION FIVE: SPEECH GROWTH—CONVERSATION, EXPRESSION, AND DRAMATIZATION

SECTION SIX: WRITING—PRINT AWARENESS AND USE

SECTION SEVEN: READING—A LANGUAGE ART

SECTION EIGHT: SETTINGS PROMOTING LITERACY— AT HOME AND SCHOOL

Preface

Early Childhood Experiences in Language Arts: Emerging Literacy is a state-of-the-art teacher-training text designed to help those working in the early childhood education field provide an opportunity-rich program full of interesting, appropriate, and developmental language arts activities. It is both a practical "how-to" manual and a collection of resources that includes a large number of classic, tried-and-true activities.

The first few chapters present a detailed account of language acquisition, young children's emerging communicative capacities, growth milestones, and age-level characteristics (infancy through preschool), along with suggested professional techniques to promote each child's self-esteem and potential. Because a comprehensive, dynamically planned early childhood language arts curriculum consists of four broad interrelated areas—speaking (oral), listening, writing, and reading—each is fully explored and described in a separate text section. It is hoped that confidence and skill gained by the reader will help to provide young children with an enthusiastic, knowledgeable teacher-companion who enjoys and encourages them in their discovery of the language arts.

Changes in this Sixth Edition emphasize the child's emerging literacy and exposure to language play. Infant and toddler units have been expanded and are intended to increase the reader's understanding of infant and toddler communication abilities, and the role of adult behavior in promoting language growth. Recent research concerning brain growth and language development connections are explained. Since the enrollment of culturally diverse children and children with special needs has dramatically increased in early education programs, additional discussion and recommended teacher techniques are provided in this edition. Special attention has been given to ways of providing the child with language-rich environments and enthusiastic, supportive teachers who are dynamic, observant companions, and collaborators offering enjoyable language arts experiences and opportunities. Designing program activities connected to the diverse backgrounds of enrolled children has been emphasized. The influence of Vygotsky's theories has been given increased attention. Scaffolding and webbing techniques are included. Fine literature and classics appropriate to the child's age level are recommended, as in the previous edition. Activity ideas and patterns for storytelling and flannel-board sets provide the student resource ideas to try out in early child classrooms. A current view of young children's progress in the understanding and use of print in daily life has been updated. The text reflects current research and theory concerning the young child's active investigation of reading. Whole-language practice and theory, as well as balanced approaches to reading instruction, are explained. Children's curiosity and their natural ability to become communicators are described to give the reader increased confidence in children's ability to learn. A discussion concerning children's intelligent pursuit of knowledge and skill helps teachers recognize and provide growth-producing comments in verbal exchanges. Parent tips to extend language and provide literacy-rich home environments are included in this edition.

Traditional learning aids, such as learning objectives and review questions have been retained from the previous edition. Student activity sections at chapter endings provide for additional study, insight, and reflection and promote lively classroom discussions with peers. An extensive appendix with numerous classroom ideas and activities and lists of additional resources appears at the end of the text.

ABOUT THE AUTHOR

The author's experience in the early childhood education field has included full-time assignment as community college instructor and department chairperson. Her duties included supervision of early childhood education students at two on-campus laboratory child development centers at San Jose City College and Evergreen Valley College, as well as child centers in the local community. Her teaching responsibilities encompassed early childhood education, child development, and parenting courses.

She received her MA from San Jose State University and her vocational community college life credential with coursework from the University of California at Berkeley. Her experience includes working as a teacher and director in public early childhood programs, parent cooperative programs, and a self-owned and operated private preschool. Ms. Machado is an active participant in several professional organizations that relate to the education and well-being of young children and their families. She is a past president of CCCECE (California Community College Early Childhood Educators), and Peninsula Chapter of the California Association for the Education of Young Children. Her authoring efforts (1997), with Dr. Helen Meyer-Botnarescue of the University of California at Hayward produced a text for student teachers entitled *Early Childhood Student Teaching*.

Currently, Ms. Machado works with teachers and young children in Cascade, Idaho.

ACKNOWLEDGMENTS

The author wishes to express her appreciation to the following individuals and agencies.

Nancy Martin, Jayne Musladin, David Palmer, Ann Lane, and Joseph Tardi Associates for the photographs

Theresa and Caryn Macri for appearing in photos for Chapter 1

The students at San Jose City College, AA Degree Program in Early Childhood Education

Arbor Hill Day Care Center, Albany, NY

San Jose City College Child Development Center Staff

Marcy Pederson of Magic Moments

Evergreen Valley College Child Development Center personnel, San Jose, CA

James Lick Children's Center, Eastside High School District, San Jose, CA

Kiddie Academy, Albany, NY

Lowell Children's Center, San Jose Unified School District, San Jose, CA

Piedmont Hills Preschool, San Jose, CA

Pineview Preschool, Albany, NY

St. Elizabeth's Day Home, San Jose, CA

Sunnymont Nursery School, Cupertino, CA

A Child's Garden, Boise, ID

W.I.C.A.P. Headstart, Donnelly, ID

Cascade Elementary School-Preschool, Cascade, ID

Erin O'Connor Traylor and the staff at Delmar Publishers

In addition, special appreciation is due the reviewers involved in the development of the Sixth Edition:

Diane E. Beals, EdD
  Washington University
  St. Louis, MO

Julia Beyeler, PhD
  University of Akron-Wayne College
  Orrville, OH

Alice D. Beyrent
  Hesser College
  Manchester, NH

Carol Bunch
  Hannibal-LaGrange College
  Hannibal, MO

Colin Ducolon, EdD
  Champlain College
  Burlington, VT

Debbie S. Dewitt, PhD
  Coastal Carolina University
  Conway, SC

Cindy Leigh, EdD
  University of Mississippi
  University, MS

Leanna Manna
  Villa Maria College
  Buffalo, NY

Terry Oliver
  Technical College of the Lowcountry
  Beaufort, SC

Joan Sanoff
  Wake Technical Community College
  Raleigh, NC

ReJean A. Schulte
  Cuyahoga Community College
  Parma, OH

TO THE STUDENT

Since you are a unique, caring individual who has chosen an early childhood teaching career, or who is currently working with children, this text is intended to help you discover and share your innate and developing language arts gifts and talents. Create your own activities; author, when possible, your own "quality" literary, oral, and writing opportunities for young children. Share your specialness and those language-arts-related experiences that excite you now and delighted you when you were a child.

In this text, I urge you to become a skilled interactor, collaborator, and conversationalist, "a subtle opportunist," getting the most possible out of each child-adult situation, while also enjoying these daily exchanges yourself.

Collect, select, construct, and practice those appropriate activities you can present with enthusiasm. Your joy in language arts becomes their joy. A file box and/or binder collection of ideas, completed sets, patterns, games, and so on, carefully made and stored for present and future use is suggested. Filling young children's days with developmental, worthwhile experiences will prove a challenge, and your collection of ideas and teaching visual aids will grow and be adapted over the years.

In this text, I attempt to help you become increasingly skilled at what you may do well and help you grow in professional competence. Suggested activities and review sections at the end of chapters give immediate feedback on your grasp of chapter main ideas and techniques. Since I'm growing too, I invite your suggestions and comments so that in future revisions I can refine and improve this text's value to students.

You can make a difference in young children's lives. Ideally, this text will help you become the kind of teacher who does.

LANGUAGE DEVELOPMENT

Emerging Literacy in the Young Child

CHAPTER 1

Beginnings of Communication

OBJECTIVES

After studying this chapter, you should be able to:

- describe one theory of human language emergence.

- identify factors that influence language development.

- discuss the reciprocal behaviors of infants, parents, and caregivers.

- list suggested child-adult play activities for infants 1 to 6 months and infants 6 to 12 months.

- explain the significance of infant signaling.

Each child is a unique combination of inherited traits and environmental influences. From birth, infants can be described as communicators interested in their surroundings.

Researchers confirm that newborns seem to assimilate information immediately. Technology can now monitor the slightest physical changes in breathing, heartbeat, eye movement, and sucking rhythm and rates. Tronick (1987) suggests that babies begin learning how to carry on conversations quickly and sucking patterns produce a **rhythm** that mimics give-and-take dialogues. He notes that infants respond to very specific maternal signals, including tone of voice, looks, and head movements. Babies gesture and make sounds and seem to hold up their ends of conversations. Infants demonstrate an alert state when body activity is suppressed, and energy seems to be channeled into seeing and hearing (Klaus and Klaus, 1985).

Gaze coupling, witnessed in young infants' eye contacts with their mothers, is seen as one of their first steps in establishing communication (Gleason, 1987). Infants can shut off background noises and pay attention to slight changes in adult voice sounds (Eyler, 1987).

The qualities a child inherits from parents and the events that occur in the child's life help shape the child's language development. Genetic givens include gender, temperament, and a timetable for the emergence of intellectual, emotional, and physical capabilities (Villarruel, Imig, and Kostelnik, 1995). In the short four to five years after birth, the child's speech becomes purposeful and adult-like. This growing language skill is a useful tool for satisfying needs and exchanging thoughts, hopes, and dreams with others. As ability grows, the child understands and uses more of the resources of oral and recorded human knowledge, and is well on the way to becoming a literate being.

Rhythm — uniform or patterned recurrence of a beat, accent, or melody in speech.

Gaze coupling — infant-mother extended eye contacts.

The natural capacity to categorize, invent, and remember information aids the child's language acquisition. Although unique among the species because of the ability to speak, human beings are not the only ones who can communicate. Birds and animals imitate sounds and signals and are believed to communicate. For instance, chimpanzees exposed to experimental language techniques (American Sign Language, specially equipped machines, and plastic tokens) have surprised researchers with their language abilities. Some have learned to use symbols and follow linguistic rules with a sophistication that rivals that of some two-year-olds (de Villiers, 1979). Researchers continue to probe the limits of their capabilities. However, a basic difference between human beings and other species exists. It is nestled separately in the human brain and encompasses a diverse set of talents, including language aptitude, symbol making, and communication abilities (Ornstein and Sobel, 1987).

Current theories suggest humans have the unique species-specific ability to test hypotheses about the structure of language, develop rules of a particular language and remember them, and use these rules to generate appropriate language (Premack, 1985).

The human face becomes the most significantly important communication factor for the infant; and the facial expressions, which are varied and complex, eventually will be linked to infant body reactions (interior and exterior). Emotional reactions often involve cardiovascular and gastrointestinal systems (Ornstein and Sobel, 1987). Parents and caregivers strive to interpret the infant's state of well-being from reading the infant's face and postures, as infants also search faces in the world around them.

Figure 1–1 identifies a number of signals used by infants and their probable meanings. Response and intentional behavior become apparent as infants age and gain experience:

> The infant . . . will respond initially with various pre-programmed . . . gestures like smiling, intent and interested looking, crying, satisfied sucking or snuggling, soon

INFANT ACTS	PROBABLE MEANING
Turning head and opening mouth	Feeling hungry
Quivering lips	Adjusting to stimuli
Sucking on hand, fist, thumb	Calming self, feeling overstimulated
Averting eyes	Tuning out awhile
Turning away	Needing to calm down
Yawning	Feeling tired or stressed
Looking wide-eyed	Feeling happy
Cooing	Feeling happy
Appearing dull with unfocused eyes	Feeling overloaded, needing rest
Waving hands	Feeling excited
Moving tongue in and out	Feeling upset or imitating

FIGURE 1–1 Born communicators

> to be followed by active demanding and attention-seeking patterns in which attempts to attract and solicit caregiver attention rapidly become unmistakable, deliberate, and intentional. (Newson, 1979)

Researchers are studying the roles of facial expressions, gestures, and body movements in human social communication. Early smile-like expressions may occur minutes after birth and are apparent in the faces of sleeping babies whose facial expressions seem to constantly change. Totally blind infants have been observed smiling as young as two months of age in response to a voice or tickling (Freedman, 1964).

Speech is much more complex than simple parroting or primitive social functioning. The power of language enables humans to dominate other life forms. The ability to use language creatively secured our survival by giving us a vehicle to both understand and transmit knowledge and to work cooperatively with others (Hoy and Somer, 1974). Language facilitates peaceful solutions between people.

Definitions

Language, as used in this text, refers to a system of intentional communication through sounds, signs (gestures), or symbols that are understandable to others. The language-development process includes both sending and receiving information. *Input* (receiving) comes before *output* (sending); input is organized mentally by an individual long before there is decipherable output.

Communication is a broader term, defined as giving and receiving information, signals, or messages. A person can communicate with or receive communications from animals, infants, or foreign speakers in a variety of ways. Even a whistling teakettle sends a message that someone can understand. Infants appear to be "in tune," focused on the human voice, hours after birth.

Influences on Development

A child's ability to communicate involves an integration of body parts and systems allowing hearing, understanding, organizing, and using language. Most children accomplish the task quickly and easily, but many factors influence the learning of language (figure 1–2).

Klaus and Klaus (1985) describe an infant's life within the womb, based on ultrasound studies, as ". . . floating in his private island . . . after sleeping he opens his eyes, yawns, kicks and rolls to his other side . . . brings his fingers to his face and sucks his thumb . . . he can hear his mother's voice . . . he stops to listen . . . ever present is the lullaby of his mother's heartbeat. . . ." And immediately after birth, "Hands are stroking and cradling him . . . He

---

Language — the means by which a person communicates ideas or feelings to another in such a way that the meaning is mutually understood.

Communication — the giving (sending) and receiving of information, signals, or messages.

FIGURE 1–2 Communication between children and family starts early in the child's life.

can hear his mother's soothing familiar heartbeat . . . voices are much clearer and closer . . . he relaxes . . . he mouths his fists making small sucking sounds." Current research suggests that babies instinctively turn their heads to face the source of sound and can remember sounds heard in utero. This has promoted mothers talking to, singing to, and reading classic literature and poetry to the unborn. Research has yet to document evidence of the benefits of these activities.

Of all sounds, nothing attracts and holds the attention of infants as well as the human voice— especially the higher-pitched female voice. "Motherese," a distinct caregiver speech, is discussed later in this unit. Rhythmic sounds and continuous, steady tones soothe some infants. A variety of sound-making soothers are now marketed and designed to attach to cribs or are placed within plush stuffed animals. Most emit a static-like or heartbeat sound or combination of the two. Too much sound in the infant's environment, especially loud, excessive, or high-volume sounds, may have the opposite effect. Excessive household noise can come from television sets, radios, and stereos. Some mothers report that at about age five to eight months their children have an interest in lively, colorful television programs, such as *Sesame Street*, and seem to watch for reasonably long periods, sitting quietly and focused while doing so. Many have described sensory-overload situations when infants try to turn off sensory input by turning away and somehow blocking that which is at the moment overwhelming, whether the stimulus is mechanical or human.

Although hearing ability is not fully developed at birth, newborns can hear moderately loud sounds, and can distinguish different pitches (Weiser, 1982). **Auditory acuity** develops swiftly (figure 1–3). Within a few weeks of birth, infants inhibit motor activity in response to strong auditory stimuli or when listening to the human voice. This is seen by some researchers as an indication that infants are "constitutionally geared to orient their whole bodies toward any signal that arouses interest" (Junker, 1979). Researchers have concluded that infants' body responses to human verbalizations are a rudimentary form of speech development.

Sensory-motor development, which involves the use of sense organs and the coordination of motor systems (body muscles and parts), is vital to language acquisition. Sense organs gather information through sight, hearing, smelling, tasting, and touching. These sense-organ impressions of people, objects, and life encounters are sent to the brain, and each **perception** (impression received through the senses) is recorded and stored, serving as a base for future oral and written language.

Newborns and infants are no longer viewed as passive, unresponsive "mini" humans. Instead,

AGE	PERCEPTIONS
By 3 months	Differentiates tonal and nontonal sounds
	Differentiates pitch and timbre
	Has auditory fixation to adult's verbalizations
	Looks for source of sound
	Soothed by soft, rhythmical sounds
By 6 months	Differentiates tones of voice
	Differentiates speech sounds
	Likes to "talk" to self
	Coos and gurgles
By 9 months	Associates sound with its source (toy or person)
	Enjoys listening to musical sounds
	Attempts "conversation"
	Babbles
By 12 months	Imitates adult vocalizations
	Responds rhythmically to music
	Knows own name
	Knows name of other persons
	Understands more than verbalizes
	Tries to comply with verbal requests

FIGURE 1–3 Auditory perception during the first 12 months *(From* Group Care and Education of Infants and Toddlers, *by M. Weiser, © 1982. C.V. Mosby Co., copyright © 1985 Merrill Publishing Co., Columbus, Ohio. Reprinted with permission.)*

Auditory — relating to or experienced through hearing.

Acuity — how well or clearly one uses senses; the degree of perceptual sharpness.

Sensory-motor development — the control and use of sense organs and the body's muscle structure.

Perception — mental awareness of objects and other data gathered through the five senses.

infants are seen as dynamic individuals, pre-programmed to learn, with functioning sensory capacities, motor abilities, and a wondrous built-in curiosity. Parents and caregivers can be described as guides who open opportunity and act *with* new-borns rather than *on* them.

A child's social and emotional environments play a leading role in both the quality and quantity of beginning language. Brazelton (1979) describes communicative neonatal behaviors that evoke tender feelings in adults:

> When the stimulus is the human voice, the neonate not only searches for the observer's face but, when he finds it, his face and eyes become wide, soft and eager, and he may crane his neck, lifting his chin gently toward the source of the voice. As he does so, his body tension gradually increases, but he is quietly inactive. A nurturing adult feels impelled to respond to these signals by picking the baby up to cuddle him.

Human children have the longest infancy among animals. Our social dependency is crucial to our individual survival and growth (Ornstein and Sobel, 1987). Much learning occurs through contact and interaction with others in family and social settings. Basic attitudes towards life, self, and other people form early, as life's pleasures and pains are experienced. The young child depends on parents and other caregivers to provide what is needed for growth and **equilibrium** (a balance achieved when consistent care is given and needs are satisfied). This

FIGURE 1–4   Care and attention in the early years influence language development.

side of a child's development has been called the **affective sphere**, referring to the affectionate feelings (or lack of them) shaped through experience with others (figure 1–4). As Halliday (1979) observes "at no stage is language an individual matter."

Textbooks often speak indirectly about the infant's need to feel loved consistently, using words like nurturance, closeness, caring, and commitment. The primary goal of parents and caregivers should be handling the infant and satisfying the child's physical needs in a way that leads to mutual love and a bond of trust. This bond, often called **attachment**, is an event of utmost importance to the infant's progress. It is formed through mutual gratification of needs and reciprocal communication influenced by the infant's growing cognitive ability. The two-way nature of the attachment process, also referred to as bonding, is emphasized by Friedrich (1986) "as a kind of wordless dialogue."

Equilibrium — a balance attained with consistent care and satisfaction of needs that leads to a sense of security and lessens anxiety.

Affective sphere — the affectionate feelings (or lack of them) shaped through experience with others.

Attachment — a two-way process formed through mutual gratification of needs and reciprocal communication influenced by the infant's growing cognitive abilities. Sometimes referred to as bonding.

The baby not only understands what the mother is communicating, or not communicating, but is trying to tell her things, if she will only listen.

The specialness an infant feels for the main caregiver later spreads to include a group of beloved family members. If an attachment bond is evident and consistent care continues, the child thrives.

Newborns seem to have an individual preferred level of arousal, a **moderation level**, neither too excited nor too bored. They seek change and stimulation and seem to search out newness. Each human may possess an optimum level of arousal—a state when learning is enhanced and pleasure peaks. Mothers serve as buffers to keep infants at moderate levels of arousal, neither too high nor too low (Kaye, 1979). One can perceive three states during an older infant's waking hours: (1) a state in which everything is all right and life is interesting, (2) a reactive state to something familiar or unfamiliar, when an observer can see an alert "what's that?" or "who's that?" response (figure 1–5), or (3) a crying or agitated state. One can observe a switch from feeling safe or happy to unsafe or unhappy in a matter of seconds. Loud noises can startle the infant and elicit distressed crying. Infants control input and turn away or turn off by moving eyes and head or body and by becoming fussy or falling asleep.

Other important factors related to the child's mental maturity or ability to think are ages, stages, and sequences of increased mental capacity that are very closely related to language development. Language skill and intellect seem to be growing independently, at times, with one or the other developing at a faster rate. The relationship of intelligence and language has been a subject of debate for a long time. Most scholars, however, agree these two areas are closely associated. Links between emotions and intellect are also being given new attention by early childhood educators. They are considering Greenspan's (1977) emphasis on infant's emotions. He believes the mind's most important faculties are rooted in emotional experiences from very early in life.

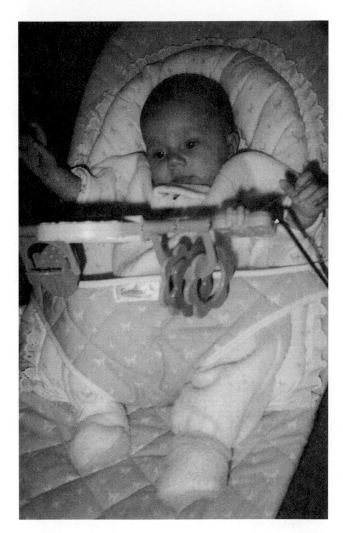

FIGURE 1–5 Look at this infant's alert, focused expression.

The natural curiosity of humans requires discussion here. Curiosity can be defined as a compulsion (drive) to make sense of life's happenings. Exploring, searching, groping, and probing by infants shift from random to controlled movements as the infant ages. White (1986) speaks about the

---

Moderation level — an individual preferred state of arousal between bored and excited when learning and pleasure peak.

period starting at about eight months of age as an age when infants possess insatiable appetites for new things—touching, manipulating, and trying to become familiar with everything that attracts them. Increasing motor skill allows greater possibilities for exploration. Skilled infant caregivers are kept busy trying to provide novelty, variety, and companionship, while monitoring safety. The curiosity of infants seems to wane only when they are tired, hungry, or ill.

Cultural and social forces touch young lives with group attitudes, values, and beliefs. These have a great impact on a child's language development. Some cultures, for instance, expect children to look downward when adults speak, showing respect by this action. Other cultures make extensive use of gestures and signaling. Still others seem to have limited vocabularies. Cultural values and factors can indeed affect language acquisition.

Theories of Language Emergence

Many scholars, philosophers, linguists, and researchers have tried to pinpoint exactly how language is learned. People in major fields of study—human development, linguistics, sociology, psychology, anthropology, speech-language pathology, and animal study (zoology)—have contributed to current theory. The following are major theoretical positions.

Behaviorist (or Stimulus-Response) Theory

As parents and main caregivers reward, correct, ignore, or punish the young child's communication, they exert considerable influence over both the quantity and quality of language usage and the child's attitudes toward communicating. Under this theory, the reactions of the people in a child's environment have an important effect on a child's language development. In other words, positive, neutral, and/or negative reinforcement plays a key role in the emergence of communicational behaviors.

The child's sounds and sound combinations are thought to be uttered partly as imitation and partly at random or on impulse, without pattern or meaning. The child's utterances may grow, seem to stand still, or become stifled, depending on feedback from others. This theory is attributed to the work of B. F. Skinner, a pioneer researcher in the field of learning theory.

Maturational (Normative) Theory

The writings of Arnold Gesell and his colleagues represent the position that children are primarily a product of genetic inheritance, and environmental influences are secondary. Children are seen as moving from one predictable stage to another with "readiness" the precursor of actual learning. This position was widely accepted in the 1960s when linguists studied children in less than desirable circumstances and discovered consistent patterns of language development. Using this theory as a basis for planning instruction for young children includes (1) identifying predictable stages of growth in language abilities and (2) offering appropriate readiness activities to aid children's graduation to the next higher level.

Predetermined Theory

Under this theory, language acquisition is considered innate (a predetermined human capacity). Each new being is believed to possess a mental ability that enables that being to master any language to which he or she has been exposed from infancy. Chomsky (1968), a linguistic researcher, theorizes that each person has an individual Language Acquisition Device (LAD). Chomsky also theorizes that this device (capacity) has several sets of language system rules (grammar) common to all known languages. As the child lives within a favorable family climate, his or her perceptions spark the device, and the child learns the "mother tongue." Imitation or reinforcement are not ruled out as additional influences.

Chomsky notes two- and three-year-olds can utter understandable, complicated sentences that they have never heard. The child has to possess either remarkable thinking skills to do so or very special skills as a language learner. Chomsky favors the latter explanation. Theorists who support this position note the infant's ability to babble sounds and noises used in languages the child has never heard.

Cognitive-Transactional Theory

Under a fourth theory, language acquisition develops from basic social and emotional drives. Children are naturally active, curious, and adaptive and are shaped by transactions with the people in their environment. Language is learned as a means of relating to people. Others provide social and psychological supports that enable the child to be an effective communicator (Harris, 1990). L. S. Vygotsky's major work, *Thought and Language* (1986), suggests children's meaningful social exchanges prepare them for uniting thought and speech into "verbal thought." This inner speech development, he theorizes, promotes oral communication and is the basis for written language. Drives stem from a need for love and care, and the need prompts language acquisition. Children are described as reactors to the human social contact that is so crucial to their survival and well-being. Children's views of the world consist of their mental impressions, built as new life events are fit into existing ones or as categories are created for new events. Language is an integral part of living; consequently, children seek to fit language into some pattern that allows understanding. With enough exposure and with functioning sensory receiving systems, children slowly crack the "code" and eventually become fluent speakers. The works of Jean Piaget, Jerome Bruner, and J. McVicker Hunt have promoted a wide acceptance of this theory by early childhood professionals.

Vygotsky (1980) believes that language learning is, in part, biological but that children need instruction in the zone between their independent language level and the level at which they can operate with adult guidance. Bodrova and Leong (1996) list four basic principles underlying Vygotskian framework:

1. Children construct knowledge.
2. Development cannot be separated from its social context.
3. Learning can lead development.
4. Language plays a central role in mental development.

The early childhood practitioner adopting Vygotsky's ideas would believe both teacher behaviors and the child's active physical manipulation of his environment influence and mediate what and how a young child learns or "constructs" mentally:

> If one teacher points out that the blocks are distinct sizes, that student will construct a different concept than the student whose teacher points out the blocks' color. (Bodrova and Leong, 1996)

In other words, without the teacher's social interaction, a child doesn't learn which characteristics are most important or what to notice and act upon (Bodrova and Leong, 1996). The teacher's role is to find out through thoughtful conversation, observation, and collaboration what concept a child holds during a jointly experienced happening, and to aid the child to further mental construction(s). Teachers, consequently, under Vygotskian theory can affect young children's cognitive processes—the way they think and use language. Other individual and societal features that affect children's thinking are family, other children and people in their lives, and society at large, including language, numerical systems, and technology.

Children learn or acquire a mental process by sharing, or using it in interacting with others (Bodrova and Leong, 1996). Once gained, the child's learning (the acquired mental tool) is used by the child in an independent manner.

Constructivism

Proponents of constructivism theorize that children acquire knowledge by constructing it mentally in interaction with the environment (Kamii, 1993). Children are believed to construct theories (hypothesize) about what they experience and put happenings into relationships. Later, with more life experiences, revisions occur and more adequate explanations are possible. Constructivists point to young children's speech errors in grammar. Internal rules have been constructed and used for a period of time but with more exposure to adult speech change to more adult-like forms. The rules young children used previously were their own construct and never modeled by adult speakers. Clay (1991) in *Becoming Literate* points out:

> We know that children operate on some kind of language rules to form plurals and the past tense of verbs and negatives, and we know that many of the rules they seem to use could not have emerged from anything they have heard adults use. They must have been constructed by children themselves.

Planning for language development and emergent literacy using a constructivist perspective would entail offering wide and varied activities while emphasizing their interrelatedness. Teachers and parents are viewed as being involved jointly with children in literacy activities from birth onward. The overall objective of a constructivist's approach would be promoting children's involvement with interesting ideas, problems, and questions. Teachers would also help children put their findings and discoveries into relationships and help them notice similarities and differences (DeVries and Kohlberg, 1990). Children's hands-on activity is believed to be paired with mental action.

Epstein, Schweinhart, and McAdoo (1996) describe the socioeconomic settings constructivists deem necessary for realizing cognitive objectives:

> A secure and noncoercive environment allows children to decenter and cooperate, develop respect for one another, exercise curiosity, gain confidence in their ability to

figure things out on their own, and become autonomous.

Other Theories

There is no all-inclusive theory of language acquisition substantiated by research; rather, there is some truth in each possibility. Many relationships and mysteries are still under study. Current teaching practices involve many different styles and approaches to language arts activities. Some teachers may prefer using techniques in accord with one particular theory. One goal common among educators is the desire to provide instruction that encourages social and emotional development while also offering activities and opportunities in a warm, language-rich, supportive classroom, center, or home. Educators believe children should be included in talk and treated as competent language partners (Schickedanz, 1986). Eveloff (1977) identified three major prerequisites for a child's development and language acquisition. They are (1) thinking ability, (2) a central nervous system allowing sophisticated perception, and (3) loving care. These all are present if children are healthy and in quality day-care and preschool facilities.

This text promotes many challenging activities that go beyond simple rote memorization or passive participation. It offers an enriched program of literary experience that encourages children to think and use their abilities to relate and share their thoughts.

This text is based on the premise that children's innate curiosity and desire to understand and give meaning to their world equips them to learn language and become literate. Language growth occurs simultaneously in different yet connected language arts areas. Children continually form, modify, rearrange, and revise internal knowledge as experience, activities, opportunities, and social interactions are encountered.

Since language arts areas are interlinked, co-occurring, overlapping, and interacting, children's inner unconscious mental structuring of experience proceeds in growth spurts and seeming regressions, with development in one area influencing another.

Research on Infant's Brain Growth

Rich early experience and time with caring and loving parents or early childhood educators has become even more important as neuroscience researchers make new discoveries about infant's and young children's brain growth. Though awed by the brain's exceptional malleability, flexibility, and plasticity during early years and its ability to "explode" with new **synapses** (connections), scientists also warn of the effects of abuse or neglect on the child's future brain function (Nash, 1997).

New technology gives researchers additional tools to study brain energy, volume, blood flow, oxygenation, and cross-sectional images. Neuroscientists have found that throughout the entire process of development, beginning even before birth, the brain is affected by environmental conditions, including the kind of nourishment, care, surroundings, and stimulation an individual receives (Shore, 1997).

Early experience has gained additional importance and attention. Life experiences are now believed to control both how the infant's brain is "architecturally formed" and how intricate brain circuitry is wired. Infant sight and hearing acuity needs to be assessed as early as possible given this new information.

Older debates about nature (genetic givens) versus nurture (care, experiential stimulations, parental teaching, and so on) are outdated (figure 1–6). The interaction and interplay between both is now viewed as critical in determining brain development and which neural pathways and circuitry will diminish, possibly disappear, or grow stronger and become permanent.

Nash (1997) describes a growth spurt that occurs in the infant's brain shortly after birth:

> After birth, the brain experiences a second growth spurt, as the axons (which send signals) and the dendrites (which receive them) explode with new connections. Electrical activity, triggered by a flood of sensory experiences, fine-tunes the brain's circuitry —determining which connections will be retained and which will be pruned . . . Each time a baby tries to touch a tantalizing object or gazes intently at a face or listens to a lullaby, tiny bursts of electricity shoot through the brain, knitting neurons into

Synapse — the gap-like structure over which the axon of one neuron beams a signal to the dendrites of another forming a connection in the human brain. Concerns memory and learning.

OLD THINKING . . .	NEW THINKING . . .
How a brain develops depends on the genes you are born with.	How a brain develops hinges on a complex interplay between the genes you're born with and the experiences you have.
The experiences you have before age three have a limited impact on later development.	Early experiences have a decisive impact on the architecture of the brain, and on the nature and extent of adult capacities.
A secure relationship with a primary caregiver creates a favorable context for early development and learning.	Early interactions don't just create a context; they directly affect the way the brain is "wired."
Brain development is linear: the brain's capacity to learn and change grows steadily as an infant progresses toward adulthood.	Brain development is non-linear: there are prime times for acquiring different kinds of knowledge and skills.
A toddler's brain is much less active than the brain of a college student.	By the time children reach age three, their brains are twice as active as those of adults. Activity levels drop during adolescence.

FIGURE 1–6 Rethinking the brain *(From* Rethinking the Brain, *by R. Shore, 1997, New York: Families and Work Institute. Reprinted with permission.)*

circuits as well defined as those etched onto silicon chips. The results are those behavioral mileposts that never cease to delight and awe parents.

Many scientists believe that in the first few years of childhood there are a number of critical or sensitive periods, or "windows," when the brain demands certain types of input in order to create or stabilize certain long-lasting structures (Nash, 1997). As Kantrowitz (1997) points out:

> Every lullaby, every giggle and peek-a-boo, triggers a crackling along his neural pathways, laying the groundwork for what could someday be a love of art or a talent for soccer or a gift for making and keeping friends.

What specifically do brain researchers recommend?

- Excellent child care for working parents
- Talking a lot to babies
- Cuddling and hands-on parenting
- Using "parentese," the high-pitched, vowel-rich, singsong speech style most adults readily undertake when interacting with babies that helps babies connect objects with words
- Giving babies freedom to explore within safe limits
- Providing safe objects to explore and manipulate
- Giving babies regular eye exams and interesting visual opportunities
- Providing loving, stress-reduced care for the child's emotional development

Cowley (1997) describes "red flag behaviors" that should alert parents to possible child learning difficulties:

- *0–3 months.* Does not turn when you speak or repeat sounds like coos.
- *4–6 months.* Does not respond to the word *no* or changes in tone of voice; does not look around for sources of sound like a doorbell, or babble in speechlike sounds such as *p, b,* and *m*.

- *7–12 months.* Does not recognize words for common items, turn when you call her name, imitate speech sounds, or use sounds other than crying to get your attention.

The idea that electrical activity in brain cells changes the physical structure of the brain during the early years tips the scales in the long-standing debate about the importance of nature or nurture in child development. Increasing focus and importance is bound to be attached to quality care in infancy and preschool years. Care should be provided by knowledgeable adults who realize that early experiences and opportunities may have long-term developmental consequences and who provide rich, language-filled experiences and opportunities.

Healy (1987) worries that "excess pressure" for inappropriate skills at early ages may cause problems for the child during later schooling. Parents' or other adults' enthusiasm for creating "superbabies" may motivate them to offer meaningless age-inappropriate activities. She suggests:

> Most babies give explicit clues about what kind of input is needed and let you know when it's overpowering or not interesting anymore. Explaining things to children won't do the job; they must have a chance to experience, wonder, experiment, and act it out for themselves. It is this process throughout life that enables the growth of intelligence. Babies come equipped with the "need to know"; our job is to give them love, acceptance, and the raw material of appropriate stimulation at each level of development.

Greenspan (1997) believes his observations make clear that certain kinds of emotional nurturing propel infants and young children to intellectual and emotional health, and that affective experience helps them master a variety of cognitive tasks. He states:

> As a baby's experience grows, sensory impressions become increasingly tied to feelings. It is the *dual coding* of experience that is the key to understanding how

emotions organize intellectual capacities and indeed create the sense of self.

Interactive emotional exchanges with caregivers and their reciprocal quality are increasingly viewed as critical to human infants' growth and development, including language development.

Communicative Beginnings in Infancy

Development of the ability to communicate begins even before the child's birth. Prenatal environment plays an important role, and factors such as the mother's emotional and physical health and nutrition can affect the development and health of the unborn. These factors may also lead to complications later in the child's language-learning capabilities.

Newborns quickly make their needs known. They cry and their parents respond. The parents feed, hold, and keep their children warm and dry. The sounds of parents' footsteps or voices, and their caring touch, often stop the babies' crying. Babies learn to anticipate. The sense perceptions they receive begin to be connected to stored impressions of the past.

Lewis and Rosenblum (1974) picture infants as very powerful in shaping relationships with significant caregivers. Newborns are a wonderful combination of development, potential development, and cognitive flexibility (Bornstein, 1992).

An infant can perceive from maternal behavior a willingness to learn from the infant and respond to his or her patterns of behavior and rhythms of hunger. This is accomplished by close observation of infant vocal and body clues, which indicate the child's state of being (Bateson, 1979). At some point, the mother notes her infant's gaze. This usually triggers a type of brief conversation:

> . . . once a pattern of mutual gazing is established, the mother tends to behave in a given way within mutual gaze episodes. This would seem to be the case with proto-conversation: mutual gazing sets the stage for maternal vocalizations which set up the

possibility of an unfolding process of learning, probably strengthened by selective attention. (Bateson, 1979)

Curry and Johnson (1990) describe two tasks that confront infants. They:

1. Regulate themselves with others. Babies begin to establish "islands of consistency" as adults soothe, hold, feed, and otherwise nurture them.
2. Interact with others. Playful encounters first occur around caregiving functions (diapering, dressing, playing "This Little Piggy") and later through play with toys (Brazelton and Als, 1979).

The infant is a noisemaker from birth. The child's repertoire includes sucking noises, lip smacking, sneezes, coughs, hiccups, and, of course, different types of cries. As an infant grows, he or she makes vocal noises, such as **cooing** after feeding. During feeding, slurping and guzzling sounds indicate eagerness and pleasure. Cooing seems to be related to a child's comfort and satisfaction (figure 1–7). During cooing, sounds are relaxed, low-pitched, and gurgly vowel sounds that are made in an open-mouthed way; for example, e (as in see), e (get), a (at), ah, and o, oo, ooo. The infant appears to be in control of this sound making. Discomfort, by comparison, produces consonant sounds, made in a tense manner with lips partly closed.

Parents who attend to infant crying promptly and who feel that crying stems from legitimate needs rather than attempts to control tend to produce contented, trusting infants. Advice for parents of colicky babies consists of holding and carrying the infant more frequently in an effort to soothe.

Infants differ in numerous ways from the moment of birth. Freedman's research (1979) concludes that significant ethnic differences and similarities exist in a newborn's reactions to various

---

Cooing — an early stage during the prelinguistic period in which vowel sounds are repeated, particularly the u-u-u sound.

FIGURE 1–7   Cooing relates to a child's comfort level.

stimuli. However, in most cases, milestones in language development are reached at about the same age and in a recognizable sequence.

Babies learn quickly that communicating is worthwhile because it results in action on the part of another. Have you ever watched a baby gaze intently into his or her parent's eyes? Somehow, the child knows that this is a form of communication and is avidly looking for clues. If the parent speaks, the baby's entire body seems to respond to the rhythm of the human voice. The reciprocal nature of the interactions aids development. Greenspan (1997) warns unless a child masters the level we call two-way intentional communication, normally achieved by an eight-month-old infant, his or her language, cognitive, and psychosexual and

social patterns ultimately develop in an idiosyncratic, piecemeal, disorganized manner. Clark-Stewart (1973) reported a high degree of relationship between a mother's responsiveness and her child's language competence. In a longitudinal study of infants from 9 to 18 months of age, the more responsive mothers promoted greater language facility and growth.

Infants quickly recognize subtle differences in sounds. A parent's talk and touch increases sound making. Condon and Sanders (1983) observed infants moving their arms and legs in synchrony to the rhythms of human speech. Random noises, tappings, and disconnected vowel sounds didn't produce that behavior.

There's a difference between people in an infant's life. Some talk and touch. Others show delight. Some pause after speaking and seem to wait for a response. The child either "locks on" to the conversationalist, focusing totally, or breaks eye contact and looks away. It's almost as though the infant controls what he or she wants to receive. Of course, hunger, tiredness, and other factors influence this behavior also and may stop the child's interest in being social.

Research continues to uncover response capabilities in both infants and their parents that have previously been overlooked. In one experiment, newborns learned to suck on an artificial nipple hooked to a switch that turned on a brief portion of recorded speech or music. They did not suck as readily when they heard instrumental music as when they heard a human voice (de Villiers, 1979). Neuman and Roskos (1993) believe that lacking speech, babies use a form of protolanguage, gestures, expressions, and voice tones, to communicate.

Signaling becomes a form of highly organized facial and body movement communication. (Signaling is discussed further later in this unit.) In early infancy, infant signals come mostly from the child. By 7 to 9 months of age they increasingly come from the caregiver. Parents and children using signaling alone can communicate efficiently about a third event by the time a child reaches one year (Emde, 1989).

The special people in the infant's life adopt

observable behaviors when "speaking" to the child, just as the child seems to react in special ways to their attention. Mothers sometimes raise their voice pitch to a falsetto, shorten sentences, simplify their syntax, use nonsense sounds, and maintain prolonged eye contact during playful interchanges. Masataka's (1992) study of mothers found their speech with infants characterized by higher overall pitch, wider pitch exclusions, more distinctive pitch contours, slower tempo, and longer pauses than in their normal adult conversations. Infants display a wide-eyed, playful, and bright-faced attitude toward their mothers and fathers (Brazelton, 1983). A mutual readiness to respond to each other appears built-in to warm relationships. The infant learns that eye contact can hold and maintain attention and that looking away usually terminates both verbal and nonverbal episodes.

Crying

Crying is one of the infant's primary methods of communication. Cries can be weak or hardy and provide clues to the infant's general health (Lester, 1983). Crying or calling out is the only way an infant or animal has of affecting its situation of need or discomfort (Buchwald, 1984). Infants begin early in life to control the emotional content of their cries. Many parents feel they can recognize different types of crying . . . sleepy, frightened, hungry, and so on, especially if infant body movements are observed concurrently. Researchers have recently discovered parents do indeed accurately infer the intensity of an infant's emotional state from the sound of the cry itself, even if the baby is not visually observed. Even adults inexperienced with infants seem to possess this ability (Hostetler, 1988).

Child development specialists advise adult alertness and responsiveness to minimize crying. Crying will take place in the best of circumstances, and current research has indicated that there are some positive aspects of crying, including stress reduction, elimination of toxin in tears, and reestablishment of physical and emotional balance (Ornstein and Sobel, 1987). However, although cry-

ing may have its benefits, it is not recommended that infants be left to cry, but rather that adults continue to attempt to soothe and satisfy infant's needs.

Lester (1983) describes the direct and indirect effects of an infant's crying on developmental outcomes.

> Direct effects are due to the cry as a measure of the integrity of the nervous system; indirect effects are due to the cry as a determinant of parent-infant interaction, which in turn affects the cognitive and socio-emotional development of the infant.

A baby's crying may cause strong feelings in some adults, including anger, frustration, irritation, guilt, and rejection. Successful attempts at soothing the infant and stopping the crying give both the infant and the caregiver satisfaction, feelings of competence, and a possible sense of pleasure. When out-of-sorts infants cease crying, usually alertness, attentiveness, and visual scanning happen and/or they fall asleep. Infant-parent interaction has been described as "a rhythmic drama," "a reciprocal ballet," and "a finely tuned symphony." All these touch on the beauty and coordination of sound-filled moments between parent and child. Crying is a helpful mechanism promoting maintenance of physical satisfaction and comfort. It releases energy and tension. There is a change in cries as the infant ages:

> In the first months, we see a change from crying as a response to physiological demands, to crying as part of the development of affective expression. Toward the end of the first year (seven to nine months), a second biobehavioral shift occurs, characterized by major cognitive and affective changes. (Lester, 1983)

Emotions are expressed frequently in crying as the infant nears his or her first birthday. Fear, frustration, uneasiness with novelty or newness, separation from loved ones, and other strong emotions can provoke crying through childhood and beyond.

Infant care providers in group programs engage

in frank staff discussions concerning infant crying. Normal and natural staff feelings concerning crying need open discussion so strategies can be devised in the best interests of both the infants and staff members. Lots of techniques exist to minimize crying and also to monitor the crying levels of individual infants so that health or developmental problems can be spotted quickly.

Smiling and Laughing

Smiling is seen in some babies who are only a few days old. Some smile in their sleep. This type of smiling seems to be tied to inner stimuli. True smiling can occur before six months of age, and it's usually associated with a caretaker's facial, auditory, or motor stimuli. Laughter may occur as early as four months of age, and is thought to be a good predictor of cognitive growth and the child's level of involvement in what the child is doing (Spieker, 1987). Spieker suggests the earlier the baby laughs, the higher the developmental level. In the second half of the first year, infants smile at more complex social and visual items. Laughter at this age may be full of squeals, howls, hoots, giggles, and grins. Incongruity may be noticed by the infant, and laughter follows. If an infant laughs when he or she sees the family dog in the driver's seat with its paws on the wheel, the child may be showing recognition of incongruity—the child has learned something about car drivers.

Responsive mothers promote infant smiling. Ainsworth and Bell (1972) concluded that **responsive mothers** (those who are alert in caring for the infant's needs) had babies who cry less frequently and had a wider range of different modes of communication. These responsive mothers created a balance between showing attention and affording the infant autonomy (offering a choice of action

---

Responsive mothers — mothers who are alert and timely in responding to and giving attention to infant needs and communications.

Echolalia — a characteristic of the babbling period. The child repeats (echoes) the same sounds over and over.

within safe bounds) when the infant became mobile. They also provided body contact and involved themselves playfully at times.

Babbling

Early random sound making is often called *babbling*. Infants the world over babble sounds they've not heard and will not use in their native language. This has been taken to mean that each infant has the potential to master any world language (Jacobson, 1968). Close inspection shows repetitive sounds and "practice sessions" present. Babbling starts at about the fourth to sixth month and continues in some children through the toddler period. However, a peak in babbling is usually reached between 9 and 12 months. Periods before the first words are spoken are marked by a type of babbling that repeats syllables over and over, as in "dadadadadada." This is called **echolalia**. Infants seem to echo themselves and others. Babbling behavior overlaps the one and two (or more) word-making stages ending for some children at about 18 months of age.

Deaf infants also babble and in play sessions will babble for longer periods without hearing either adult sound or their own sounds as long as they can see the adult responding. However, they stop babbling at an earlier age than do hearing children. It is not clearly understood why babbling occurs, either in hearing or nonhearing children, but it is felt that babbling gives the child the opportunity to use and control the mouth, throat, and lung muscles. Possibly, a child's babbling amuses and motivates the child, acting as stimulus that adds variety to the child's existence.

In time, there is an increasing number of articulated (clear, distinct) vowel-like, consonant-like, and syllabic sounds. "Ba" and "Da" are acquired early because they are easy to produce while "el" and "ar" are acquired late because sophisticated articulatory control is required. Although babbling includes a wide range of sounds, as children grow older they narrow the range and begin to focus on the familiar, much-heard language of the family. Other sounds are gradually discarded. Researchers

[handwritten margin note: Not]

[handwritten margin note: It is easier to use the same sounds]

Levitt and Uttman (1992) conclude English-learning infant's babbling contains more closed syllables than French-learning infants due to differences in their language environments.

There's a point when infant's eyes search and follow sound in their environment, and when the infant can easily turn his or her head toward the speaker. Toys are visually examined and reached for and sometimes talked to. Almost any feature of environment may promote verbalness.

Physical contact continues to be important. Touching, holding, rocking, and other types of physical contact bring a sense of security and a chance to respond through sound making. The active receiving of perceptions is encouraged by warm, loving parents who share a close relationship. Secure children respond more readily to the world around them. Children who lack social and physical contact, or live in insecure home environments, fall behind in both the number and range of sounds made; differences start showing at about six months of age.

Simple imitation of language sounds begins early. Nonverbal imitated behavior, such as tongue protrusion, also occurs. Sound imitation becomes syllable imitation, and short words are spoken near the end of the child's first year.

Infant Signaling

During the latter part of the first year, alert caregivers notice hand and body positions that suggest the child is attempting a communication. Infants as young as seven months may bang on a window to get a family cat's attention or reach out, motion, or crawl toward something or someone they want. Matheny (1992) sees infant's pointing of the arm, hand, or finger as one of his or her earliest signals. He believes the sign indicates the child's interest in some environmental feature.

Toward the end of the child's first year, pointing becomes goal oriented—the infant may want a specific object (Fogel, 1992). As time progresses, more and more infant body signaling takes place (figure 1–8). Signals are used over and over, and a

GESTURE	MEANING
Allows food to run out of mouth	Satisfied or not hungry
Pouts	Displeased
Pushes nipple from mouth with tongue	Satisfied or not hungry
Pushes object away	Does not want it
Reaches out for object	Wants to have it handed to him
Reaches out to person	Wants to be picked up
Smacks lips or ejects tongue	Hungry
Smiles and holds out arms	Wants to be picked up
Sneezes excessively	Wet and cold
Squirms and trembles	Cold
Squirms, wiggles, and cries during dressing or bathing	Resents restriction on activities
Turns head from nipple	Satisfied or not hungry

FIGURE 1–8 Some common gestures of babyhood *(From Child Development, by E. B. Hurlock, 1972. Used with permission of McGraw-Hill Company.)*

type of sign-language communication emerges. Research suggests that infants use a "signal and sound system" understood by caregivers. Halliday (1979) believes a "child tongue" develops before "mother tongue." When responded to appropriately, the infant easily progresses to word use and verbal aptitude.

Acredolo and Goodwyn's (1992) studies of gestural communication note infants with more advanced gestures had larger vocabularies and girls seem slightly more advanced in gesturing than boys. The results of their studies suggest the development of gestures is an important aspect of an infant's development.

Well-meaning parents may choose not to respond to infant gestures and signals, thinking this will accelerate or force the use of words. The opposite is thought to be true. Lapinski (1996) suggests aware parents may acquire early insights into their baby's thinking:

. . . signing and the eye contact it requires helps your baby learn that communication is a satisfying, back-and-forth process. And signing can provide parents with an early window into your baby's mind.

Alert parents who try to read and receive signals give their infant the message that communication leads to fulfillment of wishes. Successful signaling becomes a form of language—a precursor of verbal signals (words). Lapinski (1996) believes baby signers by age 2 are better at both expressing themselves and understanding others' speech, and on average, have slightly larger vocabularies than their nonsigning peers. Sitting down at the child's level at times when the infant is crawling from one piece of furniture to another may facilitate the adult's ability to pick up on signaling. Watching the infant's eyes and the direction the infant's head turns gives clues. Infants about eight months old seem fascinated with the adult's soundmaking ability. They often turn to look at the adult's lips or want to touch the adult's mouth.

Understanding

Most babies get some idea of the meaning of a few words at about 6 to 9 months. At about 10 months of age, some infants start to respond to spoken word clues. Somewhere between 8 to 13 months the child's communication, whether vocal or gestural, becomes intentional as the child makes a connection between responses, his or her behavior, and parent or early childhood educator responses. A game such as "pat-a-cake" may start the baby clapping and "bye-bye" or "peek-a-boo" brings about other imitations of earlier play activities with the

parents. The child's language is called passive at this stage, for he or she primarily receives (or is receptive). Speaking attempts will later become active (or expressive). Vocabulary provides a small portal through which adults can gauge a little of what the child knows. There is a point at which children expand nonverbal signals to true language.

Older infants communicate with their parents through many nonverbal actions; one common way is by holding up their arms, which most often means, "I want to be picked up." Other actions include facial expression, voice tone, voice volume, posture, and gestures such as "locking in" by pointing fingers and toes at attention-getting people and events.

Although infants at this stage can respond to words, speaking does not automatically follow, because, at this early age, there is much more for infants to understand. For example, Bornstein's (1992) studies point out that infants have the capacity to distinguish phonemes, the smallest significant units of sounds in words, and to understand that speech pauses indicate a "my turn-your turn" situation. When mothers used longer speech pauses, their babies did also. Changes in parents' facial expressions, voice tone and volume, and actions and gestures carry feelings and messages important to infants' well-being. Understanding the tone of parents' speech comes before understanding parents' words, and that understanding happens prior to children trying to say words.

First Words

Before an understandable, close approximation of a word is uttered, the child's physical organs need to function in a delicate unison, and the child must reach a certain level of mental maturity. At around the age of 12 months, the speech centers of the brain are poised to produce what is perhaps the most magical moment of childhood: the first word, which marks the flowering of language (Nash, 1997). The child's respiratory system supplies the necessary energy. As the breath is exhaled, sounds and speech are formed with the upward movement of air. The larynx's vibrating folds produce voice

---

Phonation — exhaled air passes the larynx's vibrating folds and produces "voice."

Resonation — amplification of laryngeal sounds using cavities of the mouth, nose, sinuses, and pharynx.

Articulation — the adjustments and movements of the muscles of the mouth and jaw involved in producing clear oral communication.

(called **phonation**). The larynx, mouth, and nose influence the child's voice quality (termed **resonation**). A last modification of the breath stream is **articulation**—a final formation done through molding, shaping, stopping, and releasing voiced and nonvoiced sounds that reflect language heard in the child's environment.

Repetition of syllables such as ma, da, and ba in a child's babbling occurs toward the end of the first year. If "mama" or "dada" or a close copy is said, parents show attention and joy. Language, especially in the area of speech development, is a two-way process; reaction is an important feedback to action.

Generally, first words are nouns or proper names of foods, animals, and toys (figure 1–9). Monolingual (one language) children utter their first words at approximately 11 months of age, the range is from about 9 months to about 16 months (Bloom, 1973). Talking alone, Reznick (1996) believes, shows no link to mental development at age 2, but a child's

FIGURE 1–9 The name of a family pet may be among the first words a child learns.

comprehension of words is paramount. Cowley (1997) points out there's no evidence that late talkers end up less fluent than early talkers. Lieven, Pine, and Barnes (1992) note that some children acquire large numbers of object names in their first 50 to 100 words. The first spoken words usually contain p, b, t, d, m, and n (front of the mouth consonants), which require the least tongue and air control (Beck, 1982). They are shortened versions, such as da for daddy, beh for bed, up for cup. When two-syllable words are attempted, they are often strung together using the same syllable sound, as in dada, beebee. If the second syllable is voiced, the child's reproduction of the sound may come out as dodee for doggy or papee for potty.

At this stage, words tend to be segments of wider happenings in the child's life. A child's word "ba" may represent a favorite often-used toy (such as a ball). As the child grows in experience, any round object seen in the grocery, for instance, will also be recognized and called "ba." This phenomenon has been termed overextension. The child has embraced "everything round," which is a much broader meaning for ball than the adult definition of the word *ball*.

Lee (1970) describes the child's development from early situation-tied first words to a broader usage:

> All words in the beginning vocabulary are on the same level of abstraction. They are labels of developing categories of experiences.

Following is a list of words frequently understood between 8 and 12 months of age (P.A.T.—*Parents As Teachers Program Planning and Implementation Guide*, 1986): mommy, daddy, bye-bye, baby, shoe, ball, cookie, juice, bottle, no-no, and the child's own name and names of family members.

A child finds that words can open many doors. They help the child get things and cause caretakers to act in many ways. Vocabulary quickly grows from the names of objects to words that refer to actions. This slowly decreases the child's dependence on context (a specific location and situation) for communication and gradually increases the child's reliance on words—the tools of abstract thought. Children learn very quickly that words not only name things and elicit action on another's part, but also convey comments and express individual attitudes and feelings (Beck, 1982).

Toddler Speech

Toddlerhood begins, and the child eagerly names things and seeks names for others. As if playing an enjoyable game, the child echoes and repeats to the best of his or her ability. At times, the words are not recognizable as the same words the parents offered. When interacting with young speakers, an adult must listen closely, watch for nonverbal signs, scan the situation, and use a good deal of guessing to understand the child and respond appropriately. The child's single words accompanied by gestures, motions, and intonations are called **holophrases**. They usually represent a whole idea or sentence.

While the child is learning to walk, speech, for a short period, may take a back seat to developing motor skill. At this time, the child may listen more intently to what others are saying (Scott, 1968).

The slow-paced learning of new words (figure 1–10) is followed by a period of rapid growth. The child pauses briefly, listening and digesting, gathering forces to embark on the great adventure of becoming a fluent speaker.

Implications for Infant-Center Staff Members

The importance of understanding the responsive, reciprocal nature of optimum caregiving in group infant centers cannot be underestimated.

Holophrases — the expression of a whole idea in a single word. They are characteristic of the child's language from about 12–18 months.

Responsive mothers—those who ignore few episodes and respond with little delay—have infants with more variety, subtlety, and clarity of noncrying communication. . . . Mothers who vocalize and smile frequently have been found to have infants who vocalize and smile frequently. (Jacobson, 1978)

Greenspan (1997), discussing the emotional base needed for intellectual growth, describes a developmental consequence:

Our observations of children suggest that even the capacities generally considered to be innate, such as the ability to learn language, require an emotional base in order to acquire purpose and function. Unless a child masters the capacity for reciprocal emotional and social signaling, her ability to use language (as well as her cognitive and social patterns) develops poorly, often in a fragmented manner. Words lack meaning, pronouns are often confused, and scraps of rote learning, such as repeating illogical phrases, dominate her speech. Her social interests remain focused on her own body or inanimate objects.

As Honig (1981) points out "caregivers who boost language are giving the gift of a great power to babies," consequently infants benefit from sensitive, alert, skilled adults. Adult caregivers need to read both nonverbal and vocalized cues, and react appropriately. They need to be attentive and loving. Learning to read each other's signals is basic to the quality of the relationship. Liberal amounts of touching, holding, smiling, and looking promote language as well as the child's overall sense that the world around him or her is both safe and fascinating. Recognizing the child's individuality, reading nonverbal behaviors, and reacting with purposeful actions are all expected of professional infant specialists. The following are suggestions that can be used to promote the infant's sound making and subsequent first-spoken words.

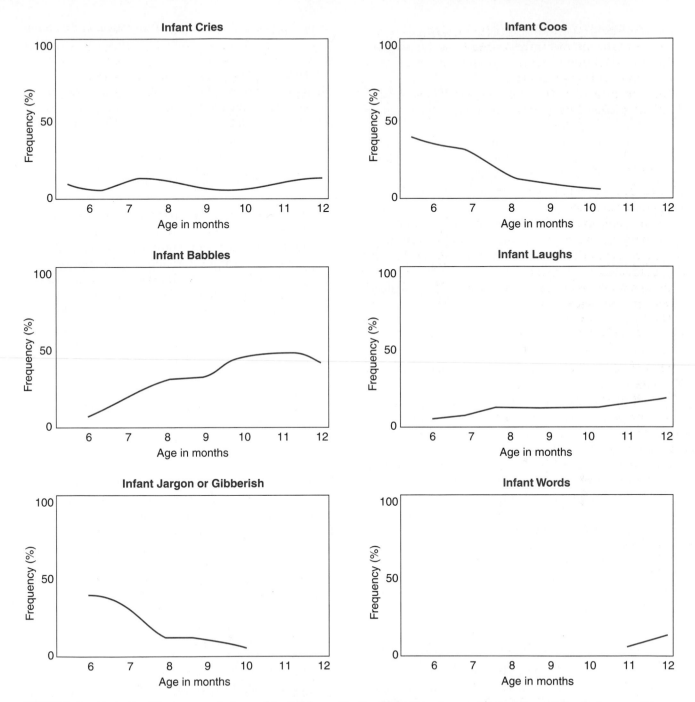

FIGURE 1–10   Estimated frequency of observable child vocalization behaviors to parent or care provider during age 6 to 12 months *(Adapted from* Prelinguistic Communication in Infancy, *by A. Ziajka, Praeger Publishers, CBS Educational and Professional Publishing, 521 Fifth Avenue, NY, NY 10175.)*

During early infancy

- Hold the infant firmly yet gently, and make soft, gentle sounds while moving smoothly and holding the infant close.
- Talk in a pleasant, soothing voice, use simple language, and make frequent eye contact (Bredekamp, 1997).
- Make a game out of the infant's smiles, sounds, and movements when the infant is responsive.
- Imitate the infant's babbling, cooing, or other sound making between 4 and 6 months of age (playfully echo).
- Whisper in the infant's ear to soothe him or her.
- Be watchful for signs that the infant may need a less stimulating setting and is emitting "escape signals."
- Use the infant's name—"Scott's toes" instead of "Baby's toes."

Especially during late infancy

- Speak clearly.
- Explain what is happening and what will happen next (Bredekamp, 1997).
- Encourage the infant to look at you while you speak.
- Don't interrupt vocal play, jargon, or self-communication.
- Engage in word play, rhyme, chants, fun-to-say short expressions.
- Be an animated speaker.
- Try simple finger plays.
- Plan concrete, participatory activities with textures, sights, and sounds.
- Encourage sound making and provide noise making and musical toys.
- Talk about sounds when you hear them—"Knock, knock, there's daddy at the door."
- Remember to pause and wait for the child's response.

Weiser (1982) suggests occasionally using "singing conversations" with infants and also urges change of pitch with expressions like "up comes the spoon." This lays the basis for both speech and later music education. Both recorded and live musical sounds are part of an auditory-rich environ-ment for infants. Tarrow and Lundsteen (1981) have identified goals and additional caregiver activities (figure 1–11).

How does a caregiver go about establishing a dialogue with an infant? First, consider the infant to be communicating from day one and expect many face-to-face opportunities. Newson (1979) provides an example of a caregiver's attempt to establish dialogue:

> The child suddenly arrests the ongoing pattern of his play activity in response to a new noise such as a car passing outside. His mother takes her cue from this shift in his attention to mark or 'comment' on his reaction by indicating that she too has noticed the intrusive noise. Perhaps she picks up the child to let him look out of the window and see the car as it disappears down the road. The maintenance of communication in an incident of this kind is only accomplished by the fact that one of the two communicating persons is socially sensitive to the effect of what is happening to the other, moment by moment.

Remember that infants are alike yet uniquely different. You'll meet sensitive infants who appear overwhelmed and require little stimuli to maintain equilibrium. Others will thrive in an environment providing a multitude of people, sights, sounds, and new activities. Each infant provides a challenge one must "puzzle out" to decide best courses of action—what works, what doesn't work, and what's best.

The individualism of infants has been described by Greenspan (1997), a child psychiatrist and researcher, as follows:

> Another aspect of this new understanding of thought and emotion is a recently discovered fact: a given sensation does not necessarily produce the same response in every individual. Inborn differences in sensory makeup can make a sound of a given frequency and loudness—say, a high-pitched voice—strike one person as exciting and invigorating while it impresses another as

LEVEL	OBJECTIVE	ACTIVITY
Birth to 1 month	1. To develop intimacy and awareness of communication based on personal contact.	1. Whisper into the child's ear.
	2. To introduce the concept of oral communication.	2. Coo at the child.
	3. To introduce verbal communication.	3. Talk to the child.
	4. To stimulate interest in the process of talking.	4. Let the child explore your mouth with his or her hands as you talk.
1 to 3 months	1. To develop oral communication.	1. Imitate the sounds the child makes.
	2. To develop auditory acuity.	2. Talk to the child in different tones.
	3. To develop the concept that different people sound different.	3. Encourage others to talk and coo to the child.
	4. To develop the concept of oral and musical communication of feelings.	4. Sing songs of different moods, rhythms, and tempos.
3 to 6 months	1. To develop the concept of positive use of verbal communication.	1. Reward the child with words.
	2. To stimulate excitement about words.	2. Talk expressively to the child.
	3. To develop the concept that words and music can be linked.	3. Sing or chant to the child.
	4. To develop the ability to name things and events.	4. Describe daily rituals to the child as you carry them out.
6 to 9 months	1. To develop use of words and reinforce intimacy.	1. Talk constantly to the child and explain processes such as feeding, bathing and changing clothes.
	2. To develop the concept that things have names.	2. Name toys for the child as the child plays, foods and utensils as the child eats, and so on.
	3. To develop the concept that there is joy in the written word.	3. Read aloud to the child, enthusiastically.
	4. To develop the concept that language is used to describe.	4. Describe sounds to the child as they are heard.
9 to 12 months	1. To develop the concept that body parts have names.	1. Name the parts of the body and encourage the child to point to them.
	2. To reinforce the concept that things have names.	2. Describe and name things seen on a walk or an automobile trip.
	3. To stimulate rhythm and interest in words.	3. Repeat simple songs, rhymes, and finger plays.
	4. To stimulate experimentation with sounds and words.	4. Respond to sounds the child makes, and encourage the child to imitate sounds.

FIGURE 1–11 Sequential objectives and activities for language development *(From* Activities and Resources for Guiding Young Children's Learning, *by S. W. Lundsteen and N. B. Tarrow, 1981. Reproduced with permission from McGraw-Hill Book Company.)*

piercing and shrill, rather like a siren. A light of a certain brightness might seem cheerful to one person but glaring and irritating to another. A gentle caress may soothe one but painfully startle another, like a touch on sunburned skin. . . . A given sensation can thus produce quite different emotional effects in different individuals— in one case pleasure, for example, but in another anxiety.

Since infants' first sensory experiences are part of emotional relationships with caregivers, caregivers' efforts to provide developmental care go hand in hand with providing positive emotional support in daily reciprocal exchanges between the child and adult. The terms *child-centered* and *child-focused* need to be coupled with reactive, observant, playful, nuturant adult sending behaviors. This type of infant care is nearly impossible when adult-infant ratios in out-of-home care are inadequate.

Generally, the types of adults who promote language are those who are alert to the child's achievements, notice them, and enjoy interacting, as well as adults who can offer novelty, assistance, and enthusiasm besides focusing on the child's interests (White, 1986). Language competence at age three is related to maternal (or caregiver) emotional and verbal responsiveness. Play opportunity and play materials also become important at age 6 months (Elardo, Bradley, and Caldwell, 1977).

Threats to early language development include:

- hearing loss,
- lack of sharing experiences with caring adults,
- failure of adults to talk frequently to preverbal infants, and
- stifling baby's curiosity (White, 1986).

Baby Games and Explorations

Infants almost daily seem to increase the ways they can explore and enjoy verbal-physical games. Many parents and infants develop a set of games of their own (Kaye, 1979). A few favorite infant play pursuits and examples of adult comment follow:

Common Activities	Possible Adult Remarks
look and watch	"See the kitty."
touch it	"Grandpa's nose."
mouth it	"Eat the cracker."
make a sound	"Ring goes the bell."
pick it up	"A rock! You found a rock."
push it or pull it	"Push the box."
drop it off	"Down goes the block."
empty it, fill it	"Out come the dish towels."
climb it	"Foot goes up."
carry it	"Robert's holding the car."
roll it	"The ball's rolling on the rug."

Curry and Johnson (1990) suggest adult interaction with older infants helps develop a joint feeling of exploration:

Display an attitude about the environment that nourishes children's curiosity and sense of wonder about themselves and objects. Think about what you are saying and how it affects baby's feelings about exploration.

Since caregivers spend considerable time supervising active infants, it usually takes little effort to supply brief running remarks. Pausing is as important as talking. Co-explorers must give the infant time to send signals and then must issue approving nods or words or reactions. Infants quickly can get the idea that conversation is a two-way process. An infant who is with a caregiver who has primarily a policing orientation that is full of "no-no's" and little else misses tremendous language opportunities.

Many mothers speak in a special way to infants and young children. No one has instructed them to do so, yet they seem to automatically shift from their adult-adult style. This has been termed "motherese" by researchers. Harris (1990) has pinpointed characteristics:

Mothers talking to young children employ shorter sentences, a lower mean length of utterance, more single words, fewer complex sentences and a more restricted vocabulary. Grammatical errors are very infrequent. Motherese tends to be produced at a slower rate with more pronounced pauses and exaggerated intonational contours.

He goes on to observe adults talk about events and objects in the immediate surroundings, and frequently focus on child objects of interest. Many self-repetitions and imitations of child language occur. Mother imitations usually extend the child's speech by providing more accurate meanings or adding new related clarification. Harris (1990) notes studies of motherese have yet to conclude how many features of this special mother talk actually contribute to or impede children's language learning. The one exception is when adults talk about objects and events in the immediate surroundings. Children benefit when adult contributions are semantically (meaningfully) related to the child's own utterance (Harris, 1990). This might be done by direct imitation or expansion of the child's utterance into a phrase or sentence that captures the child's intention by providing a novel feature or by recasting the child's meaning into a more precise form.

Social Play

It's obvious that infants six months and older watch, imitate, and attempt physical and verbal contact with other infants and children. There's a strong attraction to other "small people and animals." Most young infants prefer to be in the same room with a favored caregiver. Only as they become mobile and older do they explore adjacent rooms and areas on their own.

Music

The role of music and song in infant development has been the subject of meager research. Common sense tells us certain musical experiences enrich infant's lives and may soothe both infants and caregivers. Pick (1986) believes babies as young as three months can distinguish between certain melodies. Musical infant babbling described by Gordon (1986) includes both "tonal babble and rhythm babble." Tonal babble is defined as babbling in a single pitch, the babble sounding like a monotone singer. In rhythmic babble the child's body or voice displays a rhythmic beat or quality.

Much of the music offered infants may be accompanied by mother's singing. Nursery, cultural, and folk tunes shared by caregivers can introduce language in intimate, pleasant settings.

Garcia-Barrio (1986) suggests Bach preludes and Vivaldi's "Springtime Symphony" as good infant-listening selections.

Kucenski (1977) suggests that before the age of one year children can learn to distinguish individual songs that have been sung often and that children relate the tunes to the activities accompanying their presentations.

Favorite Movement Activities and Song Books

The following references include classic songs and movement activities for infants and toddlers:

Aliki. (1974). *Go tell Aunt Rhody*. New York: Macmillan.

Brown, M. (Ed.). (1987). *Play rhymes*. New York: Dutton.

Burton, M. (1989). *Tail, toes, eyes, ears, nose*. New York: Harper and Row.

Engvick, W. (Ed.). (1965). *Lullabies and night songs*. New York: Harper Collins Child Books.

National Gallery of Art. (1991). *An illustrated treasury of songs*. New York: Rizzoli International Publications.

Nelson, E. L. (1984). *The funny song book*. New York: Sterling.

Poston, E. (Ed.). (1972). *The baby's song book*. New York: Crowell.

Schwartz, A. (Ed). (1993). *And the green grass grew all around: Folk poetry from everyone*. New York: Harper Collins Children's Books.

Shannon, G. (1989). *Oh, I love!* New York: Bradbury Press.

Wirth, M., Stassevitch, V., Shotwell, R., & Stemmber, P. (1983). *Musical games, fingerplays, and rhythmic activities for early childhood*. West Nyack, NY: Parker.

CLASSIC LANGUAGE PLAY

The following language and body-action play has brought delight to generations of infants. The most-enjoyed play activities include tickling, bouncing, and lifting with accompanying words and rhymes. Snow, De Blauw, and Van Roosmalen (1979) see baby games as especially appropriate to language emergence:

> The way mothers talk to babies is well designed to create the feeling of effective communication, and the structure of games and other playful episodes is especially appropriate to that end.

Wolf (1994) suggests baby "oos" and "coos" need to be echoed by caregivers. In play with infants early childhood practitioners will find many opportunities to do so.

THIS LITTLE PIGGIE
(Recited while holding each toe down to the pinkie.)
This little pig went to market,
This little pig stayed home,
This little pig had roast beef,
This little pig had none,
This little piggie cried, "Wee, wee, wee, wee!" all
the way home.

PAT-A-CAKE
(Recited while helping the child imitate hand-clapping.)
Pat-a-cake, pat-a-cake, baker's man,
Bake me a cake as fast as you can.
Pat it and prick it and mark it with a "B,"
And put it in the oven for baby and me.

SO BIG
Say, *"How big are you?"* and then help the child answer by saying *"So-o-o-o-o big!"* as you raise the child's hands above the child's head. Repeat.

Say "Ah" as you slowly bring the child to your face, and then gently say *"Boo!"* Repeat. *"Ah-h-h-h-h . . . Boo!"*

from Pushaw, D. R. (1976). *Teach your child to talk*. New York: Dantree Press Inc.

WHAT HAVE WE HERE?
Here's two little eyes big and round
And two little ears to hear all sounds,
One little nose smells a flower sweet,
One little mouth likes food to eat.

Here's ten little fingers to grasp and wiggle,
Tickle ten toes and there's a giggle.
Here's a button on a tiny tummy
Around and around—that feels funny!

ROUND AND ROUND
(This is a frequently used tickling verse of English mothers.)
Round and round the garden (said slowly while circling the baby's palm)
One step, two steps (walking fingers toward a tickling spot at neck, stomach, or underarms, and said a little faster)
Tickle you there! (said very fast)

Reading to Infants

Between 6 and 12 months, some infants will sit and look at a picture book with an adult. The child will want to grab pages and test the book in his or her mouth or try to turn pages. The child's head may swivel to look at the adult's mouth. If the child has brought a book to the adult, the child will usually want to sit on the adult's lap as both go through the book. The child gets ever more adept at turning pages as a first birthday nears. The soothing sound of a human voice and close, cuddly physical contact is part of the enjoyment of book-reading settings. Familiar objects in colorful illustration and large faces seem to be particularly fascinating.

Book-reading techniques include reading with average volume and expression, using gesturing or pointing when called for, promoting child imitation, letting the child turn sturdy pages, and making animal or sound noises. A good rule of thumb is to stop before the child's interest wanes. Adults may find that many infants enjoy repeated reading of the same book during the same sitting.

Simple, colorful, sturdy-paged or cardboard books are plentiful. Reading them on a regular basis can become a pleasant activity. Cullinan (1977) recommends books of cotton fabric, heavy plastic, canvas, or cardboard, and ones with flaps to lift and peek under, soft furry patches to feel, rough sandpaper to touch, and holes to look through or stick a finger through. Homemade collections of family photographs have delighted many young children. The ideal book for babies, according to Schickedanz (1986), has simple, large pictures or designs set against a contrasting background, and is constructed to stand on its own when opened.

There exists a number of literary classics (although not all experts agree to the same titles) that most children in our culture experience. Many of these involve rhyme, rhythm, touching, motions, or hand gestures. They have, over time, become polished gems passed on to succeeding generations. Some are shared as songs, and include:

"Here We Go Round the Mulberry Bush"
"One, Two, Buckle My Shoe"
"Hush-A-Bye Baby"
"Twinkle, Twinkle, Little Star"
"Rock-a-Bye Baby"
"Ba Ba Black Sheep"

Recommended books for babies follow. Many others are in print.

Dunn, P. (1987). *I'm a baby*. NY: Random House.

Fujikawa, G. (1963). *Babies*. NY: Putnam.

MacDonald, A. (1992). *Let's play*. NY: Candlewick.

Oxenbury, H. (1981). *Dressing*. NY: Little Simon.

Oxenbury, H. (1995). *I hear*. NY: Candlewick.

Ra, C. F. (1987). *Trot trot to Boston, play rhymes for baby*. New York: Lothrop, Lee, and Shepard Books.

Shott, S. (1991). *Mealtime*. NY: Dutton.

Tafuri, N. (1987). *My friends*. New York: Greenwillow Books.

Ziefert, H. (1987). *Where's the dog?* New York: Harper & Row.

Ziefert, H., & Gorbaty, N. (1984). *Baby Ben's bow wow book*. NY: Random House.

Recordings

Growing numbers of recording tapes and videotapes are being produced for infants. Infants listen and sometimes move their bodies rhythmically. Environmental and animal sound recordings are available. Caregivers find that certain recordings are soothing and promote sleep. Infants are definitely attracted to musical sounds, and researchers are studying whether listening to music during infancy promotes listening abilities and speech production.

Early Experience with Writing Tools

As early as 10 to 12 months, infants will watch intently as someone makes marks on a surface or paper. They will reach and attempt to do the marking themselves. Chalk and thick crayons or crayon "chunks" are recommended for exploring. Large-sized paper (torn apart grocery brown bags) taped at the edges to surfaces and chalkboards work well. These activities require constant, close supervision to prevent infants from biting or chewing writing tools. The child may not realize the writing tool is making marks but may imitate and gleefully move the whole arm. Many feel it's simply not worth the effort to supervise very young children during this activity and save this activity until the children are older. Healy (1990) speculates awkward hand positions in writing may become habitual and difficult to change at a later time. She suggests waiting.

Adult help in the pencil-holding technique after the child has developed an interest in making marks with writing tools seems the prudent course of action.

Implications for Parents

Parents' attitude toward their infant's communicating abilities may influence their progress:

> Mothers who believe their babies are potential communicative partners talk to them in ways which serve both to strengthen that belief and to make it come true (Snow, De Blauw, and Van Roosmalen, 1979).

The highly simplified and repetitive "mother talk" typical of many American mothers and verbal conversations with preverbal infants are not typical in some cultures. These cultures do not view the infant as a legitimate conversational partner (Genesee and Nicoladis, 1995).

Parents' expectations and feelings shape their responses to their children. These attitudes are the early roots of the critical partnership between adult and child, and the child's sense of feeling lovable and powerful. Consequently, they influence the child's assessment of self (Curry and Johnson, 1990). In *Zero to Three* (June 1994), published by the National Center for Infants, Toddlers, and Families, it was suggested that babies' emotional exchanges with their caregivers should become the primary measuring rod of developmental and intellectual competence. Language promotion activities and behaviors are shown in figure 1–12.

Parenting techniques and home environments of children described as "resilient and capable" by researchers may provide clues to optimum language-promoting factors (Werner and Smith, 1982; Hakuta, 1986). Also, special infant projects that seem to have promoted later school success have provided information in this area as well (Parents As Teachers, 1986). Home factors mentioned from both these sources include:

- lots of attention by socially responsive caretakers;

CHILD'S AGE	ADULT EFFORT
Birth–3 months	Spends time in face to face contact.
	Repeats baby sounds.
	Talks through eating, dressing, bathing activities and touches.
	Sings and provides music.
	Encourages a "you talk" then "I talk" interaction.
	Sensitively notes when baby tunes out and discontinues talk or actions.
3 months–1 year	Names objects and actions.
	Responds to baby vocalization.
	Introduces "baby play games" such as pat-a-cake.
	Talks and touches.
	Continues "my turn," "your turn" conversations.
	Offers simple books.
	Guesses child's needs.
	Watches child's attempts to gesture and responds.
	Often talks face-to-face.
	Sings simple rhymes and songs.
	Makes sure room sound level and noise is appropriate.
	Shows delight in child sound making.
	Draws attention to happenings, objects, and so on.
	Makes sense of child verbalization (or tries to).
	Uses simple, clear speech.
	Tells simple stories.
	Looks for books that encourage children to label pictures.
	Supplies sound-making toys.
	Listens for intent, not perfection.

FIGURE 1–12   Helpful parent and adult language promotion activities and behaviors

ACTIVITIES ACTIVITIES ACTIVITIES ACTIVITIES ACTIVITIES

- little or no disruption of bonding attachment between the infant and his or her primary caregiver during the infant's first year;
- availability of space and objects to explore;
- good nutrition;
- active and interactive exchanges and play time;
- parent knowledge of developmental milestones and the child's emerging skills;
- parent confidence in infant handling;
- maintenance of the child's physical robustness; and
- positive attention and touching in play exchange.

Factors bearing little or no relationship to the child's future language competence include parent's age, education, social class, income, native language (other than English), expensive toys and equipment, number of siblings, amount of alternative care, or living in a single-parent family.

Parent (or family) stress and less-than-desirable quality in child-parent interactions seem to hinder children's language development. Since most families face stress, a family's reaction to stress, rather than stress itself, is the determining factor.

It is good practice to talk through the routines of dressing, feeding, and bathing the infant in simple sentences. Also, making statements such as "push the switch on" and "lights off," while these actions are being performed, are recorded in the child's memory. Pausing in conversations for the infant to make his or her own noises, and acknowledging these with a smile or look of recognition, will encourage the infant to continue making sounds.

Fischer (1986) has good advice for parents:

Don't worry about teaching as much as providing a rich and emotionally supportive atmosphere.

The richness to which he refers is a richness of opportunity, rather than expensive toys and surroundings. Parents may get the idea that a parent has to talk constantly, and that early infant "talkers" have parents with more competency in parenting skills. However, current research indicates that parents who spontaneously speak about what the child is interested in and who zoom in and out of the child's play as they go about their daily work are responsive and effective parents. Also, early and late "talkers" usually show little difference in speaking ability by age three. The variation between children with respect to the onset and accomplishment of most human characteristics covers a wide range when considering what is normal and expected.

....
Summary

Each child grows in language ability in a unique way. The process starts before birth with the development of sensory organs. Parents play an important role in a child's growth and mastery of language.

Perceptions gained through life experiences serve as the base for future learning of words and speech. Babbling, soundmaking, and imitation occur, and first words appear.

A number of related factors influence a child's language acquisition. Most children progress through a series of language ability stages and milestones at about the same ages (figure 1–13) and become adult-like speakers during the preschool period. The way children learn language is not clearly understood, and so there are a number of differing theories of language acquisition.

Early in life, infants and parents form a reciprocal relationship reacting in special ways to each other. The quality and quantity of parental attention becomes an important factor in language development.

The child progresses from receiving to sending language, which is accompanied by gestures and nonverbal communication. From infancy, the child is an active participant, edging closer to the two-way process required in language usage and verbal communication.

Staff members in infant-care programs can possess interaction skills that offer infants optimum opportunities for speech development.

ACTIVITIES ACTIVITIES ACTIVITIES ACTIVITIES

INFANT'S AGE	STAGES OF LANGUAGE DEVELOPMENT
Before birth	Listens to sounds. Reacts to loud sounds.
At birth	Birth cry is primal, yet individual—vowel-like. Cries to express desires (for food, attention, and so on) or displeasure (pain or discomfort). Makes eating, sucking, and small throaty sounds. Hiccoughs. Crying becomes more rhythmic and resonant during first days. Shows changes in posture—tense, active, or relaxed.
First days	Half cries become vigorous; whole cries begin to take on depth and range. Coughs and sneezes.
1 month	Three to four vowel sounds apparent. Seems to quiet movements and attend to mother's voice. Eating sounds mirror eagerness. Sighs and gasps. Smiles in sleep.
2 to 3 months	Coos and makes pleasurable noises (babbling); and blowing and smacking sounds. Most vowel sounds are present. Open vowel-like babbles may begin. Consonant sounds begin, usually the following—b, d, g, h, l, m, n, p, t. Markedly less crying. Smiles and squeals and may coo for half a minute. Peers into faces. Adults may recognize distinct variations in cries, i.e., cries that signal fear, tiredness, hunger, pain, and so on. Focuses on mother's face and turns head to her voice. May be frightened by loud or unfamiliar noise. May blow bubbles and move tongue in and out.
4 to 5 months	Sound play is frequent. Social smiling more pronounced. Can whine to signal boredom. May laugh. Reacts to tone of voice. Seems to listen and enjoy music. Likes adult vocal play and mimicking. Favorite people seem to induce verbalness. Babbles several sounds in one breath. Body gestures signal state of comfort or discomfort. Attracted to sounds. Approaching 6 months of age, may start to show understanding of words often used in household. Turns head and looks at speaking family members. Consonant sounds more pronounced and frequent.
6 to 8 months	Increased babbling and sound making; repeats syllables; imitates motions and gestures; uses nonverbal signals; vocalizes all vowel sounds; reduplication of utterances; more distinct intonation. Increases understanding of simple words. Enjoys making noise with toys and household objects. Repeats actions to hear sounds again. May blow toy horn. Delights in rhythmic vocal play interchange, especially those that combine touching and speaking. Twists and protrudes tongue, smacks, and watches mother's mouth and lips intently. May look at picture books for short period or watch children's television programs.
9 to 10 months	May make kiss sounds. Increases understanding of words like no-no, mommy, daddy, ball, hat, and shoe. May play pat-a-cake and wave bye-bye. May hand books to adults for sharing. Uses many body signals and gestures. May start jargon-like strings of sounds, grunts, gurgles, and whines. Listens intently to new sounds.
11 to 14 months	Reacts to an increasing number of words. Speaks first word(s) (usually words with one syllable or repeated syllable). Points to named objects or looks toward named word. Makes sounds and noises with whatever is available. Imitates breathing noises, animal noises (like barking dog or cat's meow), or environmental noises (like "boom," or train toot). Uses many body signals especially "pick me up" with arms outstretched and reaching for another's hand, meaning "come with me." May understand as many as 40 to 50 words. At close to 15 months, one word has multiple meanings. Jargon-like strings of verbalness continue. The child's direction of looking gives clues to what the child understands, and the child may have a speaking vocabulary of 10 or more words. Uses first pretend play gestures such as combing hair with a spoon-shaped object, drinking from a pretend cup, pretending to eat an object, and pretending to talk with another on a toy telephone.

FIGURE 1–13   Milestones in developing language behavior

STUDENT ACTIVITIES

1. What parental expectations of infants might interfere with the infant's ability to develop the idea he or she is an effective communicator? List three or four. Give examples from your own experience if possible. Compare your list with that of a classmate.

2. Observe three newborns and compare their cries.

3. Observe two infants (birth to 12 months). Note situations in which the infants make sounds and how adults (parent or teacher) react to the sound making.

4. Describe nonverbal communication that you notice or receive in any situation with a group of people, such as in a classroom, cafeteria, family group, or social group.

5. Sit with a young infant facing you. Have a note pad handy. Remain speechless and motionless. Try to determine what moment-to-moment needs the child has, and try to fulfill each need you recognize. Try not to add anything new; just respond to what you feel the child needs. Write a description of the needs observed and your feelings.

6. Rate the following adult techniques for quieting and soothing a crying infant on a scale of 1 to 15, with 15 indicating the most common technique, and 1 the least common:

   ___ feeding   ___ changing
   ___ holding   ___ swaddling
   ___ massaging   ___ caressing
   ___ rocking   ___ giving pacifier
   ___ humming or singing   ___ using a low "motor-type" noise
   ___ car riding   ___ pushing in buggy
   ___ lifting to shoulder   ___ walking the floor
   ___ using a heartbeat-sound plush toy

   Can you cite other safe, comforting techniques that might calm a crying infant?

   Compare your answers with those of a classmate.

7. Visit an infant-toddler center. Focus on an infant over six months of age. What behaviors can you pinpoint in the infant's early childhood teachers that promote future language?

8. Try sharing a colorful, simple book with an 8- to 12-month-old. What did you observe?

9. Discuss your memories, thoughts, and feelings with a partner as you read this unit's discussion of Baby Games and Explorations, and Classic Language Play.

10. Create a new game, rhyme, or movement word play, and test it on an infant 6 to 12 months of age.

11. Try the following with a 4- to 12-month-old. Touch the child as you say the words. Report the child's reactions at the next class meeting.

   Here comes a mouse
   Mousie, mousie, mouse
   With tiny light feet
   And a soft pink nose
   Tickledy tickle
   Wherever he goes
   He runs up your arm
   And under your chin
   Don't open your mouth
   Or the mouse will run in
   Mousie, mousie, mouse!

   from Watson, C. (1978). *Catch me and kiss me and say it again.* New York: Putnam Publ. Group.

12. Locate three books you feel would be appropriate for older infants, and share them with the class.

13. Review Judith Schickedanz's book, *More than the ABCs: The Early Stages of Reading and Writing.* Washington, DC: National Association for the Education of Young Children, 1986, for additional suggestions concerning book use in infancy.

14. Discuss the following quote. Decide whether today's children are close or far from this ideal. Elaborate.

   Ideally, children have one-on-one language coaches built into their lives from birth. (Healy, 1990)

15. Try the following with a 2- to 8-month-old infant.
   a. Attract the child's attention by gaining eye contact, saying his name, being close, or moving or showing an object or toy.
   b. Play out a word-movement activity or sing a simple song or rhyme.
   c. Stop and gaze expectantly into the child's eyes, letting the child initiate some reaction.
   d. Give attention to any action, gesture, vocalization, or facial expression and see if your attention prompts the child to repeat or try a new behavior. Wait.
   e. Respond for the child by moving his hand to touch your face and note his reaction.
   f. Report your experiences at the next class session. What communication skill did you give the infant a chance to display?

16. Observe three children under one year of age interacting with three adults for one 10- to 30-minute period. Take notes concerning their verbalness and interactions. What language developing techniques were present? Which child would you choose to be if you could change places with one of the observed children and why?

CHAPTER REVIEW

A. Write your own theory of language acquisition. (A child learns language . . .) Compare and contrast your theory with those on pages 8–10.

B. Finish the following: Early childhood educators working in group infant-care programs who wish to give infants opportunities to acquire language should carefully monitor their ability to . . . (list specific techniques).

C. Write definitions for:

phonation	bonding	babbling
resonation	moderation level	articulation
echolalia	infant signing	larynx

D. Discuss and finish the following: "Language is a kind of game infants learn. A game played with precise recognizable rules like . . . First, I talk; then you talk. To learn the game, it's best to have adults in your life who . . ."

E. Answer the following questions based on the information in the unit.
    1. What are the two basic factors that influence language development?
    2. How can parents help the young child develop language?
    3. What is one purpose of a child's babbling?
    4. Why is language development described as a two-way process?
    5. What are the names of the sense organs that receive and transmit messages?
    6. What is the name for impressions received through the senses?

F. Select the best answer.
    1. Environmental factors that can affect future language development start
       a. at birth.   c. during infancy.
       b. before birth.   d. during toddlerhood.
    2. The tone of a parent's voice is
       a. understood when a child learns to speak in sentences.
       b. less important than the parent's words.
       c. understood before actual words are understood.
       d. less important than the parent's actions.
    3. In acquiring language, the child
       a. learns only through imitation.
       b. is one participant in a two-part process.
       c. learns best when parents ignore the child's unclear sounds.
       d. does not learn anything by imitating.

4. Select the true statement about babbling.
   a. Why babbling occurs is not clearly understood.
   b. Babbling is unimportant.
   c. Babbling predicts how early a child will start talking.
   d. Babbling rarely lasts beyond one year of age.

5. How a child acquires language is
   a. clearly understood.
   b. not important.
   c. only partly understood.
   d. rarely a subject for study.

G. Explain the difference between language and communication.

H. Match the words in Column I with the appropriate meaning or example in Column II.

Column I	**Column II**
1. perception K.	a. random sound production
2. babbling a.	b. mama, dada, bye-bye
3. tone g.	c. the Behaviorist Theory
4. B. F. Skinner c.	d. close reproduction of alphabet letter sounds
5. imitation h.	e. zero to four words
6. speaking vocabulary at 12 months n.	f. language and thought are interrelated
7. nonverbal communication	g. the way words are spoken rather than the meaning of the words
8. deprivation j	h. repeating sounds and actions
9. repeated syllables b.	i. thumb sucking, smiling, crying
10. one of five senses m.	j. lack of warm, loving care
11. first words e	k. impressions sent from sensory organs to brain
12. recognized English language sounds d.	l. a term used describing electrical brain connections
13. authorities agree f.	m. touching
14. synapses l.	n. usually represent objects or people experienced daily

I. What is the significance of current discoveries concerning young children's brain growth for early childhood educators?

CHAPTER 2

The Tasks of the Toddler

OBJECTIVES

After studying this chapter, you should be able to:

- discuss phonology, grammar, and the toddler's understanding of semantics.

- list three characteristics of toddler language.

- identify adult behaviors that aid the toddler's speech development.

If you were amazed at the infant's and one-year-old's ability, wait until you meet the toddler! Toddlerhood marks the beginning of a critical language-growth period. Never again will words enter the vocabulary at the same rate; abilities emerge in giant spurts almost daily. When children stop and focus on things, from specks on the floor to something very large, concentration is total—every sense organ seems to probe for data. As White (1987) notes, "The one-year-old seems genuinely interested in exploring the world throughout the major portion of his day."

Toddlerhood begins with the onset of toddling (walking), a little before or after the child's first birthday. The toddler is perched at the gateway of a great adventure eager to proceed, investigating as the child goes, and attempting to communicate what he or she discovers and experiences. "The bags are packed" with what's been learned in infancy. The child will both monologue and dialogue as he or she ages, always knowing much more than can be verbally expressed. As Harris (1990) points out:

> Communication is well established *before* children begin to use words, and it seems that children's first word meanings are created by the very fact that the words they

use are embedded in social acts which already have communicative significance.

Greenspan (1997) describes an important happening during the toddler period when the child switches from primarily motor or gesture action communication to symbolic (speech) communication. He believes this happens through the maturing possibilities of the child's neurology combined with the richness of the child's affective experiences. The key, Greenspan feels, is a warm, close relationship with an adult, one in which communication becomes important enough to provide satisfaction in itself.

From a few spoken words, the toddler will move to purposeful speech that gains what is desired, controls others, allows personal comments, and accompanies play. It becomes evident that the toddler realizes the give and take of true conversation, and what it is to be the speaker or the one who listens and reacts—the one who persuades or is persuaded, the one who questions or is questioned. Toddlers become aware that everything has a name and that playfully trying out new sounds is an enjoyable pursuit. The child's meanings for the few words the child uses at the start of the toddler period may or may not be the same as common public usage (Dopyera and Lay-Dopyera, 1992):

> The task of gradually modifying the private meanings of words to coincide with public meanings continues throughout the life span.

Cambourne (1988) describes the enormous complexity of learning to talk:

> When one has learned to control the oral version of one's language, one has learned literally countless thousands of conventions. Early language spoken on the Earth today (some three or four thousand) comprises a unique, arbitrary set of signs, and rules for combining those signs to create meaning. These conventions have no inherent "rightness" or "logic" to them, just as driving on the right or left side of the road has no intrinsic rightness or logic to it. Yet each language is an amazingly complex, cultural artifact, comprising incredibly complex sets of sounds, words, and rules for combining them, with equally numerous and complex systems for using them for different social, personal, and cognitive purposes.

There are four major tasks in learning the rule systems of language that face the toddler. These are (1) understanding *phonology* (the sound system of a language), (2) learning *syntax* (a system of rules governing word order and combinations that give sense to short utterances and sentences (often referred to as grammar), (3) learning *semantics* (word meanings), and (4) learning *pragmatics* (varying speech patterns depending on social circumstances and the context of situations). The understanding of these rule systems takes place concurrently—one area complementing and promoting the other.

Rule systems form without direct instruction as toddlers grope to understand the speech of others, express themselves, and influence others both verbally and nonverbally. We can think of the toddler as a "hypothesis tester," a thinker who over time can unconsciously formulate the rules of language (Genishi, 1985).

Language emergence is but one of the toddler's achievements. Intellectually toddlers process, test, and remember language input. They develop their own rules, which change as they recognize what are and are not permissible structures in their native language (Menyuk, 1991). Other important developmental achievements intersect during late toddlerhood as children increasingly shift to symbolic thinking and language use. Gains in social, emotional, and physical development are apparent as well as issues of power and autonomy (Curry and Johnson, 1990).

....
Phonology

Toddlers learn the **phonology** of their native language—its phonetic units and its particular and sometimes peculiar sounds. This is no easy job! As Geller (1985) notes, the young language learner must sort sounds into identifiable groups and categories while he or she is possibly experiencing the speech of a variety of people in a variety of settings. Since spoken language is characterized by a continuous flow of word sounds, this makes the task even more difficult. A **phoneme** is the smallest unit of sound that distinguishes one utterance from another—implying a difference in meaning. English has 46 to 50 phonemes, depending on what expert is consulted. Harris (1990) defines language from a phonetic perspective in the following:

> . . . language might be characterized as a continuous sequence of sounds produced by the expulsion of air through the throat and mouth . . . Structures in the ear are sensitive to the airwave vibrations produced in this way and make the detection of speech sounds possible.

Phonology — the sound system of a language and how it is represented with an alphabetic code.

Phoneme — one of the smallest units of speech that distinguishes one utterance from another.

FIGURE 2–1 Toddlers spend much time looking and listening.

Languages are divided into vowel sounds and consonants. In vowels, the breath stream flows freely from the vocal cords; in consonants, it is blocked and molded in the mouth and throat area by soft tissue, muscle tissue, and bone, with tongue and jaw often working together. The child focuses on those sounds heard most often (figure 2–1). The toddler's speech is full of repetitions and rhythmic speech play. Toddler babbling of this type continues and remains pleasurable during early toddlerhood. Sounds that are combinations of vowels and consonants increase. Sounds that are difficult to form will continue to be spoken without being close approximations of adult sounds until the child reaches five or six years of age or is even slightly older. Early childhood teachers realize that they will have to listen closely, and watch for nonverbal clues to understand child speech in many instances.

It is a difficult task for the child to make recognizable sounds with mouth, throat, and breath control working in unison. Lenneberg (1971) comments on the difficulties of perfecting motor control of speech-producing muscles, noting that this sophisticated skill comes ahead of many other physical skills.

Speech, which requires infinitely precise and swift movements of tongue and lips . . . is all but fully developed when most other mechanical skills are far below levels of their future accomplishment.

Much of early speech has been called jargon or gibberish. The toddler seems to realize that conversations come in long strings of sound. Rising to the occasion, the child imitates the rhythm of the sound but utters only a few understandable words.

Toddlers hear a word as an adult hears it. Sometimes, they know the proper pronunciation but are unable to reproduce it. The child may say "pway" for play. If the parent says "pway," the child objects, showing confusion and perhaps frustration. Toddler talk represents the child's best imitation, given his or her present ability.

Baron (1989) defines adult-child talk as "special language" or "child-directed speech" that is a set of speech modifications commonly found in the language adults use to address young children. She goes on to divide adult-child language into five main categories. They are pedagogy, control, affection, social exchange, and information.

The pedagogy mode is characterized by slow adult speech that overenunciates or overemphasizes one or two words. Baron (1989) believes this type of adult speech is "tailor-made" for one- or two-year-olds trying to segment the speech stream into comprehensible units.

Parents tend to label happenings and objects with easy-to-learn, catchy variations, such as choo-choo, bow-wow, etc. Other parental language techniques include

1. labeling themselves as Mommy or Daddy, instead of I or me in speech.
2. limiting topics in sentences.
3. using short and simple sentences.
4. using repetition.
5. expanding or recasting children's one-word or unfinished utterances. If toddler says "kitty," parent offers "Kitty's name is Fluff."
6. using a wide range of voice frequencies to gain child's attention and initiate a communication exchange.
7. carrying both sides of an adult-child conversation. Parent asks questions, then answers. This technique is most often used with infants but also common during the toddler period. The parent is modeling a social exchange.

8. echoing a child's invented word. Many toddlers adopt a special word for a certain object. The whole family may use the child's word in conversational exchanges also.

Baron (1989) concludes that the use of child-directed speech fosters the child's language development and that it also benefits the parent. She feels human language grows out of a person's need to interact. The child needs to learn the formal words and constructions that make this interchange possible. When parents feel their infants and toddlers can communicate, parental actions and speech can increase children's communicative abilities and opportunities.

Not all early childhood educators agree with Baron's conclusions. While believing caregivers should treat toddlers as communicating children, they avoid child-like or cutesy expressions. They offer simple forms of speech and easy-to-pronounce words whenever possible.

Views on adult use of baby talk include the idea that the practice may limit more mature word forms and emphasize dependency. On the other hand, parents may offer simplified, easily-pronounced forms like "bow-wow" for barking poodle. They later quickly switch to adult, harder-to-pronounce forms when the child seems ready. In the beginning, though, most adults automatically modify their speech when speaking with toddlers by using short sentences and stressing key words.

Children progress with language at their individual rates and with varying degrees of clarity. Some children speak relatively clearly from their first tries. Other children, who are also progressing normally, take a longer time before their speech is easily understood. All 50 basic sounds (50 including diphthongs) are perfected by most children by age seven or eight.

Morpheme — the smallest unit in a language that by itself has a recognizable meaning.

Morphology — the study of the units of meaning in a language.

Morphology

A **morpheme** is the smallest unit of language standing by itself with recognized meaning. It can be a word or part of a word. Many prefixes (un-, ill-) and suffixes (-s, -ness, -ed, -ing) are morphemes with their own distinct meaning. The study of morphemes is called **morphology**. There are wide individual differences in the rates toddlers utter morphemes (figure 2–2). It is unfortunate if early childhood teachers or parents attempt to compare the emerging speech of toddlers or equate greater speech usage with higher ability, thus giving the quiet toddler(s) perhaps less of their time.

Between the ages of two and four years, children gradually include a variety of different morphemes in their spontaneous utterances. There seems to be a common sequence in their appearance (Brown, 1973).

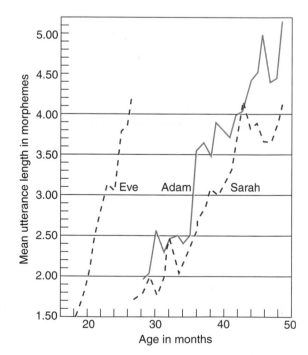

FIGURE 2–2 Individual rates in morpheme usage (*From "The child's grammar from I to III," by R. Brown, C. Cazden, and U. Bellugi-Kilma,* Minnesota Symposium on Child Psychology, *Vol. 2, John P. Hill, ed., 1969. Reprinted by permission of the University of Minnesota Press.*)

Syntax

Languages have word orders and rules, and young children speak in word order and follow the rules of their native tongue. Children typically acquire the rules of grammar in their native language with little difficulty from normal communicative interactions with adults (Snow and Tabors, 1993).

Harris (1990) points out:

> The rules for ordering words in sentences do not operate on specific words, but on classes of words such as nouns, verbs, and adjectives. This has the advantage that a relatively small number of syntactical rules can account for the production of a very large number of sentences.

In one language, the subject of a sentence follows the verb; in other languages, it precedes the verb. **Modifiers** (descriptive words) in some languages have gender (male and female forms), while in others they do not. Plurals and possessive forms are unique to each language. Young speakers will make mistakes, but adults marvel at the grammar the child does use correctly, having learned the rules without direct instruction. Donoghue (1985) compares children's mastery of **phonetics** to their mastery of **syntax**:

> In contrast to the gradual mastery of phonology, children use syntax correctly (though incompletely of course) from the very beginning. By age two, and sometimes as early as 18 months, children begin to string together two or more holophrases and have thereby arrived at telegraphic stage.

> All telegraphic speech consists of acceptable grammatical sequences which are the precursors of the sentence.

From all the perceptions received and the words spoken to and about the child, the child has noted regularities and has unconsciously formed rules, which are continually revised. Chukovsky (1963) describes this task:

> It is frightening to think what an enormous number of grammatical forms are poured over the poor head of the young child. And he, as if it were nothing at all, adjusts to all the chaos, constantly sorting out in rubrics the disorderly elements of words he hears, without noticing as he does this, his gigantic effort. If an adult had to master so many grammatical rules within so short a time, his head would surely burst.

Grammar involves the way sounds are organized to communicate meaning (Harris, 1990). With grammatical knowledge the young child can produce and understand a wide range of new, novel, grammatically correct, and meaningful sentences. Researchers of young children's brain development suspect there is a "window" or critical time period for acquiring syntactic understandings, and believe this period may close as early as five or six years of age (Nash, 1997).

Clay (1993) notes as the child learns to talk during preschool years she produces many ungrammatical sentences and uses words in unusual ways. The errors of the two-year-old disappear as the child gains more control over language, but new kinds of errors appear in three-year-olds who are trying new forms of expression. An understanding of the general rules of grammar develops before an understanding of the exceptions to the rules. Correct grammar forms may change to incorrect forms as the child learns new rules. Slobin (1971) has an interesting example of this phenomena:

Modifier — a word that gives a special characteristic to a noun (for example, a *large* ball).

Phonetic — pertaining to representing the sounds of speech with a set of distinct symbols, each denoting a single sound.

Syntax — the arrangement of words as elements in a sentence to show their relationship.

Grammar — the word order and knowledge of "marker" word meanings necessary to send communications to (and receive them from) another in the same language.

In all of the cases which have been studied ... the first past tenses used are the correct forms of irregular verbs—came, broke, went, and so on. Apparently these irregular verbs in the past tense—which are the most frequent past tense forms in adult speech—are learned as separate vocabulary items at a very early age.

Then, as soon as the child learns only one or two regular past tense forms—like helped and walked—he immediately replaces the correct irregular past tense forms with their incorrect over-generalizations from the regular forms. Thus children say "it came off," "it broke," and "he did it" before they say "it comed off," "it breaked," and "he doed it." Even though the correct forms may have been practiced for several months, they are driven out of the child's speech by the **overregularization**, and may not return for years.

In later years, during elementary school, the child will formally learn the grammar rules of his or her native language. What the child has accomplished before that time, however, is monumental. The amount of speech that already conforms to the particular syntactical and grammatical rules of language is amazing. The child has done this through careful listening and by mentally reorganizing the common elements in language that have been perceived.

The toddler's growing use of intonation and **inflection** (changes in loudness of voice) adds clarity, as do nonverbal gestures. The child is often insistent that adults listen.

Overregularization — the tendency on the part of children to make the language regular, such as using past tenses like -ed on verb endings.

Inflections — the grammatical "markers" such as plurals. Also, a change in pitch or loudness of the voice.

Semantics — the study of meanings, of how the sounds of language are related to the real world and our own experiences.

The toddler's system of nonverbal signals, body postures, and motions that he or she used in late infancy has continued and expanded, becoming part of the toddler's communication style. Many signals translated by mothers to strangers, leave strangers bewildered as to how the mother could possibly know what the child wants from what the child and the mother have both observed and heard.

English sentences follow a subject-verb-object sequence. Bruner (1966) notes three fundamental properties of sentences: verb-object, subject-predicate, and modification, and explains their universal use:

> There are no human languages whose sentences do not contain rules for these three basic sentential structures, and there are no nonhuman languages that have them.

Learning grammar rules helps the toddler express ideas (Bellugi, 1977). Understanding syntax (the arrangement of words to show relationship) helps the child to be understood:

> It is our knowledge of the rules of combination—the syntax of the language—that governs how we construct and understand an infinite number of sentences from a finite vocabulary. Syntax gives language its power.

If one listens closely to the older toddler, sometimes self-correction of speech errors takes place. Toddlers talk to themselves and their toys often. It seems to aid storage and memory. The toddler understands adult sentences because he or she has internalized a set of finite rules or combinations of words.

....

Semantics

Semantics is the study of meanings. It probes how the sounds of language are related to the real world and life experiences. The toddler absorbs meanings from both verbal and nonverbal communication sent and received. The nonverbal refers to expressive associations of words: rhythm, stress, pitch, gesture, body position, facial change, and so on.

Adults perform important functions in the child's labeling and concept formation by giving words meaning in conversations.

The toddler who comes from a home that places little emphasis on expressing ideas in language may be exposed to a relatively restricted range of words for expressing conceptual distinctions (Harris, 1990). Every early childhood center should offer opportunities for children to learn a rich and varied vocabulary to refer to various experiences and to express ideas.

In toddler classrooms, teachers have many opportunities to name objects and happenings as the day unfolds. Using gesturing along with words, (or pointing to pictures in simple picture books and magazines) helps the toddler form a connection between what he or she heard and said. Repeating words with voice stress can be done in a natural way while monitoring whether the child is still interested.

Word meanings are best learned in active, hands-on experiences rather than "repeat-after-me" situations (figure 2–3). Meanings of words are acquired through their connotations, not their denotations (Gonzalez-Mena, 1976), that is, in situations that consist of feelings and verbal and nonverbal messages with physical involvement. The word "cold," for instance means little until physically experienced.

For awhile toddlers may use one sound for a number of meanings:

> When a baby is first learning to talk, the same sound often serves for several words; for instance, "bah" can mean "bottle," "book," "bath," and "bye." And sometimes babies use one sound to name an object and also to express a more complicated thought, for example, a baby may point to the stroller and name it, but later may say the same word and mean, "I want to ride in the stroller." (Sherwin, 1987)

A **concept** is the recognition of one or more distinguishing features of a set of events, persons, or objects (figure 2–4). Some adults help the child discover similarities and differences; others may not.

The child's concept building is an outgrowth and result of a natural human tendency to try to make sense of the surroundings. Attending to and

---

Concept — a commonly recognized element (or elements) that identifies groups or classes, usually has a given name.

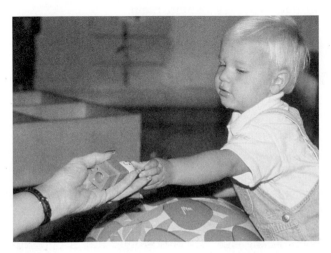

FIGURE 2–3   Hands-on experiences aid the learning of new words.

FIGURE 2–4   Focusing on a new object

pondering about the relationships, similarities, and differences in events and happenings, and mentally storing, remembering, and retrieving those ideas and impressions are all important aspects of concept development. With young children's innate curiosity, drive, and desire to explore and experience, concepts are continually being formed, reformed, and modified.

Examples of toddler behavior demonstrate that conceptual conclusions happen daily in group and home care settings. When a child blows a whistle-shaped toy, licks and bites a plastic fruit in housekeeping play, tightly clings to an adult when a dog barks, or says "hot" when pointing to a water faucet, one can see past experiences are basic to the child's behavior.

To understand how concept development is individual and based upon life experiences, ask yourself what makes a cup a cup. How many distinguishing features can you list? Ask another adult to do the same. You will both probably list similar characteristics, such as

- has a handle,
- holds liquids and substances,
- is often round on top tapering to a smaller round base or can be cylindrical,
- is used as a standard measurement in cooking (8 ounces),
- is made from clay, plastic, glass, metal, or from other solid substances; and
- can be used to drink liquids from.

Adults speaking about cups understand one another because they usually recognize the same distinguishing characteristic(s). If asked to get the cup on the shelf, they won't get a glass. A toddler using the word *cup* often means his or her personal drinking cup.

A toddler may overuse concepts in new situations. Perhaps a bandage on the tip of a brother's finger will be called a thimble. For a short time,

all men are daddies; a cow may be called a big dog; and all people in white are feared. As mental maturity and life experiences increase, concepts change; small details and exceptions are noticed. Toddlers underextend words also "by using a word to refer to a smaller category than would adults." An example of this phenomena is the toddler's use of the word *dog* only in reference to the child's pet rather than all dogs encountered.

Concepts, often paired mentally with words, aid categorizing. Concept words may have full, partial, or little depth of meaning. The toddler's level of thought is reflected in speech. When counting to three, the toddler may or may not know what "three" represents. Words are **symbols**. Huey (1965) explains their importance:

> A concept, to be communicable, must be represented by a symbol that is understood by others to carry the same meaning that the child intends. The symbol is usually a word. Symbols . . . enable the individual to reflect upon objects or situations which are not actually present.

A toddler's first-hand sensory experiences are very important. Stored mental perceptions are attached to words. Spitzer (1977) points out that words are only as rich as the experiences and depth of understanding behind them:

> Our society puts tremendous emphasis on the acquisition of a large vocabulary in young children. But few realize that words without experiences are meaningless. . . . The more experiences and meaning that back up words, the more rewarding the communication process will become.

The activities and experiences found in later chapters help the early childhood teacher enrich the child's concepts by providing deeper meanings in a wide range of language arts. Every activity for young children—a total school program—gives them a language arts background full of opportunities to explore by handling, tasting, smelling, and touching, as well as by seeing and listening.

Symbol — something standing for or suggesting (such as pictures, models, word symbols, and so forth).

Pragmatics

The subtleties of our language are many-faceted. **Pragmatics** is the study of how language is used effectively in a social context, or the practical aspect of oral communication. It's the study of "who can say what, in what way, where and when, by what means and to whom" (Hymes, 1971). Language is a tool in questioning, ordering, soothing, ridiculing, and in other social actions. One can request quiet in the form of a question such as "Can't anyone get a peaceful moment around here?" or talk longingly about the candy in a store for the purpose of obtaining it—as in "Oh, they have my favorite kind of chocolate bar!"—without making a direct request.

The language that young children use to express desires, wishes, concerns, and interests becomes a reflection of their social selves (Yawkey, Yawkey, Askov, Cartwright, DuPuis, and Fairchild, 1981). When a toddler communicates effectively, the toddler receives feedback from others. Many times, a sense of well-being elicited by positive events helps the child shape a feeling of competency and self-esteem. Not yet socially subtle in speech, the toddler has not learned the pragmatically useful or appropriate behaviors of older children. They seem to have one intent, to get messages across by gaining adult attention regardless of who is present and in what situation. The world, from the toddler's perspective, revolves around the toddler and his or her need to communicate.

Attachment and Development of Language Skills

Attachment problems can slow communicative development. Observers describe infants and toddlers in less-than-adequate care situations as fearful, apathetic, disorganized, and distraught (Curry and Johnson, 1990). If responsive social interaction and adult feedback exchanges are minimal, limited, frightening, or confusing, the infant or toddler may display a marked lack of interest in holding or obtaining adult attention. During toddlerhood these children can fall behind in speech development.

First Words

Before first words are uttered, the toddler learns what is socially expected and appropriate as those around him or her are producing examples of what is linguistically appropriate (Genishi, 1985). Lindfors (1985) describes first words as "building blocks" and "content words" (nouns, verbs) that carry a lot of meaning. They usually consist of names of important people or objects the toddler encounters daily. These single words can frequently go further than naming by representing a meaningful idea (a holophrase). The task of the adult includes both being responsive and guessing the child's complete thought. This may sound simple, but many times it's difficult and frustrating. Many factors influence the degree of adult responsiveness and talkativeness, particularly in child-care settings—room arrangements, adult-child ratios, adult job satisfaction, and other emotional and environmental factors. The greatest inhibitor of adults' talking and responding to children seems to be adults' talking to one another. The nature of the work in a group-care program can easily be described as emotion packed, and demanding, besides rewarding and challenging. On the surface, the general public may not see or understand skilled verbal interactions taking place between toddlers and caregivers. What seems to be random, natural playfulness and verbal responsiveness is really very skilled and professionally intentional behavior. The same, of course, is true regarding parent behavior.

Adults sometimes question the practice of responding to toddlers' grunts and "uhs" instead of seeking words first. Many toddlers seem to understand everything said to them and around them but get by and satisfy most of their needs

---

Pragmatics — the study of how language is used effectively in a social context; varying speech patterns depending on social circumstances and the context of situations.

with nonword utterances. The points for adults to consider are that the child is performing and learning a difficult task and that speech will soon follow. The message that responsive adults relay to children when rewarding their early attempts is that the children can be successful communicators and that further attempts at speech will get results.

From Egocentric Speech to Inner Speech

During the toddler period, observers notice words or short phrases spoken by adults are remembered and spoken out loud. The toddler's "hot," "no," "kitty," or similar words accompany the child's actions or a simple viewing of objects at hand. Vygotsky (1986) has called this "egocentric" speech, which is ultimately and usefully tied to the toddler's thinking.

As the child matures, this type of speech slowly becomes **inner speech**, part of the child's thinking process. Egocentric speech is regulatory, that is, useful in helping the child regulate (manage) his or her own behavior. As adults, we see examples of this regulatory function when we talk ourselves through particular perplexing situations. For example, "First the key goes in the lock, then turn the handle, and the bar moves to the left."

Symbolic Gesturing

It's old-fashioned to feel that real communication doesn't exist before a child's first words. Researchers have helped us understand that gestures and signs (signals) occur in tandem with early vocalizing (Acredolo and Goodwyn, 1986). Young toddlers can possess a rich repertoire of signals, and female infants tend to rely on or produce them with slightly greater frequency. Signs have been defined by Acredolo and Goodwyn (1986) as nonverbal ges-

---

Inner speech — mentioned in Vygotsky's theory as private speech that becomes internalized and is useful in organizing ideas.

tures symbolically representing objects, events, desires, and conditions that are used by toddlers to communicate with those around them. They literally can double a young toddler's vocabulary.

Grey (1996) points out toddler's interest in learning hand signals (signing) varies greatly. Conducting an infant-toddler program where signing is a regular part of the curriculum, Grey found some toddlers used 25 baby signs for various objects, feelings, and needs while other toddlers mixed only a few gestures with beginning word usage. Grey believes both displayed normal development.

The use of words and symbols to influence other people in predictable ways requires the child to represent mentally the relationship between the symbol (word or gesture), the meaning for which it stands, and the intended effect on the other person (Harris, 1990). A symbol—a word, a picture, a dance—exists because of human intention to infuse some tangible form—a sound, a mark, a *movement*—with meaning and, thereby, to comment on or take action in the social world (Dyson, 1993).

Gesturing significantly increases children's power to obtain what they are after. It enriches their contacts and communicative competence. Adult recognition and attention to toddler signs enhance, rather than impede, language growth. Acredolo and Goodwyn (1986) studied a child whose parents recognized that their child was interested in communicating and capable of learning nonverbal as well as verbal labels. The parents informally concocted signs on the spot for new events without any reference to a formal sign-language system. Figure 2–5 describes the signs and gives the age the signs appeared in the child's communicative behaviors and the age the child said the word represented by the sign. The list of signs includes the signs the child learned with and without direct parent teaching.

Gestures are integral companions of toddler verbalizations. Adults may have modeled the gestures in their adult-child interactions. Mothers' signals are "read" by toddlers, and a hand held palm up is usually read as "give it to me." Toddlers show their understanding by behaviors. Toddlers can and do invent new ones; consequently, sign-

SIGNS	DESCRIPTION	AGE OF SIGN ACQUISITION MONTHS	AGE OF WORD ACQUISITION MONTHS
Flower	Sniff, sniff	12.5	20.0
Big	Arms raised	13.0	17.25
Elephant	Finger to nose, lifted	13.5	19.75
Anteater	Tongue in and out	14.0	24.0
Bunny	Torso up and down	14.0	19.75
Cookie monster	Palm to mouth plus smack	14.0	20.75
Monkey	Hands in armpits, up-down	14.25	19.75
Skunk	Wrinkled nose plus sniff	14.5	24.00
Fish	Blow through mouth	14.5	20.0
Slide	Hand waved downward	14.5	17.5
Swing	Torso back and forth	14.5	18.25
Ball	Both hands waved	14.5	15.75
Alligator	Palms together, open-shut	14.75	24.0
Bee	Finger plus thumb waved	14.75	20.00
Butterfly	Hands crossed, fingers waved	14.75	24.0
I dunno	Shrugs shoulders, hands up	15.0	17.25
Hot	Waves hand at midline	15.0	19.0
Hippo	Head back, mouth wide	15.0	24.0
Spider	Index fingers rubbed	15.0	20.0
Bird	Arms out, hands flapping	15.0	18.5
Turtle	Hand around wrist, fist in-out	15.0	20.0
Fire	Waving of hand	15.0	23.0
Night-night	Head down on shoulder	15.0	20.0
X-mas tree	Fists open-closed	16.0	26.0
Mistletoe	Kisses	16.0	27.0
Scissors	Two fingers open-closed	16.0	20.0
Berry	'Raspberry' motion	16.5	20.0
Kiss	Kiss (at a distance)	16.5	21.0
Caterpillar	Index finger wiggled	17.5	23.0

FIGURE 2–5   Symbolic signs, in order of acquisition, produced by case study subject *(From Symbolic Gesturing in Language Development, Human Development, 28, 1985 by L. P. Acredolo and S. Goodwyn. Reproduced with permission from S. Karger A.G., Basel, Switzerland.)*

ing isn't simple, imitative behavior. Pointing is probably the most-used gesture of toddlers. Eventually words are preferred, and gesturing remains as an accompaniment of speech. We've all slipped back into a gesturing mode as we search for words in conversation, and hand gestures are used automatically to convey the word(s) that we can't quite express.

First Sentences

The shift from one word to a two- (or more) word stage at approximately 18 months is a milestone. At that time, the toddler has a speaking vocabulary of about 50 words; by 36 months, upwards of 1,000 words. It is crucial in talking about vocabulary to acknowledge that children not only acquire new words as they get older but also expand their understanding of old words (Snow and Tabors, 1993).

If one looks closely at two-word utterances, two classes of words become apparent. Braine (1973) termed the smaller group "pivot words." Examples of toddlers' two-word sentences, with pivot words underlined, are shown in figure 2–6. They are used more often than nonpivots but seem to enter the vocabulary more slowly, perhaps because pivot words are stable and fixed in meaning. In analyzing two-word toddler comments, one finds they are both subject-predicate and topic-comment in nature.

Joint attention — child's awareness that he or she must gain and hold another's focus during communicational exchanges to get his or her message understood.

TWO-WORD SENTENCES	MEANINGS
<u>Dat</u>* car	Nomination
Daddy <u>dare</u>	Location
<u>See</u> kitty	Identification
<u>More</u> cookie	Repetition, recurrence
Milk <u>allgone</u>	Nonexistence
<u>Sit</u> chair	Action—location
<u>No</u> car, <u>no</u> want dat	Negation
<u>Todd</u> shoe, <u>mine</u> toy	Possession, possessor
<u>Big</u> cup	Attribute description
Jin <u>walk</u>, truck <u>go</u>	Agent—action
<u>Kiss</u> you, <u>fix</u> car	Action—direct object
<u>Where</u> ball?	Question

*Underlined words are pivots.

FIGURE 2–6   Pivot words in toddler's two-word sentences

Frequently stressed syllables in words and word endings are what toddlers first master, filling in other syllables later. At times, toddlers use -um or -ah as place holders for syllables and words and replace these with correct syllables and words as they age.

Understanding grammar rules at this two-word stage is displayed even though many words are missing. Braine (1973) points out the frequency with which toddlers use a simple form and, almost in the same breath, clarify by expansion (by adding another word). The invention of words by toddlers is commonplace. Meers (1976) describes an 18-month-old who had her own private word for "sleep," consistently calling it "ooma." Parents trying to understand their toddler get good at filling in the blanks. They then can confirm the child's statement and can add meaning at a time when the child's interest is focused.

Toddler-Adult Conversations

Toddlers control attending or turning away in game-like, playlike episodes as do infants. At about one year, they understand many words and begin to display turn-taking in conversation, with "you talk, I answer" episodes. Weitzman (1992) believes **joint attention** starts by ten months of age:

> By 10 months, an infant has developed intentional communication and willingly shares his emotions, his intentions, and his interest in the outside world. To do this, he has to establish joint attention. In other words, he has to be sure that both you and he are focused on the same thing, and he does this by:
>
> - getting your attention
> - letting you know what he's communicating about (establishing the topic of conversation)
> - keeping his attention on both you and the topic by looking back and forth
>
> His communication consists of one or more of the following: looking, pointing, showing, giving, making sounds, and changing his facial expression.

Toddlers learn that speech deserves attention and that speech is great for getting adult attention. They seem to revel in the joint-endeavor aspect of conversations.

Toddlers are skillful communicators. They converse and correct adult interpretations, gaining pleasure and satisfaction from language exchanges. The following incident shows more than toddler persistence.

> A first-time visitor to the home of a 20-month-old toddler is approached by the toddler. The visitor eventually rises out of his chair, accompanies the toddler to the kitchen, gets a glass of water, and hands it to the child. The toddler takes a tiny drink, and returns, satisfied, to the living room. Parents were not involved. Thirst, itself, was unimportant. The pleasure gained by the child seemed to motivate his actions.

For the child to accomplish his or her ends, the following actions occurred:

Visitor behavior

1. Focuses attention on child.
2. Realizes a "talking" situation is occurring.
3. Listens and maintains a receiver attitude.
4. Corrects own behavior, guesses at child's meaning, and tries new actions.
5. Realizes conversation is over.

Child behavior

1. Stands in front of visitor, searches face to catch eye, makes loud vocalization dropping volume when eye contact made, observes visitor behavior.
2. Repeats first sound (parents understand, visitor doesn't), observes visitor reaction.
3. Grabs visitor's hand, vocalizes loudly, looks in visitor's eyes.
4. Tugs at hand, uses insistent voice tone, gestures toward the kitchen.
5. Pulls visitor to sink, uses new word (visitor doesn't understand), corrects through gestures when visitor reaches for cookie jar.

6. Corrects visitor's guess (milk), gestures towards water, holds out hand.
7. Drinks and hands back glass, smiles, and walks away.

This type of behavior has been called instrumental expression, because vocalization and nonverbal behaviors were used to obtain a certain goal.

The toddler seeks out people willing to listen and learns from each encounter. Adults modify and adapt their speech, based on the abilities they observe in the child. This is done intuitively by use of shorter and less complex comments, and it changes when adults notice increased capacity.

Cawlfield (1992) describes a time in some toddlers' lives she calls "Velcro Time." During this period, the toddler's behavior is characterized by sticking close to a primary caregiver, watching adult lips intently, decreased interest in toys or independent play, frequent bringing of objects to the caregiver, and attempting to say words. The duration and appearance of these grouped behaviors is unique to each toddler, Cawlfield believes. Parents, she notes, often worry about spoiling the child with attention during this stage; but Cawlfield urges parents to feed the child's desire to hear language, for soon the child emerges with a longer attention span and with new ideas and interests.

Characteristics of Toddler Language

The speech of young children speaking in two-word, or longer, sentences is termed **telegraphic** and **prosodic**. It is telegraphic because many words are omitted because of the child's limited ability to express and remember large segments of information; the most important parts of the sentence are usually present. "Prosodic" refers to the child's use

---

Telegraphic speech — a characteristic of early child sentences in which everything but the crucial word(s) is omitted, as if for a telegram.

Prosodic speech — the child's use of voice modulation and word stress to give special emphasis and meaning.

of voice modulation and word stress with a particular word(s) to give special emphasis and meaning. Donoghue (1985) describes telegraphic speech as follows:

> Their utterances are devoid of function words and resemble messages that adults would send by telegraph, for instance, "Jimmy truck" could represent "That truck belongs to Jimmy" or "Give me my truck." Meanings will often depend upon context and intonation of the utterance.

For additional toddler language characteristics that may appear before the child's third birthday, see figure 2–7.

Negatives

No discussion of older toddlers' language would be complete without mentioning the use of "no." There seems to be an exasperating time when children say "no" to everything—seemingly testing whether there is a choice. Young children first use "no" to indicate nonexistence (Bloom, 1970). Later it is used to indicate rejection and denial. Even when the child can speak in sentences longer than three words, the "no" often remains the first in a sequence of words. A typical example is "No want go bed." Soon, children insert negatives properly between the subject and the verb into longer utterances, as sentence length increases. Of all speech characteristics, toddlers' use of negatives and their avid energetic demands to be "listened to" stick in the memories of their caretakers.

Aids to Toddler Speech Development

The swift rate of new words entering toddlers' vocabularies indicates that caretakers should begin to become increasingly specific with descriptive terms in their speech. If a truck is blue, a comment like "The blue truck rolled in the mud" is appropriate. If an object is on the "bottom" shelf, in the "top" drawer, or "under" the table, those words

---

TODDLER LANGUAGE CHARACTERISTICS

- Uses two- to five-word sentences.
  "Baby down."
  "Baby boom boom."
  "No like."
  "No like kitty."
  "Me dink all gone."
  "See me dink all gone."
- Uses verbs.
  "Dolly cry."
  "Me going."
  "Wanna cookie."
- Uses prepositions.
  "In car."
  "Up me go."
- Adds plurals.
  "Birdies sing."
  "Gotta big doggies."
  "Bears in dat."
- Uses pronouns.
  "Me big boy."
  "He bad."
- Uses articles.
  "The ball gone."
  "Gimme a candy."
- Uses conjunctions.
  "Me and gamma."
- Uses negatives.
  "Don't wanna."
  "He no go."
- Runs words together.
  "Allgone," "gotta," "gimme," "lookee."
- Asks questions.
  "Wa dat?"
  "Why she sleep?"
- Letter sounds missing or mispronounced spoken words.
  "Iceam," "choo" (for shoe), "member" (for remember), "canny" (for candy).
- Sings songs.
- Tells simple stories.
- Repeats words and phrases.
- Enjoys word and movement activities.

FIGURE 2–7   Toddler language characteristics

FIGURE 2–8   "The *bubble* bottle is in your hand."

can be stressed. A color, number, or special quality can be inserted in simple comments (figure 2–8).

Playing detective to understand toddlers will always be part of adults' conversational style.

Holmes and Morrison (1979) offer adults advice for providing an optimum toddler environment for language stimulation:

- Expose the child to language with speech neither too simple nor too complex, but just slightly above the child's current level.
- Stay in tune with the child's actual abilities.
- Omit unreasonable speech demands, yet encourage attempts.
- Remember that positive reinforcement is a more effective tool than negative feedback.
- Accept the child's own formulation of a language concept.
- Channel progress by providing a correct model.
- Make a point of being responsive.
- Follow the child's interest by naming and simple discussion.

Other suggested pointers follow:

- Explain what you are doing as you work. Describe what's happening.
- Show excitement for the child's accomplishments.
- Talk about what the child is doing, wanting, or needing.
- Pause and listen with ears and eyes after you have spoken.
- Encourage toddler imitation of gestures and sounds.
- Imitate the child's sounds.

The following adult behaviors are included in appropriate practices identified by the National Association for the Education of Young Children (NAEYC) (Bredekamp & Copple, 1997):

Adults engage in many one-to-one, face-to-face conversations with toddlers. Adults let toddlers initiate language, and wait for a response, even from children whose language is limited. Adults label or name objects, describe events, and reflect feelings to help children learn new words. Adults simplify their language for toddlers who are just beginning to talk (instead of "It's time to wash our hands and have a snack," the adult says, "Let's wash hands. Snacktime!"). Then, as children acquire their own words, adults expand on the toddler's language.

Tarrow and Lundsteen (1981) suggest some toddler activities for corresponding objectives (figure 2–9). Additional toddler-adult activities promoted by the Parents As Teachers *Program Planning and Implementation Guide* (1986) include:

- Setting out two or three familiar objects and asking the child to get one.
- Calling attention to interesting things you see, hear, smell, taste, or feel.
- Showing and labeling your facial features and the child's in a mirror.
- Labeling and pointing to objects around a room.
- Verbally labeling items of clothing as the child is dressing and undressing.
- Labeling the people in the toddler's world.

A toddler movement play follows. Many others are available in teacher sourcebooks that can be obtained at libraries or from school-supply companies.

	OBJECTIVES	ACTIVITIES
12 to 18 months	1. To develop the ability to label things and follow directions	1. Line up various objects and, naming one, ask the child to get it.
	2. To expand vocabulary and lay the foundation for later production of sentences.	2. Act out verbs ("sit," "jump," "run," "smile," etc.)
	3. To reinforce the concept of names and the ability to recognize names and sounds.	3. Use animal picture books and posters of animals.
	4. To encourage verbal communication.	4. Let the child talk on a real telephone.
	5. To reinforce the concept of labels and increase vocabulary.	5. Describe things at home or outside, on a walk or an automobile trip.
18 to 24 months	1. To stimulate imitation and verbalization.	1. Tape-record the child and others familiar to the child, and play the tapes back for the child.
	2. To improve the ability to name objects.	2. On a walk around the home or neighborhood with the child, point out and name familiar objects.
	3. To encourage repetition, sequencing, and rhythm.	3. Play counting games, sing songs, and tell and retell familiar stories.
	4. To develop auditory acuity, passive vocabulary, and the concept of language constancy.	4. With the child, listen to the same recording of a story or song over and over.
	5. To stimulate verbalization, selectivity, and— eventually—descriptive language.	5. Cut out of magazines and mount on stiff cardboard: pictures of foods, clothing, appliances, etc. Have the child identify them as you show them. Use memorable descriptions: "orange, buttery carrots"; "the shiny blue car."
	6. To stimulate conversation.	6. With the child, prepare and eat a make-believe meal.

FIGURE 2–9   Toddler objectives and activities *(From* Activities and Resources for Guiding Young Children's Learning, *1981, by S. W. Lundsteen and N. B. Tarrow. Reproduced with permission from McGraw-Hill Book Company.)*

Take your little hands and go clap, clap, clap
Take your little hands and go clap, clap, clap
Take your little hands and go clap, clap, clap
  Clap, clap, clap your hands.
Take your little foot and go tap, tap, tap
Take your little foot and go tap, tap, tap
Take your little foot and go tap, tap, tap
  Tap, tap, tap your foot.
Take your little eyes and go blink, blink, blink
Take your little eyes and go blink, blink, blink

Take your little eyes and go blink, blink, blink
  Blink, blink, blink your eyes.
Take your little mouth and go buzz, buzz, buzz
Take your little mouth and go buzz, buzz, buzz
Take your little mouth and go buzz, buzz, buzz
  Buzz like a bumblebee.
Take your little hand and wave bye, bye, bye
Take your little hand and wave bye, bye, bye
Take your little hand and wave bye, bye, bye
  Wave your hand bye-bye.

Language through Music

Toddlers are music lovers. If a bouncy melody catches their ear, they move. There's plenty of joy in swaying, clapping, or singing along. Many can sing short, repeated phrases in songs; and some toddlers will create their own repetitive melodies. Words in songs are learned when they are sung repeatedly. Adult correction isn't necessary or appropriate. Playful singing and chanting by adults is a recommended language development technique.

Honig (1995) cites the soothing aspect of many nursery songs and how teacher singing can aid the child's understanding of daily classroom routines. She believes teacher's songs give tots "aesthetic pleasure" as they listen to the lilting notes of richly onomatopoeic poetry found in both rhymes and simple songs.

The social component in musical games is also a language facilitator. Joining the fun with others gradually attracts even the youngest children (McDonald and Simons, 1989).

A toddler's introduction to new songs, musical listening, and participation experiences adds another avenue for language growth.

Andress (1991) suggests a "tactile modeling" technique with music used along with other teacher techniques, such as verbally describing how a particular child is moving to music. ("Johnny is lifting his knees high up to his tummy.")

> Tactile modeling . . . holds great promise as a technique to encourage two-year-old children's movement to music and should be used frequently when appropriate. The adult can extend the two index fingers for the child to grip (thus allowing the child to release at any time) and then begin to gently sway or otherwise guide movements to music.

Wolf (1994) suggests criteria for selecting sing-along songs, recorded music, and songbook selections:

1. Shortness
2. Repetitive phrases
3. Reasonable range (C to G or A)
4. Simple rhythms

She also urges the inclusion of folk music diversity.

A suggested list of records and tapes is included in the Appendix.

Symbolic Play

Somewhere around 12 to 15 months, toddlers who are developing well engage in symbolic (pretend) play. This important developmental leap allows the child to escape the immediate and first-hand happenings in his or her life and use symbols to represent past experiences and imagine future possibilities (Gowen, 1995). The acts of toddler pretend play observed by teachers are widely diverse and depend in part on the child's life experiences. One can always find toddlers who will talk into toy phones, spank dolls, grab the steering wheel of toy vehicles and accompany motor movements with sounds, speech, and vrooms. Some re-enact less commonplace past experiences that are puzzling to their teachers. Gowen (1995) suggests the following teacher techniques (figure 2–10).

Learning from Mothers

Burton White's projects have influenced many early childhood educators. His writings have highlighted the importance of the environment and mothering behaviors during what's been termed "a critical childhood growth stage"—toddlerhood. White (1987), while observing mothers from all economic levels and watching their children's progress, identified maternal skills that he believed accounted for the competence in the observed children. The competence, ingenuity, and energy of this group of mothers, he felt, was commendable. White felt that mothering can be a vastly underrated occupation.

Comment on what the child is doing.

Examples:

Child pushes truck, saying, "Brummm."
Say, "I hear your truck coming."

Child puts baby bottle to doll's mouth.
Say, "You're feeding your baby. You're such a good mommy!"

Imitate the child's action.

Examples:

Child pushes truck, saying, "Brummm."
Push another vehicle and make motor sound.

Child pretends to drink from toy cup.
Pick up another cup and pretend to drink from it.

Reinforce the child's symbolic play.

Examples:

Child pretends to feed doll.
Say, "You're such a good mommy!"

Child pushes toy across floor.
Say, "Boy, you can really make that car go!"

Child puts toy dishes on table.
Say, "You've got the table all ready!"

Make indirect suggestions.

Examples:

Child is playing with toy beings.
Say, "I think your baby (this horse, this man) is hungry (is sleepy, needs a bath)."

Child fed milk to doll from toy baby bottle.
Say, "Your baby's had her dinner. I bet she's sleepy now."

Child pushes car, then stops it.
Say, "Is your car out of gas?"

Child puts plates on table.
Say, "I'm hungry. May I have a hamburger?"

Make direct suggestions.

Examples:

Pick up round, red paper scrap.
Say, "This can be our pizza, OK?"

Put rectangular block (size of a stick of butter) on the table.
Say, "Let's pretend this is our butter."

Model symbolic-play behaviors.

Examples:

Put undressed doll in box, rub square block on a piece of fabric, and pretend to bathe the doll.

Hop toy person to toy car, put it in, and say in a low voice, "I'm going shopping. See you later."

FIGURE 2–10 Techniques for promoting symbolic play through caregiver-child interaction *(From Gowen, J., 1995, Young Children, 50(3), 75–84. Reprinted with permission from NAEYC.)*

The following describes some of White's identified mother behaviors:

> Mothers talk a great deal to their children, and usually at a level the child can handle. They make them feel as though whatever they are doing is usually interesting. They provide access to many objects and diverse situations. They lead the child to believe that he can expect help and encouragement most, but not all of the time. They demonstrate and explain things to the child, but mostly on the child's instigation rather than their own. They are imaginative, so that they make interesting associations and suggestions to the child when opportunities present themselves. They very skillfully and naturally strengthen the child's intrinsic motivation to learn.

Pflaum (1986), another well-known educator, suggests home language experiences that contribute to language emergence:

> The language environment many children experience is one that contains language games during feeding and other caregiving episodes; parental understanding of correct functioning; parental acceptance of utterances; probes to elicit more talk; special baby talk to attract attention and to engage them in talk; parents recast statements to clarify language concepts and offer routines through which to practice. These are the characteristics of the setting in which children learn the vocabulary, syntax (order and structure of word combinations), sounds, and meanings of language.

Recognizing Differences in Language Growth

Early childhood teachers are better able to identify talented, normal (average), and delayed speakers at about 18 months of age (White, 1987). What causes diversity is too complex to mention here, but some factors can be inferred, and others have been previously mentioned. Mothers' and caregivers' responses to children's verbalness toward the end of the children's first year and into the second year can be a determining factor:

> Sooner or later . . . caregivers become aware of [the] child's emerging capacity of language acquisition. Some choose to feed the growth of language by going out of their way to talk a great deal to their children. Some provide language input effectively by careful selection of suitable words and phrases and by exploiting the child's interest of the moment. Others provide a great deal of input but with considerably less skill and effectiveness. Other[s] . . . show minimal attention to the language interest of . . . children or for other reasons provide negligible amounts of language input. (White, 1987)

Introducing Toddlers to Books

Toddlers show an interest in simple, colorful books and pictures and enjoy adult closeness and attention (figure 2–11). Pointing and naming can become an enjoyable game. Sturdy pages that are easily turned help the toddler. A scrapbook of favorite objects mounted on cardboard individualizes the experience. Clear contact paper and lamination will add life and protection.

Board books (usually stiff, coated, heavy cardboard) for toddlers allow both exploratory play and may offer colorful, close-up photographs or illustrations of familiar, everyday objects. These books promote the child's naming of pictures and active participation at book reading times. They are both fiction and nonfiction and the best are simple, direct, inviting, and realistic (Vardell, 1994). With durable, glossy, wipe-clean page coating and smaller-than-average picture book size, small and sometimes sticky hands can explore but rarely tear covers or pages.

Since a toddler may move on quickly to investigating other aspects of the environment, adults offering initial experiences with books need

FIGURE 2–11 Brightly illustrated books read with a parent will become favorite memories of young children.

to remember that when interest has waned, it's time to respect the search for other adventures.

NAEYC (Bredekamp, 1997) suggests that "adults frequently read to toddlers, individually on laps or in groups of two or three. Adults sing with toddlers, do finger plays, act out simple stories like 'The Three Bears' with children participating actively, or tell stories using a flannelboard or magnetic board, and allow children to manipulate and place figures on the boards."

Desirable features of toddler-appropriate books often include simple uncomplicated storylines, colorful, uncrowded illustrations or photographs, opportunities for the toddler to point and name familiar objects, predictive books (ones allowing the child to guess or predict successfully), strong, short rhymes or repetitive rhythms. "Touch and feel" books are particularly enjoyed; and sturdy, heavy board pages that can be mouthed but not torn are practical. Novelty books that make noise or pop-up books and books with sturdy moving parts capture a toddler's attention. Weiser (1982) lists "reading-related objects" that can be provided for the exploring toddler:

- Catalogs and magazines to look at, touch, finger, mouth, and otherwise investigate.
- Cloth books.
- First books, homemade or center-made on cardboard pages, protected by transparent stick-on coverings.
- Photographs or books containing photographs of people and objects in the toddler's life. (Include photos of the toddler.)
- Homemade sensory books that call for touching or smelling and that use safe materials.

Techniques for reading books to toddlers are very similar to those used in late infancy. Cozy, undisturbed settings with adults watchful of child interest and disinterest are still important. Label and point to pictures of objects, and expand on the picture a little with whatever comes to mind. If a picture of a cow is encountered, the adult might say, "Cow. The cow says 'Moo moo!'" Toddlers enjoy hearing appropriate sound effects. (Parents As Teachers, 1986). Schickedanz (1986) suggests the following adult techniques and sequence:

1. Get the child's attention.
2. Ask a labeling question.
3. Wait for the child to answer, or if necessary, provide the answer yourself.
4. Provide feedback. (Nino & Bruner, 1978)

Other book reading techniques are identified by Sherwin (1987):

Sharing books together can be one of the most satisfying experiences you can have with a young child. You don't have to stick to the text or read every word, instead, involve the child in the book by asking questions about the pictures. Your toddler might also enjoy simply turning the book's pages. Knowing when to read is important. It's true that introducing books early can lay the foundation for a lifelong love of books and reading. But pressuring or cajoling a resistant [one]-year-old to sit still and listen can have the opposite effect.

Now is the time to also share the strong rhyming rhythms of Mother Goose and introduce two classics, "Mary Had a Little Lamb" and "Pop Goes the Weasel."

Additional recommended toddler books follow:

Ahlberg, J., & Ahlberg, A. (1983). *The baby's catalogue*. Boston, MA: Little, Brown. Features objects in a toddler's environment.

Barton, B. (1986). *Trucks*. New York: Crowell. Vivid color, and objects that move.

Blegvad, L. (1986). *This is me*. New York: Random. (Board book)

Blonder, E. (1988). *My very first things*. New York: Gossett. (Board book)

Brown, M. (1985). *Hand rhymes*. New York: E. P. Dutton.

Chorao, K. (1984). *The baby's story book*. New York: E. P. Dutton.

Cousins, L. (1991). *Farm animals*. New York: Tambourine.

Davenport, Z. (1995). *Mealtime*. New York: Ticknor & Fields. Large colorful food and food-related illustrations.

Davenport, Z. (1995). *Toys*. New York: Ticknor & Fields. Common toys and objects for identification.

Dyer, J. (1996). *Animal crackers*. New York: Little, Brown. A delectable collection of pictures, poems, and lullabies for the very young.

Gomi, T. (1991). *Guess who?* San Francisco: Chronicle.

Gretz, S. (1986). *Hide and seek*. New York: Four Winds Press.

Hill, E. (1987). *Spot goes to the farm*. New York: Putnam.

Hoban, T. (1985). *One, two, three*. New York: Greenwillow.

Hoban, T. (1985). *What is it?* New York: Greenwillow.

Kunhardt, D. (1942). *Pat the bunny*. New York: Golden Touch and Feel Books.

Lynn, S. (1987). *Farm animals*. New York: Macmillan.

McCue, L. (1987). *Ten little puppy dogs*. New York: Random. (Board book)

Oxenbury, H. (1988). *Tickle, tickle*. New York: Macmillan.

Pearson, S. (1987). *The baby and the bear*. New York: Viking.

Pragoff, F. (1987). *Alphabet*. New York: Doubleday.

Prelutsky, J. (Ed.). (1988). *Read-aloud rhymes for the very young*. New York: Alfred Knopf Publishers.

Price, M., & Claverie, J. (1987). *Easy objects*. New York: Tuffy Books Inc.

Price, M., & Claverie, J. (1987). *Show and tell me*. New York: Tuffy Books Inc.

Price, M., & Claverie, J. (1987). *Simple objects*. New York: Tuffy Books Inc.

Price, M., & Claverie, J. (1988). *Happy birthday*. New York: Alfred Knopf Publishers.

Shevitt, A., & Shevitt, S. (1986). *Baby's ABC*. New York: Random. (Board book)

Siler, D. (1985). *What do babies do?* New York: Random.

Tafuri, N. (1987). *Where we sleep*. New York: Greenwillow.

Time for a rhyme. (1993). Newmarket, England: Brimax Books, Ltd. A charmingly illustrated board book featuring classic, short rhymes.

Twinkle, twinkle. (1994). Newmarket, England: Brimax Books, Ltd. Short classic rhymes. (Board book)

A number of novelty books available today "talk" or make environmental or animal noises. Pressing a picture, button, or symbol causes the book to emit a prerecorded sound or short sentence, which captures the child's attention.

What can toddlers begin to understand during the reading of picture books? Besides knowing that photographs and illustrations are between the covers of books, the toddler gathers ideas about book pleasure. As the child touches pictured objects, the child may grasp the idea that the objects depicted are representations of familiar objects.

The toddler can notice that books are not handled as toys.

Holdaway (1979) describes the very young child's reading-like behaviors:

> By far the most surprising and significant aspect of preschool book-experience, however, is the independent activity of these very young children with their favorite books. Almost as soon as the infant becomes familiarized with particular books through repetitive readings, he begins to play with them in reading-like ways. Attracted by the familiar object with which he has such positive associations, the infant picks it up, opens it, and begins attempting to retrieve for himself some of the language and its intonations. Almost unintelligible at first, this reading-like play rapidly becomes picture stimulated, page-matched, and story complete.

Near two years of age, the toddler probably still names what's pictured but may understand stories. The toddler may grasp the idea that book characters and events are make believe. If a particular book is reread to a child, the child can know that the particular stories in books don't change, and what's to be read is predictable. Sometimes the toddler finds that he or she can participate in the telling by singing, repeating character lines, and making physical motions to represent actions; for example, "knocking on the door."

Beginning Literacy

During toddlerhood, some children gain general knowledge of books and awareness of print. This is viewed as a natural process, which takes place in a literate home or early learning environment (Anbar, 1986). Toddlers learn through imitation, by reacting and constructing their own ideas, and by internalizing social action as an apprentice to others (loved ones, early childhood educators, and so on). Immersing toddlers in language activities facilitates their literacy development. It is possible to establish a positive early bonding between children and book-sharing times—a first step toward literacy. Some toddlers who show no interest in books will, when exposed to books at a later time, find them as interesting as other children. In our get-ahead society, even toddler centers are pressured to provide sit-down instruction. Parents need to understand that a literary interest can be piqued throughout early childhood. The fact that a toddler may not be particularly enamored with books or book-sharing times at a particular stage is not a matter of concern. It may be simply a matter of the child's natural, individual activity level and his or her ability to sit and stay focused in an environment that holds an abundance of features to explore.

Toys

Certain types of toys have a strong connection to toddlers' emerging language development. Musical toys, dolls and stuffed animals that make noises or talk, and alphabet toys, including magnetic alphabet letters, can be described as language-promoting toys. Noise-making toys or recordings, both audio and visual, capture the toddler's attention. Videos for toddlers are becoming increasingly available. Songs and music are also enjoyed by toddlers and offer another language-inputting opportunity; but some educators are concerned about the quantity, quality, and subject matter of audio-visuals that possibly may be replacing adult-child language interaction.

Advice to Parents of Toddlers

Verbally responsive and playful people, and a "toddler-proof" home equipped with objects and toys the toddler can investigate, are positive factors in increasing emerging toddler language. Objects and toys need not be expensive and can be designed and created at home. Social contact outside the home is important also. Toddlers enjoy branching out from the home on excursions with caring adults. Local libraries may offer toddler story hours, and play groups are increasingly popular and sponsored by a wide number of community groups. Exposing the toddler to supervised toddler play groups gives the child "peer teachers" and promotes social skill. Typically toddlers play side-by-side rather than cooperatively, but beginning attempts at sharing and short give-and-take interactions take place.

Sitting on the floor at times or on a low chair helps adults both send and receive. At this age, toddlers can drive people crazy asking for the names of things and can be insistent and impatient about demands. Words will be learned during real events with concrete (real) objects.

Regularly involving toddlers in educative conversations with educational toys and simple books prompts language growth. Patience and interest—rather than heavy-handed attempts to teach—are best. Getting the most from everyday experiences is a real art that requires an instructive yet relaxed attitude and the ability to talk about what has captured the child's attention. A skilled adult who is with a toddler who is focused on the wrapping paper rather than the birthday present will add comments about the wrapping paper. Or at the zoo, in front of the bear's cage, if the child is staring at a nearby puddle, the adult will discuss the puddle. Providing words and ideas along the child's line of thinking, and having fun while doing so, becomes second nature after a few attempts.

Skilled adults tend to modify their speech according to the child's ability but also add to sentence length and complexity, providing that which is just a little beyond the child's level. Parent talk that sensitively and effectively suggests and instructs primes the child's language growth.

Parent and teacher resource books that contain a number of adult-child interactive games follow:

Silberg, J. (1993). *Games to play with two year olds.* Bettsville, MD: Gryphon House.
Silberg, J. (1996). *More games to play with toddlers.* Bettsville, MD: Gryphon House.

Summary

Language ability grows at its fastest rate of development during the toddler period. Young children accomplish difficult language tasks. They learn their native language sounds (phonetics) and successfully produce an increasing number of sounds. Grammar rules form and reform as the child gets closer to reproducing mature speech patterns. The child listens more carefully, noticing regularities and meanings (semantics) of words and gestures.

Concepts develop, serving as categories that help the child organize life's events. Many concepts are paired with words. Word symbols aid communication and language by allowing the child to speak and to be understood. Parents' conversations and the child's first-hand exploration through sense organs give depth to new words.

Toddlers are active in conversations, speaking and listening, sometimes correcting, trying to get the message across to whoever in the family will listen. Toddlers talk to themselves and their toys in one- and then two- (or more) word sentences. These sentences are barely recognizable at first but gain more and more clarity as children age.

Differences between children's speech output may be noticed, and responsive, sensitive adults are language-promoting companions. Toddler books are enjoyed and plentiful.

STUDENT ACTIVITIES

1. Make a book for toddlers from magazine illustrations or from photographs of common objects familiar to toddlers. Pages should be sturdy. Cut away any distracting backgrounds. If desired, outline objects with a wide tip felt pen and protect pages with clear adhesive plastic or slip into page protectors. (An old binder works well to hold the pages.) Test your book on toddlers, and share your results.

2. Form a group of three fellow students. Using the following three statements, explore changing word stress, rhythm, and pitch. Analyze the changed meanings.
   a. What am I doing?
   b. It was his book.
   c. You're a fine person.

3. Try this activity with a toddler (18 to 24 months). Gather a number of different large gloves. Sit in front of the toddler facing her. Greet the toddler using her name. Put a box of gloves between you and open it and put on one glove saying, "The glove (mitten) is *on* my hand. Take it off, saying while putting it back in the box, "The glove is *in* the box." Look expectantly at the child, then down at the box. Say, "(Child's name)." Wait at least a minute. Report back to class at next meeting, including what you said and did during the rest of the glove game activity. Note how long the child's attention was captured.

4. Using only gestures, get the person sitting next to you to give you a tissue or handkerchief or to tell you that one is not available.

5. Observe three toddlers (15 to 24 months old). Write down consonant sounds you hear. Record the number of minutes for each observation.

6. Using the following scale, rate each of the following statements.

1	2	3	4	5
Strongly Agree	Agree	Can't Decide	Mildly Disagree	Strongly Disagree

   a. Toddlers can be best understood when adults analyze their words instead of their meanings.
   b. Some parents seem to have a knack for talking to young children that they probably don't realize they possess.
   c. The labeling stage is a time when children learn concepts rather than words.
   d. Learning language is really simple imitation.
   e. The study of semantics could take a lifetime.
   f. A toddler who doesn't like books isn't progressing properly.
   g. After reading this unit, I won't react to toddler grunts.
   h. Parents whose toddlers are speaking many words have purposely taught words to their children.
   i. It's a good idea to have a special place in the home where books are enjoyed with a toddler.
   j. It's best to give the toddler specific words for things, like pick-ups instead of trucks, or bonnet instead of hat.

   Talk about your ratings in a group discussion.

7. On a piece of paper, list as many toddler language milestones or accomplishments as you can remember.

8. Read the following:

   Mothers interested in developing their child's signing ability start slowly. Their goal is not to teach a complex signing system but to enrich their communicative relationship. Lapinski (1996) describes a mother's teaching technique as follows:

   > One of the best ways to teach your baby a new sign is to find as many concrete examples of it as you can. If you're trying to teach your child the sign for "cat," for example, keep your eyes open for kitties everywhere—in books, on TV, and in toy store displays as well as on neighborhood window sills. Point to these various felines as you say the word "cat" and follow up with the kitty sign—stroking the back of your hand with your other palm. Then ensure that the gesture "sticks" in your baby's memory by helping him make the sign with his own hands.

   With a classmate make a short list of common objects a toddler might encounter. Develop hand signs. Share with the class.

9. In a small group list nursery songs appropriate for toddlers.

CHAPTER REVIEW

A. Match each word in Column I with the phrase it relates to in Column II.

Column I	Column II
1. jargon	a. "Allgone cookie." "Shoe allgone."
2. phonology	b. toddler goes through a naming or labeling stage
3. grammar	c. toddler unconsciously recognizes word order
4. dis? dat?	d. though they are limited in number, many serve a double purpose
5. pivot	e. each world language has its own
6. alphabet	f. "Ibbed googa oodle."
7. symbol	g. a word represents something

B. Write a brief description of experiences that could promote a toddler's learning the word "hat." (Example: Parent points to a picture of a hat in a book, and says "hat.")

C. List five identifying characteristics of the following concepts:

van, rain, needle, giraffe

D. Return to Review Question B. How many of your examples involved the child's sensory exploration of a hat? Why would this aid the child's learning?

E. Why is the toddler period called the prime or critical time for learning language?

F. Write definitions for the following words. Check your definitions with the ones found in the Glossary at the end of the text.

syntax   phonetic   modifier   phoneme   morpheme

G. Select the best answer.

1. Most children clearly articulate all English letter sounds by age
   a. 7 or 8.
   b. 6.
   c. 5.
   d. 24 months.

2. Most concept words used correctly by toddlers are
   a. labels and imitative echoing.
   b. fully understood.
   c. used because identifying characteristics have been noticed.
   d. rarely overused.

3. From beginning attempts, children
   a. reverse word order.
   b. use full simple sentences.

    c. use stress, intonation, and inflection in speaking.

    d. are always clearly understood.

4. One should _____ insist that the toddler pronounce "tree" correctly if he or she is saying "twee."

    a. always   c. never

    b. usually   d. tactfully

5. A toddler's one word sentence, "Wawa," may mean:

    a. "I want a drink of water."

    b. The child's dog, Waiter, is present.

    c. The child's father's name is Walter.

    d. Any one or none of the above.

H. What parent behaviors are helpful in the toddler's acquisition of language?

I. Describe the characteristics of mother-to-toddler, child-directed, or special-language speaking.

CHAPTER 3

Preschool Years

OBJECTIVES

After studying this chapter, you should be able to:

- identify characteristics of typical preschool speech.

- describe differences in the language of younger and older preschoolers.

- discuss the preschooler's growth of language skill.

The preschool child's speech reflects sensory, physical, and social experiences, as well as thinking ability. Parents and teachers accept temporary limitations, knowing that almost all children will reach adult language levels.

During the preschool years, children move rapidly through successive phases of language learning. It is generally agreed that by the time youngsters reach their fifth year, the most challenging hurdles of language learning have been overcome (Geller, 1985).

Teachers should interact with the children and provide growing opportunities and activities. An understanding of typical preschool speech characteristics can help the teacher do this.

Background experiences with children and child study give a teacher insight into children's language behavior. The beginnings of language, early steps, and factors affecting the infant and toddler's self-expression were covered in Chapters 1 and 2. This chapter pinpoints language use during preschool years. Although speech abilities are emphasized, growth and change in other areas are also covered as they relate to speech.

In addition to the child's home environment, playing with other children is a major factor influencing language development. Finding friends in the child's age group is an important part of attending an early childhood center. In a place where there are fascinating things to explore and talk about, language abilities blossom (figure 3–1).

It is almost impossible to find a child who has all of the speech characteristics of a given age group, but most children possess some of the characteristics that are typical for their age level. There is a wide range within normal age-level behavior, and

FIGURE 3–1 "I bet I can catch the bubbles first!"

each child's individuality is an important consideration.

For simplicity's sake, the preschool period is divided into two age groups: early preschoolers (two- to three-year-olds) and older preschoolers (four- to five-year-olds).

Young Preschoolers

Preschoolers communicate needs, desires, and feelings through speech and action. Close observation of a child's nonverbal communication can help uncover true meanings. A raised arm, fierce clutching of playthings, or lying spread-eagle over as many blocks as possible may express more than the child is able to put into words. Stroking a friend's arm, handing a toy to another child who hasn't asked for it but looks at it longingly, and following the teacher around the room, carry other meanings.

One can expect continued fast growth and changing language abilities, and children's understanding of adult statements is surprising. Garvey (1984) discusses the child's third year:

> Talk assumes ever-increasing importance in the child's life from the first verbal exchanges with caregivers, which begin to appear before the second birthday, through the preschool period. With the beginning of formal education, new people and new experience create the need for other uses of talk. Perhaps the most dramatic changes and the most impressive achievements occur during the third year of life.

Squeals, grunts, and screams are often part of play (figure 3–2). Imitating animals, sirens, and environmental noise is common. The child points and pulls to help others understand meanings. Younger preschoolers tend to act as though others can read their thoughts because, in the past, adults anticipated what was needed. A few children may have what seems to be a limited vocabulary at school until they feel at home there.

FIGURE 3–2   Giggles and laughter are abundant during preschool years.

The words used most often are nouns and short possessives: my, mine, Rick's. Speech focuses on present events, things are observed in newscaster style, and "no" is used liberally. As preschoolers progress in the ability to hold brief conversations, they must keep conversational topics in mind and connect their thoughts with those of others. This is difficult for two-year-olds, and true conversational exchange with playmates is brief if it exists at all. Although their speech is filled with pauses and repetitions in which they attempt to correct themselves, preschoolers are adept at conversational turn taking. Garvey (1984) estimates that talking over the speech of another speaker at this age occurs only about 5% of the time.

Speech may be loud and high-pitched when the child is excited, or barely audible and muffled when the child is embarrassed, sad, or shy. Speech of two- and three-year-olds tends to be uneven in rhythm, with comments issued in spurts rather than in an even flow like the speech of older children.

There seems to be an important step forward in the complexity of content in children's speech at age two. They may begin making comments about cause and effect and sometimes use conjunctions, such as 'cause, 'ah, and 'um, between statements. Pines (1983) describes conversational topics identified in a New York research project that monitored two-year-olds' speech:

The children talked mostly about their own intentions and feeling, why they wanted or did not want to do certain things, or what they wanted other people to do.

Curry and Johnson (1990) point out:

Two-year-olds ... go through a stage of commenting on their own actions. "I'm painting." "I'm climbing on the steps!"

Much of the time very young preschoolers' play focuses upon recreating the work of the home—cooking, eating, sleeping, washing, ironing, infant care, and imitations of family events and pets. Play of slightly older preschoolers is more interactive. The child continues self-play but also explores other children, adults, environments, and actions. At that point, "what's happening" in play becomes a speech subject along with brief verbal reactions to what others are saying and doing.

A desire to organize and make sense out of their experiences is often apparent. Colors, counting, and new categories of thought emerge in their speech. There is a tendency for them to live out the action words they speak or hear in the speech of others. An adult who says "We won't run" may motivate a child to run; in contrast, an adult who says "Walk" might be more successful in having the child walk.

The Subdued Two-Year-Old

About 10% of any given group of young children may appear subdued and quiet, having a tendency toward what many might call shyness (Kagan, 1988). These children may possess a natural inclination that tends to inhibit spontaneous speech. Researchers have monitored bodily functions of a group of children identified as "shy" and found muscle tensions, including tensions in the larynx. This possibly may account for the low volume of their speech. Most preschool teachers have worked with children whose speech was difficult to hear. Often, these children seem restrained when faced with unfamiliar situations. Older preschoolers may become more outgoing and talkative or may continue to be less talkative and somewhat subdued when compared with their more boisterous counterparts. Teachers respect these children's natural inclinations and tendencies.

Verb Forms

In English, most verbs (regular forms) use -ed to indicate past tense. Unfortunately, many frequently used verbs are irregular, with past-tense forms like came, fell, hit, saw, took, and gave. Since the child begins using often-heard words, early speech contains correct verb forms. With additional exposure to language, the child realizes that past events are described with -ed verb endings. At that point, children tack the -ed on regular verbs as well as on irregular verbs, creating words such as broked, dranked, and other charming past-tense forms. This beautiful logic often brings inner smiles to the adult listeners. Verbs ending with "ing" are used more than before. Even auxiliary verbs are scattered through speech—"Me have," "Daddy did it" (Pflaum, 1986). Words such as wanna, gonna, and hafta seem to be learned as one word, and stick in the child's vocabulary, being used over and over.

A term for children's speech behavior that indicates they've formed a new internal rule about language and are using it is **regularization**. As children filter what they hear, creating their own rule systems, they begin to apply the new rule(s). An expected sequence in formed rules for past-tense verb usage follows:

- Uses irregular tense endings correctly (e.g., ran, came, drank).
- Forms an internal rule when discovering that -ed expresses past events (e.g., danced, called, played).
- Overregularizes. Adds -ed to all regular and irregular verbs that were formerly spoken correctly (e.g., camed, dided, wented, breaked).

Regularization — a child's speech behavior that indicates the formation and internalization of a language rule (regularity).

- Learns that both regular and irregular verbs express past tense, and uses both.

In using plural noun forms, the following sequence is common:

- Remembers and uses singular forms of nouns correctly (e.g., ball, dog, mouse, bird).
- Uses irregular noun plurals correctly (e.g., men, feet, mice).
- Forms an internal rule that plurals have "s" or "z" ending sounds.
- Applies rule to all nouns (e.g., balls, mens, dogs, feets, birds, mices, or ballsez, dogsez, feetsez).
- Achieves flexible internal rules for plurals, memorizes irregular plural forms, and uses plurals correctly.

Key-Word Sentences

The two-year-old omits many words in sentences, as does the toddler. The remaining words are shortened versions of adult sentences in which only the essentials are present. These words are key words and convey the essence of the message. Without relating utterances to real occurrences, meaning might be lost to the listener. Sentences at this stage are about four words long. Some pronouns and adjectives, such as pretty or big, are used. Very few, if any, prepositions (by, on, with) or articles (a, an, the) are spoken frequently. Some words are run together and are spoken as single units, such as "whadat?" or "eatem," as are the verb forms mentioned earlier. The order of words (syntax) may seem jumbled at times, as in "outside going ball," but basic grammar rules are observed in most cases.

Pronouns are often used incorrectly and are confused, as in "Me all finish milk," and "him Mark's." Concepts of male and female, living things, and objects may be only partly understood, as shown in the following example:

> And when a three-year-old says of the ring she cannot find, "Maybe it's hiding!" the listener wonders if she hasn't yet learned that hiding can be done only by an animate object. (Cazden, 1972)

Questions

Wh- questions (where, what, why, who) begin to appear in speech. During the toddler period, rising voice inflection and simple declarative utterances such as "Dolly drink?" are typical. At this stage, questions focus on location, objects, and people, with causation (why), process (how), and time (when). This reflects more mature thinking that probes purposes and intentions in others. Figure 3–3 shows one child's questioning development. Questions are frequent, and the child sometimes asks for an object's function or the causes of certain events. It is as if the child sees that things exist for a purpose that in some way relates to him or her. The answers adults provide stimulate the child's desire to know more.

Vocabularies range between 250 to over 1,000 words (figure 3–4). An average of 50 new words enter the child's vocabulary each month.

Overlapping Concepts and Underextension

Younger preschoolers commonly call all four-footed furry animals "dog," and all large animals "horse." The child has *overextended* and made a logical conclusion because these animals have many of the same features, can be about the same size, and therefore fit the existing word. This phenomenon is seen in the examples given in figure 3–5.

Underextension refers to the child's tendency to call all male adults "daddy" or all dogs by the family dog's name, even though the child can clearly recognize the difference between his or her dad and all other males and his or her dog and other dogs.

Concept development, defined in Chapter 2 as the recognition of one or more distinguishing features or characteristics, proceeds by leaps and bounds during preschool years and is essential to meaningful communication. Details, exceptions, and discrepancies are often discussed in four-year-olds' conversations. The younger preschooler can be described as a "looker and doer" who engages in limited discussion of the features of situations. The excitement of exploration and discovery, particu-

1 CHILD: AGES	YES-NO QUESTIONS	WH- QUESTIONS
Period A (28 mo.)	Expressed by intonation only: Sit chair? Ball go?	Limited number of routines: What('s) that? Where NP* go? What NP doing?
Period B (38 mo.)	Dat black too? Mom pinch finger? You can't fix it?	What soldier marching? Where my mitten? Why you waking me up?
	More complex sentences being questioned, but no development of question forms themselves, except the appearances, probably as routines, of two negative auxiliaries *don't* and *can't*.	
	Are you going to make it with me? Will you help me? Does the kitty stand up? Can I have a piece of paper?	What I did yesterday? Which way they should go? Why the Christmas Tree? How he can be a doctor?
	Development of auxiliary verbs in the child's entire grammatical system. Inversion of aux. and subject NP in Yes-No, but not in Wh- questions.	
Period C–F (42–54 mo.)	Development of tag questions from *Huh?* to mature form: I have two turn, huh? We're playing, huh? That's funny isn't it? He was scared wasn't he? Mommy, when we saw those girls they were running weren't they?	Inversion of aux. and subject NP, first in affirmative questions only: Why are you thirsty? Why can't we find the right one?
		Later, starting in Period F, negative question also: Why can't they put on their diving suits and swim?
		Development of complex questions, including indirect Wh- questions: You don't know where you're going. He doesn't know what to do. We don't know who that is.

*NP signifies noun or pronoun substitute.

FIGURE 3-3 Development of question forms (*From Child Language and Education, by C. B. Cazden. Copyright 1972 by Holt, Rinehart, and Winston, CBS College Publishing.*)

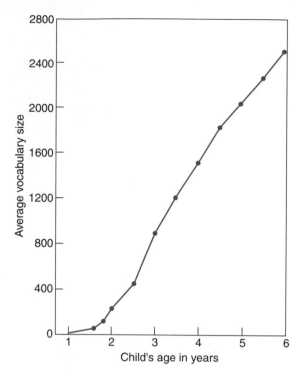

FIGURE 3–4 Growth of vocabulary

larly of something new and novel is readily apparent in preschool classrooms. Children typically crowd around to see, touch, experience, and make comments about objects and events. Teachers notice the all-consuming focusing, the long periods of watching or touching, usually followed by verbalizing and questioning an event or experience.

Running Commentaries

As children play, their actions are sometimes accompanied by running self-commentaries of what they are doing, or what is happening (figure 3–6). It can be described as a kind of verbal thought process, like mentally talking to oneself. It seems to increase in complex play situations as the child problem solves and talks it through.

Brophy (1977) offers reasons for private speech:

Children talk to themselves to give themselves directions for the same reason that they use their fingers in counting; they need sensorimotor activity as a reinforcement or "crutch" because their cognitive schemes

Word	Object or Event for Which the Word Was Originally Used	Other Objects or Events to Which the Word Was Later Applied
mooi	moon	cakes, round marks on windows, writing on windows and in books, round shapes in books, tooling on leather book covers, round postmarks, letter *O*
buti	ball	toy, radish, stone spheres at park entrance
sch	sound of train	all moving machines
em	worm	flies, ants, all small insects, heads of timothy grass
fafer	sound of trains	steaming coffee pot, anything that hissed or made a noise
va	white plush dog	muffler, cat, father's fur coat

FIGURE 3–5 Some examples of overextensions in the language of 1- and 2-year-old children
(From "Knowledge, context, and strategy in the acquisition of meaning," by E. V. Clark. In Gurt, 1975: Daniel P. Dato, ed., Developmental psycholinguistics: Theory and applications. *Copyright 1975 by Georgetown University, Washington, DC.)*

Situation:	Girls playing with water. (four- and five-year-olds)	
	Commentary	**Characteristic**
Debbie:	"Two of those make one of these." (playing with measuring cups)	Talking to self.
Debbie:	"Two cups or three cups . . . whoops it went over."	Talks about what happened.
Tifine:	"Stop it or else I'll beat you up." (said to Debbie)	Doesn't respond to another's speech.
Debbie:	"This is heavy." (holding the 2-cup measuring container full of water)	Describes perception.
Christine:	"Is it hot?" (Christine just dropped in)	
Debbie:	"Feel it and see." "It's not hot." (feeling the water)	Hears another; answers appropriately. Child talking to self.
Debbie:	"I'm finished now. Oh this is awfully heavy—I'm going to pour it into the bottle."	Talking about what she perceives and what she is doing.

FIGURE 3–6   Conversation during play activity

are not yet developed well enough to allow them to think silently.

According to Vygotsky (1978), self-talk may help children sequence actions, control their own behavior, use flexible modes of thinking, and manipulate the goals they are trying to achieve in their play.

Talking to self and talking to another can occur alternately. Toys, animals, and treasured items still receive a few words. Statements directed to others do not usually need answers. Private speech rarely considers another's point of view. A conversation between young preschoolers may sound like two children talking together about different subjects. Neither child is really listening or reacting to what the other says. When a very young preschooler does wish to talk directly to another child, it is sometimes done through an adult. A child may say, "I want truck," to an adult, even if the other child is standing close by, playing with the truck.

Researchers who have examined self-talk suggest a number of possible developmental reasons and benefits. These include:

- Practicing newly recognized language forms.
- Obtaining pleasure through play with word sounds.
- Exploring vocal capacities.

- Reliving particular significant events.
- Creating dialogue in which the child voices all people's parts, perhaps helping the child later fit into social settings.
- Experimenting with fantasy, thereby accommodating the creative urge.
- Attending objectively to language.
- Facilitating motor behavior in a task or project.

Whatever its benefits, self-talk is natural, common behavior. By the age of five, the child's self-talk is observed infrequently. As children approach the age of three, both dialogue and monologue is apparent. Observers of play conversations find it difficult to determine just how much of each is present.

Repetition

Repetition in speech occurs often. Sometimes it happens randomly at play, and at other times it is done with a special purpose. A young child may repeat almost everything said to him or her. Most young preschoolers repeat words or parts of sentences regularly. Honig (1988) suggests that children's growing language skills allow them to create repetitions that rhyme, as in "oogie, woogie, poogie bear," which greatly please them. They quickly imitate words that they like; sometimes, excitement is the cause. Chukovsky (1963) points out that rhyming words or rhyming syllables may promote enjoyable mimicking and that the younger the child, the greater the child's attraction to word repetition that rhymes. Some reasons for repetition are (1) it helps children remember things (just as adults mentally repeat new telephone numbers), (2) it reduces stress, and (3) it is an enjoyable form of sound making.

Free associations (voiced juggling of sounds and words) occur at play and at rest and may sound like babbling. Many times, it seems as though, having learned a word, the child must savor it or practice it, over and over.

Lack of Clarity

About one in every four words of the young preschooler is not readily understandable. This lack of clarity is partially caused by an inability to control mouth, tongue, and breathing and to hear subtle differences and distinctions in speech. Typically, articulation of all English speech sounds is not accomplished until age seven or eight (figure 3–7). Young preschoolers are only 40% to 80% correct in articulation. This lack of intelligibility in children can be partly attributed to the complexity of the task of mastering the sounds. Although children may be right on target in development, their speech may still be hard to understand at times.

The young preschooler may have difficulty with the rate of speech, phrasing, inflection, inten-

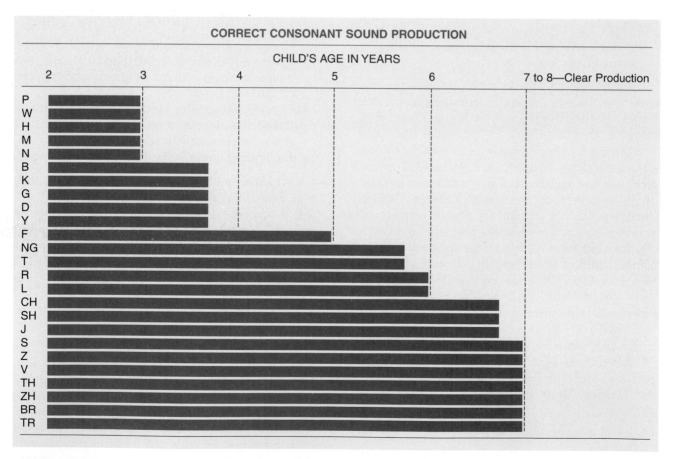

FIGURE 3–7   Correct consonant sound production

sity, syntax, and voice stress. Misarticulation and defective sound making can also contribute to the problem. The child who attempts to form the longest utterances is the one who is hardest to understand. The child who omits sounds is less clear than the one who distorts them. As a rule, expect omissions, substitutions, and distortions in the speech of two- and three-year-olds, for they will be plentiful.

Young children typically omit sounds at the ends of words, saying, for example, "ba" for ball. Middle consonants in longer words are also passed over lightly—"ikeem" for ice cream, or "telfone" for telephone. Even beginning sounds may be omitted, as in "ellow" for yellow.

Substitutions of letter sounds are also common, for example, "aminal," and "pasghetti." Until the new sound is mastered, one consonant may even take the place of another; "wabbit," "wun," and "wain" are frequently heard examples. Children who cannot yet produce all of the speech sounds accurately can generally hear the differences between *w* and *r*, or *t* and *th* when they are pronounced by others (Saville-Troike, 1980).

FIGURE 3–8 Children often imitate family members during dramatic play activities.

Dramatic Play

Short play sequences that involve acting or imitating the behavior of mom or dad begin at home and school (figure 3–8). Speech usually accompanies the reenactments. Although young children at this age play side-by-side, most of this type of play starts as solitary activity. Common play themes mentioned by Caplan and Caplan (1983) include mom on the phone, mom caring for baby, mom or dad cooking (figure 3–9). Dolls, toys, and dress-up clothes are usually part of the action and may serve to initiate this type of play. Observers of two- and three-year-olds in classrooms find it hard to determine whether children are engaged in joint planning of play or children are playing in the same area with the same kinds of playthings. Preschools purposely purchase multiple dolls so that many children can feed and rock "their babies" when they see others doing it.

FIGURE 3–9 "Here's baby's bottle!"

Advice for Parents and Early Childhood Staff Members

Parents sometimes worry about a child who stops, stammers, or stutters when speaking. Calling attention to this speech and making demands on the child cause tension, making the situation worse instead of better. All children hesitate, repeat, stop, and start in speaking—it is typical behavior. Searching for the right word takes time, and thoughts may come faster than words. Adults need to relax and wait. Speech is a complex sending and receiving process. Maintaining patience and optimism and assuming a casual "I'm listening" stance is the best course of action for the adult. Many schools routinely send home informational material to alert parents to age-level speech characteristics.

Cooper's (1993) conclusions about what teachers may feel about children's seemingly illogical speech statements coincide with what many teachers suspect. Child logic is there but teachers aren't privy to young children's inner thought processes and their past experiences. Cooper states:

> On the whole, I find that young children *intend* to be intelligible though sometimes they are unable to coordinate their words with their thoughts, which is a very different state of mind than egocentrism. If we could understand their mental references and associations, we could see that most often they are being quite logical.

Sometimes when working with the young child, the listening teachers will feel on the edge of understanding what the child is trying to say. This happens with both younger and older preschoolers struggling at times to put into words what they are thinking. Acceptance and interest are appropriate.

Attentive interaction with positive feedback is recommended for adults who live or work with two- and three-year-olds. Reacting to the intent of the child's message is more helpful than concentrating on correctness. In other words, focus on what is said rather than the way it is said. A lot of guessing is still necessary to determine what the child is trying to say. The adult's model of speech will override temporary errors as the child hears more and more of it.

Helping the children see details and relationships in what they encounter is useful if done in an unpressured manner. Connecting past events to present events may aid their understanding.

Regular checkups of children's hearing is recommended, because even a moderate hearing loss may affect speech production. Preschoolers are particularly prone to upper respiratory infections and ear problems.

As younger preschoolers get older, adults can expect the following:

- Longer sentences with more words per sentence.
- More specificity.
- More "ing" endings on verbs.
- Increased correctness in the forms of the verb "to be."
- More auxiliary verbs present.
- More facility with passive-voice verbs, including did and been.
- Changes in negative sentences, from "No want" to "I don't want."
- Changes in question forms, from "Car go?" to "Where did the car go?"

Books for Younger Preschoolers

A wide selection of picture books is available for this age group. Generally, experts suggest books that have:

- Themes, objects, animals, or people that are familiar and within their range of life experience.
- Clarity of content and story line.
- Clear, simple illustrations or photo-illustrations with backgrounds that don't distract from the intended focus.
- Themes concerning everyday tasks and basic human needs.

Most two- and three-year-olds enjoy actively participating in story reading, but they can be very good listeners as well. Participation can include pointing, noisemaking, repeating dialogue, or performing imitative body actions. Books that are repetitive and predictable offer the enjoyment of anticipating what will come next. For children who are used to being read to at bedtimes, the calming effect of listening to the human voice becomes very apparent at story-reading times. Chapter 9 covers the topic of introducing preschool children to literature.

Older Preschoolers

Between four and five years of age, most preschoolers approach adult-like speech; their sentences are longer, with almost all words present rather than only key words.

Preschoolers' play is active and vocal, and they copy each other's words and manner of speaking. A word such as "monster," or more colorful words, may swiftly gain interest and spread rapidly from child to child. Remember the joy that both younger and older children exhibited with the phrases: "zip-a-dee-doo-dah," "bibbidi-bobbidi-boo," "scoobi-scoobi-do," "blast off," "fuzzy-wuzzy," and "ooey-gooey"? Every generation of preschoolers seems to have its own favorite sayings, and new ones are constantly appearing.

Social speech and conversations of the older preschooler are heard and interpreted to a greater degree by others of the child's age. The child learns and practices the complexities of social conversation including (1) gaining another's attention by making eye contact, touching, or using words or catchphrases like "Know what?" (2) pausing and listening, (3) correcting himself or herself, (4) maintaining attention by not pausing so as not to let another speaker jump in, (5) taking turns in conversing by developing patience and trying to listen while still holding in mind what he or she wants to say.

Friendships

The young preschooler may develop a new friend or find another they prefer to play near or with. At ages two and three friendships are usually temporary, changing from day to day. Friendships of older preschoolers are more stable and lasting.

By ages four and five there seems to be a desire to remain compatible, work out differences, therefore creatively maintaining a type of play acceptable to both. Negotiation, clarification, and an open mindedness flourish during play. A friend's needs and requests are handled with sensitivity, and flexibility characterizes conversations. Needless to say, spats, "blow ups," and the crushed feelings accompanying rejection sometimes occur. Verbal interaction between children adds a tremendous amount of verbal input and also promotes output.

Group Play

Joint planning of play activities and active make-believe and role playing takes on a new depth. Adults often see themselves in the play of children. The four-year-old's main concern seems to be interacting with age mates. Twosomes and groups of play companions are typical in older preschoolers' classrooms and play yards (figure 3–10). As speech blossoms, friendships blossom and disintegrate. Speech is used to discourage and disallow entrance to play groups when running from newcomers is impossible. Speech is found to be effective in hurting feelings, as in statements such as "I don't like you," or "No girls." Children find

FIGURE 3–10 Preschoolers thrive on group play.

verbal inventiveness may help them join play or initiate play.

In group play, pretending is paramount. Make-believe play appears to be at its zenith (Caplan and Caplan, 1983). Many children grow in the ability to (1) verbally suggest new directions and avenues of fantasy, (2) engage in verbal negotiation, (3) compromise, (4) argue, and (5) become a group's leader by using the right words. Popular children seem to be those who use speech creatively and become enjoyable companions to others.

Violent statements like "I'm going to shoot you" or "cut you up" are sometimes heard, and these tend to reflect television news or drama. The reality-fantasy of some play situations may become temporarily blurred, causing some children considerable anxiety.

Older preschoolers talk "in character" as they elaborate their dramatic play. If a scenario calls for a mother talking to a baby or teenagers talking, preschoolers adopt appropriate speech. Imitations of pop singers or cartoon characters are common. Role-taking is an important skill in mature communication, indicating that social/dramatic play and improvisation are effective means of facilitating growth in communicative competence (Pinnell and Jaggar, 1992).

Four-year-olds seem to boast, brag, and make lots of noise. However, apparently boastful statements like "Look what I did" may just be the child's attempt to show that he or she is capable and to share his or her accomplishments. Although preschoolers enjoy being with their peers, they quickly and easily engage in quarreling and name-calling. Sometimes, they do battle verbally (Caplan and Caplan, 1983). Typically, three- to five-year-olds disagree over possession of objects or territory, and verbal reasons or verbal evidence may help them win arguments. Many conflicts are resolved and lead to continued play. Speech helps them settle their affairs with and without adult help.

As a child develops a sense of humor, giggling becomes part of the noise of play. As Caplan and Caplan (1983) observe, "there's a wonderful silliness." One preschool boy thought it hilarious to go up to a teacher named Alice and say "What's your name, Alice?" and then run off laughing—quite mature humor for a four-year-old! Honig (1988) cites instances in which preschoolers distort and repeat what a caregiver says, making changes in sounds and gleefully chanting the distorted message. She urges teachers who want to cultivate children's ability to understand and appreciate humor to present materials that challenge children's ability to interpret humor.

Arguing, persuading, and child statements aimed at controlling others are frequently heard during play. Older preschool children are able to state reasons, request information, give explanations, utter justifications for their behavior, and verbally defend themselves. At times, establishing authority in disagreements seems paramount to compromising.

Exploring the Conventions of Conversation

Children learn language by reinventing it for themselves, not by direct instruction. They crack the code through exposure and opportunities to converse. They actively, though unconsciously, ingest and discover the rules of the system. Their speech errors often alert adults to the inner rules of language being formed.

Conversations have unwritten rules and expectations, "You-talk-I-talk" sequence being the most apparent. Geller (1985) believes some preschoolers (three- and four-year-olds) may delight in violating or "playing" with the conventions of conversation. This, she notes, can be seen in child-child or adult-child conversations when savvy preschoolers deliberately mislead usually to tease playfully, use "taboo" bathroom talk, nonsense talk, or tone unexpectedly when capable of verbally responding at a more mature level. In the last example, most teachers sense the child is asserting independence by rejecting conversational convention. One teacher termed this "going into the verbal crazies" to reject what another child or adult is saying, therefore attempting to change or control the situation. Also, by violating conversational convention it "helps (children) clarify how it should operate" (Geller, 1985).

Relational Words

More and more relational words appear as the child begins to compare, contrast, and revise stored concepts with new happenings. The following teacher-recorded anecdote during a story-telling activity shows how the child attempts to relate previously learned ethics to a new situation:

> During story telling Michael repeated with increasing vigor, "He not berry nice!" at the parts of the story when the wolf says, "I'm going to blow your house down." Michael seemed to be checking with me the correctness of his thinking based on his internalized rules of proper moral conduct. (Busy Bee Preschool)

Perhaps because adults stress bad and good or because a young child's inner sense of what is and what is not correct is developing, teachers notice preschoolers often describe feelings and people within narrow limits. One is either pretty or ugly, mean or nice. Shades of meaning or extenuating circumstances seem yet to be understood.

Beck (1982) describes how concept's mature:

> Just as infants use single-word sentences to name and describe objects, and as the two-year-old combines words to describe the nature of a ball or dolly or truck, and three-year-old children continue to specify and describe, four-year-old children are also creatures of their senses. They are concerned with the smell of a thing, the touch of a thing, the look of a thing and the sound of a thing. What is special about four-year-old children, however, is that their sensual awareness begins to take on conceptual dimensions. They begin to notice function or use and they begin to see it comparatively. . . . They come to see relationships between several objects and/or several events, and in comparing one to the other, they are learning the principle of categorization.

Space and size relationships and abstract time relationships rarely are expressed with adult precision. Although the words "big" and "little" are common usage with preschoolers, they are overused. Many other comparison words give children trouble, and one hears "biggerer," "big-big-big," and "bestus one" to describe size. Time words elicit smiles from adults as children wrestle with present, past, and future, as in "zillion days" or "tomorrower." Number words are difficult for some children to handle, and expressions like "whole bunches" and "eleventeen" are sometimes heard.

Although four-year-olds are able speakers, many of the "plays on words," double meanings, and connotative language subtleties that are important in adult speech are beyond the children's understanding. Their creative uses of words at times seem metaphoric and poetic and are valiant attempts to put thoughts into words. Half-heard words and partially or fully learned words are blended together and are, at times, wonderfully descriptive.

Speech and Child Behavior

There is tremendous variety in the ways children can modify their voices, and they may speak in a different pitch or rhythm when speaking to different people. They can whine, whisper, change volume, and distort timing and pronunciation (Garvey, 1984).

Some children discover that by increasing volume or changing tone they can affect others' behavior. They find that speech can show anger, sarcasm, and be used aggressively to hurt others.

Preschoolers may mimic the speech of "bad-guy" television characters. Acts of aggression, clothed in the imitated speech and actions of a TV character, can become part of this type of play.

Purposeful echoing or baby talk can irritate or tease. Excessive talking is sometimes used to get one's way, and "talking back" may occur.

Some children find that silence can get as much attention from adults as loud speech. Tattling on another may be simply a way of checking for correctness, or it can be purposeful.

Through trial and error and feedback, the child finds that words can hurt, gain friends or favor, or satisfy a wide range of needs. Because preschoolers are emotion-packed human beings, their statements range from expressions of "you're my buddy" to "you're my enemy" within a matter of minutes.

What may appear to be violent statements may be just role playing or make-believe competition. To some adults, the preschooler speech may appear loud and wild. Speech seems overly nasal and full of moisture that sprays out in some words. A young child may have frequent nasal colds and congestion during this period. Preschoolers tend to stand close to others, and their volume increases when they are intense about their subjects (figure 3–11).

Impact Words

Not all speech used by older preschoolers is appreciated by adults. Name-calling and offensive words and phrases may be used by active preschoolers to gain attention and reaction from both adults and children. Children discover that some phrases, sentences, and words cause unusual behavior in others. They actively explore these and usually learn which of these are inappropriate and when they can be used. Children learn that most of this type of talk has "impact value." If certain talk makes people laugh or gives the children some kind of positive rewards, it is used over and over.

Bathroom words seem to be explored and used as put-downs and attention getters. Giggles and uproarious laughter can ensue when these words are used. Adding to the child's enjoyment, new teachers may not know how to handle these situations. The school's policy regarding this matter can be a subject for staff discussion. Generally, newly spoken bathroom talk should be ignored unless it is hurtful, or the child should be told that the place to use the word is in the bathroom. This frequently remedies the behavior, since the child's enjoyment of it is spoiled without an audience. Alternatively, it might suffice to firmly say "That's a word that hurts. His name is Michael." Rubin and Fisher (1982) advise parents that "Since so many preschoolers love using forbidden words, especially when they play together, and since you really can't control everything your child says, there's no way you can stop all toilet talk." What

FIGURE 3–11   Being deeply absorbed in a building project can temporarily depress speech.

parents and teachers can control is what is said in their presence.

Sound Words

In our culture, children are particularly fond of repeating conventionalized sounds reputedly made by animals ("arf-arf," "meow," "baa") as well as action sounds for toy vehicles ("putt-putt," "beep," "varoom") (Geller, 1985). When a child is playing the baby in home re-enactment dramatic play, "wa-wa" will be heard frequently. Rough and tumble outside play may be accompanied by cartoon strip sounds like "Pow," "Bam," and "Zap."

Created Words

Created words such as "turner-overer" for pancake turner, "mudpudders" for rain boots, or "dirt digger" for spade are wonderfully descriptive and crop up occasionally in child speech. Many cite young children's fascination with the functions of objects in their environment as the reason such words are created. Children love making up words, including nonsense words and rhymes, and revel in their newly gained abilities to do so.

Reality and Nonsense

Some preschool children can enjoy the absurd, nonsensical, and ridiculous in their experiences and find humor in the unexpected. Others, at a different stage in their cognitive development with another orientation, insist on knowing the right way—the real, the accepted, the "whys and wherefores"—and will see no humor in what confuses them or contradicts the "usual order of things."

A number of preschoolers view life and surroundings seriously, literally. Others can "play" in speech with the opposite of what they know to be true. We know this is true in some adults also. They simply don't seem to enjoy what most of us may find humorous!

Geller (1985) cautions teachers to be aware of the tendency to suppress a child's delight in absurdity by insisting upon exact or literal renditions of things. She urges teachers to encourage nonsense play by appreciating a child's inventions or nonsensical propositions as in the following example:

> During moments of chanting . . . I would sometimes say, "And the dogs go meow and cats say bow-wow." Through their laughter, my listeners would inwardly shriek, "No!" and then either correct me or join in the game, producing their own inversions. (Geller, 1985)

Myths Concerning Speech and Intelligence

A large and mature vocabulary at this age may tend to lead teachers to think a child has superior intelligence. Making conclusions about children based on language ability at this age has inherent pitfalls considering the many factors which could produce limited or advanced vocabulary particularly when one considers cultural differences, bilingualism, and the child's access to "language-rich environments." At later ages language usage does seem to be related to school success.

Common Speech Patterns

Four-year-olds frequently rhyme words in their play speech, and teachers sometimes join the fun. Older preschoolers engage in self-chatter as do early preschoolers. Older preschoolers continue to make errors in grammar and in the use of the past tense of verbs ("He didn't caught me") and in the use of adjectives ("It's biggerer than yours"), time words ("The next tomorrow"), and negatives ("I didn't did it"). But preschoolers' skills are increasing at this stage, and their use of forms of the irregular verb "to be" improve: "I am so," or "Mine are hot and yours are cold." Sentence structure becomes more adultlike, including use of relative clauses and complex and compound sentence forms. Articulation of letter sounds is still developing; about 75% of English letter sounds are made correctly. Omissions of letter sounds ('merca for America) and substitutions (udder for other) are still present.

The older preschooler may have a vocabulary of over 2,000 words. The child is very concerned about the correct names of things and can find the errors in the speech of others. Since the older preschooler is an active explorer, his or her questions still probe the "purposefulness" of objects or actions (as in "Why is the moon in the sky?"). The four-year-old becomes an active problem solver and tends to explain things through visually noted attributes; for example, "A cow is called that 'cause of its horns." Elkind (1971) describes preschoolers' inability at times to talk about their solutions:

> Although the preschooler can respond to and solve problems posed verbally, he is not able to verbalize his solutions.

The child can transform questions; for example, if asked to carry a message asking mom whether *she's* ready, the child will correctly ask her, "Are *you* ready?"

Most four-year-old children enjoy books, stories, and activities with words. More and more of their time is spent on these pursuits.

The four-year-old may still stutter and clutter and stop speech when there is stress or excitement. The less-mature speech of a best friend might be copied, and nonverbal expression is always a part of communication. However, most four- and five-year-olds are avid speakers. They are interested in exploring the real world as well as make-believe worlds. Chukovsky (1963) prizes the child's ability to fantasize, and encourages teachers and parents to accept and value it, writing, ". . . and it should be diligently nurtured from earliest childhood."

A wide range of individual speech behavior is both normal and possible. Knowing some typical behaviors can help the teacher understand young children. Some younger preschoolers may have the speech characteristics of older preschoolers; while some older preschoolers have the characteristics of younger preschoolers (figure 3–12). Each child is unique in his or her progress and rate of acquiring language skills.

....
Summary

Knowing typical and common language development characteristics helps the teacher understand that children are unique individuals. Rapid growth of vocabulary and language skills is part of normal growth. Errors in the speech of young preschoolers (aged two to three) make verbalizations partly understandable. Key words in the correct order give adults clues to what's intended. Self-talk during the child's play usually describes what the child is doing and may alternate with social comments.

Teachers can use their knowledge of early childhood language development in many ways, such as alerting the staff about a child's need for hearing tests or special help and helping parents who are concerned with their child's speech patterns.

Older preschool children (aged four to five) have almost adultlike speech. They explore words and begin to understand their power. Fantasy play peaks accompanied by speech. Some newly learned speech may be irritating to school staffs and parents, but it can indicate physical, mental, and social growth. Exploring and enjoying books occupies more of the children's time. Exploring the real and make-believe worlds with words becomes children's active pursuit during the early childhood years.

There is no "average" child when it comes to language development; individual differences exist and are treated with acceptance and optimism (figure 3–13).

	3 YEARS OLD	4 YEARS OLD	5 YEARS OLD
Average vocabulary	900 words	1500 words	2200 words
Typical sentence length	3–4 words	5–6 words	6+ words
Regular plurals	mastered	mastered	mastered
Irregular plurals	errors common	errors common	errors common
Regular verb tenses	mastered	mastered	mastered
Irregular verb tenses	errors common	errors common	errors common
Conjunctions	uses *and*	adds *but*, *because*	adds more conjunctions
Questions	uses *who*, *what*	adds *when*, *why*	
Pronunciation	mispronounces 40% speech sounds	mispronounces 20% speech sounds	mispronounces 10% speech sounds
Disfluency	common	common	common

FIGURE 3–12   Typical characteristics of language learning in preschoolers (*From* Your Preschooler, *p. 50, by R. R. Rubin and J. J. Fisher, 1982, Macmillan Publishing Co. Inc., NY.*)

CHILD'S AGE		CHILD'S AGE	
2–2½ years	Joins words in sentences of 2 or more words.		Names some colors and is interested in counting.
	Knows name and age.		Looks at books while alone and enjoys reading times.
	Has vocabulary of over 3 words.		Talks about relationships.
	Understands long spoken sentences and simple commands.		Memorizes a short song, poem, fingerplay, or story.
	Begins using plurals and past tense.		Repeats 3 digits and 2 to 3 nonsense syllables if asked.
	Changes pitch and/or loudness for specific meaning.		Uses adjectives and pronouns correctly.
	Begins using forms of verb "to be."		Can copy a recognizable circle or square well if shown a model.
	Uses a few prepositions.		Can imitate a clapping rhythm.
	Uses I, me, and you.		Starts to talk about the function of objects.
	Uses about 25 phonemes.		Can find an object in group that's different.
	Articulates about 10 to 12 vowel types and about 12 to 15 consonants.		Can find missing parts of wholes.
	Points to and names objects in pictures.		Can classify using clear, simple distinctions.
	Names 5 to 8 body parts.		Knows names of common shapes.
	Enjoys rhythm in words, nursery rhymes, finger plays, and simple stories.	**4–5 years**	Has vocabulary of over 1,500 words.
	Understands and responds to almost all of adult speech.		Uses sentences of 5 to 6 (or more) words.
	Generalizes by calling round objects ball, and so on.		May use impact, shock, and forbidden words.
2½–3 years	Negatives, imperatives, and commands occur.		May use words of violence.
	Shows variety in question types.		Argues, convinces, and questions correctness.
	Adds as many as 2 to 3 words to vocabulary daily.		Shares books with friends.
	Names items in signs and books.		Acts out story themes or recreates life happenings in play.
	Uses 3- or 4-word sentences.		Has favorite books.
	Enjoys fun with words.		Likes to dictate words.
	Follows simple directions.		Notices signs and print in environment.
	Points to body parts when asked.		Uses etiquette words, such as please, thank you, and so on.
	Names many common objects.		Enjoys different writing tools.
	Uses an increasing number of nouns, verbs, and pronouns.		Knows many nursery rhymes and stories.
	Draws lines and circular forms in artwork.		May add alphabet letters to art work.
	Knows words or lines from books, songs, stories.		Creates and tells long stories.
3–4 years	Asks why, what, where, how, and when questions.		Can verbally express the highlights of the day.
	Loves word play.		Knows many colors.
	Makes closed figures in art.		Can repeat a sentence with 6 or more words.
	Begins using auxiliary verbs.		May pretend to read books or may actually read other's nametags.
	Tells sex and age.		Holds writing tools in position that allows fine control.
	Utters compound sentences with connecting and . . er . . but, and so on.		Traces objects with precision.
	Engages in imaginary play with dialogue and monologue.		Classifies according to function.
	Says full name.		Asks what words mean.
	Follows 2- and 3-part requests.		Is familiar with many literary classics for children.
	Relates ideas and experiences.		Knows address and phone number.
	Uses adverbs, adjectives, and prepositions.		Can retell main facts or happenings in stories.
			Uses adultlike speech.

FIGURE 3–13   Developmental language-related milestones at ages 2 through 5

STUDENT ACTIVITIES

1. Observe a two-, three-, four-, and five-year-old for fifteen minute periods. (Omit children's names.) Try to write down what is said and a brief description of the setting and actions. Underline typical characteristics described in this chapter. Make comparisons between older and younger preschool children.

2. Interview two teachers. Ask if any preschool child within their care seems to have special speech or language problems. Write down the teachers' comments and compare them with typical characteristics mentioned in the chapter.

3. What rules or restrictions concerning the use of inappropriate speech (name-calling, swearing, and screaming) would you expect to find in a preschool center?

4. Write definitions for:

   egocentric speech or private speech
   running commentary
   fantasy
   overextension
   impact words

5. Finish the following adding an additional paragraph or page to the discussion: "Hearing in young children needs careful monitoring because...."

CHAPTER REVIEW

A. Associate the following characteristics with the correct age group. Some may seem to fit both categories; choose the most appropriate one. Write the characteristics under the headings Younger Preschooler (two- and three-year-olds) and Older Preschooler (four- and five-year-olds).

75% perfect articulation	nonverbal communication
"Look, I'm jumping."	2,000- to 2,500-word vocabulary
telegraphic speech	talking about what one is doing
rhyming and nonsense words	stuttering
name-calling	talking through an adult
repetitions	substitutions
omission of letter sounds	role playing
adultlike speech	planning play with others
bathroom words	arguing

B. Select the correct answers. Many questions have more than one correct response.

1. The younger preschool child (two to three years old)
   a. may still grunt and scream while communicating.
   b. always replies to what is said to him or her by another child.

   c. articulates many sounds without clarity.
   d. speaks in complete sentences at two years of age.

2. A truly typical or average child
   a. would have all the characteristics of his or her age.
   b. is almost impossible to find.
   c. is one who speaks better than his or her peers.
   d. sometimes makes up words to fit new situations.

3. Repetition in the speech of the young child
   a. needs careful watching.
   b. is common for children aged two to five.
   c. can be word play.
   d. happens for a variety of reasons.

4. Name-calling and swearing
   a. may take place during preschool years.
   b. can gain attention.
   c. shows that children are testing reactions with words.
   d. only happens with poorly behaved children.

5. A word like "blood" or "ghost"
   a. may spread quickly to many children.
   b. has impact value.
   c. can make people listen.
   d. is rarely used in a preschool group.

6. Most younger preschoolers
   a. cannot correctly pronounce all consonants.
   b. omit some letter sounds.
   c. have adultlike speech.
   d. will, when older, reach adult-level speech.

7. Stuttering during preschool years
   a. happens often.
   b. should not be drawn to the child's attention.
   c. may happen when a child is excited.
   d. means the child will need professional help to overcome it.

8. "Me wented" is an example of
   a. pronoun difficulty.
   b. a telegram sentence.
   c. verb incorrectness.
   d. the speech of some two- or three-year-olds.

9. Joint planning in play with two or more children is found more often with
   a. two- to three-year-olds.
   b. four- to five-year-olds.
   c. slowly developing children.
   d. male children.

10. Knowing typical speech characteristics is important because teachers
    a. may need to alert their director's attention to a child's difficulty.
    b. can help individual children.
    c. interact daily with young children.
    d. should be able to recognize typical age level behavior.

11. Nonverbal communication and gesturing
    a. happens less and less frequently as a child matures.
    b. continues after adolescence.
    c. indicates poor progress if used often.
    d. indicates shyness.

12. One can expect _____ two- and three-year-olds.
    a. hearing unclear speech in most
    b. hearing full sentences in most
    c. hearing incomplete but meaningful sentences in most
    d. books to interest most
    e. incorrect verb use to precede correct verb use in most

CHAPTER 4

Growth Systems Affecting Early Language Ability

After studying this chapter, you should be able to:

- describe sequential stages of intellectual development.

- list three perceptual-motor skills that preschool activities might include.

- discuss the importance of a center's ability to meet young children's social and emotional needs.

The child is a total being, and so language growth cannot be isolated from physical, mental, and social-emotional well-being. All body systems need a minimum level of movement (exercise) to keep the body in good working order and to stimulate brain growth. A proper intake of nutritious foods and living conditions that provide emotional security and balance can affect the child's acquisition of language and his or her general health and resistance to disease. A preschool, child center, or learning center intent on developing language skills focuses on satisfying both physical and emotional needs while also providing intellectual opportunity and challenge by offering a variety of age-appropriate activities (figure 4–1).

Physical Growth

Physical development limits or aids capabilities, thereby affecting children's perceptions of themselves, as well as the way they are treated by others. Early childhood teachers are aware of these fundamental physical changes that take place in young children. For instance, a slightly taller, physically active, strong, and well-coordinated child who can ride a two-wheel bike and drop-kick a football may be admired by his or her peers. These two skills are not usually witnessed during preschool years, but occasionally, a child possesses such physical skills. A wide range of physical abilities in individual children exists within preschool groups as in all developmental areas.

Preschoolers grow at the rate of two to three inches in height and four to six pounds in weight a year. At about 18 to 24 months, the child's thumb is used in opposition to just one finger. The ability to use tools and drawing markers with a degree of skill emerges. The nutritional quality of the child's diet exerts an influence on both body and neural development. Monitoring nutrient intake, height, weight gain, and emotional well-being can alert parents to possible deficiencies. *See pediatrician regularly*

Illness during accelerated growth may produce conditions affecting language development if it damages necessary body systems. Hearing loss and vision difficulties impair the child's ability to receive communications and learn his or her native language. A brain impairment may hinder the child's ability to sort perceptions, slowing progress.

Preschools and early learning programs plan a wide range of motor activities; much of the children's

FIGURE 4–1   Schools provide outdoor play in all types of climates.

time is devoted to playing with interesting equipment in both indoor and outdoor areas. The well-known benefits of a healthy mind in a healthy body should be planned for, by incorporating daily physical activities that promote well-exercised and well-coordinated muscles into young children's daily programs.

Perception

An infant's physical actions are the vehicle of knowledge. Seeing and trying to touch or act upon the environment are the work of infancy. This early physical stage precedes and develops into the child's understanding his or her world, and this makes later verbal labeling and speech possible.

As the child matures, perceptual acuity increases; finer detail is seen. Most children achieve 20/20 vision (adult optimum) at age 14. At ages two to five vision is in the 20/45 to 20/30 range (Weymouth, 1963). Hearing acuity increases from birth through ages four and five (Weiss & Lillywhite, 1981). At this point, the hearing mechanisms are essentially mature and will not change greatly except through disease or injury.

Young children are noted for their desire to get their hands on what interests them (figure 4–2). If a new child with particularly noticeable hair joins a group, hands and fingers are sure to try to explore its texture. If a teacher wears a soft, fuzzy jacket, the children will stroke it and snuggle into it.

FIGURE 4–2   Children enjoy a variety of toys.

Perceptions are gathered with all sense organs. Ornstein and Sobel (1987) believe that the main purpose of receiving, organizing, and interpreting what one encounters perceptually is to achieve constancy—a stable, constant world. Development involves changes or shifts in the way a person organizes experience and copes with the world, generally moving from simpler to more complex, from single to multiple and integrated ways of responding (Shapiro and Mitchell, 1992).

Researchers exploring infant visual preferences have pinpointed a series of changes in attention-drawing features from infancy to age five:

Two months—change from having attention captured by movement and edges of people and objects to active search and explore.

Age 2–5—change from unsystematic exploring to systematically examining each feature carefully. (Gibson, 1969)

Children get better and better at focusing on one aspect of a complex situation: they become selective in focusing their attention, and they ignore the irrelevant and distracting. Life events that cause tension and anxiety can interfere with their emerging abilities. In complex situations the child does best when perceptual distractions are minimized, allowing deep concentration (Gibson, 1969).

Individual differences have been noted in the way children explore their environment and react to problems. Kagan (1971) has described **conceptual tempo** to contrast the **impulsive** child, who answers quickly and may make mistakes, with the **reflective** child, who spends considerable time examining alternatives. A second difference in perception identifies field independence, and field-dependent styles of perceiving. Field-independent children are those good at ignoring irrelevant context, while field-dependents tend to focus on the total context.

Perceptual-Motor Skills

Sensory- (or perceptual-) motor intelligence has been defined by Jewell and Zintz (1986) as a kind of action-knowledge that is not to be confused with the intelligence involving thinking and logic. The latter grows during preschool years and beyond when children can think about and know without acting out in a physical way.

Piaget, the noted Swiss psychologist and researcher, greatly affected early childhood educators' interest in perceptual-motor activities. Piaget and others observed that reflective (automatic) movements such as crying, sucking, and grasping in infants became controlled, purposeful body movements as the child grew. He speculated that physical movement served as a base for later mental abilities. His theory (1952) includes stages in the development of human intelligence, which are condensed in the following:

1. *Sensorimotor period* (birth to 18 to 24 months). Reflex actions become coordinated and perfected by physical movement and exploration of real objects and events.

2. *Preoperational period* (18 to 24 months to 7 to 8 years). Mental symbols represent what is experienced; imitation occurs. As the child matures, meanings attached to symbols grow and become detailed and precise, and physical actions combine with mental actions.

3. *Concrete operations period* (7 to 8 years to 11 to 12 years). Child's thinking now is less dependent on physical involvement or immediate perceptual cues that aid classifying, ordering, grouping, numbering, and "inner" and "cross" sub-grouping of concepts.

Conceptual tempo — a term associated with Jerome Kagan's theory of different individual pacing in perceptual exploration of objects.

Impulsive — quick to answer or react to either a simple or complex situation or problem.

Reflective — taking time to weigh aspects or alternatives in a given situation.

During the preschool years, the development of motor skills is as important as the development of language skills. Just as there is gradually increasing control over language, movement, and body control in the preschool years, so there is a similar continuing increase in the ability to scan new material, organize one's perception of it, remember it, and perhaps refer to it by some label, or assign meaning in some other way (Clay, 1991). The close ties between motor activities and thought processes indicate that the child needs motor activity involving the five sense organs, as well as large-muscle use. Exactly how much of a child's mental activity is dependent on or promoted by physical activity is unknown. Most educators of young children feel that a definite, strong connection exists.

Motor skill develops in an orderly, predictable, head-to-toe fashion. Head, neck, and upper body muscles are controlled first (large muscles before small muscles), and center of body muscles are coordinated before extremities (fingers and toes). Handedness (left or right) is usually stable by age five or six. Clay (1991) discusses child limitations if motor experience is limited:

> The child who has had limited experience to run around, to climb, to use his body effectively in activities which demand gross motor skill, will not be ready for the finer adjustments that are required in the motor skills of eye movement and hand-eye coordination in school activities.

Montessori's approach (1967) to educating young children is noted for direct manipulation of real objects presented in sequenced form. This led to her design and construction of many tactile (touching) exploring materials for the young child. She explains her motives in the following:

> The training and sharpening of the senses has the obvious advantage of enlarging the field of perception and of offering an ever more solid foundation for intellectual growth. The intellect builds up its store of practical ideas through contact with, and exploration of, its environment. Without

such concepts the intellect would lack precision in its abstract operations.

Preschools are full of appealing equipment and programs that offer a planned approach to the development of sensory-motor skills. They are seen as integral parts of the curricula. Spitzer (1977) believes that sensory exploration and motor-skill development take place jointly.

School success in later elementary years may also be influenced by the development of perceptual-motor skill.

There seems to be no clearly accepted or defined separate place within the preschool curriculum for sensory-skill development. Some centers identify a series of sequential activities and label them perceptual or sensory-motor; their main goal is skill development. In other centers, every activity is seen as developing perceptual-motor skill. Commonly, music activities and physical games deal with physical coordination and endurance. Other programs plan for perceptual-motor activities within their language arts curriculum. What remains important is that this type of emphasis be part of every center's program.

This list of objectives designed to refine perceptual-motor skills is drawn from a number of schools' and centers' goal statements:

- Awareness of self in space.
- Awareness of self in relation to objects.
- Flexibility.
- Body coordination.
- Posture and balance.
- Awareness of spatial relationships.
- Rhythmic body movements.
- The ability to identify objects and surfaces with the eyes closed.
- Awareness of temperatures by touch.
- Ability to trace form outlines with fingers.
- Ability to discriminate color, shapes, similar features, different features, sizes, textures, and sounds.
- Ability to match a wide variety of patterns and symbols.
- Ability to identify parts of figures or objects when a small part of a whole is presented.

Good ideas!

FIGURE 4–3 Coordination, flexibility, strength, and confidence are needed to master rope climbing.

- Eye-hand coordination (figure 4–3).
- Familiarity with the following terms: same, different, long, longer, longest, small, smaller, smallest, big, little, tall, short, wide, narrow, high, low, above, below, on, in, hard, soft, sweet, salty, sour. *concepts*
- Ability to identify food by tasting.
- Ability to identify smells of a variety of items.
- Ability to identify common sounds.

Activities for Perceptual-Motor Development

It is difficult to think of one piece of preschool equipment or one activity that does not contain some aspect or component of perceptual-motor development. Figure 4–4 lists perceptual-motor development activities and equipment, gathered from a broad range of early childhood books and sources. It can serve as a beginning.

EXPERIENCES DEALING WITH:	POSSIBLE MATERIALS AND EQUIPMENT
Visual Discrimination *– See differences*	
long, longer, longest	felt or paper strips; sticks; ribbons
small, smaller, smallest	nested boxes; blocks; buttons; measuring cups
big, little	blocks; jars; buttons; balloons; toys
tall, short	felt figures; stuffed toys
wide, narrow	pieces of cloth and paper; scraps of wood; boxes
high, low	jump rope; small ball; see-saw made from small board with tiny block in middle
above, below	table-shaped piece of felt with box-on, in shaped felt pieces to place above and below box with colored stones
Auditory Discrimination *– hear differences*	
quiet, noisy	two boxes: one containing something that rattles (such as stones or beads) and one containing cloth or paper
bell sounds	bells of varying shapes and sizes for a variety of tones
falling sounds	feather; leaf; stone; block of wood; cotton
shaking sounds	maracas; baby rattle; pebbles inside coffee can
musical sounds	variety of rhythm instruments
Tactile Discrimination *– touch differences*	
textures	sandpaper; tissue; stone; waxed paper; tree bark; velvet; wool; fur; cotton
outline of shapes	thin wooden circle, square, triangle, rectangle; letters cut from sandpaper
recognition of *Ex.* objects *(Sensory bag)*	four different-shaped objects, each tied in end of sock—children guess what each is by feeling it (change objects often)
hard, soft	handkerchief; rock; cotton batting; nail; sponge
Taste Discrimination	
identifying food: sweet, salty, sour	small jars: filled with salt, sugar, unsweetened lemonade
trying new foods	variety of vegetables children may not know; samples of fruit juices; honey, molasses, maple syrup
Smell Discrimination	
identifying object by smell	cake of soap; vial of perfume; pine sprig; onion; vials of kitchen spices; orange
Kinesthetic Discrimination	
lifting, racing downhill, swinging, throwing, running, jumping, climbing, bending, stretching, twisting, turning, spinning, balancing.	yard and motor play materials

FIGURE 4–4 Perceptual activities

Cognitive Development

There are major, opposing views concerning the link between language and thought. One is that language is the foundation of thought and vital to a person's awareness of the world. Another view suggests that language is dependent on thinking; as intelligence grows, language grows, reflecting thoughts. Vygotsky (1980) has influenced early childhood educators' beliefs by theorizing that language is an actual mechanism for thinking, a mental tool. Language makes thinking more abstract, flexible, and independent from immediate stimuli (Bodrova and Leong, 1996). It is difficult to determine which of these ideas is closer to the truth. White (1987) states that "It's clear that you can't fully separate the topics." Harris (1990) takes the view that in learning to communicate, the child is also learning to represent experience and learning to think. Most educators will agree that language and thought are closely associated.

Jaggar (1985) describes the process of learning languages as follows:

> ... children, in interacting with others, construct the language system ... At the same time ... they are also using the system to construct another one, namely their picture of the world. That is, they are using language and *learning through language*. In the course of developing both systems (language and knowledge), they are also learning about language itself. They are becoming "aware" of the nature of language, of its forms and functions.

Language processing calls upon both left and right brain hemispheres (Healy, 1990). As the brain grows, it is reorganized by child experience. Some children who have been passive viewers of life (i.e., television, videos, etc.) rather than active listeners (explorers and conversationalists) may lack practice in both auditory analysis and logical, sequential,

---

Neuroscience — study and research concerned with brain growth and development.

reasoning skills (Healy, 1990). Sensitive or optimal periods of brain development are thought to exist.

The connection between brain growth and development is the subject of current **neuroscience** research. Greenspan (1997), an adult and child psychiatrist and researcher in child development, suggests that perhaps the most critical role for emotions is to create, organize, and orchestrate many of the mind's most important functions. He states:

> In fact, intellect, academic abilities, sense of self, consciousness, and morality have common origins in our earliest and ongoing emotional experiences.

Greenspan (1997) presents educators with what he perceives to be the fundamental sequential building blocks of mental growth based on human beings' capacity to experience emotions. They include the ability to:

- Attend
- Engage
- Be intentional
- Form complex interactive intentional patterns
- Create images, symbols, and ideas
- Connect images and symbols

The idea that the reciprocal emotionally charged interactions between infants and young children and caregivers influence their cognitive development is not new, but increasingly it is given close attention by anyone caring for the very young.

Classifying Information

Intellect is rooted in each particular child's stored perceptual and sensory-motor experiences. Each child interprets happenings and attempts to connect each to what the child already knows. If it fits, the child understands, and it all falls together. An example of this might be seen if one watches a nine-month-old learn to make noise come out of a toy plastic horn. At first, the child has no knowledge of how the horn works. When he or she first blows into it and it makes a toot, the child blows into it repeatedly (and usually happily). After that, the child knows how to toot the horn. Infants, toddlers, and preschoolers can be thought of as having mental groupings (classes and categories) before they have words for them. The nine-month-old above probably has no word associated with what the child knows about the horn. Each mental grouping is distinguished by a set of distinctive features, and objects yet to be **classified** are examined for the presence of these features. If the horn-blowing infant reacts by trying to blow into a new toy horn of a similar shape, one can be relatively sure the child is forming a class of "horn" mentally. One can expect that the infant above will try blowing into any horn shape that comes the child's way. Later, a word or language symbol can be attached to a class or category, which makes it possible for the child to communicate about what the class or category means to the child, or how the child feels about it.

Preschool teachers readily see differences between the feelings and meanings expressed by each child. For example, the way that a child reacts when the child meets a new large animal may demonstrate what the child knows and feels about large animals. Another child's reaction might be entirely opposite.

Putting events and experiences into classes and categories is innate—a natural mental process. The motivation to engage actively with the environment—to make contact, to have an impact, and to make sense of experience—is built into human beings (Shapiro and Mitchell, 1992). The mind yearns for order, and knowledge is built within from what is experienced. Children construct theories or hypotheses about objects and phenomena by putting things into relationships. When they put previously made relationships into relationship and become aware of their circular reasoning, they go on to construct a more adequate explanation (Kamii, Manning, and Manning, 1991). A child's knowledge is constantly changing, for children are curious and are constantly searching for a variety of experience, fighting to overcome boredom (figure 4–5). A new or novel idea or event may greatly affect a child by adding to or changing all a child knows and feels on a particular subject.

FIGURE 4–5 Working with clay is an activity that encourages creativity.

As a child's language ability develops, mental classes, categories, and concepts are represented symbolically by words. Words become an efficient shortcut that eliminates the need to act out by gesturing or signaling to make something known to another. Thoughts can be analyzed and evaluated internally as the child grows older. If there exists a common language system between the child and others, it can be used to reveal the child's unique self. Young children frequently focus attention and direct their behavior in play through the use of "self-talk" (Berk and Winsler, 1995). Most often they are unaware they are talking to themselves and expect no answering comments from other children or adults.

Piaget's (1955) terms **assimilation** and **accommodation** describe what happens when infants and children experience something new. From the time of conception, each individual unconsciously

---

Classify — the act of systematically grouping things according to identifiable common characteristics; for example, size.

Assimilation — the process that allows new experiences to merge with previously stored mental structures.

Accommodation — the process by which new experiences or events change existing ideas or thought patterns.

Sensory–motor

structures (internally builds and organizes) what is perceived. If a new experience or event is perceived, it is assimilated into what already mentally existed. If it changes or modifies those existing structures (ideas or thought patterns), the new is accommodated. In other words, children attend to features that make sense to them, and learning involves adding to what is already known or modifying (changing) what is known. As Spelke (1986) and others point out "children are born with an innate ability to divide their experiences into categories."

Jewell and Zintz (1986) explain the connections between concepts and language:

> A category system of related meaning is formed on the basis of distinguishing criteria, which each child defines. The system constantly expands as new information is encountered. This becomes the cognitive and affective stores, the schemata for operating on the world and making sense of it. Labels are attached to meanings and language emerges.

Smith-Burke (1985) gives an example of a child trying to make sense of her experience in the following:

> ... after a visit to the hospital to see her dying great-grandmother who was 101, Abby (age 4) commented, "Ya know, Dad, the Brooklyn Bridge is pretty old. It's going to die soon!" In her struggle to understand life and death, Abby had made a connection between the Brooklyn Bridge, the celebrations of its centennial, and her great-grandmother.

Although children use words adults know and recognize, the knowledge behind children's words often carries quite a different meaning and understanding.

Different Levels of Maturity

The human brain's cortex contains two differently specialized hemispheres. Each hemisphere appears designed for unique functions, different abilities, and styles of thought, including verbal and spatial thinking. Different brain areas are well defined and possess a rich concentration of certain abilities that are not equal among children (Ornstein and Sobel, 1987). Research indicates that between ages two and four, there is a period when brain-growth spurts increase the child's ability to attain new levels of learning and accept cognitive challenges (Soderman, 1984). Naturally, the brain structures of some children may be developing more slowly than others, which might affect their ability to learn and may cause teachers to compare them unfairly with children of the same age who have developed more quickly. Consequently, teachers need to pay special attention to how they act when comparing children. Competitive, pressurized lessons can create an unhealthy "I'm not good (smart) enough" attitude that can be self-perpetuating.

Preschool children's statements that seem to be "errors in thinking" on the surface can, on deeper analysis, be seen as quite mature and understandable, not just random guesses. When a child says a camel is a horse with a hump, he or she should be given credit for seeing the similarity rather than merely corrected.

The child's fantasy world, which appears and is expressed in speech, should be seen as a giant intellectual leap. Make believe is internal intellectual creation and/or recreation. A preschooler may say he or she is someone else—most often this someone else is a hero of sorts or an admired personage usually from the movies or television or real life. There may be days when the child wishes to assume the name and identity of a friend or animal.

Many children during preschool can readily follow story sequences and identify with book characters. An in-depth discussion of preschoolers and books is found in Chapter 9.

Teachers need to realize that there are differences between adult concepts and child concepts. The child's view of the world is usually based on immediate, present happenings and beginning thought processes. A child's speech is full of many unique misconceptions, conclusions, and errors (as judged by adult standards). These errors arise because of each child's unique way of sorting out experiences—a continuous process of trying to make sense and order out of daily events. Errors based on just a few happenings may be quite logical conclusions. For example, a child may conclude that milk comes from the store, or, when looking at an *n*, that it is a "baby *m*."

Teacher's Role

Teachers who work with infants, toddlers, and preschoolers realize sensory-motor experiences and opportunities with people, toys, and room environments are early intellect-building events. Exploring and experimenting is enhanced by adult provision of materials and equipment. At some point, teachers realize some actions look as though the child thought first and then acted. At about 10 months some infants seem to be majoring in dropping and emptying. They drop things from high-chair trays and watch the objects fall or put things into containers, drawers, or boxes and empty and refill these over and over. One has to smile and think of very young infants as active scientists. The work of Vygotsky (1980) has influenced educators' ideas of how they should verbally interact with young children to increase what children learn from new experiences. When working with two-year-olds and young three-year-olds, teachers notice a good deal of voiced external speech that accompanies play. Vygotsky theorizes that this speech helps the child order and organize thoughts, plan and develop solutions, and come to conclusions. A "zone of proximal development" is what Vygotsky calls the area between what the child can solve alone when faced with problems and experience and what the child can possibly solve or come to know with the help of adults or more experienced, knowing children. When adults name and explain happenings and talk about relationships, this is seen as a stimulant to both language and mental growth. A teacher trying to put into practice Vygotsky's theories would try to talk with children, becoming a catalyst who names, discusses, and prompts the child's exploration and expression of what he or she has discovered or formulated. It also means that adults

must know when not to interrupt children's thoughts when they're deeply emerged in play. Dialogue makes much more sense when children seek adult help or when they are companions in activities.

In promoting what children will store (learn and remember), teachers deal with both meaning and feelings. Each intellect building encounter and interaction with children starts with the adult's supportive acceptance and caring. Purposeful teacher dialogue is often part of child-teacher exchanges. Its goal is to advance further discovery or to help put the discovery or experience into words. A teacher listens and observes closely. This listening may expose aspects of the child's thinking, logic, inner concepts, and feelings.

Working with children on a daily basis, teachers strive to understand the logic and correctness behind children's statements. The balance a teacher maintains between gently correcting false impressions and having children discover the misconceptions for themselves is not easy to maintain. Piaget (1952) encourages teachers to concentrate on discovery techniques:

> Each time one prematurely teaches a child something he could have discovered for himself, that child is kept from inventing it and consequently from understanding it completely.

Skillful questioning and sensitive responses from the teacher preserve a child's feelings about expressing worthwhile ideas and makes the child more willing to speak and share. These are some examples:

- "I can see you want to have a turn talking too, Becky, and I want to hear you."
- "Would you tell us, Mark, about the boat you put together this morning?"
- "You thought of a different way to make a hole in your paper; perhaps your friends would like to hear about it."
- "Did anyone see what happened to Tim's shoe?"
- "I wonder if there's a way for three people to share two pairs of scissors?"

Huey (1965) lists suggestions for teaching young children that promote use of both cognitive and language abilities:

1. Set the stage for abundant sensory experiences that are varied so as to encourage children to discriminate among these and to make associations.
2. Provide abundant opportunities for self-selected learning activities, especially of the manipulative and experimental types.
3. Provide many opportunities for children to observe work activities of adults so that they will have experiences to think about.
4. Encourage children with toys, other play accessories, conversation, and art materials to symbolize their experiences through play, art, and language.
5. Direct children's attention to learning opportunities they may miss, to opportunities to use their previous associations, and to opportunities for abstracting common elements (e.g., "all blue things").
6. Provide an environment of simple language that helps clothe children's experiences with language while they are absorbing the experiences.
7. Encourage children to use the language that they have to clothe their own experiences in their own language.
8. Plan opportunities or experiences that will help children discover new concepts, redefine familiar concepts and differentiate between concepts (figure 4–6).
9. Provide opportunities for vicarious experiences through stories, pictures, and conversations that relate to recent direct experiences.
10. Pace learning opportunities, not too many at one time, for the group and for the individual child, so that clear images are possible, new learnings are

FIGURE 4–6   This child is finding out how high he can make his tower.

reinforced to the point of usefulness, and the hazard of overstimulation is avoided.

While keeping these suggestions in mind, look at figure 4–7, which illustrates how the preschooler's ability to process information is improving and expanding during this period.

Social and Emotional Growth

Interaction with other people is always a major factor in the child's language learning. Children who have positive feelings about themselves—feelings of self-value and security—speak frequently. New contacts with adults outside the home run smoothly as the child branches out from the home.

1. Seeking information. (Focusing)
2. Seeking word labels. (Concept building)
3. Naming, classifying, categorizing, and grouping experiences mentally—objects, ideas, etc. (General to specific; revising concepts)
4. Responding and remembering. (Memorizing and recalling)
5. Comparing and contrasting information. (Abstracting)
6. Making inferences and predicting in general ways. (Predicting)
7. Generalizing. (Inductive thinking)
8. Applying known information to new situations. (Transferring)
9. Making hypotheses (educated guesses) and predicting in specific ways. (Deductive thinking)

FIGURE 4–7 The child's emerging intellectual skills

Feelings and emotions are part of each human conversation. A child's feelings toward adults are generalized to teachers in early school years. The parent-child bond and its influence on language learning has been described by Douglass (1959):

> The feeling relationships between parents and child appear to be a tremendous factor in the child's learning of language. The child who avoids talking because he fears lack of acceptance, the child whose feelings are not understood, the standards of eating, toilet training, and behaviors which are imposed too soon, and emotional tensions existing in the home, can create surface symptoms produced by a child who attempts to cope with an unsatisfying and hostile world.

During preschool years, children form ideas of self-identity. It becomes difficult for children to believe in themselves—or their language abilities—if self-esteem is constantly undermined. Figure 4–8 suggests teacher behavior and response in communicating with children to promote social growth.

Erikson (1950) identified a series of social-emotional developments in the young child:

In communication, the teacher:
- cares and is ready to give of self.
- listens, intent on understanding.
- adds simple words when the child cannot.
- doesn't correct speech when this might break down willingness to speak further.
- is available for help in clarifying ideas or suggesting new play and exploring possibilities.
- senses child interests and guides to new real experiences.
- is available when problems and conflicts happen.
- enjoys time spent in child activities.
- establishes friendships with each child.
- talks positively about each child's individual uniqueness.
- is an enthusiastic and expressive communicator.
- offers friendly support while redirecting undesirable social behavior or stating rules.
- notices and respects each child's work.

FIGURE 4–8 Teacher behaviors helpful to the child's social growth

- (Infants) *Trust vs. Mistrust.* Trust develops from consistent care, which fulfills basic needs (food, warmth, physical contact, and so on), leading to stable and secure feelings rather than anxiousness. A positive view of life forms.
- (Toddlers and two-year-olds) *Autonomy vs. Shame and Doubt.* Children get to know themselves as separate persons. What they control, decisions they can make, and freedom they may have while still being very dependent become apparent. Awareness of inabilities and helplessness is sensed. Behavior may be testing and full of the word "no."
- (Preschoolers) *Initiative vs. Guilt Feelings.* Experimentation and active exploration of new skills and directions occur. There are strong emotions at times in resistance to authority figures and rules, yet children are still dependent on adult approval.

Werner and Smith (1982) have studied what they describe as "resilient children," those who thrive and succeed despite what could be termed "at-risk" childhoods. As children, they displayed positive self-concepts and well-developed identities. As adults, they became socially well-integrated, confident, and autonomous—adults who "worked well, played well, loved well, and expected well."

Social development must not be ignored in planning and conducting language activities or in trying to manage groups. Structure and rules are necessary for group living. An individual child's status in the eyes of the group can be enhanced through the sharing and appreciation of the child's ideas and accomplishments and by providing frequent opportunities for the child to lead or help lead the group in activities, which is almost always a confidence- and status-building experience.

Teachers should be concerned with a child's *social connectedness*—a term defined by Ornstein and Sobel (1987) as characteristic of people with stable, secure lives, supportive families and friends, and close ties to community and accepted as a worthy part of a group and able to weather life's stresses with a sense of individual identity. A teacher is in control of a school's atmosphere and works with the home and community.

Preschoolers begin to learn labels for feelings such as happy, sad, jealous, fearful, and so on. They begin to think of others' feelings. The conscience is forming and interest in right and wrong is expressed. Teachers who speak of their own feelings as adults set an example and provide a climate in which children's feelings are also accepted and understood (Greenberg, 1969).

Most children explore social actions and reactions, figure 4–9. Strong emotions accompany much of children's behavior; their total beings speak. When a child feels left out, life becomes an overwhelming tragedy, while a party invitation may be a time to jump for joy.

The following activities can help children develop a sense of self. These are just a few suggestions; many more are possible.

- Activities using mirrors.

FIGURE 4–9   These boys enjoy each other's company.

- Activities using children's photographs and home movies.
- Tracings of the child's outline.
- Making nametags and placing names on belongings, drawings, lockers, and projects.
- Activities that identify and discuss feelings.
- Activities concerned with personal opinions.
- Activities that show both similarity to others and individual diversity.
- Activities that build pride or membership in a group.
- Activities that identify favorite pursuits, objects, or individual choices.

Based on research of outstanding and well-developed two- and three-year-olds (24 to 36 months), White (1986) identified social abilities that he feels serve as a strong foundation for future schooling:

- Being able to get and hold the attention of adults in a variety of socially accepted ways.
- Being able to express affection or mild annoyance to adults and peers when appropriate.
- Being able to use adults as resources after determining that a task is too difficult to handle alone.

language skills

- Being able to show pride in achievement.
- Being able to lead and follow children of the same age.
- Being able to compete with age mates.

White (1986) goes on to say:

If a three-year-old has acquired this pattern of abilities, we believe she (he) has had a "superior education" during her first years. Furthermore, such a foundation probably goes a long way toward ensuring that a child will enter school well-prepared for future development.

Teachers strive to supply a center atmosphere in which a sense of trust and security thrives. Danoff, Breibart, and Barr (1976) feel this is crucial to each child's opportunity to learn.

Basic to the learning process is children's ability to trust themselves and the adults who teach them. This is totally interactional. Children must trust people in their world, or else they reject all that these people want to teach them. They learn to have faith in those who respect them and accept their feelings. In turn, they learn to trust themselves. In a climate that engenders trust, they want to learn and are able to learn.

Securely attached infants, those who have received responsive and developmentally appropriate care, emerge as confident, energetic toddlers with beginning awareness of self as a person. Imitative play, self-pretending play, and play that models emotions (hugging or spanking dolls) appear during the child's second year. Empathy for others who are hurt or crying may also be displayed.

As children age, self acts can be talked about and judged by the child. The author once met a young three-year-old boy who would sit himself in a chair if he felt he had misbehaved (i.e., purposely bumped another with a bike, pushed another, taken another's toy). He would sit only a few moments then happily resume play. This type of guidance technique was not used by the staff, but at home sitting in the "thinking chair" was a common occur-rence. The center staff respected the child's behavior, and watchfully intervened when behavior warranted urging the child's use of words to solve problems. The child's self-discipline slowly disappeared as he gained both social and language skill.

Whether or not young children see themselves as "valued identities" depends on their interactions with their care providers and families. As Curry and Johnson (1990) point out:

. . . all individuals need a great deal of responsive, supportive adult investment throughout childhood to enable them to construct valued identities in the complex, changing, diverse yet increasingly interactive world in which we live.

The child whose confidence stems from the security of feeling loved, valued, and appreciated as an individual is a child who continues to communicate. Adults contribute greatly to the ever-maturing view the child has of himself or herself.

Summary

Physical, intellectual, and social-emotional growth is proceeding as is the child's speech. Understanding these growth systems promotes appropriate teacher techniques and behaviors. Danoff, Breibart, and Barr (1976) identify child characteristics and needs in figure 4–10, and suggest teacher activities.

Perceptual-motor activities are an integral part of many centers' language arts programs. Many educators feel that there is a strong correlation between physical activity during this period and mental growth.

Adults need to react to and sense the correctness of what seem to be errors in children's thinking. Guiding the child's discovery of concepts is an integral part of early childhood teaching.

A child who trusts can learn. Teachers must accept children's feelings and concentrate on establishing bonds between themselves and the children. This encourages growth of abilities. The feeling tone that lies beneath each human contact and conversation creates a setting for learning.

INTELLECTUAL CHARACTERISTICS	NEEDS	SUGGESTIONS FOR THE CLASSROOM TEACHER
Are curious: learn best through active involvement through their senses, and through direct experiences with things in the environment.	Opportunities to have sensory experiences—to see, touch, taste, smell and hear things around them. Opportunities to handle materials and make their own discoveries.	Provide firsthand experiences. For example, bring a guinea pig to the classroom and provide enough time and space for a small group of children to sit around and watch and handle the animal. Questions will most likely come from the children. For instance: "What is this?" "Where do guinea pigs come from?" The teacher is there to provide clear and simple explanations as well as to ask questions when necessary.
Are concerned primarily with things that affect them personally.	Opportunities to investigate things that they see around them or experience in their everyday lives. Opportunities to see their names, their photographs, and their work as part of the classroom materials and displays.	Provide activities that enable the children to explore familiar materials like water, soap, and plastic containers. Classroom meetings may include discussions about the children's families and the work their parents do. Snacks can include many foods that the children also eat at home. The children can also make their own snacks—like French toast or pancakes—and can be encouraged to observe and discuss each step in the process. Books can be made about the children's experiences, including names of people they know.
Are concerned primarily with the present.	Opportunities to distinguish between reality and "make-believe."	Stories should be concerned with feelings and experiences that are familiar to the children.
Are increasing their attention span.	Opportunities to have a variety of experiences that are interesting to children.	For younger children, provide many different materials for similar learning experiences. Schedule group activities for relatively short periods of time. Provide games and toys which are open-ended (have more than one way of being played or played with) or which require a relatively short amount of time. Gradually introduce activities that require a longer attention span.
Are developing a sense of time.	Opportunities to recall experiences. Opportunities to plan and organize play.	At snack time the children can be asked what they did earlier in the morning. Classroom discussions on Monday morning should include what the children did over the weekend. The children should be asked to choose where they want to work each day—for example, a child might choose the block area. Block structures can be left intact and added to each day for as long as the children are interested.

FIGURE 4–10   Chart of teaching ideas, matching child's needs and intellectual abilities to appropriate activities (*From* Open for Children, *by Danoff et al., 1976. Used with permission of McGraw-Hill Book Company.) (continues)*

INTELLECTUAL CHARACTERISTICS	NEEDS	SUGGESTIONS FOR THE CLASSROOM TEACHER
Are developing the ability to "symbolize" experiences.	Opportunities to express ideas in a variety of ways. Opportunities to symbolize their experiences through art, language, dramatic play, music, and movement. Opportunities to use materials imaginatively and creatively.	If the children take a trip, they can be encouraged to discuss the experience, and the teacher can write down some of what they say. They can also reproduce some of the sounds they heard with rhythm instruments, or they can make a mural of their visual impressions, or recreate the experience with blocks.
Are developing the ability to deal with complex, abstract ideas.	Opportunities to note similarities and differences between things around them. Opportunities to sort, group, categorize, and classify the things around them.	At a group time, the children can be asked, "Who is wearing pants today?" "Who is not wearing pants?" The children can be asked to compare any two pieces of clothing from the housekeeping area in terms of color, size, or function. A box full of clothes can be sorted in many different ways. For instance, the children can put together all the things that are worn on the head or all the clothes that have stripes.

FIGURE 4–10   *continued*

STUDENT ACTIVITIES

1. Observe young children (two to four years old) in a public place (restaurant, laundromat, grocery store, park, bus, department store). What do the children seem to notice, and how do they investigate what they notice? Write down those environmental objects, people, and so on, and what features capture children's interest (for example, sound, color, texture).

2. Using the chalkboard or a large piece of newsprint (or shelfpaper) list, with a small group of other students, the teacher behaviors that might develop a sense of trust in children on the first day of school.

3. Plan and conduct two activities with preschool children that concentrate on a perceptual-motor skill. Report your successes and failures to the group.

4. Describe your reactions to the following statements from children:
   a. "Milk comes from a truck."
   b. "You're ugly!"
   c. "You like her best!"
   d. "He always gets to be first!"
   e. "I don't like Petey." (another child)
   f. "Don't touch me!"
   g. "My dad kills all our bugs."

   What would you say in response to each child?

5. With your eyes closed, identify three objects given to you by another person.

6. Pair with another student. Each take three personal articles and place them on the table or desk in front of both of you. Try to categorize these articles. How many objects can you put in the same category? Can you find a category that includes all of the items?

CHAPTER REVIEW

A. Give a definition of:

abstract   motor development   conceptual tempo   tactile

concept   assimilation   identity

B. Write a brief description of Piaget's stages of intellectual development or Erickson's stages of social-emotional development.

C. Choose the category that fits best, and code the following words with the headings (a) perceptual-motor development, (b) social-emotional development, or (c) mental development.

1. trust
2. concepts
3. tasting
4. self-awareness
5. self-image
6. categorizing
7. predicting
8. avoiding people
9. eye-hand skill
10. body image
11. security
12. generalizing
13. balance
14. conscience
15. abstracting

D. Read the following teacher behaviors and verbalizations. Write the numbers of those you feel would help a child develop healthy social-emotional skills.

1. Recognizing each child by name as he or she enters.

2. Pointing out (to others) a child's inability to sit still.

3. Telling a child it's all right to hate you.

4. Keeping a child's special toy safe.

5. Encouraging a child's saying "I'm not finished" when another child grabs his or her toy.

6. Saying, "Jerome (child) thinks we should ask the janitor, Mr. Smith, to eat lunch with us."

7. Saying "Hitting makes me angry. It hurts."

8. Planning activities that are either "girls only" or "boys only."

9. Encouraging children who show kindness to others.

10. Allowing a child to make fun of another child without speaking to the first child about it.

11. Changing the rules and rewards often.

12. Ignoring an irritating behavior that seems to be happening more frequently.

E. Discuss children's vision and hearing acuity during preschool years.

F. Why is it important to know young children may have differences in perceiving?

G. Choose the best answer.

1. Most centers agree that perceptual-skill development belongs
    a. somewhere in the program.
    b. in the language arts area.
    c. in the music and physical education area.
    d. to a separate category of activities.

2. The younger the child the more he or she needs
    a. demonstration activities.
    b. to be told about the properties of objects.
    c. sensory experience.
    d. enriching child conversations.

3. Trust usually _____ being able to risk and explore, when considering early childhood school attendance.
    a. follows
    b. combines
    c. is dependent upon
    d. comes before

4. Young children's thinking is focused on
    a. first-hand current happening.
    b. abstract symbols.
    c. pleasing adults for rewards.
    d. the consequences of their behavior.

5. There is a _____ relationship between language and thought.
    a. well-understood
    b. well-researched
    c. clear
    d. cloudy

6. Resilient, able two- and three-year-olds have been described in this chapter as children who
    a. don't let others take their toys.
    b. are assertive and smart.
    c. have a strong sense of identity and self-worth.
    d. speak frequently and use "mature" language.

DEVELOPING LANGUAGE ARTS PROGRAMS

CHAPTER 5

Understanding Differences

OBJECTIVES

After studying this chapter, you should be able to:

- discuss standard and nonstandard English.

- describe the teacher's role with children who speak a dialect.

- discuss early childhood centers' language programs for second language learners.

- identify common speech problems.

The United States is becoming a multicultural society. During the 1990s it will shift from being a predominantly white society rooted in Western culture to a world society characterized by three large racial and ethnic minorities (Villarruel, Imig, and Kostelnik, 1995). As Garcia and McLaughlin (1995) note we are a country of incredible cultural and linguistic diversity. Remarried, never-married, single-parent, and cross-cultural families are quickly becoming the dominant family structure in the United States (Villarruel, Imig, and Kostelnik, 1995).

Many preschool teachers encounter a wide range of linguistically and culturally diverse young children, figure 5–1. Early childhood programs as well as elementary schools are examining older, traditional curriculum and teaching techniques. Quite simply, our school populations have changed, becoming much more diverse. Many educators believe as does Burchfield (1996):

Old models and traditional structures for teaching and learning are not working well for all children entering our school doors, nor are these approaches challenging children to reach their full potential so that they may succeed in school, the work place, and in life.

As with other educators, you will be searching for ways to meet young children's varied educational needs.

Play opportunity for many language-limited or language-diverse young children opens the child to expression and is an integral part of any early childhood program. As Wiltz and Fein (1996) explain:

Young children have numerous ways of expressing themselves. Through play, language, movement, and stories, they reveal their feelings and thoughts, usually with ease and spontaneity. Language is one mode of expression, and play is another.

Speech is improved when these children keep talking or trying to communicate, particularly communication in which the child attempts to express his or her own needs and intentions (Harris, 1990).

Child-Focused and Child-Sensitive Approaches

Program planners are experimenting and refining instructional models. These new approaches can

LINGUISTIC DIVERSITY IN THE USA

The latest Census found that 2.9 million U.S. households —3.2% of the nation's total — are linguistically isolated. This means, in these households, no person above age 14 speaks English fluently. What they speak:

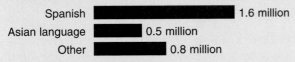

Spanish	1.6 million
Asian language	0.5 million
Other	0.8 million

31.8 million people above age 4 speak a language other than English at home. The 10 most common languages in 1990 and the percentage of change from 1980:

Number in Millions	Change
Spanish 17.3	+50.1%
French 1.7	+8.3%
German 1.5	–3.7%
Italian 1.3	–19.9%
Chinese 1.2	+97.7%
Tagalog. 0.8	+86.6%
Polish 0.7	–12.4%
Korean 0.6	+127.2%
Vietnamese. . . 0.5	+149.5%
Portuguese . . . 0.4	+19.0%

FIGURE 5–1 Linguistic diversity in the USA *(Source: U.S. Census Bureau)*

include offering young children:

- Multi-age activities and classrooms
- Developmentally appropriate educational experiences
- Group and project activities
- Meaningful printing (printscript) activities
- Opportunities to understand their world through musical, kinesthetic, special movement, and cooperative collaborative interaction with peers

In a safe classroom environment, one respecting differences and uniqueness, the environment energizes young children's ability to communicate desires, fears, and understandings (Wiltz and Fein, 1996).

The National Association for the Education of Young Children (NAEYC, 1996) has recommended:

> For the optimal development and learning of all children, educators must accept the legitimacy of children's home language, *respect* (hold in high regard) and *value* (esteem, appreciate) the home culture, and *promote* and *encourage* the active involvement and support of all families, including extended and nontraditional family units.

As Noori (1996) notes, recent perspectives in education encourage teachers to celebrate diversity and reflect on their own teaching behaviors and practices. Young children explore, question, predict, discover, and interact with their early childhood teachers who are bent on fostering natural curiosity by serving as co-explorers, feedback agents, providers of opportunity, and facilitators of children's emerging language abilities.

Teachers realize that children whose language skills or patterns are different are just as intelligent and capable as those who speak in standard English. Before discussing language differences, it is important to clarify the intent of this book. The purpose here is to help teachers (1) help the children and (2) help in such a way that it won't actually make matters worse. The teacher's sensitivity to and knowledge of a particular cultural group and different language patterns can aid a particular child's growth. Preserving the child's feelings of adequacy and acceptance is the teacher's prime goal; moving the child toward the eventual learning of standard forms is a secondary goal. Meers (1976) clearly states our primary goal:

> . . . to ensure that his idea of himself is positive; of helping the child see himself as a rich source of ideas, as an inventive, resourceful, problem-solving person who can function successfully in personal relationships; at work; in his leisure; as a full member of his community.

With today's busy, working parents and perhaps some homes that lack language interaction, it is increasingly important that schools and child care programs provide "language-filled," interactive, quality environments and skilled care providers. Many children who experience difficulties with language and communication may have had limited opportunities to engage in social routines in which language is natural and appropriate (Harris, 1990).

Early childhood educators strive, through professional associations and individual efforts, to increase program quality. In doing so, each center needs to examine its program to ensure language learning is not seen as occurring only at language time but from the moment teachers greet each child at the beginning of the day. Every child-adult interaction holds potential for child language learning. The key question is whether each child is receiving optimum opportunity during group care to listen and speak with a savvy adult skilled in natural conversation that reinforces, expands, and extends.

Bartoli (1995) describes problems facing teachers intent on helping children become literate:

> ... we have a growing underclass of educationally, socially, emotionally, and economically disenfranchised children and youth who will make up one-third of the population of the 21st century ... in our inner-city schools over half of attending students fail to learn how to read adequately.

It is particularly important that every individual have equal access to educational and economic opportunity, especially those from groups who have consistently been found on the bottom of the educational, social, and economic heap—African American, Latino, Mexican American, and Native American people (Bartoli, 1995).

Standard English

Standard English is the language of elementary schools and textbooks. It is the language of the majority of people in the U.S. The child whose speech reflects different past experiences and a cultural (or subcultural) outlook that is different from the majority is found in increasing numbers in preschool programs. By practicing and copying his or her group's way of speaking and becoming aware of his or her group's values, attitudes, food preferences, clothing styles, and so on, the child gains acceptance as a group member. Some theorize that the child's manner of thinking about life's experiences has also been influenced.

Phillips (1988) believes one of the goals of preschool teachers is to offer language instruction that helps all racial and cultural groups have equal access to opportunities for quality lives and power over their own lives. Standard English usage is advantageous, and possibly, as Jespersen (1945) states, a unifying force that brings together cultures within cultures, thereby minimizing class differences.   —6 dialects

Dialect, as used here, refers to language patterns that differ from standard American English. Dialects exist in all languages and fall into categories: (1) regional and geographic and (2) social and ethnic (Yawkey et al., 1981). Diverse dialects include African-American English, Puerto Rican English, Appalachian English, varieties of Native American English, Vietnamese English, and others. Dialects are just as highly structured, logical, expressive, and complex as standard English.

Washington and Craig's (1995) study of African-American preschoolers who speak **Black English** found the children used advanced syntax such as linking two clauses 12 percent of the time, while their standard-English speaking peers used complex syntax only 6 percent of the time. African-American

---

Standard English — substantially uniform formal and informal speech and writing of educated people that is widely recognized as acceptable wherever English is spoken and understood.

Dialect — a variety of spoken language unique to a geographical area or social group. Variations in dialect may include phonological or sound variations, syntactical variations, and lexical or vocabulary variations.   _word usage_

Black English — a language usually spoken in some economically depressed black homes. A dialect of nonstandard English having its own rules and patterns.

English, Black English, and the term **Ebonics** refer to a grammatically consistent speech whose key features include not conjugating the verb "to be" and the dropping of some final consonants from words, figure 5–2. Current debate focuses on whether African-American English is a distinct **language** or a **dialect** (Leland & Joseph, 1997). Elevating African-American English to the status of a language has evoked emotional reaction nationwide from both African-Americans and others. Early childhood professional have mixed opinions. Many educators believe the professional teacher's primary task is to preserve children's belief that they are *already* capable speakers and also provide the opportunity for children to hear abundant standard English speech models in classrooms. Linguists and educators do agree on the desperate need to teach some African-American children standard English, but there is little agreement on how best to do so (Hale, 1997). It should be pointed out here that many African-American children speak standard English not African-American English.

Actually, only relatively minor variations in vocabulary, pronunciation, and grammatical forms are apparent in most dialects as Jaggar (1980) explains:

> Most variations occur in pronunciation. For example, nonstandard speakers may not pronounce the "rr" and "l" sounds and the consonant cluster at the ends of words. . . .

Ebonics — a nonstandard form of English, a dialect often called Black English that is characterized by not conjugating the verb "to be" and by dropping some final consonants from words.

(Joiner, 1979, p. 343)	Examples
1. The use of the verb <u>be</u> to indicate a reality that is recurring or continuous over time.	1. <u>He be working</u> = He is working everyday.
2. The deletion of some form of the verb <u>to be</u>.	2. <u>Cleo sick today</u> = Cleo is sick today.
3. The use of the third person singular verbs without adding the <u>s</u> or <u>z</u> sound.	3. <u>My mama she talk all the time</u> = My mama she talks all the time.
4. The use of the <u>f</u> sound for the <u>th</u> sound at the end of a word.	4. <u>mouf</u> = mouth <u>wif</u> = with
5. The use of an additional word to denote plurals rather than adding an <u>s</u> to the noun.	5. <u>Two boy left for home</u> = Two boys left for home or boys left for home.
6. Non-use of <u>s</u> to indicate possessives.	6. <u>Mr. Green truck got smashed</u> = Mr. Green's truck got smashed.
7. The elimination of <u>l</u> or <u>r</u> sounds in words.	7. <u>hep</u> = help <u>doe</u> = door
8. The use of words with different meanings.	8. <u>bad</u> = great/good
9. The lack of emphasis on the use of tense in verbs.	9. <u>They already walk to the store</u> = The already walked to the store.
10. The deletion of final consonants.	10. <u>toll</u> = told <u>fine</u> = find
11. The use of double subjects.	11. <u>George he here now</u> = George is here now.
12. The use of <u>it</u> instead of <u>there</u>.	12. <u>It ain't none left</u> = There isn't any left.

FIGURE 5–2   Some features of Black English *(From "Memorandum Opinion and Order: Martin Luther King Junior Elementary School Children et al. V. Ann Arbor School District Board" (473 F. Supp. 1371 (1979), by C. W. Joiner. Reprinted in* Black English and the Education of Black Children and Youth, *E. G. Smitherman. Detroit, MI: Wayne State University Center for Black Studies, 1981.)*

The pronunciation rules thus produce different homonyms in children's language, just as *their* and *there* and *pail* and *pale* do in standard English. These and other differences are shared by many regional standard dialects and should not interfere with communication. The context should be sufficient to reveal the child's meaning. There are fewer dialectical differences in grammar than in pronunciation, but these differences are the more stigmatizing. ... Moreover, if we examine the grammatical variations we find they are relatively minor, surface differences in language ...

Speakers of a particular dialect form a speech community that reflects the members' life-styles or professional, national, family, or ethnic backgrounds. Certain common features mark the speech of the members, and no two members of a particular community ever speak alike because each person's speech is unique (Donoghue, 1985). The term "dialect" unfortunately can connote to some people less than correct speech. In the U.S. today, the major regional dialect areas are identified as Northern, Southern, South Midland, Gulf Southern, North Midland, and Plains Southern (Conklin and Lourie, 1983). In describing speakers from these areas, many would describe them as having a speech accent. Dialects differ from one another in a number of ways and are fully formed systems. As Farr (1992) points out, children from nonmainstream groups enter school with a set of linguistic and cultural resources that in some respects differ from, and even conflict with, rather than resemble, those of the school culture.

Dialects evolve naturally over time and possess an element of regularity and systematic usage. Jones (1990) points out a language dialect provides social identity and cultural cohesion. Clay (1991) describes child acquisition of dialectic speech and its importance:

Some children acquire through parents and neighborhood what has been called a "nonstandard" dialect. It is an intimate possession, understood by loved ones. It reflects their membership in a particular speech group and identifies them with that group. It is personal and valuable and not just an incorrect version of a standard dialect.

Individuals react to dialects with prestige, acceptance, ambivalence, neutral feelings, or rejection, based on value judgments.

Dialect-speaking teachers, aides, and volunteers (working with children and families of the same dialect) offer children a special degree of familiarity and understanding. A standard-English speaking teacher may sound less familiar but affords the child a model for growth in speaking the dominant language of our society, which is important to his or her life opportunities.

Although a dialect (or accent) may be an advantage in one's community, it may be a disadvantage outside of that community. Farr (1992) believes:

To learn mainstream language and cultural patterns, then, is tantamount to denying one's identity and joining forces with those who are rejecting one's group.

Just as a child who meets another child from a different part of the country with a different accent might say, "You sound funny!" so others may think of dialectic speech as crude or reflecting lack of education. Early childhood teachers are urged to celebrate diversity and remain nonjudgmental.

Accented speech, for this discussion, is defined as distinctive, typical speech habits of an individual or group of individuals associated with a geographic location or region. One can speak standard English with an accent, but a dialectic speaker is a nonstandard-English speaker.

Working with Dialect-Speaking Families

Many centers employ staff members who have dialects that the children can easily understand, so children feel at home. Teachers who speak the children's dialect may be eagerly sought and in short supply. Additional insight into the child's culture and the particular meanings of their words is often an advantage for teachers who have the same dialect as the children. They may be able to react and expand ideas better than a standard-English-speaking teacher.

It is important for teachers to know whether the children are speaking a dialect and to understand dialectic differences. The four most common dialectic differences between standard English and some common dialects occur in verb forms. These differences occur in the following areas.

- subject-verb agreement
- use of the verb "to be"
- use of present tense for past tense
- use of got for have

In some areas where a language other than English is spoken, part of the rules of the second language may blend and combine to form a type of English, different from the standard. Examples of this are (1) English spoken by some Native American children, and (2) English spoken in communities close to the Mexican/American border.

There are differing opinions about the teaching of preferred standard English in early childhood centers. In most centers, however, preserving the child's native dialect while moving slowly toward standard English usage is considered more desirable than immediate, purposeful instruction in standard forms. Joint parent and center discussions can help clarify program goals.

The Teacher's Role

Understanding dialectic differences is important to the teacher's understanding of each child. In order to give young children the best model possible, the teacher should speak standard English. On the other hand, many successful teachers have speech accents and also possess other characteristics, abilities, and useful techniques that aid young children's development of language and literacy. It matters very little to children whether the teacher speaks a bit differently from the way they speak. The teacher's attitude, warmth, and acceptance of the dialect and

FIGURE 5–3 Staff attitude and behavior can build each child's feelings of self-confidence.

the children themselves is a very important consideration (figure 5–3).

Kiefer (1985) observes teachers are in a unique position to build bridges rather than walls between cultures. Villarruel, Imig, and Kostelnik (1995) feel the teacher's essential task is to create new and shared meanings between the teacher and children—new contexts that give meaning to the knowledge and skills being taught. The challenge is to find personally interesting and culturally relevant ways of creating new contexts for children, contexts in which school skills are meaningful and rewarding.

As Strickland (1994) points out, competence is not tied to a particular language, dialect, or culture.

Galda, Cullinan, and Strickland (1993) clarify the correct techniques to encourage the child's use of standard English:

Encourage standard English through exposure to a variety of oral and written texts and oral language activities. Keep in mind that while competence in standard English is a worthy goal for all children, it must not mean a rejection or replacement of one language and culture with another. Rather, it should be viewed as language expansion and enrichment of the student's home language to include standard English, giving them the opportunity and the *choice* to communicate with a broader speech community.

Teachers may receive little instruction (teacher training) in the types of language behaviors to expect from diverse speakers, or little help in how to effect growth in language competencies. Kiefer suggests that with meager research on diversity at the present time, teachers themselves will need to do their own classroom observation and research to identify variations and differences. Young preschoolers have learned the social speech expectations of their homes and possibly their communities. They know when to speak and when to be silent. At school they make inferences about what's appropriate based on what they hear and observe there. When children begin to use a second language or second dialect, they tend to use words in syntactic constructions found in their native speech or dialect. Since quite a few cultures, including Chinese, Vietnamese, and some Native American communities, expect children to learn from listening, these young children may be relatively silent when contrasted with children encouraged to be verbal from birth. Hawaiian children observed by researchers often did not like to be singled out for individual attention, and tended to give minimal answers when questioned.

Since impact words and swear words are said with emotion and emphasis, it's not uncommon for these words to be learned first and used at the wrong time. In some cultures children may be encouraged to use "yes" and interrupt adult speech to signify they are in tune with the speaker.

Some facial expressions or gestures acceptable in one culture may be highly insulting in another (Kiefer, 1985). Even the acceptable distance between speakers of different languages varies. Teachers may interpret various child language (or lack of it) as disrespectful without considering cultural diversity. Misunderstandings between children, humorous as they may be to teachers, will need sensitive handling.

A child may be a very good speaker of his or her particular dialect or language, or he or she may be just a beginner. Staff members working with the young child should respect the child's natural speech and not try to stop the child from using it. The goal is to promote the child's use of natural speech in his or her native dialect. Standard English can be taught by having many good speaking models available at the center for the child to hear. Interested adults, play activities, other children, and a rich language arts program can provide a setting where children listen and talk freely.

The teacher should know what parts of the center's program are designed to increase the child's use of words. Teachers can show a genuine interest in words in their daily conversations with the children. The teacher can also use the correct forms of standard English in a casual way, using natural conversation. Correcting the children in an obvious way could embarrass them and stop openness and enthusiasm. Careful listening, skillful response, and appropriate questions during conversations help the child learn to put thoughts into words. The child thinks in terms of his or her own dialect or language first and, in time, expresses words in standard English.

Preschool teachers must face the idea that children's accents and dialects may affect their attitudes about those children and, consequently, teacher behaviors. A teacher may tend to seek out and communicate with those children whose speech is most similar to the teacher's speech. Extra effort may be necessary to converse and instruct. Staff-parent meetings and additional planning is a must to meet the needs of children with diverse language patterns. Pronunciation guides helping teachers say children's names correctly are gathered from parents at admitting interviews. This is just a small first step.

Working with culturally diverse children means lots of teacher observation ("kid watching"). This may give clues to each child's preferred or learned style of language interaction.

Sensitive, seasoned teachers won't put some children on-the-spot with direct questions or requests at group times. They may include additional storytelling or demonstration activities with young children whose native cultures use this type of approach. "Rappin," chanting, and words-to-music may appear to a greater extent in some child programs. Drama may be a way to increase language use in other classrooms. To be sure, with the great diversity in today's early childhood classrooms, teachers will be struggling to reach and extend each child's language competence. This is not an easy task!

Farr (1992) urges teachers who work with non-mainstream children to:

- understand that their own views of the world, or ways of using language in that world, are not necessarily shared by others.
- be aware of the extent to which they believe their own cultural and linguistic patterns are natural or logical, and realize how they may tend to interpret others' behavior according to their cultural norms.
- realize indirectness in language or other behavior can signify respect or politeness in one culture and dishonesty in another.
- understand communication between teacher and student is crucial to effective teaching and learning.

Soto's (1991) suggestions are based on recent research. They follow:

1. Accept individual differences with regard to language-learning time frames. . . . Avoid pressures to "rush" and "push" children. . . . Young children need time to acquire, explore, and experience second language learning.
2. Accept children's attempts to communicate, because trial and error are a part of the second language learning

process. . . . Children should be given opportunities to practice both native and newly established language skills. Adults should not dominate the conversations; rather, children should be listened to. . . .
3. Recognize that children need to acquire new language skills instead of replacing existing linguistic skills. Afford young children an opportunity to retain their native language and culture. . . .
4. Provide a stimulating, active, diverse linguistic environment with many opportunities for language use in meaningful social interactions. Avoid rigid . . . grammatical approaches with young children. . . .
5. Valuing each child's home culture and incorporating meaningful active participation will enhance interpersonal skills, and contribute to academic and social success.
6. Use informal observations to guide the planning of activities, interactions, and conversations for speakers of other languages.
7. Provide an accepting classroom climate that values culturally and linguistically diverse young children.

Additional Teacher Tips

A teacher should guard against:

- Correcting children in a way that makes them doubt their own abilities.
- Giving children the idea that they are not trying hard enough to correct or improve their speech.
- Discouraging children's speaking.
- Allowing teasing about individual speech differences.
- Interrupting children who are trying to express an idea.
- Hurrying a child who is speaking.
- Putting children on stage in an anxiety-producing way.

Second-Language Learners

Garcia (1991) defines language-minority children (second-language learners) as children who:

1. Participate extensively in non-English-speaking social and cultural contexts out of school.
2. Have developed the communicative competence required for participation in those sociocultural contexts.
3. Are being introduced, in substantive ways, to an English-speaking environment.

Grant (1995) describes the two categories of second-language learners as follows:

> In educational settings, young learners who speak no or very little English fall into two categories. The first includes those children who come to this country at a very young age or are born here to immigrants who have lived in areas of the world where language as well as the culture, systems of government, and social structures are quite unlike those of the United States. The second category comprises learners who are native born, such as Native Americans or Alaskan natives, yet enjoy different languages, personal histories, and cultures.

The following terms may be used in reading and research to describe second-language learners:

- Bilingual learner
- English as a second language student
- Students with limited English proficiency
- Language-minority learner
- English language learner
- Linguistically diverse student (Grant, 1995)

Weitzman (1992) defines simultaneous bilingualism as a child younger than three years of age who learns two (sometimes more) languages at the same time and sequential bilingualism as a child who learns a second language after age three.

Children, just learning, may possess different degrees of proficiency in two or more languages. Genesee and Nicoladis (1995) discuss the vocabulary development of young preschoolers in the following:

> That bilingual children initially might have smaller vocabularies when each language is considered separately should not be surprising when one considers a couple of facts. The memory capacity of young children is limited and presumably restricts their rate of vocabulary acquisition, even if only one language is involved. Bilingual children have equally limited memory capacities but two sets of vocabularies to learn. Thus, at any particular point during development, one would expect them to know fewer vocabulary items in each language but approximately the same number when both languages are taken together.

White (1986) suggests that if more than one language is spoken in the home and both languages are spoken well, the baby should be exposed to both from the beginning. But if, as is so often the case, the first language is spoken exclusively in the home, research indicates the child should be encouraged to develop expertise in a wide range of language functions in the first language, in the expectation that these will easily transfer to the second language (English).

The most immediate question the teacher of a bilingual child must face is deciding how well the child is progressing in all the languages the child is learning. A full language assessment with respect to the child's first language and with respect to the child's knowledge of English will probably show the child's difficulties are limited to the acquisition of English.

Children raised in bilingual settings have demonstrated that, not only do they acquire their first language with ease, but they can simultaneously learn a second language (Allen, 1992). When working with second-language learning preschoolers, Allen suggests:

> . . . it is important that the learner receive input that is not only comprehensible but just slightly beyond his or her current level of competence.

Pressure tactics by over-eager teachers that cause young children anxiety actually delay second-language acquisition.

Wong-Fillmore (1976) has identified several strategies that children used to learn English as a second language:

1. They assumed that what people are saying is directly related to the ongoing situation.
2. They learned a few stock expressions or formulaic speech, and started to talk.
3. They looked for patterns that recurred in the language.
4. They made the most of the language they had.
5. They spent their major effort on getting across meaning and saved the refinement for later.

She estimates that most second-language learning children will require from four to six years to be competent users of English, and some will take as long as five to eight years.

Garcia and McLaughlin (1995) suggest effective early childhood curricula should provide:

- abundant and diverse opportunities for speaking and listening
- **scaffolding** to help guide the child through the learning process
- encouragement to take risks, construct meaning, and reinterpret knowledge within compatible social contexts

Neuroscience researcher's findings support the idea that the ability to learn a second language is highest between birth and the age of six, then undergoes a steady inexorable decline (Nash, 1997).

A variety of plans and methods to help bilingual children are adopted in most early childhood centers (figure 5–4). Techniques are often researched and studied by individual staff members and are frequently part of a center's in-service education. Home-school instructional programs have provided books, audiotapes, "borrowed" tape players (recorders) for use in homes with limited access to English language models and storybooks (Blum, Koskinen, Tennant, Parker, Straub, & Curry, 1995).

FIGURE 5–4 A program rich in experiences is planned.

Many educators believe as Soto (1991) does:

Immigrant children from diverse, developing nations . . . are entering classrooms which are usually unprepared to receive them.

Soto describes the optimal early childhood bilingual program as supportive, natural, with a language-rich environment, affording acceptance and meaningful interactions.

Scaffolding — a teaching technique helpful in promoting languages, understanding, and child solutions. It includes teacher-responsive conversation, open-ended questioning, and facilitation of children's initiatives.

Being unable to understand or to be understood may be one of the problems facing the bilingual child. Like monolingual speakers, bilinguals make inferences about social and linguistic appropriateness, based on continued interaction in diverse social settings (Genishi, 1985). Learning a second language includes a number of difficult tasks. The child must:

- Produce sounds that may not be used in the native language.
- Understand that native speech sounds or words may have different meanings in the new (second) language.
- Learn and select appropriate responses.
- Sort and revise word orders.
- Learn different cultural values and attitudes.
- Control the flow of air while breathing and speaking.

Weitzman (1992) has also identified three stages of second-language learning, figure 5–5.

An important technique—admitting and recognizing that a child is a classroom resource when it comes to explaining other ways of naming and describing objects or other ways of satisfying human needs—should be understood by teachers (Clement, 1981). Printed word cards in both languages can be added to the classroom to reinforce this idea.

The preschooler's language capacity helps the child who learns two languages during the early years. In preschool work, it is common to meet children who can quickly switch fluent conversation between two languages.

U.S. News and World Report (July 1986) points out that the number of American preschoolers who are learning to speak two and three languages is on the rise, because many experts, brain researchers, and parents believe that learning foreign tongues stimulates a child's mental development. Research has promoted the idea that bilingual youngsters are more imaginative, better with abstract notions, and more flexible in their thinking than monolingual children. Some educators point out that even if a child after learning two languages well discontinues use of one, the unused language is stored

Stage 1:

The child becomes involved in social interactions with speakers of the second language.

During this stage, the child relies on whole, memorized phrases and sentences—e.g., "Know what?" or "All right, you guys." She also uses nonverbal communication—e.g., pointing, and a number of key words which are useful in social situations. In general, she tries to act as if she knows what's going on and guesses a lot at what people mean.

Stage 2:

The child communicates with second-language speakers in the second language.

The principle at this stage seems to be "Start talking." The child begins to create her own sentences, which may include memorized phrases and some new vocabulary. She communicates as best she can, even if the way she expresses herself is not correct. Children who are risk-takers learn the language quicker than those who don't talk much for fear of making a mistake.

Stage 3:

The child attempts to speak correctly, using correct vocabulary, grammar, and pronunciation.

The child looks for patterns in sentences, just as she did when learning her first language, and then works out the rules.

FIGURE 5–5 Three stages of second language learning that seem to motivate and guide second language learners after age 3. (*From* Learning Language and Loving It, *by C. Weitzman, 1992. Reprinted with permission from The Hanen Centre, 252 Bloor St. W, Ste. 3–390, Toronto, Ontario, Canada M5S 1V5.*)

for future reference and makes that language or another easier to learn at a later age (Lambert, 1986). Researchers have noticed that bilingualism improves many children's self-esteem and strengthens family ties, figure 5–6.

Most early childhood educators ask themselves "How can I best address the needs of speakers of other languages?" (Soto, 1991).

Researchers studying second-language learners believe second-language preschoolers are able to communicate in peer-appropriate ways using verbal

FIGURE 5–6   Bilingual children are fluent in two languages.

children's everyday, first-hand exploration of the environment.

Additional suggested teacher techniques follow:

- Provide a safe, accepting classroom environment.
- Listen patiently, maintaining eye contact.
- Give attention to child attempts.
- Respond to meaning rather than speech technicalities or specifics.
- Promote sharing and risk-taking.
- Make classroom activities inviting, interesting, meaningful, and successful.
- Help the child realize he or she is unique and special, exactly "as is."

Arenas (1978) feels that successful programs for bilingual/bicultural children should:

- Provide an environment that reflects the language and culture of the children it serves. Staff members and program resources should be representative of the group's racial and cultural mixture.
- Build on the strengths that bilingual/bicultural children bring to a new learning situation. The children have a language, and with it a rich cultural background with values and expectations—a strong base for learning.
- Continue the development of the first language and facilitate the acquisition of a second. Children should be made to feel that their language or dialect is both acceptable and welcome. Show children the pleasure and necessity of communication in both languages.
- Be aware of the child's home values and expectations; involve parents in various aspects of the program.
- Integrate both languages into all areas of the curriculum in an atmosphere of respect and appreciation for cultural diversity. If both languages are part of the regular classroom environment, children will help each other learn both languages. All children will benefit from understanding that there are many ways of speaking and different ways of behaving.

and nonverbal skills when in play situations but not as successfully in cognitive/academic tasks (Skutnabb-Kangas and Toukomaa, 1976). Cummins (1979) theorizes a cognitively and academically beneficial form of bilingualism can be achieved only on the basis of adequately developed first-language skills. Early childhood practitioners following this theory would strongly promote and support parental provision of literacy-rich activities in the child's home language and also attempt to recruit teachers aides and classroom volunteers who speak the child's native tongue.

The value of second-language learning children's exposure to quality books can't be overlooked. Story times and one-to-one, adult-child book readings can supply vocabulary and meaning in a way that conversational models alone cannot accomplish. Songs and music can also present language learning opportunities. Print use in the center environment can also promote literacy development. Opportunities for abundant play and interaction with English-speaking children is another important aspect of all early childhood programs handling second-language learners.

The most successful methods for teaching a second language include the same features mentioned in the child's learning of his or her first language—warm, responsive, articulate adults involved with

Since many centers deal with children who speak a language other than English, or who speak very little English, a center has many decisions to make. The first concern should be the child's adjustment to school. Every effort should be made to make the child feel at ease.

Elementary schools teaching reading have relied on a variety of methods. Two common strategies are used:

1. Delay reading instruction until the child has mastered English, or

2. Teach reading in the child's native language (dialect) and switch to English during a later grade in school.

Preschools that encourage children to use two languages are given suggestions by Flores (1980). (Ms. Flores focuses on the Spanish-speaking child, but the comments and suggestions could be applied to other language groups.)

- *Let the children hear both languages.* Speak both languages throughout the day so that children feel comfortable with the second language.
- *Identify the languages being spoken.* When two languages are being used, identify each language to confirm the child's notion that more than one language is being spoken.
- *Acknowledge and encourage a child's attempt to speak a second language.* Children eventually will experiment with the sounds and intonations of a second language. Encourage them and comment on what they are doing: "That sounds a lot like Spanish, Mark." When a child addresses you in gibberish, answer in the language they are imitating and then translate. This gives the child the feeling that talking and being understood in the second language is possible.
- *Let a child hear you speak his or her second language to another child.* For example, read a story in Spanish to a Spanish-speaking child so that an English-speaking child nearby can overhear.
- *Occasionally, give simple commands to the whole group in one language without translating.* "Let's clean up now."
- *Once you get along well with a child in his or her first language, talk to that child for short periods in the second language.* A child may not under-

stand at first, but by hearing a lot of the second language in a variety of situations, the child will eventually begin to notice, play with, and grasp intonation patterns and sounds.

Children whose spoken language is not English, or whose variety of English is not similar to regional standard, and/or whose parents have not read to them extensively before they get to school, find themselves immediately behind the literacy eight-ball (Brause & Mayher, 1991). Teachers should not focus on relatively minor differences, but rather on the common potential.

Teachers faced with a portion of their enrollment speaking another language face unique problems. An interpreter may be necessary, and a concerted effort should be made to understand the family's culture. Consultants and parents are invaluable. Bilingual teachers or aides are required in a number of centers that serve newly arrived populations. Designing room features and planning curriculum activities that welcome and show acceptance are important staff tasks.

Gestures aid communication. Pairing words with actions when speaking and naming distinctly helps children understand.

Both teachers and children can be expected to experience some frustration. Touching and nonverbal behaviors are important cues in communication. The teacher will find that his or her speech slows and sentences shorten to one or two words when speaking to the nonEnglish speaking child. Children will rely heavily on gestures as they try to communicate and speak. However, preschoolers' language ability is amazing, and teachers will notice more and more understanding of English, then hesitant naming, followed by beginning phrases. If the teacher tries to learn the child's language, the same sequence is apparent.

Cultural Differences

Cultural differences in communicating are important for a teacher to understand since cross-cultural communication abounds in many early childhood classrooms. MacDonald (1992) points out that diversity represents the richness and uniqueness of human life. It is something we value and share with the children we work with.

Multicultural education hopes to prepare children for a diverse society where differing languages are spoken and customs and values differ. Its goals include communicating despite differences, cooperating for mutual good, fighting bias and discrimination, respecting others' values, and dignity and fair treatment for all. Garcia and McLaughlin (1995) suggest early childhood education leaders must embrace our culturally diverse children, adopt them, nurture them, celebrate them, and challenge them.

A study of cultural differences can help teachers receive accurate messages. Gestures and body language of the cultural groups attending a center may differ widely in meaning.

Little research is available to guide early childhood educators who work with children from widely diverse cultural backgrounds. However, Wong-Fillmore's (1986) findings point out opportunities for Hispanic children to interact with English-speaking peers is an important factor in helping them acquire both speaking and comprehension skills. For some Chinese children, on the other hand, interactions with the teacher seemed more beneficial. Hispanic children in Wong-Fillmore's study did well when teacher instructions were clear and well organized, but they became inattentive when the teacher was unclear. Chinese children in the same study became even more attentive in situations in which understanding was difficult. Native American children seem to benefit when demonstrations accompany teacher verbalization (Phillips, 1972).

Teachers interested in studying the culture(s) of enrolled children might use Saville-Troike's (1978) identified components of culture. Components include family structure, definitions of stages, periods, or transitions during a person's life, roles of adults and children, their corresponding behavior in terms of power and politeness, discipline, time and space, religion, food, health and hygiene, history, traditions, holidays, and celebrations. Questions teachers could ask themselves concerning both their own culture and attending children's culture follow:

- How is a family defined? Is it extended or intergenerational? Two or more families in one residence? A family authority figure?
- Roles of child? Adults?
- Guidance techniques?
- Punctual? Are tasks completed slowly?
- Religion? Topics that shouldn't be discussed at school?
- Food preferences?
- Person(s) who treats family illness?
- Are there observances of historical events or well-known figures from their country of origin? What traditions exist? Holidays observed?
- Feelings concerning proper education of males, females, children?
- Typical conversational style(s)?
- Gestures common in country of origin?

The ways in which language is used in different situations vary from one culture to another. People from different cultural groups transact business in different ways; converse with one another in different ways; praise, criticize, and greet one another in different ways; and so on (Genesee and Nicoladis, 1995). Variations in the ways cultures organize the use of language reflect differences in cultural beliefs, values, and goals concerning social roles and relationships in their group (Crago, 1992).

In some cultures, it is believed that children are not appropriate conversational partners for adults and that the ability to learn language is not associated with the child's active use of language (Genesee and Nicoladis, 1995). Children may not be encouraged to initiate conversations about themselves or their interests, and adult talk may not be child-centered. Children may have learned not to look directly at adults when talking. Some children grow up learning that cooperation is more highly valued than competition and others the reverse (Villarruel, Imig, and Kostelnik, 1995).

Cultures are complex and changing, so understanding cultural similarities and differences can be a life's study in itself. Culture is defined here as all the activities and achievements of a society that individuals within that society pass from one generation to the next. Garcia and McLaughlin (1995) have an expanded definition:

> When we speak of "culture" to which an individual belongs, our reference is generally to the system of understandings (value, prescriptions, proscriptions, beliefs, and other constructs) characteristic of that individual's society, or some subgroup within his or her society—that is, ethnic minorities, social classes, countercultures, generations, genders, and occupational groups. . . . Most definitions of culture include another social dimension, the notion that culture is something that members of a group share in common.

Ethnic origin is often a basic ingredient in subcultural groupings. Subculture is defined as other than a dominant culture. Class structure also exists in societies consisting of upper, middle, and lower income groups. Often, patterns of child rearing vary between cultures and classes (Broman, 1978). Families may express attitudes and values peculiar to their class or culture. Attitudes and feelings of an impoverished group, for instance, often include futility, anger, violence, and loss of trust in anyone or anything.

Teachers try to determine the backgrounds of their attending families, noting the individual nature of children's home communities—housing, income, general numbers, and types of cultural groups—in an attempt to better understand children and provide language-developing experiences. Their

ability to respond and relate to what attending children verbalize is enhanced.

What cultural differences can inhibit child speech? Adult models' lengths of sentences or their inability to modify their speech to child levels, neutral or negative environments, family arrangements that require children to be alone for long periods or in which children are expected to be quiet or cannot gain adult attention, lack of books or early reading experiences are all factors that can affect speech growth. Hall (1982) states that parents are the primary language teachers in the early years and that language competence grows out of familiar situations such as seeking help or establishing joint attention—situations that provide frameworks in which children learn to make their intentions plain and to interpret the intentions of others.

Promoting Acceptance

Teachers need to remember bilingual children generally exhibit more rapid progress and more ability in whichever language predominates in their social environment (Genesee and Nicoladis, 1995).

Practitioners may have to field questions from children about another child's speech. Answering in an open, honest fashion with accurate information gives the adult an opportunity to affirm diversity and perhaps correct a child's biased ideas. Negative stereotypes can be diminished or dismissed. Before answering it is a good idea to clarify what the child is really asking. Examples of teacher statements follow:

> "Yes, Paloma speaks some words you don't understand. Her family comes from Guatemala and they speak the Spanish language. Paloma is learning lots of new words at school in the language of her new country—English."

> "Quan doesn't talk to you because he doesn't know our words yet. He speaks a different language at his house. He is listening, and one day he will speak. While he is listen-

---

Culture — all the activities and achievements of a society that individuals within that society pass from one generation to the next.

Subculture — an ethnic, regional, economic, or social group exhibiting characteristic patterns of behavior sufficient to distinguish it from others within an embracing culture or society.

ing and learning words to speak, he wants to play. Show him with your hands and words what you want him to do. He will understand."

Teachers working with culturally diverse children need to watch and listen closely. Children's behavior and movements will give clues to their well being and feelings of safety in the group. Teachers may need to ease into situations where unpleasant remarks or actions are directed at a newly enrolled child who speaks a different language and express sadness such as:

"Ricardo has heard some unkind and unfriendly words from you boys in the loft. He is new at school and doesn't know what our school is like. I'm going to try and help Ricardo enjoy his first day in our room."

Working with culturally diverse children also means that educators will guard against alienating children from their own cultural values. As Cummins (1986) points out, when they are not alienated, they do not experience widespread school failure.

Early childhood educators must realize besides learning a new language children are being socialized to literacy. They are developing literacy behaviors, such as knowing when and how to be part of a group, ask questions, offer ideas and reactions to literacy events, and so on.

Teachers need to remember the ability to learn a second language and the syntax of that language is highest between birth and the age of six (Nash, 1997). The same experiences and responsive care that gave rise to language in infancy will work—lots of language activities, labeling activities, listening to picture books, musical activities, play with peers, and the adult's time and confidence in the child's grasp of new-for-him language usage. As repetition of experience was needed in infancy, it will again be needed.

Identifying quality multicultural and multiethnic picture books is discussed in Chapter 9. Room displays, bulletin boards, and learning centers should also reflect the cultural diversity of attending children.

Planning Programs and Activities

In planning language activities of all types, every effort must be made to make children aware of cross-cultural similarities and to explore differences. Genesee and Nicoladis (1995) urge language arts programming to draw on the linguistic, cultural, and personal experiences of language-diverse children when planning instructional activities so that opportunities are provided that are familiar to them. Parents and extended family members can be invited to share family stories and artifacts relating to theme units, learning centers, or other program components.

Young children can be exposed to the idea that people eat, sleep, wear clothing, celebrate, dance, sing, live in groups, speak to one another in common languages, and that they do these things in ways that may be either the same as or different from the ways their families do these things. Planned activities can make comparisons treating diversity with the dignity it deserves. Skin color, hair styles, food preferences, clothing, and music are starting points for study. Modeling friendship and cooperation between cultures and planning activities showing dissimilar individuals and groups living in harmony is a good idea. Stories exist in all languages and in most dialects. Two resources for multicultural books follow:

Beilke, P. F., & Sciara, F. J. (1986). *Selecting materials for and about Hispanic and East Asian children and young people.* Hamden, CT: Shoe String Press/Library Professional Publications.

Rollock, B. (1984). *The black experience in children's books.* New York: New York Public Libraries.

It is important to plan language arts programs that incorporate different cultural styles of dramatic play, story-telling, and chanting (IBFC Bulletin, 1983). Librarians can help teachers discover picture books and other materials written in dialects or two language translations.

Each center designs its own activities, giving each child a chance to accomplish new skills. There are many possible program activities. Most program plans emphasize the following:

FIGURE 5–7 Preschools try to provide toys, activities, and events that expand the children's experiences.

- Activities that develop sensory skills—visual, auditory, and tactile (touch), as well as discriminatory, relational, and sequential abilities (figure 5–7).
- Activities that facilitate problem solving and concept development—classifying, organizing, and associating.
- Activities that deal with the language arts and vocabulary and comprehension development—listening, speaking, printing words, and using symbolic forms.
- Activities that promote children's biliteracy.

Planning for Play

Unfortunately young children who lack social skills may miss out on peer play interactions, which are important in language learning. This can have a tremendous impact on both development and social skill growth. Through play and its resultant conversations, peers are teachers. The child who cannot sustain play interactions with peers needs to learn skills associated with maintaining play relationships, which is sometimes tough enough for fluent child speakers. The acts of conflict resolution, sharing, cooperating, collaborating, and negotiating all involve use of language and are typical parts of preschool peer play.

Children who are learning English, have easily identifiable communication deficiencies (such as hearing loss, visual impairment, or speech impairments), and language delay often find they are left out of vital play experiences with others. Planning play opportunity and experiences is an important teacher task in program planning. This involves observing individual children during play periods and promoting play groups for children experiencing difficulties.

Planning program activities and goals with parents and community leaders and hiring staff members from the same ethnic and language-minority groups as attending children is a plan of action followed in some preschool programs.

Translating to parents the school's respect for

the culture and language of the parent is not an easy job. Knowledgeable educators realize the child's long range advantage as a future bilingual and bicultural job seeker. Every effort should be made to support parental efforts to acquaint their children with the parents' native culture and its language, literature, history, beliefs and values, and heritage.

Feeling at home at school and having opportunities to engage in mainstream language, book language, and a center's provision of a literate school environment are all factors to consider.

When working in communities with newly arrived immigrant populations, teachers have to devote considerable time and study to understanding the families and lives of attending children. A strong connection between home and school should exist, with parents playing a role in program planning and as assistants or teachers in classrooms. Parents can help teachers understand the many areas of similarity and diversity that possibly exist. When parent literacy rates are less than desirable, teachers have to proceed carefully with suggestions concerning reading to their children. Wordless books and parent storytelling are alternatives. Family literacy programs are discussed in Chapter 19.

Program Types

Controversy exists concerning which type of program is best suited to the child learning English as a second language. Commonly found programs include:

Bilingual program.
   Two languages are used for instructions.

Transitional bilingual program.
   Children's first language is used as a medium of instruction until they become fluent enough to receive all their instruction in English.

Maintenance bilingual program.
   Instruction in two languages is continued throughout the child's schooling experience to fully develop fluency and literacy in two languages.

English program only.
   Child attends a monolingual, English program.

Immersion program.
   The class is monolingual (English) but the teacher understands the child's native language and plans according to child's needs.

Tutor assisted program.
   Special tutor (or teacher) works with a child for a portion of the school day. (Allen, 1992)

Some classrooms combine approaches and program types.

Wong-Fillmore (1982), studying kindergarten classrooms, found children made better progress in English when teachers shaped their language to meet the learners' needs, simplified their language, used gestures, linked talk to a strong context, involved children in talk, and judiciously used the child's native language when necessary.

Visuals and images (pictorial representations) used while the teacher is talking almost always improves student listening comprehension and reduces recall errors (Chung, 1994).

The role of peers as teachers in preschool classrooms is important. Teachers are urged to organize programs that encourage children to work together on tasks that involve purposeful talk based on their own interests. Developing a buddy system in classrooms that pairs a newly arrived immigrant child with a long-term second-language resident is suggested (Grant, 1995).

The second-language child may associate more with other children speaking his or her native language, while monolingual peers present a better English model. When grouping is planned, teachers need to recognize and be sensitive to non-English-speaking children who work well with other speakers and those who still need the security of a buddy who speaks the native language. Encouraging child friendships among children has extra meaning to teachers working with non-English speakers.

Allen (1992) suggests second-language learners need classrooms in which children:

- Acquire the language naturally, using the language for real purposes.

- Receive linguistic input that is made comprehensible by a strong supportive context.

- Experiment with, hypothesize about, and try out language in low anxiety settings.

- Work with English-speaking peers on meaningful tasks that create opportunities and real reasons to talk, write, and listen to books together.

- Use language for a broad variety of functions, both social and academic.

Assessment

Assessment is usually undertaken when teachers suspect a child has difficulty communicating and could profit from specialized instruction. The goal is to identify whether a child's language is less advanced than other children his or her age (delayed language) or is deficient when compared with performance on social and/or intellectual tasks (language deficit) or whether the child fits both categories. Screening tests should be conducted by trained professionals.

In attempting to assess children with suspected language impairment during early childhood years, the staff needs to remember that children learn the language of their particular community. One needs to ask "What kind of language is appropriate for this child's home?" and "Is this child's ability consistent with his or her experience and the expectations of those around him or her?" (Harris, 1990).

Hearing disorders — characterized by an inability to hear sounds clearly. May range from hearing speech sounds faintly or in a distorted way, to profound deafness.

Speech and language disorders — communication disorders that affect the way people talk and understand and range from simple sound substitutions to not being able to use speech and language at all.

Children with Special Needs

Special language-development preschool centers with expert personnel are available in most communities for children with easily identifiable communication deficiencies such as hearing loss, visual impairment, and obvious speech impairments. Other children in need of special help may not be identified at the preschool level and function within the wide range of children considered to be average or normal for preschool ages. Most programs are reticent to label children as having language learning problems because of their lack of expertise to screen and evaluate children in a truly professional manner. Referral to speech-language pathologists or local or college clinics is suggested to parents when a question exists concerning a particular child's progress. Dumtschin (1988) points out that early childhood teachers are not speech or language pathologists and should therefore not be expected to diagnose language problems or to prescribe therapy. The National Association for Hearing and Speech Action (NAHSA) (1985) divides communication disorders into two main categories:

Hearing disorders. These are characterized by an inability to hear sounds clearly. Such disorders may range from hearing speech sounds faintly or in a distorted way, to profound deafness. See figure 5–8, a parent resource published by the American Speech-Language-Hearing Association (ASLHA) (1988).

Speech and language disorders. These affect the way people talk and understand and range from simple sound substitutions to not being able to use speech and language at all.

Speech-Language Disorders

About 11 to 13 million people in the U.S. have some kind of expressive speech disorder, the most frequent problem involving articulation—an estimated 75% (Weiss and Lillywhite, 1981). The rest, approximately 25%, have language, voice, and fluency disorders, or a combination of these. Most articulation

check one ✓		Hearing and Understanding	Child's Age	Talking	check one ✓	
YES	**NO**				**YES**	**NO**
		Does your child hear and understand most of what is said at home and in school? Does everyone who knows your child think he/she hears well (teacher, baby sitter, grandparent, etc.)? Does your child pay attention to a story and answer simple questions about it?	**4½–5 YEARS**	Does your child communicate easily with other children and adults? Does your child say all sounds correctly except maybe one or two? Does your child use the same grammar as the rest of the family?		
				Does your child's voice sound clear like other children's? Does your child use sentences that give lots of details (e.g., "I have two red balls at home")? Can your child tell you a story and stick pretty much to the topic?		
			4–4½ YEARS			
		Does your child hear you when you call from another room? Does your child hear television or radio at the same loudness level as other members of the family? Does your child answer simple "who," "what," "where," "why" questions?	**3–4 YEARS**	Does your child talk about what he/she does at school or at friends' homes? Does your child say most sounds correctly except a few, like *r*, *l*, *th* and *s*? Does your child usually talk easily without repeating syllables or words? Do people outside your family usually understand your child's speech? Does your child use a lot of sentences that have 4 or more words?		
		Does your child understand differences in meaning ("go–stop"; "in–on"; "big–little"; "up–down")? Does your child continue to notice sounds (telephone ringing, television sound, knocking at the door)? Can your child follow two requests ("get the ball and put it on the table")?		Does your child have a word for almost everything? Does your child use 2–3 word "sentences" to talk about and ask for things? Do you understand your child's speech most of the time? Does your child often ask for or direct your attention to objects by naming them?		
			2–3 YEARS			
		Can your child point to pictures in a book when they are named? Does your child point to a few body parts when asked? Can your child follow simple commands and understand simple questions ("Roll the ball," "Kiss the baby," "Where's your shoe?")? Does your child listen to simple stories, songs, and rhymes?	**1–2 YEARS**	Is your child saying more and more words every month? Does your child use some 1–2 word questions ("where kitty?" "go bye-bye?" "what's that?")? Does your child put 2 words together ("more cookie," "no juice," "mommy block")? Does your child use many different consonant sounds at the beginning of words?		
		Does your child recognize words for common items like "cup," "shoe," "juice"? Has your child begun to respond to requests ("Come here," "Want more?")?	**7 MONTHS–1 YEAR**	Does your child have 1 or 2 words (bye-bye, dada, mama, no) although they may not be clear?		
		Does your child enjoy games like peek-a-boo and pat-a-cake? Does your child turn or look up when you call his or her name? Does your child listen when spoken to?		Does your child's babbling have both long and short groups of sounds such as "tata upup bibibibi"? Does your child imitate different speech sounds? Does your child use speech or non-crying sounds to get and keep your attention?		
		Does your child respond to "no"? Changes in your tone of voice? Does your child look around for the source of new sounds, e.g., the doorbell, vacuum, dog barking? Does your child notice toys that make sound?	**4–6 MONTHS**	Does your child's babbling sound more speech-like with lots of different sounds, including *p*, *b*, and *m*? Does your child tell you (by sound or gesture) when he/she wants you to do something again? Does your child make gurgling sounds when left alone? When playing with you?		
		Does your child turn to you when you speak? Does your child smile when spoken to? Does your child seem to recognize your voice and quiet down if crying?	**0–3 MONTHS**	Does your child repeat the same sounds a lot (cooing, gooing)? Does your child cry differently for different needs? Does your child smile when he/she sees you?		
		Does your child listen to speech? Does your child startle or cry at noises? Does your child awaken at loud sounds?	**BIRTH**	Does your child make pleasure sounds? When you play with your child, does he/she look at you, look away, & then look again?		
		Total		**Total**		

INSTRUCTIONS: Read each question through your child's age group and check yes or no. Add the total and see below.

ALL YES: GOOD—Your child is developing hearing, speech, and language normally.

1–2 NO: CAUTION! Your child may have delayed hearing, speech, and language development. Look at the "Reminders" section in this brochure.

3 OR MORE NO: ACTION! Take your child for professional help. See "Where to get help" section.

FIGURE 5-8 Speech and hearing ages *(From "How Does Your Child Hear and Talk?" Reprinted with permission from the American Speech-Language-Hearing Association.)*

problems not caused by physical, sensory, or neurological damage respond to treatment. Nonorganic causes of problems can include:

- lack of stimulation
- lack of need to talk
- poor speech models
- lack of or low reinforcement
- insecurity, anxiety, crisis

Language Delay

Language delay is characterized by a marked slowness in the development of the vocabulary and grammar necessary for expressing and understanding thoughts and ideas (NAHSA, 1985). It may involve both comprehension and the child's expressive language output and quality. A complete study of a child includes first looking for physical causes, particularly hearing loss, and other structural (voice producing) conditions. Neurological limitations come under scrutiny, as do emotional development factors. Home environments and parental communicating styles are examined when a thorough study by speech-language pathologists takes place. Referral to experts is considered if a child falls two years behind his or her peers or when a sudden change in a well progressing child is noticed. Dumtschin (1988) has identified possible noticeable behavior of language-delayed children:

> Language-delayed children may display limited vocabularies, use short, simple sentences, and make many grammatical errors. They may have difficulty maintaining a conversation, talk more about the present and less about the future, and have difficulty in understanding others and in making themselves understood.

> In addition to strictly linguistic problems, language-delayed children may also have difficulty classifying objects and recognizing similarities and differences. They may spend little time in dramatic play with others and may exhibit general difficulties

in the classroom. The extent of concern would necessarily differ according to the age of the child.

Other behaviors a teacher might notice include:

- less variety in sentence structure
- simple two- and three-word sentences
- less frequent speech
- plays alone frequently
- participates less adeptly in joint planning with age mates

Teachers might readily agree with the following description of a language-delayed child: "Speaks markedly less well than other children of the same age and seems to have normal ability in intellectual, motor, sensory, and emotional control areas."

Indication of language delay mentioned by NAHSA (1985) includes a child's not using words by the age of two years, or not being able to speak in short sentences by age three. Another indication would be a child's inability to respond to simple requests, such as "sit down" or "come here," by age two.

Teachers working with language-delayed children use the following interactive techniques:

- gaining attention with tempting, interest-catching activities
- being at eye level, face-to-face, if possible
- establishing eye contact
- displaying enthusiasm and playfulness
- establishing a play activity involving my turn, your turn interaction
- verbalizing single words, short phrases, or short sentences depending on child's verbal level
- pausing, waiting, and looking expectantly, encouraging the child's turn to talk
- repeating teacher statements and pausing expectantly
- copying the child's actions or verbalizations
- following the child's focus of interest with joint teacher interest
- probing the child's interest with logical questions
- maintaining close, accepting physical contact and a warm interactive manner

Dumtschin (1988) suggests that preschool teachers provide language-rich environments that effectively support language-delayed children and regard the children as active learners, encouraging communicative attempts in an accepting atmosphere, using interaction techniques that are related to the children's focus of attention, and capitalizing on spontaneous language-teaching opportunities.

The Cloistered Child

Some teachers and educators describe children with inadequate language due to lack of human interactive environments (Healy, 1990; O'Rourke, 1988; Costa, 1988). To be "cloistered" connotes isolation, separation, limited experience, meager human contact, a narrow view of the world, small or sparsely furnished living quarters, plus a time-consuming devotion to spiritual contemplation and prayer. In the cloistered child the spiritual contemplation and prayer has been replaced with the passive pursuit of hours and hours of undiscussed television and/or video watching.

The cloistered child is thought to display one or many of the following characteristics:

- limited attention span
- unable to express ideas
- limited language and vocabulary
- unable to draw on past knowledge
- unable to listen
- impulsive (says first thing that pops into mind)
- lacks perseverance ("It's work. It's too hard.")
- blunted interest and curiosity
- disorganized
- expects learning to be fun
- impatient, can't wait
- poor conversation skill

The curriculum recommended to develop what is seen as "missing language and missing experience" includes lots of talk, active involvement, time and play with other children, and exposure to literature. Benard (1993) would recommend opportunities to plan, which facilitates seeing oneself in control, and promoting child resourcefulness in seeking help from others.

Articulation

Articulation disorders involve difficulties with the way sounds are formed and strung together, usually characterized by substituting one sound for another, omitting a sound, or distorting a sound.

If consonant sounds are misarticulated, they may occur in the initial (beginning), medial (middle), or ending positions in words. It's prudent to point out again that normally developing children don't master the articulation of all consonants until age seven or eight.

Most young children (three to five years old) hesitate, repeat, and re-form words as they speak. Imperfections occur for several reasons: (1) A child does not pay attention as closely as an adult, especially to certain high-frequency consonant sounds; (2) the child may not be able to distinguish some sounds; (3) a child's coordination and control of his or her articulatory mechanisms may not be perfected. For example, he or she may be able to hear the difference between Sue and shoe but cannot pronounce them differently. About 60% of all children with diagnosed articulation problems are boys (Rubin, 1982).

Articulation characteristics of young children include:

- *Substitution.* One sound is substituted for another, as in "wabbit" for rabbit or "thun" for sun.
- *Omission.* The speaker leaves out a sound that should be articulated. He or she says "at" for hat, "ca" for cat, "icky" for sticky, "probly" for probably. The left out sound may be at the beginning, middle, or end of a word.
- *Distortion.* A sound is said inaccurately but is similar to the intended sound.
- *Addition.* The speaker adds a sound, as in "li-it-tle" for little and "muv-va-ver" for mother.
- *Transposition.* The position of sounds in words is switched, as in "hangerber" for hamburger and "aminal" for animal.
- *Lisp.* The s, z, sh, th, ch, and j sounds are distorted. There are from 2 to 10 types of lisps noted by speech experts.

Articulation problems may stem from a physical condition such as a cleft palate or hearing loss, or they can be related to problems in the mouth such as a dental abnormality. Many times, articulation problems occurring without any obvious physical disability may involve the faulty learning of speech sounds.

Some children will require special help and directed training to eliminate all articulation errors, and others seem to mature and correct articulation problems by themselves.

Teacher behavior that aids the situation includes not interrupting or constantly correcting the child and making sure that others don't tease or belittle the child. Modeling misarticulated words correctly is a good course of action. Simply continue your conversation and insert the correctly articulated word in your answering comment.

Voice Disorders

Teachers sometimes notice differences in children's voice quality, which involves pitch, loudness, resonance, and general quality (breathiness, hoarseness, and so on). The intelligibility of a child's speech is determined by how many of the child's words are understandable. One can expect 80% of the child's speech to be understandable at age three.

Stuttering and Cluttering

Stuttering and cluttering are categorized as fluency disorders. Stuttering involves the rhythm of speech and is a complicated many-faceted problem. Speech is characterized by abnormal stoppages with no sound, repetitions, or prolonged sounds and syllables. There may also be unusual facial and body movements associated with efforts to speak (NAHSA, 1983). This problem involves four times as many males as females and can usually be treated. All young children repeat words and phrases, and this increases with anxiety or stress. It is simply typical for the age and is not true stuttering. A teacher should wait patiently for the child to finish expressing himself or herself and should

resist the temptation to say "slow down." An adult talking at a slow, relaxed rate and pausing between sentences can give a child time to reflect and respond with more fluency. Keeping eye contact and not rushing, interrupting, or finishing words is also recommended (Kay, 1996). Classmates should be prohibited from teasing a stutterer.

The causes for stuttering are felt to be different for different people. Teachers need to listen patiently and carefully to what the child is saying, not how he or she is saying it. A speech-language pathologist is the appropriate person to evaluate and plan improvement activities.

Cluttering is more involved with the rate of speaking and includes errors in articulation, stress, and pausing. Speech seems too fast with syllables and words running together. Listener reaction and good speech modeling are critical aspects in lack of fluency. Bloodstein (1975) suggests that adults who work with young children should:

- Refrain from criticizing, correcting, helping the child speak, or otherwise reacting negatively or calling a speech problem to the child's attention.
- Improve parent-child relationships if possible.
- Eliminate any factors or conditions that increase problems in fluency.
- Strengthen the child's expectation of normal fluency and self-confidence as a speaker.

Approximately 25% of all children go through a stage of development during which they stutter (Kay, 1996). A child who appears to be having a problem may be going through periods of normal disfluency associated with learning to speak.

About 1 in every 13 four year olds evaluated by their parents in the U.S. Department of Education's *National Household Education Survey* (1993) stutters, stammers, or speaks in a way not understandable to a stranger.

Selective (Elective) Mutism

Occasionally, early childhood teachers encounter silent children. Silence may be temporary or lasting, and will be a matter for teacher concern. Children with **selective (elective) mutism** are described simply as children who *can* speak but don't. They display functional speech in selected settings (usually at home) and/or choose to speak only with certain individuals (often siblings or same-language speakers). Researchers believe selective mutism, if it happens, commonly occurs between ages 3 and 5 years. Since child abuse may promote delayed language development or psychological disorders that interfere with communication such as selective mutism, teachers need to be concerned (Angelou, 1969). School referral to speech professionals leads to assessment and individual treatment programs. School directors prefer parents make appointments and usually provide parents with a description of local resources.

Teachers can help professionals by providing observational data to describe the child's behavior and responses in classroom settings. So many factors can possibly contribute to a particular child's silence or reduced speech. Consequently, teachers are cautioned to avoid a mutism diagnosis. Children's teasing or embarrassment of a child with language or speech diversity should be handled swiftly and firmly by preschool staff members.

At the beginning of the school year or a child's enrollment, some children may prefer to watch and observe rather than interact. Speakers of languages other than English may choose to play and speak only to those children and adults who understand their language. These behaviors change as English usage grows and the child feels comfortable and secure at school.

Other Conditions Teachers May Consider Problems

Frequent Crying

Occasionally frustrated children will cry or scream to communicate a need. Crying associated with adjustment to a new situation is handled by providing supportive attention and care. Continual crying and screaming to obtain an object or privilege,

on the other hand, calls for the following kinds of teacher statements:

> "I don't understand what you want when you scream. Use words so I will know what you want."

> "Sara does not know what you want when you cry, Billy. Saying 'Please get off the puzzle piece,' with your words tells her."

This lets the child know what's expected and helps the child see that words solve problems.

Avid Talkers and Shouters

Occasionally children may discover that talking incessantly can get them what they want. In order to quiet children, others give in. This is somewhat different from the common give and take in children's daily conversations or children's growing ability to argue and state their cases.

Language becomes a social tool. A child may find that loudness in speech can intimidate others and will out shout the opposition. It is prudent to have the child's hearing checked.

Questioners

At times, children ask many questions, one right after another. This may be a good device to hold or gain adults' attention: "Why isn't it time for lunch?" or "What makes birds sing?" or "Do worms sleep?" The questions may seem endless to adults. Most of the questions are prompted by the child's natural curiosity. Teachers help children find out as much as possible and strive to fulfill the needs of the individual child. Along the way, there will be many questions that may be difficult or even impossible to answer.

Selective mutism — a behavior that describes child silence or lack of speech in select surroundings and/or with certain individuals.

Hearing

A screening of young children's auditory acuity may uncover hearing loss. The seriousness of the problem is related both to the degree of loss and the range of sound frequencies that are most affected (Harris, 1990). The earlier the diagnosis, the more effective the treatment. Since young children develop ear infections frequently, schools alert parents when a child's listening behavior seems newly impaired.

Otitis media is a medical term that refers to any inflammation of the middle ear. There are two types of otitis media: (1) a fluid-filled middle ear without infection and (2) an infected middle ear. Many preschoolers have ear infections during preschool years, and many children have clear fluid in the middle ear that goes undetected (NAHSA, 1985). Even though the hearing loss caused by otitis media may be small and temporary, it may have a serious effect on speech and language learning for a preschool child. Teele, Klein, and Rosner (1989) believe only the common cold outranks child ear infection, and a teacher can expect one child in three to be affected on any given day.

If undetected hearing distortion or loss lasts for a long period, the child can fall behind. General inattentiveness, wanting to get close to hear, having trouble with directions, irritability, or pulling and rubbing the ear can be signs a teacher should heed. Other signs to look for include:

- difficulty hearing word endings such as -ed, -ing, -s
- problems interpreting intonation patterns, inflections, and stress
- distractibility
- inattentiveness
- asking adults to repeat
- confusion with adult commands
- difficulty repeating verbally presented material

Otitis media — inflammation and/or infection of the middle ear.

Deaf — children whose hearing is so impaired that they are unable to process auditory linguistic information, with or without amplification.

- inappropriate responses to questions
- watching for cues from other children
- complaints about ears
- persistent breathing through mouth
- slow to locate source of sounds
- softer or "fuzzier" speech than others
- aggressiveness
- loss of temper

Barrio-Garcia (1986) estimates 84,000 children under the age of six have hearing impairments. Hearing loss can be temporary or permanent. Early detection and treatment is important, and newborns test with reasonable accuracy.

Preschool staff members who notice children who confuse words with similar sounds may be the first to suspect auditory perception difficulties or mild to moderate hearing loss.

Mild hearing impairment may masquerade as:

- stubbornness
- lack of interest, or
- a learning disability.

With intermittent **deafness**, children may have difficulty comprehending oral language. Limited exposure to common sentence structures used in "story book" English can also occur (Clay, 1991).

Severe impairment impedes language development and is easier to detect than the far more subtle signs of mild loss. Most infected ears cause considerable pain, and parents are alerted to the need for medical help. However, if the ear is not infected or if the infection does not cause pain, the problem is harder to recognize.

Seeking Help

If a child's speech or language lags behind expected development for the child's mental age (mental maturity), school staff members should observe and listen to the child closely to collect additional data. When speech is unusually difficult to understand—rhythmically conspicuous, full of sound distortion, or consistently difficult to hear—this indicates a serious problem. Professional help is available to parents through a number of resources. Most cities have speech and hearing centers and public and private practitioners specializing in speech-language pathology and audiology. Other resources include:

- universities and medical schools
- state departments of education offices
- The American Speech-Language-Hearing Association Directory (found by checking local medical societies).

A center's director can be alerted to observe a child whom the teacher feels may benefit from professional help. It is important to have a referral system in place at a school or center to assist parents in finding appropriate testing and therapy for their children. Directors can establish a relationship with a therapist or agency before a referral is needed. Speech-language pathologists have master's degrees or doctoral degrees in speech-language pathology and, in many states, hold licenses.

Experts give the parents of hearing-impaired children the following advice:

- Help the child "tune" into language.
- Talk.
- Provide stimulation.
- Read picture books.
- Enroll the child in an infant-stimulation program during infancy.
- Schedule frequent doctor examinations for the child.
- Join parent organizations with a hearing-impairment focus.
- See the child simply as a child rather than "a hearing-impaired child." (Coffman, 1986)

The Reluctant Child

Occasionally teachers encounter a reluctant and unresponsive preschooler. Emotional upset can be the cause and when the child finds engaging activity choices he or she slowly emerges.

Other seemingly withdrawn children can be afraid of failure! Lack of confidence from past experience is coloring behavior. Clay (1991) points out that coaxing that is not carping, support that is not demanding, and confidence in the child that does not deny the reality of the child's sense of inadequacy are considerations that should underlie the teacher's behavior and attitude.

Advanced Language Achievement

Each child is unique. A few children speak clearly and use long, complex, adultlike speech at two, three, or four years of age. They express ideas originally and excitedly, enjoying individual and group discussions. Some may read simple primers (or other books) along with classroom word labels. Activities that are commonly used with kindergarten or first-grade children may interest them. Just as there is no stereotypical average child, language-talented children are also unique individuals. Inferring these language precocious children are also intellectually gifted isn't at issue here. Teachers will encounter young children with advanced language development. They may exhibit many of the following characteristics.

- Attend to tasks in a persistent manner for long periods of time.
- Focus deeply or submerge themselves in what they are doing.
- Speak maturely and use a larger-than-usual vocabulary.
- Show a searching, exploring curiosity.
- Ask questions that go beyond immediate happenings.
- Demonstrate avid interest in words, alphabet letters, numbers, or writing tools.
- Remember small details of past experiences and compare them with present happenings.
- Read books (or words) by memorizing pictures or words.
- Prefer solitary activities at times.
- Offer ideas often and easily.
- Rapidly acquire English skills, if bilingual, when exposed to a language-rich environment.
- Tell elaborate stories.
- Show a mature or unusual sense of humor for age (Kitano, 1982).
- Possess an exceptional memory.
- Exhibit high concentration.
- Show attention to detail.
- Exhibit a wide range of interests.
- Demonstrate a sense of social responsibility.
- Show a rich imagination.
- Possess a sense of wonder.

- Express feelings and emotions, as in storytelling, movement, and visual arts.
- Use rich imagery in informal language.
- Exhibit originality of ideas and persistence in problem solving.
- Exhibit a high degree of imagination.

Preschoolers may recognize letters early and show an early focus on printed matter. They may be interested in foreign languages and also exhibit correct pronunciation and sentence structure in their native language. Young children may show an advanced vocabulary and may begin reading before they start preschool.

Kitano (1982) recommends planning activities within the regular curriculum that promote advanced children's creative thinking. Suggestions include providing the following opportunities:

- *Fluency opportunities.* Promoting many different responses, for example, "What are all the ways you can think of to . . . ."
- Flexibility opportunities. Having the facility to change a mind set or see things in a different light, for example, "If you were a Christmas tree, how would you feel . . . ."
- *Originality opportunities.* For example, "Make something that no one else will think of."
- *Elaboration opportunities.* Embellishing of an idea or adding detail, for example, presenting a doodle or squiggle and asking "What could it be?"

Schwartz (1980) notes that teachers can help ward off problems for advanced students and recommends:

- Grouping children with others of high ability or shared interests.
- Arranging situations in which the child's gifts or talents are seen as a group asset.
- Using special assignments and varied projects.

If teachers believe as does Gardner (1993) in the theory of multiple intelligences (one of which is linguistic intelligence) and in the occurrence of "crystallizing experiences," those teachers will notice the young children who take particular inter-est in and react overtly to some attractive quality or feature of a language arts activity. These children will tend to immerse themselves and focus deeply. This may be the child who loves to act roles in dramatic play, collects words, is fascinated with books or alphabet letters, creates daily rhymes, or display similar behaviors. The child may persist and spend both time and effort on his chosen pursuit and displays a definite intellectual gift.

Renzulli (1986) defines the talented child's behavior as

> . . . evident when a child displays three basic characteristics . . . above-average ability, creativity, and "task commitment," that special drive and motivation that causes some individuals to persist at something when others would quit.

Summary

Teachers work with children who may differ greatly in language development. One of the teacher's roles is to carefully work toward increasing the child's use of words, while providing a model of standard English through activities and daily interaction. Teachers are careful not to give children the impression that their speech is less worthy than that of others.

Program goals should be clearly understood, as should the needs and interests of children who have developed a language that differs from the language of the school. Cultural differences exist, and teachers need to be aware of them in order to understand the young child. The teacher can provide activities that start at the child's present level and help the child to grow, know more, and speak in both standard English and his or her native speech.

Speech differences require observation and study by a center's staff. There are a variety of language behaviors that are considered speech and language disorders. Parents can be alerted to whether their children may need further professional help.

STUDENT ACTIVITIES

1. List and describe dialects found in your community. Give a few sentence examples of each.

2. In small groups, discuss what you feel are essential factors to language growth that may be missing in a disadvantaged child's background.

3. Interview the director of a center that cares for bilingual and/or economically deprived young children. Ask what techniques are used to increase a child's language ability. If there is no early childhood center in your community, give examples of goals or techniques used to increase a child's language ability that you have found from research at a library.

4. If possible, have a speech therapist or speech-correction specialist speak with the class.

5. Observe a "silent-at-group-time" child at play and lunch period. Try to assess when or under what circumstances this child is more verbal. Take written notes.

6. Develop a list of community resources or agencies that offer services to children with speech or hearing problems.

7. Tape record your voice in a five-minute conversation with a friend. Have the recording analyzed for dialect, accent, and standard English usage.

8. Consider the following children. Which children would you suggest to the center's director as possibly needing further staff observation and expert assessment and help?
   a. Trinh seems roughly two years behind his age mates in vocabulary.
   b. Rashad turns his head toward speakers frequently.
   c. Barbara rubs one ear constantly.
   d. Doan cups his hand behind his ear when spoken to.
   e. Tisha is three, and one can't understand her words.
   f. Bill says "Why did his folks call him Rocky, when he can't say it? He says his name is Wocky Weed!"
   g. Maria is always stressed and extremely tense when she has to speak.
   h. Ben has a monotonal quality to his voice.
   i. Becky reads difficult books without help.

9. What cultural or ethnic artifacts or objects does your family possess? Are there family stories that are culturally significant? Share with a group of classmates, then report to the whole group.

10. React to the following quote concerning Ebonics: "Certainly, cultivating pride and self-respect is a worthwhile goal, but that self-respect should be rooted in achievement. Students already at an education disadvantage should not be provided with false pride in the misuse of language." (Cose, 1997)

11. Observe three preschool children (one at a time) for a period of 10 minutes each. Write down exactly what each child says. Include a description of gestures and nonverbal communications. Analyze your notes. Are there any examples of common speech errors or dialectic differences?

12. Compare two languages. What are the differences? What are the similarities?

13. In Chapter 9 find three additional culturally-sensitive picture books. Share titles with the class and evaluate the quality of the books.

CHAPTER REVIEW

A. Answer the following questions.

1. How can a teacher learn about the cultural background of a child?

2. What should be the teacher's attitude toward children whose speech is different from the teacher's?

B. One of the responsibilities of a teacher is to act as a model to the child for correct forms of speech. Another responsibility is to increase the child's ability to express ideas in words. Quality of responses is more important than just talking. In the following exchanges between teachers and small children, why did the child stop speaking?

1. *Teacher:*   How are you today, Mary?
   Child: Fine.

2. *Child:*   Mrs. Brown, Johnny hit me!
   Teacher: I saw you grab the truck he was playing with. That wasn't nice!
   Child: (Silence)

3. *Child:*   Teacher, I want crayon.
   Teacher: Do you know how to use a crayon?
   Child: Yes.
   Teacher: Tell me how to use a crayon.
   Child: To color.
   Teacher: Say, "To make colored marks on the paper."
   Child: (Silence)

4. *Child:*   I found a bug.
   Teacher: That's nice.

5. *Child:*   Fellow one?

   Teacher: It's yellow, not fellow.

   Child: Fellow one.

   Teacher: You want the yellow one. A fellow is a man, Lindy.

   Child: (Silence)

6. *Teacher:*   Jason, what's your favorite ice cream flavor?

   Child: Huh?

   Teacher: What's your favorite ice cream flavor?

   Child: Flavorite?

   Teacher: Don't you like ice cream?

   Child: Yah.

   Teacher: What's your favorite ice cream flavor?

   Child: (Silence)

C. Define these speech terms.

   1. dialect   4. auditory   7. otitis media

   2. bilingual   5. cluttering   8. subculture

   3. stuttering   6. articulation   9. standard English

D. Listed below are comments made by children. Give an example of the response that a teacher could make in order to encourage more thought and stimulate growth on the part of the child.

   1. Child with ball says, "Me play."

   2. Child remarks, "I done went to get a red crayun."

   3. Child says, "I got this thing."

   4. Child says, "I like chitchun choop!"

   5. Child asks, "No run in street?"

   6. Child exclaims, "I don't wanna play with them childruns."

E. Select the correct answer. Some items have more than one correct answer.

   1. Standard English is
      a. the language of textbooks.
      b. often taught slowly to nonstandard speakers.
      c. often different from English spoken in a dialect.
      d. needed for success in any line of work.

   2. Early childhood centers try to
      a. teach children standard English during the first days of school.
      b. make sure each child feels secure.
      c. plan activities in which language-different children have an interest.
      d. provide for each child's development of word use in his or her own dialect.

3. Teachers should be careful to guard against
   a. correcting children's speech by drawing attention to errors.
   b. thinking that only standard English is correct and therefore better than English spoken in a dialect.
   c. giving children the idea that they speak differently or "funny."
   d. feeling that children who come from low-income homes are always disadvantaged when compared with children from middle-income homes.

4. Young children with speech errors
   a. rarely outgrow them.
   b. may need special help.
   c. often do not hear as well as adults.
   d. can hear that what they say is different but do not have the ability to say it correctly.

5. Bilingualism in the young child is
   a. always a disadvantage.
   b. sometimes a disadvantage.
   c. a rewarding challenge to the teacher.
   d. a problem when schools make children feel defeated and unaccepted.

6. A disadvantaged child may
   a. also be hyperactive and aggressive.
   b. be more independent and talkative than a middle-class child.
   c. talk a lot but have a smaller vocabulary than the average middle-class child.
   d. need teachers who not only model standard English but also model problem solving with words.

7. Considering the vocabularies of young second-language learners, one would expect:
   a. their vocabulary to be equal to native English-speaking children of the same age.
   b. their vocabularies to outdistance those of native English speakers.
   c. the vocabulary in their native language plus their second language to be equal in number to native English-speaking same-aged children.
   d. depressed vocabularies in both languages.

F. Explain why designations such as Asian or Hispanic do not accurately describe a child's culture.

G. List teacher techniques appropriate and useful in classrooms enrolling second-language learners.

H. What classroom materials, displays, and activities might make an ethnically or culturally diverse child feel at-home in a classroom?

I. Describe the speech characteristics of children who speak African-American English.

CHAPTER 6

Achieving Language and Literacy Goals Through Programming

OBJECTIVES

After studying this chapter, you should be able to:

- define literacy.
- describe emerging literacy in early childhood.
- discuss programming early childhood language arts activities.
- describe assessment's role in program development.
- write an activity plan for a language arts activity.

This text divides language arts into four inter-related areas: listening, speaking, writing, and reading. Increasing the child's understanding of how language arts combine and overlap in every-day preschool activities helps to increase language use and literacy.

Stanchfield (1994) discussed the interrelatedness of literacy skills:

I believe the most important thing we have learned in the last 30 years about the teach-ing and learning of reading is dynamically concerned with the interrelatedness of the literacy skills of listening, speaking, think-ing, reading, and writing. For the last 15 years, I have been convinced that read-ing cannot be taught in isolation, but rather as a part of the whole—the "gestalt" of the literacy. Students who can listen, discuss, and think with words are going to learn to read more effectively. Conversely, students who have meager vocabularies, limited sentence structure, short attention spans, and little experience with expressive lan-guage may have almost insurmountable difficulties in learning to read. Today, most educators stress the word literacy rather than reading.

To that end, a unified approach is recommended, one in which the teacher purposefully shows and stresses connections between areas (figure 6–1).

Past practice and program planning in schools attempted to promote literacy by dividing (seg-menting) language arts into separate skills. Educa-tors, convinced by evidence from researchers, believe that only the use of language for real and worthwhile purposes can make a significant dif-ference in language development (McKenzie, 1985).

The ages of the children and their past life expe-riences will decide the literacy activities one plans and presents and the techniques and adult-child interaction one deems appropriate. MacDonald (1992) observes:

Literary development happens within rela-tionships. When you acknowledge an infant turning the page of a book or a toddler turn-ing a picture book right-side-up, you are encouraging their interest in literacy. When you listen intently as a preschooler reads you the scribbles she carefully made on a sheet of paper, and encourage a school-age child to explain to a friend how he figured out the meaning of an unfamiliar word, you are helping children feel good about themselves as readers and writers.

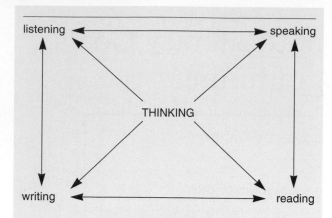

Listening (receptive language)

  One hears speech.

  One can listen to another reading orally.

  One can listen and write what one hears.

Speaking (oral expressive language)

  One can speak to a listener.

  One can put speech into written form.

  One can read orally.

Writing

  One can write what's spoken and heard.

  One's writing can be read.

  One's writing can be read and spoken.

Reading

  One can read written words.

  One can listen to another reading.

  One can read speech when it's written.

FIGURE 6–1   Interrelation of early childhood language arts

Literacy — involves complex cognitive interactions between readers and their texts and between background knowledge and new information. It involves both skill and knowledge and varies by task and setting. Different types of literacy are described—prose, document, quantitative, academic, workplace, and functional.

Literacy Goals—Skill and Knowledge

Any discussion of **literacy** begins with a working definition. Hillerich (1976) defines it as a:

> . . . demonstrated competence in communication skills which enables the individual to function, appropriate to age, independently of society and with a potential for movement in society.

Young children usually progress to this level of literacy by developing what Gordon Wells (1981) termed "a knowledge of literacy," which includes oral language skill, and an awareness that written (graphic) marks and words carry meaning. Wells feels that early superficial understandings about picture books and being read to lead to a much deeper understanding of the purpose of reading. Psycholinguistic theory focuses on the unique nature of human language, humans' innate search for order, structure, and meaning (Itzkoff, 1986). Using this theory as a basis, one can see how children will initiate their own first steps toward literacy when exposed to language-rich environments in which positive attitudes develop toward language arts activities.

Cambourne's (1988) definition of literacy stresses one's ability to use language in daily life.

> . . . literacy is a word which describes a whole collection of behaviours, skills, knowledge, processes and attitudes. It has something to do with our ability to use language in our negotiations with the world. . . . Reading and writing are two linguistic ways of conducting these negotiations. So are talking, listening, thinking, reflecting, and a host of other behaviours related to cognition and critical thinking.

Formerly, educators believed literacy was only attained through elementary school completion. Literacy is now seen as "emerging" in early childhood with children constructing meaning from infancy onward.

The term emergent literacy refers to young preschool children's language arts behaviors, concepts, and skills that precede and can develop into a literacy that includes reading, conventional writing, and a larger body of literary knowledge at later ages.

The act of printing shapes with an underlying logic and children's "pretending to read" behaviors are viewed as early forms of reading and writing (Kantor, Miller, Fernie, 1992; Goodman, 1986; Ferreiro, 1985).

Itzkoff (1986) describes early awareness of written forms:

Children gradually learn that certain marks— lines, circles, etc.—stand for another set of meanings in the world. The idea is born in the child's mind even while these marks are still "mysterious" that they have a special brand of meaning.

Literacy is a complex and multifaceted phenomenon involving attitudes, assumptions, and expectations about writing and reading, and about the place and value of these activities in one's life (McLane & McNamee, 1990). It is a social and cultural achievement, and an individual intellectual accomplishment that encompasses a body of cultural knowledge enabling people to participate in a range of groups and activities involving writing and reading (McLane and McNamee, 1990). Roskos and Neuman (1994) have identified literacy performance indicators for the early years in figure 6–2.

Early home-life activities start children's literacy development by providing early experiences, including parent models and attitudes. A home environment can be stimulating or drab, rich in literate activities or deficit. Children actively search for meaning, and many have lives in which print surrounds them and picture books are familiar. If children have observed and participated in home reading or writing activities, they frequently enter group care with interest and positive attitude and an emergent head start in literacy. They are able to enjoy symbolic dramatic play and eventually attempt symbolic representation in art, block

PROCESSES	PERFORMANCE INDICATORS
Rudimentary writing processes	Grasps and manipulates writing implements
	Records ideas through pictures, words, and/or sentences her or his "own way"
	Writes and recognizes own name
Concepts about print	Shows awareness of print permanency (Words in print remain the same from one reading to the next.)
	Shows awareness that text is read from left to right and from top to bottom (in English)
	Shows development of print-meaning associations: recognizes environmental print; assigns verbal labels to letter symbols or words
	Uses pictures and print to label and tell a story
Literature and sense of story	Enjoys listening to and engaging in rhyme, rhythm, songs, poetry, and storytelling
	Plays with rhyming sounds and words, showing increasing ability to discrimiate and identify sounds
	Expresses interest and attends to stories and informational text
	Displays increasing ability to retell a story, including characters and actions, demonstrating a basic understanding of story sequence (beginning, middle, and end)

FIGURE 6–2 Literacy processes and performance indicators: The early years *(From "Of Scribbles, Schemas, and Storybooks," by K. A. Roskos and S. B. Neuman, 1994,* Young Children, *49(2), p. 79. Reprinted with permission from NAEYC.)*

Emergent literacy — the speaking, listening, print awareness, and reading alphabet letters and words skills that evolve into literacy in a particular society.

[Handwritten note at bottom: You establish literacy skills at birth - Very important to read from the start.]

building, and a variety of other preschool pursuits. They communicate ideas, discuss meanings, and probe adults and other children for information.

Children's growing awareness and "knowledge of literacy" is evident and can include all language arts areas—reading, writing, speaking, and listening.

Becoming literate is an extension and companion of language arts skill. Most children acquire spoken language without sit-down instruction; they all become speakers, although at different rates, unless disease, illness, or trauma interferes. Literacy, on the other hand, isn't attained unconsciously or by all in our society. Literacy requires a shared body of understanding, much of which involves a common exposure to oral and written material and a level of listening, speaking, reading, and writing proficiency. Literacy acquisition involves a commitment of time and mental energy plus opportunity. At the preschool level, this commitment is a teacher's commitment to presenting a program that both promotes language arts skills and furnishes a shared body of understandings appropriate to preschoolers.

Elementary school reading textbooks in the early part of this century were collections of classics. The idea of reading levels was not in vogue but rather the goal was to have every child learn information and skills that were common to the democratic literate public electorate of the time and necessary to the development of a truly educated man or woman. Literacy today is still seen by some as only referring to reading and writing, but many researchers and early childhood educators are concerned with the taproots of literacy, which may be developed during the preschool period.

Great concern over our society's literacy rates by numerous popular writers including Hirsch (1988) and Kozol (1985) have caused alarm:

> The evidence is clear that our national literacy has been declining not only among disadvantaged children but also among our top students (Hirsch, 1988).

As society enters the age of electronic information processing, meaningful participation is increasingly dependent on literacy (Daniel, 1995). Stedman (1996) notes few researchers deny that millions of adult Americans are severely hampered by literacy problems and that minorities and the poor are disproportionately affected.

> The largest number of illiterate adults are white, native-born Americans. In proportion to population, however, the figures are higher for blacks and Hispanics than for whites. Sixteen percent of white adults, 44% of blacks, and 56% of Hispanic citizens are functional or marginal illiterates. (Kozol, 1985)

To be considered functionally literate, one must have a knowledge of shared, common information that is neither set down on paper nor explicitly stated in oral communication and that provides the basis for understanding what is heard or read. This idea is well illustrated by a similar phenomenon that occurs when outsiders listen to an in-group whose members have learned a specialized technical vocabulary. For instance, suppose we are having a difficult time understanding a group of computer buffs. We would know they are speaking our language, but we cannot understand the bulk of their conversation. As they chat about bits, bytes, or modems, they do not make any sense to us. We would then consider ourselves functionally illiterate in computer terminology.

Hirsch (1988) feels that learning language arts skills should not be the primary goal of early childhood instruction. He theorizes that skill alone does not guarantee literacy. He feels that preschools should pay attention to *culturally significant information* (information that most beginning reading materials assume that beginning readers know). He points out that different children come to school knowing different things and suggests that "preschool is not too early for starting earnest instruction in literate national culture." The necessary cultural background knowledge one possesses to be considered literate changes over time; the early childhood professional intent on promoting literacy should be aware of this and update the curriculum periodically.

Healy (1990) believes real access to concepts of cultural heritage comes from extended, personally meaningful conversations with adults, books read aloud at home, and children reading by choice for pleasure.

In programming, an integrated language/literacy approach that emphasizes child comprehension is suggested by current research. It is one of the goals of this textbook.

Philosophies

The staff of each early childhood center drafts a program based on the unique mesh of their staff's personal theories about what they feel is appropriate and effective. If a language arts program focuses on the correct form(s) of language, such as the sequential learning of letter names, sounds, etc., the program could be described as *traditional* or conventional. This text urges an approach to teaching language arts that is *meaning-based*, *functional* for children, *literature-rich*, and taught in a natural, interrelated fashion emphasizing a "whole" rather than a "parts" philosophy. This type of program approach believes child learnings in language arts are reinforced and made meaningful when the reading, writing, listening, and speaking aspects of daily activities are encountered concurrently. A developmentally appropriate program first considers the unique group of children enrolled, their needs, their abilities, their interests, and their parents' wishes concerning desirable educational outcomes.

Excellent advice program designers need to keep in mind has been offered by Healy (1990):

If we encourage children to make choices from a selected variety of available challenges, both environmental and intellectual, we are no doubt following the wisest course.

No discussion of philosophies concerning literacy would be complete without study of Cambourne's (1988) model of learning and the processes involved. Cambourne's work clarifies not only what but how programs could *engage* young children in learning. Cambourne (1988) states:

Reading, writing, speaking and listening, while different in many respects, are but parallel manifestations of the same vital human function—the mind's effort to create meaning. The fact that speaking and listening are tied to the production and/or comprehension of patterned sequences of sound, while reading and writing are tied to the reception/production of graphic marks, is not of such great importance at the level of how the brain goes about creating meaning with them.

Program planners using Cambourne as a guide would plan a wide variety of language arts activities and demonstrations of language arts uses.

Two additional theories concerning how young children learn need mentioning. DeVries and Kohlberg (1987) outline four steps in effective learning situations: awareness, exploration, inquiry, and utilization. Holdaway's (1986) natural-learning model also offers a sequence of four learning conditions: demonstration, participation, practice, and performance. Teachers using either theory to plan developmental activities would build into their plans ways to:

- gain child attention and interest
- provide aspects of hands-on, first-hand exploration and participation
- use demonstrations when appropriate
- promote questioning and discussion
- provide practice opportunities
- help children relate information or skill to children's lives and be of practical usefulness
- provide time and activities to perform or demonstrate what they have learned
- provide activities in which previous understanding, skills, and attitudes are used

Figure 6–3 offers an additional possible sequence of children's language learning in both planned and unplanned classroom activities.

Child has experiential background observing and participating in a rich language arts school environment.

Child gives attention to classroom activities, demonstrations, behaviors modeled by others, new happenings, teacher presentations, or other classroom events. Child perceives activity to be useful, interesting, or worthwhile.

Child feels comfortable and safe in this situation, and feels capable and likely successful. Understands teacher expects appropriate classroom behavior.

Child continues focus and concentration on activity that is unfolding and progressing.

Child gathers and selects information and data. Develops beginning ideas. May ask questions. Looks, listens, touches as if investigating or trying to find out.

Child may see or state relationships and form hypotheses or conclusions. May discuss points of view.

Child may test ideas or check ideas with teacher or others present.

Child may receive feedback from teacher and/or other children. May be uncertain or puzzled.

Child may develop a definite idea and "fit" the newness experienced in the activity into what he or she already knows. Learning occurs.

FIGURE 6–3   Possible sequence in language learning

Language Use in All Curriculum Areas

Every planned preschool activity uses language in some way. Past experience is basic to all language arts, because a child's success often depends on his or her understanding of what is happening. Language helps children learn, retain, recall, and transmit information (Lerner, 1976). Messages are received through words and nonverbal means. The teacher's speech, behavior, and use of words in planned activities are discussed in the following units.

Daily routines, play with peers, and unplanned happenings stimulate language as well as the center's planned program. Teachers use every opportunity to add meanings in a natural, conversational way during the preschool day. This generally begins with the teacher's personal greeting or affectionate physical contact as the child enters the early childhood center. The "hello" and comments are part of the rituals in preschools that aim to recognize each child's presence each arrival time.

Daily routines are the regular features of a school's program that occur about the same time every day—snacks, toileting, and group activities—in which language is an associate function (figure 6–4).

Group times range from short announcement times to planned child language arts (or other content area) experiences. Instruction may take place with one child, a few, or with a group.

Planned activities should have a purpose children can understand and connect in some way to what they already know. As Moon (1996) points out, most if not all learning can be made applicable to the child's life. Early childhood practitioners provide real, hands-on experiences in their classrooms when possible. Secondhand activities are second best.

McLane and McNamee (1990) suggest:

> Children learn about literacy most easily when writing and reading are embedded in daily classroom activities and have a purpose children can understand.

In an activity planting spring seeds, signs or labels adjacent to planted seeds have a practical

FIGURE 6–4 Snack time is talking time.

purpose. The teacher could read the seed packet instructions to the children to find out about planting particulars. If individual planting pots are used, the children or teachers could print their names to label them.

Language Arts Programming

Preplanned language arts programs develop from identified goals: the knowledge, skills, and attitudes that the school intends to teach. Early childhood teachers also base teaching techniques on what they feel is best, right, appropriate, and prudent. This, in turn, is connected to views they hold about how, what, when, and where children learn to communicate and use language. The following views about language learning are commonly expressed or implied by staff members involved in planning language arts programs:

- Language permeates all planned and unplanned activities.

- A dynamic, rich-in-opportunity classroom stimulates communication and exchanges of ideas.
- Real experiences are preferred to vicarious ones when practical and possible.
- The reciprocal nature of exploring and discovering together should be promoted by teachers.
- Play provides many opportunities to learn language.
- Teachers' instructional techniques should be skilled and alert to child readiness.
- Stressing relationships between objects, events, and experiences is a useful teaching technique.
- Individual planning, as well as group planning, is desirable.
- Program activities should center on the child's interests.
- Literary classics (preschool level) are an important planned-program component.
- The entire teaching staff should be committed and enthusiastic about their planned program, and understand stated objectives.
- An integrated approach to language arts instruction helps children experience the "connectedness" of language arts areas.

Schools and child centers have given special attention to the last goal in light of recommendations made by The Commission on Reading (1985) in the report entitled "Becoming a Nation of Readers," which emphasizes the need to view all language processes—listening, speaking, reading, and writing—as interrelated and mutually supportive.

McLane and McNamee (1990) list preschool programming elements that promote literacy:

1. child opportunities for fantasy (dramatic) play;
2. extended open-ended conversations with teachers (group and individual talk and expression);
3. books and writing material access;
4. a comfortable reading area;
5. well-equipped writing and drawing (art) room centers; and
6. when children are read to using a variety of materials, and stories are shared and told daily.

In any planned language arts program Healy (1990) cautions educators to think first about the priority of "interactive talk." She believes, as do most childhood teachers, that the preschool period is the apex of the brain's sensitive period for language acquisition.

What is the best type of program? According to Healy (1990) an early childhood program attempting to enrich should emphasize language understanding and expression, basic reasoning skills, interesting experiences, and positive attitudes toward learning. Parent outreach and involvement was also deemed important.

Classroom Environment

Yetta Goodman (1990) describes a literacy environment as follows:

> Classrooms need to reflect the rich literate environments in which children are immersed outside of school. There need to be signs that label materials for children to use; labels for areas where children store their belongings; books and magazines to read; and various sizes, shapes, and colors of paper that children can write on in appropriate ways in their play, their cooking, and their independent time activities.

> All learning experiences need to be organized so that they invite children to participate in literacy events.

> *and*

> Authentic literacy events need to become the focus of the school day as children:

- are signed in daily so that the teacher knows who has arrived in school;
- put away their materials in an appropriate setting, using the signs in the room or their names on their cubbies;
- read recipes and menus as they cook, eat, and learn about healthy nutritional activities;

- write prescriptions at the play hospital or take phone messages in the house corner; and
- read storybooks, write letters, and record observations (Goodman, 1990).

Culturally Diverse Musical Experience

The songs and music of childhood are a part of our cultural heritage. The folk songs and ballads that have survived to the present day and the regional tunes parents and teachers offer are part of each child's cultural literacy. Early childhood programs attempt to provide the music of various ethnic groups. Most of these musical experiences give young children the opportunity to form beginning ideas concerning the music and language of diverse peoples.

Musical activities have gained new status and are no longer viewed as just fun and enjoyable. Research suggests definite connections to academic learning. Growth seems to take place in special and separate parts of the brain. Other studies conclude that in cultures where musical play is actively encouraged, children acquire heightened competencies in motor and communication skills at early ages (Jaffe, 1992).

Determining Program Effectiveness

Goals pinpointed through staff meetings and solicited parent input can be finalized in written form to serve as a basis for planning. For one child or many, goals are achieved when teachers and staff plan interesting and appropriate activities for daily, weekly, monthly, or longer periods. In addition to the actual program, materials, and classroom equipment and arrangement, teacher techniques and interactions and other resources aid in goal realization.

Teacher observation and assessment instruments—teacher-designed and commercial—add extra data that helps in planning programs. In any attempts to gather data, preschool staffs carefully examine which methods or instruments best suit a program planning group's needs and the reliability and suitability of each proposed course of action.

Testing at the beginning of the child's first group experience can contribute to inaccurate results caused by the child's unfamiliarity with test procedures and inability to display the necessary response behaviors.

Carefully planned, recorded, and well-conducted teacher observation is an assessment tool that's hard to beat. Standardized tests all too often do not tell observant teachers anything they don't already know about children (Bredekamp, 1988). Neuman and Roskos (1993) add:

> To detect patterns of language and literacy behavior, then, the assessing we do must include multiple sources of information which are gathered over some period of time. And it is our close examination of these diverse indicators of behavior that enhances the credibility of the interpretations we make about children's language and literacy growth.

There are many different types of assessments. A developmental checklist for two-and-a-half- to five-year-old children is included in the Appendix. Some assessments attempt to determine ability and accomplishment in a number of language and communication areas; others may be limited to one language skill.

Teacher Observation

Many child centers encourage teachers to continually observe the language skills of attending children. Each child and group may have different needs, and the center attempts to fulfill needs and offer a language arts program that will be growth producing and enriching. Many different observation methods and instruments can be employed. Some may be school-designed; others may be commercially produced.

A teacher who is a keen observer and listener gathers information, which guides teacher actions and planning. In their efforts to make an activity relevant, teachers observe attending children's needs,

desires, and interests, and make individual judgments regarding children's already acquired knowledge, attitudes, and language skills. As teachers observe, some try to answer the following questions:

- What individual language characteristics are present?
- How can activities be planned that capture and hold children's interest and enthusiasm?
- How do my actions and behaviors affect the children's language arts behaviors?
- Which children are interested in which indoor and outdoor areas?
- What patterns of behavior have I noticed?
- What do children seem eager to talk about or explore? And with whom?
- What can I do to provide experience or exploration just beyond what they already know?
- Which children readily express themselves? Or rarely do so?
- How can I possibly help the language arts growth of each and every child?

Assessment is a continual, on-going process (Glazer and Burke, 1994).

Observation information is confidential and often useful in program planning. Running accounts of child conversations are difficult to obtain because an adult's presence may affect a child's spontaneity. Also, the child's attention span and mobility make it almost impossible to capture more than a few minutes of speech with preschoolers. Many teachers note a few phrases or speech characteristics on a writing pad they carry with them throughout the day. For many teachers, having time just to observe children is considered a luxury. However, observation is important and can be considered an on-going teacher responsibility in all areas of instruction.

To ensure a language program's quality, plans are changed, updated, and revised based on both the children's progress and staff members' evaluations and observations. Keeping a planned language arts program vital, dynamic, appealing, and appropriate requires continual revision and overhaul of the program.

Individual center and school staff members decide whether identification of children's abilities through testing and assessment will take place. Unfortunately testing emphasizes children's scores rather than the school's ability to offer a program suitable for each attending child. One of the great challenges in teaching is to present what each child needs in a way that turns the child on to additional school and home experiences and activities.

Each center's goals are concerned with (1) attending children's needs, (2) parental and community input, and (3) the personalities, training, and experience of staff.

Goal Statements

A particular center may have many or few goal statements, which can be both general and specific.

In infant and toddler centers, the following specific objectives might be included in goal statements:

- Making comfort and discomfort sounds.
- Following an object with eyes and reaching for it.
- Smiling and laughing.
- Turning head in a sound's direction.
- Anticipating consequences of a heard sound.
- Recognizing familiar people.
- Picking up small objects.
- Babbling with vowels and consonants.
- Making physical response to words.
- Gesturing in response, as in waving bye-bye.
- Engaging in vocal play.
- Imitating sounds made by others.
- Mimicking nonverbal actions.
- Using jargon suggestive of meaning.
- Using one-word sentences.
- Pointing to body parts when requested.
- Pointing to objects to elicit object's name.
- Using telegram speech.
- Using an 8- to 10-word spoken vocabulary.
- Knowing name.

Goal statements for preschoolers two-and-a-half to five years old are usually categorized into the four language arts areas and can include goals dealing with imaginative and creative use of language. *Auditory skill* (listening—receptive language) in-

cludes awareness, discrimination, memory, comprehension, and direction following. Possible goal statements follow:

- Listens to stories.
- Is able to retell short parts of stories: plot particulars, main ideas, and character traits.
- Hears rhyme.
- Becomes increasingly understandable, less dependent on context in speech.
- Gives attention to verbal instructions.
- Replies in a relevant fashion to others' remarks.
- Identifies familiar sounds from the environment.
- Describes past listening experience.
- Discriminates sounds.
- Possesses a sense of the rhythm, sequence, and patterns of something heard.
- Evaluates and considers comments on what is heard in a thoughtful manner.

Expressive speaking skills for two-and-a-half to five-year-olds may include the following:

At two-and-a-half

- Uses correct word order most of the time.
- Averages at least 75 words per hour during play.
- Uses two- to three- (or more) word sentences.
- Uses pronouns such as I, me, mine, it, who, and that.
- Uses adjectives and adverbs at times.
- Names common objects and pictures.
- Repeats two or more items from memory.
- Announces intentions before acting.
- Asks questions of adults.

At three

- Gives name.
- Tells simple stories.
- Uses plurals and some prepositions.
- Can describe at least one element of a picture.
- Talks about past and future happenings.
- Uses commands, is critical at times, and makes requests.
- Uses wh- questions and offers answers.

At three-and-a-half

- Uses four- to five- (or more) word sentences.
- Averages over 200 words per hour in play.

- Tells experiences in sequential order at times.
- Recites simple rhymes or finger plays or sings simple songs.

At four

- Speaks in adultlike sentences.
- Repeats nine-word sentences from memory.
- Enjoys and uses nonsense words at times.
- Exaggerates and uses imaginative speech at times.
- Often requests the reasons for things.
- Uses "why."
- Can tell a simple story with picture clues.
- Evaluates own activities in words periodically.

At four-and-a-half

- Uses compound or complex sentences.
- Problem solves in language with peers.
- Creates simple stories.
- Dramatizes simple stories with others.
- Is 85% to 95% fluent in speech.
- Speaks mainly in complete sentences.
- Listens to others, raises questions, and speculates out loud in class.
- Possesses a substantial passive vocabulary.

Writing Goals

In the process of literacy development, young children can profit from an understanding of the role of the printed word. The uses of writing, including recording and transmitting information, recording self-authored creations, and providing entertainment, are important to the quality of human life. A knowledge of writing uses may lead to a realization of the value of learning to read. Writing and reading open each individual to the thoughts, creations, and discoveries, of multitudes of people, living and deceased. This discussion is not intended to promote early printing instruction but rather to point out that there are basic ideas about writing that must be considered when planning a language arts curriculum that promotes literacy (figure 6–5).

There is a strong connection between the child's familiarity with books (and his or her book-reading experiences) and literacy. Illustrations of the reasons

FIGURE 6–5   This child may be signaling an interest in making shapes that look like the letter *e*.

for writing and how writing can satisfy everyday needs can be incorporated into any center's goals for promoting literacy growth.

Most schools concentrate on exposing children to printed words rather than starting actual writing practice in alphabet letter formation. The following are common child-center activities that involve writing skills:

- Tracing.
- Cutting.
- Using marking tools.
- Dictating words or sentences.
- Contributing to group dictation on charts, experience stories, and so on.
- Creating short books with dictated print and illustrations.
- Attempting simple dot-to-dot drawings.
- Making lines and simple shapes.
- Discussing uses of writing in everyday life.

Reading Goals

Reading skills are multiple and complex, and often involve the coordination of other skills and abilities. Some reading goals that will facilitate later reading skills follow:

- Reads pictures.
- Shows an interest in and enjoyment of stories and books.
- Is able to arrange pictures in a sequence that tells a story.
- Finds hidden objects in pictures.
- Guesses at meanings based on contextual cues.
- Reads own and others' names.
- Predicts events.
- Recognizes letters of own name in other words.
- Senses left-right direction.
- Guesses words to complete sentences.
- Chooses favorite book characters.
- Treats books with care.
- Authors own books through dictation.
- Sees finely detailed differences.
- Recognizes and names alphabet letters at times.
- Shows interest in libraries.
- Shows interest in the sounds of letters.
- Watches or uses puppets to enact simple stories.
- Has background in traditional literature appropriate for age and ability.

Some schools are under considerable pressure to begin teaching reading skills rather than plan a program of activities that fully develops all areas. A carefully planned language arts program provides children with basic experiences that can help make future reading both successful and pleasurable. Reading skill is certainly a key skill in elementary schooling, but no more so than the child's possessing a positive view of his or her own competence, a positive attitude toward reading and books, and a body of general knowledge. Preschoolers need a wealth of important exploration and discovery activities based on their own choice and agenda.

Goals That Promote Emerging Literacy

There seems to be some debate over whether "relevant" language arts materials and activities should take precedent over "traditional" ones. Most early childhood educators feel that goal statements should include both when planning programs, and

this usually presents no problem. Hirsch (1988) notes that there has been a disappearance of traditional literate culture in the early school curriculum, and others feel early reading skill practice has taken precedence over traditional literature.

Preschool teachers planning and conducting programs that promote language development in young children try to provide a "classic" literary experience, featuring age-level appropriate materials collected from many cultures and eras. Such a curriculum would serve as a basis of human cultural understanding and would include a wide range of oral and listening materials and activities: books, poetry, language games, puppetry, and story telling. Most teachers feel that early exposure to and familiarity with literary classics can help the child understand what might be encountered later in literature, media, or schooling.

At present, a widely circulated list of classics for preschool children has not been available, but a list of these works has existed in the minds and hearts of individual teachers. Mother Goose stories are undisputed classics. Two other classic stories have been identified by Anderson, Hiebert, Scott, and Williams (1985):

> Even for beginners, reading should not be thought of simply as a skill subject. It is difficult to imagine, for instance, that kindergartners could be called literate for their age if they did not know *Goldilocks and the Three Bears* or *Peter Rabbit*. For each age there are fables, fairytales, folk tales, and classic and modern works of fiction that embody the core of our cultural heritage.

Whether a story, play, rhyme, or song is considered a "classic," however, is usually a matter of judgment by individual teachers.

Jewell and Zintz (1986) have compiled a list of suggestions that can help promote literacy and possibly ease the sometimes burdensome task of learning to read. These activities and provisions can be incorporated into center goals and planning if they aren't already present.

- Read to children that which they cannot read for themselves.
- Read from a variety of materials with a high interest level—stories, poems, and so forth, that are fun.
- Provide a reading environment by having an abundance of reading materials readily available.
- Tape stories and store cassettes for children to use in a listening center.
- Provide flannel boards with appropriate cutouts for children to tell stories to themselves or to others. Teachers should also tell stories.
- Have writing materials readily available.
- Have a scrap or "attic box" filled with a collection of odds and ends for children to sort through, touch, and talk about in whatever way they choose.
- Provide time to engage in all of the above activities (figure 6–6).
- Provide a multitude of hands-on experiences for children to do and to talk about.
- With the emergence of reading behaviors, provide information and help as the child requests.
- Begin to prepare language experience stories by recording child talk about experience in the classroom.

FIGURE 6–6 There are always planned times for child selection of favorite activities.

- Provide time for them to read and look at books.
- Continue to share books with the whole group by reading daily. Your own attitude and commitment to reading is a model that demonstrates that reading is an enjoyable, worthwhile activity.

Sociocultural Language Goals

Are there important goals teachers need to consider in a democratic society? Powell (1992) suggests the following:

> *Goal #1.* All students are able to communicate effectively with all persons within a multicultural, diverse society.
>
> *Goal #2.* All students learn to value linguistic diversity and celebrate the cultural expressions of those who are different from themselves.
>
> *Goal #3.* All students see the value of language and literacy for their own lives. . . .

Early childhood educators can lay the groundwork and monitor attitudes and feelings that in any way degrade other than mainstream language speakers.

A language arts curriculum should include language activities that celebrate cultural diversity. Family and community literacy activities are important considerations. Family stories and literacy-promoting activities and events can be included in center planning. Collaboration with parents reinforces the unique contributions families and neighborhoods make to child literacy growth. Bartoli (1995) notes:

> . . . we can go beyond programs that attempt to make parents more like the white middle class to programs that empower them (parents) to better understand and transform their own communities, their own lives, and the lives of their children.

Increasingly, schools' efforts to ensure young children's developing literacy and cognitive skills will involve children's parents in that process. Literary-based early childhood programs must be aware of home languages and culture.

Language Arts Curriculum

Schools and centers differ widely in **curriculum** development; however, two basic approaches can be identified. First a unit or thematic approach emerges from identified child interest and teacher-selected areas, such as families, seasons, animals, and so on. Using this approach, some centers use children's books or classic nursery rhymes as their thematic starting topic. Others introduce a proposed theme (unit) topic to small child discussion groups. This offers input from attending children and lets teachers explore children's past experience, knowledge, and interests. Questions children ask and vocabulary used may aid teachers' thematic unit development. Staff and parent group discussion can also uncover attitudes and resources. Goals are considered, and activities are then outlined and scheduled into time slots. Many teachers feel this type of program approach individualizes instruction by providing many interrelated and, consequently, reinforced learnings while also allowing the child to select activities.

The second common instructional approach is to pinpoint traditional preschool subject areas, such as language arts, science, mathematics, art, cooking, and so forth, and then plan how many and what kind of planned activities will take place. This can be done with or without considering a unifying theme. Some teachers feel that this is a more systematic approach to instruction.

In both approaches, the identification of goals has come before curriculum development. Ages of children, staffing ratios, facility resources, and other particulars all have an impact on planning. After

planned curriculum activities take place, teachers evaluate whether goals were reached, and modifications and suggestions are noted. Additional or follow-up activities may be planned and scheduled for groups or individual children.

Thematic Inquiry Approach to Language Instruction

Imagine a classroom turned into a pizza parlor or a flower garden. There would be a number of activities going on simultaneously—some for small groups, others for large groups, and some for individuals. Teachers would be involved in activities, and classroom areas might be set up for continuous, or almost continuous, child exploration. Art, singing, number, movement, science-related, health-and-safety-related, and other types of activities would (or could) be preplanned, focusing on the two themes mentioned above. The sensory activities could be included so that children could experience the smells, sounds, sights, tastes, and so on, associated with each theme. Planning language arts instruction using this approach allows teachers to use creativity and imagination. It also requires planning time to gather and set up material that might not be found in the school storeroom or supply area. It is easy to see that there could be many opportunities for children's use of speech, listening, reading, and writing, and the natural connection among these activities might be more apparent to the children. Most teachers feel using a thematic approach is an exciting challenge that is well worth teacher time and effort. They see this approach as one that encourages child-teacher conversations that expand both language usage and knowledge.

Nunnelly (1990) suggests teachers not limit their program to traditional themes but also explore and discover beyond the familiar. She urges teachers to follow children's curiosity and their own childhood interests. Many centers believe as does Moon (1996) that real teaching is found when each staff member gives children what he or she individually has to offer from the heart as well as the mind.

Develop exciting topics by using a planning strategy with three steps: (1) brainstorming, (2) design-

---

Curriculum — an overall plan for the content of instruction to be offered in a program.

ing a theme's implementation, and (3) planning specific activities for groups and learning centers.

In constructing a theme, the following steps are usually undertaken:

1. Observing and recording a child's interest and/or teacher drawing from own past experience.
2. Identifying a topic. (Could be a book, poems, drama, or category.)
3. Try to discover what children know and want to know.
4. Imagining possible activities (in and out of school).
5. Deciding on attempted goals of instruction.
6. Pinpointing range, scope, vocabulary, main ideas, and activities.
7. Discussing room environment, staffing, visitors, and helpers. (What will take place in classroom or yard learning centers?)
8. Making specific plans for individual and group activities.
9. Listing necessary materials and supplies.
10. Deciding on a culminating activity. (Usually a recap or "grand finale.")
11. Setting a time table if necessary. (Daily schedules may be prepared.)
12. Pinpointing evaluation criteria.

Burchfield (1996) describes a unit of study designed by practitioners who consider Gardner's (1983, 1986) theory of multiple intelligences:

> . . . allow children to experience a concept or skill in a variety of ways and demonstrate their learning and understandings by using their strong suits and by being challenged to develop their ability in areas identified (by parents, teachers, and even children) for more emphasis and improvement.

To promote literacy, teachers think about how each theme activity involves listening, speech, reading and writing, and how to logically connect these areas during on-going activities.

The thematic approach has claimed more advocates since the trend toward whole-language instruction has captured the interest of a growing number of elementary school teachers and early childhood teachers. Many early childhood teachers who work with children who are younger than kindergarten age have used a unit (or thematic) approach to instruction for many years.

Thematic/Literacy-Based Instruction

Literature-based instruction, now mandated or recommended in elementary schools in many states, is very similar to what early childhood educators call thematic instruction. Both levels realize the value of literature and its relationship to literacy. A theme in early childhood could be any topic of interest to children. A literacy-based approach would use a classic book or informational book as its central core, figure 6–7. A preschool educator would have no problem using a book as a starting place, and could plan discussions, drama, art, music, puppetry, and other language arts activities to strengthen various concepts encountered.

Curriculum Webs and Webbing

The use of curriculum webs in program planning is popular with some preschool teachers. A web can be thought of as a graphic overall picture of what might be included in a theme or unit approach to instruction. Figure 6–8 shows a skeleton web designed for the study of dogs. Under the box "care and needs" one can think of a number of items that could be listed. In fact, the web could become highly detailed as the teacher using it listed concepts associated with the subject—dogs. The object of creating a web is for the teacher to define and refine the web based on the interests and needs of his or her particular enrolled group. The plan (web) is then translated into planned daily happenings with children's active exploring and participation. The goal is to offer activities to engage the students' interest, imagination, and spark their desire

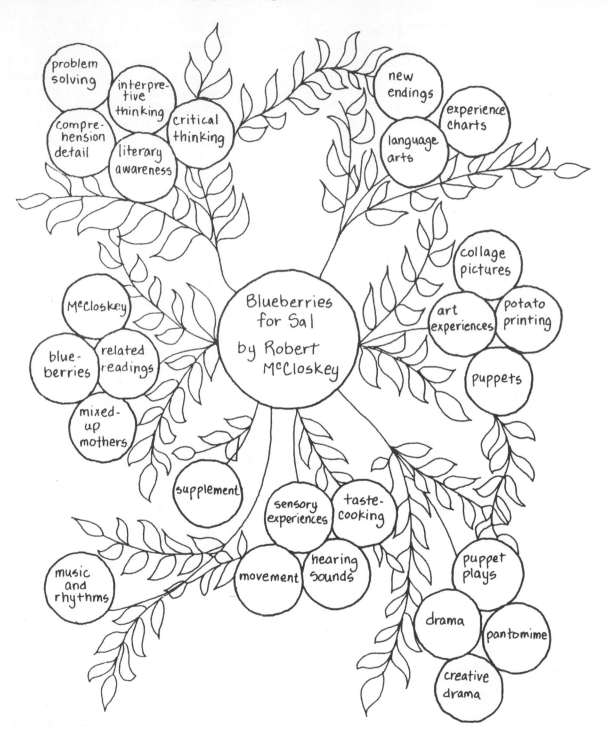

FIGURE 6–7 Example of webbing using a children's book *(From* Learning to Love Literature, *L. Lamme, ed. Copyright 1981 by the National Council of Teachers of English. Reprinted with permission.)*

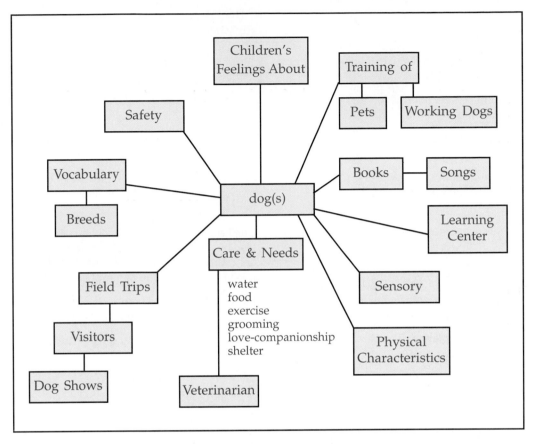

FIGURE 6–8 Topic Web—Dog(s)

to seek out answers, ponder questions, or create responses. One of the rewards of teaching is to present or set up an activity that children eagerly select, and perhaps ask a million questions about; in other words, one that has "captured" them and engaged their minds.

Reggio Emilia

Early childhood educators studying the Reggio Emilia approach to program planning are reexamining their curriculum. Gandini (1997) describes the teacher's role in the Reggio Emilia approach:

> To know how to plan or proceed with their work, teachers observe and listen to the children closely. Teachers use the understand-

ing they gain in this way to act as a resource for them. They ask questions and discover the children's ideas, hypotheses, and theories. Then the adults discuss together what they have recorded through their own notes, or audio or visual recordings, and make flexible plans and preparations. Then they are ready to enter again into dialogues with the children and offer them occasions for discovering and also revisiting experiences since they consider learning not as a linear process but as spiral progression.

For Hendrick's (1997) comparisons of American and Reggian schools see figure 6–9. A reading list for those exploring the Reggio Emilia approach is found in the Appendix.

AMERICAN	REGGIAN
"Projects" or themes are short-lived, extending a day or a week.	"Projects" may be brief but often continue for weeks or months.
"Topics" are used to provide information and (possibly) practice in midlevel thinking skills.	"Topics" are used to pose problems and provoke thought.
Children acquire a shallow smattering of information on many subjects.	Children acquire in-depth knowledge about fewer subjects (i.e., "know more about less").
Inquiry learning focuses on science tables; some problem solving encouraged.	Pronounced emphasis on "provoking" children to propose reasons why things happen and possible ways to solve problems.
Children may show what they know by talking to teacher about it.	Children show what they know by talking about it but also by using many different media: models, graphics, bent wire, dance, and so forth to explain their ideas: "You don't know it until you can explain it to someone else."
The individual is emphasized; autonomy, self-responsibility, independence are valued.	Existence within the group is emphasized; sense of community and interdependence are valued.
Children select whatever they wish to participate in each day.	Children select what they want to do but are also encouraged to work in consistent small groups based on their continuing interests.
Time is highly regulated and scheduled.	Time flows easily in an unhurried way.
Record keeping is typically limited to results rather than work in progress—shows what children have learned (checklists, portfolios, observations) or do not know.	Record keeping—Documentation boards record what children "know" at beginning and during, as well as end of project; boards used for everyone to re-visit and re-cognize their work as it progresses.
Teacher changes at least once a year.	Teachers remain with children for 3 years.
Staffing is teacher, or teacher plus aide.	Staffing is two teachers of equal rank plus services of a *pedagogista* and *aterlierista*.
Hierarchy of staff positions (i.e., director, teacher, aide).	There are no directors; everyone accepts various responsibilities.
Confrontation is avoided.	Debate and "confrontation" with different points of view between adults and with children are favored methods of learning for everyone.
Teachers tend to be isolated; policy about and regularity of staff meetings varies.	Close collaboration between *all* teachers occurs regularly and frequently.

FIRST STEPS TOWARD TEACHING THE REGGIO WAY by Joanne Hendrick, © 1988. Reprinted by permission of Prentice-Hall, Inc., Upper Saddle River, NJ.

FIGURE 6–9   A sampling of some additional comparisons of American and Reggian schools

Whole-Language Movement

Whole-language advocates are influencing many early childhood educators. General assumptions used by whole-language practitioners as a basis for curriculum decisions mesh well with early childhood developmentally appropriate curriculum statements. The whole-language movement has been closely identified with elementary school reading methods. (See Chapter 17.)

Flooding whole-language classrooms with children's literature to expose them to an integrated speaking, reading, writing approach is part-and-parcel of the movement. Whole-language theorists predict children will then become captured by the possibilities of reading and writing and *eventually* master reading and writing. This eventual happening is on a time table of its own and may or may not immediately raise test scores. As a reaction to low child reading test scores when phonics and word decoding skills are overlooked, many professionals now urge a "balanced" approach to reading instruction rather than an exclusive whole-language instructional model.

A teacher following a whole-language thematic philosophy might offer a unit on valentines along the lines that follow.

- Discuss valentines.
    "What do you know about valentines?"
    "Where can I find a valentine?"
    Talk about valentines you have received.
    "Why would someone send a valentine?"
- Write children's answers and comments on a wall chart.
- Provide each child with a box to use as a mailbox.
    Child chooses sticker to identify box.
    Write child's name on box.
- Teacher and children examine envelopes that come to school.
    Point out lines and words across stamp.
    Use word "cancelled."
    Teacher talks about unused stamps.
    Discuss letter carriers. Use pictures of letter carriers to promote conversation.

- Conduct a field trip to the post office.
    Share a book about receiving mail.
    Set up a work center with stamps (any kind), envelopes, writing tools, and lists of names.
- Set up a work area complete with materials used for making valentines.
- Introduce a list of all the names of people in the class.
- Introduce songs about valentines.
- Share a poem about valentines.

A beginning teacher can see from this barebones outline that the teacher is identifying possible learning activities associated with the valentine theme. Each teacher or school using a theme or whole-language approach may develop a unit on valentines that has similarities and differences. Many of the differences arise from the teacher's knowledge of what is appropriate for the teacher's particular group of children and the goals that have been identified. On further planning and when presenting this unit to the class, the whole-language teacher would look for opportunities to state and show relationships among language arts areas.

The Project Approach

Based on the writings of Katz and Chard (1989), the project approach involves integrated teaching and learning. It encourages meaningful, first-hand, relevant study of child-teacher developed and chosen units. This program approach is valued by teachers for its flexible and creative aspects, which fit diverse child groups and geographical communities. Children are involved in decision making, program planning, implementation, and evaluation through active teacher-child shared discussion,

---

Whole language — a philosophy and reading-instruction approach integrating oral and written language. Advocates believe that when children are given literature-abundant and print-rich environments they will follow their natural curiosity and learn to read as they learned to speak. A thematic focus is used. Teachers seize opportunities to connect and interrelate language arts areas.

brainstorming, and unit outlining. Teachers also plan activities and experiences. Children are urged to explore and investigate and become testers of ideas as individuals and in study groups. Educators believe that the key to child interest and motivation and their desire to know or want to find out in the project approach is children's role as curricular decision makers and teacher collaborators. Teachers using thematic unit instruction may feel the project approach best suits kindergarten and elementary-aged children.

Commitment to Goals and Objectives

A number of factors determine whether goals are met:

- Enthusiasm and commitment of staff
- Staffing ratios
- Staff ingenuity, resourcefulness
- Methods and techniques used
- Resources available
- General feeling or tone of center
- Examination of sequence (easiest to complex)
- Parental and community support

Effort and staff creativity translate goals into daily activities.

Daily Activity Plans

Recognizing child interests stimulates activity-planning ideas based on what captures and holds the child's attention. Part of the challenge and excitement of teaching is finding ways to be creative in daily activity planning.

Although two staff members work toward the same goal, they may approach the task in a different way. Lesson plans are more frequently used in schools using approaches other than the thematic (unit) approach described above but can also be used for individual teacher-conducted activities within theme planning.

Lesson plans enable teachers to foresee needs—settings, materials, and staffing. The time that children spend waiting can be minimized. Some

teachers pinpoint exactly what words and concepts will be emphasized or what questions asked; other teachers prefer a more spontaneous approach.

Some activities in language arts may require teacher practice beforehand. Others may require visual aids or materials that must be gathered in advance. Planning time is time well spent. Preparation reduces teacher tension and results in child activities that run smoothly.

Teachers must strive to be always aware of child safety and comfort. They must also try to maintain a reasonable level of stimulation somewhere between not very interesting or overly exciting activities, so that children are encouraged to process information in a manner that is both pleasurable and efficient. Experienced teachers know when children are interested and are actively participating. Many teachers say this is one of the greatest joys of teaching.

Group size is an important factor in planning. It is easier for teachers to plan for an entire class group, and sometimes staffing demands it. However, many teachers have explored ways to keep children occupied and supervised while working with small groups. Small groups allow greater intimacy, conversational depth, and opportunity for feedback. Research substantiates the idea that both children and adults feel more comfortable sharing their thoughts when in small groups. "Instant replays" with small groups can be planned and coordinated. Beginning preschool teachers may not have seen many small-group activities modeled by other teachers, but this text recommends them.

The three examples in figures 6–10 through 6–12 illustrate different types of activity planning.

Detailed written lesson plans help beginning teachers feel prepared and relaxed (figure 6–13, page 153). After a period of time, teachers internalize lesson-planning components and discontinue detailed written plans, although they continue to use lists and outlines.

Watching the class carefully, keeping a notebook in a handy pocket, and writing down small observations can help a teacher to remember the interests of a young group. A good guide to unearthing new subjects of interest for a particular class is to

UNDERSTANDING LOCATIONAL WORDS

Note: This is a self-selected child activity set up during a unit study of transportation for a class of three- and four-year-olds. A waiting list is available, so children are assured a turn.

Purpose: Child will be able to place vehicle "under," "over," "behind," and "in front of" when given verbal directions after becoming familiar with the words in the play situation.

Materials: Streets and a highway drawn on a large sheet of paper taped to a table. Toy vehicles (car, truck, school bus, van, etc.); blocks, a box, or cardboard to make a highway overpass.

Procedure:

1. Place box with toy vehicles inside in front of child. "Tell me about what you find in the box." Verbally label each vehicle if child does not.

2. Pause and let child talk about toy vehicles. Introduce overpass and discuss "under" and "over" the bridge.

3. "We're going to take turns. First I'm going to ask you to put the vehicles in different places. Then you tell me where you want me to place one of the vehicles."

4. "Can you drive the car *under* the bridge?" Encourage child if necessary. Pause. "Which vehicle do you want me to drive *under* the bridge? The bus?"

5. "My turn. Drive the truck *over* the bridge." Pause. "Which one do you want me to drive *over* the bridge?"

6. "Put the bus in front of the car." "Which one do you want me to move *in front of* the bus?"

7. Proceed until all four locational words are introduced and demonstrated. Then "Tell me where you choose to drive or park the toys. I'll watch you."

8. Allow child time to play as he or she wishes. As the child continues with the activity add comments when appropriate, such as "You drove the van *under* the bridge."

FIGURE 6–10 Example 1—individual activity

VISUAL PERCEPTION

Purpose: Matching identical stockings

Materials: Enough matching pairs of stockings for each child in the group. (More pairs if possible.) Use socks of the same size but different in pattern. Two bags. (Separate, putting one sock of each pair in bags.)

Procedure:

1. "Here's a pair of stockings. Tell me how they are the same. Yes, these are blue and they have white stripes. If your stockings at home were all mixed together in a basket, raise your hand if you think you could find all the stockings that are the same and put them in pairs." (Let discussion flow.) "We're going to play a game. Pretend you've lost one stocking at school and I found it."

2. "I'm going to take all the stockings I've found at school and put them in a pile." Empty one bag making a pile on a low table. "(Child's name), I saw your hand raised. Take one stocking out of this bag (second bag) and see if you can find its mate on the table. Its mate looks the same. Tell how those two stockings are the same. Yes, they are both red and have dots."

3. Place paired socks side-by-side.

4. Continue until all children have had several turns.

Reinforcement Activities:

1. Turn this group activity into an individual activity in which one child can pair all the socks. A standing clothes rack or a clothesline can be used.

2. Mittens or shoes can also be matched in a similar group activity. The closer the distinctions, the more difficult the match.

3. To exercise visual perception, use seasonal items, such as matching leaves, ornaments, valentines, jack-o-lanterns, etc. made by the teacher. Differences should be subtle.

FIGURE 6–11 Example 2—group activity

notice what has already captured the children's attention. What do the children talk about most often? What do they crowd around? Does the activity promote children's interested questions? What has the longest waiting list? Are children eager to explore a particular object with their hands? Who wants to share something discovered or created? For example, if butterflies interest a group, planned butterfly experiences can add depth to the curriculum.

NOTE: This is a portion of a longer description. The words in italics show how the teacher works toward a variety of goals.

This episode is an account of a sequence of planned activities culminating in a cooking experience for four 4-year-old children. Part 1 of the episode details the preparation in the classroom for the purchase of the food and the group's trip to a local store. Part 2 describes the cooking.

The fresh pears at lunch evoked the excited comment "Apples!" from Spanish-speaking Fernando.

"Well, this is a fruit," said Miss Gordon, encouragingly, "but it has another name. Do you remember the apples we had last week?"

"They were hard to bite," said Joey.

"And we made applesauce," said Rosina.

"This fruit is called a pear, Fernando; let's taste this pear now. We'll have apples again."

The teacher responds to what is correct in the child's response, valuing his category association. First, she wants to support communication and willingness to experiment with language; later she gives the correct name. The children strengthen the experience by relating it to previous experience in which they were active.

"Mine's soft," said Joey.

"Can we make applesauce again?" begged Rosina.

The teacher replied, "Perhaps we could do what Janice wanted to do. Remember? To take some home to her family?"

"To my mommy, and my grandma, and Danny."

"Not to my baby," said Rosina. "He's too little. Him only drink milk."

"Tomorrow we'll buy lots of apples," said Miss Gordon.

The teacher is building a sense of continuity by recalling earlier intentions that had been expressed by the children.

She rarely corrects use of pronouns for four-year-olds. She knows the child will learn through greater social maturity and hearing language.

After rest, Miss Gordon asked the children how they could take home their applesauce. "What can we put it in?"

Rosina ran to the house corner and returned with two baby food jars. "I bringed lots," she said. Miss Gordon remembered that Rosina had come to school lugging a bag full of baby food jars, many of which she had put away. "A good idea! And your mommy said she would keep more for us. Let's write a note to tell her we need them tomorrow."

Rosina dictated a note: "I got to bring bunches of jars to school. We are going to make applesauce. I love you, Mommy." Rosina painted her name with a red marker.

The teacher helps children to think ahead to steps in a process.

The use of a tense form, though incorrect, represents learning for the child. The teacher does not correct at this moment, when she is responding to the child's pleasure in solving the practical problem that had been posed. She is strengthening the connection between home and school.

The teacher helps the children learn that writing is a recording of meaning and a way of communicating.

The next day was jar washing and arranging time. Each of the four children put his jars on a tray on which there was a large card with his name.

Janice put on one jar for her mother, one for her grandmother, one for her brother, and after a pause, one for herself.

Rosina changed her mind. "My baby can have a little tiny bit," she said. So she needed a jar for her father, her mother, her baby and herself.

Joey and the teacher figured out that he needed six, and that Fernando needed nine!

The children are actively involved in the steps preparatory to the planned activity—an experience in organization which has personal meaning.

The teacher's plan calls for recognition of one's own name and one-to-one counting of family members.

The teacher turned their attention to a chart near the cooking corner. She had made a recipe chart, pasting colored (magazine) pictures next to the names of the items they would need to make the applesauce and had taped a stick of cinnamon to the chart.

Miss Gordon said, "Let's look at the recipe chart. I have a list so we can remember to buy everything."

The children said, "Apples."

Miss Gordon checked her list.

Then, "Sugar."

The children were silent as they looked at the stick of cinnamon taped to the chart.

Miss Gordon suggested, "Smell it. Have we had it before?"

Joey remembered: "Toast! What we put on toast!"

"Yes," said Miss Gordon, and then gave the word, "cinnamon."

The children are having a dual experience—pictorial representation and formal symbol usage.

The teacher supplies the word after the children have revived their direct experience with the phenomenon (Biber, Shapiro, Wickens, 1977).

FIGURE 6–12   Example 3—multiple-goal approach

LANGUAGE ACTIVITY PLAN GUIDE

1. Language activity title _____
    _____

2. Materials needed _____
    _____
    _____

3. Location of activity (To be used when plan is developed for a particular classroom or area) _____
    _____

4. Number of children _____

5. Language goal or objective _____
    _____

6. Preparation (Necessary teacher preparation, including getting materials or objects, visual aids, etc., ready) _____
    _____
    _____

7. Getting started (Introductory and/or motivational statement) _____
    _____
    _____

8. Show and explore (Include possible teacher questions or statements that promote language ability) _____
    _____
    _____
    _____
    _____

9. Discussion key points (What vocabulary and/or concepts might be included?) _____
    _____
    _____
    _____
    _____
    _____

10. Apply (Include child practice or application of newly learned knowledge or skill when appropriate) _____
    _____
    _____
    _____

11. Evaluation: (1) Activity, (2) Teacher, (3) Child participation, (4) Other aspects such as setting, materials, outcomes, etc.
    _____
    _____
    _____
    _____
    _____

FIGURE 6–13   Sample activity plan form

Activities based on teacher enthusiasm for life and growth, skills, talents, hobbies, and pursuits can fit beautifully into language arts goals. Parent and community resources, including borrowed items and field trips increase the vitality of programs.

Evaluation

Thinking back over planned activities helps teachers analyze the benefits and possibly leads to additional planning along the same line or with the same theme. Oversights in planning always occur, and activities may develop in unexpected ways. Hindsight is a useful and valuable tool in evaluating activities.

Often centers evaluate their planned programs by asking themselves questions such as:

- Do children share personal interests and learning discoveries with teachers and/or other children?
- Can teachers enter conversations without diminishing children's verbal initiative?
- Do children become involved in planned activities and room centers?
- Are there times when children listen with interest?
- Are language arts areas (speaking, writing, reading, listening) connected in a natural way during daily activities?
- Is child talk abundant?

Summary

Preschool professionals are concerned with the literacy of preschoolers and believe attention to beginning literacy should be reflected in the planning of the language arts curriculum. Three factors, skill, a shared body of common knowledge, and attitude, promote emerging literacy. Beginning literacy is believed to exist in children who demonstrate beginning competence in language.

Language is part of every preschool activity. This text recommends an integrated approach to early childhood language arts—that is, a program that involves listening, speaking, writing, and reading.

Centers identify language arts goals through a group process. Activities are then planned based on these goals. Daily plans carry out what is intended. Assessment instruments are evaluated, and decisions are made concerning whether these instruments are to be used or not used. Staff observation provides data on children's abilities, interests, and skill levels, as well as additional insights that are useful in activity planning. Every center has a unique set of goals and objectives, so designing child experiences is done in a variety of ways. Since attending children change in any particular school, plans change according to children's needs and interests.

Evaluating a planned activity after it is presented can pinpoint strengths and weaknesses. This also serves as the basis for further activity planning.

STUDENT ACTIVITIES

1. Define literacy in your own words. Share with class.
2. List 10 reasons for illiteracy in the United States. Then, list 10 ways preschool centers can help a preschooler's emerging literacy. Ask for a volunteer to make a chart on a large surface that everyone in the classroom can see, listing the reasons for illiteracy that are given by students. Put tallies after ideas so that the class can see what was the most frequently thought of reason. Make a second large listing of the group's ideas concerning how preschools can promote emerging literacy.

3. Describe an activity(ies) that might interest young children based on your own personal experience, a talent or skill you possess, a family possession or article, or an interesting field trip. Don't forget clothing you own for special purposes or hobbies or collections or people you know who might share their talents or possessions.

4. Form a discussion group with a few fellow students. Take out one item from your pocket or purse. Describe an activity you could use with children to promote the following skills:
   a. Memory (naming or recalling)
   b. Discrimination
   c. Problem solving
   d. Perceptual-motor skill

   Be aware that each activity planned should
   — be interesting and enjoyable.
   — help children feel competent and successful.
   — stimulate children to discover.
   — promote sensory exploration.
   — include learning by doing.
   — promote language by promoting expression of what the child experienced or discovered.

   Go on to discuss what activities could be planned that would promote the same four skills (a through d) using a box of paper clips or a doll.

5. Design an activity plan form that includes:
   a. Title (What?)
   b. Materials and tools needed (With what?)
   c. An objective (language arts) (Why?)
   d. A preparation section
   e. Setting or location description
   f. Number of children who are to participate at one time
   g. Identification of child skills and abilities necessary for success
   h. A statement that introduces the activity to children
   i. A description of how the activity will proceed (How?)

6. Invite teachers to describe their center's language arts curriculum. Try to invite a teacher using the whole-language philosophy to share the teacher's curriculum plans.

7. Using any activity plan form, make a written plan for a language development activity. Share your plan with others at the next class meeting. Rate the quality of your participation in the discussion using the following scale, or write a beginning outline for a unit of your own choosing or one you feel is of interest to a group of four-year-old children. Share your unit ideas at the next class meeting.

No Input	Very Little	Contributed About As Much As Classmates	A Fair Amount	Offered Lots of Ideas

8. Ask a practicing early childhood teacher to speak about the use of assessment instruments in the language program where the person is employed.

9. With a group of peers design an activity. Offer the activity with some in your group playing the role of children. Use figure 6–3 to evaluate the activity. Share with class.

10. Look back into your own childhood before age six. What classics, songs, rhymes, language activities were part of your childhood? If you do not remember, answer this alternative question: Which literacy-promoting language activities should not be missed by any child? Be specific, and name poems, books, rhymes, stories, or other literary experiences.

11. After reading the following passage, discuss the ability of musical activities to promote cultural understanding.

    Music has often been termed "the universal language." It offers one of the most direct and accessible ways of experiencing the aesthetic style and feeling of a particular culture. Incorporating the music of a child's own culture into an early childhood setting creates a more homelike environment in which a child will feel more secure and validated (Jaffe, 1992).

12. Look for additional information at the library about Brian Cambourne's ideas regarding language learning. Report your findings and reactions to the class. Discuss how Cambourne's writings might affect your program planning.

CHAPTER REVIEW

A. Name the four interrelated language arts areas, arranging them in what you feel is their order of appearance in young children.

B. Compare lesson plan Examples 2 and 3 (figures 6–11 and 6–12) in this unit. How do they differ? In which ways are they similar?

C. Write three language arts goal statements (what you would want children to have the opportunity to experience and learn). These should be statements that would be included in a program where you were (or will be) employed.

D. Select the correct answer. Each item may have more than one correct answer.
   1. Assessment instruments can be
      a. a checklist.
      b. a child interest inventory.
      c. counted on to be valid.
      d. teacher made.

2. Compiling and identifying a center's goal statements ideally involves
   a. children's input.
   b. staff.
   c. parents.
   d. interested community members.

3. Early childhood language arts should be offered to children using
   a. an approach that helps children see relationships between areas.
   b. techniques that promote the child's realization that spoken words can be written.
   c. separate times of day to explore reading and writing without combining these skills.
   d. identified goal statements as a basis for activity planning.

4. When goals are identified, a school (or center) could
   a. retain its flexibility in activity planning.
   b. lose its ability to fulfill children's individual needs if the same activity plans are used from year to year.
   c. keep its program "personal" by continually evaluating and updating.
   d. periodically take a close look at goals to see whether staff commitment is strong or weak.

5. Literacy as defined in this chapter included
   a. both skills and general knowledge.
   b. the ability to enjoy written language.
   c. the idea that there can be literate preschoolers.
   d. the idea that cultural literacy changes over time.
   e. the idea that reading skill instruction is necessary during preschool years if a child is to become literate.

6. Using commercial assessment instruments
   a. is questionable because reliability varies.
   b. serves as the basis of professional programming.
   c. can mean using teacher-designed assessments is out of the question.
   d. is a group decision.

7. "There is only one correct way to plan and present activities to children." This statement is
   a. true.
   b. false.
   c. partly true because each individual strives to find the one plan that helps planned activities run smoothly and successfully.
   d. incorrect because the plan itself doesn't ensure success or goal realization.

8. Evaluating an activity is
   a. rarely necessary if it is well planned.
   b. admitting that teachers can learn a lot through hindsight.
   c. busywork with little value.
   d. necessary if teachers wish to improve their abilities.

9. Test results are
   a. always valid if a test is standardized.
   b. used primarily to judge children's inherited ability.
   c. used to help teachers plan child growth experiences.
   d. always reliable if the teacher has studied the publisher's instructions.

10. Although language arts goals may be identified, language
    a. is part of every activity.
    b. can be taught through music activities.
    c. of children will grow whether planned activities are offered or not offered.
    d. activities offered daily cannot assure that goals attempted will be attained.

CHAPTER 7

Promoting Language and Literacy

OBJECTIVES

After studying this chapter, you should be able to:

- list three roles of a teacher in early childhood language education.

- discuss the balances needed in teacher behavior.

- describe ways a teacher can promote language growth.

A good description of a skilled early childhood educator is a "responsive opportunist" who is enthusiastic and enjoys discovery, and who is able to establish and maintain a warm, supportive environment. When a reciprocal relationship between a child and an adult or between children is based on equality, respect, trust, and authentic dialogue (real communication), child language learning is promoted. Teachers need to create a classroom atmosphere where children can expect success, see the teacher as a significant person, are allowed choice, and are able to make mistakes. Ideally, children should join in planned activities eagerly. These activities should end before the child's capacity to focus is exhausted. The child should be able to expect the teacher to listen and respond to the child's communication in a way that respects the child's sense of the importance of the communication.

There are three specific teaching functions that encourage the development of language arts and literacy:

1. The teacher serves as a *model* of everyday language use. What is communicated and how it is communicated are important.

2. The teacher is a *provider* of experiences. Many of these events are planned; others happen in the normal course of activities.

3. The teacher is an *interactor*, sharing experiences with the children and encouraging conversation (figure 7–1).

These three functions should be balanced, relative to each child's level and individual needs.

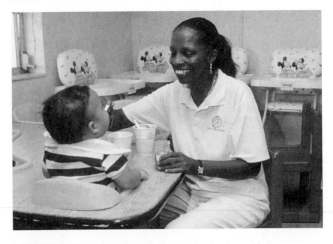

FIGURE 7–1 As the teacher interacts in everyday experiences, a smile is a way of showing interest.

The teaching role requires constant decision making: knowing when to supply or withhold information to help self-discovery and when to talk or listen. Basically, sensitivity and predictable behavior can make the teacher the child's best ally in the growth of language skills.

The teacher's role as an observer is an on-going responsibility that influences all daily teacher-child exchanges and allows the teacher to decide on courses of action with individual children. Knowing children's interests, present behaviors, and emerging skills helps the teacher perform the three above-mentioned functions, based on group and individual needs.

Observing all elements of a program as well as children's behavior and progress involves watching, listening, and recording. This can be the most difficult part of teaching because of time constraints and supervisory requirements. With so much to supervise and provide, teachers can view observation time as a luxury. In-depth observation is best accomplished when a teacher is relieved of other responsibilities and can focus without distractions. Many teachers who do not have duty-free observation time must observe while on duty. Observation often unearths questions regarding children's difficulties, talents, and a wide range of special needs that can then be incorporated into plans and daily exchanges.

Listening intimately is highly advisable. Providing growth depends partially on being on a child's or group's wavelength. Conversations are more valuable when teachers try to converse and question based on the child's line of thought. Activities provided should increase children's ability to think and rethink and therefore make sense from what they encounter. Carter and Jones (1995) remind teachers to keep in view the goals they might have for any adult-child communication:

> Part of the task is helping teachers think through the goals they might have for any given communication with children. If your

goal is to test for right answers or to stop certain behavior, you will probably say things differently than if you are trying to build verbal expression or self-confidence.

Unplanned teacher talk can be viewed as less important than talk in teacher-guided activities. If a teacher feels this way, it can limit a teacher's ability to support problem-solving, child discovery, and child expression of events important to the child. The **listening** and *observing* behavior of teachers increases the quality and pertinence of teachers' communicative interactions.

The Teacher as a Model

Teachers model not only speech, but also attitudes and behaviors in listening, writing, and reading. Children watch and listen to the adult's use of grammar, intonation, and sentence patterns and imitate and use the adult as an example.

Consider the different and similar ways teachers verbally interact with young children (figure 7–2). After studying British families, Bernstein (1962) theorized that a recognizable style of verbal interaction based upon social class exists. Working class speakers, Bernstein believed, used a restricted code type of speech, while middle class speakers, used both elaborated code and restricted code speech in some verbal exchanges. Restricted code speech characteristics are described as follows:

- specific to a current physical context
- limited
- stereotyped
- condensed
- inexact
- nonspecific
- short sentence length
- vague and indefinite expressions used

Elaborate code speech, in Bernstein's view, is:

- more differentiated
- more precise
- not specific to a particular situation or context and afforded opportunities for more complex thought

---

Listening — recognizing and interpreting sounds and oral symbols.

Example A

Child: "It's chickun soup."

Teacher: "That's right."

Example B

Child: "It's chickun soup."

Teacher: "Yes. I see chicken pieces and something else."

Child: "It's noodles."

Teacher: "Yes, those are long, skinny noodles. It's different from yesterday's red tomato soup."

Child: "Tastes good. It's 'ellow."

Teacher: "Yellow like the daffodils in the vase." (Pointing.)

Example C

Child: "Baby cry."

Adult: "Yes, the baby is crying."

Example D

Child: "Baby cry."

Adult: "You hear the baby crying?"

Child: "Uh-huh."

Adult: "Maybe she's hungry and wants some milk."

Child: "Wants bottle."

Adult: "Let's see. I'll put the bottle in her mouth."

Child: "Her hungry."

Adult: "Yes, she's sucking. The milk is going into her mouth. Look it's almost gone."

FIGURE 7–2 Adult verbal styles

Speakers' styles of communication were seen by Bernstein as powerful determining factors in the young child's development of cognitive structures and modes of communication. He believed that young children exposed exclusively to restricted code speakers are at an educational disadvantage in school settings where elaborated code speech predominates. The major assumption behind this view is that middle-class ways of talking with children support literacy development, while working-class ways inhibit it.

Many other researchers such as Sigel (1982) and Snow (1991) have investigated verbal exchanges between parents and children to pinpoint connections between adult talk and its relationship to child speech, thinking ability, and literacy. Sigel (1982) described parental high-level and low-level distancing strategies in verbal exchanges. High-level distancing strategies include:

- drawing conclusions
- inferring cause-and-effect relationships
- planning
- evaluating consequences
- evaluating effect

Low-level distancing strategies include labeling, producing information, and observing. Sigel hypothesized that social class alone does not predict children's cognitive and linguistic outcomes. Early childhood educators observing young children would agree.

Beals (1993) suggested that preschool teachers focus on studying their ability to use **explanatory talk** in child-teacher verbal exchanges. Explanatory talk consists of conversation concerning some connection between objects, events, concepts and/or conclusions that one speaker is pointing out to another. Preschool teachers commonly and typically explain their intent and actions to children and provide explanations in response to child comments and questions. This is a preferred behavior in early childhood teachers' verbal interactive exchanges.

"The blocks go on the shelf. We will know were to find them when we want to use them, and no one will trip on them."

"The window was open, and the wind blew and knocked over the small cups where our seeds were planted."

"I'm putting my snack dish in the tub on the table when I'm finished. Mrs. Gregorio will come and get the tub after snack time. She'll wash our snack plates."

Explanatory talk — a type of conversation characterized by a speaker's attempt to create connections between objects, events, concepts, or conclusions in order to promote understanding in the listener.

This explanatory style sometimes carries over into teachers' personal lives. Teachers report family members often say to them, "Yes, I know why you're doing that!"

Adults should use clear, descriptive speech at a speed and pitch easily understood. Articulation should be as precise as possible. Weiss and Lillywhite (1981) describe appropriate models during infancy and toddlerhood. These teacher characteristics are also desirable in teachers of preschoolers.

> But being a good model involves more than merely speaking clearly, slowly, and appropriately. A good model uses a variety of facial expressions and other forms of nonverbal communication; associates talking with love, understanding, affection; provides happy, pleasant experiences associated with talking; demonstrates the importance of clearly spoken words. A good model takes advantage of various timely situations. . . .

and speaking further about infancy:

> A good model imitates what the child says or echoes the sounds the child makes and provides many opportunities for the child to experiment with the vocal mechanism and rewards these early efforts.

Preschool teachers also need to be sure that reward in the form of attention is present in their teaching behavior as they deal with young children's attitudes, skills, and behaviors in language arts activities, figure 7–3. Teachers should use language patterns with which they feel comfortable and natural and should analyze their speech, working toward providing the best English model possible. Familiar language patterns reflect each teacher's personality as well as ethnic culture (Weir and Eggleston, 1975). Knowing what kind of model one presents is important, so knowing that there is room for improvement can help a teacher become more professional. Hutinger (1978) suggests:

> Record your own language . . . Listen to your questions, to your sentence structure, your pronunciation.

FIGURE 7–3 Giving attention can be a form of reward for some children.

Modeling the correct word or sentence is done by simply supplying it in a relaxed, natural way rather than in a corrective tone. The teacher's example is a strong influence; when a teacher adds courtesy words (please and thank you, for instance), they appear in children's speech. Finishing an uncompleted word by adding an ending or beginning may be appropriate with very young speakers. (The child may say; "na na;" the teacher would provide, "banana.") Completing a phrase or offering complete sentences in standard English suits older speakers. Though adult modeling has its limits in facilitating spontaneous language, it is an essential first step in learning language (Cole, 1989).

After hearing corrections modeled, the child will probably not shift to correct grammar or usage immediately. It may take many repetitions by teachers and adults over a period of time. What's important is the teacher's acceptance and recognition of the child's idea within the verbalization and the addition of pertinent comments along the same line.

If adults focus on the way something was said (grammar) rather than the meaning, they miss opportunities to increase awareness and extend child interest. Overt correction often ends teacher-child conversation. Affirming is appropriate; emphasize the child's intended message.

Adults can sometimes develop the habit of talking and listening to themselves rather than to the children; it is hypnotic and can be a deterrent to really hearing the child. If one's mind wanders or if one listens only for the purpose of refuting, agreeing, or jumping to value judgments, it interferes with receiving communication from others. Weiss and Lillywhite (1981) urge teachers to not be afraid of silences and to pause slightly when necessary before answering. They make the following listening suggestions to teachers:

- Work as hard to listen as you do to talk.
- Try to hear the message behind the words.
- Consciously practice good listening.

One teaching technique that promotes language skill is simple modeling of grammar or filling in missing words and completing simple sentences. This is called **expansion**. It almost becomes second nature and automatic after a short period of intentional practice. While using expansion, the teacher can also promote wider depth of meaning or spark interest by contributing or suggesting an idea for further exploration. Additional conversation usually occurs.

The teacher is a model for listening as well as speaking. Words, expressions, pronunciations, and gestures are copied as is listening behavior. A quiet teacher may have a quiet classroom; an enthusiastic, talkative teacher (who also listens) may have a classroom where children talk, listen, and share experiences. The way children feel about themselves is reflected in their behavior. When teachers listen closely, children come to feel that what they say is worthwhile.

Modeling good printscript form (classroom or center manuscript print) should result after studying upcoming chapters in this text. Since children seem to absorb everything in their environment, it is necessary to provide correctly formed alphabet letters and numerals on children's work, charts, bulletin boards, and any displayed classroom print.

Teachers' use and care of books are modeled, as well as their attitudes toward story and nonfic-tional book experiences. Through their observations of teachers' actions, children begin to develop ideas about how books should be handled and stored.

One teacher who wanted to model storytelling of personal stories divided a large paper into eight sections; in each section she drew a picture of different stages in her life. She showed this to her class and asked them to pick a picture, which she then related in storytelling (Mallan, 1994). Teachers also model poetry reading and its use, dramatization, puppet play, and many other language arts activities.

Covey's (1989) statement, "What *we are* communicates far more eloquently than anything we say or do," wasn't written expressly for teachers of young children; nonetheless it is a good finale to this discussion.

The Teacher as Provider

As providers, preschool teachers strive to provide experiences that promote literacy. As Kate Briggs (1988) points out:

> . . . children are our richest natural resource, thus all efforts should be aimed at making certain we have a 100% literate population, starting with our children.

Fortunately, the number of interesting language arts activities one can offer children is almost limitless. Teachers rely on both their own creativity and the many resources available to plan experiences based on identified goals. Early childhood resource books, other teachers, teacher magazines, workshops, and conferences all contribute ideas.

Gathering activity ideas and storing them in a personal resource file is suggested, since it is almost impossible to remember all the activity ideas one comes upon. An activity file can include new or

---

Expansion — a teaching technique that includes the adult's (teacher's) modeling of word(s) or grammar, filling in missing words in children's utterances, or suggesting ideas for child exploration.

tried-and-true activity ideas. Developing a usable file starts with identifying initial categories (file headings) and adding more heads as the file grows. Some teachers use large file cards, others use binders or file folders. Whatever the file size, teachers find that files are very worthwhile when it comes to daily, weekly, and monthly planning. Often, files are helpful when ideas on a certain subject or theme are needed or when a child exhibits a special interest.

A large number of activity ideas are presented in following chapters. Your creativity can produce other ideas. Suggestions for separate file headings (categories) follow.

- Audiovisual Activities
- Bulletin Board Ideas
- Child Drama Ideas
- Children's Books
- Circle Time Ideas
- Classroom Environment Ideas
    Reading Centers
    Writing Centers
    Listening Centers
- Dramatic Play Stimulators
- Dramatic Play Theme Ideas
- Experience Stories
- Field Trip Ideas
- Flannel Board Ideas
- Finger Plays
- Free and Inexpensive Material Resources
- Language Game Ideas
- Listening Activities
- Listening Center Ideas
- Magazine (Child's) Activities
- Patterns
- Poetry
- Perceptual-Motor Activities
- Printscript Ideas
- Puppets
- Reading Readiness Ideas
- Rebus Stories
- Seasonal Ideas
- Speaking Activities Ideas
- Stories for Storytelling
- Visitor Resources

As a provider of materials, a teacher must realize that every classroom object can become a useful program tool to stimulate language. From the clock on the wall to the door knob, every safe item can be discussed, compared, and explored in some way. Since most school budgets are limited, the early childhood teacher finds ways to use available equipment and materials to their fullest.

Each teacher is a unique resource who can plan activities based on personal interests and abilities. Most teachers are pleasantly surprised to see how avidly their classes respond to the interests of their teachers.

When the teacher shares enthusiasm for out-of-school interests, hobbies, projects, trips, and individual talents, he or she can help to give children an introduction to important knowledge. Almost anything appropriate can be presented at the child's level. Whether the teacher is an opera buff, a scuba diver, a gourmet cook, stamp collector, or violin player, the activity should be shared in any safe form that communicates special interest and love of the activity, and the specific vocabulary and materials relating to the activity should be presented. Enthusiasm is the key to inspired teaching.

Providing for Abundant Play

Abundant opportunities for play are important to the child's language acquisition. Considerable research shows that child's play is in fact more complex than it is commonly believed to be. It provides a rich variety of experiences: communication with other children, verbal rituals, topic development and maintenance, turn taking, intimate speech in friendships, follower-leader conversations, and many other kinds of language exchanges. Peer play helps to develop a wide range of communicative skills (Garvey, 1977). Except where the children's safety is in question, children's natural ability to pretend should be encouraged, and the flow of this kind of play should proceed without the teacher's interference. Children will want to talk to teachers about their play, and the teacher's proper involvement is to show interest and be playful themselves at times.

Some preschool teachers tend to give play a priority above teacher-child conversations (Cazden, 1981):

> Many school conversations seemed to be rapidly terminated, not by other demands being made on the teacher, but by her suggestion to the child to start or continue a play activity.

If a child has chosen to engage a teacher in conversation instead of play, or during play, the teacher should be both a willing listener and a competent, skillful conversationalist. Opportunities for play and opportunities to engage both children and adults in extended, warm, and personal conversations should be readily and equally available to the child.

Young children explore constantly. They want to do what they see others doing. Play opportunities usually involve manipulating something. When deeply involved in play, children may seem to be momentarily awe struck in their search for meanings, but soon they will approach adults with questions or comments.

When one observes preschoolers at play, it is obvious that they learn a great deal of language from each other (figure 7–4). They may even argue over correct language use. Some observers believe that the majority of language teaching that takes place in the four-year-olds' classroom is child-to-child teaching.

A resourceful teacher will strive to provide a variety of play by regarding all of a center's area (and furnishings) as a possible place (or object) for safe and appropriate play. Creative use can be made of each foot of floor space.

Providing Accurate and Specific Speech in All Content Areas

Although this text concentrates on teacher-child interactions in the subject field, language arts, other content areas, such as mathematics (numbers), social studies, health and safety, art, music, movement, and so on, will be subjects of teacher-child conversations and discussions. The same teacher techniques that are useful in building children's language competence and vocabulary in language arts are equally useful for other content areas. Every subject area has its own vocabulary and common terms that can overlap other fields of study. For example, the teacher may discuss "applying" paints during an art activity and "applying" an antibacterial on a wound or scratch. If children are focused on the number of muffins on a tray, or whether there are enough scissors to go around, then teacher comments include number words.

Teacher comments should be as accurate, and specific as possible in light of what the teacher feels the children might already know or have experienced. Purposeful teacher conversation adds a little more information than the children know and reinforces and adds depth to words already in the children's vocabulary. When working with numbers or other subjects, the teacher should use terminology that is appropriate to the subject area but at a level the children will understand. For example, the teacher might say "Let's count the muffins" or "The tool in your hand is a wire whip" or "The metal cylinder attached to the wall is a fire extinguisher. Fire extinguishers have something inside that can be sprayed out to put out fires." In movement or music activities, many descriptive

---

From 3 years onwards, children should demonstrate most of the following behaviors with peers:

- getting a peer's attention
- being the leader in an activity
- imitating a peer
- expressing affection toward a peer
- expressing hostility toward a peer
- following or refusing to follow a peer's request
- negotiating an acceptable solution
- playing in a group for a relatively long time

FIGURE 7–4 Behaviors demonstrated by preschoolers with their peers *(From* Learning Language and Loving It, *by C. Weitzman, 1992. Reprinted with permission from The Hanen Centre, 252 Bloor St. W, Ste. 3–390, Toronto, Ontario, Canada M5S 1V5.)*

terms can be added to teacher demonstrations and conversations. Terms like hop, jump, and stretch or soft, loud, high, and low are easily understood when the child is in the process of experiencing them.

The teacher prompts children's use of the words that the teacher provides. Sometimes a teacher is careful to define new words immediately after using the new terms. In number activities, number words are used in the presence of a corresponding number of objects. In movement activities, types of movement are discussed with quick demonstrations.

It is important to introduce new terms in a natural conversational tone rather than within the framework of an obvious lesson. Leading a child or groups of children to new discoveries offers the teacher an opportunity to use specific and accurate terms and also makes children feel like partners in the discoveries.

In the theme (unit) approach to instruction, often there is identifiable terminology attached to the theme. Teachers sometimes outline the terms that might be encountered in a particular unit and try to include these specific terms in conversations. A unit on birds could include many terms and specific names that a teacher might need to research.

The Teacher as Interactor

An interactor can be defined as a person who is always interested in what a child is saying or doing (figure 7–5). This person encourages conversation on any subject the child selects. An interactor is never too busy to talk and share interests and concerns. Time is purposely planned for daily conversations with each child. These private, personal, one-on-one encounters build the child's feelings of self-worth and open communications. Conversations can be initiated with morning greetings such as:

"Alphonse, I've been waiting to talk to you. Tell me about your visit to Chicago."

or

"How is your puppy feeling today, Andrea?"

or

FIGURE 7–5 As an interactor, the teacher enjoys participating in an activity that interests the child.

"Those new blue tennis shoes will be good for running in the yard and for tiptoeing, too."

Tough (1977) claims that the listening, alert, and knowledgeable teacher can consciously influence children's talk and help them pursue ideas and develop new meanings. Her study found where teachers were warm and accepting but offered children little invitation to talk:

Teachers found it quicker and easier to anticipate students' needs and thus failed to seize opportunities that would make children want and need to talk.

She suggests teachers may need to raise their own awareness of their interactions with children, in other words, rate themselves on their ability to expand children's verbalness. Clay (1991) alerts preschool educators to the importance of adult-child language interactions:

For the first five years the child's language growth is entirely dependent on what people say to him—on how much they speak to him, about what things, in what dialect or language, and in what manner, whether gentle and explaining or peremptory and imperative.

Clay believes:

Through the things a preschool teacher attends to she reveals to children what she values.

and

Such valuing of preschoolers' efforts and involvements is continuous, individual, personal, and powerful.

In looking at individual children, Covey (1989) reminds us of what we know in our hearts to be true, fair, and compassionate. Each child is to be valued for his or her identity as a person and for his or her unique individuality, separateness, and worth. Comparisons between children cloud our view. Traits teachers may see as negative can be fostered by the environment we offer and our own perceptions of correct student behavior. An educator's job, according to Covey, is to recognize potential, then coddle and inspire that potential to emerge at its own pace. Weitzman (1992) urges teacher waiting behavior:

When you wait, you give the child time to initiate or to get involved in an activity. You are, in effect, giving her this message: "You're in control—I know you can communicate, so you decide what you want to do or say. I'll give you all the time you need."

and

Studies of adult-child interactions have shown that adults give children approximately one second in which to respond to a question. After one second, the adult repeats and rephrases the question or provides the answer. One second! Most children need much longer than one second to process the question and figure out their response.

Adult speech containing a relatively high proportion of statements or declaratives has been associated with accelerated language development in young children (Harris, 1990). Adult-child conversations tend to last longer if adults add new relevant information. If adults verbally accept and react to children's statements with "yes," "good," "that's right," "oh, really?" or "I see," additional conversation seems to be promoted.

When a teacher answers a child by showing interest, this rewards the child for speaking. Positive feelings are read internally as an automatic signal to continue to do what we are doing (Ornstein and Sobel, 1987). Vygotsky's (1980) work suggests teachers should guide and collaborate to promote children's independent problem solving in any given situation. Most often teachers show their attention by listening to, looking at, smiling at, patting, or answering a child, or by acting favorably to what a child has said or done.

In figure 6–12, in the previous chapter, the teacher and children were planning and participating in an activity. Children displayed interest and enthusiasm. This figure illustrates the teacher's thinking. She is guiding, providing, and interacting in a way that promotes children's verbalness and use of writing. It's easy to see that children exposed to this type of interaction with an adult are learning far more than language. In the example, language and thought are paired. There are obvious growth opportunities in both. How many similar situations in joint planning and joint problem solving are possible in the average classroom? The opportunities are limitless!

Note also that in figure 6–12 not once did the teacher interact in a test-like manner by asking "What color are apples?" or "What is this called on the recipe chart?" Rather, her verbal comments provoked children's discovery. When she prompted and it was obvious children were unfamiliar with a word, the teacher offered it (for example, cinnamon).

Teachers trying to determine their skills as interactors can ask themselves the following:

- How often do I respond to child-initiated comments? 100% of the time? 50% of the time?
- Do I keep to the child's topic and include it in my response?
- Do I purposefully prompt the children to see or discover an aspect that they might not have perceived or discovered?
- Are most of my verbalizations directives that sound like commands?

- Am I aware of favorite subjects and interests of individual children and topics that will stimulate talk?
- Are my comments appropriate in light of the children's developmental levels?
- Do children seek me out to share their accomplishments and concerns, or do they turn primarily to other available adults?
- Do I often react to child comments using teacher echolalia?

> *Child:*   "I went to the zoo."
> *Teacher:* "Oh, you went to the zoo."

Or would my answer more likely be "What animals did you see?"

The following additional questions are suggested by Mattick (1981):

- Are conversations two-way interactions, or are they monologues on my part?
- Do I encourage the children to engage me in conversation?
- Are my questions open- or close-ended?
- Are my questions thought-inducing or are they merely seeking correct answers?
- Who does most of the talking, the child or me?
- What is the level of specificity in my responses?
- Am I moralizing, telling children how they should be thinking and feeling instead of accepting the way they think or feel?
- Is my language production geared to the children's understanding and at the same time expanding the child's existing language, giving new words for more complex operations?
- Do I finish my sentences, or do I leave the children hanging in midair?
- Do I avoid using pat phrases over and over again?
- Do I involve children in activities that promote, or even necessitate, verbal interactions?
- Is there maximum opportunity for children to converse with each other?
- Do I take action to involve children in verbal communications when there is the opportunity?
- Is verbal interaction related to the real world and, more important, to the child's world?

- Does the interaction take place in the context of mutual trust and respect, a mutual trust and respect based on my genuine friendliness, unconditional acceptance, warmth, empathy, and interest?

Tough (1973) offers teachers interactional techniques to extend conversations:

- Invite children to speak by developing a relationship that encourages talking through being a good listener—smiling, nodding, and saying "mm," "yes," and "really" tell the child to go ahead and you're listening.
- Reflecting back on what the child has said, showing your understanding.
- Using questions that are indirect and give the child the choice of answering or not.
- Letting the child know it's ok not to answer your question such as: "Do you want to tell me about . . . ?", or "If you'd like, I'd like to know how. . . ."
- When the child is eager to talk, use more direct open-ended questions—"What do you see?"

Teachers often act as interpreters, especially with younger preschoolers. The child who says "Gimme dat" is answered with "You want the red paint." Don't worry about faulty teacher interpretations! Most children will let teachers know when they have interpreted incorrectly by trying again. Then the teacher has the opportunity to say, "You wanted the blue paint, Taylor."

Harris (1990) has identified a number of language-developing, teacher speech interactions that may be used in conversations with young children:

1. Use language slightly more complex than the child's.
   > *Child*:   "Those are cookies."
   > *Teacher*: "Yes, they're called gumdrop mountains because they come to a point on the top."
2. Speak with young or limited-language children by referring to an action, object, person, and/or event that is currently happening.
   > *Teacher*: "You're climbing up the stairs."

3. Base your reactive conversation on the meaning the child intended. There are three ways to do this: (a) *repetition* ("Pet the dog" to child's "Pet dog"); (b) *expansion* (the child says, "play bath," and the teacher expands with "You want to play with your toys in the bath tub;" and (c) *recasting* (The child says, "You can't get in" and the teacher responds, "No, I can't get in, can I?")

4. Use "I see," "Yes," or a similar expression to indicate you are listening.

She also suggests that conversations be adult-like, allowing children to make comments, tell about happenings and how they feel, and exchange information. This is possible throughout the preschool day (figure 7–6).

A teacher may find it harder to interact verbally with quiet children than with those children who frequently start conversations with the teacher (Monaghan, 1971). The teacher should be aware of this tendency and make a daily effort to converse with all attending children.

FIGURE 7–6 Sitting on a child-sized chair puts adults at a level to engage in intimate conversation.

Teachers shift to more mature or less mature speech as they converse with children of differing ages and abilities. They try to speak to each according to his or her understanding. They use shorter, less complex utterances and use more gestures and nonverbal signals with infants, toddlers, and speakers of foreign languages. Generally, the ability to understand longer and more complex sentences increases with the child's age.

At times it will be prudent for the teacher to refrain from speaking. Young children who are talking to themselves, directing their actions with self-talk, will appear to be in their own little world. Intrusion by an adult is not expected by the child, nor is it necessary. Children usually think out loud while they are deeply absorbed in self-pursued activities. Adult talk at these times can be interruptive.

The teacher who interacts in daily experiences can help to improve the child's ability to see relationships. Although there is current disagreement as to the teacher's ability to promote cognitive growth (the act or process of knowing), attention can be focused and help provided by answering and asking questions. Often, a teacher can help children see clear links between material already learned and new material. Words teachers provide are paired with the child's mental images that have come through the senses. Language aids memory because words attached to mental images help the child to retrieve stored information.

Intellectually valuable experiences involve the teacher and parent as active participants in tasks with the child. Adults can label, describe, compare, classify, and question, supporting children's intellectual development (Stevens, 1981). An example of this type of interaction follows:

> Sonja (24 months old) says something about a circus. Mother: "No, you didn't go to the circus—you went to the parade." Sonja: "I went to the parade." Mother: "What did you see?" Sonja: "Big girls." Mother smiles. "Big girls and what else?" Sonja: "Trumpets." Mother: "Yes, and fire engines. Do you remember the fire engines?"

Sonja: "You hold my ears a little bit." Mother smiles. "Yes, I did, just like this," and puts her hands on Sonja's ears. Sonja laughs. (Carew, 1980)

As the teacher interacts by supplying words to fit situations, it should be remembered that often a new word needs to be repeated in a subtle way (figure 7–7). It has been said that at least three repetitions of a new word are needed for adults to master the word; young children need more. Teachers often hear the child repeating a new word, trying to become familiar with it. Teacher speech should be purposefully repetitive when a new word is encountered.

There are times when a teacher chooses to supply information in answer to direct child questions. There is no easy way for the child to discover answers to questions like "What's the name of today?" or "Why is that man using that funny stick with a cup on the end?" A precise, age-level answer is necessary, such as "Today is Monday, May 9" and (while demonstrating) "It's a stick, called a plunger. It pushes air and water down the drain and helps open the pipes so that the water in the sink will run out." As a provider of information, the teacher acts as a reference and resource person, providing the information a child desires. If the teacher does not wish to answer a question directly, he or she may encourage the child to ask the same question of someone else or help the child find out where the answer is available.

> Child: "What's lunch?"
>
> Adult: "Come on, we'll go ask the cook."
>
> or
>
> "I'll have to go and read our posted menu.
>
> Come on, let's go see what it says."

A teacher can help the child focus on something of interest. The child's desire to know can be encouraged. Repetition of words and many first-hand activities on the same theme will help the child

FIGURE 7–7   As director of classroom activities teachers often need to give verbal instructions.

to form an idea or concept. The child may even touch and try something new with the teacher's encouragement.

The teacher's reaction supplies children with feedback to their actions. The teacher is responsible for reinforcing the use of a new word and gently ensuring that the children have good attitudes about themselves as speakers.

Every day, the teacher can take advantage of unplanned things that happen to promote language and speech. Landreth (1972) provides an illustration:

> While children were sitting in a story group, John noticed that a mobile, hung from the ceiling above, was spinning. "Look," said John pointing, "it's moving!" "How come?" said another child. "Someone must have touched it," said Mary. "Stand up, Mary, and see if you can touch it," added the teacher, standing up and reaching, herself, "I can't reach it either." "Maybe it spins itself," contributed Bill. "No, it can't spin itself," said another child. "Let's see," said the teacher. She got a piece of yarn with a bead tied to the end and held it out in front

of the children. It was still. Then she held it near the mobile, which was in a draft of a window. The string swayed gently. "The window, the window is open," suggested the children. "Yes, the wind is coming through the window," said John. "And making it move," said all the children, pleased with their discovery. The teacher held the string so the children could blow at it. "Look, I'm the wind" said one of them. That afternoon, outside, the children were given crepe paper streamers to explore wind direction. They were also read *Gilberto and the Wind*, which tells what happens when wind blows the sail of a boat, the arm of a windmill, the smoke from a chimney, and a child's hat and hair.

Being able to make the most of an unexpected event is a valuable skill. Moving into a situation with skill and helping the child discover something and tell about it is part of promoting word growth.

Scaffolding

Curry and Johnson (1990) describe scaffolding as support with challenge. This refers to a teaching technique that includes responsive conversation, open-ended questions, and facilitation of the child's initiatives. The concept of scaffolding identified with the work of Vygotsky (1987) suggests adults can estimate the amount of necessary verbal support and provide challenging questions for child growth in any given situation. The idea is to promote the child's understanding and solutions. As the child ages, the autonomous pursuit of knowledge will need less adult support. The author is reminded of the four-year-old who described the workings of a steam locomotive. His knowledge and train terminology was way above that of other children his age and even this teacher. Someone in this child's life had supplied the type of "scaffolding" (support with challenge) that allowed the child to follow an interest in trains.

Vygotsky (1978) suggests inner speech develops as children learn to use language, first to think

and then to reason inside their own mind. Language scaffolding by teachers helps children use inner speech and may clarify their thinking. Interactive teachers provide verbal assistance and nudge discovery based on the individual child's degree of sophistication.

It's felt children need experiences and educational opportunities with adults who carefully evaluate, think, and talk daily occurrences through.

What specific teacher verbalizations and behaviors are suggested in scaffolding? Ones that:

- offer responsive and authentic conversation;
- offer a facilitation of the child's initiatives;
- offer open-ended questions;
- prompt;
- promote language by using modeling of slightly more mature language forms, and some language structures that are new to children;
- offer invitations for children to express thoughts and feelings in words;
- promote longer, more precise child comments;
- invite divergent responses;
- offer specific word cues in statements and questions that help children grasp further information, i.e., what, who, why, because, so, and, next, but, except, if; when, before; after, etc.;
- provoke lively discussions and quests for knowing more about subjects that interest them; and
- increase collaborative communication with adults and other children.

Scaffolding is not as easy as it first may appear to teachers. What is opportunity and challenge for one child may not be for the next. In scaffolding, teacher decision making is constant and complex.

An educator using scaffolding believes understanding, discovery, and problem solving can be guided. Rather than always being dependent on adults for help, the child actually is moved towards becoming an independent thinker. Adults who accompany children at home or at school can use a scaffolding approach to talk through and plan ahead activities as simple as setting the table, cleaning the sink, getting an art area ready for finger painting, or taking care of the needs of the school pet.

Langer and Applebee (1986) have identified additional instructional scaffolding. Child ownership of ideas is encouraged. What is right or wrong becomes less important than the child's expression of his or her own conclusions. The child is encouraged to verbalize the "whys" of his or her thinking. For example, "Royal thinks the rabbit eats paper because he saw Floppy tearing paper into small pieces inside the cage."

Valuable teacher collaboration with children sustains the momentum of the search, actions, or exploration. Small group projects are often a natural part of children's block area play, and can also be promoted in other aspects of daily play and program. For example, a lemonade stand can be managed by a small group, or a present or card can be designed for a sick classmate at home then completed and mailed by a small group of children.

Teacher Interactive Styles

A central task for the educator is to find a balance between helping a child consolidate new understanding and offering challenges that will promote growth (Shapiro and Mitchell), 1992).

Barnes (1976) suggests there are two teaching styles—transmission and interpretation. Transmission teaching is the traditional, believing child knowledge is acquired through teacher talking, sharing of books, and explaining classroom events and experiences. Interpretation teaching is based on the understanding that children reinterpret information for themselves; and consequently, the teacher's role involves dialogues that support the children's efforts to verbalize their ideas and actual experiences.

One can easily see how easy it is to become a transmission teacher. It's overwhelmingly modeled in a teacher's own schooling. An interpretation teacher really listens and doesn't monopolize conversations by a display of what the teacher knows. Achieving balance between these two styles is the key. Educators both transmit and interpret.

In promoting developing language arts and literacy in early childhood, an interpretation style would help children not only talk about what they know but also help them put ideas and impressions in print through dictation. Healy and Barr (1992) suggest the teacher's role is to provide the occasions, resources, and enabling climate for the pursuit of individual meaning.

Teachers can be fun-filled and playful interactors at times, exhibiting their love and enthusiasm for life and child company. This side of teachers comes naturally to some adults and less easily to others. Perhaps some of us remember adults from our own childhood years who were able to engage themselves in adult-child interactions that could be described as joyful playing. Early childhood practitioners bent on language development are careful not to dominate conversations at these times but rather to be responsive companions.

Interaction in Symbolic Play Situations

Pretend play (symbolic play) teacher interactions take both understanding and finesse. The teacher may wish to preserve the child's chosen play direction and not encroach upon self-directed imaginative activity, but at the same time promote the child activity by giving teacher attention, and therefore status, to the child's pursuit. There will definitely be many times when teacher interaction may be deemed intrusive because of the child's deep involvement. At those times teachers simply monitor at a distance. In other instances, particularly with younger preschoolers, teacher interaction may enrich the child's experience.

Stressing Language Connections

The teacher interested in stressing connections between classroom language arts events and activities, as is done in an integrated approach or a whole-language approach, may often purposefully make the following comments.

"I am writing down your ideas."

"This printing I am reading says 'please knock.'"

"Do you want me to read what is printed on the wall?"

"I can print that word."

"What does the sign for your parking garage need to say?"

"You seemed to be listening to the story I was reading."

"Yes, *s* is the first alphabet letter in your name."

"You want me to print your name on your work, right?"

"I can read what this small printing on the box says."

Accepting Approximations

Just as parents accept and celebrate inaccurate and incorrect language and writing attempts because they are seen as signs of growth, teachers also give attention to beginning attempts and provide encouragement. Lively, interesting environments and experiences where children offer their ideas and comments, feeling safe from criticism and insensitive grammatic correction, help children risk and push ahead.

Handling Interruptions

Children often interrupt adults during planned activities. When an idea hits, they want to share it. Their interruptions can indicate genuine involvement and interest, or they can reflect a variety of unrelated thoughts and feelings. Teachers usually acknowledge the interruption, accept it, and may calmly remind the interruptor that when one wants to speak during group activities, one should raise one's hand first. Other teachers feel preschoolers' enthusiasm to speak is natural and characteristic. These teachers feel that teaching children to raise their hands during group discussions is best reserved for a later age. Interruptions give the

teacher an opportunity to make a key decision that affects the flow of the activity. Will the interruption break the flow of what's going on, will it add to the discussion, or is it best discussed at a later time? If the teacher decides to defer a comment, one of the methods suggested below may be employed. Or, the teacher may accept being sidetracked and briefly digress from the main subject, or develop the interruption into a full blown teacher-group discussion, as was the case in the Landreth (1972) example above. Additional examples follow:

Situation: The teacher is telling a flannel board story about a squirrel preparing for winter by hiding nuts in a tree.

Child: "My cat climbs trees."

Teacher: "Michael I've seen cats climb trees."
(short acknowledgment)

or

Teacher: "Michael's cat climbs trees, and the squirrel is climbing the tree to hide the nuts he is storing away for winter."
(acknowledges, but refers listener back to the story line.)

or

Teacher: "Michael, you can tell me about your cat that climbs trees as soon as we finish our story."
(Defers discussion until later.)

Incorporating the children's ideas and suggestions into group conversations, and giving children credit for their ideas, makes them aware of the importance of their expressed ideas.

"Kimberly's idea was to . . ."
"Angelo thinks we should . . ."
"Christal suggests that we . . ."
"Here's the way Trevor would . . ."

Using Sequential Approaches to Instruction

Teachers need a clear understanding of how children learn words and concepts. The chart in figure 7–8 includes guidelines for the teacher's words and actions to accompany the child's progress toward new learning.

One approach to teacher interaction during structured, planned, or incidental activities, described by Maria Montessori (1967), is called three-stage interaction. It shows movement from the child's sensory exploration to showing understanding, and then to verbalizing the understanding. An example follows:

Step 1: Associating sense perception with words

A cut lemon is introduced and the child is encouraged to taste it. As the child tastes, the adult says, "The lemon tastes sour," pairing the word *sour* with the sensory experience. Repetition of the verbal pairing strengthens the impression.

Step 2: Probing understanding

A number of yellow cut fruit are presented. "Find the one that tastes sour," teacher suggests. The child shows by his or her actions his or her understanding or lack of it.

Step 3: Expressing understanding

A child is presented with a cut lemon and grapefruit and asked, "How do they taste?" If the child is able to describe the fruit as sour, he or she has incorporated the word into his or her vocabulary and has some understanding of the concept.

When using the three-step approach, Montessori (1967) suggests that if a child is uninterested, the adult should stop at that point. If a mistake is

CHILD ACTIVITY	TEACHER ACTIONS
• Focuses on an object or activity.	• Name the object, or offer a statement describing the actions or situation. (Supplies words)
• Manipulates and explores the object or situation using touch, taste, smell, sight, sound organs.	• Try to help the child connect this object or action to child's past experience through simple conversation. (Builds bridge between old and new)
• Fits this into what he or she already knows. Develops some understanding.	• Help the child see details through simple statements or questions. (Focus on identifying characteristics)
	• Ask "Show me . . . " or "Give me . . . " questions that ask for a nonverbal response. (Prompting)
	• Put child's action into words. (Example: "John touched the red ball.") (Modeling)
	• Ask the child for a verbal response. "What is this called?" "What happened when . . . ?" (Prompting)
• Uses a new word or sentence that names, describes, classifies, or generalizes a feature or whole part of the object or action.	• Give a response in words indicating the truth factor of the response. "Yes, that's a red ball." or "It has four legs like a horse, but it's called a cow." (Corrective or reinforcing response)
	• Extend one-word answers to full simple sentence if needed. (Modeling)
	• Suggest an exploration of another feature of the object or situation. (Extend interest)
	• Ask a memory or review question. "Tell me about . . . " (Reinforcing and assessing)

FIGURE 7–8 Language learning and teacher interaction

made, the adult remains silent. The mistake only indicates the child is not ready to learn—not that he or she is unable to learn.

This verbal approach may seem mechanical and ritualistic to some, yet it points out clearly the sequence in a child's progress from not knowing to knowing.

The following example of a variation of the Montessori three-step approach includes additional steps. In this teaching sequence, the child asks the teacher how to open the tailgate of a dump truck in the sandbox.

Teacher Intent	Teacher Statements
1. Focus attention.	"Look at this little handle."
2. Create motivation, defined as creating a desire to want to do or want to know. (Note that in this situation this isn't necessary because the child is interested.)	"You want the tailgate to open." Pointing.
3. Provide information.	"This handle turns and opens the tailgate." Demonstrating.
4. Promote child attempt or practice.	"Try to turn the handle."
5. Give corrective information or feedback or positive reinforcement.	"The handle needs to turn. Try to push down as you turn it." (Showing.)
	or
	"You did it; the tailgate is open."

Steps 1 through 5 are used in the following situation in which the teacher wants the child to know what is expected in the use of bathroom paper towels.

1. "Here's the towel dispenser. Do you see it?"
2. "You can do this by yourself. You may want to dry your hands after you wash them."

3. Demonstration. "First take one paper towel. Dry your hands. Then the towel goes into this waste basket."

4. "You try it."

5. "That's it. Pull out one towel. Dry your hands. Put the towel in the basket."

"Now you know where the dirty paper towels go. No one will have to pick up your used towel from the floor. You can do it without help now like some of your classmates."

Statements of this kind help the child learn both the task and vocabulary. The ability to provide information that the child needs, without talking too much, is one of the skills required of a really excellent teacher. Some theorists believe that the successful completion of a task is a reward in itself. Others feel an encouraging verbal pat on the back is in order.

The same dump truck scene above could be handled using a discovery approach, instead of a teacher-directed sequence, with the following types of questions. "Did you see anyone else playing with this dump truck? Is there a button to push or a handle to turn that opens the tailgate? What happens if you try to open the tailgate with your hand?"

Prompting in a child-adult conversation intends to encourage the child to express ideas perhaps more precisely and/or specifically. It is used slightly different with younger preschoolers, as shown in the following examples:

Young preschooler. *Child:* "Cookie."
Adult: "You want a cookie?"
Child: "Dis cookie."
Adult: "You want this brown cookie?"

Older preschooler. *Child:* "I want that cookie."
Adult: "You want one of these cookies. Which kind, chocolate or sugar?"

Child: "The chocolate one."

Adult: "Help yourself. You can sit here or you can choose to sit in the chair next to Myra."

Can teachers really make a difference in the level and quality of children's language development?

Very significant correlations were found between both the frequency of informative staff talk, the frequency with which the staff answered the children, and the language comprehension scores of the children. (Tizard, 1972)

Interaction does require teachers to "wonder out loud." They express their own curiosity while at the same time noticing each child's quest to find out what makes others tick and what the world is all about.

How can teachers interact skillfully?

- Expand topics in which the child shows interest.
- Add depth to information on topics of interest.
- Answer and clarify child questions.
- Help the child sort out features of events, problems, and experiences, reducing confusion.
- Urge the child to put what's newly learned or discovered into words.
- Cue children into routinely attending to times when the adult and child are learning and discovering together through discussion of daily events.

Dealing With Children's Past Experiences

As an interactor, a teacher encounters a wide range of children's perceptions as to how the children should communicate with adults. A child's family or past child-care arrangements may have taught the child to behave in a certain way. With this in mind, the teacher can almost envision what it means to be a conversationalist in a particular family or societal group. Some families expect children to interrupt; others expect respectful manners. Wild, excited gesturing and weaving body movements are characteristic of some children, while motionless, barely audible whispering is typical of others. Teachers working with newly arrived children from other cultures may see sharp contrasts in communication styles. Some children verbally seek help, while others find this extremely difficult. Some speak their feelings openly; others rarely express their feelings.

To promote child learning, teachers need to consider both styles and how they interface:

Because learning means connecting new ideas to what is already known, pupils must have opportunities to verbalize their unique understandings in order to create the context that encourages further learning. (Healy and Barr, 1992)

Past child-care experiences may have left their mark. A four-year-old child named Perry seemed to give one teacher considerable understanding about how speech can be dramatically affected by past undesirable child-care arrangements (Busy Bee, 1989). The following is that teacher's observation and conclusions.

Perry sat quietly near the preschool's front door, ignoring all play opportunities, and holding his blanket until his mom's return on his first day at school. He only spoke or looked up when teachers tried repeatedly to engage him in conversation. He sat on adults' laps silently when they tried to comfort him, and ate food quickly and then returned to his waiting place near the door. The real Perry emerged a few weeks later as a talkative, socially vigorous child. Our verbal and behavioral interactions concentrated on rebuilding trust with adults and other children; only later was language developing interaction possible.

It can be difficult for a child to engage an adult in conversation as was the case with Perry. As Garvey (1977) notes, "Seeking the availability of a teacher and assuring one's right to her attention and reply often calls for persistence and ingenuity." Perry may have long before given up trying.

Children's Inquisitive Honesty

Young children rarely limit their questions or modify their responses to the teacher for the purpose of hiding their ignorance as older children sometimes do. During conversations, young children intent on answers will probe enthusiastically for what they want to know. Teachers actively promote guesses and appreciate error-making in an atmosphere of trust. They interact in conversations by focusing child attention, posing questions, pointing out problems, suggesting alternatives, and providing information at the teachable moment (Smith-Burke, 1985).

Interacting With Vygotsky's Theory in Mind

A teacher examining Vygotsky's ideas of children's language acquisition might interact in a particular fashion in a preschooler classroom. Believing social interaction builds language learning, the teacher would attempt to stretch above what the child seems to know and say and build on child strengths. Vygotsky (1980) suggests:

> What the child can do in cooperation today he can do alone tomorrow. Therefore the only good kind of instruction is that which marches ahead of development and leads it.

In Vygotsky's social interaction model the child engages in meaningful interaction with others, and through this interaction inner language unfolds (Bartoli, 1995).

The Teacher as a Balancer

In all roles, the teacher needs to maintain a balance. This means:

- Giving, but withholding when self-discovery is practical and possible.
- Interacting, but not interfering or dominating the child's train of thought or actions.
- Giving support, but not hovering.
- Talking, but not overtalking.
- Listening, but remaining responsive.
- Providing many opportunities for the child to speak.
- Being patient and understanding. As Fields and Lee (1987) point out, "When adults already know an answer, we find it hard to be patient as children go through the process of figuring the answer out for themselves."

To maintain such a balance, the teacher is a model, a provider, and an interactor, matching his or her behavior and speech to the ability of each child. As a model, the teacher's example offers the child a step above—but not too far above—what the child is already able to do. In doing this, the teacher watches and listens while working with individual children, learning as much from the child's misunderstandings or speech mistakes as from correct or appropriate responses and behavior. This does not mean that the motive is always to teach, for the teacher also enjoys just talking with the children. It means the teacher is ready to make the most of every situation, as teacher and child enjoy learning together.

There's an old story about two preschool boys who discover a worm in the play yard.

First child: "Boy it tickles! Look at him!" (Holding worm in hand.)

Second child: "Let's show it to teacher."

First child: "No way—she'll want us to draw a picture of it and make us print 'worm'!"

A teacher's attitude toward child growth in language should be one of optimism; provide the best learning environment and realize the child will grow and learn new language skills when he or she is ready. Early childhood centers plan for as much growth as possible in language abilities with teachers who model, provide, and interact during activities (figure 7–9).

Minuchin (1987) identifies what is to be considered in trying to offer a balanced developmentally based curriculum.

- Material to be explored.
- Time and space so a child has choice, free time, and a variety of social experiences.

FIGURE 7–9 "Look at me, teacher!"

- Teacher guidance in (1) acquiring knowledge and relating it to the environment, (2) making connections between present experiences and remembered ones, and (3) comparing similarities and differences.
- Teacher questions that raise questions and lead to investigation and answers.

Sheldon (1990) urges teachers to thoughtfully use comments and conversation free of sexist, male-oriented attitudes. If a teacher is talking about a stuffed teddy bear or the school's pet guinea pig (whose sex is yet to be discovered), "it," rather than "he" or "she," is recommended.

Shapiro and Biber (1972) offer an additional suggestion:

> The provision of many ways to re-express what is felt and what is learned: through blocks, paints, dramatic play, and the creation of stories that can be written down and read back.

Summary

Teachers function as models, providers of opportunities for language growth, collaborators, and interactors. Children copy behaviors and attitudes of both adults and peers. Teacher skills include extending and expanding child conversations. Conversations are a key factor in the child's growing language competence. Extending means adding new information, and expanding means completing a child's statement so that it is grammatically complete.

Words are symbols for objects, ideas, actions, and situations. The teacher can increase the learning of new words and ideas by helping children to recognize links between past and present.

Teachers observe and listen closely so teacher comments are pertinent and timely. An atmosphere of adult-child trust and acceptance of child ideas whether valid or incorrect is recommended.

The three teacher roles discussed in this chapter are model, provider, and interactor. A delicate balance exists in teaching functions. Decisions are made that affect children's learning opportunities.

STUDENT ACTIVITIES

1. Observe a teacher interacting with a preschool child. Note the type of teacher speech and behavior that makes the child feel that what he or she says is important.

2. Pretend you are having a conversation about a teacher's car that the children observed being towed away for repair. You are attempting to extend the topic of conversation, wringing as much out of the experience as possible while monitoring child interest and knowledge. Create possible teacher conversational comments in b to g after reading the example in a.
   a. Recap what you noticed and promote children's remembrance.
      Example. "I saw a tow truck driver climb out of the tow truck cab."
   b. *Explain* some aspect of the situation by giving reasons.
   c. Describe a cause-and-effect feature of the situation.
   d. Compare this situation with another.
   e. Talk about what might happen to the teacher's car.
   f. Comment about what the teacher could do in this situation besides calling a tow truck.
   g. Ask how the children would feel if it were their parent's car.
   h. List six other aspects of the situation that could be discussed.

   Compare your answers with a group of classmates. Now discuss further teacher-planned activities that could increase and expand children's comments, questions, or understanding. Share with the entire group.

3. Listen intently to three adults. (Take notes.) How would you evaluate them as speech models (good, average, poor)? State the reasons for your decisions.

4. Describe what is meant by the following terms:
   standard English   image   example
   symbol   motivation   cognitive
   positive reinforcement   interactor

5. Record a conversation with another classmate. Have the recording analyzed for standard English speech usage.

6. Tape record or videotape your interaction with a group of young children for a period of 15 minutes. Analyze your listening, questioning, sentence structure, extending ability, and pronunciation.

7. Interview two preschool teachers. Ask that they describe their roles as models, providers, interactors, and collaborators with young children. Ask how they maintain a balance in these teaching behaviors. Share with the class.

8. In groups of four or five, develop a listing (on a wall chart or chalkboard) of language-stimulating classroom visitors. Prepare a one-page visitor information sheet to help the visitor understand how to structure the visit to offer a literacy-rich classroom experience. Choose two members of the group to role play a situation in which the head teacher or director and a guest visitor discuss the visitor information sheet.

9. Consider the following slogans. Explain and elaborate their meanings.
   Intent not correctness.
   Your topic not mine.
   The wrong answer is right.
   Logic not mechanics.
   Give them eyes and ears.
   Responsive opportunist here!
   Shh! Here comes the teacher.

10. Read the following quote. Discuss its relationship to child language growth.

    The small Zulu also didn't have just one daddy. He had the dadoos, his father's brothers and other male adults who talked to him about hunting, showed him how to make a little bow and arrow and all of this kind of stuff. They spent time with him and they "joyed in his presence," as someone once defined love. So on into adult life there was for both the boys and the girls this abundance of love and affection and attention and tenderness. (Lair, 1985)

11. How could the following teachers provide for child awareness and involvement in their special interests: An opera buff, a stamp collector, a gourmet cook, a scuba diver, a cashier, a gardener, a clock collector?

12. Fill out the checklist in figure 7–10, and compare your ratings with those of your classmates.

	AGREE	CAN'T DECIDE	DISAGREE
1. Every center happening should encourage speech.			
2. It takes considerable time and effort to have personal conversations with each child daily.			
3. Each child is entitled to a personal greeting and goodbye.			
4. "How are you?" is a good opening remark.			
5. A child who bursts out with something to say that has nothing to do with what's presently happening must have something important on his or her mind.			
6. Pausing silently for a few moments after speaking to a shy child is a good idea.			
7. Most new vocabulary words are learned at group times.			

FIGURE 7–10 Opinion poll *(continues)*

The interrelatedness of

Listening

Speaking

Print

Reading

is emphasized to promote concurrent learning in all language arts areas.

Dramatic play areas are often identified by printscript signs. This sign includes three languages.

Speech is an integral part of play. Children and adults talk to each other in play situations.

Teachers ease in and out of children's dramatic play, often adding words and ideas as children listen.

Without directing or dominating play, teachers verbalize activity choices for children's consideration. Discussion ensues.

Props are suggested or provided to extend play and promote children's speech interactions.

Print is everywhere.

Print is connected to daily classroom life.

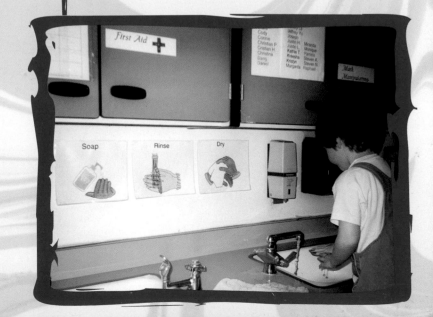

Preschoolers experiment with writing as a natural result of seeing it used in their environments.

Blowing Bubbles

Dip your ⟶ and gently
◐◐ the tiny ○ grow
○ and ◯ ,round and fat,
⌒⌒ - colored, and then -
○ SPLAT !

VALENTINE
VALENT
VALENT

Writing
Area

Nói
Tập Viết

Reading a picture book involves skill.

Techniques include:

- Sparking children's curiosity about illustrations, story line, print, and other book features
- Questioning
- Scaffolding dialogue and responses
- Offering supportive, positive attention to children's interests and comments
- Extending information
- Clarifying
- Restating children's discoveries
- Directing discussion
- Prompting the sharing of personal reactions
- Pausing to elicit guesses
- Developing phonetic awareness through rhyme, alliteration, or word play
- Drawing on children's life experiences
- Enjoying
- and

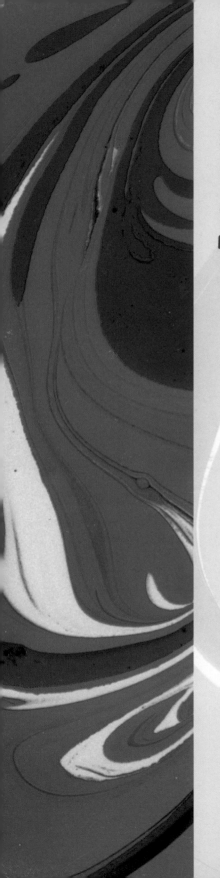

...emphasizing the interrelatedness of listening, speaking, and print to the act of reading

	AGREE	CAN'T DECIDE	DISAGREE
8. Saying "John stepped over the green block" is unnecessary, for the child knows what he has done.			
9. All children have home interests that teachers can discuss with them.			
10. At mealtimes, it's best to remain quiet while children enjoy their food.			
11. If the child talks about a bathroom function, ignore it.			
12. When Phil says, "Girls can't drive trucks," tell him he's wrong.			
13. Teachers really need to talk more than they listen.			
14. Saying "Tell him you don't like it when he grabs your toy" is poor technique.			
15. I don't think it's possible to use a lot of language-building techniques and still speak naturally and comfortably with a child.			
16. Teachers should model a playful attitude at times.			

FIGURE 7–10 *continued*

CHAPTER REVIEW

A. Name the three basic functions of the early childhood teacher.

B. List five examples of each of the functions you listed for question A.

C. Following is an observation of a teacher and children. After reading it, indicate what you feel was appropriate behavior and inappropriate behavior on the part of the teacher in regard to language development.

Situation: Teacher is conducting a sharing time with Joey, Mabel, Maria, and Chris.

Teacher: "It's time for sharing. Please sit down, children."

Joey: "I want to share first!"

Teacher: "You'll have your turn. You must learn to wait."

Mabel:	"I can't see."
Teacher:	"Yes you can. Maria, you're sitting quietly and not talking. You may go first."
Maria:	"This is a book about Mickey. Mickey clips."
Joey:	"What's clips, teacher?"
Teacher:	"You're next, Joey."
Joey:	"Mickey on TV, teacher. Tomorrow I went to the fire station. The firefighter let me wear his badge, like this."
Chris:	"Firefighter's truck red. Goes whee-whee."
Teacher:	"It's Joey's turn, Chris. Would you wait to talk?"
Mabel:	"I want to go, now!"
Teacher:	"Mabel, you must have your turn to share before you can go."
Mabel:	"I see a butterfly on the window."
Teacher:	"Later, Mabel. You can go outside later."

D. What two factors should be considered by the teacher in trying to keep the main functions of teaching in balance?

E. Select the correct answers. All have more than one correct reply.

1. The teacher is a model for
    a. speech.
    b. attitudes.
    c. speech more often than parents may be.
    d. speech only during planned activities.

2. It is more important for young children to
    a. like to speak than to speak correctly.
    b. participate than sit quietly.
    c. speak than to listen.
    d. have the teacher tell them about something than to explore it themselves.
    e. feel comfortable with a teacher than speak clearly.

3. Teachers reinforce learning by
    a. using speech to solve problems.
    b. giving attention to the child's use of a new word.
    c. motivating the child's "wanting to know."
    d. linking the old with the new ideas.

4. When speaking, the teacher should
    a. attempt to use natural language patterns.
    b. speak in full sentences.
    c. make sure each child responds by speaking.
    d. refrain from "overtalking."

5. Preschool children
    a. are also speech models.
    b. rarely teach others new words.
    c. play and use words in play.
    d. have growing vocabularies only when teachers act appropriately.

6. Words are
   a. symbols for real happenings.
   b. related to stored images.
   c. learned through the senses.
   d. not labels for concepts.

F. Write a short ending to the following: "A teacher who is not speaking standard English should . . ."

G. Robert D. Hess and V. C. Shipman have shown that different adults have different styles of communicating with young children. The following is a comparison of two mothers trying to teach the same task to their child.

> *First Mother:* "All right, Susan, this board is the place where we put the little toys; first of all, you're supposed to learn how to place them according to color. Can you do that? The things that are all the same color you put in one section; in the other section you put another group of colors, and in the third section you put the last group of colors. Can you do that? Or would you like to see me do it first?"
>
> *Child:* "I want to do it."
>
> *Second Mother* (introducing the same task): "Now I'll take them all off the board; now you put them all back on the board. What are these?"
>
> *Child:* "A truck."
>
> *Second Mother:* "All right, just put them right here; put the other one right here; all right, put the other one there."
>
> From R. D. Hess & V. C. Shipman, Early experience and the socializations of cognitive modes in children. *Child Development*, 1966.

Write a brief comparison of the two mothers, but pretend they are two teachers.

H. Finish the following statement. "Simple expansion of child comments to make full sentences is not as valuable as extending conversations because . . ."

I. Choose the one best answer.

1. Briana is staring at the wall clock. The teacher might say
   a. "You're wondering what time it is."
   b. "That's our class clock. It tells us what time it is."
   c. "Tell me about the clock."
   d. "You've noticed our clock. Do you have one at your house?"

2. Scaffolding in teacher-child conversations is
   a. encouragement and laddering.
   b. supportive assistance to help the child express and try out language.
   c. supplying data and information.
   d. telling the child his or her right and wrong conclusions.
   e. letting the child work things out independently.

LISTENING

Literate Beginnings

CHAPTER 8

Developing Listening Skills

OBJECTIVES

After studying this chapter, you should be able to:

- list five types of listening.

- discuss teaching techniques that promote good listening habits.

- demonstrate how to plan an activity that promotes a listening skill.

- present a listening activity to a group of preschoolers.

- tell a story that involves purposeful child listening.

The world, with its many sounds, bombards children. Although no one formally teaches an infant to listen, certain sounds become familiar and take on meanings from this mass of confusion. The child has begun to listen.

Listening skill is the first language arts skill learned, and it develops before a child speaks. Many children develop the ability to listen carefully to the speech of others during early childhood; others do not. Since language growth has been described as a receiving process followed by a sending process, a child's listening ability is important to speaking and future reading and writing success (Donoghue, 1985).

Hearing and listening are quite different. Hearing is a process involving nerves and muscles that reach adult efficiency by age four to five. Listening is a learned behavior, a mental process that is concerned with hearing, attending, discriminating, understanding, and remembering. It can be improved with practice. Listening affects social interactions, one's level of functioning, and perhaps one's overall success in life (Weiss and Lillywhite, 1981). Nichols (1984) estimates that we listen to 50% of what we hear and comprehend only 25% of that.

Listening skill can be described as passive and receptive but involves active thinking and interpretation. Lively conversations between adults and young children who feel free to verbalize reactions to life's happenings promote listening and speaking. Children offer more verbal comments in school settings in small, relaxed groups in which comments are accepted and appreciated. Young children sometimes learn that it's best to keep quiet in some classrooms. In other classrooms, every child's opinion counts, and classroom discussions are frequent and animated.

There are usually many opportunities to listen in early childhood centers. Teacher-planned or child-created play is a source of many sounds (figure 8–1). A quality program sharpens a child's listening and offers a variety of experiences. Listening is not left to chance; planned programs develop skills.

FIGURE 8–1   Teacher-planned or child-centered play is a source of many sounds.

Research on Listening

Although limited current research has been done on both listening and whether direct instruction in listening skill is effective, studies conducted in the 1950s and 1960s showed listening instruction led to measurable gains in listening comprehension. Active involvement following listening activities may help more than passive activities (Pinnell & Jaggar, 1992).

Horrworth (1966) suggests listening is not a discrete skill or generalized ability, but a cluster of specific abilities closely related to those needed in the reading task.

Types of Listening

Listening occurs in a variety of ways. A person does not always listen for knowledge but may also listen to a sound because it is pleasing to hear. The first time children discover the sounds made by pots and pans, they are fascinated. Preschoolers often make their own pleasurable or rhythmic sounds with whatever is available.

The human voice can be interesting, threatening, or monotonous to a child, depending on past experience. Silence also has meaning. Sometimes teachers suspect that a child has a hearing problem, only to find that the child was inattentive for other reasons.

Children may listen but not understand. They may miss sound differences or listen without evaluating what they hear. Listening involves a variety of skills and levels. In order to provide growing opportunities, teachers should be aware of various listening levels, as shown in figure 8–2.

Appreciative listening. The child finds pleasure and entertainment in hearing music, poems, and stories. It is best to begin with this type of listening because it is passive, but personal, for each child.

Purposeful listening. The child follows directions and gives back responses.

Discriminative listening. The child becomes aware of changes in pitch and loudness. Sounds become differentiated in the environment. Eventually, the child is able to discriminate the speech sounds.

Creative listening. The child's imagination and emotions are stimulated by his listening experiences. Thoughts are expressed spontaneously and freely through words or actions, or both.

Critical listening. The child understands, evaluates, makes decisions, and formulates opinions. To encourage this critical listening, the teacher may pose such questions as: "What happens when we all talk at once?" "What if everyone wanted to play in the playhouse at the same time?" The child must think through the responses, decide the most logical solution to the problem, and present a point of view.

FIGURE 8–2   Some of the ways a child listens *(From* Learning Time with Language Experiences, *by Louise B. Scott, New York: McGraw-Hill Book Co., 1968.)*

RESPONDING TO STIMULI	ORGANIZING THE STIMULI	UNDERSTANDING THE MEANING
Awareness	Sequencing and	(Classification;
Focus	Synthesizing	Integration;
Figure-Ground	Scanning	Monitoring)
Discrimination		

←————————————— Memory —————————————→

Stage 1—Responding to stimuli: Was there sound? Where was it? Which sound was it? Was there more than one sound? Were the sounds the same?

Stage 2—Organizing the stimuli: What was the sequence of the sounds? What was the length of time between sounds? Have I heard that sound before? Where have I heard it?

Stage 3—Understanding the meaning: What do the sounds and words mean?

FIGURE 8–3   Stages of the listening process

The goal of a good program in early childhood language arts is to guide the young child toward development of these listening levels. The listening process contains three stages the child moves through in efficient listening (figure 8–3).

When a sound occurs, it is remembered by thinking about its features: direction, pitch, intensity, newness, and so on.

Toddler Listening Experiences

Parents and center staff members can engage toddlers in a number of activities to stimulate listening. Body-action play of the old "coo-chee-coo" variety, "this little piggy," and simple rhymes and repetitions are recommended. Connecting noises and sounds with toys and objects and encouraging the child to playfully imitate show the child that joy and sound-making go hand in hand. Rhythmic clapping, tapping, and pan beating in sequence or patterns can be enjoyable. Musical toys and records add variety and listening pleasure. Encouraging children to watch facial expressions as different human sounds are produced and locating environmental sounds together are additional tech-

niques in developing children's listening skills.

Adults exercise care in sound volume, and quality; at all age levels, extra loud, shrill, vibrating, or emergency alert sounds can be frightening.

Purposeful Listening Activities

The intent of purposeful listening practice is to increase the child's ability to follow directions and instructions, perform tasks, or respond appropriately in some fashion. Teachers can use a three-step method to help very young preschoolers gain skill in this type of listening:

1. Tell the children what you are going to tell them.
2. Tell the children.
3. Tell the children what you told them.

Example

1. "I'm going to give you an envelope, and tell you where to take it."
2. "Take the envelope to the cook, Mrs. Corelli, and then come back to our classroom."
3. "You took the envelope to Mrs. Corelli and returned. Thank you."

Purposeful, attentive listening takes concentration. Teachers can perfect a "what I'm going to say next is important" tone and consequently create a desire in children to listen. A statement such as "You might want to know how" or "You can listen closely to find out" or "If you'd like a turn, watch and listen" may also provide the motivation to listen closely.

Planned, purposeful listening activities can include activities that encourage children to listen in order to:

- Do something for themselves.
- Tell another how to do something.
- Operate some type of toy or equipment.
- Carry a message.
- Recall details.
- Put objects in a special order or sequence.
- See how many names or facts they can remember.
- Learn new skills, such as singing new songs or chanting or doing finger plays.

Appreciative Listening Activities

Appreciative listening deals with light listening when enjoyment or pleasure is paramount. A wide variety of recorded and live appreciative listening experiences is possible. Background music can accompany favorite preschool pursuits. Chanting a remembered selection of words gives the children a double treat of hearing voices in unison and feeling part of a group. Some appreciative listening builds moods, touches emotions, and adds another dimension to experience. The world is full of beautiful and not-so-beautiful sounds.

Possible appreciative listening activities include:

- Moving to music.
- Discussing music, rhythms, and sounds.
- Talking about favorite sounds.
- Talking about happy, sad, or funny feelings that sounds produce.
- Tapping, clapping, or moving to music or rhythmic speech.

Cole (1989) lists the benefits of introducing a music curriculum to young children:

> Music provides another means of oral expression for children. . . . building vocabulary, establishing a sense of internal rhythm, developing an awareness of pitch and intonation in voice, and creating an understanding of language concepts such as loud, soft, fast, and slow. Providing practice in singing promotes the development of syntax and memorization skills.

Research suggests a predictable pattern in children's learning of any song. Words are learned first, then rhythms and other elements (McDonald and Simons, 1989). Traditional nursery songs are plentiful, appropriately pitched, and contain repetition of melodic and rhythmic patterns. Music has been called a "language builder" (Bayless and Ramsey, 1978.)

Favorite Traditional Songs

Old MacDonald Had a Farm
Dinah
Teddy Bear
Eensy, Weensy Spider
I'm a Little Teapot
Hot Cross Buns
The Bus
Twinkle, Twinkle, Little Star
Yankee Doodle
Did You Ever See a Lassie?
If You're Happy
Ring Around a Rosy
Oh, Dear, What Can the Matter Be?
Skip to My Lou
Down by the Station
Looby Loo
Bingo
The Bear Went Over the Mountain

Partial List of Language Features

Vocabulary
Predictability
Story line and sequence

Rhyming
Repetition
Cultural literacy significance
Rhythmic beat
Concept development
Appreciative listening
Purposeful listening
Discriminative listening
Creative listening
Coordination of words and physical movement

Critical Listening Activities

Critical listening requires the children's evaluation of what's heard and comprehended. It requires contemplation and reflection, and some preschoolers develop considerable skill in this area and use it frequently. These children seem able to weigh the new against what they already know and feel and are eager to discuss differences. Other children seem rarely to hold any opinion or particular viewpoint and are reticent to share thoughts. Activities that involve critical thinking can be ones in which:

- A problem is discussed and solutions are offered and evaluated.
- A probable outcome or guess is prompted.
- A real or make-believe feature is pinpointed using some criteria.
- Personal preferences or dislikes are discussed.
- Group votes are reviewed, and outcomes are anticipated.
- Errors of some type are discovered or detected.
- Feelings of others are predicted.

Teacher Skills

Good listening habits are especially important in school situations. Teachers need to assess their own listening habits and abilities in their daily work with children. If they expect undivided attention from children, they must also give undivided attention to them (Jalongo, 1996). Most of us have been told in teacher training to bend or lower ourselves to child eye level when we speak to children, but how often do we do this when we listen to them?

Instructions from teachers should be clear and simple, with a sequence of what comes first, next, and last. Usually instructions need not be repeated when given clearly and simply. Often, when the attention of the group is required, a signal is used. Any distinctive, easy-to-hear, pleasant sound or visual signal can alert children that it is time to listen. The silent pause before beginning an activity can be used effectively to focus attention on listening.

Teachers also use a short song, finger play, or body-movement activity to stimulate interest and draw the group together. This helps children focus on what is to follow.

Encouragement and smiles at any time of the day can reward individual listening. Positive, specific statements such as "Michael, you listened to what Janet had to say before you started talking" or "It's quiet, and now we can all hear the beginning of the story" give children feedback on expected listening behavior.

These are sample teacher statements that can promote a group's ability to listen:

At the Beginning

- "When I see everyone's eyes, I'll know you're ready to hear about. . . ."
- "We'll begin when we can all hear the clock ticking."
- "I'm waiting until everyone can hear before I start. We need to be quiet so everyone can hear about . . ."
- "It seems everyone is listening; it's time to begin."
- "We take turns speaking. Bill is first, then. . . ."

During Activity

- "Jack had his hand up. Would you like to tell us about your idea?"
- "It's Maria's turn to tell us. . . ."
- "We can hear best when just one person is talking. Louis, you go first, then Cristalee."

- "Bill, it's hard to wait when you want to talk. Gloria is talking now; you can be next." (Later add, "Bill, thank you for waiting for Gloria to finish. Now we will hear what you wanted to tell us.")
- "Everyone wants to tell us about their own pets. Raise your hand—I'll make a waiting list so we can hear everyone." (Make the list quickly and hold it up.) "Isaac, your name is first."

At Activity's End

- "We listened so quietly. We all heard every word of that story."
- "Everyone listened to what their friends said."
- "We listened and found out a lot about. . . ."

Additional examples of teacher talk that promotes listening:

- "We are going to do two things right now. Listen. Pick up your rug square; that's the first thing to do. Then put your square right here on this pile on the table. You were listening Polly, thank you."
- "Listen and then you'll know who will hold the door open. Today it's Rudy's job. Whose job is it? Right, it is Rudy's job today."
- "When we can hear the clock ticking, I'll know everyone is listening."
- "Eyes open. Lips closed. It's listening time."
- "I can't hear when everyone is talking. Mario tell us what you said. Michelle you need to wait. We will listen to you next."
- "It's Adrian's time to talk now. That means no one else is talking."
- "Let's wait until it is quiet, then we are all ready to listen to the story."
- "When I see everyone's eyes looking in my eyes, I'll know you are ready to listen."
- "That was attentive listening. Everyone was quiet while Joni told us about her painting."
- "Josh has something important to say. Let's listen so we all hear what he is going to tell us."
- "I know it's hard to wait, Cleota, but Rick is talking now. Wait. It will be your turn next."

- "What are we going to do after we pour the milk in the bowl? Yes, Brenda, we said we had to stir with the spoon. Good listening, Brenda."
- "Now let's think of another sound we might hear if we go to the window and listen."
- "My turn to talk. Your turn to listen."

Rewarded behavior is usually repeated and becomes a habit. Teachers should consistently notice correct listening behavior and comment favorably about it to the children.

Auditory Perception

Ears respond to sound waves. These sounds go to the brain and become organized in relation to past experience. The same process is used in early childhood and later when the child learns to read. Language development depends on the auditory process.

Educational activities that give practice and help perfect auditory skills usually deal with the following objectives:

- Sustaining attention span.
- Following directions or commands.
- Imitating sounds.
- Identifying and associating sounds.
- Using auditory memory.
- Discriminating between sounds (intensity, pitch, tempo).

The intensity of a sound is its degree of force, strength, or energy. Pitch is the highness or lowness of sound. Tempo is the rate of speed of a sound, in other words, the rhythm of the sound that engages the attention.

Auditory Activities

A wide range of auditory activities can be planned. The following goals often serve as the basis for planning. Simple skills come before more difficult ones:

- Recognizing own name when spoken.
- Repeating two nonsense words, short sayings,

chants, poems, finger plays, or any series of words.

- Reporting sounds heard at home.
- Imitating sounds of toys, animals, classroom, rain, sirens, bells.
- Telling whether a sound is near or far, loud or soft, fast or slow, high or low, same or different.
- Identifying people's voices.
- Identifying and repeating rhythms heard.
- Retelling a story, poem, or part of either.
- Trying to perform first one- and then two-part directions.
- Recalling sounds in sequence.
- Coordinating listening skills with body movements in a requested way.
- Enjoying music, stories, poems, and many other language arts, both individually and in groups.

Settings for Listening

When preparing listening activities, the teacher can plan for success by having activities take place in room areas with a minimum of distracting sounds or objects. Screens, dividers, and bookcases are helpful. Heating and lighting are checked, and comfortable seating is provided. Decisions concerning the size of a group are important. In general, the younger the children, the smaller the group, and the shorter the length of the activity.

Listening cannot be forced, but experiences can be provided that create a desire to listen (figure 8–4). Some schools offer children the choice of joining a group listening activity or playing quietly nearby. Teachers find that an interesting experience will attract children who are playing nearby. When activities are enjoyable and successful, the child who was hesitant may look forward to new experiences. A teacher can turn on or turn off attention by ending, changing, or modifying activities when necessary. The teacher should watch carefully for feedback; this will help to develop active listening in the child. A skillful teacher will complete the learning activity before the group becomes restless. When an activity is planned for which listening is required, it is important to consider that an active

FIGURE 8–4   A teacher promotes active speech and tries to motivate listening too.

preschooler may have to struggle to remain seated for any length of time.

Talk-Listen Group Times

Kindergarten and some early childhood programs are offering older preschoolers "talking-listening" social skill groups. The goal of this activity is to give children who desire to participate the chance to discuss child- and teacher-selected topics in a social setting. This structured activity promotes active listening. In elementary school, this group experience is usually termed "active listening" time or "community circle" (Curran, 1991).

Children are seated in a circle so they can look at the person speaking and easily hear everyone's comments. In preschools, the circle times are kept short and intimate, with small groups of children.

Teachers structure this type of talking-listening time as follows:

1. Teacher announces a talk-listen circle as a choice of activity.

2. Teacher names the topic or elicits one from the group. It might be *cats* because a picture book has been shared, or *worms* because one has been found, or an open-ended statement like "After school I like to go home and . . ."

3. A chart depicting expected talk-listen circle child behavior is introduced or reviewed. "We'll be looking at the person speaking. We'll listen with our ears." The teacher may choose to introduce only looking at others during children's first circle, and listening another time.

4. Teacher states, "Each of us will have a turn to speak. If you don't want a turn to speak, you can say 'pass.'"

5. Teacher speaks first, modeling a short sentence—"My cat is gray and likes to sleep in a sunny window." Then she proceeds around the circle.

6. A very short group evaluation can take place when all have had a turn: Was it easy to wait for your turn? Did you see others' eyes while you were talking? (Children's answers are given in turn.)

Teachers may continue if discussion is still of interest with statements such as "We've all had a turn. Raise your hand if you've something more to tell. Anyone can choose to leave our talking-listening time."

A number of common behaviors occur at preschool discussion times. An egg timer might have to be used with the child who drones on and on. The same children may pass day after day or the same children may choose to participate in circle discussions. A child may not stick to the announced topic, but all comments are accepted and appreciated by the teacher.

Since listening closely and group discussion may be new to preschoolers and because individual developmental levels vary, children may either quickly or slowly grasp the social and listening skills offered.

Of course, many unplanned discussions take place in most preschool classrooms. This type of structured group time encourages young children's social discussion—a skill useful in future classrooms.

Listening Centers

Special listening areas, sometimes called listening posts, can become a part of early childhood classrooms. Enjoying a quiet time by oneself or listening to recorded materials fascinates many children. Headsets plugged in to a jack or terminal help to block out room noise. Partitions cut distractions. Clever listening places where children can settle into become favorite spots, such as:

- large packing boxes lined with soft fabrics and pillows;
- old, soft armchairs; or
- a bunk or loft.

Phonographs, cassette tape recorders, photographs, picture sets, and books offer added dimensions to listening centers. Recordings of the teacher reading a new or favorite story can be available at all times for children's use. These recordings are sometimes called read-alongs, and are also available from commercial sources. Their quality varies widely, so it is recommended that they be reviewed before they are purchased.

When teachers realize how much future educational experience depends on how well language is processed through children's listening, listening activities and listening centers gain importance. As Healy (1990) points out, many of today's children have passively listened to considerable TV but may be particularly lacking in the practice of auditory analysis and logical sequential reasoning.

Children can record, with adult help, their own descriptions of special block constructions together with accompanying drawings or photos. "Why I like this book" talks can be made about a special book. Children can record comments about their own pieces of art. A field-trip scrapbook may have a child's commentary with it. Recorded puppet scripts and flannel board stories can be enjoyed while the child moves the characters and listens. The child can explore small plastic animals while listening to a prepared cassette tape story. Possibilities for recorded activities are limited only by preparation time and staff interest.

Children's ages are always a factor in the use of audio-visual equipment. Listening centers need teacher introduction, explanation, and supervision.

Recordings

Some companies specialize in recordings for children that improve listening skills. These recordings involve children in listening for a signal, listening to directions, or listening to sounds. Some recordings include body-movement activities along with listening skills.

Not all recordings contain appropriate subject matter for young children. Before purchasing one for children, the teacher should listen to it. The following criteria may be used to judge a recording's worth:

1. Is the subject matter appropriate for young children?
2. Is it clearly presented?
3. Is it interesting to young children?
4. Does it meet the teaching objective?

Many recordings have been made of children's classics. These can also help to improve children's listening skills.

Tape Recorders

Tape recorders can both fascinate and frighten children. They can be valuable tools for listening activities. Under the teacher's supervision, children can explore and enjoy sounds using tape recorders.

Children's Books with Listening Themes

Books with themes concerned with listening are good springboards to discussion about listening skills. Examples follow:

Borten, Helen. (1960). *Do You Hear What I Hear?* New York: Abelard-Schuman. Describes the pleasures to be found in really listening.

Brown, Margaret Wise. (1951). *The Summer Noisy Book.* New York: Harper and Row. Can be easily made into a "guess what" sound game.

Fisher, Aileen. (1988). *The House of a Mouse.* New York: Harper and Row. Mouse poems can be read in a tiny teacher voice. Rhyming text.

Glazer, Tom. (1982). *On Top of Spaghetti.* New York: Doubleday. Teacher sings a silly story.

Guilfoile, Elizabeth. (1957). *Nobody Listens to Andrew.* Chicago: Follett. The no-one-ever-listens-to-me idea is humorously handled.

Johnson, LaVerne. (1967). *Night Noises.* New York: Parents Magazine Press. Listening to noises in bed at night.

Lloyd, David. (1986). *The Sneeze.* New York: Lippincott. The child listens to questions.

Novak, Matt. (1986). *Rolling.* Riverside, NJ: Bradbury Press. The sounds of a storm dominate this story.

Showers, Paul. (1961). *The Listening Walk.* New York: Thomas Y. Crowell. Good book to share before adventuring on a group sound walk.

Spier, Peter. (1971). *Gobble Growl, Grunt.* New York: Doubleday. Lots of variety in animal sounds with brilliant illustrations.

Zolotow, Charlotte. (1980). *If You Listen.* New York: Harper and Row. A touching tale of a child who, missing her father, turns to listening.

Are There Differences in Children's Listening Abilities?

Yes, wide differences. As teachers become familiar with the children enrolled in their classes, they may notice that some children display abilities that allow them to note fine differences in sounds. Other children, who are progressing normally, will not acquire these skills until they are older.

Some researchers feel that boys have a slight edge in one particular area, listening vocabulary (Brimer, 1969). Theories attempting to explain this difference suggest that boys speak later than girls and consequently depend on discriminative listening for a longer period and gain more skill. Other researchers suggest that mothers respond more frequently to male infant vocalizations, giving males greater vocal input. Chances are that preschool teachers will not notice any significant difference between their male and female students.

LISTENING ACTIVITIES

Listening activities are used to increase enjoyment, vocabulary, and skill. In this chapter, the activities focus on the development of auditory skills through listening and response interactions. Activities that further develop these skills through the use of books and stories are found in later chapters.

Chapter 14 gives a great deal of encouragement and helps you conduct circle or group activities. If you will be trying out activities in this chapter, it is best to skip ahead and read chapter 14 first.

One of your first tasks will be gathering an interested group. Every classroom has some signal that alerts children to a change in activities or a new opportunity. This can range from a few notes on a classroom musical instrument to more creative signals. Usually a short invitational, and attention-getting statement will be used to pique children's curiosity such as:

- "Gail has a new game for you in the rug area today."
- "Time to finish what you are doing and join Madelyn in the story-time center with a book about Clifford, the big, red dog."
- "Our clapping song begins in two minutes; today, we are going to be jack-in-the-boxes."

In some centers, children are simply requested to finish up what they are doing and join their friends in a particular room area. The enjoyment of already-started finger plays, chants, songs, or movement captures their attention and they are drawn in. This is a great time to recognize all children by name, as in the following: (To the tune of "She'll Be Coming Round the Mountain.")

"Susie is here with us, yes, yes, yes."
(Clap on yes, yes, yes.)

"Larry's here with us, yes, yes, yes."
(Continue until all children are recognized, and end with the following.)

"We are sitting here together,
We are sitting here together,
We are sitting here together, yes, yes, yes."

Note: The following activities will have to be evaluated for age-level appropriateness and use with a particular group of children. They are provided here as examples of listening activities, but may or may not be appropriate for your teaching situation.

Recognizing Voices Guessing Game

Objective

To practice discriminative listening and auditory memory skills

Materials

Individual snapshots of school personnel. A tape recording of different school staff members' voices reading sequential paragraphs in a story or describing the work they perform.

Introduction and Activity

Line up snapshots in view of the children after each is identified. "Here are some snapshots of people we know. Now we're going to listen and try to guess who's talking. Raise your hand if you think you know." When a child guesses the voice correctly, have him or her turn the snapshot face down or put it into a box on your lap. Proceed to the next voice.

At the conclusion of the activity, show the photos one by one and name each. A great follow-up is guessing children's voices using the same game format.

Build a Burger

Objective

To practice purposeful listening

Materials

Cutouts of foods that are added to hamburger buns—onion slices, lettuce, tomato slices, cheese slices, pickles, meat patties, bacon, mayonnaise, mustard, and catsup. Cut out paper buns or make clay bun halves.

Introduction and Activity

Ask the children what kinds of food they like on their hamburgers. After the group discusses the things they like, say "I'm going to show you pictures of some of the things you've said you liked on your hamburger and some things I like. Here are onion slices; Marion said she liked them." Go on to show and name all the cutouts. Select three children to start the activity and have them sit facing the others. One child holds two bun halves, the next holds a flat box lid with all the hamburger parts, and the third child names all the things the first child selected when his or her hamburger is completed. The second child hands the first child the cutouts he or she names and places between the bun halves. At various times, the teacher asks different children in the large group whether the second child has selected the item that the first child has named, or the children can be encouraged to chant "Hamburger, Hamburger, yum, yum, yum. I want that hamburger here on my tongue." After each hamburger is completed and food items are named, second-round children are selected by first-round children.

Sound Cans

Objective

To match similar sounds by using discriminative listening skills

Materials

Cans with press-on or screw-off lids. Cards large enough to hold two cans. Outline circles of can bottoms with dark pen. Two circles for each card. Large different color index cards work well. It is best to use cans that are impossible for children to open or to securely tape cans shut. Fill pairs of cans with same materials, such as sand, paper clips, rocks, rice, beans, nuts, and bolts.

Introduction and Activity

This is a solitary activity or one that children can choose to play with others. It can be used in a learning center. An introduction like the following is necessary. "Here are some cans and cards. The way you play this game is to shake one can and then shake all the rest to find the one that sounds the same as the first can. Let's listen to this can." Shake it. "Now I'm going to try to find the can that sounds just like this one when I shake it." Pick up another and ask "Does this sound the same to you?" Shake the first and second cans. "No, this sounds different, so I'm going to shake another can." Go on until the mate is found and placed beside the first can on the card.

This activity is a classic one, and many sound sets are found in preschool programs. (Sets are also commercially manufactured.)

"Can You Say It as I Do?"

Objective

To imitate sounds

Materials

None

Introduction and Activity

The teacher says, "Can you change your voice the way I can?"

"My name is (teacher softly whispers his or her name)." With changes of voice, speed, and pitch, the teacher illustrates with a loud, low, or high voice, speaking fast or slow, with mouth nearly closed or wide open, when holding nose, and so on.

The teacher then asks for a volunteer who would like to speak in a new or funny way. "Now, let's see if we can change our voices the way Billy does. Do it any way you want, Billy. We'll try to copy you."

The teacher then gives others a turn. This activity may be followed up with a body-action play with voice changes, like the "Mr. Tall and Mr. Small" activity in Chapter 16.

What's Crunchy?

Objective

To practice discriminative listening and auditory memory skills

Materials

Small celery sticks, carrot sticks, cotton balls, miniature marshmallows, uncooked spaghetti

Introduction and Activity

Put materials in a bag behind your back. Reach in and show a celery stick as you start to sing "Celery is long and green, long and green, long and green" (to the tune of "Mary Had a Little Lamb"). Repeat the first line. "When you eat it, it goes crunch." Pass out a celery stick to each child who wants one, and sing the song again, crunching the celery when you reach the end of the song. Follow up with, "What else is crunchy?" Sing the song substituting celery with the child's suggestion. Then introduce the following lyrics, passing out items from your bag to each child:

- "Carrot sticks are long and orange. When you eat them, they go crunch."
- "Cotton balls are soft and white. When you touch them, they feel soft."
- "Spaghetti is long and thin. When you break it, it goes snap."
- "Marshmallows are small and white. When you squeeze them, they pop back."

Variation

Try children's names next, if group is still with you: "Jayne is a girl who's four." Repeat. "When you

ask her she says ..." (pause, waiting for child to finish sentence; if the child doesn't finish, add "Hello" and try other children).

Parakeet Talk

Objective

To imitate sounds

Materials

Popsicle sticks and colored construction paper. Cut out parakeets from colored construction paper and paste them on Popsicle sticks. All forms can be traced and cut from one pattern.

Introduction and Activity

Discuss birds that imitate what people say. Distribute parakeet forms. Begin with something like, "We can pretend to be parakeets, too."

Teacher: Hi, parakeets!
Children: Hi, parakeets!

Teacher: Pretty bird.
Children: Pretty bird.

Teacher: Now let's hear from Julie, the yellow parakeet. Can the blue parakeet (Mike) say whatever the green parakeet (Sue) says? Let's see."

This activity is a good lead-in to a record with children pretending to be flying. Suggest that the children flap their wings through a door to an outdoor area, or take a walk to listen for bird sounds.

"Listen, Oops a Mistake!"

Objective

To associate and discriminate among word sounds and objects

Materials

Four or five common school objects (such as a pencil, crayon, block, toy, cup, and doll) and a low table

Introduction and Activity

Talk about calling things by the wrong name, being sure to discuss how everyone makes mistakes at times. Begin with something like, "Have you ever called your friend by the wrong name?"

> *Teacher:* When you call your friend by the wrong name, you've made a mistake. Look at the things on the table. I am going to name each of them. (Teacher names them correctly.) All right, now see if you can hear my mistakes. This time I'm going to point to them, too. If you hear a mistake, raise your hand and say, "Oops, a mistake!" Let's say that together once: "Oops, a mistake!" Are you ready? Listen: crayon, ball, doll, cup.

Change objects, and give the children a chance to make mistakes while others listen (figure 8–5). This activity can later be followed with the story *Moptop* (by Don Freeman, Children's Press), about a long-haired red-headed boy who is mistaken for a mop.

FIGURE 8–5   Give children a chance to make mistakes in front of their peers.

Errand Game

Objective

To follow verbal commands

Materials

None

Introduction and Activity

Start a discussion about doing things for parents. Include getting objects from other rooms, from neighbors, and so on. Tell the children you are going to play a game in which each person looks for something another has asked for.

> *Teacher:* "Get a book for me, please."
> "Can you find a leaf?"

Items to ask for include a rock, a blade of grass, a piece of paper, a block, a doll, a crayon, a toy car, a sweater, a hat, clothes, a hanger, a blanket, and so forth. Send children off one at a time. As they return, talk to each about where he or she found the item. While the group waits for all members to return, the group can name all the returned items. Put them in a row, ask children to cover their eyes while one is hidden, and then ask the children to guess which item was removed, or chant "We're waiting, we're waiting for (child's name)."

If interest is still high, the teacher can make a request that the items be returned and repeat the game by sending the children for new items.

Blind Walk

Objective

To depend on listening to another child's verbal directions

Materials

Scarfs, bandanas, or cloth strips

FIGURE 8–6   This teacher is using a scarf as a blindfold.

FIGURE 8–7   The blindfolded child is depending on her guide's verbal directions.

Introduction and Activity

Discuss blindness and guide dogs. Pair children and blindfold one child. Ask the guide to hold the blindfolded child's hand and take a classroom walk. Ask the guide to talk about where children are going, and urge the blindfolded child to use hands to feel objects, etc. Change blindfolds giving guide a chance to also go on a guided walk (figure 8–6 and figure 8–7). (Some children may object to blindfolds or act fearful. Respect their wishes.) Conduct a brief follow-up discussion.

Courtesy of WICAP Headstart, Donnelly, Idaho.

Jack-in-the-Box

Objective

To discriminate sounds by listening for a signal and responding to it

Materials

None

Introduction and Activity

Recite the following rhyme in a whispered voice until the word "pop" is reached. Using hand motions, hide your thumb in your fist and let it pop up each time the word "pop" is said.

Jack-in-the-box, jack-in-the-box, where can you be?
Hiding inside where I can't see?
If you jump up, you won't scare me.
Pop! Pop! Pop!

Suggest that children squat and pretend to be jack-in-the-boxes. Ask them to listen and jump up only when they hear the word "pop." Try a second verse if the group seems willing.

Jack-in-the-box, jack-in-the-box, you like to play.
Down in the box you won't stay.
There's only one word I have to say.
Pop! Pop! Pop!

Pin-On Sound Cards (Animals and Birds)

Objective

To associate and imitate sounds and use auditory memory

Materials

Safety pins or masking tape, file cards (3" × 5") or self-stick memo paper with pictures of birds and animals (gummed stickers of animals and birds are available in stationery stores and from supply houses). Suggestions: duck, rooster, chick, owl, goose, woodpecker, horse, cow, cat, dog, sheep, lion, mouse, turkey, bee, frog, donkey, seal.

Introduction and Activity

Have a card pinned on your blouse or shirt before the children enter the room. This will start questions. Talk about the sound that the animal pictured on your card makes. Practice it with the children. Ask who would like a card. Have the children come, one at a time, while you pin on the cards. Talk about the animal and the sound it makes. Imitate each sound with the group. Have one of the children make an animal noise and have the child with the right card stand up and say "That's me, I'm a (name of animal)." Children usually like to wear the cards the rest of the day and take them home, if possible.

Guess What?

Objective

To identify and discriminate common sounds

Materials

A bell, hand eggbeater, paper bag to crumple, baby rattle, tambourine, drum, stapler, any other noisemaker; a room divider, screen, table turned on its side, or blanket taped across a doorway. (This activity also works with a prerecorded cassette tape.)

Introduction and Activity

Ask children to guess what you have behind the screen.

Teacher: "Listen; what makes that sound?"

Note that with younger children, it is best to introduce each item with its name first. Ask different children to come behind the screen and make the next noise.

Variation

Clap simple rhythms behind the screen and have children imitate them. Rhythms can be made by using full claps of the hands with light claps and pauses at regular intervals; for example, a loud clap followed by two light ones and a pause repeated over and over.

Ask a child to sit in the "guessing chair" with his or her back to the group. From the group, select a child to say, "Guess my name." If the first child answers correctly, he or she gets a chance to select the next child who is to sit in the guessing chair.

Play Telephones

Objectives

To focus on listening and responding

Materials

Paper, blunt toothpicks, string, two small tin cans with both ends removed (check for rough edges).

Introduction and Activity

Cover one end of each tin can with paper. Make a

small hole. Insert a long string in the hole. Tie the string around blunt toothpicks. (Paper cups can be substituted for the tin cans.) Make enough sets for the group. Demonstrate how they work.

Sound Story

This story contains three sound words. Every time one of the words is mentioned, the children should make the appropriate sound.

Say, "When you hear the word *spinach*, say 'yum, yum, yum.' When you hear the word *dog*, bark like a dog. When you hear the word *cat*, meow like a cat." Then, recite the following story.

> Once upon a time, there was a little boy who would not taste SPINACH. Everyone would say, "Marvin, why won't you taste SPINACH?" Marvin would say, "I think SPINACH is yuk!!!" Marvin's DOG Malcolm loved SPINACH. Marvin's CAT Malvina loved SPINACH. If Marvin didn't eat his SPINACH, Malcolm the DOG and Malvina the CAT would fight over who would get the SPINACH. The DOG and CAT would make so much noise fighting over the SPINACH that everyone in the neighborhood would say, "If you don't stop that noise, you will have to move away from here." Marvin loved his house and he didn't want to move away from the neighborhood. Malcolm the DOG loved his house and he didn't want to move away from the neighborhood. Malvina the CAT loved her house and she didn't want to move away from the neighborhood. What could they do?

Let the children tell you the answer. This game is a great deal of fun, and the children never tire of hearing the story. You can make up your own sound stories. You can also add rhythm instruments to make the sounds instead of voices (Weissman, 1979).

Author's Chair or Child Picture Book Sharing

Early childhood programs that promote poetry, child dictation, storytelling, and authorship can institute an author's chair, a listening and discussion activity. Usually the child-sized chair is specially decorated and used at one time of the day or a sign is affixed—Author's and/or Reader's Chair. Children are invited to share their own efforts or share a favorite or brought-to-school picture book. Teachers may find a need to establish time limits for ramblers or suggest audiences can choose to leave quietly when they wish.

Listening Riddles for Guessing

Animal Riddles

A tail that's skinny and long,
At night he nibbles and gnaws
With teeth sharp and strong.
Beady eyes and tiny paws,
One called Mickey is very nice.
And when there's more than one
We call them _____. (mice)

He has a head to pat.
But he's not a cat.
Sometimes he has a shiny coat.
It's not a hog, it's not a goat.
It's bigger than a frog.
I guess that it's a _____. (dog)

No arms, no hands, no paws,
But it can fly in the sky.
It sings a song
That you have heard.
So now you know
That it's a _____. (bird)

Sharp claws and soft paws,
Big night eyes, and whiskers, too.
Likes to curl up in your lap,

Or catch a mouse or a rat.
Raise your hand if you know.
Now all together, let's whisper its name very slowly
_____. (cat)

Riddle Game

Children take turns calling on others with raised hands.

I'll ask you some riddles.
Answer if you can.
If you think you know,
Please raise your hand.
Don't say it out loud
'Til _____ calls your name.
That's how we'll play
This riddling game.

A beautiful flower we smell with our nose.
It's special name is not pansy but _____. (rose)

I shine when you're playing and having fun.
I'm up in the sky and I'm called the _____. (sun)

If you listen closely you can tell,
I ring and chime because I'm a _____. (bell)

You've got 10 of me, I suppose,
I'm on your feet and I'm your _____. (toes)

I'm down on your feet, both one and two
Brown, black, blue, or red, I'm a _____. (shoe)

I sit on the stove and cook what I can
They pour stuff in me, I'm a frying _____. (pan)

It is helpful to have magazine pictures of a rose, the sun, toes, shoes, and a pan, plus a real bell to ring behind you as you speak. These are appropriate for young children who have little experience with rhyming.

Body Parts Riddle

If a bird you want to hear,
You have to listen with your _____. (ear)

If you want to dig in sand,
Hold the shovel in your _____. (hand)

To see an airplane as it flies,
Look up and open up your _____. (eyes)

To smell a pansy or a rose,
You sniff its smell with your _____. (nose)

When you walk across the street
You use two things you call your _____. (feet)

If a beautiful song you've sung,
You used your mouth and your _____. (tongue)

All these parts you can feel and see
Parts are always with you on your _____. (body)

Tracing hands or drawing any body part they choose (on a picture with missing hands, feet, and so forth) is a fun follow-up activity for four-and-a-half-year-olds.

Listen and Follow Directions—Stories and Games

Sit-Down/Stand-Up Story

Say to the children, "Let's see if you can stand *up* and sit *down* when I say the words. Listen: Stand *up!* You all are standing. Sit *down!* Good listening; we're ready to start." Then, tell the children the following story.

When I woke *up* this morning, I reached *down* to the floor for my slippers. Then I stood *up* and slipped them on. Next, I went *down*stairs to the kitchen. I opened the refrigerator, picked *up* the milk and sat *down* to drink. When I finished drinking, I tried to stand *up*, but I was stuck in the chair. I pulled and pulled, but I was still sitting.

"Don't sit on the chairs," my dad called from *up*stairs. "I painted them."

"It's too late! I'm sitting *down*," I answered. "Hurry *down* here and help me."

Dad pulled and pulled, but I didn't come *up*.

"I'll go get our neighbor, Mr. Green. Maybe he can pull you *up*," Dad said. Dad and Mr. Green pulled and pulled. "What'll I do?" I said. "The children will be waiting at school for me." Then I got an idea. "Go get the shovel," I said. Well, that worked. They pushed the shovel handle *down* and I came *up*.

You know, I think I'm stuck in this chair, too. Look, I am. _____ (child's name) and _____ (child's name), please help me. Everyone else please sit.

After my story, let's see if just _____ (child's name) and _____ (child's name) can show us with their hands which way is *up*, and which way is *down*.

A good follow-up is to talk about what can be seen in the room that is up above the children's heads and down below their heads, or say this poem together:

When you're up—you're up,
And when you're down—you're down.
But when you're halfway in between,
You're neither up nor down.

Funny Old Hat Game

Gather a bag of old hats (such as new or discarded paper party hats). Pass the hats out to the children, or let the children choose them.

Say, "We're ready when our hats are on our heads. We're going to put our hats in some funny places and do some funny things. Listen."

Put your hat between your knees.
Put your hat under your arm.
Put your hat over your shoes.
Put your hat under your chin.
Touch the top of your hat.
Sit on your hat.
Stand on your hat.

Encourage the children to choose a place to put the hat, and then say, "Where's the hat? Where's the hat, (child's name). Can you see the hat, hat, hat?" (This can be chanted.) "Under the chair, under the chair—I can see the hat, hat, hat."

See If You Can Game

Collect objects from around the classroom (for example, scissors, ruler, eraser, cup, chalk). Put them on the floor on large paper. Say, "I'm not going to say its name. See if you can tell me what object I am talking about. Raise your hand if you know." (Keep giving hints until the children guess.)

"What has two circles for two fingers?" (scissors)
"It's long and thin with numbers printed on one side." (ruler)
"What makes pencil marks disappear?" (eraser)
"You can fill it with milk." (cup)
"What's white and small and writes on the chalkboard?" (chalk)

Make up some of your own.

Additional Listening Activities

- Make a sound chart. Four or five times a day, gather children and ask them to listen. Divide the chart into inside sounds and outside sounds columns. Ask children what they hear and then list the response and the child's name next to his or her comment. Follow up on another day and compare charts by asking children to listen to find out whether the sounds present on the first chart are absent or still present.
- After a sound walk or field trip, ask children to remember sounds. List and post child comments.
- Record animal or environmental sounds and have fun mimicking them with the group of children.
- Obtain a box of sound makers—rattles, bells, clickers, poppers, and so on. Have children decide if two sounds made inside the box (out of sight) are the same or different. At the activity's end, make a list for children to take turns playing with the box of sound makers. Encourage children to play in pairs.

- Try a What-Comes-Next? Sequencing Sound Game after collecting sound makers or introducing sounds to children. Instruct children to predict which sound will come next. You will have to repeat the pattern a few times before you stop and ask, "What comes next?" Then do the pattern together when the answer is found. Suggested sound sequences follow:
  - Clap, clap, stomp, stomp, clap, clap,?
  - Bell, whistle, whistle, drum, drum, drum, bell,?
  - Moo, bark, meow, meow, moo,?
  - Walk to the door, knock, say hello, say goodbye, walk to the door,?

  With a xylophone or other musical instrument:
  - High sound, low sound, high sound, low sound,?
  - Share the book *Riddle Rhymes* by C. Ghigna, 1995, Hyperion.

Music as a Listening Activity

A type of listening Wolf (1992) calls "focused listening" occurs in many music activities. Children may be attending to specific sounds and words that give directions. Singing games often call for child response or child silence (or pause). To remember and sing a song (or parts of songs), staying in tune and rhythm, entails not only focused listening but also auditory discrimination and intellectual processing. Suggestions for music activities in early childhood centers follow:

- Songs and records that give directions

- Songs and records that contain certain sounds that serve as a cue for response in speech, movement, or both
- Music that highlights particular rhythm instruments, drums, bells, sticks, etc.
- Music with environmental sounds
- Music or songs that promote creative child response
- Background music accompanying play and exploration

See the Appendix for Wolf's (1992) suggested records and tapes.

Summary

Listening skill is learned behavior. The ability to listen improves with experience and exposure, although young children vary in their ability to listen. Listening ability can be classified by type—appreciative, purposeful, discriminative, creative, and critical.

Planned activities, teacher interaction, and equipment can provide opportunities for children to develop their auditory perception skills.

Listening cannot be forced, but experiences can be provided so that a desire to listen is increased. Signals and attentive teacher encouragement can help to form habits. Settings that limit stimuli and control the size of groups are desirable. When teachers are watchful and act when children seem restless or uninterested during planned activities, listening remains active. One of the responsibilities of the teacher is to plan carefully so that young children consistently want to hear what is being offered.

STUDENT ACTIVITIES

1. Choose one of the listening activities found in this chapter, one from another source or one you create. Present the activity to a group of preschoolers, modifying the activity to suit the child group if necessary. Then answer the following questions.
   a. Was the activity interesting to the children?
   b. Were they able to perform the auditory perception tasks?
   c. Would you change the activity in any way if you presented it again?

2. Find or create five additional listening activities. Provide information regarding the source, name of activity, materials needed, description of activity, and objective. After citing the source, state the title of the book where you found the activity idea. If the idea is original, indicate this by using the word "self."

3. Select a popular children's television program to watch. Study the following questions before watching the program. Answer them after viewing the program.
   a. What is the name of the program, and the time and date of viewing?
   b. Were there attempts to build listening skills? If so, what were they?
   c. Do you have any criticism of the program?
   d. Could teachers of early childhood education use any techniques from the show in their auditory perception activities?

4. Practice the listening story in this chapter entitled "Sit-down/Stand-up Story," or find another listening story. At the next class meeting, tell the story to a classmate. Share constructive criticism.

5. Create a tape-recorded activity in which children will in some way analyze what they hear and share response(s) with the teacher. An activity that requires logical or sequential listening could also be attempted. Share your tape and accompanying objects and/or visuals at the next class session.

6. With a small group of classmates, discuss some of the ways a home or school environment can make young children "tune out."

7. Watch a listening activity in a preschool center, and then answer the following questions.
   a. How did the teacher prepare the children for listening?
   b. What elements of the activity captured interest?
   c. How was child interest held?
   d. Did the teacher have an opportunity to recognize children's listening skill?
   e. Did children's listening behavior during the activity seem important to the teacher?
   f. Was this the kind of activity that should be repeated? If so, why?

8. Observe preschoolers in group play. Write down any examples of appreciative, purposeful, discriminative, creative, or critical listening.

9. Plan a listening activity. Describe the materials needed, how the activity will start, what is to happen during the activity, and the auditory perception skills that are included in your plan.

10. In a paragraph, describe the difference between encouraging a child to listen and trying to force a child to listen.

11. Find a source for recorded stories in your community.

12. Plan five activities that deal with children's personal preferences.

13. Bring one read-along book and recording from a commercial source to class. Check with a library in your area to see whether they are available. With a small group of classmates, develop a rating scale to judge the quality of the read-alongs. Rate and share results with the class.

14. Discuss in groups of five to six people the factors that might be present when a preschooler reacts to only about half of the things said to him or her. Share with the total group.

15. Do talk-listen circle times seem overly structured to you, or do you feel they may be appropriate for today's generation of "television-saturated" children? Elaborate.

CHAPTER REVIEW

A. Five types of listening have been discussed. After each of the following statements, identify the listening type that best fits the situation.

1. After hearing an Indian drum on a record, Brett slaps out a rhythm of his own on his thighs while dancing around the room.

2. During a story of *The Three Little Pigs*, Mickey blurts out "Go get 'em wolfie!" in reference to the wolf's behavior in the story.

3. Kimmie is following Chris around. Chris is repeating "Swishy, fishy co-co-pop," over and over again; both giggle periodically.

4. Debbie tells you about the little voice of small Billy Goat Gruff and the big voice of Big Billy Goat Gruff in the story of the *Three Billy Goats Gruff*.

5. Peter has asked whether he can leave his block tower standing during snacktime instead of putting the blocks away as you requested. He wishes to return and build the tower higher. He then listens for your answer.

B. Name five objectives that could be used in planning listening activities for auditory perception.

C. Select the correct answers. All have more than one correct reply.

1. Most parents unconsciously teach preschoolers
   a. to develop auditory perception.
   b. attitudes toward listening.
   c. to listen to their teachers.
   d. many words.

2. A teacher can promote listening by
   a. demanding a listening attitude.
   b. using a signal that alerts children and focuses attention.
   c. encouraging a child.
   d. telling a child he or she is not listening.

3. Critical listening happens when the
   a. child relates what is new to past experience.
   b. child disagrees with another's statement.
   c. child makes a comment about a word being good or bad.
   d. teacher plans thought-provoking questions, and the child has the maturity needed to answer them.

4. Children come to early childhood centers with
   a. individual variation in abilities to listen.
   b. habits of listening.
   c. all the abilities and experiences needed to be successful in planned activities.
   d. a desire to listen.

5. Children's ability to follow a series of commands depends on
   a. their auditory memory.
   b. how clearly the commands are stated.
   c. how well their ears transmit the sounds to their brains and how well their brains sort the information.
   d. how well they can imitate the words of the commands.

D. Explain what is meant by intensity, pitch, and tempo.

E. Assume the children are involved in an activity when they are suddenly distracted by a dog barking outside the window. List four things you could say to the children to draw their attention back to the activity.

   If you wished to use their focus on the barking for a spontaneous listening activity, how would you proceed?

F. What elements of music might promote listening skills?

G. Describe three listening activities, stating the objective of each activity and giving a description of the activity.

RESOURCES FOR ADDITIONAL LISTENING ACTIVITIES

Engel, R. C. (1972). *Language-motivating experiences for young children*. Van Nuys, CA: Educative Toys and Supplies.

Mayesky, M. (1995). *Creative activities for young children*. Albany, NY: Delmar Publishers.

INTRODUCING LITERATURE

CHAPTER 9

Children and Books

After studying this chapter, you should be able to:

- state three goals for reading books to young children.

- describe criteria for book selection.

- demonstrate suggested techniques for reading a book to a group of children.

- design a classroom library center.

- explain quality book features.

- discuss multicultural and multiethnic book use.

Picture books are an important beginning step on the child's path to literacy, as well as an excellent source of listening activities for the young child. Seeing, touching, and interacting with books is part of a good quality program in early childhood education. Books play an important role in language development. *Becoming a Nation of Readers* asserts that reading aloud is the single most important activity for creating the background necessary for eventual success in reading (Anderson, Hiebert, Scott, and Williams, 1985).

Cox (1981) describes the child's first home being-read-to experience as a curriculum:

It is a curriculum rich in pleasant associations: a soft lap, a warm bath, a snugly bed . . . This initial literature curriculum makes possible the impossible, uses common words in uncommon ways, titillates the senses, nurtures curiosities, stretches the memory, and the imagination.

When they are handled with care, reading experiences at home and at school can create positive attitudes toward literature and help to motivate the child to learn to read. A positive attitude towards literacy is most easily established early in life (Bettelheim and Zelan, 1981). Even older infants and toddlers can enjoy having picture books read to them, as discussed in Chapters 1 and 2.

Many parents read to their children at home; others do not. A teacher may offer some children their first contact with stories and books (figure 9–1). Teacher and child can share the joy of this very pleasant experience. Trelease (1995) discusses reading to young children and the possible significance to the child and parent:

Next to hugging your child, reading aloud is probably the longest-lasting experience that you can put into your child's life. Reading aloud is important for all the reasons that talking to children is important—to

FIGURE 9–1   Children may have their first experiences with picture books at a child care center.

inspire them, to guide them, to educate them, to bond with them and to communicate your feelings, hopes and fears. You are giving children a piece of your mind and a piece of your time. They're more interested, really, in you than they are in the story—at least in the beginning.

Early childhood teachers agree that book-sharing sessions are among their favorite times with children. Teachers introduce each new group of children to favorite books that never seem to lose their magic.

There will be times when young children are rapt with enjoyment during picture-book readings, and at such times the lucky reader will understand the power of literature and realize his or her responsibility as the sharer of a vast treasure. The value of offering thoughtfully selected books in a skilled way will be readily apparent.

What, exactly, do picture books offer young children? They open the door to literacy and create the opportunity to:

- Build positive attitudes about books and reading.
- Explore, re-create, and obtain meaning in human experience. *Gives meaning to experience.*

- Come in contact with the diversity and com- *exposure to* plexity of life.
- Feel the texture of others' experiences. *Gives a sense of*
- Look at vulnerability, honesty, and drama in a unique literary form (Hoggart, 1970).
- Experience in well-conveyed literature an art that leaves a lasting radiance *impression* (Sebesta and Iverson, 1975).
- Gain a sense of well-being.
- Experience the concise charm of heightened language and form (Lewis, 1976). *Exposes them to various forms of language*
- Experience that sense of deepened self— children might call good feelings—that come from involvement with important human emotions (Lewis, 1976). *Emotion*
- Unearth human truths.
- Nurture and expand imagination (Norton, 1994).
- Understand, value, and appreciate cultural heritage (Norton, 1994).
- Develop language, stimulate thinking, and develop socially (Norton, 1994).
- Gain facts, information, and data (nonfiction).
- Experience visual and aesthetic variety.
- Hear the rhythm and sound qualities of words.
- Gain reading skills.
- Sharpen listening.
- Understand what is acceptable and admirable and what is undesirable or deplorable (Dopyera and Lay-Dopyera, 1992).
- Experience a rich set of perspectives for thinking about their own feelings and behaviors (Dopyera and Lay-Dopyera, 1992).
- Experience vocabulary enrichment (Dopyera and Lay-Dopyera, 1992).
- Develop real readers and writers; develop one's sensibilities and compassion, stretch one's imagination, and "dwell in possibility" (Huck, 1992).

Clay (1991) notes another advantage:

Preschool children learn to respond to the messages in children's stories which are told or read to them and in doing this they use the kind of language and thought processes that they will use in learning to read later on.

As you read through this chapter, other benefits of reading aloud to children will occur to you, and you will clarify your thoughts about the benefits you consider of primary and secondary importance.

Cullinan (1992) suggests story form is a cultural universal; stories help us to remember by providing meaningful frameworks. Stories make events memorable.

A special kind of language is found in books. Oral language differs from written language in important ways. Though many young children communicate well and have adequate vocabularies, they don't construct sentences in the same manner found in their picture books. Knowing the way books "talk" makes them better predictors of words they will discover in their early reading attempts.

Each child gets his or her own meaning from picture-book experiences. Books cannot be used as substitutes for the child's real life experiences, interactions, and discoveries, because these are what help to make books understandable. Books add another dimension and source of information and enjoyment to children's lives.

Age and Book Experiences

Careful consideration should be given to selecting books that are appropriate to the child's age. Children under three (and many over this age) enjoy physical closeness, the visual changes of illustrations, and the sound of the human voice reading text. The rhythms and poetry of picture books intrigue them. Beck (1982) points out that very young children's "syntactic dependence" is displayed by their obvious delight in recognized word order. The sounds of language in picture books may be far more important than the meanings conveyed to the very young child. Teachers of two- and three-year-olds may notice this by observing which books children select most often. Four-year-olds are more concerned with content and characterization, in addition to what they previously enjoyed in picture books. Fantasy, realism, human emotions, nonfiction, and books with a variety of other features attract and hold them.

Brief History of Children's Literature

The idea that children need or deserve entertainment and amusement is a relatively new development. Until the mid-eighteenth century books for children instructed and aimed to improve young children, particularly their moral and spiritual natures.

Folk tales were sung and told in primitive times, and stories of human experience were shared. Storytellers often attempted to reduce anxieties, satisfy human needs, fire the imagination, and increase human survival among other aims. Orally handed down, tales appeared in most of the world's geographic locations and cultures. Much of today's literature reflects elements of these old tales and traditional stories.

Early American children's literature was heavily influenced by English and Puritan beliefs and practices. Books that existed before William Caxton's development of printing in fifteenth-century England were hand copied adult books that children happened to encounter in private wealthy households. Caxton translated *Aesop's Fables* (1484) from a French version and printed other adult books literate English children found interesting. *Aesop's Fables* is considered the first printing of talking animal stories. Themes of other books in Victorian England included romances of chivalry and adventure, knights in shining armor, battles with giants, and rescue of lovely princesses and other victims of oppression (Muir, 1954).

Victorian families read to their children, and minstrels and troubadours were paid to sing narrative verses to the families of rich patrons. The English Puritans were dedicated to a revolution founded on the deep conviction that religious beliefs form the basis for the whole of human life (Muir, 1954). Writers such as Bunyan, author of *A Book for Boys and Girls* (1686), were intent on saving children's souls.

Chapbooks (paper booklets) appeared in England after 1641. Initially they were intended for adults, but eventually fell into children's hands. They included tiny woodcuts as decoration, and later woodcuts to illustrate text. Salesmen (chapmen) traveled England selling these small, 4" × 2½" editions to the less affluent. Chapbooks written to entertain and instruct children followed, as sales and popularity increased. Titles included *The Tragical Death of an Apple Pie* and *The History of Jack and the Giants*.

John Newbery and Thomas Boreman are recognized as the first publishers of children's books in England. Chapbooks, though pre-dated, are considered booklets. Most of these newly printed books were instructional (Nelson, 1972); but titles like *A Little Pretty Pocket-Book* (Newbery, 1744) were advertised as children's amusement books (figure 9–2). In 1765, Newbery published *The Renowned History of Little Goody Two Shoes, Otherwise Called Mrs. Margery Two Shoes*. The book chronicles Goody's rise from poverty to wealth. Newbery prospered. Other publishers followed with their own juvenile editions, many with themes designed to help children reason and use moral judgment to select socially correct courses of action.

Books used as school readers in early America also contained subject matter of both a religious and moral nature.

By the mid-1800s adventure stories for older boys gained popularity with Mark Twain's *Adventures of Tom Sawyer*, published in 1876. Louisa May Alcott had created *Little Women* in 1868, as a girl's volume.

Picture Books

Toward the end of the nineteenth century some picture books became artistic (Bader, 1976). English and French publishers produced colorful illustrations of charm, quality, and detail. The books of Randolph Caldecott, Maurice Boutet de Monvel, and Kate Greenway had captivating drawings that over-

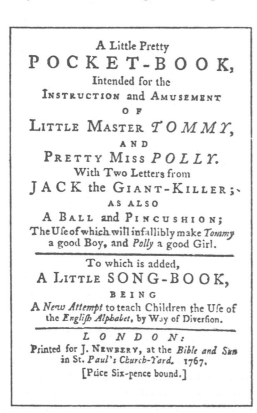

FIGURE 9–2 Excerpts from *A Little Pretty Pocket-Book*, published by John Newbery, 1744

shadowed the drab and homely illustrations that were typically found in American picture books.

Though not intended or recommended for children, comic picture sequences, like those of A. B. Frost, appeared in American magazines from 1880–1890. Their humor was shared by families. Two American picture books resembling Frost's slapstick humor gained acceptance from American librarians: Gelett Burgess's *New Goops and How to Know Them* (Lippincott, 1928), and Palmer Cox's *Brownies* (1927).

E. Boyd Smith, an American, created illustrations for *The Story of Noah's Ark* (Houghton Mifflin, 1905), which are described as both artistic and humorous. The books Smith created delighted children and adults with colorful panoramic illustrations. Librarians speaking of Smith's illustrative work used words such as honest, true, "better than any done by an American artist" (Bader, 1976). The cost of full color printing escalated and illustrative color in picture books was not to reappear in the U.S. and become widely affordable until the later 1920s and 1930s. Little Golden Books became popular, and European books with colorful illustrative art were imported to the U.S. for those who could afford them.

Extraordinary black and white illustrations drawn by Wanda Gag in *Farm Sale* (Coward-McCann, 1926), *Millions of Cats* (Coward-McCann, 1928), and a lithographic technique used in her other books captured both children's fancy and book reviewers' praise. Her drawings complemented and reinforced her text. Together the effect was polished and eminently suitable for her folk tales. As Bader (1976) notes, the combination of Wanda Gag's text, drawings, and format constitute its lasting distinction.

American picture books for children began to reflect a world view of children's literature. Colorful illustrations appeared in school readers. Stories for young children set in foreign countries were widely acclaimed during the 1930s. *Madeline* (Simon & Schuster, 1939), by Ludwig Bemelmans, is still found on most suggested early childhood reading lists.

The child-study movement and research at numerous universities and institutions during the late 1920s and 1930s led some well-known researchers to believe small children's interests focused on "the-here-and-now." This was translated as home objects and environments, community settings, airplanes, trains, local workers and professionals, and "everyday matters." Approved and recommended book lists guided parents' selection of preschool books as early as 1913.

It's felt Russian information and "how-to" books of the 1940s and 1950s increased nonfiction picture-book production in the U.S. Books concerning machines and how they worked, insects, and science concepts became abundant. Illustrations included photographs.

Some of the changes in picture-book publishing during the 1960s occurred because several individuals, including Nancy Larrick (1965), spotlighted the lack of African Americans in storylines and illustrations. The civil rights movement affected the social consciousness of many teachers and parents.

Only a few research surveys conducted in the 1970s and 1980s attempted to pinpoint the numbers of picture-book representations for Mexican Americans, Asian Americans, or Native Americans. It is reasonable to say they were minimal in number.

Although published multicultural literature for young children increased and became an important part of language arts education (Bishop, 1990), cultural accuracy that helps young children gain a "true" sense of the culture depicted (a so-called insider's view) is a relatively recent development. This type of picture book is eagerly sought by most early childhood educators.

Picture books dealing with the reality of young children's daily lives, their families and living problems (stress, fear, moving, appearance, etc.) began appearing in larger numbers in the 1970s and 1980s broadening subject matter felt appropriate and of interest to children. These books, many classified as "therapeutic," often attempted to build self-esteem or help young children cope in difficult situations. Characters in picture books always had problems to be solved by creative thinking and self-insight; but these new stories dealt more frequently with life situations children could not change themselves.

Literacy concerns and the whole language movement (1980s–1990s) have dramatically increased educators' ideas of the importance of quality literature in early childhood curriculum. More and more activities are based on children's reactions to books and language arts activities offered by their teachers.

Today's picture books have historical roots. Some have outlived the generation of children for whom they were produced and are classics of quality. It is those you as a teacher of young children will endeavor to find and share along with the "classics of the future."

Where to. Start

This chapter contains a list of picture books (pages 226 and 243) to be considered merely as a starting point. Since the quality of a book is a subjective judgment, your favorites may not appear on this list. There are many other books of quality; each teacher should develop a personal collection. Librarians and bookstore salespeople can offer valuable suggestions and advice.

Quality

Judging quality means reading and viewing a picture book to find out whether it contains something memorable or valuable. For every good book you discover, you may wade through a stack that makes you wonder whether the authors have any experience at all with young children. Remember, appropriate material for a four-year-old may not suit a younger child.

Each book you select may have one or more of the following desirable and valuable features:

- characterization
- color
- an example of human courage, cleverness, or grit
- aesthetic appeal
- a gamelike challenge
- word play
- listening pleasure
- nonsense
- onomatopoeia (the naming of a thing or action by a vocal imitation of the sound associated with it, as in buzz and hiss)
- suspense
- humor or wit
- fantasy
- surprise
- repetition
- hope
- charm
- sensitivity
- realistic dialogue
- cultural insight
- action
- predictability

The preceding is only a partial listing. A book can excel in many different ways. An outstanding feature of many good stories is that they can cause the reader to smile with recognition and think "life is like that" or "I've been there myself."

The theme of respect for individual differences in Bill Peet's *Huge Harold*, the gentleness of Uri Shulevitz's *Rain, Rain, Rivers*, or the tenderness of Charlotte Zolotow's *My Grandpa Lew* may fit your criteria of quality. The runaway fantasy of Frank Asch's *Popcorn* and Tomie de Paola's *Strega Nona* might tickle your fancy.

The panoramic scenes of Mitsumasa Anno's *Anno's Counting Book*, the patterns and contrasts in Ezra Jack Keat's *Snowy Day*, or the fun of discovery in Janet and Allan Ahlberg's *Each Peach Pear Plum* might help a book become one of your favorites because of visual appeal.

For humor and wit, you might choose Steven Kellogg's *Can I Keep Him?*, Leah Komaiko's *Annie Bananie*, Robert Kraus's *Leo the Late Bloomer*, James Marshall's *George and Martha*, Mercer Mayer's *What Do You Do With a Kangaroo?*, or a selection of others that may make you laugh. You might never forget the way you trip over your tongue while reading about Jack, Kack, Lack, Mack, Nack, Quack, Pack, and Quack in Robert McCloskey's *Make Way for Ducklings* or Arlene Mosel's *Tikki-Tikki Tembo*. If you enjoy surprise or an ending with a twist, you might be delighted by Brinton Turkles' *Deep in the Forest* or Jimmy Kennedy's *The Teddy Bears' Picnic*. The sound pleasure in Wanda Gag's *Millions of Cats* or the onomatopoeia in Mabel Brass's *The Little Engine That Could* might make these books memorable.

You might relive your experience of city living in *Tell Me a Mitzi* by Lore Segal. Perhaps discovering the facts through the colorful, precise artwork in Ruth Hellers' *Chicken's Aren't the Only Ones* will attract you to the world of nonfiction. Unforgettable characters like Leo Lionni's Frederick, Don Freeman's Corduroy and Beady Bear, Gene Zion's Harry The Dirty Dog, or Ludwig Bemelman's demure individualist, Madeline, may be counted among your friends as you search for quality. Jewels will stand out, and you will be anxious to share them with children.

You will be looking for fascinating, captivating books. Some captivate by presenting believable characters. "Character-drawing is like a tremendous, complicated conjuring-trick. Appealing to imagination and goodwill, diverting attention by sheer power of technique, the writer persuades us (for the period of reading and sometimes for long afterwards) to accept the identity of certain people who exist between the covers of his book" (Fisher, 1975). Some fascinate to the extent that worries are forgotten, and the child lives in the fantasy world of the story during its reading and beyond (Bettelheim and Zelan, 1981).

Speaking about a true literature-based curriculum, Cooper (1993) identifies quality books:

> Teachers need to watch for stories that "catch on," stories that fulfill some deep understanding of human intentions, or express a developmental concern, or arouse our curiosity: these are the stories that should lead a curriculum of hearing stories, knowing them, and—if they appeal—reliving them through writing, drama, or retelling.

You'll want to choose classics so that from the very beginning the child has a chance to appreciate literature. Not everyone will agree with what is a modern-day classic. *Where The Wild Things Are*, by Maurice Sendak, continues to cause arguments among adults about whether it is truly a classic. Martinez (1987) notes that "adults don't like it very much, but nearly all the children really respond to it—Sendak is just on the kids' wavelength."

Award Winning Books

Each year the Association for Library Services to Children (American Library Association) recognizes the *artist* it feels has produced "the most distinguished American picture book for children" with the Caldecott Medal and Honor awards. Early childhood educators look for these and other award winning books. Other awards given to books include:

- Newbery Medals
- International Reading Association Children's Book Awards
- Coretta Scott King Awards
- National Jewish Book Awards
- Catholic Book Awards
- Newspaper awards
- Magazine reviews and recognitions found in *Book Links* (American Library Association) and *Language Arts* (National Council of Teachers of English)
- Local public library awards or recognitions

Illustrations

In many quality picture books, the story stands well by itself. The illustrations simply visualize what is written. In others, illustrations play a dominant role and are an integral part of the entire action (Freeman, 1967). Picture books are defined by Glazer (1986) as "those books that rely on a combination of illustrations and narrative with both being integral to the complete work." Fortunately many picture-book illustrations are created by highly talented individuals. A wide range of artistic styles exists in picture-book illustration, including line drawings, woodcuts, water colors, collage, photography, among others. Poltarnees (1972) describes the true artist as one who is able to enter the realm that his or her work evokes and move as freely there as if it were the kingdom of his birth. As a consequence, the artist can show us things that we would not have seen as mere visitors.

Illustrations help give words reality. For young children, illustrations promote visual literacy. Cox (1981) lists additional benefits:

1. provision of pleasure
2. nourishment of the imagination
3. promotion of creative expression
4. development of imagery
5. presentation and exploration of a variety of styles and forms for the communication of ideas
6. awareness of the functions of languages
7. acquisition of metalinguistic awareness (defined as a sense of what printed language is all about)

Picture-book illustrations are often familiar objects in life-like settings, and publishers are careful to emphasize figures rather than backgrounds. In addition to the simple, true-to-life depictions preferred by young preschoolers, illustrations of pure fantasy and illustrations that contain more detail appeal to older preschoolers.

Format

A book's format is defined as its overall and general character, that is, the way it is put together. Decisions concerning format by book publishers and author/illustrators include the size and shape of the cover and interior pages, paper quality, printing colors, typesetting, content of each page, and binding. A book's format can enhance its narrative, appeal, and subsequent enjoyment, or it can confuse, frustrate, and alienate the reader. A book can reflect a thoughtful attempt to create a classic volume of enduring worth and value or represent a sacrifice of quality for the sake of quick profit.

Genre, another way of categorizing books, concentrates on a book's content. Narrative is considered to be poetry or prose. Prose can be further classified as fiction or nonfiction. The category of fiction includes excursions into sheer fantasy as well as more plausible stories about people or situations that could be, could have been, or might be. The latter group is classified as realistic fiction.

If Only They Would Choose Books and Book-Related Activities

Many early childhood teachers are worried that busy parents and money-tight families haven't the time or resources to make books part of children's lives. Consequently, they are expending extra effort and attention to books and book-related activities. Emergent literacy research has alerted educators to the idea that preschoolers who are read to and who are interested in stories and books are more successful students in the beginning years of elementary school and in accomplishing reading (Holdaway, 1979; Clay, 1991; Dumbro, 1992; Goodman, Y., 1986b). Raines and Isbell (1994) suggest educators monitor how many children select classroom book-related activities, library areas, and also the amount of time spent.

Teacher planning and thoughtful analysis can increase child interest. Thinking of classroom schedules and book reading times more critically can initiate change and creative and imaginative presentation of activities. Time spent reading to children can be viewed as only one part of a book's introduction. What precedes and what follows is equally important. Practitioners need to ask themselves, "How is this book relevant to children's lives?" What can I do to increase child involvement and interest? What will make children eager to be part of story times? How can I discover child thoughts about what has been read and then build in further experiences? What can follow this story time, and will children give me clues? In other words, how can this book become part of their lives and at the same time be highly enjoyed? After attempting to answer these and other teacher questions, one can see simply reading to children may not be enough to reach a teacher's true goals.

Goals

Because children can gain so much from books, the teacher's way of presenting them is very important.

DeLawter (1992) urges language and literature teachers to become "explorer" teachers:

As student responses are validated and extended, their sophistication with language and literature grows, and the journey into literature becomes an exploration of life itself.

Becoming this type of teacher requires the teacher to view children as active, individual learners. In previewing Tomie de Paola's picture book *Strega Nona* (Prentice-Hall, 1975) for a group reading, a teacher might think as follows:

What past experiences has this group had with pasta?

What follow-up, extending activities, could be planned?

What teacher questions would guide a discussion that probes children's feelings and ideas?

How can I make the "overflowing," "too much," concept a real experience?

The teacher's goal should be to lead each child to understand that books can be fun and interesting, can hold new experiences, and can be enjoyed alone or in the company of others.

Creating a positive attitude towards reading experiences should be a prime concern. If a child does not enjoy being read to, he or she might avoid all similar situations in the future. Children who enjoy being read to will seek out books. Fraiberg (1987) urges preschool teachers to think of the preschool years as "... a critical period for becoming addicted, the time when urges are felt as irresistible and objects that gratify the urge are also experienced as irresistible. The educator who wishes to capitalize on the addictability of the child at this age must insure early and repeated gratifications from stories told and stories read."

Books you may review and reject you'll recognize as inappropriate or missing their mark with young children. You may judge them as having no redeeming social value, to be dull and uninteresting, contain violence, unfortunate representations, unclear messages, or poor models of behavior. A book's construction and format may be undesirable. Of the nearly 69,000 children's books currently

in print, many will not come up to the quality standards you set.

Most educators are eager to learn more about new children's books and are already quite knowledgeable (Cullinan, 1992). Picking books for a specific child's interest, and selecting books to suit some unique classroom situation or event is an ongoing teacher task.

In a diverse society, offering multicultural and ethnically representative literature is a must for young children. Though age-recommended lists are available, most teachers actively pursue additional publications. Librarians, publishers, and children's book stores are excellent resources. Anti-bias themes and sex equity themes are also eagerly sought to ensure book models give young children every chance to value themselves as individuals.

Sales of children's books to affluent parents, who want to give (perhaps literally) their child every educational advantage, are growing. Yet, no one is really sure who—if anyone—is actually reading the books (Healy, 1990).

It is the teacher's responsibility to encourage the children's interest (figure 9–3), because not every child in preschool is interested in books or sees them as something to enjoy. Although children cannot be forced to like books, they can acquire positive feelings for them. Part of the positive feelings

FIGURE 9–3   Teachers encourage book exploration.

depends on whether children feel successful and competent during reading time. This, in turn, depends on how skillfully the teacher acts and reacts and how well the book sessions are planned. The key is to draw reluctant children into the story by making story times so attractive and vital that children simply cannot bear to stay away.

An important additional goal in reading books to children is the presentation of knowledge. Books can acquaint the child with new words, ideas, facts, feelings, and happenings. These are experienced in a different form than spoken conversation. In books, sentences are complete; in conversation, they may not be. Stories and illustrations follow a logical sequence in books.

Teachers ought to be concerned with whether the child comprehends what is read. To ensure comprehension, the books must offer significant content, something that relates to the child's everyday experience. Humor and fantasy, for example, are commonplace in favorite picture books. Usually, these books aren't merely frivolous. A closer reading will often reveal that they deal with universal human emotions or imaginations. Comprehension is aided by open discussion. Children should be free to ask questions that will help them connect the book's happenings to their own past experiences. The more outgoing and talkative children often clear up misunderstandings of the whole group when books are discussed. Those who work with young children often notice children's innate tendency to try to make sense and derive meaning from the happenings in their lives.

Teachers can show that books may also be used as resources. When a child wants to find out about certain things, teachers can refer to dictionaries, encyclopedias, or books on specialized subjects. The teacher can model the use of books to find facts. When a child asks the teacher a question about some subject of special interest and the teacher says, "I don't know, but I know where we can find out," the teacher can demonstrate how books can be used for finding answers. The teacher tells where to look and follows through by showing the child how the information is found. The joy of discovery is shared, and this opens the door to seeking more answers.

Another goal of the teacher should be to encourage the development of listening skills. During listening times, children's attention can become focused. Many different types of listening—discriminative, appreciative, purposeful, creative, and critical—can all be present in one reading experience.

In contrast, "pressure-cooker" programs, which promise to have four-year-olds reading before kindergarten, often feature drill sessions designed to develop technical reading skills (such as decoding words). When these drill sessions, which are usually meaningless and boring to young children, are connected to picture-book readings, they could endanger the young child's budding love affair with books. A further discussion of this problem can be found in Chapter 17.

Many children pick up reading knowledge and reading skills naturally, as they notice books and become more familiar with their features. They will see regularities and differences in the book's illustrations and text that will aid them in their eventual desire to break the code of reading. An early type of reading has been witnessed by all experienced preschool teachers. Paul Copperman (1982) calls it "imitative reading." He defines this behavior as "reading the story from pictures, sometimes speaking remembered text that precisely follows the book for a page or more." Certain techniques can be used to encourage imitative reading:

- Reading picture books to children daily.
- Planning repeated reading of new and old favorites.
- Reliving enjoyed parts in discussions.
- Being attentive to children's needs to be heard "reading."
- Issuing positive encouragement about your enjoyment of what the children have shared.
- Expecting some creative child deviation from the actual story.
- Suggesting or providing additional ways children could "read" a book (for example, into a tape recorder).
- Viewing the children's activity as emerging literacy and behavior to value as a milestone.

Another goal to consider when planning a program is to encourage children to learn how to care for books and where and how they can be used. Attitudes about books as valuable personal possessions should be instilled during early childhood. A number of emerging behaviors and skills will be noticed as children become fond of books. Learning to read is a complex skill that is dependent on smaller skills, some of which children develop during story times and by browsing through books on their own.

Using Literature to Aid Conflict Resolution Skills

Concerned with rising levels of violence in our society, early childhood teachers are attempting to use picture books and stories to help children identify and define problems, a first step in conflict resolution. Books can be a valuable tool. Illustrations and book text may help child visualization, build empathy, provide nonviolent resolution to story line disputes, portray different types of conflicts, and give examples of peacemaking at work (Schomberg, 1993).

Book Selection

Teachers are responsible for selecting quality books that meet the school's stated goals; often teachers are asked to select new books for the school's collection. Book selection is not an easy task for teachers. McCord (1995) points out:

> As caregivers or teachers, we have the responsibility to select each book with much thought to its content and relevance to particular children. We must be sensitive to how children might personalize a story we have selected. An awareness of family situations, cultures, religions, and social biases of the "smaller community" in our classrooms must be developed with respect as we choose which stories to tell.

Some books may fill the needs completely; others may only partially meet the goals of instruction. The local library offers the opportunity to borrow books that help keep story-telling time fresh and interesting, and children's librarians can be valuable resources.

One child may like a book that another child does not like. Some stories appeal more to one group than to another. Stories that are enjoyed most often become old favorites. Children who know the story often look forward to a familiar part or character. MacDonald (1992) points out that selected books should match your children's needs:

> Children need books that reflect their changing interests. They need books that range from simple to more difficult. They need books that are relevant to the social and cultural reality of their daily lives and our multi-cultural, multi-ethnic, multi-racial world.

Professional books and journals abound with ideas concerning the types of books that young children like best. Some writers feel that simple fairy-tale picture books with animal characters who possess lifelike characteristics are preferred (Beck, 1982). Others mention that certain children want "true" stories. Most writers agree with Self (1987):

> Much of the . . . success of any book for young children depends on its presentation of basic human tasks, needs, and concerns from their perception and at a level at which they can respond. They do not need books which are condescending, which trivialize their concerns and efforts, and which present easy answers to complex problems. Rather, young children need adults and books, and other materials which support their right to be children, their efforts to meet both their common and their individual needs, and their efforts to create meaning in the world.

Bettelheim (1976) advises that both fairy tales and realism should be offered to young children:

When realistic stories are combined with ample and psychologically correct exposure to fairy tales, then the child receives information which speaks to both parts of a budding personality—the rational and the emotional.

Many parents and educators have concerns about the violent nature of some folk and fairy tales. Others believe children already know the world can be a dangerous and sometimes cruel place. Tunnell (1994) explains many old stories involve justice—good things happening to people with good behavior and bad things happening to people with bad behavior. Tunnell points out:

> The old stories have existed for centuries mainly because they speak to us on a deep level concerning the human experience. Because good and evil are the most basic of human traits, children are concerned from an early age with the ramifications of good and bad behavior. In classic fantasy stories, there are few gradations of good and bad—evil characters are truly evil and cannot be swayed toward good. Likewise, the pure in heart remain pure. These stories, then, are a study in justice.

Individual teachers and staff groups may decide some folk tales are too violent, gory, or inappropriate for the age or living circumstances of attending children. Each book needs examination. It is likely that at times staff opinions will differ.

Some beginning teachers worry about book characters such as talking bears and rabbits. Make-believe during preschool years is an ever-increasing play pursuit. Beck (1982) advises:

> Children don't mind if bears talk if the message of their speech is something with which they can identify. On the other hand, they will reject stories that seem realistic if the problems the characters face have little to do with their own emotional lives.

The clear-cut story lines in many folk and fairy tales have stood the test of time (Pines, 1983) and are recommended for a beginning teachers' first attempts at reading to preschoolers. Bettelheim and Zelan (1981) feel "good literature has something of meaning to offer any reader of any age, although on different levels of comprehension and appreciation." Each child will interpret and react to each book from an individual point of view, based on his or her unique experience.

You will want to introduce books with excellent language usage, ones that enchant and create beautiful images using the best grammatical structure, vocabulary, and imaginative style—in other words, memorable quality books.

Kinds of Books

Children's book publishing is a booming business. Many types of books are available, as illustrated in figure 9–4, which lists various categories in the left column. The figure identifies the major genre classifications and formats of children's books used in preschool classrooms, but excludes poetry, which is discussed in another chapter. Many books do not fit neatly into a single category; some books may fit into two or more categories.

A vast and surprising variety of novelty books are also in print: floating books for bath time; soft, huggable books for bedtime; pocket-sized books; jumbo board and easel books (Scholastic); lift-the-flap books; movielike flipbooks (Little, Brown & Co.); books that glow in the dark; sing-a-story books (Bantam); potty training books (Barron's); and even books within books.

Oversized Books (Big Books)

Big, giant, and jumbo (24" × 36") are descriptors used to identify oversized books. Publishers are mass producing this size book due to their increased popularity with both early childhood educators and whole-language curriculum advocates.

Because they are easily viewed by groups of children, oversized books have been added to teacher curriculum collections. New and classic titles abound. Since the text is large, it's not overlooked by young children. Found in soft and hard

TYPES	FEATURES TEACHERS LIKE	FEATURES CHILDREN LIKE

Story books (picture books)
• Family and home
• Folktales and fables
• Fanciful stories
• Fairy tales
• Animal stories
• Others
	Shared moments
	Children enthusiastic and attentive
	Making characters' voices
	Introducing human truths and
	   imaginative adventures
	Sharing favorites
	Easy for child to identify with small
	   creatures
		Imagination and fantasy
		Identification with characters'
		   humanness
		Wish and need fulfillment
		Adventure
		Excitement
		Action
		Self-realization
		Visual variety
		Word pleasure

Nonfiction books (informational) also
   referred to as *content books*
	Expanding individual and group
	   interests
	Developing "reading-to-know" attitudes
	Finding out together
	Accurate facts
	Contains scientific content
		Facts, discovery of information and
		   ideas
		Understanding of reality and how
		   things work and function
		Answers to "why" and "how"
		New words and new meanings

Wordless books	Promote child speech, creativity, and
	   imagination
		Supplying their own words to tell
		   story
		Discovery of meanings
		Color, action, and visual variety

Interaction books (books with active child participation built in)	Keeping children involved and attentive Builds listening for directions skills	Movement and group feeling Individual creativity and expression Appeal to senses Manipulative features
Concept books (books with central concepts or themes that include specific and reinforcing examples)	Promotes categorization Presents opportunities to know about and develop concepts Many examples	Adds to knowledge Visually presents abstractions
Predictable books (books with repetitions and reinforcement)	Permits successful guessing Builds child's confidence Promotes ideas that books make sense	Opportunity to read along Repetitiveness Builds feelings of competence

Reference books (picture
dictionaries, encyclopedias, special
subject books)
	Opportunity to look up questions with
	   the child
	Individualized learning
		Getting answers
		Being with teacher
		Finding a resource that answers their
		   questions

Alphabet and word books (word
books have name of object
printed near or on top of object)
	Supplies letters and word models
	Paired words and objects
	Useful for child with avid interest in
	   alphabet letters and words
		Discovery of meanings and names of
		   alphabet letters and words
		Names what is illustrated

Novelty books (pop-ups, fold-outs,
stamp and pasting books, activity
books, puzzle books, scratch and
sniff books, hidden objects in
illustrations, talking books)
	Adds sense-exploring variety
	Stimulates creativity
	Comes in many different sizes and shapes
	Motor involvement for child
		Exploring, touching, moving, feeling,
		   smelling, painting, drawing,
		   coloring, cutting, gluing, acting
		   upon, listening to a mechanical
		   voice, and getting instant feedback

FIGURE 9–4   Categories of children's books   *continues*

TYPES	FEATURES TEACHERS LIKE	FEATURES CHILDREN LIKE
Paperback books and magazines (Golden Books, Humpty Dumpty Magazine)	Inexpensive Wide variety Many classics available	Children can save own money and choose for themselves
Teacher- and child-made books	Reinforces class learnings Builds understanding of authorship Allows creative expression Records individual, group projects, field trips, parties Promotes child expression of concerns and ideas Builds child's self-esteem	Child sees own name in print Shares ideas with others Self-rewarding
Therapeutic books (books helping children cope with and understand things such as divorce, death, jealousy)	Presents life realistically Offers positive solutions and insights Presents diverse family groups Deals with life's hard-to-deal-with subjects	Helps children discuss real feelings
Seasonal and holiday books	Accompanies child interest May help child understand underlying reasons for celebration	Builds pleasant expectations Adds details
Books and audiovisual combinations (read-alongs)	Adds variety Offers group and individual experiencing opportunities Stimulates interest in books	Projects large illustrations Can be enjoyed individually
Toddler books & board books (durable pages)	Resists wear and tear	Ease in page-turning
Multicultural and cross-cultural books (culturally conscious books)	Increases positive attitudes concerning diversity and similarity	Meeting a variety of people
Oversized books (Big Books)	Emphasizes the realities in our society Extra-large text and illustrations	Easy-to-see in groups Giant book characters

FIGURE 9–4 *continued*

cover versions with brilliant-colored illustrations, some have accompanying audio-cassette tapes and small book editions. Teachers use chalkboard gutters or art easels as book holders.

Strickland and Morrow (1990) recommend the use of big books, and suggest:

> Enlarged texts allow groups of children to see and react to the printed page as it is being read aloud, a factor considered key to the effectiveness of shared reading between parent and child. Many teachers regard Big Book experiences as the closest approximation to family storybook reading one can offer in the classroom.

Active participation and unison participation can be encouraged. Teacher underlining the words with his or her hand while reading gives attention to print and its directionality.

Nonfiction Books

Teachers may encounter and share nonfiction books that answer child questions, are related to a curriculum theme, or serve another teaching purpose such as providing pictorial information. Moss (1995) points out that nonfiction books can teach concepts and terms associated with a variety of topics, people, places, and things children may never encounter in real life. A book with a simplified explanation of how water comes out of a faucet serves as an example. Vardell (1994) points out that nonfiction (books) may be perceived as more appropriate for older grades, and a real revolution has occurred in recent years in the writing and production of nonfiction books for young children.

Examples of nonfiction books follow:

Arnosky, J. (1985). *Watching foxes*. New York: Lothrop Lee and Shepard Books.

Coats, L. (1987). *The oak tree*. New York: Macmillan.

Hirschi, R. (1987). *What is a bird?* New York: Walker.

Stein, S. (1985). *Mouse*. New York: Harcourt Brace Jovanovich.

Yabuuchi, M. (1985). *Whose footprints?* New York: Philomel Books.

Story Songs

A growing number of favorite books put to music and favorite songs published as books are increasingly available. An adult sings as pages are turned. Teachers can introduce this literary experience and encourage children to join in. The added advantage of visual representations helps induce child singing. The novelty of teacher singing a book also offers a possible incentive for the child to select this type of book because of his or her familiarity with an already memorized and perhaps enjoyed song. Word recognition is sometimes readily accomplished.

Popular books of this type include:

de Paola, T. (1984). *Mary had a little lamb*. New York: Holiday House.

McNalley, D. (1991). *In a cabin in a wood*. New York: Cobblehill/Dutton.

Kovalski, M. (1987). *The wheels on the bus*. Boston: Little Brown.

Criteria for Selection

Consider the attention span, maturity, interests, personality, and age of children you are targeting when selecting books. Developing broad literary and artistic tastes is another important idea.

The following is a series of questions a teacher could use when choosing a child's book.

1. Could I read this book enthusiastically, really enjoying the story?
2. Are the contents of the book appropriate for the children with whom I work?
   a. Can the children relate some parts to their lives and past experience?
   b. Can the children identify with one or more of the characters?
      Look at some children's classics such as Mother Goose. Almost all of the stories have a well-defined character with whom children have something in common. Teachers find that different children identify with different characters—the wolf instead of one of the pigs in "The Three Little Pigs," for example.
   c. Does the book have directly quoted conversation?
      If it does, this can add interest; for example, "Are you my mother?" he said to the cow.
   d. Will the child benefit from attitudes and models found in the book?

Many books model behaviors that are unsuitable for the young child. Also, consider the following questions when analyzing a book for unfavorable racial stereotypes or sexism:

- Who are the "doers" and "inactive observers"?
- Are characters' achievements based on their own initiative, insights, or intelligence?
- Who performs the brave and important deeds?
- Is value and worth connected to skin color and economic resources?
- Does language or setting ridicule or demean a specific group of individuals?
- Are individuals treated as such rather than as one of a group?
- Are ethnic groups or individuals treated as though everyone in that group has the same human talent, ability, food preference, hair style, taste in clothing or human weakness or characteristic?
- Do illustrations capture natural looking ethnic variations?
- Does this book broaden the cross-cultural element in the multicultural selection of books offered at my school?

- Is the book accurate and authentic in its portrayal of individuals and groups?

3. Was the book written with an understanding of preschool age-level characteristics? See Kathryn Galbraith's *Katie Did!* (Atheneum, 1983).
   a. Is the text too long to sit through? Are there too many words?
   b. Are there enough colorful or action-packed pictures or illustrations to hold attention?
   c. Is the size of the book suitable for easy handling in groups or for individual viewing?
   d. Can the child participate in the story by speaking or making actions?
   e. Is the fairy tale or folktale too complex, symbolic, and confusing to have meaning? See *East of the Sun and West of the Moon* (Norway) or "Beauty and the Beast" (France) (examples of traditional folktales with inappropriate length, vocabulary, and complexity for the young child). Although some educators debate offering "life's realities" to young children, others think folktales may help them face fears.

4. Is the author's style enjoyable?
   a. Is the book written clearly with a vocabulary and sequence the children can understand? See Mercer Mayer's *There's a Nightmare in My Closet* (Dial, 1969). Are memorable words or phrases found in the book?
   b. Are repetitions of words, actions, rhymes, or story parts used? (Anticipated repetition is part of the young child's enjoyment of stories. Molly Bang's *Ten, Nine, Eight* (Greenwillow, 1983) contains this feature.)
   c. Does the story develop and end with a satisfying climax of events?
   d. Are there humorous parts and silly names? The young child's humor is often slapstick in nature (pie-in-the-face, all-fall-down type rather than play on words). The ridiculous and far-fetched often tickle them. See Tomie de Paola's *Pancakes for Breakfast* (Harcourt, Brace, Jovanovich, 1978), a wordless book.

5. Does it have educational value? (Almost all fit this criteria.)
   a. Could you use it to expand knowledge in any special way? See Maureen Roffey's *Home, Sweet Home* (Coward, 1983), which depicts animal living quarters in a delightful way.
   b. Does it offer new vocabulary? Does it increase or broaden understanding? See Masayuki Yabuuchi's *Animals Sleeping* (Philomel, 1983), for an example.

6. Do pictures (illustrations) explain and coordinate well with the text? Examine Jane Miller's *Farm Counting Book* (Prentice Hall, 1983) and look for this feature.

Some books meet most criteria of the established standards; others meet only a few. The age of attending children makes some criteria more important than others. Schools often select copies of accepted old classics (figure 9–5). These titles are considered to be part of our cultural heritage, ones that most American preschoolers know and have experienced. Many classics have been handed down through the oral tradition of storytelling and can contain archaic words, such as stile and sixpence. Most teachers try to offer the best in children's literature and a wide variety of book types.

Culturally Conscious and Culturally Diverse Books

Yokota (1993) defines multicultural children's literature as literature that represents *any* distinct cultural group through accurate portrayal and rich detail. She urges teachers to evaluate multicultural children's literature using two criteria: (1) literary quality and (2) cultural consciousness.

Cai and Bishop (1994), searching for a definition of multicultural literature, found that numerous definitions agree that multicultural literature is about some identifiable "other," a person or group, that differs in some way (for example, racially, linguistically, ethnically, culturally) from the Caucasian American cultural group.

A PARTIAL LISTING

Ba, Ba, Black Sheep	Little Girl With a Curl	Rock-A-Bye Baby
Chicken Little	Little Jack Horner	Row, Row, Row Your Boat
The Crooked Sixpence	Little Miss Muffet	Silent Night
Goldilocks and the Three Bears	Little Red Hen	Simple Simon
Here We Go Round the Mulberry Bush	Little Robin Redbreast	Sing a Song of Sixpence
Hey Diddle, Diddle (the Cat and the Fiddle)	London Bridge is Falling Down	Take Me Out to the Ball Game
Hickory, Dickory, Dock	Mary Had a Little Lamb	The Three Bears
Humpty Dumpty	Mary, Mary, Quite Contrary	The Three Billy Goats Gruff
Jack and Jill	Old King Cole	The Three Blind Mice
Jack and the Beanstalk	Old Mother Hubbard	The Three Little Pigs
Jack Be Nimble	The Old Woman Who Lived in a Shoe	To Market
Jack Sprat	Peter Piper	Twinkle, Twinkle, Little Star
Little Bo Peep	Pop Goes the Weasel	Ugly Duckling
Little Boy Blue	Ride a Cock Horse (Banbury Cross)	You Are My Sunshine

FIGURE 9–5   Stories, songs, rhymes, and poems considered classics for preschoolers. Many can be found in picture book form.

The National Council of Teachers of English (1994) estimates multicultural and multiethnic themes, settings, and characters in children's literature constitute only 3 to 4 percent of the 15 to 18 thousand new books published during the years 1990 to 1992. As NCTE points out:

> Literature educates not only the head, but the heart as well. It promotes empathy and invites readers to adopt new perspectives. It offers opportunities for children to learn to recognize our similarities, value our differences, and respect our common humanity. In an important sense, then, children need literature that serves as a window onto lives and experiences different from their own, *and* literature that serves as a mirror reflecting themselves and their cultural values, attitudes, and behaviors.

The books listed in figure 9–6 not only include African Americans, Asian Americans, Hispanic Americans/Latinos, and Native Americans but also subgroups of different and distinct groups under each heading. Other world groups are also included. Books recommended in figure 9–6 need teacher previewing for age-level appropriateness because books for both younger and older preschoolers are included.

When offering multicultural and multiethnic books to young children, no attempt to give these books special status is suggested. Child questions and comments that arise are discussed as all interesting books are discussed. These books aren't shared only at certain times of year or for recognized celebrations but are included as regular, standard classroom fare.

Harris (1993) believes the following characteristics are part of authentic multiethnic/multicultural literature:

- Books include the range of character types or people found within the culture, though not necessarily in one book. The characters should not be idealized, but neither should stereotypes predominate. There should be doctors, teachers, truck drivers, cooks, and individuals with other occupations.

Armstrong, J. (1995). *Wan Hu is in the stars.* New York: Tambourine. Traveling the heavens on a homemade rocket.

Arnold, T. (1987). *No jumping on the bed!* New York: Dial Books. Depicts apartment house living.

Ashley, B. (1991). *Cleversticks.* New York: Crown. Multiracial class with Chinese American child who questions his capabilities.

Bang, M. (1986). *Ten, nine, eight.* New York: Greenwillow. A counting book depicting African Americans.

Bruchac, J., & Ross, G. (1995). *The story of the Milky Way.* New York: Dial Books. Presents a Cherokee legend with colorful illustrations.

Buchanan, K. (1994). *This house is made of mud/Esta casa está hecha de lodo.* Flagstaff, AZ: Northland. In both Spanish and English poetic language about a home made of mud.

Caines, J. (1998). *I need a lunch box.* New York: Harper & Row. Young child in African American family wishes for a lunch box like his older sister has.

Carlstrom, N. (1992). *Northern lullaby.* New York: Philomel Books. A poetic lullaby set in Alaska featuring native people. (For older preschoolers.)

Chocolate, D. M. (1992). *My first Kwanzaa book.* New York: Scholastic. For older four- and five-year-olds.

Clark, A. N. (1941). *In my mother's house.* New York: Viking. Poetic Pueblo lifestyles.

Cummings, P. (1991). *Clean your room, Harvey Moon.* New York: Bradbury Press. African American family life.

Dale, P. (1987). *Bet you can't.* Philadelphia: Lippincott. African American brother and sister clean room at bedtime.

Daly, N. (1986). *Not so fast Songololo.* New York: Margaret K. McElderry Books. Explores family life in South Africa.

Emberley, R. (1990). *Taking a walk: A book in two languages/Caminando: Un libro en dos linguas.* Boston: Little Brown. A colorful book with identifying labels in English and Spanish.

Falwell, C. (1992). *Shape space.* New York: Clarion Books. Geometric shapes are encountered with an African American dancer.

Feeney, S. (1980). *A is for aloha.* Honolulu, HI: University of Hawaii Press. Active Hawaiian preschoolers.

Galbraith, K. (1987). *Waiting for Jennifer.* New York: Margaret K. McElderry Books. Ethnic diversity in story characters.

Giovanni, N. (1996). *The genie in the jar.* New York: Holt. Rhythmic read-aloud with a message of self-esteem and self-discovery.

Greenfield, E. (1991). *I make music.* Inglewood, CA: Black Butterfly Children's Books. Rhythmic and rhyming, this book encourages young children to join in.

Greenfield, E. (1991). *My doll Keshia.* Inglewood, CA: Black Butterfly Children's Books. A predictable text about a child and doll play.

Greenspun, A. A. (1991). *Daddies.* New York: Philomel Books. Photographs of dads and children of diverse cultures.

Hale, I. (1992). *How I found a friend.* New York: Viking. Interracial friendship.

Hale, S. J. (1990). *Mary had a little lamb.* New York: Scholastic. Child attending a racially mixed school visits a farm in Maine.

Hill, E. S. (1990). *Evan's corner.* New York: Viking Penguin. African American family life.

Hoffman, M. (1987). *Nancy no-size.* New York: Oxford University Press. A middle child's self-concept in an urban African American family is examined.

Hughes, S. (1985). *When we went to the park.* New York: Lothrop, Lee & Shepard Books. Multiethnic theme and illustrations.

Hutchins, P. (1993). *My best friend.* New York: Greenwillow. Friendship between African American children.

Johnson, J. (1986). *Police officers: A to Z.* New York: Walker. Multiethnic photographs.

Joose, B., & Lavelle, B. (1991). *Mama do you love me?* San Francisco: Chronicle Books. Child questions the love of her Inuit mother.

Keats, E. J. (1964). *Whistle for Willie.* New York: Viking Press. A well-known classic featuring an African American child.

Kleven, E. (1996). *Hooray, a pinata.* New York: Dutton. A diverse way to celebrate birthdays and other special days.

MacKinnon, D. (1992). *My first ABC.* Hauppauge, NY: Barron's Educational Series. Multiethnic photographs, nonsexist, and displays both upper- and lowercase alphabet letters.

Marcellino, F. (1996). *The story of little Baboji.* New York: Harper Collins/Michael di Capua. An authentic tale set in India.

FIGURE 9–6   Multiethnic, multicultural book list   *continues*

McMillan, B. (1991). *Eating fractions.* New York: Scholastic Books. Math concepts interestingly presented while presenting interracial friendship.

Mora, P. (1992). *A birthday basket for Tia.* New York: Macmillan. A Mexican American family celebrates a special aunt's birthday.

Morris, A. (1992). *Tools.* New York: Lothrop, Lee and Shepard Books. Around the world encountering tool use.

Roe, E. (1991). *Con mi hermano/With my brother.* New York: Bradbury Press. A loving relationship between Mexican American brothers.

Russo, M. (1992). *Alex is my friend.* New York: Greenwillow. Child's disability handled with feeling.

Sage, J. (1991). *The little band.* New York: Margaret K. McElderry Books. A multiethnic band in a multicultural town depicts racial harmony.

Samton, S. W. (1991). *Jenny's journey.* New York: Viking Penguin. Interracial friendship.

Say, A. (1991). *Tree of cranes.* Boston: Houghton Mifflin. Japanese boy is introduced to Christmas.

Schaefer, C. L. (1996). *The squiggle.* New York: Crown. Asian child delights in imaginative play.

Schertle, A. (1985). *My two feet.* New York: Lothrop, Lee and Shepard Books. Explores the commonality of everyone's use of their feet.

Sierra, J. (1996). *Nursery tales around the world.* New York: Clarion. An international collection of folktales.

Simon, N. (1976). *All kinds of families.* Morton Grove, Il: Albert Whitman. Portrays diverse families and family life.

Waters, K., & Slovenz-Low, M. (1990). *Lion dancer: Ernie Wan's Chinese New Year.* New York: Scholastic. Color photographs capture a Chinese New Year celebration in New York.

Weiss, N. (1992). *On a hot, hot day.* New York: P. Putnam's Sons. Multicultural setting deals with ways to cool off in extra heat.

Williams, V. B. (1990) *"More more more," said the baby.* New York: Greenwillow Books. Love and life with multiethnic families with babies.

Yolen, J. (Ed.). (1992). *Street rhymes around the world.* Honesdale, PA: Boyds Mill Press/Wordsong. Children's rhymes and counting songs from a wide range of countries.

Young, R. (1992). *Golden bear.* New York: Penguin. A golden bear is this African American child's friend. Text rhymes.

Zalben, J. (1988). *Beni's first Chanukah.* New York: Henry Holt. Family traditions are experienced by a small child.

FIGURE 9–6   *continued*

- Illustrations should not consist of caricatures of a group's physical features. Rather, the illustrations should reflect the variety found among members of any group.

- Speech adopted by characters should have linguistic authenticity.

- Names of characters should reflect cultural traditions of a group.

- Food should not be used as a shorthand signifier of a group; for example, *rice* is not a code word for Asian or Asian American.

- The beliefs and values of characters as well as their world views should reflect the diversity found in the group's communities.

- Writers should understand pivotal family roles and family configurations.

- Members of groups should portray members as intelligent problem solvers.

- Authenticity derives from insider knowledge about a culture acquired as a member or through extensive study, observation, and interaction.

Because of the increasing cost of books and book buying increasingly becoming a middle- and upper-class phenomenon, educators will have to lead the movement for ensuring that working-class and poor children have opportunities with books that reflect their cultures, are popular, and are deemed classics (Harris, 1993).

Parents interested in book purchase can be urged to buy through school-sponsored book clubs and to investigate local library book sales, used book stores, thrift shops, yard sales, and less expensive paperback classics.

Bishop (1990) has observed a shift in the content in picture books depicting African Americans:

... more ... folk tales, more picture books retelling family stories and family histories, more books for the very young ... and more books which include people from the Caribbean.

As Reimer (1992) points out, "Hispanic" children's literature does not refer to one culture but rather a conglomerate of Central and South American cultures. Hispanics, though one of the largest and fastest growing populations in the U.S., are poorly represented in children's literature. Books that exist are often folktales or remembrances of an author's childhood. Books always need to be screened thoroughly for classism, sexism, and portrayals of helpless, passive caricatures.

In picture books classified as depicting the Asian culture, one may find Chinese, Japanese, Korean, Taiwanese, Laotian, Vietnamese, Cambodian, and Filipino cultural experiences depicted. Increasingly, published books about Asians deal with Asian assimilation into the American mainstream. One can find numerous books dealing with Asian folktales. Yet to be written are plentiful picture books from the Vietnamese, Cambodian, and Laotian cultures.

Books concerning Native Americans can be easier to locate. Most are folktales, but some deal with rituals, ceremony, everyday life, family joys, and problems. Again, the teacher needs to screen for stereotypical characteristics.

Teacher resources for finding multicultural books follow:

Beilke, P. F., & Sciara, F. (1986). *Selecting materials for and about Hispanic and East Asian children and young people.* Hamden, CT: Shoe String Press/Library Professional Publications.

Council on Interracial Books for Children, 1841 Broadway, New York, NY 10023.

Gilliland, H. (1980). *Indian children's books.* Billings, MT: Montana Council For Indian Education.

Jenkins, E. C., & Austin, M. C. (1987). *Literature for children about Asians and Asian Americans.* New York: Greenwood Press.

Lindgren, M. V. (Ed.). (1991). *The multicolored mirror: Cultural substance in literature for children and young adults.* Fort Atkinson, WI: Highsmith Press.

Manna, A., & Brodie, C. S. (Eds.). (1992). *Many faces, many voices: Multicultural literacy experiences for youth.* Fort Atkinson, WI: Highsmith Press.

Marantz, K., & Marantz, S. (1993). *Multicultural picture books: Art for understanding others.* Worthington, OH: Linworth Publishing, Inc.

McCann, D., & Woodward, G. (Eds.). (1985). *The Black American in books for children* (2nd ed.). Metuchen, NJ: Scarecrow Press.

Miller-Lachmann, L. (Ed.). (1992). *Our family, our friends, our world: An annotated guide to significant multicultural books for children and teenagers.* New Providence, NJ: R. R. Bowker.

Multicultural Big Books. New York: Macmillan Publishers.

Schon, I. (1978). *Books in Spanish for children and adults: An annotated guide.* Metuchen, NJ: Scarecrow Press.

Slapin, B., & Seale, D. (1988). *Books without bias: Through Indian eyes.* Berkeley, CA: Oyate Press.

Bibliotherapy

Bibliotherapy, literally translated means book therapy. Teachers, at times, may seek to help children with life problems, questions, fears, and pain. Books, some professionals believe, can help children cope with emotional concerns. At some point during childhood, children may deal with rejection by friends, ambivalence toward a new baby, divorce, grief, or death, along with other strong emotions (Smith and Foat, 1982).

Fairy tales can reveal the existence of strife and calamity in a form that permits children to deal with these situations without trauma (Bettelheim and Zelan, 1981), and these tales can be shared in a reassuring, supportive setting that provides a therapeutic experience. A small sampling of books considered to be therapeutic in nature follows:

Alexander, M. (1971). *Nobody ever asked me if I wanted a baby sister.* New York: Dial. (Jealousy)

Blegvad, L. (1985). *Banana and me*. New York: Margaret K. McElderry Books. (Fear)

Brown, M. B. (1960). *The first night away from home*. New York: Franklin Watts, Inc. (Security)

Dragunwagon, C. (1976). *Wind rose*. New York: Harper and Row. (Birth)

Hazen, B. S. (1987). *Fang*. New York: Atheneum. (Bravery)

Le Tord, B. (1987). *My Grandma Leonie*. New York: Bradbury Press. (Death)

Mayer, M. (1968). *There's a nightmare in my closet*. New York: The Dial Press. (Fear)

Noonan, J. (1971). *The best thing to be*. Garden City, NY: Doubleday. (Feelings about being small)

Udry, J. M. (1961). *Let's be enemies*. New York: Harper. (Vacillating friends)

Viorst, J. (1973). *The tenth good thing about Barney*. New York: Atheneum. (Death of a pet)

A much wider selection of such titles is in print. The following resource books are helpful to preschool teachers looking for books dealing with strong feelings:

Bernstein, J. E. (1977). *Books to help children cope with separation and loss*. New York: R. R. Bowker. (A listing of book titles)

Dreyer, S. (1980). *The book finder*. Circle Pines, MN: American Guidance Services Inc. (Books are listed by their themes; synopsis and author/illustrator information is included.)

Gillis, R. J. (1978). *Children's books for times of stress*. Bloomington, IN: Indiana University Press. (An annotated bibliography categorized under headings covering anger, overweight, hospital stays, illness, rivalry, guilt, fear, bravery, hate, rejection, along with other feelings and problem areas.)

Griffin, B. K. (1986). *Special needs bibliography: Current books for/about children and young adults regarding social concerns, emotional concerns, the exceptional child*. DeWitt, NY: The Griffin.

Bernstein (1977) urges parents and teachers to use books to open conversations in which children express grief:

It is from adults that they learn their behavior patterns for the future; whether grieving is normal and permissible or whether it is forbidden and wrong and a source of discomfort. Perhaps the most important aspect of helping young people cope with loss is the willingness of adult guides to expose their own grief while at the same time encouraging children to express theirs. For the way in which adults handle trauma determines youngsters' abilities to survive, physically and mentally, and they can come forth from crisis strong and ready once again to celebrate life.

Reading Books to Young Children

Teachers read books in both indoor and outdoor settings, to one child or to many. If a child asks for a story and a teacher is available, the book is shared. Planned reading, called story times, are also part of a quality early childhood program.

Because of the importance of reading to children, teacher techniques need to be carefully planned and evaluated. Most of us have seen well-meaning adults use reading techniques that are questionable and defeat the adult's purpose in reading. Bettelheim and Zelan (1981) emphasize the importance of teaching methods in the following:

If we wish to induce children to become literate persons, our teaching methods should be in accordance with the richness of the child's spoken vocabulary, his intelligence, his natural curiosity, his eagerness to learn new things, his wish to develop his mind and his comprehension of the world, and his avid desire for the stimulation of his imagination ... in short, by making reading an activity of intrinsic interest.

The burden of making reading interesting falls on the teacher. Building positive attitudes takes skill. A step-by-step outline is helpful in conducting group story times.

Step 1

Think about the age, interests, and special interests of the child group and consider the selection criteria mentioned in this chapter. Read the book to yourself enough times to develop a feeling for characters and the story line. Practice dialogue so that it will roll smoothly. For example, you might not be able to read *The House That Jack Built* unless you have practiced the incremental refrain (Stewig, 1977). In other words, analyze, select, practice, and prepare.

Step 2

Arrange a setting with the children's and teacher's comfort in mind. The illustrations should be at children's eye level. A setting should provide comfortable seating while the book is being read. Some teachers prefer small chairs for both children and teachers; others prefer rug areas. Avoid traffic paths and noise interruptions by finding a quiet spot in the classroom. Cutting down visual distractions may mean using room dividers, curtains, or furniture arrangements.

Step 3

Make a motivational introductory statement. The statement should create a desire to listen or encourage listening: "There's a boy in this book who wants to give his mother a birthday present"; "Monkeys can be funny, and they are funny in this book"; "Have you ever wondered where animals go at night to sleep?"; "On the last page of this book is a picture of a friendly monster." Then briefly introduce the author and illustrator.

Step 4

Hold the book to either your left or right side. With your hand in place, make both sides of the page visible. Keep the book at children's eye level.

Step 5

Begin reading; try to glance at the sentences and turn to meet the children's eyes as often as possible, so your voice goes to the children. Also watch for children's body reactions. Speak clearly with adequate volume, using a rate of speed that enables the children to both look at illustrations and hear what you are reading. Enjoy the story with the children by being enthusiastic. Dramatize and emphasize key parts of the story but not to the degree that the children are watching you and not the book. Change your voice to suit the characters, if you feel comfortable doing so. A good story will hold attention and often stimulate comments or questions.

Step 6

Answer and discuss questions approvingly. If you feel that interruptions are decreasing the enjoyment for other children, ask a child to wait until the end when you will be glad to discuss it. Then do it. If, on the other hand, most of the group is interested, take the time to discuss an idea. Sometimes, children suck their thumbs or act sleepy during reading times. They seem to connect books with bedtime; many parents read to their children at this time. By watching closely while reading, you will be able to tell whether you still have the attention of the children. You can sometimes draw a child back to the book with a direct question like "Debbie, can you see the cat's tail?" or by increasing your animation or varying voice volume. Wondering out loud about what might happen next may help.

Step 7

You may want to ask a few open-ended discussion questions at the end of the book. Keep them spontaneous and natural—avoid testlike questions. Questions can clear up ideas, encourage use of vocabulary words, and pinpoint parts that were especially enjoyed. "Does anyone have a question about the fire truck?" You will have to decide whether to read more than one book at one time. It helps to remember how long the group of children can sit before getting restless. Story times should end on an enthusiastic note, with the children looking forward to another story. Some books may end on such a satisfying or thoughtful note that discussion clearly isn't appropriate; a short pause of silence seems more in order. Other times, there may be a barrage of child comments and lively discussion.

Many children's comments incorporate the story into their own personal vision of things and indicate that the text has meaning for them (Miller, 1990). Personal meanings are confirmed, extended, and refined as children share their interpretations with others (Golden, Meiners, Lewis, 1992). The focus in after-book discussions is on meaning, and the goal is to "make sense of the text" (Goodman, 1986).

Independent Reading

Teachers should examine daily programs to ensure children time to pursue favorite books and new selections. It is ridiculous to motivate then not allow self-selection or time for children to spend looking at and examining introduced books page by page at their own pace. Most rooms have book areas or libraries.

Additional Book-Reading Tips

- Check to make sure all of the children have a clear view of the book before beginning.
- Watch for combinations of children sitting side by side that may cause either child to be distracted. Rearrange seating before starting.
- Pause a short while to allow children to focus at the start.
- If one child seems to be unable to concentrate, a teacher can quietly suggest an alternative activity to the child. Clear understanding of alternatives or lack of them needs to be established with the entire staff.
- Moving a distracted child closer to the book, or onto a teacher's lap, sometimes works.
- When an outside distraction occurs, recapture attention and make a transitional statement leading back to the story: "We all heard that loud noise. There's a different noise made by the steam shovel in our story. Listen and you'll hear the steam shovel's noise."
- Personalize books when appropriate: "Have you lost something and not been able to find it?"

- Skip ahead in books, when the book can obviously not maintain interest, by quickly reading pictures and concluding the experience. It's a good idea to have a backup selection close by.
- Children often want to handle a book just read. Plan for this as often as possible. Make a quick waiting list for all who wish to go over the book by themselves.
- Plan reading sessions at relaxed rather than rushed or hectic times of day.
- Handle books gently and carefully.
- Remember it is not so much what you are reading but how you read it (Jaronczyk, 1984).
- Choose material to suit yourself as well as the group. Select a story type that you like. Practice projecting your voice (Jaronczyk, 1984).
- Lower your voice or raise your voice and quicken or slow your pace as appropriate to the text. Lengthen your dramatic pauses, and let your listeners savor the words and ideas (Dopyera and Lay-Dopyera, 1992).
- Periodically point to things in illustrations as the text refers to them, and sweep your fingers under sentences to emphasize the left-to-right pattern of reading (Dopyera and Lay-Dopyera, 1992).
- Read a book a child has brought to school before you read it aloud to children. (Share suitable "parts" only if necessary.) (Glazer, 1981)
- Handle a child comment such as, "I've heard it before" with a recognizing comment such as, "Don't tell how it ends," or "See if you see something different this time." (Glazer, 1981)

Child Interruptions During Story Time

A slight debate exists as to the degree that child questions and comments during story time mar or enhance the experience for all group members. One position holds that a book should be enjoyed without any loss of flow that diminishes the book's intent and effect. The other position is expressed by Bos (1988): "It's important that we keep conversation going even if we never get to the end of the story." Teachers and schools have arrived at a number of techniques, which follow. It's a good idea to discuss courses of action at a school where you are employed, volunteering, or student teaching. Teachers can decide to:

- save all comments until the end, or
- answer and accept comments up to the point that they feel the story is being sacrificed, or
- make certain books "taboo" for discussion: "This book is one we won't talk about until the end."

Studies of young children's questions during storybook review show, in general, that questions about the book's pictures predominate, while questions about the meaning of the story rank second (Schickedanz, 1993).

Paraphrasing Stories

Paraphrasing means putting an author's text into one's own words. By tampering with the text, the a teacher may interfere with a book's intent, message, and style. Many professionals find this objectionable and urge teachers to read stories exactly as they are written, taking no liberties, respecting the author's original text. When a book doesn't hold the interest of its audience, it should be saved for another time and place, perhaps another group. Some teachers feel that maintaining child interest and preserving the child's positive attitude about books supersedes objections to occasional paraphrasing.

Building Participation

Children love to be part of the telling of a story. Good teachers plan for child participation when choosing stories to read. Often books are read for the first time, and then immediately reread, with the teacher promoting as much participation as possible. Some books hold children spellbound and usually take many readings before the teacher feels that it is the right time for active involvement other than listening. Copperman (1982) believes that listening skills are encouraged to develop when "children contribute to read-aloud sessions" and become active, participating listeners.

Miller (1990) believes group readings have five distinct benefits: (1) they encourage discussion of the text; (2) discussions help generate meaning and serve as checks on the meaning constructed by individuals; (3) they cause a social experience to develop around the sharing of literature; (4) children share knowledge with one another; and (5) classmates answer questions as well as the teacher.

Miller (1990) points out three-year-olds take a while to settle into appropriate and expected story-time behaviors. A young group may, as Miller observes, "reach out physically in territorial battles over pillows, places for feet, or stuffed toys. Later they reach out with questions, ideas, and comments."

Nonfiction books may not provide as much material for child involvement.

Examining story lines closely can give the teacher ideas for children's active participation. Many of the benefits young children derive from adult-child readings come through active child participation and adult reading strategies:

> Several strategies have proven particularly helpful to children: prompting their responses, scaffolding or modeling responses for them, getting them to relate responses to real experiences, asking them questions, and offering positive reinforcement for their comments and questions. (Strickland and Morrow, 1989)

Here is a list of additional ways to promote child participation and active listening:

1. Invite children to speak a familiar character's dialogue or book sounds. This is easily done in repeated sequences: "I don't care," said Pierre.

2. Pantomime actions: "Let's knock on the door."

3. Use closure: "The cup fell on the . . ." (floor). When using closure, if children end the statement differently, try saying "It could have fallen on the rug, but the cup in the story fell on the floor."

4. Predict outcomes: "Do you think Hector will open the box?"

5. Ask opinions: "What's your favorite pie?"

6. Recall previous story parts: "What did Mr. Bear say to Petra?"

7. Probe related experiences: "Emil, isn't your dog's name Clifford?"

8. Dramatize enjoyed parts or wholes.

Younger preschoolers, as a rule, find sitting without active motor and/or verbal involvement more demanding than older ones.

Reading to Individual Children

Teachers without aides and/or volunteers in their classroom may never have undivided time to share books with individual children. One-on-one readings can be the most beneficial and literacy-developing times of all. The dialogue possible and the personalized interaction exceeds group readings. In large groups, some children are reluctant to speak, and consequently receive less appreciation and feedback. (Small groups are recommended.)

Busy parents can tend to rely on schools to offer books. Many centers have been clever in promoting home reading. Bulletin boards, lending arrangements, or mandating parent classroom participation are among the most common tactics.

It's not the simple "I-read-you-listen" type of adult-child interaction with books that really counts. It's the wide-ranging verbal dialogue the adult permits and encourages that gives children their best opportunity to construct a full knowledge of how people use books (Smolkin and Yaden, 1992). Schools consequently include and share reading techniques in their communications with parents.

Teachers should plan times to be in the classroom's book center, book corner, library, book-reading area (whatever it's called!). A teacher's presence models interest and allows for individual child readings, questions, and interactions other than at planned group book times.

Rereading Stories

It never ceases to amaze teachers and parents when preschoolers beg to hear a book read over and over.

Beginning teachers take this statement to mean they've done a good job, and even veteran teachers confess it still feels good. Ornstein and Sobel (1987) note that young children enjoy repetition more than older children or adults. A teacher who can read the same book over and over again with believable enthusiasm, as if it were his or her first delighted reading, has admirable technique and dedication. Children often ask to have stories reread because, by knowing what comes next, they feel competent, or they simply want to stretch out what's enjoyable. The decisions that teachers make about fulfilling the request depends on many factors including class schedules and children's desire but lack of capacity to sit through a second reading. It is suggested that books be reread often and that teacher statements such as "I'd like to read it again, but . . ." are followed by statements such as "After lunch, I'll be under the tree in the yard, if you want to hear the story again."

Holdaway (1991) believes the request to "read it again" arises as a natural developmental demand of high significance and an integral part of book exposure. The child's behavior alerts adults to which book(s) hold and preoccupy them. Teachers can think of the behavior as children selecting their own course of study. Multiple copies of favorite books may be deemed necessary and advantageous.

A curious response occurred when the same story books were read and reread to four-year-olds in Martinez and Roser's study (1985). The researchers attempted to identify the consequences of rereading familiar and enjoyed stories. Children in the study made more detailed comments centering on characters, events, titles, story themes, settings, and the book's language with rereadings. Other results suggest as children understand particular aspects of stories (gained through numerous rereadings) they shift focus and attend to additional story dimensions overlooked in initial readings.

Spencer (1987) suggests additional possible benefits in adult's rereading of child favorites. Children experience:

- story schema
- the structure of plots
- anticipation of events

- memory of what happened from a previous reading
- the way in which language is used to create the effects of surprise, climax, and humor

In a related study, Morrow (1988) found that participation in one-to-one, read-aloud events increased the quantity and complexity of the children's responses.

Following this line of research, early childhood educators intent on literacy development would plan to reread familiar, favorite story books to both groups and individual children.

"I Can Read" Teacher!

Early childhood practitioners with any experience have encountered children who want to "read" to their teacher or peers. Teachers often smile, hypothesizing that the child is using rote memory, but often the child tells the story in his or her own words. Holdaway (1991) points out that detailed study of this child behavior suggests some of these children displayed a deep understanding of and response to central story meanings. Comparing older and younger children displaying "I-can-read" behavior, both older and younger children told stories using their own level of spoken language, not by memorizing the book's vocabulary or word-for-word grammar but rather by memorizing the book's meaning.

Using Visuals During Story Times

There are a number of reasons teachers decide to introduce books with objects or other visuals. A chef's hat worn by a teacher certainly gets attention and may motivate a group to hear more about the chef in the picture book. A head of lettuce or horseshoe may clarify some feature of a story. The possibilities are almost limitless. Currently, with the popularity of theme or unit approaches to instruction, a picture book may expand or elaborate a field of study or topic that has already been introduced. If so, some new feature mentioned in a book may be emphasized by using a visual.

When the teacher wears an article of clothing, such as the hat mentioned above, it may help him or her get into character. Since children like to act out story lines or scenes, items that help promote this activity can be introduced at the end of the story. Previewing a picture book may make it easier to find an object or person that could add to the story-telling experience.

A teacher at one center wanted to enlarge illustrations in a book that was a classroom favorite. She first used an overhead projector and outlined the enlarged figures on chart paper. She displayed these as she read the book. The experience was enjoyed, and she found posting the enlarged characters around the room drew child interest. Another favorite book was photographed and made into slides. Reading the book in a darkened area with a flashlight while projecting the slides held the children spellbound. One child asked if they could "go to the movies" again.

After-Reading Discussions

How soon after a story is read should discussion, which promotes comprehension of stories, take place? It is obvious that a discussion might ruin the afterglow that occurs after certain books are shared. Teachers are understandably reluctant to mar the magic of the moment.

A number of researchers, including Roser and Martinez (1985), conclude teachers can promote children's growth as "responders to literature." Cochran-Smith (1984) sees the teacher's role during storybook readings as acting as a "mediator" who assists children in two ways: (1) by helping them to learn to take knowledge they had gained outside of book-reading experiences and use this knowledge to understand the text, (2) by helping them apply the meanings and messages gained from books to their own lives. Teachers often wonder what type of questions to ask to stimulate book discussions. Open-ended questions work well: "What do you think Asam should do?" "How would you try to find the lost shoe?" "In what ways are your toys different from Ling's toys?" Questions concerning how children feel about book features are helpful. Inviting child responses, and reacting with close accepting listening is suggested. The teacher who conjectures, connects, appreciates, muses, challenges, and questions shows the child how the mature responder interacts with text (Martinez and Roser, 1992).

Hansen and Graves (1992) urge teachers to build on what children say rather than trying to impart or transmit information. The teacher's focus in asking questions in an after-book discussion is not to check children's knowledge, but rather to learn from the child. Cochran-Smith (1984) describes preschool teacher's story-reading discussions as negotiated, non-focused interactions in which teachers become aware of the "sense-making" children express.

The process depends on what children say about their confusions, interpretations, and what they understand together with the teacher's response to the meaning the group seemed to make of the story. Teachers who believe children "construct" their own knowledge will be more apt to try this type of after-book discussion.

After children listen and participate at story-time, the teacher can assume children have both understandings and questions. Langer (1992) suggests responding to literature involves the raising of questions. Discussion after a book, if teacher deems it appropriate, can focus on student responses and questions. Langer (1992) suggests the following teacher questions: "How did you feel at the end of the story (book)?" "Is there anything you want to talk about?" or "Are there any questions about the pictures you saw in the book?"

Research suggests that a discussion of the literal meaning of storybook text may foster beginning literacy development (Dickinson and Snow, 1987). Anderson (1988), referring mainly to elementary school reading, states that "there needs to be a strong emphasis on teaching comprehension," and early childhood teachers could at times consider asking what Anderson calls "artful questions" that draw attention to major elements of characterization and plot and the moral or deeper implications of a story, if appropriate. The solution that many teachers favor is to wait until children seem eager to comment, discuss, and perhaps disagree, and only then act as a guide to further comprehension. The opportunity may present itself after repeated readings of favorites or after a first reading. Teachers hope children will think out loud, sharing their ideas with the discussion group. All present are given the opportunity to respond or add comments and cite personal experiences. Those children more interested in other pursuits can be allowed to drift away. Discussion is akin to a small community (with teacher included) sharing ideas. Teachers using post book-reading discussions believe book content, word meanings, and ideas are best remembered if talked about.

Teachers should take special care to avoid asking testlike questions at the conclusion of book readings, because it discourages open and natural discussion. Unfortunately, many adults have had this kind of questioning in their own elementary schooling, so they automatically and unconsciously copy it.

Some centers designate a time after a story is read as "story time talk" (Roser, Hoffman, Labbo, Forest, 1992). It's described as a time when children's ideas are recorded by teacher on a "language chart" made of chart paper or butcher paper. This activity gives importance to children's ideas. Names by contributions afford additional status. Children's art related to the book can be appended. Other schools make basket collections of inexpensive small plastic or other material figures of story characters, animals, houses, story objects, and so on to go along with a book. These are so popular one teacher made home-sewn story dolls for the school basket collection.

Story or Book Dramatization

Some early childhood educators encourage child dramatization of favorite picture books and stories. Research suggests young children's recollection of literal story details and their comprehension of story features is enhanced.

Planning for book enactment means teachers start with simple enactments, and display various props, objects, costumes, etc. to serve as motivator and "get-into-character" aids. In previewing picture books or oral stories for story times, teachers become accustomed to looking for material with repeated words, sentences, or actions. These are the books or story parts that are easy to learn. In the telling of *The Three Little Pigs*, most children will join in with "then I'll huff, and I'll puff and I'll blow your house down!" after just a few tellings.

Picture Books as the Basis for Theme Instruction

Early childhood centers are experimenting with using picture books as the basis for theme programming. Under this approach to program planning, instruction branches out from the concepts and vocabulary present in the book. Usually, the meaning of the story is emphasized, and a number of different directions of study and activities that are in some way connected to the book are conducted. Eric Carle's *The Very Hungry Caterpillar* is a favorite theme opener.

The classroom setting can be transformed into the cabbage patch that Peter Rabbit was so fond of exploring. Activities such as counting buttons on jackets, singing songs about rabbits or gardens, field trips to vegetable gardens, and science experiences in vegetable growing are a few examples of associated activities. A "Stuffed Toy Animal Day" invites children's own favorite to class for story time. Memorable experiences connected to classic books can aid literacy development, and an increasing number of preschools are using this approach in language arts programming.

Literature-Based Curriculum

Literature-based reading instruction is sweeping the nation. Many states have either recommended or mandated this elementary school approach. Advocates, such as Huck (1992), have identified a comprehensive literature program as permeating the curriculum. It includes reading aloud to children,

making use of informational books, and encouraging children's response to books using drama, art, and child-dictated writing.

Can an early childhood teacher implement a "literature-based" language arts program? Most early childhood teachers would answer "Yes, if activities are developmentally appropriate, literature can permeate program planning."

From Books to Flannel (Felt) Boards and Beyond

Teachers find that a number of books can be made into flannel board stories relatively easily; Chapter 12 is devoted to these activities. Five books that are particular favorites have been adapted:

- *The Very Hungry Caterpillar* by Eric Carle
- *The Carrot Seed* by Ruth Kraus
- *Jony and His Drum* by Maggie Duff
- *My Five Senses* by Aliki
- *Brown Bear, Brown Bear, What Do You See?* by William Martin

Books often open the door to additional instruction through activities or games on the same subject or theme. Whole units of instruction on bears, airplanes, families, and many other topics are possible.

Teachers have attempted to advertise particular books in creative ways. Enlarged book characters might be displayed, or displays of the book of the week or book of the day may be placed in a special spot in a classroom. An attending child's mother or father may be a special story-time book reader. Bev Bos (1988), in discussing morning greetings to children, states "Many times I may have a new book in my lap and then share the cover to set the excitement about story time."

Library Skills and Resources

A visit to the local library is often planned for preschoolers. Librarian-presented story hours often result in the children's awareness of the library as a resource. Selecting and checking out one's choice can be an exciting and important milestone. Most preschools also do their best to encourage this parent-child activity.

Many libraries have well-developed collections and enthusiastic and creative children's librarians who plan a number of activities to promote literacy. Along with books, you may find computers, language-development computer programs, audio and video tape cassettes, records, book and tape combinations, slides, films, children's encyclopedias, foreign language editions, pamphlet collections, puzzles, and other language-related materials and machines.

Finding out more about the authors of children's books can help to provide teachers with added insights and background data. One goal of language arts instruction should be to alert children to the idea that books are created by real people. Most children find a photograph of an author or illustrator interesting, and discussions about authors and authorship can help to encourage children to try their hand at writing books.

Becoming more familiar with authors such as Margaret Wise Brown, often called the "Laureate of the Nursery," helps a reader appreciate the simplicity, directness, humor, and the sense of the importance of life that are found in her writings. The following books give helpful background data on authors:

Doyle, B. (1971). *Who's who in children's literature.* New York: Schocken.

Hopkins, L. B. (1969). *Books are by people.* New York: Scholastic Magazine.

The following resources include autobiographical and biographical sketches:

de Montreville, D., & Crawford, E. D. (Eds.). (1978). *Fourth book of junior authors and illustrators.* New York: Wilson.

Hoffman, M., & Samuels, E. (1972). *Authors and illustrators of children's books.* New York: R. R. Bowker Co.

Kirkpatrick, D. L. (1978). *Twentieth-century children's writers.* New York: St. Martins Press.

Some early childhood centers set up author displays, celebrate author/illustrator birthdays, and encourage visiting authors and illustrators. Letters to authors might be written with child input.

A teacher who has done some reading and wants to mention or quote the children's favorite authors might use items like the following that were found in the preceding resources:

- from Steven Kellogg, author/illustrator of *Can I Keep Him?* "I particularly loved (as a child) drawing animals and birds."

  or

  "I made up stories for my younger sisters." (*Fourth Book of Junior Authors and Illustrators*)
- from Mitsumasa Anno, author/illustrator of *Anno's Alphabet*, "The imaginative eye is the source of all the books I have made for children." (*Fourth Book of Junior Authors and Illustrators*)
- from Eric Carle, author/illustrator of *The Very Hungry Caterpillar*, "I remember large sheets of paper, colorful paints and big brushes" (speaking of childhood). (*Authors and Illustrators of Children's Books*)
- from Leo Lionni, author/illustrator of *Little Blue and Little Yellow,* "I like to write about birds because I have birds at home: parrots, pigeons, chickens and finches." (*Authors and Illustrators of Children's Books*)

Child- and Teacher-Authored Books

Books authored by children or their teachers have many values.

- They promote interest in the classroom book collection.
- They help children see connections between spoken and written words.
- The material is based on child and teacher interests.
- They personalize book reading.
- They prompt self-expression.
- They stimulate creativity.
- They build feelings of competence and self-worth.

If a child-authored book is one of the school's books, the book corner becomes a place where the child's accomplishment is exhibited. Teachers can alert the entire group to new book titles as the books arrive and make a point to describe them before they are put on the shelves.

Child-made books require teacher preparation and help. A variety of shapes and sizes (figure 9–7) add interest and motivation. Covers made of wallpaper or contact paper over cardboard are durable. The pages of the books combine child art and child-dictated words, usually on lined printscript paper. Staples, rings, yarn (string), or brads can bind pages together (figure 9–8). Child dictation is taken word for word with no teacher editing.

The following book, dictated by a four-year-old, illustrates one child's authorship.

The Window

Page 1: Once upon a time the little girl was looking out the window.
Page 2: Child's Art
Page 3: And the flowers were showing.
Page 4: Child's Art
Page 5: And the water was flushing down and she did not know it.
Page 6: Child's Art

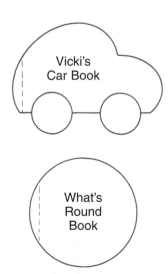

FIGURE 9–7

BOOKBINDING

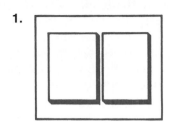

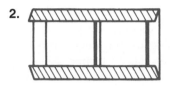

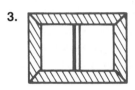

FIGURE 9–8

Teacher-authored books can share a teacher's creativity and individuality. Favorite themes and enjoyed experiences can be repeatedly relived. Books containing the children's, teachers', staff's, parents', or school pets' names are popular. Photographs of familiar school, neighborhood, or family settings are great conversation stimulators. Field trips and special occasions can be captured in book form.

Lentz and Burris (1985) suggest using what they call caption books with young children. Their caption books carefully place the print in the top left of the page, include photographs that give clues to the print message on the same page, and use short meaningful sentences that repeat on succeeding pages. These writers also suggest teacher-made books that record nature walks, seasonal events, and holiday celebrations. An additional suggestion from Lentz and Burris (1985) involves urging children to illustrate their favorite stories with their own art.

Group authorship is another idea. Books in which every child has contributed one or more pages are enjoyable projects and discoveries.

Book Areas and Centers

Classrooms with inviting book storage areas beckon curious browsers. Books should be at the child's eye level with book front covers in sight. Book-jacket wall displays and life-size book characters (drawings made by using overhead projectors to increase size then tracing on large sheets of paper) have their own appeal. Comfort and color attract. Softly textured rugs and pillows, comfortable seating, and sprawling spaces prolong time spent in book areas. Low round tables and plump pillows used as seating can also be inviting. Quiet, private spaces that are shielded from outside distractions and sounds and that have good lighting increase the child's ability to stay focused (figure 9–9). Hideaways where friends can escape together and experience a book that has captured their attention are ideal.

Guidelines that outline the rules and responsibilities of book handling should be developed by

FIGURE 9–9   Hiding away to read

the school. Rules should be designed to encourage children to return books to shelves, turn pages carefully, and respect the quietness of the area. Well-defined boundaries of library centers help books stay put. Teachers should promote the idea that using the area is a privilege and monitor book centers frequently when younger preschoolers who may have had little past experience with book collections and libraries enter the area.

What kind of collection should a well-stocked classroom library center have? Collections often reflect a school's budget and priorities. The purchase of classroom favorites and classics should be the first priority; after that, a well-rounded collection that includes a lot of different topics and categories is recommended.

Rotating books by removing and storing some books from time to time and providing a different, previously stored set of books will make the area more interesting. Library books supplement the school's collection and may have special, classroom-handling rules. Seasonal and holiday books are provided when possible. Paperbacks round out some collections, and multiple copies are considered for younger preschoolers' classrooms. Constant book repair is necessary in most classrooms because of heavy use.

Teachers should browse in book centers, modeling both interest and enthusiasm when time and supervision duties permit.

Settings

Most classrooms have areas suitable for picture-book reading in groups, besides areas for individual, self-selected browsing and places where children can be in the company of a few others. If these areas are not available, staff members can create them (figure 9–10). The reading or library area should be comfortable and well lit and as far removed from interruptions and distractions as possible. Generally, lighting that comes from behind the children is preferred. Intense, bright light coming from behind the book can make it hard to see. During group readings, one center put a floor lamp in the reading area, and dimmed the overhead lights. This setup worked well to cut distrac-

FIGURE 9–10 One school acquired a giant stuffed bear for children to sit on and lean on while looking at books with friends.

tions and focus the group on the reading. Another teacher brought a large packing case into the classroom, hooked up a light, added comfortable pillows, made a door, and called it the "Reading Box." A large, horseshoe-shaped floor pillow can increase child comfort. Many centers use small carpet sample squares for comfort and to outline individual space. A shady spot in the play yard may be a good site for teacher's reading on a warm day.

The number of children in groups is an important consideration; as the size of the group increases, intimacy, the child's ease of viewing, and the teacher's ability to be physically close and respond to each child decrease. The ideal group size for story time ranges from 5 to 10 children. Unfortunately, staffing ratios may mandate a much larger group size. Some preschools do "instant replays"—they have many small reading groups in succession, rather than large group reading sessions.

Care and Storage of Books

By setting an example and making clear statements about handling books, the teacher can help children form good book-care habits. However, with time and use, even the sturdiest books will show wear.

Teachers are quick to show their sadness when a favorite book is torn, crayoned, or used as a building block. Some classrooms have signs reading "Books are friends—Handle with Care" or "Books are for looking, talking about, and sharing." Teachers are careful to verbally reward children who turn pages gently and return books to shelves or storage areas.

Resources for Finding Reading Materials

Public Libraries

Many libraries have book lists of suggested early childhood editions. Often, seasonal books are together in special displays. Ask the librarian about new books, special services, or resources that include films or slides.

Children's Book Stores and Toy Stores

Many stores carry popular new and older titles. Some stock as many as 15,000 titles.

Teacher Supply Houses and School Supply Stores

Often a wide selection is stocked, sometimes at school discount prices.

Children's Book Publishers

Catalogs listing new titles, with summaries of contents, are available for the asking.

Teacher Resource Books

Teacher resource books are good sources for finding titles on specific topics or themes.

Resources for Teacher Authors

The following provide tips on writing and publishing children's books:

Writing children's books. (1993). New York: The Children's Book Council.
Publishing children's books in America, 1919–1976. (1987). New York: The Children's Book Council.
Teacher as writer, Karin L. Dahl (Ed.). (1990). NCTE, 1111 Kenyon Road, Urbana, IL 61801.

Book Clubs

Book clubs offer monthly selections of a wide variety of titles. These clubs usually reward schools with free books and teacher gifts that include posters and teaching visuals. Enough order forms for each child's parent are sent on a monthly basis. This offers parents an easy way to order books for their children by having school personnel send and receive orders.

Children's Periodicals

A helpful reference book that describes and evaluates nearly 90 children's magazines is *Magazines for Children: A Guide for Parents, Teachers and Librarians* by Selma Richardson, published by the American Library Association.

Book Week

The Children's Book Council has sponsored National Children's Book Week since 1945 (1989 marked its seventieth anniversary) to promote reading and encourage children's enjoyment of books. Mobiles, materials, posters, bookmarks, and book-week kits can be ordered from:

The Children's Book Council Inc.
67 Irving Place
New York, NY 10003

Book Services to Parents—School Lending Libraries

Preschools that have overnight and weekend book borrowing privileges promote book use and home enjoyment of books. Manila folders or envelopes, preprinted with the center's name, protect books in transit. Book pockets and cards are available at stationery or school-supply stores. This service can operate with minimal teacher supervision. Parents can help their children pull cards on selected titles, if they thoroughly understand the school's system and rules for book borrowing.

Favorite Children's Books

Generally, children's favorites become your favorites. There is really only one way to develop your own list. Preview books and then try them with children. Figure 9–11 provides a list of books that are young children's favorites. Lay-Dopyera and Dopyera (1982) urge beginning teachers to consider the following:

You can help children learn the value of reading first by getting "hooked" on books yourself and then by developing your repertoire for sharing that enjoyment with children.

Brown, M. W. (1938 and 1965). *The dead bird.* New York: Young Scott Books. Deals tenderly with the death of a bird.

Carle, E. (1969). *The very hungry caterpillar.* Collins World. The hungry caterpillar eats through the pictures and emerges as a butterfly on the last page.

Chorao, K. (1977). *Lester's overnight.* New York: E. P. Dutton. Family humor in a child's overnight plans and his teddy bear.

Ets, M. H. (1955). *Play with me.* New York: Viking Press. A lesson to learn on the nature of animals.

Flack, M. (1932). *Ask Mr. Bear.* New York: Macmillan. The search for just the right birthday present for a loved one.

Freeman, D. (1954). *Beady bear.* New York: Viking Press. Meet Beady and his courage, independence, and frailty.

Freeman, D. (1968). *Corduroy.* New York: Viking Press. The department store teddy who longs for love.

Gag, W. (1928). *Millions of cats.* New York: Coward-McCann, Word pleasure and magic—a favorite with both teachers and children.

Guilfoile, E. (1957). *Nobody listens to Andrew.* New York: Scholastic Book Services. An "adults often ignore what children say" theme.

Hazen, B. S. (1974). *The gorilla did it.* New York: Atheneum Press. A mother's patience with a fantasizing child. Humorous.

Hoban, R. (1964). *A baby sister for Frances.* New York: Harper and Row. Frances, "so human," deals with the new arrival.

Hutchins, P. (1968). *Rosie's walk.* New York: Macmillan. A fox is outsmarted.

Hutchins, P. (1976). *Good-night owl!* New York: Macmillan. Riddled with repetitive dialogue: a delightful tale of bedtime.

Hutchins, P. (1971). *Changes, changes.* New York: Macmillan. Illustrations of block constructions tell a wordless story of the infinite changes in forms.

Keats, E. J. (1967). *Peter's chair.* New York: Harper and Row. A delightful tale of family life.

Kraus, R. (1973). *Leo the late bloomer.* New York: Dutton. Wonderful color illustrations and a theme that emphasizes individual development.

Kraus, R. (1945). *The carrot seed.* New York: Harper and Row. The stick-to-it-tiveness of a child's faith makes this story charming.

Leonni, L. (1949). *Little blue and little yellow.* New York: Astor-Honor. A classic. Collages of torn paper introduce children to surprising color transformations, blended with a story of friendship.

Marshall, J. (1989). *Goldilocks and the three bears.* New York: Dial Books for Young Readers. Humorous illustration of old classic in a new setting.

McCloskey, R. (1948). *Blueberries for Sal.* New York: Viking Press. The young of the two species meet.

McMillan, B. (1988). *Growing colors.* Fairfield, NJ: Lothrop, Lee, and Shepard Books. Color photographs of bountiful nature.

Mosel, A. (1968). *Tiki tiki tembo.* New York: Holt, Rinehart, and Winston. A folktale that tickles the tongue in its telling. Repetitive.

Potter, B. (1987). *Peter Rabbit's ABC.* Bergenfield, NJ: Frederick Warne. Clever alphabet letter presentation.

Raskin, E. (1975). *Nothing ever happens on my block.* New York: Atheneum Press. The child discovers a multitude of happenings in illustrations.

Scott, A. H. (1972). *On mother's lap.* New York: McGraw-Hill. There's no place like mother's lap!

Schulevitz, U. (1969). *Rain rain rivers.* New York: Farrar, Straus and Giroux. Illustrative fine art.

Segal, L. (1970). *Tell me a Mitzi.* New York: Farrar. New York city life.

Slobodkina, E. (1947). *Caps for sale.* New York: William R. Scott. A tale of a peddler, some monkeys, and their monkey business. Word play and gentle humor.

Stevens, J. (1987). *The town mouse and the country mouse.* New York: Holiday House. One's own house is best.

Viorst, J. (1971). *The tenth good thing about Barney.* New York: Atheneum. Loss of family pet and positive remembrances.

Viorst, J. (1976). *Alexander and the terrible, horrible, no good, very bad day.* New York: Atheneum Press. Everyone relates to the "everything can go wrong" theme.

Zion, G. (1956). *Harry the dirty dog.* New York: Harper and Row. Poor lost Harry gets so dirty his family doesn't recognize him.

Note: A listing of predictable children's books is included in Chapter 19.

FIGURE 9–11 Favorite children's books—beginner's book list

Parental Influences on Children's Reading-Like Behaviors

Parental influences on the attitudes young children hold about books and book reading times must be considered. When a first book reading time is announced, a newly enrolled child's behavior can reflect unexpected reactions. Under the right circumstances, young children who have developed a liking for books may be similar to the children Doake (1985) describes in the following:

> By being read to regularly from very early in their lives, children soon begin to demonstrate their growing enjoyment of the experience. Their attention span increases, their repertoire of favorite stories expands, and they begin demanding that these be read over and over. Their avid listening to stories in the secure and close proximity of a loved parent becomes a deeply rewarding, warm, human experience for the children and their parents. . . . The children soon begin to develop very high expectations for books and reading.

> Children begin to see books as sources of personal pleasure and derive from them a type of personal satisfaction they can secure in no other way.

Doake (1985) gives insight into parental reading techniques and book selection criteria that facilitate both development and positive child attitude:

> When a powerful inner drive to want to learn and a natural aptitude for learning are coupled with parents who not only select highly predicable stories (Rhodes, 1981) to read to their children, but who read in a way that invites children to participate, then learning to reproduce stories through reading-like behavior becomes a relatively simple process. This learning becomes even easier when it is permitted to operate in a non-corrective no-fail environment where children are encouraged to experiment and approximate in their attempts to "read." When these conditions prevail, children have the opportunity to take the initiative and direct their own learning.

Parental techniques in the previous quote are also used effectively by teachers, especially when reading with very small groups or in one-to-one classroom reading situations. What exactly are the techniques pinpointed by Doake (1985)?

1. a non-corrective, no-fail environment
2. invited child participation
3. encouraging the child to experiment and approximate in their attempts to "read"

And the types of books selected? Predictive.

Reading-like child behavior can include "reading" the book to themselves or others, mumbling words as they page through a book, joining in with the parent on select pages, passages, and/or book character's verbalizations, offering rhyming, repetitive guesses during an adult reading, echoing by "reading" slightly behind the adult. Children may also embellish or deviate from a known familiar story, and then return to the original text.

Doake (1985) mentions another reading-like behavior termed "completion reading," which occurs when a reader pauses and the child completes the sentence or story. Parents seem to know intuitively where to pause in order to invite their children to complete a sentence or phrase.

Reading-like behavior may include early child knowledge of print. Parents may have pointed to print in picture books explaining "it says that here" or "this word is . . ." Early elementary school teachers and some parents may move their hands under words as they read, consequently drawing attention to print. This also gives clues to the direction words are read. A parent may point and ask "What does this say?" Children also may point to words in books asking readers the same question. Many young children come to realize the print in books is significant and connected to what the reader is saying. At this point, children may struggle to understand and some children actually accomplish the unbelievable feat of the real reading of many words. A few children can read simple books and primers before kindergarten, leaving their teachers in awe of the tremendous capacity of some young minds.

Summary

The teacher has certain goals when reading books to young children:

- Promoting child enjoyment and attitude development.
- Acquainting children with quality literature.
- Presenting knowledge.

- Developing children's listening skills.
- Encouraging emerging literacy (figure 9–12).

A careful selection of books makes it easier to reach these goals and gives reading activities a greater chance for success. Books vary widely in content and format. Teachers who are prepared can interact with enthusiasm by showing their own enjoyment of language; this helps promote the children's language growth.

Good book-reading technique requires study and practice. Professional interaction is crucial to achieving goals and instilling a love of books.

Settings for group times need to be free of distraction, with optimal comfort and lighting. Book care is expected and modeled by teachers.

YOUNGER PRESCHOOLERS (Ages 2 to 3)

- Able to sit and maintain interest while a quality picture book is skillfully read.
- Able to browse through a book from cover to cover.
- Has a favorite book.
- Points to and talks about objects, people, or features of illustrations when in individual reading sessions.
- Can name one book character.
- Brings a book to adults to read.

- Wants to be present at most book-reading times.
- Brings a book to school to share.
- Discusses or acts out story parts at times.
- Handles book gently.
- Enjoys library trips.
- May point to words or letters.
- Wants name on his or her work.

OLDER PRESCHOOLERS (Ages 4 to 5)

- Obviously enjoys story times.
- Asks about words.
- Picks out own nametag.
- Knows beginning letters of a few words.
- Wants his or her ideas and comments written down.
- Has favorite books and book characters.
- Can put book events in sequence.
- Realizes books have beginnings, middles, and endings.
- Understands authoring.
- Explains a number of functions of printed words and signs.
- Asks about the names of letters of his or her own name.
- Can tell a book story from memory.
- Handles and cares for books properly.

- Discusses and shares books with others.
- Finds similar letters in different words.
- Knows spaces exist between words.
- Recognizes a few words.
- Tries to decipher words in books.
- Knows stories in books don't change with rereadings.
- Interested in alphabet games, toys, and activities.
- Tries to copy words or letters from books.
- Knows alphabet letters represent sounds.
- Interested in machines or toys that print words or letters.
- Wants to make his or her own book.
- Knows books have titles and authors.
- Creates own stories.

FIGURE 9–12 Emerging literacy indicators

STUDENT ACTIVITIES

1. Select, prepare, and present three books to children. Evaluate your strong points and needed areas of growth.

2. Read a children's book to two classmates or to a video camera; take turns evaluating the presentations.

3. Form two or more groups for a debate. The topic is "Technical reading-skill development during story times—should it take place?" An example of technical reading-skill development activities would include finding similar alphabet letters, phonics, reading sight words, and so on.

4. Visit a preschool classroom new to you. After observing, develop a book list (10 books) for the class, indicating why each was selected.

5. Interview a local librarian concerning the children's book collection and library services.

6. Pretend you are to make a presentation about the desirable elements and formats of picture books to a sixth, seventh, or eighth grade class interested in creating and then sharing their picture book creations with a small group of preschoolers. What would be your key points? What guidelines or tips concerning reading to preschoolers would you present? List your answers.

7. Create a self-authored picture book. Share it with a small group of young children. Share results, outcomes, and your feelings with fellow students.

8. Visit the local library. Using the form for analyzing a children's book (figure 9–13), review five books.

9. Do you believe as does Harris (1993) that to author authentic multicultural or multiethnic literature the author either has to have "lived" the experience or studied it deeply? Participate in a class discussion after first listing your main points.

10. Develop an annotated book list (10 books) using short descriptions, as follows:
    Zion, Gene. *Harry the Dirty Dog*. New York: Harper and Row Publishers, 1956. About a family dog who gets so dirty his family doesn't recognize him.
    Select books published after 1990.

11. Make a list of five nonfiction books that could be used with preschoolers.

12. Find a picture book that could be used with a group of children that might lead to a discussion of peace making, negotiation, conflict resolution, or identification of a conflict situation. Share with class.

13. Present a short oral report about Caldecott and Newbery Medal books.

14. Read the following quotation from Barbara Elleman:

    My subject today, however, is stereotypes less noticeable and less noticed that have surfaced over my many years of reading and writing about children's books. Or, perhaps they are noticed after all. In my March editorial, "Intergenerational Relationships," I mentioned that children today most likely have grandparents who are younger and more active than those depicted in most stories, who seem to be closer in age and physical

Name _____   Date _____

Name of Book _____

Author _____

Illustrator _____

Story Line

1. What is the book's message? _____

_____

_____

2. Does the theme build the child's self-image or self-esteem? How? _____

_____

_____

3. Are male and female or ethnic groups stereotyped? _____

4. Why do you consider this book quality literature? _____

_____

Illustrations

1. Fantasy? True to Life? _____

2. Do they add to the book's enjoyment? _____

_____

General Considerations

Could you read this book enthusiastically? Why?

How could you involve children in the book? (besides looking and listening)

How could you "categorize" this book? (i.e., firefighter, alphabet book, concept development, emotions, and so on)

On a scale of 1–10 (1—little value to 10—of great value to the young child) rate this book. _____

FIGURE 9–13   Form for analyzing a children's book

condition to the grandparents of those writing and illustrating the books. The resulting chorus of agreement has made me realize that I am not alone in being bothered by these skewed portrayals of the elderly.

This, in turn, triggered thoughts about another stereotype of the elderly that is perpetrated without much comment. An older character who is scruffily dressed, eccentric, and has a sinkful of unwashed dishes, dust an inch high, and a menagerie of dogs or cats in tow is almost always depicted as warm, caring, thoughtful, and sympathetic. But let a character be neatly dressed and coifed, keep a tidy house and yard, and be meticulous in lifestyle, and the resulting image is nearly always that of, at the least, a disagreeable person.

For some reason, the orderliness-equals-nastiness equation is often associated in children's books with affluence. In addition to being very meticulous, the wealthy are nearly always depicted as mercenary, arrogant, and unscrupulous schemers. And as for offspring of affluent parents, they are too-often portrayed as conceited, haughty, and vain. What books do you know that find the wealthy kid on the block the nice one?

Books containing these or any stereotypes shouldn't necessarily be dismissed because of their failings; instead, portrayals should be talked about with children. They should know that one can be neat and still be nice, that affluence isn't always corrupt, that someone from a monied family isn't necessarily a snob. Stereotypes won't disappear by sweeping them under the rug; they are best met head-on through discussion and sharing. It's another reason to read with and to children." (Elleman, 1995)

Discuss with a group of peers. Report the group's comments.

15. Review an issue of *Book Links* and report your findings, opinions, and comments to the class at its next meeting. Use notes and be specific about book titles, authors, magazine articles, and the publication date of the issue you selected.

16. Record yourself reading a favorite story. A book and tape can fit into a flapped large manila envelope with a pictorial representation of the book's main character on the envelope's front. Share your recording with a classmate.

17. Obtain two copies of an inexpensive paperback picture book. Make stick puppets out of characters, objects, and buildings by cutting them out of one copy. Read the book to a small group of preschoolers, and introduce the stick puppets. Put the book and puppets together in a box or basket. Ask which children would like a turn. Have paper and pencil available for a waiting list. Report your experiences to the class.

18. Write a one-page autobiography about your own young childhood experiences with books, magazines, or comics. Name specific books you remember and/or the people who read them to you. Try to capture your feelings. If you have few preschool memories, concentrate on formal reading instruction in elementary school, and/or teachers who read to you and what they read.

19. In a group of 3 to 5 classmates share a wordless book. Read and react to the following quote. Report your group's comments to the total class.

Wordless books demand that readers take more responsibility for making predictions and constructing plot than books with predictable texts do.

(From Galda, L., Carr, E., & Cox, S. (November 1989). The plot thickens. *The Reading Teacher*, *43*(2). Newark, DE: IRA, 160–164.

20. Janine, a student teacher, made the following observation of her cooperating teacher's story time.

Every child was seated on a carpet square cross legged with hands in laps. Mrs. Cordell asked all to "zip their lips and open their ears." Mrs. Cordell started reading the first page with enthusiasm and expression. She used theatrical talent, changing her voice to fit character dialogue. Josh asked a question and Mrs. Cordell simply put her finger to her lips shushing him and then went ahead with her dramatic presentation that included a loud voice which mesmerized the children. She stopped once to ask Ryan to sit still on his carpet square and a few times to praise individual children for their attention. Children focused on Mrs. Cordell spellbound but seemed later to start wiggling toward the book's end. They bolted from the reading circle after Mrs. Cordell excused them. I was surprised none of them wanted to talk about the book. I felt I'd seen a teacher performance I couldn't match and dreaded the future when I'd read a picture book and she'd watch me.

React with written notes to be used for a class discussion. Write questions about the student teacher's observation that you'd like answered in the class discussion.

21. Design a preschool classroom library center. Include materials and furnishings and show room features such as windows and doors and adjacent activity areas.

22. Review three all-time best-sellers: *The Tale of Peter Rabbit* by Beatrix Potter; *The Real Mother Goose* published by Rand McNally; and *Pat the Bunny* by Dorothy Kunhardt. Give reasons for the popularity of these books.

23. Observe a classmate reading to a small group of preschool children. Complete figure 9–14.

CHAPTER REVIEW

A. Read the following comments by a teacher who is reading to children. Select those comments that you feel would help the child accomplish a goal mentioned in this chapter.

1. "Sit down now and stop talking. It's story time."

2. "Kathy, can you remember how the mouse got out of the trap?"

3. "What part of this story made you laugh?"

4. "John, I can't read any more because you've made Lonnie cry by stepping on her hand. Children, story time is over."

5. "Children, don't look out the window. Look at the book. Children, the book is more interesting than that storm."

6. "Donald, big boys don't tear book pages."

7. "Was the dog striped or spotted? If you can't answer, then you weren't listening."

8. "Mary, of course you liked the story. Everyone did."

9. "Tell me, Mario, what was the boy's name in our story? I'm going to sit here until you tell me."

10. "No, the truck wasn't green, Luci. Children, tell Luci what color the truck was."

	Yes	Can't Determine	No

1. Reader's name: _____
2. Brief description of group (age, number, etc.): _____
3. Location: _____
   Setting: _____
4. How was group gathered? _____
   _____

5. Seating comfort considered? _____
   All saw and heard? If not, explain. _____
   _____
   _____

6. Interesting introduction? _____
7. Title and author mentioned? _____
8. Reader's voice appropriate? _____
   If not, describe problem. _____
   _____

9. Read with expression?
   Appropriate? If not, explain. _____
   _____

10. Book suitable for group?
    If not, explain. _____
    _____

11. Book familiar enough for reader to read with ease? _____
12. Did reader give attention and expression to "special" or
    "unique" words, phrases, sentences, or dialogue? _____
    _____

13. How did reader initiate group discussion of story? _____
    _____

14. Were child comments respected and accepted?
    If not, explain. _____

15. Any unusual child reactions to book?
    If yes, explain. _____

16. What reader skills impressed you? _____
    _____

17. What reader skills need attention? _____
    _____

18. How would you rate this book's holding power on a scale
    of 1 (low) to 10 (high)? _____

FIGURE 9–14 Picture book reading rate sheet

11. "Take your thumb out of your mouth, Debbie; it's story time."

12. "You all looked at the book and told me what was in each picture."

13. "One book is enough. We can't sit here all day, you know."

14. "Children, we have to finish this book before we can go outside. Sit down."

15. "That book had lots of colorful pictures."

16. "Well, now we found out who can help us if we ever lose mama in a store."

B. Answer the following questions:

1. Why is it important for the teacher to read a child's book before it is read to the children?

2. How can a teacher help children learn how books are used to find answers?

3. Why should a teacher watch for the young child's reactions to the story while reading it?

C. Select the best phrases in Column II that apply to items in Column I.

Column I	**Column II**
1. fairy tales	a. before teacher starts reading to the group
2. first step in planned reading	
3. arrange setting with comfort in mind	b. when children show interest in a subject
4. stop storytelling to discuss it	c. a book with violence
5. not appropriate for early childhood level	d. book may not be appropriate for this age level
6. children become restless	e. may be too frightening
7. directly quoted conversation	f. "Tick-tock," said the clock
8. "And I'll huff and I'll puff and I'll blow your house down."	g. teacher reads the book beforehand
	h. repetition in "The Three Little Pigs"
9. "So they all had a party with cookies and milk." The End.	i. identification
10. "The rabbit is just like me, I can run real fast."	j. a satisfying climax to a story
	k. in an upright position with the front cover showing
11. a book should be read and held	l. at children's eye level
12. books are more inviting when stored this way	

D. Describe in step-by-step fashion how you would plan and conduct a group story time.

E. Choose the true statements. Each question may have none or more than one true statement.

1. A book's format
   a. is defined by its content.
   b. includes paper weight.
   c. includes size and shape.
   d. can frustrate children.

2. A teacher's goals when sharing books with children can include
   a. to give information.
   b. to promote literacy.
   c. to build attitudes.
   d. to make them aware of print.
   e. to teach listening behavior.

3. Bibliotherapy refers to books that are
   a. nonfiction.
   b. focused on life's happy moments.
   c. helpful in promoting reading skills.
   d. colorful and well illustrated.
   e. written by people with problems.

4. When it comes to different types of books for young children,
   a. most are suitable.
   b. many contain exceptional art.
   c. the fewer words, the greater the enjoyment.
   d. a wide variety exists.
   e. there are more factual than fantasy books published.

5. When preparing to read a picture book to a group of young children, the following was recommended:
   a. Be prepared to dramatize so that children watch you closely.
   b. Skip over old-fashioned words.
   c. Practice until it easily rolls over your tongue.
   d. The larger the audience the more vivid the experience.
   e. Speak in character dialogue, if it's comfortable for you.

6. Multicultural picture books are
   a. offered to children only at special times and during celebrations.
   b. treated the same as other classroom books.
   c. difficult to obtain depicting a wide variety of ethnic groups.
   d. widely available and account for about 30 percent of children's picture books published after 1990.

F. What types of resources are available to teachers who want books with specific themes for young children? List.

G. Describe a prudent way to handle books children bring to school for the teacher to read aloud.

H. Why should teachers read and then reread books to young children?

RESOURCE

McCord, S. (1995). *The storybook journey*. Columbus, OH: Merrill.

CHAPTER 10

Storytelling

OBJECTIVES

After studying this chapter, you should be able to:

- describe how storytelling can help language growth.

- list teacher techniques in storytelling.

- demonstrate the ability to create a story that meets suggested criteria.

- describe promotion of child-created stories.

Storytelling is a medium that an early childhood teacher can develop and use to increase a child's enjoyment of language. When good stories are told by a skilled storyteller, the child listens intently; mental images may be formed. Storytelling enables teachers to share their life experiences and create and tell stories in an individual way. It is a teacher's gift of time and imagination (Gage and Cooksey, 1992).

Rivers (1996) describes the individuality and improvisations possible in storytelling:

> You know you have to hit certain key points in the story, but how you get there is up to you.

Beginning teachers need not worry that their version of a favorite or any story differs from others.

Breneman and Breneman (1983) offer the following definition of storytelling:

> ... the seemingly easy, spontaneous, intimate sharing of a narrative with one or many persons: the storyteller relates, pictures, imagines, builds what happens, and suggests characters, involving him- or her-

self and listeners in the total story—all manifested through voice and body.

Storytelling is the act that essentially makes humans human. It defines us as a species (Moore, 1991). We are shaped by the stories we hear (Schram, 1993). In storytelling, children leave the "here and now" and go beyond what's seen and at hand. They experience the symbolic potential of language with words themselves the main source of meaning independent of the time and place they are spoken (Wells, 1985).

Early childhood teachers recognize the importance of storytelling in a full language arts curriculum. Good stories that are well told have fascinated young listeners since ancient times. Chambers (1970) feels that storytelling is a form of expressive art.

> The art of storytelling remains one of the oldest and most effective art forms. The oral story, be it aesthetic or pedagogical, has great value. It seems to be a part of the human personality to use it and want it. The art of the storyteller is an important, valuable ingredient in the lives of children.

The art of storytelling is enjoying a renaissance. The National Storytelling Festival's three-day celebration held in Jonesborough, Tennessee drew 8,000 people in 1996. Storytelling festivals occur in 40 states (McLeod, 1996). America is rediscovering the magic of storytelling. Regional, intergenerational, multicultural, and multiethnic story themes delight audiences.

In many cultures, oral stories have passed on the customs, accumulated wisdom, traditions, songs, and legends. Storytelling is as old as language itself.

The teacher's face, gestures, words, and voice tell the story when books or pictures are not used. Eye contact is held throughout the storytelling period. The child pictures the story in his or her mind as the plot unfolds.

How could one describe skilled storytellers? Sawyer (1969) describes them as gloriously alive, those who live close to the heart of things and have known solitude and silence and have felt deeply. They have come to know the power of the spoken word. They can remember incredible details about a good story that interests them (Bartoli, 1995). Preschool teachers may know silence only at naptimes, but they indeed live close to the heart of young children's forming character and personality and growing intellect.

Storytelling and Literacy

The promotion of oral literacy is an important consideration for preschool program planners. Oral literacy involves a shared background and knowledge of orally told stories plus a level of competence. Being able to tell a story well depends on a number of factors, including observation of techniques. Natural storytellers, if they exist, are overshadowed by storytellers who have practiced the art. Some adult job hunters find telling a story is a requested part of their job interview and is used to assess intelligence, communication ability, and literacy.

Preschools are sure to offer picture-book readings, but storytelling may be neglected. Some teachers shy away from the activity for a variety of reasons, including not being able to hold their child audience. Young children may be so used to illustration and pictures (books and television) that initial storytelling experiences are foreign to them.

Teachers can increase their skills by observing practiced storytellers, taking classes, or self-study. The best suggestion for skill development is starting by relating short, significant happenings in their daily lives—keeping it lively and working with four-year-olds rather than younger children.

As children observe and listen to teacher's storytelling, they notice common elements, including beginnings, middles, and story endings. They discover stories vary little between tellers. They imitate techniques using hand and body gesturing, facial expression, and vocal variation; they speak in character dialogue, and they may even copy dramatic pause. They also may attempt to make their audience laugh or add suspense to their stories.

Wells (1986), author of *The Meaning Makers*, studied 32 children in a longitudinal study lasting 15 years. In six case studies, which concentrated on the children's later educational achievement, she found stories are the way that children make sense of their lives. Stories, she observed, gave meaning to events by making connections between them and the real world. The number of stories children heard before schooling had a lasting effect.

Trousdale (1990) sees an additional benefit that is fostered by adult storytelling—child storymaking.

> Storytelling offers ways to bring children into the act of storymaking, ways of creating stories *with* children not just *for* or *to* children.

Much current research is encouraging teachers to promote child dictation of child-created stories and subsequent dramatization. The teacher then reads the child's work to child groups. Besides the obvious benefits of the speaking and writing involvement in this activity, it is based on child-relevant material. It is believed to open children's inner feelings and thinking processes to change and growth, and increase child self-awareness and awareness of self in relation to others. All in all it is a powerful language arts approach.

Telling Stories Without Books

Chapter 9 described the merits and uses of picture books with young children. Storytelling without books has its own unique set of enjoyed language pleasures. Storytelling is direct, intimate conversation. Arbuthnot (1953) points out the well-told story's power to hold children spellbound (figure 10–1).

> It is the intimate, personal quality of storytelling as well as the power of the story itself that accomplishes these minor miracles. Yet in order to work this spell, a story must be learned, remembered, and so delightfully told that it catches and holds the attention of the most inveterate wrigglers.

Teachers observe children's reactions. A quizzical look on a child's face can help the teacher know when to clarify or rephrase for understanding. A teacher's voice can increase the story's drama in parts when children are deeply absorbed.

Many people have noted how quickly and easily ideas and new words are grasped through storytelling. This is rarely the prime goal of early childhood teachers but rather an additional benefit. Stories are told to acquaint young children with this enjoyable oral language art. Obvious moraliz-ing or attempts to teach facts by using stories usually turns children away.

Storytelling may occur at almost any time during the course of the day, inside or outside. No books or props are necessary. Teachers are free to relate stories in their own words and manner. Children show by their actions what parts of the story are of high interest. The storyteller can increase children's enjoyment by emphasizing these features.

Goals

A teacher's goal is to become a skilled storyteller so he or she can model storytelling skill while providing another avenue to development of oral competence. Another goal is to acquire a repertoire of stories that offer children a variety of experiences.

The teacher's goals include:

- Increasing children's enjoyment of oral language.
- Making young children familiar with oral storytelling.
- Encouraging children's storytelling and authorship.
- Increasing children's vocabulary.
- Increasing children's confidence as speakers.
- Increasing children's awareness of story sequence and structure.

An additional goal by Cooper (1993) follows:

> . . . through stories young children can confront their personal and imaginative worlds so that they may come to understand them.

Storytelling is a wonderful way to promote understanding of audience behaviors, and performer behaviors. Teachers experience rewarding feelings when their technique and story combine to produce audience enjoyment and pleasure. Child storytellers gain tremendous insights into the performing arts, their own abilities, and the power of orally related stories. Most reading experts agree that oral competence enhances ease in learning to read and promotes understanding of what is read.

Thoughtful writers have questioned the wisdom of always exposing children to illustrations at

FIGURE 10–1 Children listen intently to a good story.

story time. By not allowing children to develop mental images, they feel we have possibly distracted children from attaining personal meaning (Bettelheim, 1976).

Using Picture Books for Storytelling

At times, a picture book is the source for storytelling. The teacher later introduces the book and makes it available in the classroom's book center for individual follow-up. Used this way, storytelling motivates interest in books.

There are many picture books, however, that do not lend themselves to storytelling form because illustrations are such an integral part of the experience (figure 10–2). Books that have been successfully used as the basis for storytelling can be handled in unique ways. Schimmel (1978) relates her storytelling experiences with *Caps for Sale* by Slobodkina:

> I like to make it an audience participation story. I shake my fist at the monkeys, and the audience, with only the slightest encouragement, shakes its fists at the peddler.

She recommends the following for use with young children:

The Fat Cat by Jack Kent, New York: Parents Magazine Press, 1971

The Journey, Mouse Tales by Arnold Lobel, New York: Harper & Row Publishers, 1972

The Old Woman and Her Pig by Paul Galdone, New York: McGraw Hill Book Company, 1961

The Three Billy Goats Gruff by P. C. Asbjornsen, New York: Harcourt, Brace, Jovanovich Inc., 1972

An increasing number of classrooms promote acting out stories after they are read. Immediately following this acting experience children are urged to create their own stories. These can be taped and later written by adults. These child stories can also be enacted with the story's author or teacher selecting his or her actors or with actor volunteers.

FIGURE 10–2   Some picture books cannot be used as sources for oral storytelling.

Sources for Stories

A story idea can be found in collections, anthologies, resource books, children's magazines, films, story records, or from another storyteller. A story idea can also be self-created.

A teacher-created story can fill a void. In any group of young children there are special interests and problems. Stories can expand interest and give children more information on a subject. Problems can possibly be solved by the stories and conversations that take place.

New teachers may not yet have confidence in their storytelling abilities, so learning some basic techniques for selecting, creating, and telling stories can help build confidence. This, together with the experience gained by presenting the stories to children, should convince the teacher that storytelling is enjoyable for preschoolers and rewarding to the teacher.

Teachers telling children personal stories about their lives actually "model" storytelling. They also let children know that their actions and words are the stuff of stories too (Jones, 1995). Gestures, facial expressions, body language, and variety in tone of voice is observed. This type of storytelling is a natural part of social interaction. With young children, short anecdotes and humorous life incidents work well.

Story Songs

Many stories can be introduced through song. Some of us remember the delightful folk story song that begins "A fox went out on a chilly night," and tells of the animal's adventures. These types of songs may include opportunities for children's oral, physical, and creative expression, or child involvement in the storytelling. A creative teacher can use story songs to complement, extend, and reinforce a multitude of classroom learnings. Vocabulary meanings are often more apparent to children when learned in the context of a story song.

Simple, quick definitions by teachers are offered in a conversational tone. Imagine the fun involved in a story song about the saga of a lump of dough becoming a loaf of bread: ". . . and they pushed and pulled me. Oh, how they pushed and pulled" or "it's warm in here. I'm getting hot. Look at me I'm growing and turning golden brown."

Selection

The selection of a story is as important as the selection of a book, since stories seem to have individual personalities. Searching for a story that appeals to the teller and can be eagerly shared is well worth the time. A few well-chosen and prepared stories suiting the individual teacher almost ensures a successful experience for all. The following selection criteria are commonly used.

Age-Level Appropriateness

Is the story told in simple, easily understood words? Is it familiar in light of the child's life experiences? Is it frightening? Can the child profit from traits of the characters?

Plot

Does the setting create a stage for what is to come? Is there action? Is there something of interest to resolve? Does the story begin with some action or event? Does it build to a climax with some suspense? Does it have a timely, satisfying conclusion? Are characters introduced as they appear?

The stories you'll be searching for will have one central plot; a secondary plot may confuse children. Action-packed stories where one event successfully builds to another holds audience attention.

Style

Does the story use repetition, rhyme, or silly words? Does it have a surprise ending? Does it include directly quoted conversations or child involvement with speaking or movements? Does the mood help the plot develop?

Values

Are values and models presented that are appropriate for today's children? Screen for ethnic, cultural, and gender stereotypes that would lead you to exclude the story or discuss the issue with children.

Memorable Characters

Look for a small number of colorful characters who are distinct entities that are in contrast to the main character and each other. One should be able to identify and recognize character traits.

Sensory and Visual Images

The visual and sensory images evoked by stories

add interest. "Gingerbread cookies, warm and golden" rather than "cookie" and the "velvet soft fur" rather than "fur" create different mental images. Taste, smell, sight, sound, and tactile descriptions create richness and depth.

Additional Selection Criteria

Elements that make stories strong candidates include:

- An economy of words—a polished quality
- A universal truth
- Suspense and surprise

Themes and Story Structure

Many well-known and loved stories concern a problem that is insightfully solved by the main character. They begin by introducing a setting, and characters and have a body of events that moves the story forward to a quick, satisfying conclusion. The story line is strong, clear, and logical. One category of stories described as cautionary seems to have been designed to keep children safe by teaching a truth or moral, consequently helping children make wise decisions.

Storyteller Enthusiasm

Is the story well liked by the teller? Does the teller feel comfortable with it? Is it a story the teller will be eager to share?

Finding a story you love may make it easier for the child to enjoy the story you tell:

The easiest door to open for a child is one that leads to something you love yourself. All good teachers know this. And all good teachers know the ultimate reward: the marvelous moment when the spark you are breathing bursts into a flame that henceforth will burn brightly on its own (Gordon, 1984).

Types of Stories

Some stories, particularly folktales and fairy tales, have been polished to near perfection through generations of use. Classic tales and folktales may contain dated words and phrases, but these might be important story parts that add to the story's charm. In retelling the story to young children, a brief explanation of these types of terms may be necessary.

Fables are simple stories in which animals frequently point out lessons (morals), which are contained in the fable's last line.

Many great stories seem to have opportunities for active child participation and the use of props. Props, such as pictures, costumes and other objects, may spark and hold interest. A cowboy hat worn by the teacher during the telling of a western tale may add to the mood and can later be worn by children in play or during a child's attempt at story-telling.

Repetitive phrases or word rhythms are used in all types of stories, and chanting or singing may be necessary in the telling. Most stories have problems to be solved through the ingenuity of the main character. This sequence can be explored in teacher's self-created stories.

Story Ideas

Teachers often begin by telling stories from classic printed sources.

Classic Tales

Goldilocks and the Three Bears
Little Red Riding Hood
The Three Little Pigs
Billy Goats Gruff
The Little Red Hen
The Gingerbread Boy

From Aesop's Fables

The Lion and the Mouse

The Hare and the Tortoise
The Ant and the Grasshopper

Traditional Stories

Hans Christian Andersen, *Ugly Duckling*
Arlene Mosel, *Tiki, Ticki Tembo*
Florence Heide, *Sebastian*
Beatrix Potter, *Peter Rabbit*

Practice and Preparation

When a teacher has selected a story, a few careful readings are in order. Try to determine the story's main message and meaning. Next, look closely at the introduction that describes the setting and characters. Study figure 10–3 and analyze how the selected story fits this pattern. The initial setting often sets up a problem or dilemma. The story can be outlined on a 4" × 6" (or larger) cue card to jog your memory during practice sessions (see figure 10–4). Memorizing beginning and ending lines and interior chants or songs is suggested.

Once the story rolls out effortlessly, practice dialogue, pauses, gesturing, and facial expressions. Particular attention should be given to the rising action in the story's body so that one event builds on another until a quick, satisfying conclusion is reached.

In many cultural rituals, an air of magic, soft flickering embers, were part of the storytelling experience. African storytellers would begin, "A story, a story, let it come, let it go" (Sivulich, 1977). Ritual can mean entering a particular "distraction-free" classroom area, lighting a candle, a special teacher hat, dimming lights, a chant, or a special finger play that settles and brings anticipation. One clever teacher created a story sack, and reached inside and slowly raised her hand to her mouth before beginning. Another teacher found only short action-packed stories containing many move-the-body features appealed to his group of three-year-olds.

Sivulich (1977) has advice for early childhood storytellers:

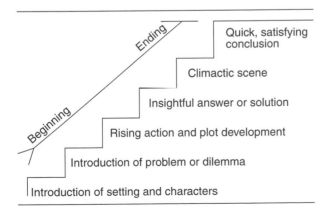

FIGURE 10–3 Common and classic story pattern form

Intro. "Once upon a time, there were four little rabbits, Flopsy, Mopsy, Cottontail, and Peter. They lived with their mother in a sand-bank, underneath the root of a very big fir tree."

Theme. Mind your mother.

Problem. Peter disobeys and goes into McGregor's garden.

Rising action.

Peter squeezes under garden gate and eats a lot.
McGregor sees him.
McGregor chases him, and he loses a shoe.
Peter gets caught in a gooseberry net and loses his jacket.
Peter hides in the tool shed in a can full of water.
Peter sneezes, almost gets caught, but jumps out a window.
Peter cries and sees cat (another danger).
Peter makes a dash for the gate and gets free.
Gets home without clothes and shoes, goes to sleep, and misses dinner. Mother serves Peter tea.

Ending lines.

"But Flopsy, Mopsy, and Cottontail had bread and milk and blackberries for supper. And that's the end of the Tale of Peter Rabbit!"

FIGURE 10–4 Cue and file card example

Having learned a story that you like and that is suited to your group, the next step is to "live" it. The most important part of the process is the desire or urgency to tell the story . . . in a sense, you can think of storytelling as "literary gossip!"

Stewig (1977) suggests the following steps in preparing a story:

The first is to divide the story into *units of action*. As you read the story, you will notice that most divide into an easily definable series of actions or episodes; these can be summarized in brief form, and then the sequence can be learned. The second task is to identify those sections which do need to be memorized verbatim. This may include some words, some repeated phrases, or perhaps some larger sections. A discerning storyteller learns verbatim these repeated sections, because the repetition encourages children to join in as the teller recites the lines.

Additional Techniques

The following techniques and tips should be kept in mind:

- Guard against sounding mechanical. Tell the story in your own personal way.
- Become familiar with the key ideas. Know the key happenings and their order of appearance in the story.
- Practice before a mirror or with another staff member.
- Enjoy and live the story as you tell it in your own words. Use gestures.
- Maintain eye contact by scanning the group during the telling; watch for children's interest or restlessness.
- Pace the storytelling by going faster during exciting or fast-action parts and slower in serious parts.

- Use a clear, firm voice. Try changing voice volume and tone to fit the story; in some parts of the story a whisper may be most effective. Change your voice to fit the characters when they speak.
- Make gestures natural complements of the story (large and descriptive for younger children).
- Involve the children often, especially with repetitions, rhymes or actions, silly words, or appropriate questions, if the story lends itself to this.
- Sit close to the group; make sure all are comfortable before beginning.
- Include teacher's and children's names and familiar places in the community to clarify meanings or add interest in teacher-created stories.
- Start by telling little personal stories about your family, pets, and daily happenings, if you're a novice; then move on to simple stories with lots of repetition.
- Investigate the cultural backgrounds of children in your care and see if you can find stories that reflect these backgrounds (Leone, 1986).
- Seek out talented storytellers in your community to observe your storytelling or to appear as guest storytellers in your classroom.
- Become very familiar with any pronunciations, including proper names and foreign or unfamiliar terms in stories.
- Use dramatic pauses to build suspense, after an exclamation, or to facilitate transitions between story events.
- Try to communicate characters' attitudes and motivations.
- Use a different tone of voice for dialogue only if you feel comfortable doing so.
- Consider the flavor and language of the particular tradition from which the story comes (Peck, 1989).
- Storytelling comes from the imagination. Let it unfold like a movie in your mind (Moore, 1991).
- Slow down. Tales are best shared when spoken at half of normal conversation speed (Moore, 1991).

Even the best storytellers have an occasional flop. If the storyteller senses that the children are restless, the story may be ended very quickly and tried at a later time, using a revised version.

Teacher storytelling is far from a one-way affair. While engaged in the telling the teller is sensitive to audience reaction. Listeners' facial expressions, body language, or oral responses such as laughter, gasps, and sighs are indicators that guide the timing, pitch, and volume of the teller's voice (Peck, 1989).

Teacher-Created Stories

Many teachers find that they have a talent for creating stories and find that a popular character in one story can have further adventures in the next. Don't forget that "bad guys" in stories are enjoyed as much as "good guys." Having a problem that needs to be resolved serves as the basis for many well-known classics.

Whenever a teacher cannot find a story that seems tailor-made for a particular group of children, he or she can create a story. As teachers use their own stories, they tend to cut and add to them based on the reactions of the children. Take care that themes do not always revolve around "mother knows best" episodes, and watch for sexism and stereotypes when creating a story.

Child-Created Stories

Storytelling is probably the first situation in which the child must sustain a monologue without the support of a conversational partner (Stenning and Mitchell, 1985). It's a complex cognitive endeavor that involves a kind of "story sense" and "story grammar." To be coherent, a child's story needs to be more than an unrelated series of events, as is often the case with beginning child storytellers. As children are exposed to stories told and stories read, they construct their own ideas about the linguistic features of narrative storytelling. They use their stories as a way of expressing certain emotionally important themes that preoccupy them and of symbolically managing or resolving

these underlying themes (Nicolopoulou, Scales, Weintraub, 1994).

Cooper (1993) believes despite our best efforts, we just don't reach young children on the inside, where they hide their stories. She states:

> The real tragedy in failing to reach even the youngest children in our care does not stem from the children, or their much publicized "lack of preparation" for school, or their "unreadiness to learn" but from our lack of response to their personal and developmental histories—in other words, to who they are and how they think.

Watching children's dramatic play, teachers will see stories "acted out" rather than told. They will be spontaneous, creative, natural, and seemingly much easier and enjoyable than the act of child storytelling. Teachers can appreciate children actors in dramatic play situations for they create their own script, improvise, develop characters in the roles they have chosen or been assigned. At times, dramatic play may seem a series of unrelated events, but surprisingly the teacher will witness many logically flowing scenarios . . . stories in action . . . preschool "soaps."

Encouraging child authorship and child storytelling goes hand-in-hand with teacher storytelling. It is an excellent way to develop fluency and elaborated language usage (Hough, Nurss, Wood, 1987). One suggestion is to offer activities in which pictures or props are used as motivators (figure 10–5). Children's attempts aren't edited or criticized but simply accepted. Logic should not be questioned, nor should the sequence of events be corrected. Each story is special. Teachers can think of dictated child stories as print awareness activities. Young children may have had limited experiences with adults printing their ideas. Child story dictation presents another use of print—a personal important use. Cooper (1993) gives teachers added insights into the possible benefits:

> The fact is that beginning writers don't write because they have something they

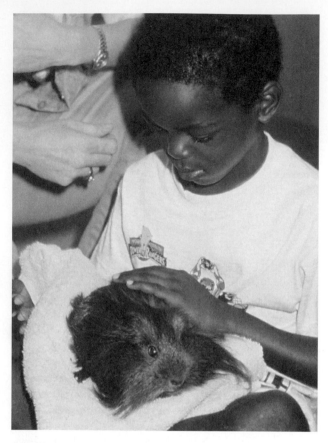

FIGURE 10–5   A visiting small animal might promote child storytelling.

for child volunteers to retell stories to other children works in some programs; an announcement may be made that Mark or Susie will be sitting in the storyteller's chair after snack. Teachers tactfully remind children before the volunteer starts his or her story that questions or comments will be saved until the story is over. An adjacent box of story-telling props may help a child get in character. If teacher has told *Goldilocks and the Three Bears* using three stuffed bears, a yellow-haired doll, three doll beds, three doll house chairs, chances are children will want to use the same props for their own telling of the story.

Clipboards can be used to list the stories that are created throughout the day. The creation of stories is given status, and sharing these stories is a daily occurrence. Sharing takes place with the child's permission, and the child chooses whether he or she or the teacher will present the story to the group.

Children's first storytelling attempts often lack sequence, have unclear plots, ramble, and involve long, disconnected events; as children mature and are exposed to stories and books, authorship improves. The goal is not to produce child storytellers but to encourage a love for and positive attitudes toward oral storytelling.

Strickland and Feeney (1992) trace the development of child storytelling:

> . . . the first evidence of the developing sense of story in children is their use of language to create a special or private world. This is thought to be the forerunner to the child's use of language to create a world of make-believe, involving dramatic play . . . and leading to the gradual acquisition of the specific conventions that constitute a sense of story. As children mature, their stories increase in length and complexity. . . . Children gradually gain greater control over the events in their stories, moving from a loose collection of related events to tightly-structured narratives which link a set of events to each other and to a common theme. (Applebee, 1978)

want to say, they write in order to discover what they have to say, just as they play with blocks, and on the playground, letting ideas flow. This is why I see dictation as so valuable to the young storyteller. Subtly and over time, dictation helps teach the child-author that a written story is merely an oral one put into print.

If recorded or dictated, the story should be taken verbatim. Some teachers initiate discussions that allow the children to tell what they liked best about a story to alert children to desirable story features. Egg timers may be useful if rambling, long-winded children leave little time for others. Asking

Successful Dictation

The following teacher techniques when taking dictation are suggested by Weitzman (1992):

- Do encourage storytelling in unstructured situations; e.g., during free play, sensory-creative activities, outdoor play, and meal and snack time.
- Do listen carefully to stories.
- Do invite all children to tell stories.
- Do make leading statements that invite children to tell a story.
- Do make comments that relate to the child's story. You can encourage children to continue their story with comments such as "That must have been so scary, getting lost in the supermarket!"
- Do ask a sincere question to help the child continue with his story.
- Do ask questions to make the child aware of information which is unclear or missing.
- Don't make children's storytelling a large group activity.
- Don't interrupt or change the topic.
- Don't turn the story into a "lesson" or "test."

Cooper (1993) suggests teachers act in the dual role of scribe and facilitator, a role she describes as complicated. Asking questions to clarify and help the child express ideas is deemed appropriate. Younger children seem to run out of steam after ten or more minutes of storytelling, and some are done in less than two minutes.

Statements that help children start dictating stories follow:

- "Tell me the words you want me to write down on the paper. I'll write them down."
- "Do you have a story to tell?"
- "I'll write down your words."
- "Let's write down what you said about your new puppy."
- "What is the story you would like to tell me?"
- "What are the words to your story?"

Preschool classrooms that announce teacher or volunteers are available and start a waiting list for a dictated child storytelling time find children accept and look forward to the opportunity. The success of the dictation activity relies on the promise of dramatization, Cooper (1993) believes. Linking dictation to children's opportunity to jointly act out before peers what the children have written is believed to be the key (Paley, 1981). Young children's interest in a concrete representation of their stories (the drama or action) coincides with young children's emotional need to establish their individual identity within the group (Cooper, 1993). Figure 10–6 gives an example of a dramatization of two-and-a-half-year-old Michael's story.

Teacher: Michael's story is about his horses. It goes like this: "These horsies are looking for hay. They're eating it. The palomino got out! The horse got out. The palomino jumped out! Real high!" Michael, which horse do you want to be in the play?

Michael: The palomino.

Teacher: Choose someone to be the other horse who eats hay with you.

[Michael chooses William.]

Teacher: William, will you be a horse in Michael's play?

[William nods "yes."]

Teacher: Okay. Now, Michael and William get on the stage.

[Michael and William stand in the center of the circle.]

Teacher: Can you boys pretend to be horses looking for hay? Good. "The palomino gets out!"

[Michael jumps up.]

Teacher: "The horse got out."

[William jumps up.]

Teacher: "The palomino jumped out. Real high!"

[Michael jumps again.]

Teacher: Good acting. You boys looked just like horses jumping.

[Michael and William grin and sit down.]

FIGURE 10–6 An example of dramatizing a child-created story *(Reprinted from* When stories come to school *by P. Cooper by permission of Teachers & Writers Collaborative, 5 Union Square West, New York, NY 10003. Copyright 1993.)*

Nicolopoulou, Scales, and Weintraub (1994) studied the content of four-year-olds' dictated stories and found differences in boys' and girls' tales. Boys' stories were far less likely than girls' to have either a stable cast of characters or a well-articulated plot; nor did they develop their themes in the steady and methodical manner of many girls' stories. While girls' stories focused on creating, maintaining, and elaborating structure, the boys' focused on generating action and excitement. Boys' main characters were often big, powerful, and frightening, while girls depicted realistic stable family life. Girls' stories created animals that were soft, cute creatures, while boys' animals typically were violent, wild, and scary.

Cooper (1993) informs teachers that bathroom-type stories appeared at times in child dictation and were censored with a light touch.

Storytelling with Young Limited-English Children

Pantomimes of eating dinner, going to bed, dressing, washing face and brushing teeth, opening a door with a key, rocking a baby to sleep, and other pantomime activities intrigue limited-English speakers. Pantomimes can include words in English and other languages enacted by children and adults. Props are sometimes useful. Guessing is half the fun. Using pantomimes can introduce and enhance the world of storytelling.

SUGGESTED STORIES

The following stories are suggested for the beginning storyteller.

The Little Red Hen

See the Appendix for story text. Trousdale (1990) relates her experiences with this story as follows:

To encourage interactive telling . . . I have taken with me stuffed animals for each character. After the story has become thoroughly familiar to the children, the stuffed hen, dog, cat, and rat are given to individual children. I continue to "tell" or narrate the story, but when each character speaks, the child who is holding the hen, or dog, or cat, or rat, speaks that character's words. Holding the animals seems to give the children a sense of security and authority.

In early childhood many repetitions of the story may be necessary before children remember individual character's lines.

The Little House with No Doors and No Windows and a Star Inside

Author Unknown

(Plan to have an apple, cutting board, and a knife ready for the ending. A plate full of apple slices is sometimes enjoyed after this story.)

Once there was a little boy who had played almost all day. He had played with all his toys and all the games he knew, and he could not think of anything else to do. So he went to his mother and asked, "Mother, what shall I do now?"

His mother said, "I know about a little red house with no doors and no windows and a star inside. You can find it, if you go look for it."

So the little boy went outside and there he met a little girl. He said, "Do you know where there is a little red house with no doors and no windows and a star inside?"

The little girl said, "No, I don't know where there is a little red house with no doors and no windows and a star inside, but you can ask my daddy. He is a farmer and he knows lots of things. He's down by the barn and maybe he can help you."

So the little boy went to the farmer down by the barn and said, "Do you know where there is a little red house with no doors and no windows and a star inside?"

"No," said the farmer, "I don't know, but why don't you ask Grandmother. She is in her house up on the hill. She is very wise and knows many things. Maybe she can help you."

So the little boy went up the hill to Grandmother's and asked, "Do you know where there is a little red house with no doors and no windows and a star inside?" "No," said Grandmother, "I don't know, but you ask the wind, for the wind goes everywhere, and I am sure he can help you."

So the little boy went outside and asked the wind, "Do you know where I can find a little red house with no doors and no windows and a star inside?" And the wind said, "OHHHH! OOOOOOOOOOOO!" And it sounded to the little boy as if the wind said, "Come with me." So the little boy ran after the wind. He ran through the grass and into the orchard and there on the ground he found the little house—the little red house with no doors and no windows and a star inside! He picked it up, and it filled both his hands. He ran home to his mother and said, "Look, Mother! I found the little red house with no doors and no windows, but I cannot see the star!"

So this is what his mother did (teacher cuts apple). "Now I see the star!" said the little boy. (Teacher says to children) "Do you?"

The Pancake Who Ran Away

(a folk tale)

Once upon a time there was a mother who had seven hungry children. She made a delicious light and fluffy golden pancake.

"I'm hungry," said one child. "I want some pancake."

Then all the other children said the same thing, and the mother had to cover her ears because they were so loud.

"Hush, Shush!" said the mother. "You can all have some as soon as the pancake is golden brown on both sides."

Now the pancake was listening and did not want to be eaten, so it hopped from the pan and rolled out the door and down the hill.

"Stop, pancake!" called the mother. She and all her children ran after the pancake as fast as they could. The pancake rolled on and on.

When it rolled a long way, it met a man.

"Good morning, pancake," said the man.

"Good morning Mandy-Pandy-Man!" said the pancake.

"Don't roll so fast. Stop and let me eat you," said the man.

"I've run away from the mother and seven hungry children and I'll run away from you Mandy-Pandy-Man." It rolled and rolled down the road until it met a hen clucking and hurrying along.

"Good morning, pancake," said the hen.

"The same to you, Henny-Fenny-Hen."

"Pancake don't roll so fast, stop and let me eat you," said the hen.

"No, no," said the pancake. "I've run away from the mother and the seven hungry children, Mandy-Pandy-Man, and I'll run away from you." And it rolled on and on.

It met a rooster.

"Good morning, pancake," said the rooster.

"The same to you, Rooster-Zooster," said the pancake.

"Stop so I can eat you," said the rooster.

"I've run away from the mother and the seven hungry children, Mandy-Pandy-Man, Henny-Fenny-Hen, and I'll run away from you," said the pancake. And it rolled on and on until it met a duck.

"Good morning, pancake," said the duck.

"The same to you, Quacky Duck," said the pancake.

"Stop so I can eat you," said the duck.

"I've run away from the mother and the seven hungry children, Mandy-Pandy-Man, Henny-Fenny-Hen, Rooster-Zooster, and I'll run away from you," said the pancake. And on and on it rolled until it met a goose.

"Good morning, pancake," said the goose.

"The same to you, Goosey-Loosey," said the pancake.

"Stop so I can eat you," said the goose.

"I've run away from the mother and the seven hungry children, Mandy-Pandy-Man, Henny-Fenny-Hen, Rooster-Zooster, Quacky Duck, and I'll run away from you." And on and on it rolled until it met a pig at the edge of a dark wood.

"Good morning, pancake," said the pig.

"The same to you Piggy-Wiggy," said the pancake.

"That wood is dark, don't be in such a hurry! We can go through the wood together. It's not safe in there," said the pig.

The pancake thought that was a good idea, so they went along together until they came to a river. The pig was so fat he could float across, but the pancake had no way of crossing.

"Jump on my snout," said the pig, "and I'll carry you across." So the pancake did that. "Oink!" said the pig as he opened his mouth wide and swallowed the pancake in one gulp. And that's how it was . . . pancakes are for eating, and the pig had his breakfast.

A Lump the Shape of a Hump

Maxwell woke up one bright morning, and saw a brown bird walking on his window sill, and that's not ALL he saw! There was a lump the shape of a hump under the covers at the foot of his bed. Maxwell squeezed against the headboard, folded up his knees, and stared at the lump the shape of a hump. It's Bellflower the Beagle, my dog, Maxwell thought, but Bellflower bounded into the bedroom and barked at the lump the shape of a hump at the foot of the bed. It's Tootie, my brother, he thought, but Tootie came into the bedroom and blew his horn, toot-toot at the lump the shape of a hump at the foot of the bed. "Must be Bubbles, my baby sister," Maxwell said to himself, but just then Bubbles crawled into his room. Maybe it's Toady, my best friend, Maxwell thought, but then he remembered Toady (who was called Toady because he loved to play leapfrog) had gone to visit his grandmother. "What's that lump the shape of a hump?" Maxwell's dad said as he walked into the bedroom. "I think it's my pillow," Maxwell said, but they both saw Maxwell's pillow on the floor. "My teddy?" Maxwell said. "Nope," said Maxwell's dad, "Teddy's sitting over there in the chair."

Just then the lump wiggled. It shook from side to side. Tootie blew his horn. Bellflower barked. Maxwell squeezed against the headboard afraid to move. "There is something strange going on here!" Maxwell's dad said.

Then the lump made a sound like a croak. Maxwell grabbed the covers and pulled and pulled. There was Toady all doubled up ready to play leapfrog, and he was laughing and croaking. "Grandma was sick, so I sneaked into your bed," Toady said. "Let's play leapfrog!" So they did. Maxwell, Tootie, Bellflower, and Toady played leapfrog while Dad and Bubbles watched.

Participation Stories

Just Like Metoo!

(Children imitate what Metoo does. Metoo does things a little faster each day. Metoo was always late for school. Speedee was always on time.)

Once upon a time, Metoo came to live at Speedee's house. He thought, "I'd like to do what Speedee does, but I can't learn everything at one time. Each day I'll do one new thing."

On Monday, when the alarm went off, Metoo jumped out of bed just like Speedee and washed his hands and face at 7:30 in the morning. (Jump up, wash hands and face. Sit down.)

On Tuesday, when the alarm went off, Metoo jumped out of bed and washed his hands and face and brushed his teeth at 7:30 in the morning. (Jump up, wash hands and face, brush teeth. Sit down.)

On Wednesday, when the alarm went off, Metoo jumped out of bed just like Speedee and washed his hands and face, brushed his teeth, and dressed himself at 7:30 in the morning. (Jump up, wash hands and face, brush teeth, dress self, sit down.)

On Thursday, when the alarm went off, Metoo jumped out of bed just like Speedee, washed his hands and face, brushed his teeth, dressed himself, and ate his breakfast at 7:30 in the morning. (Jump up, wash hands and face, brush teeth, dress self, eat breakfast, sit down.)

On Friday, when the alarm went off, Metoo jumped out of bed, just like Speedee, washed his hands and face, brushed his teeth, dressed himself, ate his breakfast, and waved goodbye to Speedee's mother who was on her way to work at 7:30 in the morning. (Very rapidly, jump up, wash hands and face, brush teeth, dress self, eat breakfast, wave goodbye, sit down.) Speedee and Metoo walked to school together. Metoo wasn't late for school!

On Saturday, when the alarm went off, Metoo turned over and shut it off. (Move right arm across body slowly, as if shutting off alarm.) He had heard Speedee say, "This is Saturday. Nobody goes to school on Saturday."

To Grandmother's House

(Before beginning this story, draw the picture in figure 10–7 on the chalkboard or on a large sheet of paper. During the telling let your finger show Clementine's travels.)

One day Clementine's mother said, "I'm making cookies. I need some sugar. Please go to Grandma's house and borrow a cup of sugar." "Yes, Mother, I'll go right away," said Clementine.

Clementine climbed up the first mountain. Climb, climb, climb. (Make climbing motions with arms.) Climb, climb, climb.

When she got to the top of the mountain she slid down. (Make sliding motion with hands.)

At the bottom of the mountain was a wide, wide lake. Clementine jumped in and swam across. Swim, swim, swim. (Make swimming arm motions.)

Clementine climbed the next mountain. Climb, climb, climb. (Make climbing hand motions.) Then

she slid down the other side. (Make sliding motions.)

Next, Clementine crossed the bridge. Tromp, tromp, tromp. (Make feet move up and down.) Tromp, tromp, tromp.

Clementine climbed the third mountain. Climb, climb, climb. (motions) Then she slid down the other side. (motions)

Clementine's grandmother was standing next to her house. "Hello, Grandmother, may I have a cup of sugar? My mother's making cookies." "Yes, dear," said Grandmother, and she came out of the house with a little bag.

"Goodbye, Grandmother," Clementine said. Climb, climb, climb. She slid down the other side and crossed the bridge. Tromp, tromp, tromp. She climbed the middle mountain. Climb, climb, climb (motions). Then she slid down the other side (motions). She swam the lake with the bag in her teeth and her head held high. Swim, swim, swim (motions). Next, she climbed the mountain. Climb, climb, climb (motions). Then she slid down the mountain (motions) to her house.

When she went into the house, she gave her mother the sugar. Her mother said, "This is brown sugar. I wanted white sugar." "I'll go to Grandmother's," said Clementine.

Clementine climbed the first mountain. Climb, climb, climb (motions). She slid down the other side (motions). Then she swam the lake. Swim, swim, swim (motions).

She climbed the second mountain. Climb, climb, climb (motions). She slid down the other side

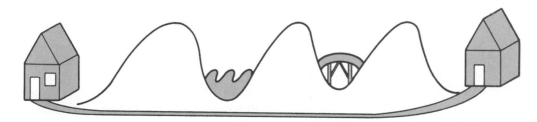

FIGURE 10–7 Clementine's travels

(motions) and crossed the bridge. Tromp, tromp, tromp (motions).

She climbed the third mountain. Climb, climb, climb (motions). Then she slid down the other side (motions).

Grandmother was working in her garden. "Hello, Grandmother," said Clementine. "Two visits in one day. How nice," said Grandmother.

"But I can't stay this time either. Mother needs white sugar instead of brown," said Clementine.

Grandmother went into her house and came out with a little bag.

"You look so tired, Clementine!" said Grandmother.

"I am," said Clementine.

"Take the shortcut home," said Grandmother.

So Clementine did. She walked straight home on the path at the foot of the mountains.

This story can be lengthened by having the mother request additional ingredients and by Clementine taking cookies to Grandmother after they are baked.

What Was Behind the Door?

Dog—"Bow Wow"	Bird—"Peep Peep"
Cat—"Meow"	Lion—"Grrrr"

(Teacher says the following to children: "I need you to help me tell this story! Do you suppose that you can remember all of the sounds that we have talked about? In this story, you can make the animal noises that Granny hears. When the story says, Granny heard a dog, say, 'Bow Wow!' (and so on). Listen carefully.")

Granny sat in a big armchair knitting Tommy a sweater. All of a sudden she heard a dog say "_____" (Bow Wow).

"Gracious!" said Granny. "I do believe there's a dog behind the door. Should I have a dog in the house?"

"Oh yes," answered the dog behind the door. "I'm a good dog. I don't jump on people."

"Very well," said Granny, and she went on knitting the sweater for Tommy. All of a sudden Granny heard a cat say "_____" (Meow).

"Gracious!" said Granny. "I do believe that there is a cat behind the door. Should I have a cat in the house?"

"Oh yes," answered the cat. "I am a good cat. I do not scratch the furniture."

"Very well," said Granny, and she went on knitting Tommy's sweater. All of a sudden Granny heard a bird say "_____" (Peep Peep).

"Gracious!" said Granny. "I do believe that I heard a bird behind the door. Should I have a bird in the house?"

"Oh yes," answered the bird. "I am a good bird. I sing very sweetly."

"Very well," said Granny, and she went right on knitting a sweater for Tommy.

All of a sudden, Granny heard a lion say "_____" (Grrrr).

"Gracious!" said Granny. "I do believe that there is a lion behind the door. This is too much!" Carefully, Granny opened the door, because she wasn't sure she liked having a lion in the house.

And what do you think she found hiding behind her door? There was Tommy. He had been making those noises after all!

Suggest: "Can you all make the noises Tommy made?"

Dog = Bow Wow
Cat = Meow
Bird = Peep Peep
Lion = Grrrr

"What other animal sounds do you know?"

A Cut-and-Tell Story

Clever teachers have created cut-and-tell stories that readily capture child attention. While telling these stories, the teacher cuts a paper shape relating to the story line. The *Boy in the Boat*, an example, follows. The Appendix includes another story of this type.

Preparation

Step 1

Fold a 9 × 12 inch (or larger) paper in half.

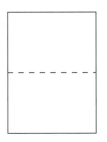

Step 2

Fold top corners down toward the middle.

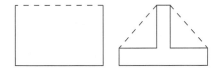

Step 3

Fold single sheet up over triangles.

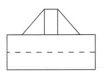

Step 4

Turn over and fold single sheet up.

Those who know how to fold a sailor's hat will recognize the pattern. Tell the story with scissors handy.

Once there was a boy (or girl) who wanted to be a sailor. He had a sailor's hat. (Show hat shape.) *And he had a boat.* (Turn the hat so it becomes a boat.) *One day he climbed in his boat and floated to the middle of a big lake. It was very hot for the sun was bright. He took off his shirt and pants and threw them into the water. He had a swimming suit on under his clothes, and he felt much cooler. His boat hit a large rock and the front of his boat fell off.* (Cut off front of boat.)

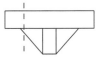

Then a giant fish took a bite out of the bottom of the boat. (Cut off the bottom.)

The back of the boat came off when a big bird flew down and sat on it. (Cut off the back of the boat.)

The boy didn't have but a little boat left and water was reaching his toes so he jumped overboard and swam to the shore. He watched his boat sink. Then he saw something white floating towards him. What do you think it could be? (Unfold what's left of the boat.)

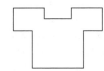

His shirt!

Resources

Many metropolitan areas have storytelling clubs and associations. Increasingly apparent are individuals and groups bent on preserving cultural and ethnic stories and techniques. One well-known resource for storytelling is The National Association for the Preservation and Perpetuation of Storytelling, P.O. Box 309, Jonesboro, TN 37659.

Additional Resources

Baker, A., & Greene, E. (1987). *Storytelling: Art and technique* (2nd ed.). New York: Bowker.

MacDonald, M. R. (Ed.). (1986). *Twenty tellable tales: Audience participation folktales for the beginning storyteller*. New York: H. W. Wilson.

Pellowski, A. (1984). *The story vine: A source of unusual and easy-to-tell stories from around the world*. New York: Macmillan.

Parents, Volunteers, and Community Storytellers

It is surprising how many parents, volunteers, and community elementary school-aged children, teenagers, and adults will rise to the occasion when asked to tell fictional stories or stories concerning significant life experiences. Guidelines of suitability will need to be discussed.

Intergeneration storytelling and its benefits have been given attention and need mentioning here. After briefing possible volunteers and older storytellers on appropriate time length, settings, story features, etc., grandparents and other seniors might relate stories from their own unique backgrounds. Stories about contemporary happenings are also valuable. Many of these stories might involve a rich array of multicultural and multigenerational themes and offer wisdom accumulated through many years of living. Stories might also be told in the authentic language of the storyteller.

(Additional stories like the following are included in the Appendix.)

Little Duck Lost
(full of sounds and action)

Cow—"Moo Moo"	Cat—"Meow Meow"
Horse—"Neigh Neigh"	Duck—"Quack Quack"
Pig—"Oink Oink"	Mouse—"Squeak Squeak"
Dog—"Bow Wow"	Rooster—"Cock-a-doodle-do"

The animals on the farm were noisy one morning. The rooster (Cock-a-doodle-do) was crowing. The cow (Moo Moo) was mooing. The dog (Bow Wow) was barking, and the cat (Meow Meow) was meowing. Everybody was looking for little duck. Little Duck was gone. The cow (Moo Moo) looked all through the sweet clover in the pasture but no Little Duck (Quack Quack). The horse (Neigh Neigh) galloped into the next field, but no Little Duck. The fat, fat pig (Oink Oink) pushed all the mud out of his puddle. He could not find Little Duck.

Then the animals hurried down to the pond once more to look for Little Duck. They all called him. (Everybody calls "Little Duck.") There was no Little Duck. The animals were quiet as they walked back to the barn. They had looked everywhere, but could not find Little Duck.

Suddenly, a little mouse (Squeak Squeak) came scurrying out of the barn. How he squeaked! He led the animals back into the barn and over to his nest in a quiet corner and there was Little Duck asleep on the mouse's (Squeak Squeak) nest. What a shout the animals gave! (Everybody calls "Wake up!") They had found Little Duck. They woke him with their shouting. Little Duck (Quack Quack) was rushed back to the duck pond, where, after all, little ducks (Quack Quack) belong.

Summary

Teachers offer orally told stories to promote literacy and encourage children's language enjoyment and development of oral abilities.

One goal of storytelling is achieving a feeling of togetherness and enjoyment through the words of a story. Building listening skills, vocabulary development, and expanding interest are other important goals.

Stories for storytelling can be found in printed sources or borrowed from other teachers. A story can also be created by the teacher. By following suggested techniques and criteria, a successful activity for both children and teachers is possible.

Stories are told in the teacher's own words with key events clearly in mind. Watching the children's interest and reactions keeps the teacher aware of how well the experience is accepted. Any skill takes practice; storytelling skills improve with use.

Teachers promote child storytelling by encouraging children and recognizing their efforts.

STUDENT ACTIVITIES

1. Create a story. In outline form, write the beginning, middle, and ending. Practice telling it to a fellow student. Use your own title or select one of the following:

The Giant Ice Cream Cone	The Mouse Who Chased Cats
Magic Shoes	The Police Officer and Mike
The Dog Who Wouldn't Bark	The Fastest Bike
Billy Found a Dollar	I've Got a Bug in My Pocket
The Big Birthday Present	

2. Tell a story to a group of children. Write an evaluation of both the story and your skill.
   a. What parts interested the children the most?
   b. What would you change if you told it again?
   c. What techniques were used to hold interest?

3. Create a story song. Share it with your classmates.

4. Find an ethnic story that could be told to young children. Cite your source and be ready to share the story with fellow classmates.

5. Design an evaluation (rating form) to assess a storyteller's skill.

6. Invite a librarian or experienced teacher who tells stories during story hours to share favorite stories with the class.

7. Tell a story and have it recorded on videotape. Play it back. Look for strong points and areas for growth in skill.

8. Read the following kindergarten teacher's description of an oral storytelling situation.

   > Once they were drawn in, they became intensely focused during the story. I couldn't help but notice the deep interest in their faces, and they begged for more. They especially liked stories with jokes about themselves, and with issues that weren't too close to home. For example, they wouldn't have enjoyed a vivid description of an angry mother, but they adored the story in which the janitor had mistakenly replaced their table chairs with those from the toddler room (Cooper, 1993).

   Knowing preschoolers enjoy a slapstick type of humor, create a story for teacher storytelling. What vivid descriptions would you avoid including in tales to preschoolers—ones you feel are "too close to home"?

9. Have a child under the age of five dictate a story to you. Try a "I'll tell you my story, and you tell me your story technique." Share the results with the class.

10. Listen to a commercial storytelling record. List the techniques used to hold children's interest.

11. Create a story in which the children's names for a particular class are woven into the story. Share with children, and share children's reactions with your fellow students.

12. List important reasons for teacher storytelling.

13. Discuss how you would provide for child storytelling in your classroom.

14. Using the cue card example (figure 10–4), tell a fellow student *The Tale of Peter Rabbit*.

15. Comment on a teacher who introduces a storytelling experience by saying "Today's story will be . . ."

16. Obtain a copy of *The Mitten* (A Ukranian folktale) retold and illustrated by Jan Brett or another author. Practice, gather props, and share it with a group of preschoolers. Report your experiences to classmates.

17. Find a story suitable for telling from a minority culture or ethnic source. Share with the class.

CHAPTER REVIEW

A. Column I lists common preschool characteristics. Select the appropriate storytelling technique or criteria from Column II that matches each item in Column I.

Column I	**Column II**
1. likes to move frequently	a. selects stories without cruel monsters or vivid descriptions of accidents
2. has had experiences at home, school, and in community	b. "Ducky-Ducky and Be-Bop-Boo went to the park to meet Moo-moo the cow"
3. has fear of large animals and bodily harm	c. stories contain familiar objects and animals
4. likes play with words	d. "What did big bird say to baby bird?"
5. likes to be part of the group	e. "Help Tipper blow out the candle. Pretend my finger is a candle and try to blow it out!"
6. likes to talk	f. "Stand up and reach for the moon like Johnny did. Now close your eyes; is it dark like night? You couldn't reach the moon, but can you find your nose with your eyes closed?"

B. Briefly answer the following questions.

1. Why should storytelling take place often in early childhood centers?

2. Name three resources for stories.

3. What are stereotypes?

C. Select the correct answers. Each item has more than one correct answer.

1. In storytelling, the storyteller not only uses words but also uses
    a. the hands.
    b. the face.
    c. the eyes.
    d. gestures.

2. Recommended techniques used by storytellers are
    a. changing the voice to fit the character.
    b. changing the personality of a character during the story.
    c. stopping without ending a story so that children will listen quietly the next time.
    d. watching children closely and emphasizing the parts they enjoy.

3. Criteria for story selection includes
    a. believable characters.
    b. a plot with lots of action.
    c. a possible problem to be resolved.
    d. making sure the story is one that can be memorized.

4. Teachers should not
    a. let children be inattentive during their story.
    b. feel defeated if a story occasionally flops.
    c. put bad guys in stories.
    d. tell the story word for word.

5. During storytelling time, the
    a. child can form his or her own mental pictures.
    b. teacher can share interesting personal life experiences.
    c. teacher models correct speech.
    d. teacher models creative use of words.

D. Write a paragraph or two describing appropriate teacher reactions to child-created stories.

E. Give two examples of words, phrases, or sentences that must be memorized when storytelling a particular story. Include story title.

RESOURCES

Cowley, G. (1997, Spring/Summer). Off to a good start [Special edition]. *Newsweek*.
Kantrowitz, B. (1997, Spring/Summer). Off to a good start [Special edition]. *Newsweek*.
McLeod, M. (1996, November 24). Once upon a time [Florida supplement]. *Orlando Sentinel*.
Rivers, K. (1996, November 24). Once upon a time [Florida supplement]. *Orlando Sentinel*.

CHAPTER 11

Poetry

OBJECTIVES

After studying this chapter, you should be able to:

- discuss poetry elements.

- demonstrate the ability to present a poem.

- create a poem with features that appeal to young children.

Children's poetry is an enjoyable vehicle for developing listening skills. Activities that involve poetry hold many opportunities to promote language and literacy by associating pleasure with words. Poetry has a condensed quality that makes every word important. It prompts imagery through its sensory descriptions and can introduce enchanting tales. Nonsense verse appeals to the preschoolers' appreciation for slapstick.

Glazer and Burke (1994) believe:

> The repetitive format of rhymes makes them "rote-able." Repetition is a strategy for learning with pleasure. Expectancies are set up and gloriously materialize. The desire to hear more is intensified.

> *and*

> The language of rhyme becomes easily fixed in memory; it can become part of a child's linguistic and intellectual resources for life.

Appropriate children's poetry is plentiful and varied. In addition to fast action and mood building, there is the joy of the rhythm of the words in many poems. Some rhythms in classic rhymes are so strong that they can motivate children to move their bodies or clap. The nursery rhymes "Jack and Jill" and "Twinkle, Twinkle, Little Star," and "The Little Turtle" (Lindsay, 1920) are good examples. Norton (1983) notes that "Rhythm encourages children to join in orally, experiment with language, and move to the rhythmical sounds." Some poems appeal to the emotions; others to the intellect (figure 11–1).

FIGURE 11–1 Poetry can captivate an audience.

A preschool child with beginning literacy might be described as a child familiar with Mother Goose rhymes and other contemporary and classic poems, and one who knows rhyming words sound alike.

Learning Opportunities

Poetry provides an opportunity for a child to learn new words, ideas, and attitudes and to experience life through the eyes of the poet. To remember how many days there are in a month, many people still recite a simple poem learned as a child. If you are asked to say the alphabet, the classic ABC song of childhood may come to mind.

Poetry has form and order. It is dependable and also easy to learn. Simple rhymes are picked up quickly, as most parents have seen from their children's ability to remember television commercials. Children in early childhood centers enjoy the accomplishment of memorizing short verses. They may ask to share the poems they have learned with the teacher, just as they ask to sing songs they know that are often poems set to music.

The teacher should provide encouragement, attention, and positive comments to the child who responds to poetry. As with picture-book reading, storytelling, and other language activities, the goal of the teacher in regard to poetry is to offer children pleasure and enjoyment of the language arts, while expanding the children's knowledge and interest.

Poetry, then, is used for a variety of reasons, including:

- Familiarizing and exposing children to classic and contemporary poetry that is considered to be part of our literary heritage.
- Training children to experience the pleasure of hearing sounds.
- Providing enjoyment through the use of poems with silly words and humor.
- Stimulating children's imaginations.
- Increasing vocabulary and knowledge.
- Building self-worth and self-confidence.
- Encouraging an understanding of rhyming.

Poetry and Early Reading Ability

Poems, rhymes, and chants acquaint young children with language in repeated pleasant patterns and with catchy rhythms, such as the "Grand Old Duke of York." Drop the words in this rhyming chant (found on page 367). Use da-Da, da-Da, da-Da, etc., and see how easy it is to isolate and sense the accented words and syllables.

Experts believe children's ability to discriminate, create rhyming words, and sense the rhythm of words is closely related to early reading ability (Healy, 1990).

Maclean, Bryant, and Bradley (1987), researchers who conducted a 15-month longitudinal study starting with children age three, found a strong and specific relationship between knowledge of nursery rhymes and the development of phonological skills, particularly the detection of rhyme and alliteration. Repetition of consonant sounds in lyrics like "cock-a-doodle-doo, dee-doodle-dee doodle-dee doodle-dee-doo" certainly demonstrates alliteration.

Selection

Poetry introduces children to characters with fun-to-say names such as:

> Jonathan Bing by Beatrice Curtis Brown
>
> Mrs. Peck Pigeon by Eleanor Farjeon
>
> Godfrey Gordon Gustavos Gore by William Rands

The characters can live in familiar and far-fetched settings:

> Under the toadstool, from "The Elf and the Dormouse" by Oliver Herford
>
> Straight to the animal store, from "The Animal Store" by Rachel Field
>
> In a little crooked house, from Mother Goose

And they have various adventures and difficulties:

> "The kids are ten feet tall," from "Grown-Up-Down Town" by Bobbi Katz

"Christopher Robin had wheezles and sneezles," from "Sneezles" by A. A. Milne

"Listen, my children, this must be stopped," from "The Grasshoppers" by Dorothy Aldis

Teachers select poetry that they can present eagerly and that they feel children will like. Delight in words is a natural outcome when the poem suits the audience. Teachers look for poems of quality and merit. Donoghue (1985) suggests that three elements exist in good poetry: *distinguished diction, carefully chosen words and phrases* with rich sensory and associated meanings, and *significant content*. Much of classic poetry has a song quality and a melody of its own. Norton (1983) suggests that teachers should examine a poem's subject matter, because in addition to delighting children, poetry can say something to them, titillate them, recall happy occasions or events, or encourage them to explore.

Geller (1985), working with three-year-olds, found traditional eighteenth-century nursery rhymes still popular with today's children. Favorite rhymes with strong four-beat couplets ("Humpty Dumpty" and others) were repeated with the teacher exaggerating the beat (as children do). This technique held group interest.

Categories of verse popular with most preschoolers have one or more of the following characteristics (Geller, 1985):

1. Simple story line ("Jack Be Nimble")

2. Simple story line with finger play ("This Little Piggie")

3. Story in song with repeated chorus ("London Bridge")

4. Verse/story with nonsense words ("Hey, Diddle, Diddle")

5. Descriptions of daily actions ("Little Jack Horner")

6. Choral reading in which youngsters could join in with rhymed words ("To Market")

No child should miss the fun, wit, and wisdom of Mother Goose. Literacy, in part, depends on a child's exposure to cultural tradition. Mother Goose is an American tradition. Make a list of Mother Goose characters. You'll be surprised at how many you'll remember.

Galda (1989) shares poetry selection criteria in the following:

. . . begin with poems which are sure to please: poems which have strong rhythm and rhyme, poems which play with sound, poems which are humorous, tell stories, and are about children and the things that make up their lives. . . . Once children have been bitten by the poetry bug, . . . focus on rhythm and rhyme, and explore how various poets use sound devices such as alliteration or onomatopoeia.

Types of Poetry

Types of poetry are described as follows:

Lyric. Melodic, descriptive poetry that often has a song quality.

Narrative. Poetry that tells a story or describes an event or happening.

Limerick. A poem with five lines of verse set in a specific rhyming pattern that is usually humorous.

Free verse. Poetry that does not rhyme.

Nonsense. Poetry that is often ridiculous and whimsical, figure 11–2

Poetry Elements

A particular poem's rhythm is influenced by sounds, stress, pitch, and accented and unaccented syllables. Manipulation of one or all of these features creates a particular idea, feeling, or message. Some rhythms are regular; others are not. The enjoyable quality of the Mother Goose rhymes stems from their strong rhythm and cadence. In poetry, authors

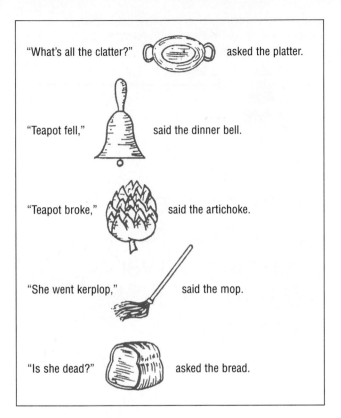

"What's all the clatter?"   asked the platter.

"Teapot fell,"   said the dinner bell.

"Teapot broke,"   said the artichoke.

"She went kerplop,"   said the mop.

"Is she dead?"   asked the bread.

FIGURE 11–2 A whimsical poem delights many children. *(From "I Can't" Said the Ant by Polly Cameron. Copyright 1961, 1989 by Polly Cameron. Reprinted by permission of Coward, McCann, and Geohegan Inc.)*

use rhythm to emphasize words or phrases, consequently capturing children's immediate attention. Exciting, dramatic rhythms and relaxed, soothing rhythms can be included in the same poem. Poetry's rhythm is capable of making children feel that they are actively participating rather than merely listening.

Children's literature is full of rhyming words and rhyming names. Poetic rhyme can occur within sentences or at line endings. Children often rhyme on their own, spontaneously, during play. Nonsense rhymes have given joy to generations of children; sayings like stomper-chomper, icky-sticky, and Dan, Dan elephant man, can spread immediately among children.

Alliteration (defined as the occurrence of two or more words having the same initial sounds, assonance, or vowel sounds) is often used in poetry. All types of repetition are characteristic of children's poetry.

Visual images are stimulated by the poet's use of sensory words and figurative language (nonliteral meanings). A poet may provide a new way of looking at things by comparing previously unconnected objects or events. Similes (direct comparisons between two things that have something in common but are essentially different) or metaphors (implied comparisons between two things that have something in common but are essentially different) are often found in poetry. Giving human characteristics and emotions to inanimate objects and animals (personification) is also commonplace, and talking dishes, trains, birds, bears, and pancakes are plentiful in children's poems.

The format of printed poetry (type size and style, page layout, punctuation, and capitalization) has been used to heighten enjoyment and highlight the subject matter. One can find poems printed in the shape of a tree or in one-word, long, narrow columns.

Teacher Techniques

If a poem is read or recited in a conversational manner, rather than in a sing-song fashion, the rhyme is subtle and enjoyable. Sing-song reading and recitation may become tiresome and difficult to understand.

Most teachers know that reciting from memory requires practice, so the poems they memorize are a few favorites. However, memorization can create a mechanical quality, as the teacher focuses on remembering rather than enjoyment. Often, poetry is shared through teacher readings from lap cards. A poem should be read smoothly without uncalled for hesitation. This means the teacher has to prepare by reading the poem enough times for it to roll off the tongue with ease, savoring the words in the telling.

The enjoyment of poetry, like other types of literature, can be increased by an enthusiastic adult (Norton, 1983). Glazer (1986) suggests a careful reading of poetry because of poetry's compactness, making every word count.

When encouraging children to join in and speak favorite poetry lines, sensitive handling is in order. A teacher can suggest, "Let's say it together" or "Join me in saying this poem if you like." A child should not be singled out or asked to recite without volunteering. Some gregarious children will want to share poems that they've learned. A number of repetitions of a favorite verse may be needed before it is totally remembered. Children usually start with a few words or phrases.

Stewig (1977) offers the following preparatory tips:

> . . . give careful attention not only to pitch and stress, but most importantly to juncture. That is, where we make the breaks in poetry will make or break our presentation. The natural tendency is to break at the end of the printed line. In poetry, this may lead to artificial segmenting, not intended by the poet.

Look at figure 11–3. Read the first two lines as one sentence without pausing at the word *tree*. Now, read the poem stopping at each line's end and you'll see what Stewig means.

A technique that works well for "a change of pace" is suggested by the work of John Kinderman Taylor (1993). Background music without lyrics but with a strong repeated beat is used as a backdrop for poems or teacher-created rhymed lines. The result is chant-like, rap-like, and promotes children's joining in and at times also clapping.

Poetry charts hanging on a chart stand next to the teacher are a helpful device for capturing attention and freeing a teacher's eyes to meet those of the children. When reading from a chart, quickly glance at a line and then turn so that the words are transmitted to the children. The poetry chart in figure 11–4 was teacher created and posted near the storage of classroom books. Children were

FIGURE 11–3   A rhyming chart

encouraged to think of other things a book might say about book care and handling. The teacher wrote these child thoughts and posted them at the chart's bottom and identified them with the child's name.

Young children sometimes create their own rhymes. The teacher can jot them down for display or to be taken home by the children. "Amber, pamber, big fat bamber," created by a child, may interest other children, and the teacher who has recorded it might share it at group time as a rhyme created by a playmate.

Poems dictated by children should be recorded verbatim, with no editing or teacher suggestions. Each creation is regarded as special. Lionni's *Fred-*

A POETRY CHART

Be gentle	Sticky hands
Turn pages slow	Make a mess
I don't want to	When I'm clean
Rip you know!	I look my best.
I fall apart	My printed words
In the rain	Will make you laugh
Pages crinkle	This book's about
It's a pain!	A funny giraffe.
If after you hold me	Don't walk away
You put me back	I'm lonely today
Others will find me	Look at me
On the book rack.	Before you play.
Inside my cover	When you hold me
A story hides	In your hands
Pick me up	And turn my pages
And look inside	I feel grand.
If you've never	I'm not safe
Been to the zoo	On the floor
Animals inside	Where feet kick
Might frighten you.	And make me sore.
by Sierra	by Bradford

FIGURE 11–4 If books could talk what would they say?

erick, a wonderful picture book, helps children understand rhyming. This book's last two lines read:

"But Frederick," they said, "you are a poet!"

Frederick blushed, took a bow, and said shyly, "I know it."

Ways to Introduce Children to Poetry

Posting poems in conspicuous places may help to create interest, particularly if pictures or illustrations are placed adjacent to the poems. A poetry tree, made by placing a smooth tree limb in plaster of paris, can have paper leaves with poems on the back that can be selected at group times. A poem of the day (or week) bulletin board has worked well in some classrooms.

Pictures and flannel boards can be used in poetry presentation to interest and help children focus on words. Other props or costumes that relate to the poem (such as a teddy bear or police officer's hat) will gain attention. Some of the best collections of poems have no pictures; others have an illustration for each poem.

A poem can be enjoyed indoors or outdoors, or between activities as a fill-in when teacher or children are waiting.

Mounting cut magazine pictures and trying to think up words that rhyme with what's pictured is a rhyming activity many teachers favor. For example, "Here's a cake, let's give it to. . . ."

Sources

A fine line divides finger plays, body and movement games, chants, songs, and poems. All can involve rhyme and rhythm. Poetry given later in this chapter is primarily the type that children would merely listen to as it is being recited, although some do contain opportunities for child participation.

Many fine picture books contain rhymed verse and can enhance a center's poetry program. Collections, anthologies, and books of children's poetry are available at the public library, book stores, school supply stores, and in children's and teachers' magazines.

Teachers also can create poetry from their own experiences. The following suggestions for creating poems for young children help the teacher-poet by pointing out the special features found in older classics and quality contemporary poetry.

- Include mental images in every line.
- Use strong rhythms that bring out an urge to chant, move, or sing.
- Use frequent rhyming.
- Use action verbs often.
- Make each line an independent thought.
- Change the rhythm.
- Use words that are within the children's level of understanding.
- Use themes and subjects that are familiar to the young child.

Teacher-created poems promote child-created poems.

Many teachers search for ethnic poems that allow them to offer multicultural variety. Jenkins (1973) points out:

> No one cultural group has a corner on imagination, creativity, poetic quality, or philosophic outlook. Each has made important contributions to the total culture of the country and the world.

Recalling the poems and verses of one's own childhood may lead a teacher to research poems by a particular poet. Remembering appealing poetry elements may also help a teacher find poetry that may delight today's young child.

The following volumes are recommended:

Brady, L., Meirelles, R., & Nikoghosian. (1987). *The best of Mother Goose.* Hanford: RozaLinda Publications.

Brown, M. (1985). *Hand rhymes.* New York: E. P. Dutton.

Carle, E. (1989). *Animals, animals.* New York: Philomel.

Carlstrom, N. W. (1989). *Graham cracker animals 1–2–3.* New York: Macmillan.

de Paola, T. (1985). *Tomie de Paola's Mother Goose.* New York: G. P. Putnam's Sons.

Gander, F. (1985). *Nursery rhymes.* Santa Barbara: Advocacy Press.

Ghigna, C. (1995). *Riddle rhymes.* New York: Hyperion.

McClosky, P. (1991). *Find the real Mother Goose.* New York: Checkerboard Press.

Prelutsky, J. (1983). *The Random House book of poetry for children.* New York: Random House.

Prelutsky, J. (Ed.). (1983). *Read-aloud rhymes for the very young.* New York: Knopf.

Prelutsky, J. (1986). *Ride a purple pelican.* New York: Greenwillow.

Scott, L. B. (Ed.). (1983). *Rhymes for learning times.* Minneapolis, MN: T. S. Denison & Co. Inc.

Silverman, J. (1988). *Some time to grow.* Menlo Park, CA: Addison-Wesley.

······································

Suggested Poems

The poems that follow are examples of the type that appeal to young children.

IF I WERE AN APPLE
> *If I were an apple*
> *And grew on a tree,*
> *I think I'd drop down*
> *On a nice boy like me.*
>
> *I wouldn't stay there*
> *Giving nobody joy;*
> *I'd fall down at once*
> *And say, "Eat me, my boy!"*

Old Rhyme

GOOD MORNING
> *One day I saw a downy duck,*
> *With feathers on his back;*
> *I said, "Good-morning, downy duck."*
> *And he said, "Quack, quack, quack."*
>
> *One day I saw a timid mouse,*
> *He was so shy and meek;*
> *I said, "Good-morning, timid mouse,"*
> *And he said, "Squeak, squeak, squeak."*
>
> *One day I saw a scarlet bird,*
> *He woke me from my sleep;*
> *I said, "Good-morning, scarlet bird,"*
> *And he said, "Cheep, cheep, cheep."*

Muriel Sipe

Reprinted by permission of Muriel Sipe (Mrs. David Russ) and the Association for Childhood Education International, 11141 Georgia Avenue, Suite 200, Wheaton, MD 20902, © 1935 by the Association.

ANIMAL CRACKERS
> *Animal crackers, and cocoa to drink,*
> *That is the finest of suppers, I think;*
> *When I'm grown up and can have what I please*
> *I think I shall always insist upon these.*
>
> *What do you choose when you're offered a treat?*
> *When Mother says, "What would you like best*
> *to eat?"*

Is it waffles and syrup, or cinnamon toast?
It's cocoa and animals that I love the most!

The kitchen's the coziest place that I know:
The kettle is singing, the stove is aglow,
And there in the twilight, how jolly to see
The cocoa and animals waiting for me.

Daddy and Mother dine later in state,
With Mary to cook for them, Susan to wait;
But they don't have nearly as much fun as I
Who eat in the kitchen with Nurse standing by:
Having cocoa and animals once more for tea!

"Animal Crackers," © 1917, 1945 by Christopher Morley. From *Chimneysmoke* by Christopher Morley. Reprinted by permission of Harper & Row Publishers, Inc.

ONE STORMY NIGHT
 Two little kittens,
  One stormy night
 Began to quarrel,
  And then to fight.

 One had a mouse,
  The other had none;
 And that's the way
  The quarrel begun.

 "I'll have that mouse,"
  Said the bigger cat.
 "You'll have that mouse?
  We'll see about that!"

 "I will have that mouse,"
  Said the eldest son.
 "You shan't have the mouse,"
  Said the little one.

 The old woman seized
  Her sweeping broom,
 And swept both kittens
  Right out of the room.

 The ground was covered
  With frost and snow,
 And the two little kittens
  Had nowhere to go.

 They lay and shivered
  On a mat at the door,

 While the old woman
  Was sweeping the floor.

 And then they crept in
  As quiet as mice,
 All wet with the snow,
  And as cold as ice.

 And found it much better
  That stormy night,
 To lie by the fire,
  Than to quarrel and fight.

       Traditional

WHAT IS RED?
 Red is a sunset
 Blazy and bright.
 Red is feeling brave
 With all your might.
 Red is a sunburn
 Spot on your nose.
 Sometimes red
 Is a red, red rose
 Red squiggles out
 When you cut your hand.
 Red is a brick and
 A rubber band.
 Red is a hotness
 You get inside
 When you're embarrassed
 And want to hide.

From *Hailstones and Halibut Bones* by Mary O'Neill, © 1961 by Mary LeDuc O'Neill. Reprinted by permission of Doubleday and Company, Inc.

COUNTING
 Today I'll remember forever and ever
 Because I can count to ten;
 It isn't an accident any more either,
 I've done it over and over again.

 I used to leave out five and three
 And sometimes eight and four.
 And once in a while I'd mix up nine
 Or seven and two, but not any more.

I count my fingers on one hand first,
And this little pig is one,
And when old thumb goes off to market
That's five, and one of my hands is done.

So then I open my other hand
And start in counting again
From pick up sticks to big fat hen,
Five six seven eight eleven nine ten!

From *Windy Morning,* © 1953 by Harry Behn; renewed 1981 by Alice Behn Goebel, Pamela Behn Adam, Prescott Behn, and Peter Behn. Reprinted by permission of Marian Reiner.

THE ANIMAL STORE

If I had a hundred dollars to spend,
  Or maybe a little more,
I'd hurry as fast as my legs would go
  Straight to the animal store.

I wouldn't say, "How much for this or that?"
  "What kind of dog is he?"
I'd buy as many as rolled an eye,
  Or wagged a tail at me!

I'd take the hound with the drooping ears
  That sits by himself alone,
Cockers and Cairns and wobbly pups
  For to be my very own.

I might buy a parrot all red and green,
  And the monkey I saw before,
If I had a hundred dollars to spend,
  Or maybe a little more.

Rachel Field

From *Taxis and Toadstools* by Rachel Field, © 1926 by Doubleday and Company. Reprinted by permission of the publisher.

I HAVEN'T LEARNED TO WHISTLE

I haven't learned to whistle
I've tried—
But if there's anything like a whistle in me
It stops
Inside

Dad whistles,
My brother whistles
And almost everyone I know.

I've tried to put my lips together with wrinkles,
To push my tongue against my teeth
And make a whistle
Come
Out
Slow—

But what happens is nothing but a feeble gasping
Sound
Like a sort of sickly bird.

(Everybody says they never heard
A whistle like that
And to tell the truth
Neither did I.)

But Dad says, tonight, when he comes home,
He'll show me again how
To put my lips together with wrinkles,
To push my tongue against my teeth,
To blow my breath out and really make a whistle.

And I'll try!

Myra Cohn Livingston

Myra Cohn Livingston, "I Haven't Learned to Whistle" from *O Sliver of Liver.* Text © 1979 by Myra Cohn Livingston. Reprinted with the permission of Atheneum Publishers.

FEET

There are things
Feet know
That hands never will:
The exciting
Pounding feel
Of running down a hill;

The soft cool
Prickliness
When feet are bare
Walking in
The summer grass
To most anywhere.

Or dabbling in
Water all
Slip-sliddering through toes—
(Nicer than
Through fingers, though why
No one really knows.)

"Toes, tell my
Fingers," I
Said to them one day,
"Why it's such
Fun just to
Wiggle and play."

But toes just
Looked at me
Solemn and still.
Oh, there are things
Feet know
That hands NEVER WILL.

Dorothy Aldis

"Feet" by Dorothy Aldis. Reprinted by permission of G. P. Putnam's Sons from *Everything and Anything*, © 1925–1927, Renewed, 1953–1955 by Dorothy Aldis.

MAYTIME MAGIC
A little seed
For me to sow . . .
A little earth
To make it grow . . .

A little hole,
A little pat . . .
A little wish,
And that is that

A little sun,
A little shower . . .
A little while,
And then—a flower!

Mabel Watts

Permission granted by Mabel Watts, 1988.

THE GRASSHOPPERS
High
Up
Over the top
Of feathery grasses the
Grasshoppers hop.
They won't eat their suppers;
They will not obey
Their grasshopper mothers

And fathers, who say:
"Listen, my children,
This must be stopped—
Now is the time your last
Hop should be hopped;
So come eat your suppers
And go to your beds—"
But the little green grasshoppers
Shake their green heads.
"No,
No—"
The naughty ones say,
"All we have time to do
Now is play
If we want supper we'll
Nip at a fly
Or nibble a blueberry
As we go by;
If we feel sleepy we'll
Close our eyes tight
And snoozle away in a
Harebell all night
But not
Now
Now we must hop
And nobody
NOBODY
Can make us stop."

Dorothy Aldis

"The Grasshoppers" by Dorothy Aldis. Reprinted by permission of G. P. Putnam's Sons from *All Together* by Dorothy Aldis. Copyright 1925,1926,1927,1928,1934,1939, 1952 by Dorothy Aldis.

I BOUGHT ME A ROOSTER
I bought me a rooster and the rooster pleased me.
I fed my rooster on the bayberry tree,
My little rooster goes cock-a-doodle-doo,
  dee-doodle-dee doodle dee doodle dee doo!

I bought me a cat and the cat pleased me.
I fed my cat on the bayberry tree,
My little cat goes meow, meow, meow.
My little rooster goes cock-a-doodle-doo,
  dee-doodle-dee doodle dee doodle dee doo!

I bought me a dog and the dog pleased me.
I fed my dog on the bayberry tree,
My little dog goes bark, bark, bark.
My little cat goes meow, meow, meow.
My little rooster goes cock-a-doodle-doo,
  dee-doodle-dee doodle dee doodle dee doo!

Traditional

Note: This is a cumulative poem that takes teacher practice; additional verses include as many animals as you wish.

THE CHICKENS

  Said the first little chicken,
    With a queer little squirm,
  "I wish I could find
    A fat little worm!"

  Said the next little chicken,
    With an odd little shrug:
  "I wish I could find
    A fat little bug!"

  Said the third little chicken
    With a small sign of grief:
  "I wish I could find
    A green little leaf!"

  Said the fourth little chicken,
    With a faint little moan:
  "I wish I could find
    A wee gravel stone!"

  "Now see here!" said the mother,
    From the green garden patch,
  "If you want any breakfast,
    Just come here and scratch!"

Anonymous

TALKING ANIMALS

  "Meow," says cat.
  "Bow-wow," says dog.
  "Oink," says pig.
  "Croak," says frog.
  Hen says, "Cluck."
  Lamb says, "Ba."
  Cow says, "Moo."
  and babies "Wah."

  Lion says, "Roar."
  Mouse says, "Squeak."
  Snake says, "Ssssis."
  Chick says, "Peep."

  Crow says, "Ca."
  Bears growl.
  Sheep bleat.
  Wolves howl.

  Pig says, "Squeal."
  Owl says, "Hoot who."
  Toad says, "Ree deep."
  Cuckoo says, "Cuckoo."

  Donkey says, "Hee Haw."
  Horse says, "Neigh Neigh."
  Turkey says, "Gobble."
  And we all say, "HOORAY!"

Note: Last line can also read, "And we say 'Happy Birthday!'"

OVER IN THE MEADOW

  Over in the meadow, in the sand in the sun,
  Lived an old mother frog and her little froggie
    one.
  "Croak!" said the mother; "I croak," said the one,
  So they croaked and were glad in the sand in the
    sun.

  Over in the meadow in a pond so blue
  Lived an old mother duck and her little ducks two.
  "Quack!" said the mother; "we quack," said the
    two,
  So they quacked and were glad in the pond so
    blue.

  Over in the meadow, in a hole in a tree,
  Lived an old mother robin and her little birdies
    three.
  "Chirp!" said the mother; "we chirp," said the
    three,
  So they chirped and were glad in the hole in a tree.

  Over in the meadow, on a rock by the shore,
  Lived an old mother snake and her little snakes
    four.
  "Hiss!" said the mother; "we hiss," said the four,
  So they hissed and were glad on a rock by the
    shore.

Over in the meadow, in a big beehive,
Lived an old mother bee and her little bees five.
"Buzz!" said the mother; "we buzz," said the five,
So they buzzed and were glad in the big beehive.

Traditional

LITTLE BOY BLUE

Little Boy Blue,
Come, blow your horn!
The sheep's in the meadow,
The cow's in the corn.
Where's the little boy
That looks after the sheep?
Under the haystack, fast asleep!

Mother Goose

THE CAT AND THE FIDDLE

Hey, diddle, diddle!
The cat and the fiddle,
The cow jumped over the moon;
The little dog laughed
To see such sport,
And the dish ran away
With the spoon.

Mother Goose

THE LITTLE GIRL WITH A CURL

There was a little girl
Who had a little curl
Right in the middle of her forehead;
When she was good
She was very, very good,
And when she was bad she was horrid.

Mother Goose

The following are poems written by early childhood students who created them to use with young children. These beginning attempts show that most teachers are capable of writing enjoyable and interesting poetry to use for language pleasure.

A SLEEPY PLACE TO BE

Oh, it was a yawning day
That nobody wanted to work or play
And everybody felt the very same way.

There was a duckling who quacked and quacked
He had soft down upon his back.
He was tired of swimming and everything,
So he put his head down under his wing.
And there under the shadowy shade tree
He slept until it was half-past three.

A little old pig gave a big loud squeal
As he ate every scrap of his noonday meal.
And under the shadowy shade tree
He slept as quietly as could be.

A butterfly blue, green and red
Sat with her wings above her head
Up on a branch of the shadowy tree.
Oh, what a sleepy place to be.

Debbie Lauer-Hunter

LITTLE KITTY

Pretty little Kitty
With fur so soft and sweet,
You tiptoe oh so softly
On your tiny little feet.

Fluffy little Kitty
With eyes so big and round,
I never hear you coming,
You hardly make a sound.

Silly little Kitty
Playing with a ball
Listen! Someone's coming!
You scamper down the hall.

Lazy little Kitty
Tiny sleepy head
Curled up, sleeping soundly
In your cozy little bed.

Bari Morgan-Miller

THE PUMPKIN NO ONE WANTED

Out in the pumpkin patch, sad and forlorn,
Sat a funny little pumpkin, shaped like a horn.
He sat and he waited, through the day and the night,
For his own special person, someone just right.

He was thin by his stem,
Fat on the bottom,
Sitting in the corner,
Alone and forgotten.

Along came a Doctor, searching through the vine
  Looking for some pumpkins, seven, eight, nine.
She saw the funny pumpkin, sad and forlorn,
  She laughed and said, "You are shaped like a
      horn."

      He was thin by his stem,
      Fat on the bottom,
      Sitting in the corner,
      Alone and forgotten.

Along came a teacher, walking down the row,
  He came to the pumpkin, laughed and said
        "No . . .
For a jack-o-lantern, you won't do at all.
  Here you're thin, there you're fat,
    you're much too tall."

      He was thin by his stem,
      Fat on the bottom,
      Sitting in the corner,
      Alone and forgotten.

Along came a little girl, all by herself.
  She wanted a jack-o-lantern to sit on a shelf.
She looked for a pumpkin, round, smooth and fat.
  She saw the funny pumpkin and said,
  "Not one like that."

      He was thin by his stem,
      Fat on the bottom,
      Sitting in the corner,
      Alone and forgotten.

Along came a tall boy, walking all alone,
  Looking for a pumpkin to take to his home.
He saw the funny pumpkin, shaped like a horn,
  Over in the corner, sad and forlorn.

      He was thin by his stem,
      Fat on the bottom,
      No longer in the corner,
      Alone or forgotten.

                                    Mary Sheridan

Summary

Poems and verses provide an important literary experience, and exposure to classics is something no child should miss. They can be a source of enjoyment and learning for young children. Rhythm, word images, fast action, and rhyme are used to promote listening skill.

Short verses, easily remembered, give children self-confidence with words. Encouragement and attention is offered by the teacher when the child shows interest.

Poems are selected and practiced for enthusiastic, smooth presentations. They can be selected from various sources or can be created by the teacher. Props help children focus on words. Poems are created or selected keeping in mind the features that attract and interest young children.

STUDENT ACTIVITIES

1. Share with the class a poem you learned as a child.
2. Select five poems from any source. Be ready to state the reasons you selected them when you bring them to the next class meeting.
3. Make a list of 10 picture books that include children's poetry. Cite author, title, publisher, and copyright date.
4. Create a poem for young children. Go back and review the features most often found in classic rhymes.
5. Present a poem to a group of preschoolers. Evaluate its success in a few sentences.

6. Find poetry written in free verse that you feel might be successful with preschool children.

7. Form groups of three to six students. Using a large sheet of newsprint tacked (or taped) to the wall and a felt pen, list clever ways to introduce poetry to young children; for example, Poem of the Day. Discuss each group's similar and diverse suggestions.

8. Discuss poetry's visual images. Cite examples.

9. Find a source of ethnic children's poetry and share it with class members.

10. Earlier in this chapter it was suggested that you list remembered Mother Goose characters. In a group of four or five classmates, compare your list with others, then with other groups. The group with the longest list then asks other groups with shorter lists to recite a Mother Goose rhyme in unison.

11. What kind of activity could you plan using the rhyme that follows?

> *Bus is comin' down the road, yes it is.*
> *Bus is comin' down the road, yes it is.*
> *Bus just turned the corner.*
> *Now it has come to a stop.*
> *Hear the doors open and pop.*
> *Hear the doors open and pop.*

CHAPTER REVIEW

A. List a few reasons why poetry is used with young children.

B. Select from Column II the term that matches each item in Column I.

Column I	**Column II**
1. poetry	a. an action verb
2. rhyme	b. self-confidence
3. beat	c. a rhythmic measure
4. order and form	d. mental pictures
5. images	e. words with like sounds
6. remembered	f. consistent and dependable
7. interest	g. teacher attention
8. goal	h. after practice
9. presentation	i. enjoyment
10. reciting	j. promotes listening skill
11. classics	k. never forced
12. song	l. library
13. props	m. Mother Goose rhymes
14. run	n. musical poem
15. source	o. focus attention

C. List the numbers of the statements that you feel agree with the suggestions mentioned in this chapter.

1. Young children must learn to recite.

2. Emphasizing the beat of poetry as you read it always increases the enjoyment.

3. Repeat the poem over and over until a child learns it.

4. Describe to children the mental pictures created by the poem before reading the poem to the children.

5. It really isn't too important for young children to memorize the poems they hear.

6. Memorizing a poem can help a child feel competent.

7. Most poems are not shared because teachers want children to gain the factual information the poem contains.

8. Poetry's rhythm comes from its form and order.

9. Memorizing a poem always causes awkward teacher presentation.

10. Teachers may try to author some of their own children's poetry.

D. List elements of poetry that can be manipulated to evoke emotion in listeners.

E. Write an example using a line of poetry or free verse for the following: alliteration, personification, simile, and figurative language.

F. Comment on a poetry reader's tendency to pause at the end of each line when reading poetry aloud.

RESOURCES

Adoff, A. (Ed.). (1984). *My black me*. New York: Dutton.

Base, G. (1990). *My grandma lived in Gooligulch*. New York: Harry N. Abrams.

Cole, J. (1989). *Anna Banana: 101 jump rope rhymes*. Illustrated by Alan Tiegreen. New York: Morrow.

Cole, J., & Calmenson, S. (Eds.). (1988). *The read-aloud treasury: Favorite nursery rhymes, poems, stories and more for the very young*. Illustrated by Ann Schweninger. New York: Doubleday.

Hopkins, L. B. (Ed.). (1992). *Flit, flutter, fly: Poems about bugs and other crawly creatures*. Illustrated by Peter Palagonia. New York: Doubleday.

Prelutsky, J. (Ed.). (1991). *For laughing out loud: Poems to tickle your funnybone*. Illustrated by Marjorie Priceman. New York: Knopf.

Prelutsky, J. (Ed.). (1983). *The Random House book of poetry for children*. Illustrated by Arnold Lobel. New York: Random House.

Stevenson, R. L. (1990). *My shadow*. Illustrated by Ted Rand. New York: Putnam.

Wood, A. (1992). *Silly Sally*. San Diego, CA: Harcourt Brace.

CHAPTER 12

Flannel (Felt) Boards and Activity Sets

OBJECTIVES

After studying this chapter, you should be able to:

- describe flannel boards and types of flannel board activities.

- make and present three flannel board activities.

- describe teacher techniques in flannel board story presentation.

Flannel (or felt) board activities are a rewarding experience for both the child and teacher. Since the attention of young children is easily captured, the teacher finds the use of flannel-board activities very popular and effective. Children are highly attentive during this type of activity—straining to see and hear—looking forward to the next piece to be put on the flannel board.

Stories to be used with flannel-board activities are selected by the same criteria used for storytelling; see Chapter 10. In addition to stories, poetry, and songs, other listening and learning activities can be presented with flannel boards.

Flannel Board Construction

Boards of different sizes, shapes, and designs are used, depending on the needs of the center. They may be freestanding or propped up in the chalkboard tray, on a chair, or on an easel. Boards can be covered on both sides in different colors. Many are made by covering a sheet of heavy cardboard, display board, pre-stretched artist's canvas, (figure 12–1), styrofoam, or wood with a piece of solid-colored flannel or felt yardage (figure 12–2). The material is pulled smooth and held by tacks,

tape, glue, or wood staples, depending on the board material. Sometimes an under padding is added.

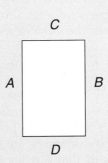

A pre-stretched *artist canvas* can be obtained at an art and craft store, or through artist's supply catalogs. Flannel or felt is available in navy blue or black in 45" widths.

Purchase ¾ yard of 45" yardage to cover a 24" × 36" canvas. Place the flannel or felt on a flat surface, and place the artist canvas face down on the material. Fold over and staple material onto the wood frame in this manner: First, staple side *A*. Pull the material snugly, and staple side *B*, then sides *C* and *D* making four hospital corners. Trim.

FIGURE 12–1 Directions for artist's canvas flannel board. *(Courtesy of Hey Diddle Diddle Publications, 1993.)*

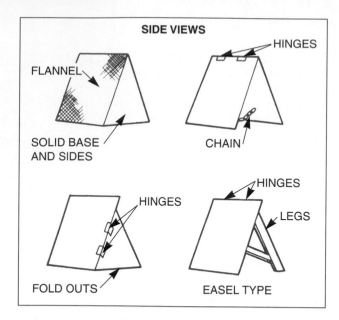

SIDE VIEWS

FLANNEL

HINGES

SOLID BASE
AND SIDES

CHAIN

HINGES

FOLD OUTS

HINGES

LEGS

EASEL TYPE

FIGURE 12–2   Freestanding boards

Putting wire mesh or a sheet of metal between the under padding and the covering material makes pieces with magnets adhere. Since all metal does not attract magnets, the mesh or metal needs testing before purchase.

Decisions on which materials to use in flannel board construction are often based on the intended use of the flannel board, material cost, and tools or skills needed in construction. Styrofoam is a good choice if having a light-weight board is important; however, wood-based boards are durable.

Making a board that tilts backward at a slight angle is an important consideration for a free-standing flannel board, because pieces applied to a slanted board stick more securely. Stores and companies that sell school supplies have premade boards in various price ranges.

Although flannel and felt are popular coverings for boards, other materials also work well. Almost all fuzzy textured material is usable. The nap can be raised on flannel or felt by brushing it with a stiff brush. It is a good idea to press a small piece of felt or pellon (fabric interfacing) to a fabric to see how well it sticks before buying the fabric.

Some boards have pockets in the back so that flannel pieces can be lined up and ready for use (figure 12–3). Some early childhood centers have parts of walls, dividers, and backs of pieces of furniture covered with flannel or felt. A simple homemade freestanding board holder is shown in figure 12–4.

A tabletop flannel board can be made from a cardboard box (see instructions and necessary materials in figure 12–5). One clever idea is using a secondhand attache case. Using a case that opens to a 90° angle, glue a large piece of flannel to the inside of the top lid. When open, the flannel will be in view. The case is used for storing sets, and the handle makes it easy to carry.

Display fabrics exist to which three-dimensional objects will adhere. Special adhesives and tapes are needed for this type of flannel board.

The size of the flannel board's front surface is important. Consider making or purchasing a board no smaller than 24" × 30" inches. The attache case could be used for individual child's play or for small groups but may be too small for larger groups. Most centers obtain or construct both a child's flannel board and a staff flannel board.

Activity Sets

Pieces for flannel activity sets can be made in a number of ways and from a number of fabrics and papers. Pellon and felt, because of their low cost and durability, are probably the most popular. Heavy-paper figures with flannel backing or felt tape also stick well. Commercial tape, sandpaper, fuzzy velour-flocked wallpaper, velcro, and used foamlike laundry softener sheets are other possibilities for backing pieces. Premade flannel or felt board sets are available at school-supply stores and at most teacher conferences. Most communities have at least one teacher who is a small business entrepreneur specializing in making flannel sets for other teachers.

Shapes and figures can be traced from books, magazines, coloring books, self-drawn and created,

Construction:

Obtain a piece of cardboard, of the size you desire for the back of your flannel board, and a large sheet of flannel or heavy wrapping paper. The flannel (or paper) should be several inches wider than the cardboard and about twice as long as the finished chart size. One-inch deep with a back 3 inches high is a good pocket size.

Measure and mark both sides of flannel (paper) at intervals of 3 inches and 1 inch, alternating. Using accordion folds, the first 1-inch section is creased and folded forward over the second 3-inch section, and so on. Pull tight and secure ends.

A pocket chart conveniently holds set pieces in sequence for flannel-board stories and can be useful in other child activities with flannel set pieces.

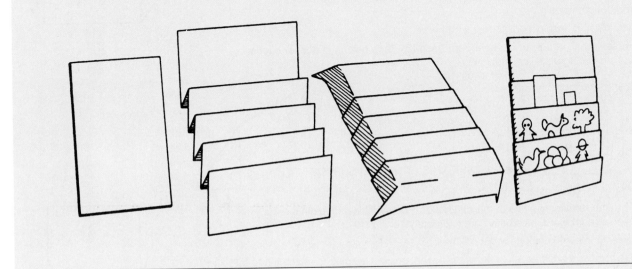

FIGURE 12–3 Pocket chart

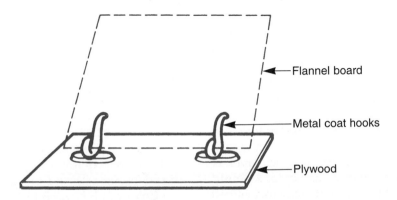

FIGURE 12–4 Two metal coat hooks screwed to a piece of heavy plywood make a good flannel-board holder.

Materials:

cardboard box
art knife or cardboard cutter
adhesive paper
cloth, plastic, or bookbinder's tape
tacky glue (or white school glue)
felt yardage (large enough to cover box)

Directions:

1. Using the cardboard cutter, remove top of box so that only the 4 sides and bottom remain.

2. As indicated in A, cut box in half lengthwise.

3. Preserve half of box for flannel-board base (B). Tape bottom of box for support. Cut sides diagonally, as shown in C.

4. From the remaining piece of the original box, cut off sides to obtain a rectangular piece of cardboard, measuring approximately 16" × 12".

5. Fit rectangle into diagonally cut box half.

6. Use adhesive shelf paper to decorate flannel board. Use glue to attach felt to the front of the box.

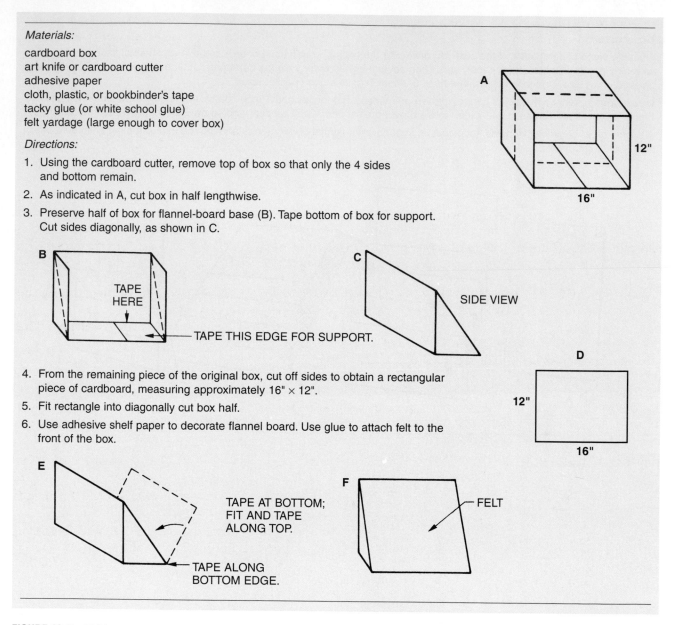

FIGURE 12–5   Tabletop cardboard box flannel board

or borrowed from other sources. Tracing paper is helpful for this purpose. Tracing can be done simply by covering the back of a paper pattern with a heavy layer of pencil lead. Soft art pencils work best. The pattern is then turned over and traced. Another method is cutting the object out, tracing its outline, and then drawing details freehand. Tracing pencils and pens are commercially available and come with directions for use and are found at craft stores.

Color can be added to set pieces with felt markers, oil pastels, acrylic or poster paint, embroidery pens, crayons, paints, and colored pencils. Sets take time to make but are well worth the effort. Favorites will be presented over and over again. Pieces can be covered with clear contact paper or can be laminated (fronts only) for durability.

Teachers can be creative with flannel-board sets by decorating pieces with:

- layered felt
- wiggly eyes (commercially available at variety stores)
- hand-stitched character clothing
- imitation fur fabric
- liquid glitter
- commercial fluorescent paint or crayons.

Many of the newer copy machines have the ability to enlarge figures or shrink them. Set pieces that are too small are difficult to handle and see. Narrow parts on set pieces should be avoided, because they tend to tear with use. Also, try to preserve the size relationship between characters (such as between a mouse and a human figure) as well as the cultural and ethnic diversity of characters.

Pattern transfer books are plentiful and available from craft and sewing supply stores. Patterns can be ironed on cloth quickly, and it is possible to obtain multiple copies. Publishers of transfer books include Dover Publications, New York, NY, and Craftways, Richmond, CA.

Some schools buy inexpensive picture books and use the illustrations as flannel-board set pieces. After the pieces are cut, they are glued to oak tag, and backed with some of the materials mentioned above.

Proper storage and care will preserve pieces and prolong their usefulness. A flat stocking box or large mailing envelope or manila folder is practical for storage. If pieces become bent, a warm iron makes most kinds flat again. Sets can be stored in plastic page protectors used in three-ring binders (available in stationery stores). Large zip-lock plastic household bags, as well as plastic envelopes available at teacher supply stores, can also be used to protect pieces.

Presentation

Like most other listening activities, a semisecluded, comfortable setting should be chosen for presentation. The activity begins with the teacher starting to place pieces on the board in proper sequence as the story or activity unfolds, always focusing on the children's reactions. In this activity, as in many others described in this text, the teacher may be presenting but also watching for reaction. Since pieces are usually added one at a time, they should be kept in an open flat box or manila folder in the teacher's lap, or, better yet, behind the board, stacked in the order they will appear. This is hard to do if the story or activity is not well in mind.

The teacher should periodically check to see whether the set has all its pieces, particularly in large centers where many staff members use the same sets. If pieces are missing or damaged, the teacher or volunteers can make new pieces. New sets are always appreciated by the entire staff and can be developed to meet the needs and interests of a particular group of children.

In order to present activities with ease, the beginner should note these steps:

- Read the story (or activity sequence) and check the pieces to be used.
- Practice until there is a smooth coordination of words and placement of pieces on the board.
- Set up the flannel board.
- Check and prepare pieces in order of their appearance.
- Place pieces out of view, behind the board within easy reach, or in a lap folder.
- Gather children. Make seating adjustments if necessary. Respond to children's needs. Group size should be considered carefully; the smaller the group, the more intimate and conversational the experience. As with other language arts presentations, consider two tellings to reduce group size.
- Introduce the activity with a statement that builds a desire to listen.
- Tell the story (or present the activity), watching for reactions from the children. Create drama and suspense with pauses, speaking in characters' voices, and moving pieces across the board's surface, if the story calls for this. Let your personality guide you.

- Discussion for language development or comprehension is optional. Teachers ask questions or discuss story particulars to elicit children's ideas and comments.
- Keep pieces flat, store them properly, returning sets where other staff members expect them to be.
- Children enjoy doing their retelling with a flannel board and their own activity sets. Most centers construct one set for teachers and another set for child exploration and activity.

In addition to storytelling activities, sets may be used for songs, poetry, numbers, language development, and other activities.

SUGGESTED STORIES AND ACTIVITIES

There are many resources for story ideas. Stories created by teachers can be enjoyed as much as commercial sets and classic stories. Sets can improve listening skills and enhance vocabulary and concept development, often within one activity. The visual shapes or pieces are linked to words and ideas. Occasionally, a child's picture book can be presented as a flannel-board activity before the book becomes part of the school's book collection.

An available flannel board placed at children's eye level with an adjacent open box of figures or shapes quickly encourages use and creativity (figure 12–6). Remembered words, lines, and whole stories are relived in children's play. They often go beyond the familiar, devising their own events. Even sturdy felt pieces will need to be ironed flat occasionally and replaced because of frequent and vigorous use by children. As suggested above, children's play with the flannel board often follows a teacher presentation but can also be a free choice activity at other times of the day.

Many centers include flannel boards and sets in their language centers along with alphabet letter cutouts. Teachers can use alphabet letter cutouts in daily activities, and many centers routinely have set pieces, such as a flower shape, labeled with the cut out alphabet letters underneath the shape on the flannel board for viewing. A flannel board with the word "closed" on it may be used to block entrance to a play area or other section of the room.

FIGURE 12–6   The children are placing pellon story pieces on a board covered with flannel.

Suggested books that lend themselves to flannel-board presentations:

Flack, M. (1971). *Ask Mr. Bear*. New York: Macmillan.

Martin, B. (1972). *Brown Bear, Brown Bear, what do you see?* New York: Holt, Rinehart, and Winston Inc.

Slobodkina, E. (1947). *Caps for sale*. Glenview, IL: Addison Wesley Publishing Company.

Young, E. (1992). *Seven blind mice*. New York: Philomel Books.

Zuromskis, D. (1978). *The farmer in the dell*. Boston: Little, Brown & Company.

Sets and activity ideas can be obtained from the following sources:

Betty Lukens, (800) 541-9279

Childwood, 8873 Woodbank Dr., Bainbridge Island, WA 98110. Manufactures magnet-backed figures for classic tales.

Community Careers Flannelboard Set, Instructo Corp., can be ordered through The Women's Action Alliance Inc., Dept. C, The Non-Sexist Child Development Project, 370 Lexington Avenue, New York, NY 10017

The Flannelboard, 3700 South Calvin Drive, West Valley City, UT 84120

Holiday Kits for Flannelboards, The Sunshine Factory, Box 650, Elizabethville, PA 17023

The Storyboard, P.O. Box 2650, Chino, CA 91708

Storytell, 48 Basswood Ave., Agoura Hills, CA 91301

The Story Teller, (800) 801-6860

Many urban school districts allow private preschool teachers in their community to use their central office curriculum centers, which may also hold flannel-board resources. Additional resources are listed at the end of this chapter and additional flannel-board stories and patterns may be found in the Appendix.

The following activities and stories are suggested as a start for the beginning teacher. They may also be used to add variety and ideas for new sets. Many of the set pieces that follow will need to be enlarged; if a copy machine with enlargement capability is not available for this purpose, try using an overhead projector.

The Lion and the Mouse

Author Unknown (a classic story)

Pieces: lion, sleeping   rope
         lion, awake   mouse
         tree   two hunters

(On the board, place the sleeping lion next to the tree. Place the mouse near the lion's back, moving it slowly toward the lion while speaking in a soft voice.)

There once was a little mouse who saw a big lion sleeping by a tree. "Oh, it would be fun to climb on top of the lion and slide down his tail," thought the mouse. So—quietly, he tiptoed close to the lion. When he climbed on the lion's back, the fur felt so soft and warm between his toes that he began running up and down the lion's back.

The lion awoke. He felt a tickle upon his back. He opened one eye and saw the little mouse, which he then caught in his paw.

(Move mouse under lion's paw.)

"Let me go—please!" said the mouse. "I'm sorry I woke you from your nap. Let me go, and I'll never bother you again. Maybe you and I could be friends—friends help each other, you know."

This made the lion laugh. "A little mouse like you, help me? I'm big, I'm strong, and I'm brave!" Then the lion laughed again, and he let the mouse go.

(Take the mouse off the board.)

The mouse ran away, and he didn't see the lion for a long time. But, one day when the mouse was out looking for seeds for dinner, he saw the lion tied to a tree with a rope, and two hunters near him.

(Remove sleeping lion. Add awake lion, placing it next to tree, with rope on top. Put the two hunters on the other side of the tree.)

One hunter said, "Well, this rope will hold the lion until we can go get our truck and take him to the zoo." So the hunters walked away.

(Remove the hunters.)

The mouse ran up to the lion as soon as the hunters were out of sight. He said, "Hello, lion."

(Add mouse.)

The lion answered, "Well, I guess it's your turn to laugh at me tied to this tree."

"I'm not going to laugh," said the mouse, as he quickly started to chew on the rope.

(Move mouse close to rope.)

The mouse chewed, and chewed, and chewed. The rope fell apart, and the lion was free.

(Remove rope.)

"You are a good friend," said the lion. "Hop on my back and hold on. Let's get away from here before those two hunters come back."

(Place lion in running position with mouse on lion's back.)

"OK," said the mouse. "I'd like that."

So you see, sometimes little friends can help big friends. The size of a friend isn't really too important.

Cut line

Fortunately-Unfortunately

Pieces:
boy	haystack	shark
plane	pitchfork	tiger
parachute	water	cave
snake	birthday cake	

Once upon a time there was a little boy. Fortunately, he received an invitation to a birthday party. Unfortunately, the party was in Florida, and he was in New York City.

Fortunately, he had a plane. Unfortunately, the plane caught fire. Fortunately, he had a parachute. Unfortunately, the parachute had a hole in it. Fortunately, there was a haystack. Unfortunately, there was a pitchfork in the haystack.

Fortunately, he missed the pitchfork. Unfortunately, he missed the haystack. Fortunately, he landed in the water. Unfortunately, there was a shark in the water.

Fortunately, he could swim, and he swam to the shore. Unfortunately, there were tigers on the land. Fortunately, he could run. Unfortunately, so could the tigers.

Fortunately, he found a cave. Unfortunately, there were snakes in the cave. Fortunately, he found a way out of the cave. Unfortunately, it led him to the middle of a formal ballroom.

Fortunately, there was a party going on. Fortunately, it was for him. And, fortunately, it was his birthday!

Remy Charlip, *What Good Luck, What Bad Luck* (New York: Scholastic Book Services, 1969).

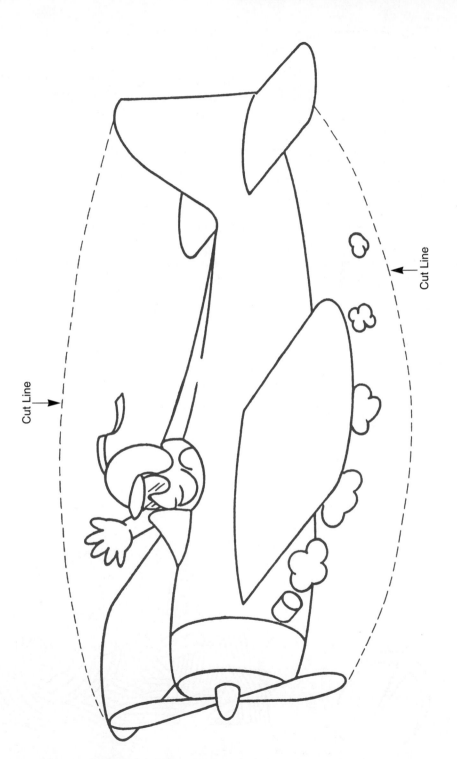

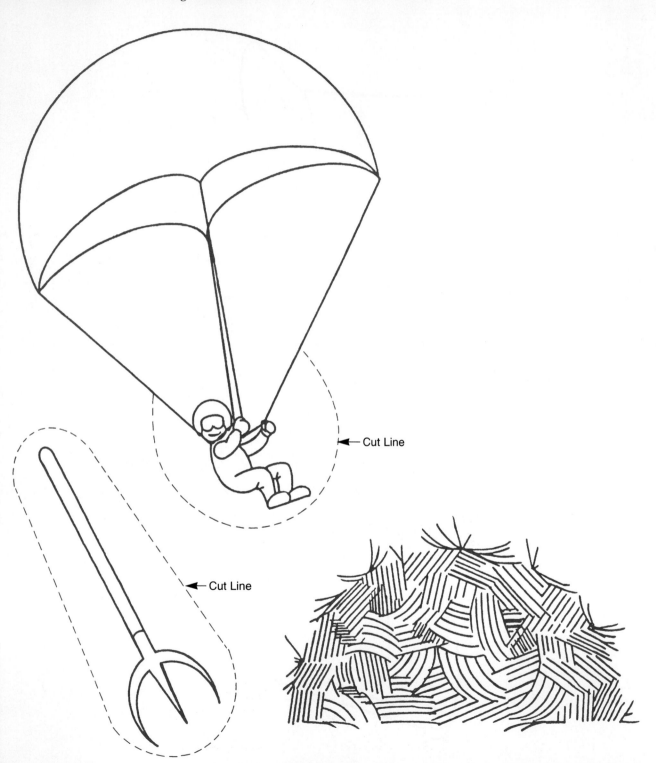

← Cut Line

← Cut Line

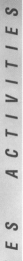

Cut Line ▶

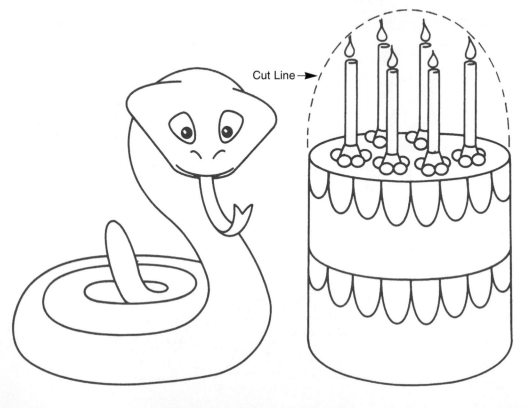

The Pumpkin That Grew

(A Halloween flannel–board story/poem)

Pieces: green leaves for vine (five or six)
              large vine
              finished pumpkin
              (green stem, orange face)

              pumpkins in three different sizes:
                  small (dark green)
                  medium (light green)
                  large (yellow)

Once there was a pumpkin
  And all summer through
It stayed upon a big green vine
  and grew, and grew, and grew.

It grew from being small and green
  To being orange and bright
And then it said unto itself,
  "Now I'm a handsome sight."

And then one day it grew a mouth
  A nose and two big eyes;
And so that pumpkin grew into
  A Jack O'Lantern wise!

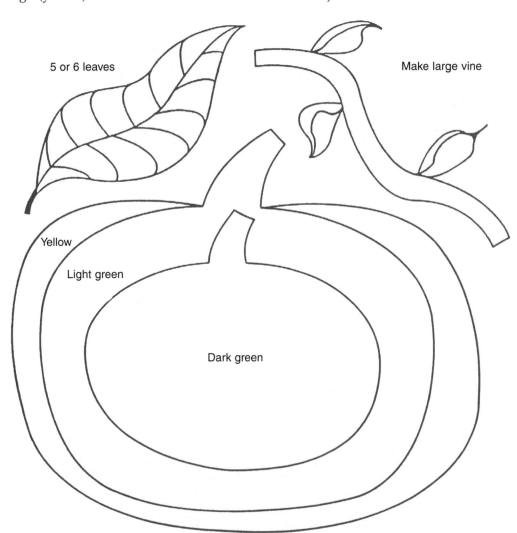

5 or 6 leaves

Make large vine

Yellow

Light green

Dark green

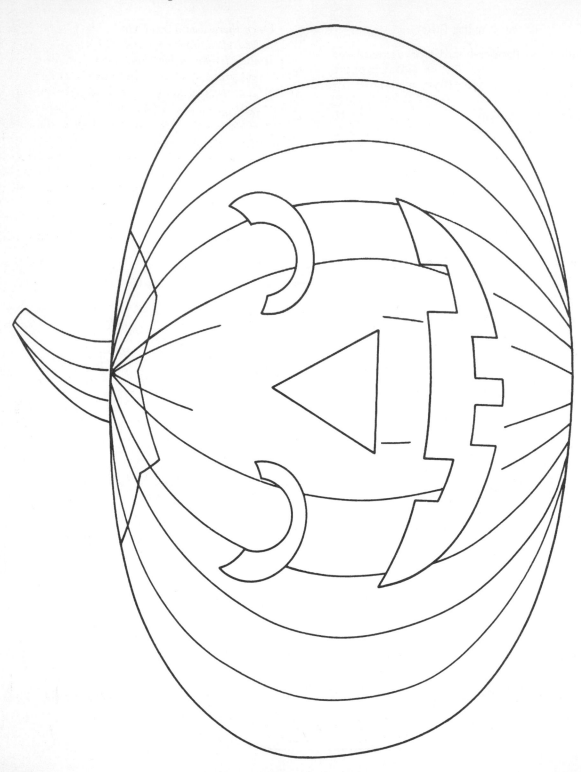

The Seed

Margie Cowsert
(While an ECE student)

Pieces: small roots   leaves
         green shoot   beaver
         deer   bird
         Mr. Man   large trunk
         apples (five or more) large leaves
         seed   large roots
         small trunk

Once upon a time, there was a seed named Abraham. He didn't know what kind of plant he would be, so he asked Mr. Bird. Mr. Bird didn't know but wanted to eat Abraham. Abraham asked him to wait until after he found out what he would be, and the bird agreed to wait.

Abraham grew small roots and green shoots. He asked Mr. Deer if he knew what he would grow up to be. "Do you know what I'll be when I grow up?" Mr. Deer said, "No," but wanted to eat the tender green shoot. Abraham said, "Please wait." So Mr. Deer decided to wait.

Abraham grew a small trunk and leaves. He was glad he was a tree but still didn't know what

Cut as one piece.

Cut as one piece.

kind. He asked Mr. Beaver, "Do you know what I'll be when I grow up?" Mr. Beaver didn't know but wanted to eat Abraham's tender bark. He decided to wait also.

Abraham grew big roots, a big trunk, and more leaves, but still didn't know what kind of tree he was. He asked Mr. Man, "Do you know what I'll be when I grow up?" Mr. Man didn't know, but he wanted to chop down Abraham to make a house. He decided to wait.

Abraham grew apples. Hooray! He knew that he was an apple tree. He told Mr. Bird he could eat him now. Mr. Bird said Abraham was too big, but that he would like one of the apples. Mr. Deer thought the tree was too big, too, but he did want an apple. Mr. Beaver took any apples that fell to the ground home to his family. Mr. Man loved apples, so he told Abraham Tree that he wouldn't chop him down.

Abraham Apple Tree was so happy to know what he was and that no one was going to eat him or chop him down that he grew lots of apples.

Just Like Daddy

Pieces: little brown bear
little brown bear's
    blue vest
flower
brown father bear
red boots for
    father bear
yellow coat for
    father bear
purple vest for
    mother bear

green fish (large)
green fish (small)
brown mother bear
red boots for little
    bear
blue vest for
    father bear
yellow coat for
    little bear

When I got up this morning, I yawned a
big yawn . . .
    Just like daddy.

I washed my face, got dressed, and had a
big breakfast . . .
    Just like daddy.
And then I put on my yellow coat and blue vest
and my red boots . . .
    Just like daddy.
And we went fishing—Daddy, Mommy, and me.
On the way, I picked a flower and gave it
to my mother . . .
    Just like daddy.
When we got to the lake, I put a worm on
my hook . . .
    Just like daddy.
All day we fished, and I caught a big
fish . . .
    Just like mommy!!!

Little bear's blue vest (cut 1)

Flower (cut 1)

Little brown bear (cut 1)

Brown father bear (cut 1)

Green fish (cut 2)

Small green fish (cut 1)

Brown mother bear (cut 1)

Red boots
for father bear
(cut 2)

Red boots
for little bear
(cut 2)

Yellow coat
for father bear
(cut 1)

Blue vest
for father bear
(cut 1)

Yellow coat
for little bear
(cut 1)

Purple vest
for mother bear
(cut 1)

The Tree in the Woods

Pieces: grass   bird's nest
          treetop   bird's egg
          tree trunk   bird
          tree limb   wing
          tree branch   feather

(The flannel board can be used to build the song by placing first the grass and then the treetop, trunk, limb, branch, nest, egg, bird, wing, and feather, as each verse calls for them.)

Now in the woods there was a tree,
The finest tree that you ever did see,
And the green grass grew all around,
  around, around,
And the green grass grew all around.

And on that grass there was a trunk,
The finest trunk that you ever did see,
And the trunk was on the tree,
And the tree was in the woods,
And the green grass grew all around,
  around, around,
And the green grass grew all around.

And on that trunk there was a limb,
The finest limb that you ever did see,
And the limb was on the trunk,
And the trunk was on the tree,
And the tree was in the woods,
And the green grass grew all around,
  around, around,
And the green grass grew all around.

And on that limb there was a branch,
The finest branch that you ever did see,
And the branch was on the limb,
And the limb was on the trunk,
And the trunk was on the tree,
And the tree was in the woods,
And the green grass grew all around,
  around, around,
And the green grass grew all around.

And on that branch there was a nest,
The finest nest that you ever did see,
And the nest was on the branch,
And the branch was on the limb,

And the limb was on the trunk,
And the trunk was on the tree,
And the tree was in the woods,
And the green grass grew all around,
  around, around,
And the green grass grew all around.

And in that nest there was an egg,
The finest egg that you ever did see,
And the egg was in the nest,
And the nest was on the branch,
And the branch was on the limb,
And the limb was on the trunk,
And the trunk was on the tree,
And the tree was in the woods,
And the green grass grew all around,
  around, around,
And the green grass grew all around.

And on that egg there was a bird,
The finest bird that you ever did see,
And the bird was on the egg,
And the egg was in the nest,
And the nest was on the branch,
And the branch was on the limb,
And the limb was on the trunk,
And the trunk was on the tree,
And the tree was in the woods,
And the green grass grew all around,
  around, around,
And the green grass grew all around.

And on that bird there was a wing,
The finest wing that you ever did see,
And the wing was on the bird,
And the bird was on the egg,
And the egg was in the nest,
And the nest was on the branch,
And the branch was on the limb,
And the limb was on the trunk,
And the trunk was on the tree,
And the tree was in the woods,
And the green grass grew all around,
  around, around,
And the green grass grew all around.

And on that wing there was a feather,
The finest feather that you ever did see,

And the feather was on the wing,
And the wing was on the bird,
And the bird was on the egg,
And the egg was in the nest,
And the nest was on the branch,
And the branch was on the limb,

And the limb was on the trunk,
And the trunk was on the tree,
And the tree was in the woods,
And the green grass grew all around,
  around, around,
And the green grass grew all around.

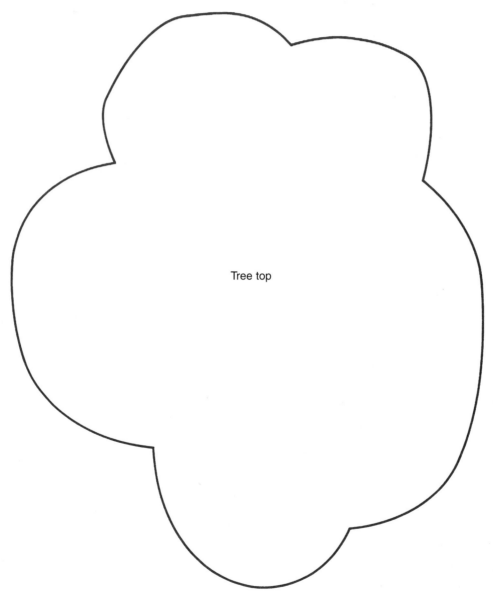

Tree top

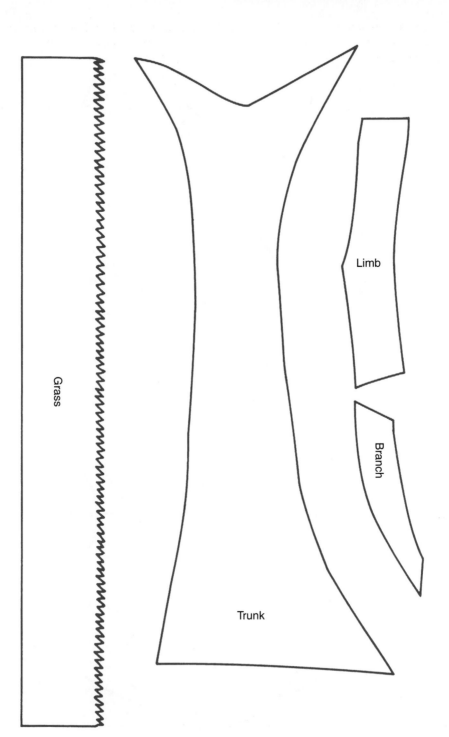

Grass

Trunk

Limb

Branch

Feather

Wing

Egg

Nest

Board assemblage—for tree in the woods

Tree top

Grass

Riddle

Pieces: Triangles of felt in red, blue, yellow, green, purple, orange, brown, black, and white

Teacher: Riddle, riddle, ree.

What color do I see?

_____ (child's name) has it on his or her

_____ (shirt, pants, and so forth).

What color can this be?

(When the color is identified, the following is said.)

Group: It's _____, _____, _____

(Example: red, red, red)

Mary (instead of Mary substitute name of child who named the color) did say.

Let's see what colors we can find today.

(Teacher puts triangle of same color on flannel board. Child whose name was mentioned is asked whether he or she, or a friend of the child's choice, is going to guess the name of the color. Each child is asked whether he or she wants to guess the color. Activity ends with line of triangles that group names as each triangle is removed.)

One, Two, Buckle My Shoe

Pieces: Numerals 1 through 10   crossed sticks
           shoe   straight sticks
           door   hen

One, Two,
Buckle my shoe;
Three, four,
Knock at the door;
Five, six,
Pick up sticks;
Seven, eight,
Lay them straight;
Nine, ten,
Big fat hen.

Cut line

This Old Man

Pieces: old man   tree
        shoe*   two clouds (heaven)
        door*   thumb
        sticks*   hive
        gate   vine
        10 bones   hen*
        dog   numerals 1 through 10*

1. This old man, he played one, he played knick-knack on my thumb.

    With a knick-knack paddy-whack, give a dog a bone.

    This old man came rolling home.

2. This old man, he played two, he played knick-knack on my shoe.

    With a knick-knack paddy-whack, give a dog a bone.

    This old man came rolling home.

3. This old man, he played three, he played knick-knack on my tree.

    With a knick-knack paddy-whack, give a dog a bone.

    This old man came rolling home.

4. This old man, he played four, he played knick-knack on my door.

    With a knick-knack paddy-whack, give a dog a bone.

    This old man came rolling home.

5. This old man, he played five, he played knick-knack on my hive.

    With a knick-knack paddy-whack, give a dog a bone.

    This old man came rolling home.

6. This old man, he played six, he played knick-knack on my sticks.

    With a knick-knack paddy-whack, give a dog a bone.

    This old man came rolling home.

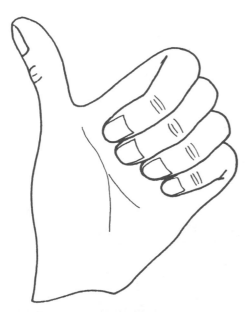

*Use patterns from One, Two, Buckle My Shoe.

7. This old man, he played seven, he played knick-knack up in heaven.

   With a knick-knack paddy-whack, give a dog a bone.

   This old man came rolling home.

8. This old man, he played eight, he played knick-knack on my gate.

   With a knick-knack paddy-whack, give a dog a bone.

   This old man came rolling home.

9. This old man, he played nine, he played knick-knack on my vine.

   With a knick-knack paddy-whack, give a dog a bone.

   This old man came rolling home.

10. This old man, he played ten, he played knick-knack on my hen.

    With a knick-knack paddy-whack, give a dog a bone.

    This old man came rolling home.

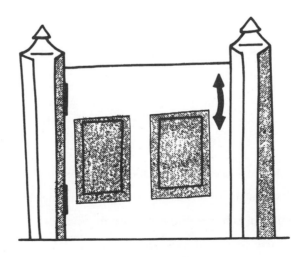

Summary

A flannel-board presentation is one of the most popular and successful listening activities for the young child. Stories are told while figures and shapes are moved on the board. The children can learn new ideas and words by seeing the visual model while listening to the story.

Beginning teachers practice presentations with words and pieces until the activity flows smoothly. The children's feedback is noted. Flannel-board activities in many other learning areas besides language development take place in early childhood centers.

A wide variety of fabrics is available for both boards and pieces; felt and flannel are the most commonly used materials for boards.

STUDENT ACTIVITIES

1. Visit a center to watch a flannel-board presentation, or invite a teacher to present an activity to the class.

2. Give a presentation to a small group of classmates. The classmates should make helpful suggestions in written form while watching the presentation, trying to look at the presentations through the eyes of a child.

3. Write an original story for the flannel board on ditto masters. Masters can be purchased from a stationery or office supply store. Include patterns for your pieces on ditto masters.

4. If videotape equipment is available in your classroom, give a flannel-board presentation and evaluate yourself.

5. Make three flannel-board sets, using any materials desired. Check the appendix.

6. Visit a school supply store and price commercial flannel boards. Compare costs for constructing a flannel board, and report at the next class meeting.

7. Make a personal flannel board.

8. Research stories and sets with multicultural variety.

CHAPTER REVIEW

A. List the types of materials used in board construction.

B. Name the kinds of materials used to make flannel-board pieces.

C. In your opinion, what is the best way to color pieces for flannel boards?

D. Why is the use of visual aids valuable?

E. Place in correct order.

   1. Give a flannel-board presentation.

   2. Set up area with board.

   3. Check pieces.

   4. Practice.

   5. Place pieces in order of appearance.

   6. Gather children.

   7. Place pieces out of sight.

   8. Discuss what happened during the activity with children (optional).

   9. Store set by keeping pieces flat.

   10. Introduce the set with a motivational statement if you wish.

F. What color flannel (or felt) would you use to cover your own board? Why?

G. Finish the following statements.

   1. A board is set up slanting back slightly because _____.

   2. A folding flannel board with handles is a good idea because _____.

   3. If children touch the pieces during a teacher presentation, the teacher should say _____.

   4. The main reason teachers like to store set pieces in a flat position is _____.

   5. One advantage of a flannel board made from a large styrofoam sheet is _____.

   6. One disadvantage of a flannel board made from a large styrofoam sheet is _____.

RESOURCES

Anderson, P. (1972). *Storytelling with the flannel board*, Book One and Book Two, T. S. Denison and Co., 9601 Newton Avenue S., Minneapolis, MN. (Useful as a source of additional stories and patterns)

Jumbo seasonal patterns. (1995). Newbridge Educational Program, P.O. Box 938, Hicksville, NY.

Kohl, D. M. (1986). *Teaching with the flannel board*. Minneapolis, MN: T. S. Denison.

Peralta, C. (1981). *Flannel board activities for the bilingual classroom*. La Arana Publishers, 11209 Malat Way, Culver City, CA 90232. (A collection of Latin-American traditional stories for the flannel board; patterns included)

Scott, L. B., & Thompson, J. J. (1984). *Rhymes for fingers and flannel boards*. Minneapolis, MN: T. S. Denison and Co. Inc.

Taylor, F., & Vaugh, G. (1980). *The flannel board storybook*. Humanics Learning, P.O. Box 7447, Atlanta, GA 30309.

Westcott, N. B. (1987). *Peanut butter and jelly: A play rhyme*. New York: Dutton.

Wilmes, L., & Wilmes, D. (1987). *Felt board fun*. Dundee: Building Books.

SPEECH GROWTH

Conversation, Expression, and Dramatization

CHAPTER 13

Realizing Speaking Goals

OBJECTIVES

After studying this chapter, you should be able to:

- state five goals of planned speech activities.

- describe appropriate teacher behavior in daily conversations with children.

- give three examples of questioning technique.

- explain the role of the teacher in dramatic play.

- describe activities that promote children's speaking abilities.

In a well-planned classroom, a child has many opportunities to speak. While some activities are planned, others just happen. Classroom discussion is paramount; throw away most or all of your ideas about quiet classrooms and instead aim for a dynamic room where discussion reigns. In this type of atmosphere, true literacy emerges. Help children see the uses of speaking in social interactions in their daily lives and tie speech to print and reading activities when possible. According to Clay (1991), preschool children do a wonderful job of learning to communicate and the more they talk the more their talking improves.

Activities can be divided into two groups: structured and unstructured. Structured activities are those that the teacher plans, prepares, and leads. The teacher is, for awhile, at the center of all action—motivating, presenting ideas, giving demonstrations, eliciting child ideas and comments, and promoting conversation. Unstructured activities, on the other hand, may still be prepared by the teacher, but the children decide the action through self-directed play, and the teacher is cast primarily in the role of cohort, confidant, and interested party. The teacher remains conversational and supportive. For optimal child learning, teachers need to appre-

ciate and offer authentic dialogue and real human communication in a reciprocal relationship between learner and teacher rooted in equality, respect, and trust (Bartoli, 1995).

Program Goals

Each center contains a unique group of children and adults. A center has its own geography, and its children come from different segments of society, so the goals and priorities of one program may differ from others. There are, however, some common factors among centers. The following goals are acceptable to most programs. They give the teacher a basis for planning speaking activities and daily conversational exchanges. Each child should be helped to attain:

- Confidence in the ability to use speech with others.
- Enjoyment of speaking experiences in play, conversations, and groups.
- Acceptance of the idea that another's speech may be different.
- A higher level of interest in the meaning of new words.

And each child should be helped to increase his or her skill in:

- Using speech for ideas, feelings, and needs.
- Using speech to solve problems.
- Using speech creatively in play situations.
- Coordinating speech and body actions.
- Waiting for a turn to speak.

The overall goal in the development of speech communication in language arts is to increase each child's ability to use the speech he or she already possesses, and to help the child move, when ready, toward the use of standard English. Program goals can be realized mainly through (1) the planning of daily activities, (2) daily staff-child and child-child interaction, and (3) the use of equipment and materials.

Skarpness and Carson (1987) note that appropriate child behavior in kindergarten is aided if certain speaking and listening skills have been acquired:

> Children who are encouraged to express themselves, practice their speaking skills, and listen carefully to others are likely to adjust more readily to changing situations within the classroom.

A wide variety of different experiences can provide many learning opportunities. An activity can follow, review, and add depth to a previous one. One has to consider how much practice time is available, as Dumtschin (1988) points out "children need to practice language skills to perfect them, just as they practice walking or riding a bicycle."

The special interests or needs of each child are considered when planning daily programs. Programs then become more valuable and meaningful.

Daily Conversations

Daily teacher-child conversations become amazingly easy when teachers focus on "children's agenda." Teachers defeat their purpose when the objective is always to teach, or add a new word to the child's vocabulary. The key is to identify the child's inter-

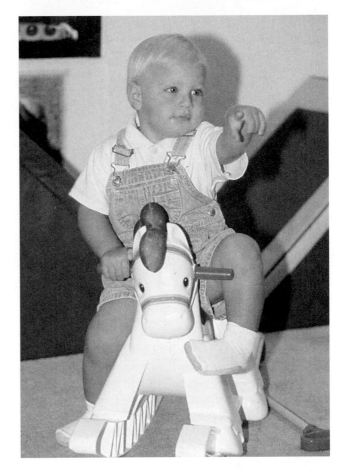

FIGURE 13–1 There should be both a desire and a need to speak.

ests; words then become meaningful (figure 13–1). When the child is engrossed, he or she will connect the teacher's words with what has fascinated him or her (Nelson, 1985).

Ginott (1972) advises teachers to treat all children with respect, as though they already are the persons they are capable of becoming. Excellent teachers make their students feel valuable, competent, and worthwhile. These are the attitudes and behaviors every would-be teacher should cultivate in conversation:

- Concern for each child's well-being.
- An unwillingness to interrupt a child's conversation to respond to an adult.

- A willingness to share the small moments of child accomplishment, sometimes even recognizing a child's achievement in a nonverbal way across a busy classroom.
- Consideration of children's verbal comments as worthy contributions and respect for individual opinions.
- Respect of each child's potential.
- Special regard for children as future leaders and discoverers.

Kiefer (1985) believes actions, questions, or statements that indicate the listener's genuine interest may elicit a wealth of oral language.

Some of the best activities happen when the teacher notices what the child or group is focusing on and uses the opportunity to expand interest, knowledge, and enjoyment. A rainbow, a delivery truck, or any chance happening can become the central topic of active speaking by the children (figure 13–2).

Whether limited or advanced, a child's speech is immediately accepted and welcomed. Teachers carefully guard and protect each child's self-confidence. By waiting patiently and reading nonverbal clues, teachers become understanding listeners.

Every effort should be made to give a logical response, showing the child that the teacher finds value in the communication. Touching, offering a reassuring arm or hand, and giving one's whole attention to the child often seem to relax him or her and increase speech production.

Children are more willing to speak when the proper classroom atmosphere is maintained:

- The tone of the room is warm and relaxed, and children have choices.
- Speaking is voluntary, not mandatory.
- The speaking group is small.
- The group listens attentively.
- Any speaking attempt is welcomed.
- Effort and accomplishments are recognized.

A teacher's willingness to engage in light-hearted dialogue may make the child more open to talking for the fun of it. When the mood is set for discovery, the teacher becomes active in the quest for answers, carefully guiding children through their exploration and expression.

Adults who emphasize the reasons for events and who take a questioning, thoughtful, and systematic approach to problems become model explorers. Thinking out loud while sharing activities is a useful device. "I wonder what would happen if you put the block there?" a teacher might ask. In their speech, young children often deal with the reality of what is happening around them; teachers' speech should also be based on this concept.

In reacting to young children's sometimes awkward, fractured, or incorrect speech, adults intuitively provide useful corrective feedback (Dopyera and Lay-Dopyera, 1992). The child's "posta put in" would automatically be accepted and corrected with, "Yes, the blocks go on the shelf." Seasoned teachers listen for content, the ideas behind words, and matter-of-factly model correct usage so smoothly the child isn't made to feel that his or her speech usage was in any way deficient. The teachers must know how to make alert, sensitive comments that ensure that the children will continue to see the teacher as a responsive, accepting adult.

Halliday (1973) has researched human speech development and classified differing "functions" of human speech. His classifications follow. Teachers

FIGURE 13–2   Children speak and listen while they play.

observing children will notice the young child's increasing use of speech in social situations.

- *Instrumental* speech satisfies wants and needs.
- *Regulatory* speech helps children control others.
- *Interactional* speech establishes and maintains contact with others.
- *Personal function* speech expresses and asserts individuality.
- *Heuristic function* speech helps children learn and describe.
- *Imaginative function* speech creates images and aids pretending.
- *Representational* speech informs.

Teachers trying to facilitate children's use of Halliday's speech classifications will want to study figure 13–3. All of these speech functions are present in the average preschool classroom.

What are young children fond of talking about? Themselves and what they are doing! They have their own views and opinions about the world around them. As their social contact increases, they exchange their ideas with other children (figure 13–4). When they become older preschoolers, they typically engage in criticism, commands, requests, threats, and questions and answers (Singer and Revenson, 1979). As a teacher listens to child-to-child conversations, he or she can make out both self-interest speech and speech that indicates social-intellectual involvement. Quite a lot of child conversation reflects the children's active, exploring, questioning minds and their attempts to try, test, manipulate, control, and discover what speech can do for them. Flights of fantasy and make-believe play are also evident.

Certain teacher behaviors and planned programs enhance children's speaking abilities. Are there factors that work counter to the realization of goals? Hough, Nurss, and Goodson (1984) compared everyday interactions in two child centers and found one center they describe as lacking language stimulation. They reported that the children spent most of their time in teacher-directed large-group activities and that most of the children's language behavior was receptive, such as listening to and following teachers' directions. Although teachers provided adequate oral language models, they were not active listeners, did not encourage curiosity, and did not spontaneously expand on children's vocabulary or concepts.

During interactions, children need their conversational partners to provide them with information that relates to the topic of the conversation, and is relevant and appropriate to their language level so they can use it to build upon what they already know (Weitzman, 1992). Teachers should try to avoid the following behaviors, because they discourage healthy speech development:

- Inappropriate or irrelevant teacher comments.
- Talking at rather than with children.
- A controlling and commanding mode of interaction.
- Repeating oneself often.
- Criticizing child speech.
- Speaking primarily to other classroom adults.

Children's Conversational Styles

Weitzman (1992) urges early childhood practitioners to observe and notice children's conversational styles. She points out that young children vary in their ability to spontaneously approach others, initiate communicative interactions, and respond. She believes conversational styles evolve from children's past life experiences and interactions with others as they form their own views of themselves as communicators. From your own experience with young children, what types of communication styles have you noticed? Eager, shy, self-conscious, self-confident, articulate, silent, questioning, repetitive, loud, advanced, and others? One child may need multiple descriptors; being social yet unclear, or shy but verbal when approached, for example. As one works daily with young children, one makes mental notes (or written ones) to help one decide what possible activities and adult interactions will provide opportunities for speech growth. Beginning teachers need to be aware of teacher tendencies to converse and spend time with children with whom they feel comfortable, perhaps because of that child's particular conversational style, cultural background, ethnic origin, or personality.

Personal Speech Expressing Individual Ideas, Feelings, Concerns

Teacher actions include:

1. Providing time and opportunity for adult-child and child-adult sharing of personal thoughts and feelings.
2. Eye-level listening and impromptu conversations throughout the school day.
3. Accepting individual child ideas and feelings and expressing your own.
4. Encouraging family visitation, participation, and interaction in classroom activities and affairs.
5. Sharing literature that elicits children's personal speech responses.

Speech Helping Children Obtain and Satisfy Wants and Needs

Teacher actions include:

1. Listening and responding to children's requests.
2. Encouraging children's ability to ask for wants and needs.
3. Increasing children's opportunities to help other children by giving verbal directions.
4. Explaining in step-by-step fashion the sequence needed to obtain desired results (i.e., how to get a turn with a favorite bike).

Speech That Promotes and Maintains Interaction

Teacher actions include:

1. Planning for shared use of materials, areas, or adult help.
2. Planning for small group discussion, problem solving, and planning.
3. Including a mix of child ages and gender in planned activities.
4. Celebrating and socializing between children and adults in classrooms.
5. Devising activities in which self-worth and diversity are valued.
6. Devising activities where negotiating and compromise are possible.

Speech That Expresses Imaginative Ideas

Teacher actions include:

1. Planning for creative individual child and group response.
2. Designing activities to promote pretending.
3. Prompting child description of creative ideas, action, and solutions.
4. Offering dramatizing, play acting, and role playing classroom opportunities and providing areas and furnishings.

5. Being playful with language and appreciating children's playful language.
6. Encouraging children's creative play by providing props and giving teacher attention.
7. Audio or visual taping or group enactment of child creativity to preserve, give status, and promote discussion and provoke additional creativity.

Speech That Enhances Children's Verbal Descriptions and Learning

Teacher actions include:

1. Providing child activities to capture child interest and spark curiosity.
2. Creating child and group verbal problem solving opportunities.
3. Putting phrases such as the following in daily teacher speech:

   "I wonder what. . . ."
   "What would happen if. . . ."
   "Let's see if. . . ."
   "That's one way, can anyone think of another?"
   "What do we know about . . . ?"
   "Can we try a new way?"
   "What did we see when . . . ?"

4. Suggesting real rather than contrived problems to solve.
5. Listening closely to child discoveries and prompting children to put ideas into words.
6. Noticing child interests. Building interest by following up with further activities.

Speech That is Representational or Informative

Teacher actions include:

1. Keeping record charts with children.
2. Planning activities that involve observing carefully and analyzing or drawing conclusions.
3. Eliciting additional or more precise information from children.
4. Recording memorable classroom events, celebrations, and other happenings.
5. Posting child birthdays, individual attributes, milestones, or other facts and data enhancing child self-worth or dignity.
6. Graphing class composition factors (i.e., height and weight graphs, food preference, and so on). Or presenting simple mapping activities involving school or neighborhood.
7. Comparing time-related classroom factors.
8. Providing activities that report individual child experiences to the group.

FIGURE 13–3 Suggested teacher strategies to promote child speech in differing classifications of human speech

FIGURE 13–4 Often conversations increase understanding of word meanings.

The Authentic Teacher

"Authentic" teachers are quick to issue appreciative comments about a child's persistence at tasks, creative or new elements in child activities, solutions to problems encountered, or other features of children's actions or behaviors. They are good at spotting every child's advances and accomplishments. They also provide honest criticism when necessary (Curry and Johnson, 1990), and this can be done with specific, detailed words that expand children's understanding. They promote children's ability to put their own feelings into words daily in conflict situations, empowering children in the process.

Of prime importance to most educators is the goal of enhancing each child's growth of self-esteem and feelings of worth and value. Teachers work daily toward this. They attempt to stretch language skills and realize a confident child will converse freely and risk new experiences.

In social conflict situations, teachers channel child problems back to the conflicting parties so that verbal solutions between children are possible. They quietly stand near, hoping confrontations can come to satisfactory solutions and only intercede when child communication breaks down.

It's obvious to teachers that many young children seek validation of their abilities. Children's "Look at me" or "Look what I did" requests can be answered in ways that are both language expanding and self-worth building. "Oh, that's nice" or "Yes, I see" are weak adult statements. A specific comment is more effective. "Your long blocks are standing on their small ends. You built your bridge very carefully, or to make your cat's tail you had to cut a long thin piece of paper. It looks like a cat's tail because it comes to a small point on the end." These are valuable teacher comments.

Integrating Children into Social Groups

Because adults know children are teachers of other children, they want all children to obtain skills in social interaction. Teachers promote child friendships. The fragile friendships of two- and three-year-olds blossom and stabilize around age four. The conversation of children in group play is a joy to overhear. A reluctant child is encouraged. Books, puppets, and other language arts media can offer friendship themes and empathy-building models. The story "Lion and the Mouse" is a good example and usually increases child comments concerning what it means to be a friend. The story ends with the line "Little friends can help big friends, too, you know!"

Suggested Interaction Guides

A teacher is a speech model for children. The following guides for teachers in daily verbal conversations are based on understanding the level of each child, since preschoolers range in abilities. These guidelines help develop speaking ability when dealing with young nonverbal, or slightly verbal, children.

- Let the child see your face and mouth clearly.
- Bend your knees and talk at the child's eye level.
- Use simple gestures. Show meanings with your hands as well as with your eyes as you talk.
- If possible, let the child touch, feel, smell, taste, and see whatever is interesting as you listen. Talk in simple sentences.
- Watch for nonverbal reactions; the child's face or body actions may show interest, fear, or other emotions. Supply words to fit the situation: "Here's the ball." "The dog will not hurt you." "Do you want a cracker?"
- Talk to the nonverbal child slowly, stressing key words such as nouns and verbs. Repeat them if the child does not seem to understand.
- If you cannot understand a word, repeat it back to the child in a relaxed way. Say, "Show me, Mary," if the child tries again and you still cannot understand the word.
- Accept a child's attempt to say a word. If a child says "lellow," say, "Yes, the paint is yellow." Articulation will improve with age and good speech modeling.
- Answer **expressive jargon** (groups of sounds without recognizable words) or jabbering with suitable statements such as "You're telling me," or "You don't say." Go along with the child's desire to put words together in a sentence.
- Play games in which the child copies sounds or words; make games fun. Stop before the child loses interest.
- Watch for the child's lead. If he or she is interested in some activity or object, talk about it in simple sentences, such as, "The kitty feels soft" or "Pet the kitty" or "Bobby's going down the slide."

- Make commands simple: "It's time to go inside." Use gestures with the words: "Put the toys in the box." (Indicate actions as you say the words.)
- Encourage the child's imitations (whether verbal or nonverbal) with a smile or touch or words. Show that the effort is appreciated.
- Pause and wait patiently for the child's response.

The following guidelines help develop speaking ability when dealing with children who speak in one-word phrases or simple sentences.

- Enlarge a child's one-word sentences into meaningful simple sentences, for example, "ball" to "The ball bounces."
- Use naming words to describe objects and actions: "The red ball is round" (figure 13–5). "The dog wants to lick your hand."
- Use conjunctions (and, but, so, also, or), possessives (mine, theirs, ours, Billy's, yours, his, hers), and negatives (is not, will not, do not, isn't, don't, won't, am not).
- Help the child talk about his or her feelings.
- Use previously learned words with new words: "The black candy is called licorice." "Your dog is a poodle; this dog is a beagle." "It's a kind of hat called a baseball cap."

FIGURE 13–5 *Teacher:* "You are talking to grandma on the telephone."

Expressive jargon — a term describing a child's first attempts at combining words into narration that results in a mimic of adult speech.

- Ask simple questions that help the child to find out and discover while his or her interest is high: "Where did you find that round rock?"
- Play labeling games with pictures and objects.
- Correct speech errors such as "wented" or "goed" by matter-of-factly saying the correct word in a sentence: "Yesterday you went to the store." (Omit any corrective tone of voice.) The child may answer by saying it the same as before, but you have modeled correct usage, and in time it will be copied.
- Accept hesitant speech and stuttering in a patient, interested way. When a child is excited or under stress, ideas may not develop into words properly.
- Wait patiently while a child tries to speak; silently hold eye contact. The thought may get lost, but if you're a good listener, and if you respond with interest to what is said, the child will try again.

When the child speaks in sentences and comes close to mature speech, the teacher should:

- Include appropriate classifications or categories in sentences to help children form concepts: "Dogs and cats are animals."
- Ask questions that help the child pinpoint identifying characteristics (figure 13–6): "Does it have a tail?"
- Ask questions that help the child see what is alike and what is different.
- After modeling a sentence pattern in conversation, ask a simple question so that the child can imitate the proper form while it is still fresh in his or her mind: "I think this lemon tastes sour. How does the lemon taste to you?"
- Help the child keep ideas in order. What happened first? What happened next? What came last?
- State instructions clearly, building from one- to two- or three-part directions: "First wash your hands; then you can choose a cracker."
- Use prepositions in your speech. Say them with gestures: "Put the toy on the shelf. Thank you. The blocks go inside the box." (Use your hand to show position as you speak.)

FIGURE 13–6 "What else is the color yellow?"

- Use adjectives (big, little, bright, red, soft, and so forth) and comparatives (more, less, lighter, heavier, shorter, tallest): "Tell me about the rubber doll." "Yes, this pink doll is bigger."
- Ask the child to take simple verbal messages to another staff member: "Tell Mrs. Brown it's time to fix the snack." Alert other staff members to the fact that you are trying to promote verbal memory and self-confidence.
- Help the child discover cause and effect: "Teacher, I'm afraid of bugs." "Why do bugs make you afraid, Billy?"
- Remember that what you say in response to the child helps the child in many ways. Really listen. Answer every child if possible. When children talk at the same time, say "I want to hear each one." "Mary, please say it again." "John, you can tell us next."
- Give ownership to the ideas children contribute: "Yesterday Nancy told us ..." "Kate's idea is ..."

Dumtschin (1988) mentions a technique in adult-child conversation from the work of Fujiki and Brinton (1984) that is termed recasting. This is very similar to expansion and feedback, previously mentioned. Recasting fills in what's missing or gently changes the child's incorrect usage in the adult's answering comment and extends the child's idea. If a child says, "I like apples," for example, the teacher could respond, "Apples taste good, don't they?" or "I like green ones, don't you?"

When teachers actively listen and observe, questions and teacher responses can better suit individual children. Teachers can grow to understand speech and conceptual errors, miscues, misconceptions, and the ways certain children express themselves with greater depth. With close observation, teachers begin to build a personal and cultural history of attending children. Some preschool children may have traveled extensively, while others haven't left their neighborhoods. Both can have rich, full vocabularies but completely different fields of reference. In a conversation about tree blossoms brought into the classroom, teacher might ask "Where have you seen trees blossom in your neighborhood?," or "Tell me how the blossoms feel when you rub them gently on your cheek like this," or "What do you see if you look very closely at the blossom in your hand?"

Goodman (1985) has suggestions regarding teacher's verbal interactions with children. They follow:

1. When a child achieves success in some communicative setting, the teacher may find ways to extend this to a new and different setting.
2. When children are involved in exploratory activities, the teacher might raise questions such as "I wonder why this is so?" or "What do you think is happening here?"
3. When children are observed to be troubled with an experience, the teacher can move in and talk about the situation with them and lead them to what they cannot yet do by themselves.
4. Teachers need to trust in children's learning and in their own ability to learn along with their children.

Weitzman (1992) pinpoints a number of teacher options in figure 13–7.

When you are having a conversation with a child, you have a number of options for extending the topic:

Inform
- Give information about past or present.
- Provide details.
- Compare/contrast two things.
- Relate present experience to past experience.

Explain
- Give reasons.
- Explain outcomes.
- Describe cause-effect relationships.
- Draw conclusions.
- Justify actions, opinions.
- Recognize problems and provide solutions.

Talk About Feelings
- Talk about how one feels.
- Talk about opinions, impressions.

Project
- Project into other people's lives, experiences.
- Project into situations never experienced (What might it be like to . . . ?).

Talk About the Future
- Talk about what will happen.
- Talk about what might happen.
- Predict what will happen.
- Anticipate possible problems and possible solutions.
- Consider alternative ways of handling a situation.

Pretend/Imagine
- Talk about imaginary things.
- Play a pretend role.
- Create an imaginary "story" (based on real life or fantasy).

FIGURE 13–7 Extending the topic (*From* Learning Language and Loving It *by C. Weitzman, 1992. Reprinted with permission from The Hanen Centre, 252 Bloor St. W, Ste. 3–390, Toronto, Ontario, Canada M5S 1V5.*)

Awareness of Intelligent Behavior

Over time a number of researchers have tried to identify effective thinking and intelligent behavior indicators. Would-be teachers observe children and conjecture how young children "come-to-know" rather than remember or state what they already know. Most classrooms enroll children whom teachers would call "successful students." By closely observing children, teachers can note behaviors that indicate children's reasoning abilities, insightfulness, strategies, perseverance, creativity, and craftsmanship.

Many indicators are best observed in children's speech behavior. Costa (1991) outlines intelligent behavior characteristics, but also notes the listing may be incomplete:

1. *Persistence*: Persevering when a solution to a problem is not immediately apparent. In preschool some children ask abundant questions, others try various and different approaches to reach goals. A child might ask all other teachers in a room if one teacher admits he/she doesn't know the answer to the question. Many children probe the reasons behind happenings and are persistent in getting more and more data to explain happenings.
2. *Decreasing impulsivity*: A thoughtful pause rather than a quick answer or action may be observed in some preschoolers.
3. *Listening to others with understanding and empathy*: Some young children hear others' points-of-view and can paraphrase another's ideas. Others may not be able to "overcome ego-centrism" at this age as Piaget observes. Both groups are displaying developmentally appropriate behavior. The first group has achieved a maturity in thinking processes, and are usually slow to ridicule, laugh at, or put down other children's ideas.
4. *Flexibility in thinking*: No matter what a teacher or parent tells a child on a certain subject, the child may not believe or accept the information. This isn't flexibility in thinking. As children age, however, many will at least consider new possibilities and doubt their previous ideas. Some check out new ideas with others with questions like "Do daddies cook?"
5. *Metacognition: Awareness of one's own thinking*: Preschoolers may be able to describe the steps they took to achieve some desired outcome, but rarely can they put into words what went on inside their heads or describe their strategies. More often when asked "How did you do that?" they will be silent or say "I just did it." This is a developmentally appropriate answer.
6. *Checking for accuracy and precision*: The child who shows a printed form to teacher saying "I made an A" may be simply stating a truth as he sees it. With another child who says "That's not an A. Is it, teacher?" The child is checking for accuracy. In discussions a child may seek a correction. Many teachers have learned this lesson with the child who's a dinosaur buff for the child has learned the distinguishing characteristics of each dinosaur well, and may be better informed than the teacher.
7. *Questioning and problem posing*: This is a characteristic of many preschoolers who inquire about the "whys" of things and are alert to discrepancies and uncommon phenomena.
8. *Drawing on past knowledge and applying it to new situations*: At times, teachers have difficulty trying to understand what common element in a present situation the child is connecting to the past. Other connections are readily apparent as when a child reacts negatively to a worker dressed in white.
9. *Precision of language and thought*: Young children use an increasing number of

descriptive words and analogous comments when exposed to adult language that is not vague or imprecise.

10. *Using all the senses*: Young children readily probe, manipulate, and savor the sensory opportunities presented to them.

11. *Ingenuity, originality, insightfulness, creativity*: Early childhood professionals treasure child attempts and behaviors in this area, and most teachers can immediately cite examples they've observed.

12. *Wonderment, inquisitiveness, curiosity, and enjoyment of problem solving—a sense of efficacy as a thinker*: Child attitudes toward problems, thinking games, guessing and obstacles can enhance or impede their quest for knowledge and solutions. Adults may model attitudes of "giving up" or "it's too hard" or "I'll never get it right" rather than the preferred "let's find out," "let's see what we can do." Adults can also model enjoyment when in the pursuit of solving some task or dilemma.

How can early childhood teachers support children's emerging intellectual abilities? From Costa's list, there are many clues. A teacher begins by having faith in the ability and intelligence of all children, and acknowledges that all children's homes (or all teachers) don't value intelligent behavior. Intelligent child behavior can be recognized and appreciated.

Children can absorb the idea that often there is more than one solution or answer or way of doing something and that pausing, gathering more data and "thinking things over" are good strategies. Children can be asked to share their plans and outcomes on chosen activities. Day-to-day happenings and real dilemmas can be talked about and problems solved through actions and discussions where every child's ideas are valued.

The teacher can rig classroom activities to promote children's thinking, problem solving, creative ideas, and imagination. Children can develop the attitude that what they contribute is worthwhile.

When teachers listen, paraphrase children's comments, clarify, and try out student ideas, children feel what they say is meaningful. "Maybe the school's pet bird does eat paper, or maybe it just tears it up. If we watch carefully we can find out, can't we?"

Providing a continually interesting classroom full of exploring opportunities is a must. Classrooms rich in first-hand manipulative experiences and responsive adults is a widely accepted goal in preschool practice.

One of the chief causes for failure in formal education is that we begin with language rather than with real and material action (Costa, 1991). At preschool level this means some teachers have a tendency to tell children about reality rather than "providing" reality—real exploring experiences encountered together. Teachers also need to model their own intelligent behaviors and enthusiasm for learning. Nothing works as well as an example.

Settings for Preplanned Speaking Activities

Speaking activities occur when children are inside or outside the classroom or when they are on the move. Preplanned activities are more successful when both children and teachers are comfortable and unhurried and when there are no distractions. Peers will be a valuable source of words and meanings.

Close attention should be given to group size and the seating space between children at group times. It is easier to create an atmosphere of inclusion and intimacy in a small discussion group than in a large group, thereby promoting children's willingness to share thoughts. Lighting and heating in the room must also be considered. Soft textures and rugs add warmth and comfort. A half-circle seating arrangement, with the teacher in the center, provides a good view of both the teacher and what is to be seen.

Ease of viewing depends on eye level and seating arrangement. Whenever possible, the objects children are to look at should be at their eye level. Teachers often sit in child-sized chairs while conducting language arts experiences. Screens, dividers, and bookcases can help to lessen distractions.

Questioning Skills

A teacher's questions often prompt children to ponder and wonder. Questions checking whether the teacher has understood the child's comment are common. They provide the child feedback concerning the teacher's attention and interest, and clarify whether the child's intended message was understood. This gives the child the opportunity to correct the teacher and send further data or explanation or clear up miscommunication. Questions can also help keep conversations afloat and show that the teacher is interested in child pursuits.

Questions can help children see details they would otherwise have missed. Sometimes questions help a child form relationships between objects and ideas; they may prompt the child to speak about both feelings and thoughts; they can lead the child to a new interest. Skill in questioning is an important teaching ability. Questions asked by a teacher can often lead children to discovery.

Goodman (1990) suggests teachers need help and specific training in questioning strategies so they can aid children's ability to see contradictions, move them toward rethinking, and assist concept development. Teachers need to ask questions that are readily understood and require easy responses for the very young child and more challenging, thoughtful responses from language-capable preschoolers. This means modifying questions depending on language levels.

In a situation in a classroom when a window has blown shut and one of the children says "Someone hit that window, Teacher!" a skillful question like "Is anyone standing near the window?" or "Could anyone reach that window from down on the ground?" or "Can you think of something else that might slam a window shut, something that could push it? Let's look out the window and see if other things are being pushed around." This could lead the child to a new conclusion.

The following example illustrates the teacher's role in stimulating the thought process that emerges from play. The teacher, who has created the climate for learning by supplying and arranging the equipment, sees a child playing with cars on ramps that he has constructed with blocks. She knows that if a car is placed on a slope made with blocks, the speed with which it descends and the distance it goes are affected by the slope and length of the ramp. She asks, "Johnny, did this blue car go faster than the red one?" She also introduces new words to his vocabulary—slant, ramp, slow, faster, above, below, under, tall, smaller than—and uses and elicits this vocabulary in conversation (Danoff, Breitbart, and Barr, 1977).

Teachers need to be sensitive to the anxiety that some children may have. In past experiences, if a child's answers have been overcorrected, or if adults' questions are associated with punishment, teacher's questions can cause children to be silent and tense.

Teachers use "choice" questions at times. It allows them to slip specific, descriptive words into their speech while the child is focused: "Do you want the red paint (pointing) or the blue paint (pointing)?"

Also important in asking questions is the teacher's acceptance of the child's answers. Since each child answers a question based on his or her own experience, children may give very different answers. The following conversation (observed at the San Jose City College Child Development Center) shows how a teacher handled an unexpected answer.

Teacher: (Conversation has centered around television sets.)
"Where could we go to buy a television set?"

Frank: "Macy's."

Chloe: "At a pear store."

Wanda: "The TV store."

Teacher: "Frank says Macy's sells television sets. Chloe thinks we could buy one at a 'pear' store. Wanda thought at a TV store. Maybe we could go to three places to buy one. Chloe, have you seen television sets at the 'pear' store?"

Chloe: "The pear store has lots of 'em."

Teacher: "You've been to a 'pear' store?"

Chloe: "Our TV broke, and we took it to the 'pear' store."

Teacher: "The repair shop fixed my broken television set, too. Yes, sets can be for sale at a repair shop."

The teacher's task is to keep the speech and answers coming, encouraging each child's expression of ideas. Sometimes a question can be answered with a question. When a child says, "What does a rabbit eat?" the teacher might say, "How could we find out?" The teacher knows that a real experience is better than a quick answer.

When using questions, the level of difficulty should be recognized. Early childhood teachers can use carefully asked questions to find the child's level of understanding. Teachers try to help each child succeed in activities while offering a challenge at the same time. Even snack time can be a time to learn new language skills.

Open-ended questions are very useful and teachers try to increase their ability to ask them. *Open-ended questions* are defined as questions with many possible answers.

Almy (1975) points out:

> Some teachers are so intent on imparting information to children that they forget to assess the ways it may be assimilated. Thus answers to open-ended questions—"Can you tell me about . . . ?" "What do you think about . . . ?"—are often more revealing than answers to questions with a more specific focus. They can be followed by "Tell me more." "Some people think that . . ." "What do you think?"

Teachers' questions can be classified into eight main types:

- *Recall:* Asks child to remember information, names, words, and so forth. Recall questions are the type most often asked. Gall (1984) reports about 60% of teachers' questions require students to recall facts; about 20% require students to think; and the remaining 20% are procedural. Teachers emphasize fact questions,

whereas research indicates an emphasis on higher, cognitive questions would be more effective. The student activities section of this chapter asks you to conduct an observational study concerning this point. Could it be this type of question was modeled constantly in most teachers' own elementary schooling? Example: What color is this ball?

- **Convergent:** Asks child to compare or contrast similarities or differences and seek relationships. Example: How are these two toy cars alike?
- **Divergent:** Asks child to predict or theorize. Example: If the boy steps on the marble, what might happen?
- *Evaluation:* Asks child for a personal opinion or judgment or asks child to explore feelings. Example: What would be on your plate if you could have your favorite food?
- *Observation:* Asks child to watch or describe what he or she senses. Example: What's happening to the ant on the window sill?
- *Explanation:* Asks child to state cause and effect, reasons, and/or descriptions. Example: The clay feels different today. What do you think happened to it?
- *Action:* Asks child to move body or perform a physical task. Example: Can you show us how to walk like a duck?
- *Open ended:* Many answers are possible. Example: How do children get from their homes to their school in the morning?

Strickland (1977) advises teachers to limit "low quality" questions that center on isolated bits of knowledge and are designed to test what's learned or remembered. Unfortunately, teachers and teacher test question behavior have been paired in the minds of some adults. They doggedly ask continual questions of children, believing this is age-old and appropriate behavior for all "good" teachers. When an adult approaches a young child playing in the sand box with questions like "What are you doing?" or "What are you making?," the child may wonder why the adult can't see for himself, or whether he is supposed to be making something. It may be hard for this adult to really focus on the

---

Convergent thinking — moving toward a single, acceptable, conventional solution to a problem.

Divergent thinking — differing lines of thinking and possible searching for a new idea(s).

child's activity and make pertinent comments like, "That's a big mountain of sand you've just made" or to pick up a sand toy cup and say, "Please pour some sand in my cup."

Preschool teachers have many opportunities through questioning to explore children's imaginative responses to books, events, and classroom happenings. Their questions can be "child-centered," promoting creative and interpretive child responses. Teachers can improve their ability to stop, listen, and learn from what their charges are saying.

The way questions are phrased may produce short or longer answers. Questions using "what" or "where" usually receive one-word or word-phrase answers. Many questions, such as Do you? Did you? Can you? Will you? Have you? Would you? can be answered by yes or no. This type of question fits the level of the very young.

Questions that help a child compare or connect ideas may begin with:

> What would happen if . . . ?
> Which one is longer?
> How are these two alike?
> Why did you say these were different?
> What happened next?
> If it fell off the table, what would happen to it?
> Can you guess which one will be first?
> Could this ball fit inside this can?
> I wonder why that is like that?
> What do you think is happening?

The following are examples of questions that encourage problem solving or stimulate creative thought:

> If you had a handful of pennies, what would you buy?
> Could you tell me what you are going to do when you're as big as your dad?
> Can you think of a way to open this coconut?
> How could we find out where this ant lives?

These questions can be answered by the more mature speakers. Through close listening and observation, the teacher can form questions that the child will want to answer.

Using a Vygotskian or Constructivist Approach

According to Bodrova and Leong (1996), a teacher using a Vygotskian approach with younger and older children should:

- Make her actions and the children's actions verbally explicit. Label her own actions as she carries them out. Label the child's actions for him as they occur. "Hand me the blue blocks."
- Model her thinking and strategies aloud. As she solves a problem, talk about what she is thinking about. "I could put them together."
- When introducing a new concept, be sure to tie it to actions. "When we want to measure something to see how long it is, we put the ruler at the end of the object and read the numbers here."
- Use thinking while talking to check children's understanding of concepts and strategies. Get children used to talking about what they think and how they solve problems.
- Encourage the use of private speech. This type of self-talk has meaning for the child and should not be discouraged. Coach the child on what he might say to himself as he does something, "The knob turns, and then press the button."

Speech in Play and Routines

Children's play opportunities in early childhood centers are planned for, promoted, and wide ranging. Benefits described here relate primarily to language arts growth.

Dyson (1990) describes play as a "canvas" in which young children can symbolize ideas and feelings through gestures and speech, and collaborate with friends.

In play, children reexamine life experiences, adding their imagination and at times manipulating happenings, settings, and people, consequently learning about their world (figure 13–8).

FIGURE 13–8 Children and teacher engaged in active conversational play.

Play

Play stimulates much child-to-child conversation, and some kinds of play promote talking more than others. Quiet activities such as painting or working puzzles may tend to limit speech while the child is deeply absorbed.

If teachers observe children's play sequences, they will note many child-initiated play situations that involve print, acting, drawing, "reading," and "writing." Props are improvised on-the-spot as dramas unfold. With writing, art, or construction materials handy, children will incorporate these into child-created and child-directed situations. Dyson (1990) points out that connections made in play, especially when symbols are used, contribute to literacy.

Teachers plan opportunities for children to play by themselves and with others in small and large groups. Play with another child or a small group almost always requires children to speak. Toddlers may play near each other in a nonverbal, imitative manner using sounds, squeals, and sometimes screams. Interaction with other children promotes the growth of speaking ability.

Early in life, children act out and repeat the words and actions of others. During preschool years, this is called **dramatic play**, and the staffs in early childhood centers plan and prepare for it. Research suggests that dramatic play has important benefits for children (Fein, 1981) and holds many learning opportunities. It helps children to:

- Develop conversational skills and the ability to express ideas in words.
- Understand the feelings, roles, or work of others.
- Connect actions with words—actions and words go hand-in-hand in dramatic play.
- Develop vocabulary.
- Develop creativity—children imagine, act, and make things up as play progresses.

Dramatic play — acting out experiences or creating drama episodes during play.

- Engage in social interaction with other children.
- Cope with life, sometimes through acting out troubling situations, thus giving an outlet for emotion (for example, almost every doll in an early childhood center gets a spanking periodically when children play house).
- Assume leadership and group-participant roles.

Griffing (1983) describes dramatic play after observing it closely:

> The play was rich in symbolic activity—the transformations of self, objects, and situations into characters, objects, and events that existed in imagination only. The play was cognitively complex in its organization, consisting of sequences of related ideas and events rather than isolated pretend behaviors. There was extensive social interaction and verbal communication with children taking roles and carrying them out cooperatively.

Pretending is an enjoyable play activity that helps speech growth. When playing house, the child can start out as the grandfather and end up as the baby or the family dog. Much time and effort is devoted to this type of play in childhood. The child engages in this type of activity often and has the ability to slide easily from the real world into the make-believe world.

Teachers watch dramatic play develop from the simple imitative actions of toddlers and younger preschoolers to the elaborate dramatic play of four-year-olds in which language use blossoms. Teachers support each step along the way by providing the necessary objects and materials that enhance dramatic episodes and by offering assistance. To be effective, teachers must observe and be aware of the adult actions and situations that capture child interest enough to prompt reenactment. One surprised student teacher who dreamed up a shaving activity, complete with mirrors, shaving cream, and bladeless razors, found that the boys rolled up their pants legs and shaved their legs. This points out two interesting items: first the wisdom of letting razors, even bladeless ones, become play items, and second, how dramatic play often enlightens teachers. Child safety is always the first criterion used to evaluate whether an activity is appropriate.

Four-year-olds engage vigorously in superhero play. As cowboys and Indians, good guys and bad guys, or monster or ghost enactments captured the imaginations of past generations of American children, new heroes have appeared in television cartoons and movies. Robots and space creatures are very common dramatic play themes for four-year-olds. The children become the chosen power figures in actions and words. Segal (1987) probes the possible reasons for the popularity of this type of play.

> . . . Superhero play is the child's way of restructuring his world according to his own rules. By dubbing himself a superman, a four-year-old can instantaneously acquire major powers and awesome strength. This strength represents access to a powerful force that is missing in their adult-controlled everyday lives.

Many teachers feel ambivalent when they witness the violence enacted in some of these play episodes, which can require special handling and supervisory decisions to keep children safe. Most teachers set up times for group dialog about superheroes, so that reality and fantasy come under group discussion. Discussions can also be seen and handled as possible learning opportunities for the entire class or group. Other teachers worry about the perceived lack of child creativity in this type of play, because the same theme and action are generally repeated over and over.

Rich home and school experiences (going places and doing things) serve as building blocks for dramatic play. One would have a difficult time playing "restaurant" or "wedding" if there had been no previous experience with either. Early childhood centers can provide activities and objects that promote dramatic play, such as:

- Field trips (figure 13–9)
- Discussions and readings by visitors and guest speakers

FIGURE 13–9   A trip to the fire station can promote firefighter play.

- Books
- Discussions based on pictures
- Films, filmstrips, and slides
- Kits (boxed sets), equipment, and settings for dramatic play
- Parent career presentations

In dramatic play, children often use symbols and language to represent objects that aren't actually present. An oblong block may become a baby bottle, a pie plate the kitchen clock, etc. The enactment of role-appropriate behavior in a make-believe situation is a major step toward literacy (Wagner, 1992). Researchers such as Pellegrini (1980) suggest a significant relationship exists between kindergartners' symbolic play and reading achievement.

Children with symbolic dramatic play skills had increased ability to comprehend words and understand a variety of syntactic structures. The test Pellegrini used to determine child differences was the Metropolitan Reading Readiness Test.

Smilansky and Shefatya (1990) list growth areas promoted and possible in dramatic play. They include verbalization, vocabulary, language comprehension, attention span, imaginativeness, concentration, impulse control, curiosity, problem solving strategies, cooperation, empathy, and group participation. Vygotsky's work (1986) has given greater emphasis to the intellectual component of child's play:

> In play the child is always behaving beyond his age, above his usual everyday behavior: in play he is, as it were, a head above himself. Play contains in a concentrated form, as in the focus of a magnifying glass, all the development tendencies: it is as if the child tries to jump above his usual level.

Dramatic Play Settings

A playhouse area with a child-size stove, refrigerator, table, and chairs encourages dramatic play. An old boat, a service station pump, and a telephone booth are examples of other pieces of equipment that children enjoy using in their play.

Furniture found at early childhood centers can be moved into room arrangements that suggest a bus, a house, a tunnel, or a store. Large cardboard boxes may become a variety of different props with, or without, word labels. Large paper bags, ropes, blankets, and discarded work clothes or dress-up clothing (figure 13–10) also stimulate the child to pretend. Items for dramatic play can be obtained from commercial school supply companies, secondhand stores, flea market sales, garage sales, and other sources.

Dramatic Play Kits

Items that go together and suggest the same type of play can be boxed together, ready for use. A

FIGURE 13–10   Dress-up time

shoe-shine kit, complete with cans of natural shoe polish, a soft cloth, a shoe brush, play money, and a newspaper or a magazine, is very popular. Children catch on to the activity quickly. Unfortunately, not many have seen a shoe-shine stand, so a teacher demonstration of this kit may be necessary.

Community theme prop boxes such as bakery, flower shop, etc. are suggested by Myhre (1993). She believes children using them make decisions about what community people think and do.

Boutte, Van Scoy, and Hendley (1996) urge teachers to consider multicultural and nonsexist prop boxes (kits), which present multiple opportunities to discuss diversity and model acceptance of differences. For example, photographs and pictures in beauty shop kits can display nonsexist hairstyles and multicultural models. Multicultural clothing as

well as nonsexist clothing is a natural part of almost all play collections. Breadmaking prop boxes can have a variety of cultural bread types. Other ideas for kits to be used in dramatic play follow.

Post office. Large index cards, used postcards and letters, stamp pads, stampers, crayons or pencils, stamps (Christmas or wildlife seals), mail boxes (shoe box with slot cut in front and name clearly printed), old shoulder bag purses for mailbags, and men's and women's shirts.

Cleaning set. Several brooms, mops, sponge mops, dust cloths, dustpans, sponges, plastic bottles and spray bottles with water, and paper toweling for windows.

Tea party. Set of cups and saucers, plastic pitchers, napkins, vase, tablecloth, plastic spoons, small empty food packages such as cereal boxes, and clay or plastic cookies or biscuits.

Doctor. Stethoscope, bandages, masking tape, red stickers for play wounds, tongue depressors, play thermometer, paper pad and pencil for prescriptions, billing forms for bill, adhesive tape, cotton balls, armband with a red cross on it, bag to carry, paper hospital gowns, white shirt, and multiethnic photographs of doctors.

Teacher. Notebooks, pencils, plastic glasses, chalk, bell, chalkboard, flannel board with sets, book about the first day at school.

Washing babies. Large pieces of toweling to cover the table, several small washable dolls, some sets of toy bathroom furniture, individual plastic pitchers or plastic tubs with soapy water (can be made from plastic bleach bottles), small pieces of toweling, cotton balls, individual talcum cans filled with cornstarch, diapers (smallest size), empty plastic soap bottles, doll clothes, clothesline, and clothespins.

Supermarket. Cash register, play money, paper pads and pencils or crayons, hole punch, paper sacks, empty food cartons, wax fruit, play grocery cart or rolling laundry cart, and purse or wallet.

Hair salon. Plastic brushes, combs, cotton balls, powder, scarves, colored water in nail polish bottles, old hair dryer (no cord or plug), curlers, water spray bottle, hairpins, and mirror.

Service station. Tire pump, pliers, cans, sponges and bucket, short length of hose and cylinder (for gas pump), hat, squirt bottle, paper towels, paper and pencil, and sign "gas for sale."

Fishing. Hats, bamboo lengths (about three feet) with string and magnet at the end, a basin, and small metal objects such as paper clips for the fish or cutouts for fish shapes with a paper clip attached to each (to attract the magnet).

Gift wrap. Old wallpaper books, assorted empty boxes or blocks to wrap, used bows, tape, scissors, gift cards, ribbon, crayons, calendar.

Camping. Old pots and pans, backpacks, blankets, foam pads, flashlight, short lengths of logs, red cellophane, large box for tent, food, old camp stove, canteen, portable radio.

Airplane. Chairs in rows, trays, plastic utensils, play food, headphones, little pillows, blankets, tickets, magazines, rolling cart, cups, plastic bottles, napkins, airline attendant clothing.

More kits can be made for the following:

TV repair person	mail carrier
baker	firefighter
painter	car wash
picnic	pilot
restaurant	circus
wedding	birthday party
police officer	astronaut
construction worker	airport

The ideas for play kits that have been suggested are based on a few of the many possible themes.

Sorenson (1981) discusses additional ideas for dramatic play props in the following:

Children love props of all kinds. "Make-believe" can happen with a scarf, an umbrella, or an old pair of glasses . . .

Sorenson suggests collecting props for favorite stories and putting them in a storage bag or container that has a picture or illustration on the front of that story. Her example for *Stone Soup* (Brown, 1947) follows:

Materials Needed: large pot, large stone, long-handled spoon, assorted vegetables, aprons for cooks, hats for travelers, three-cornered hats for soldiers.

Costumes

Costumes and clothing props let a child step into a character quickly (figure 13–11). Strong, sturdy, child-manageable ties and snaps increase self-help. Elastic waistbands slip on and off with ease. Clothing that is cut down to size (so it doesn't drag) can be worn for a longer time. Items that children enjoy are:

- hats of all types (*Note:* The use of hats, wigs, and headgear may not be possible in some programs where head lice has occurred.)

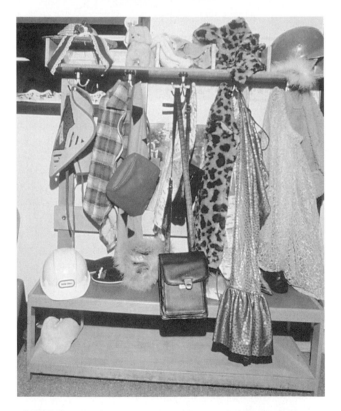

FIGURE 13–11   The center should provide the necessary equipment for dramatic play.

- shoes, boots, slippers
- uniforms
- accessories, such as ties, scarves, purses, old jewelry, aprons, badges, key rings
- discarded fur jackets, soft fabrics, and fancy fabric clothing
- wigs
- work clothes

A clever idea for a child-made costume is using a large-handled shopping bag. Once the bottom of the bag is cut out, the child can step into it, using the bag handles as shoulder straps. The child can decorate the bag and use it as a play prop.

The Teacher's Role in Dramatic Play

Dramatic play is child directed instead of teacher directed. Play ideas come from the child's imagination and experience.

Teachers can motivate dramatic play before they withdraw to remain in the background. They are watchful but don't hover. Sometimes a new play direction is suggested by a teacher to divert the children away from unsafe or violent play. The flow of play preferably is decided by the children. Teachers' close presence and words can stop or change behavior when the situation becomes unsafe or gets out of hand. If things go smoothly, the ideas, words, and dramatic play actions are those of the children.

Periodic suggestions by the teacher and introduction of material may extend and enrich play. Care is taken not to dominate but rather to be available as a friendly resource.

Play is where reading and writing begin (McLane and McNamee, 1990). In dramatic play, children understand its pretend or make-believe nature. (Although, in certain play situations, an occasional child may confuse play with reality.) McLane and McNamee (1990) have identified two potential links to the development of literacy in the following:

(1) As a symbolic activity, pretend play allows children to develop and refine their capacities to use symbols, to represent experience, and construct imaginary worlds, capacities they will draw on when they begin to write or read. (2) As an orientation or approach to experience, play can make the various roles and activities of people who read and write meaningful and hence more accessible to young children.

Older preschoolers' dramatic play becomes increasingly mature, involved, complex, and riddled with abstract symbolic representations.

Dramatic Play as an Intellectual Reaction to Book Events

Harvey, Mcauliffe, Benson, et al. (1996) suggest that children's dramatic play and role playing are ways to synthesize and connect what has been presented in picture books and in their own lives. Any observant teacher knows children's dramatic play mirrors their significant life experiences. The child who first says, "Did you bring home any money?" in a play scenario in which the child playing father enters the play situation has observed or experienced a background event(s).

What then could be the benefit of dramatic play acting a book? Besides the recreating (retelling) of book parts or themes, the experience offers a number of intellectual and literary benefits. Deeper or clearer meaning might be achieved. Early childhood practitioners can conclude that this activity helps children construct knowledge on a number of levels.

Props like hats, clothes, and objects, and settings connected to the picture book can be created using teacher ingenuity. A teacher can examine a book before presenting it for features that lead to easy enactment such as *The Three Billy Goats Gruff*. It's easy to set up a bridge with the materials and equipment found in most preschools.

Most observant teachers find children reliving favorite or captivating picture books with or without their help in groups or as individuals. It's as if in the reliving, the reenactment, the picture book's message becomes 'fitted' into what they already know.

Reenacting a picture book with a teacher's help may surprise the teacher, for as children reenact they will usually insert objects and events from their own lives into the story context (Ferguson and Young, 1996).

Books that lend themselves to child reenactment follow:

Eastman, P. (1960/1993). *Are you my mother?* New York: Harper Collins.

Flack, M. (1971). *Ask Mr. Bear.* New York: Young Readers Press.

Mora, P. (1992). *A birthday basket for Tia.* New York: Macmillan.

Williams, S. (1989). *I went walking.* San Diego, CA: Harcourt Brace Jovanovich.

Daily Routines

Periods designed especially for conversation are included in the program of an early childhood center. A gathering or group time at the start of the day is used to encourage individual recognition and speaking. Snack and lunch periods are set up to promote pleasant conversation while eating. Activities are planned and structured to provide for as much child talk as possible (figure 13–12).

Show-and-Tell

One of the most common daily routines is show-and-tell time. It must be noted here that some early childhood educators feel that this routine is outdated and overused and prefer to eliminate it from their daily schedules. In contrast, show-and-tell advocates feel that this activity encourages children to talk about their special interests in front of others. The child can bring something from home or share something made or accomplished at school. Here are some helpful hints for conducting show-and-tell.

FIGURE 13–12   Quiet outdoor play is an ideal forum for a pleasant, relaxed conversation.

- Encourage, don't force, children to speak. If they don't want to talk, they can just show what they brought.
- Let the child who is showing something to the group stand or sit near the teacher. A friendly arm around the child's shoulders may help.
- Stimulate the other children to ask the child questions: "Mark, you seem to want to ask Gustavo about his blue marble."
- Limit the time for overly talkative children by using an egg timer.
- Limit the time for the activity so that the children do not become bored.
- Thank each child for his or her participation.
- Try something new such as:
  a. Display all articles and have the group guess who brought them.
  b. Have children swap (if possible) what they have brought so that they can talk about each other's items.
  c. Bring in a surprise item to share with the children.
  d. Make a caption for each item and display it on a table (for example, Betty's Green Rock).

e. Have the child hide the object behind his or her back while describing it to the others. Then the other children can guess what the object is.

f. Be sensitive to ethnic and cultural communication styles.

Oken-Wright (1988) points out show-and-tell times can be tedious and stressful, but when well-conducted, they can also be:

- An activity for closure (ending activities on a satisfying note) and evaluation and for clarification of feelings,
- A forum for expressive and receptive language development,
- A session for brainstorming, idea catching, and idea expanding,
- An opportunity to reflect and engage in group problem solving,
- A source for curriculum ideas and materials, and
- A window into children's thoughts and feelings.

Show-and-tell items are usually kept out of children's reach to prevent the loss of a valued or favorite toy. The teacher can divide the class into groups and name the days on which each group can bring in items, or the teacher may prefer to allow the children to share whenever they wish. Show-and-tell helps children develop vocabulary, responsibility, and the ability to speak in front of others. When making these goals known to parents, teachers explain that the children have choices in these sharing times, and that items do not have to be brought to school on a daily or regular basis.

One kindergarten teacher (Edwards, 1996) initiated sharing time topics related to her classroom theme instruction and alerted parents beforehand. Sharing time consequently became focused, less rambling. Children who brought in objects unrelated to the topic could be given time after topic-centered sharing.

Some schools encourage at-home overnight visits of the school's stuffed animal collection. They stipulate host children will be able to talk about the animal's adventures at their home. Books of the school's animal experiences in different homes can be compiled by teachers by recording child-dictated comments. Photographs taken at home by parents and children's artwork are both interesting additions to "Teddy Bear's Adventures."

The Daily News or Recap Times

Many centers engage in a daily news or recap group time that focuses on important or interesting events of the day. Teachers and children share news, anecdotes, and happenings in both their home and school life. The teacher can initiate this activity with statements such as the following:

> "Keith told me about something new at his house. Would you like to share your news, Keith?"

> "Aliki and Todd built something today that I've never seen before! Tell us about it, Todd, or would you like me to tell your classmates?"

As with all other group times, the teacher must be aware of group reaction and response. On some days, there may be excited response and conversation; on others, there may be little response, and the activity should be kept brief. To give children an opportunity to talk about problems and their solutions, recap times can be partially devoted to children's verbalizing success or lack of it in proposed courses of action and projects.

> "Ryan was going to try to make a spaceship today. Ryan, do you want to tell us about it?"

> "Megan finished making her book today. Would you like to tell us what happened, Megan?"

Promoting Speech Daily

The following are suggestions that can promote more child speech in daily programs.

- Have children give verbal messages or directions to other children often: "Petey, please show Flynn our dustpan and hand broom. Tell him how we empty it." (Then follow through by thanking him.)

- Let children describe daily projects: "Danielle, tell us about your rocket ship. I know you worked hard making it. What did you do first?"
- Relate present ideas and happenings to the children's past when possible: "Shane had a new puppy at his house, too. Did your puppy cry at night? What did you do to help it stop? Kathy has a new puppy who cries at night."
- Promote child explanations: "Who can tell us what happens after we finish our lunch?"
- Promote teacher-child conversations where the teacher records children's words on artwork, constructions, or any happenings or project.
- Periodically make pin-on badges (for teachers and interested children) like the ones shown in figure 13–13.
- Play "explaining games" by setting up a group of related items on a table and having the children explain how the items can be used. For example, three groups of items might be (1) a mirror, comb, brush, washcloth, soap, and basin of water; (2) shoes, white shoe polish, and new shoelaces; and (3) nuts, nutcracker, and two

bowls. Encourage child volunteers to explain and demonstrate the use of the items by facing the group from the other side of the table. Other possibilities include items to demonstrate peeling an orange, making a sandwich with two spreads, or making a telephone call.
- Design and create games that encourage children to speak.

GAMES

The following games may promote children's expression of ideas.

Suitcase Game

Teacher: I'm going on a vacation trip. I'm putting suntan oil in my suitcase. What will you put in your suitcase?

Child: A swimming suit.

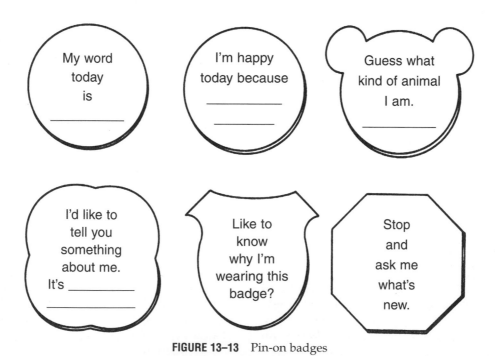

FIGURE 13–13   Pin-on badges

Child: Candy.

Teacher: (After the group has had an opportunity to contribute.)

Let's see how many items we can remember that people wanted to bring on vacation.

Grocery Store Game

Have a bag handy with lots of grocery items. Pull one out yourself and describe it. Have the children take turns pulling out an item and describing it. Teacher can make a shopping list of items named and explain a shopping list's use.

Letter Game

Provide a large bag of letters. Pull one letter out. Talk about a letter you are going to send to a child in the group. "I'm going to give this pretend letter to Frankie and tell him about my new car," or "I want to send this thank-you card to Janelle because she always helps me when I ask for cleanup helpers. Who would like to pull out a letter from this bag and tell us the person they would like to send it to?"

Guess What's in the Box

Collect small boxes with lids. Put small items inside, such as paper clips, erasers, bottle tops, plastic toys, leaves, flowers, and so forth. Have a child choose a box, guess its contents, open it, and talk about what is in the box.

Describe a Classmate

Choose a child out of the group to stand beside you. Describe or list three of the child's characteristics, for example, red shoes, big smile, one hand in pocket. Ask who would like to choose another classmate and tell three things about that person.

Guessing Photograph Happenings

Use photographs showing a sequence of actions. Help children express their ideas of what is depicted. Examples: Digging in the garden, planting bulbs, a flowering tulip; mixing pancake batter, frying pancakes, eating pancakes.

The Mystery Bag

An activity children enjoy in small groups is called the mystery bag. The teacher collects a series of common objects. Turning away from the group, the teacher puts one of the objects in another bag. The game starts when a child reaches (without looking inside) into the second bag and describes the object. It is then pulled out of the bag and discussed: "What can we do with it? Has it a name? It's the same color as what else in the room?" The group should be small, since it is hard for a young child to wait for a turn. Examples of objects that could be used include a rock, comb, orange, pancake turner, feather, plastic cup, sponge, hole punch, flower, toy animal, and whistle.

Parts-of-the-Body Guessing Game

I can see you with my _____ (eyes).

I can smell you with my _____ (nose).

I can chew with my _____ (teeth).

I can hear with my _____ (ears).

I can clap with my _____ (hands).

I walk on my _____ (feet).

I put food in my _____ (mouth).

This is not my nose, it's my _____ (point to ears).

This is not my eye, it's my _____ (point to nose).

This is not my mouth, it's my _____ (point to eye).

Leading Activities

A child can be chosen to lead others in activities if he or she is familiar with the routines and activities. The child can alert the others by saying the right words or calling out the names of the children who need items or who are next for a turn at something. One or more children can be at the front of the group, leading songs or finger plays. (Finger plays will be discussed in the next chapter.) Often, children can be chosen as speakers to direct routines with words. Also, teachers can promote speaking by asking one child to tell another child something: "Tell Billy when you want him to pass the wastebasket," or "If you're through, ask Georgette whether she wants a turn."

A watchful teacher uses many ways of encouraging the children to speak. The children tend to speak more if their speech is given attention and if speech helps them achieve their ends. It is helpful during group times to point out that the teacher and the other children want to hear what everyone says and, because of this, children should take turns speaking.

Summary

Each early childhood educational program is based on goals. Goals state the attitudes and abilities that a center wishes to develop in children. Planned activities and daily teacher-child conversations help the school reach its goals.

Teachers plan for both group and individual needs. They converse skillfully with children of varying degrees of fluency. There are specific teacher techniques that promote children's expression of ideas.

Questions are asked by both children and teachers. By observing, listening, and interacting, teachers are better able to encourage speaking abilities.

When there is a relaxed atmosphere with interested teachers and many activities, more talking takes place. Playing with others helps vocabulary development and language acquisition in settings where children interact in real and make-believe situations.

The teacher's role in dramatic play is to set the stage but remain in the background so that the children can create their own activities. Dramatic play settings and kits are made available, and some are boxed and collected by the teacher.

Part of a teacher's work is to encourage children to share their ideas and give children opportunities to lead speaking activities. Teachers ensure that children are talked with rather than talked at. Teachers plan for conversational group times and conduct games and activities that promote verbal comments.

STUDENT ACTIVITIES

1. List five speaking area goals in your own order of priority.
2. Interview a preschool teacher (or teachers). Ask the question, "If you could do only one thing to help young children's speaking ability, what would that be?"
3. Observe a preschool group. What differences do you notice in the children's ability to solve problems with words? Cite specific examples.
4. Observe a preschool classroom. Write down the teacher's questions (word for word). Using the eight question types from this chapter, tell which recorded questions fit which category. Report your findings to the class. Were more recall questions asked?

5. Pair off with another student. Try to find some object (from your pocket or book bag, for example) that might interest a preschool child. Alternate asking each other two recall, two convergent, two divergent, and two evaluation questions about the objects. Then try asking observation, explanation-seeking, or prediction questions. Which questions were easy to formulate? Which were difficult?

6. List what you feel to be two additional characteristics of intellectual behavior not found on Costa's outline of intelligent behavior characteristics on pages 335–336. How could these behaviors be supported and encouraged as they emerge in a preschool child?

7. Visit a center and record all instances of dramatic play. Note all equipment that seems to promote speaking.

8. With a classmate, describe a dramatic play-kit idea on a theme that was not included in this chapter. List the items for this theme that you feel would be safe and would promote dramatic play. Share with the class. Vote on one play kit created by classmates in this exercise that you feel would be popular with children. Give the reason(s) for your vote.

9. Review dramatic play items commercially produced by looking in school supply catalogs. Report on the cost of three items.

10. Discuss your position concerning show-and-tell time.

11. Observe a full morning program in a center. List the activities or routines in which there was active speaking by most of the children.

12. Pretend you have acquired an extra-large cardboard packing case, big enough for children to crawl into and stand. In what way would this case enhance dramatic play? In what play situations could the case be used?

13. Read the following observed child behavior. Using Costa's characteristics of intelligent behavior, identify child behaviors that match Costa's listing. With a small group of classmates, write teacher statements that might support and appreciate the child's quest. Don't include possible teacher control or behavior-change-attempt statements.

> Damian watched intently as Ariela pushed a wheeled popper toy across the floor. Brightly colored wooden balls danced and flew within the toy's transparent dome. Searching for a stuffed animal, Damian selected a green rabbit. With rabbit in hand, he stood in front of Ariela saying "What's up, Doc!" while moving the rabbit in jumping motions. Slyly he grabbed the handle of the popper toy. Ariela tried to scoot around Damian. Damian held on and Ariela howled. As the teacher approached, Damian said, "She won't give me a turn!" Teacher gently removed Damian's hand and said "Let's go find another toy." Damian instead flees to the painting easel. He paints but concentrates on Ariela and the toy by peering over the top of the easel. Ariela, aware of Damian, sees her friend Bettina, and they proceed to push the popper toy back and forth in front of Damian's easel. Damian makes loud zooming noises with his paintbrush as he strokes vigorously up and down.

Bettina becomes interested and walks around to see Damian's artwork. Ariela follows. Damian quickly drops the brush and picks up the popper toy. The girls then paint together at a second easel. The teacher notices Damian has forgotten to take his wet artwork to the drying area, so asks him to do so. With popper toy under his arm, he complies and holds the popper between his knees as he pins the wet painting on the drying line. Damian spends about ten minutes pushing the toy and watching colored balls pop upward. His fingers try to pull off the plastic cover to no avail. He slips outside to the yard to an out-of-sight corner. Teacher notices he is seated bent over the toy. She sees Damian pick up a stick and try to wedge off the plastic top using considerable pressure. She approaches and says "Damian, that's an inside toy." Damian shrugs, picks up the toy, and heads for the classroom.

14. Observe a teacher-planned group time. Describe the activities, discussion, and discussion topics. Identify children's attending and participating behaviors mentioned in this chapter. Analyze possible factors influencing these behaviors. Share with a small group of classmates and report your group's finding to the class.

15. Decide what questions an early childhood practitioner might ask a small group who just returned from a zoo.

16. Read and react to the following:

I have a difficult time not correcting children's speech mistakes overtly rather than subtly. Maybe the problem is my adult fear of children's mistakes leading to bad habits. I think that's part of our Puritan heritage or what adults did in correcting my speech errors when I was a child. I need to learn to trust children and realize if I let them correct themselves in their own good time they'll attain literacy.

17. Examine the following conversation between Josh and his teacher, Mrs. Hidalgo. How did Mrs. Hidalgo modify her initial questions to extend the conversation?

Josh: My dad got a new car.

Mrs. Hidalgo: What kind of car?

Josh: A new car.

Mrs. Hidalgo: Is it a nice color?

Josh: Yeah, it's red.

Mrs. Hidalgo: Is it your favorite color?

Josh: Nah.

Mrs. Hidalgo: What color car would you choose?

Josh: A black one.

Mrs. Hidalgo: I'd like to have a shiny black car too. Did you go for a ride?

Josh: Yep.

Mrs. Hidalgo: What's the dashboard look like?

Josh: It's got buttons and red lights.

Mrs. Hidalgo: My car's dashboard does too and a gas gauge—so I know if the car is full of gas or nearly empty.

Josh: We went to the station and my dad put gas in.

Do you have any advice for Mrs. Hidalgo?

18. Read and analyze the following from "What's Wrong with this Show-and-Tell?" by Oken-Wright (1988):

> Fifteen four-year-olds are seated in a sprawling group. "Today it's Todd's, Teddy's, Joyce's and Karen's turn," says the teacher. "Todd, did you bring anything for us? You always forget, don't you? You need to start remembering when it's Tuesday, that's your day." When it's her turn, Karen drones on in a monotone for five minutes about a plastic bracelet her mother bought her at the mall. Stevie interrupts many times trying to get the teacher's attention to tell about the frog he caught in the morning. After several warnings, the teacher tells Stevie that he has lost his turn to tell on Wednesday because of his discourteous behavior during Karen's turn today. The teacher says, "This way you don't have too many on any one day and they can talk as long as they like."

19. Discuss the following with a group of classmates. "Show-and-tell time is the only time a teacher has to sit back and rest and let the children do the talking. It's a planned time that takes little planning and preparation . . . it fills program time."

20. Make a dramatic play prop box collection for a child's picture book. On the outside of the storage container put a book illustration or character illustration. Introduce it to a group of preschoolers. Share the results with your classmates.

CHAPTER REVIEW

A. Explain each of the following terms:

1. structured activities
2. possessives
3. negatives
4. prepositions
5. comparatives

B. Answer the following questions related to speaking goals.

1. How can the goals of a program be met?

2. When children are interested in an object or event, what should the teacher do in order for the children to learn while they are motivated?

3. Where should visual material be placed for viewing with a group of children?

C. Define dramatic play.

D. Choose the factors that can help young children develop speaking abilities.

1. Equipment

2. Staff members

3. Parents

4. Making a child ask correctly for what he or she wants

5. A relaxed atmosphere

6. Interesting happenings to talk about

7. Lack of play with other children

8. Asking a child if he or she wants to tell something

9. A child's need or desire

10. A teacher's ignoring the child's nonverbal communication

11. Daily speaking routines

12. Teacher attention to speech

13. Teacher rewarding children's speech

14. Planned speaking activities

E. Answer the following questions.

1. What is a dramatic play kit?

2. Name some of the things a teacher does not want to happen during show-and-tell time (for example, one child talking too long).

F. Select the correct answers. Each item may have more than one correct answer.

1. When children say "wented,"
    a. correct them.
    b. ignore them.
    c. repeat their message correctly.
    d. have them practice "went."

2. In daily conversations, the teacher should
    a. answer or respond to nonverbal messages.
    b. pair new word meanings with words the children already know.
    c. listen to children who yell in anger.
    d. patiently accept stuttering and hesitant speech.

3. If a child says "richlotti-gongo" to you,
   a. repeat it back if you can, hoping the child will show you what he or she wants to say.
   b. ignore it and wait until you understand the message.
   c. go along with the statement saying, something like "Really, you don't say."
   d. ask the child to speak more clearly.

4. In using questions with young children,
   a. suit the question to the children.
   b. always give them the answer.
   c. insist that they answer correctly.
   d. answer some of the children's questions with your own questions, when appropriate.

5. Planned activities are based on
   a. goals only.
   b. children's current interests only.
   c. goals and children's interests.
   d. knowledge instead of attitudes.

G. Name three ways a teacher can give children confidence in their speaking abilities.

H. Select the appropriate teacher response to the children's comments.

Child	**Teacher**
1. "Dolly"	a. "Did the door hit you? And then what happened?"
2. "Where do this go?"	
3. "I fell down. The door hit me." (Child is unhurt.)	b. "Yes, they are. They both have four legs."
4. "Horses are big like cows."	c. "They taste good; here's a carrot stick to try."
5. "Dem er goodums."	d. "Where does the block go? The block goes on the top shelf."
6. "That's a mouse, teacher."	e. "You can play with this dolly."
	f. "It has fur like a mouse; it's small like a mouse; but it's called a hamster."

I. From the four question types listed, choose the type that matches questions 1 through 8.

   Recall   Divergent   Convergent   Evaluative

1. What would happen if we left this glass full of ice on the table?

2. If your shoes and socks are the same color, would you please stand up?

3. Who can tell me this puppet's name?

    4. If you had a dollar, how would you like to spend it?

    5. What do we need to make a birthday cake?

    6. Why did the basket fall over?

    7. Did the door open by itself?

    8. Who has the smallest cup?

J.   Write down teacher questions that could lead a child to a discovery and promote the child's verbal expression of the discovery in the following situations.

    1. A bird's nest is found in the yard.

    2. The wheel on a bike squeaks.

    3. A flashlight is taken apart.

K.   SITUATION. Formulate appropriate teacher comments in the following situations (1–3). What might a teacher say in response?

    1. Child is complaining that easel paint drips and doesn't stay where he wants it.

    2. It's cleanup time, and Sharie (child) says, "Scott and Keith never put anything away!"

    3. Carter is talking about the way water is disappearing in the sun.

NOW WORK ON CONVERGENT TYPE QUESTIONS. Formulate a possible teacher question.

    4. Megan noticed a bug on the floor.

    5. Christa says, "Dana has new shoes!"

    6. Ryan brings a toy truck to share at group time.

PLAN EVALUATION QUESTIONS. In 7, 8, and 9, plan evaluation questions that a teacher might use.

    7. "I don't like peanut butter," Romana says.

    8. "This is my favorite book," Linsay declares.

    9. Teacher is introducing a new toy with plastic boats.

L.   List Costa's characteristics of intelligent behavior.

M. Select the terms that best define the teacher's role in dramatic play.

    1. Interactor

    2. Background observer

    3. Provider of settings

    4. Provider of props

    5. One who redirects unsafe play

    6. Active participant

    7. Suggestor of ideas during play

8. Provider of many words
9. Gatherer of dramatic play items

N. Write a short paragraph that finishes the following:

The reasons some teachers do not actively plan programs with children leading activities in front of the child group . . .

O. In the following description of calling the roll, identify those parts that might make a child feel pressured and tense rather than relaxed. Discuss the attitude of the teacher as well.

"Good morning, children. Everyone say, 'Good Morning, Mrs. Brown.' That's good. Bonnie, you didn't say it. You were playing with your hair ribbon. Say it now, Bonnie.

I'm going to say everyone's name. When I say your name I want you all to say, 'I'm here, Mrs. Brown.' Susie Smith. 'I'm here, Mrs. Brown.' Speak louder, Susie, we can't hear you. Brett Porter. Not 'I'm present,' Brett, say 'I'm here, Mrs. Brown.' David Martinez. Answer please, David. David Martinez. David, you must answer when I call your name! Andy Smith. No, Andy, say 'I'm here, Mrs. Brown,' not 'I'm here' and that's all.

I don't know what's the matter with all of you; you did it right yesterday. We're going to stay here until we all do it the right way. Dana Collins. I can't understand what you said, Dana; say it again. Mark Jefferson. Mark, that's very good, you said it the right way. Chris Wong. No, it's not time to talk to Ronnie now; it's time to speak up. What are you supposed to say, children? I give up. You'll never learn. Let's all go outside now and work out all of our wiggles."

CHAPTER 14

Group Times

OBJECTIVES

After studying this chapter, you should be able to:

- describe circle and group-time speaking activities.

- perform a finger play with children.

- discuss ways to promote child involvement in simple plays, chants, and circle times.

- plan and lead a group time.

The activities in this chapter give children many speaking opportunities. Children involved in the activities have the opportunity to imitate speech, to use creative speech, and to express their own ideas and feelings. However, you should realize that it is difficult to classify activities as listening or speaking activities, because they often overlap.

Groups

Circle and group times are chances for children to develop understanding about themselves as group members. They enjoy language together by using familiar songs, favorite finger plays, chants, and a wide variety of activities. Children gain self-confidence, feelings of personal worth, and group spirit (figure 14–1).

School administrators and teachers need to clarify their priorities concerning group times. Since it is difficult to conduct intimate conversations and discussions with large groups, many schools prefer working with small groups of children so that con-

versations can flourish. But decisions regarding group size may hinge on staffing considerations. Sometimes large groups can be temporarily divided so that there can be "instant replays" of activities for smaller groups.

FIGURE 14–1 Group time—together time

When presenting new material during group sessions, teachers should allow time to receive and react to children's comments and questions. One pitfall in conducting group activities is the tendency for teachers to remain the center of attention, assuming the role of the great dispenser of knowledge. When this occurs, child feedback is ignored. This is further discussed under the heading entitled "Circle-Time Pitfalls." As Johnson (1987) puts it, "oral language runs a great risk in school of being eliminated or being frowned upon so heavily that children don't feel comfortable. 'Be quiet' is an admonition heard entirely too often in school. Some of the excitement of discovery has to be shouted out. Talk, after all, is the hallmark of humanity."

Language activities add sparkle and liveliness to circle times. The following is a list of words that can be used to describe a successful group experience.

active
Children's participation includes motor and speech involvement.

enthusiastic
The teacher's commitment in making a presentation is communicated by the teacher's facial expressions and manner.

prepared
All necessary materials are at the teacher's fingertips and are used with smooth verbal presentations.

accepting
The teacher is open to children's ideas and feelings and is appreciative of children's contributions.

appropriate
The activity suits the particular group.

clear
The teacher provides purposeful clarification of new concepts.

comfortable
The seating and light source are appropriate.

familiar
The activity includes previously learned and enjoyed material.

novel
New ideas and material are presented.

relaxed
The activity does not pressure or threaten children.

sharing
All children are invited to take turns in participating in the activity.

Groups of Younger Preschoolers

Two- and three-year-olds participating in group times are learning social interaction. Their group time participation may depend on their feelings of trust and security. After adjustments to seating comfort, teacher welcoming each child by name or singing their names, or teacher starting a simple song or finger play, teachers watch for child focus and involvement. Often active participation grows slowly as watchers become doers. In well-conducted circle times, children can choose their own level of activity. Teacher flexibility and preplanning, together with the teacher's obvious enthusiasm and delight in each child's presence, breeds social acceptance and success.

Time will determine whether a teacher decides to expand highly enjoyed circles or cut others short because of children's feedback signals.

Since younger children's classrooms usually are staffed with more adults and volunteers, non-leading adults can sit near or beside children to encourage child participation. An inviting group time may draw in all attending children after it is in progress.

Group time for very young preschoolers can be described as "loose and light" formations or groupings. Children choose to be present and choose their level of involvement. Teacher counts on child curiosity and desire to be part of the action. Think of yourself in a new social situation: Wouldn't you watch briefly before entering conversations with strangers and approach those who seem most open and welcoming? And wouldn't you move on if conversations were boring, irrelevant, or obtuse?

Planning Small Group Time

After considering child capacity to remain involved, a group can be planned to occupy a specific time period. What happens and when it happens is roughly outlined. A gathering together activity can be a song, a finger play, or a recording followed by any number and type of activities. A planned closing and transition ends the experience and moves the group in an orderly fashion on to other classroom pursuits. If group time is of considerable length, then standing and moving activities are interspersed with seated ones.

Circles

A circle activity (usually, a semicircle seating arrangement) is begun by capturing group attention. A signal or daily routine can be used. To make sure all children are focused, a short silence (pause) adds a feeling of anticipation and expectation.

Occasionally varying the signals keeps one signal from becoming old hat. A visual signal, a xylophone ripple, a tap on a musical triangle, an attention-getting record, a puppet announcing a group activity, or reminder stickers placed on children's hands related to the theme of the activity are a few alternatives.

A musical recording can set the mood as children form a group. As MacDonald (1988) observes, singing can serve as a magnet that pulls the group together, and a quiet song is a great means of relaxing and bonding a group.

Opening activities that recognize each child help to build group spirit. Such recognition is a way of communicating to each child that "You're an important person; we're happy to have you with us." The children can then begin group activities on the right note.

No One Said Leading Groups Would Be Easy

Harker and Green (1985) describe one teacher's decision-making and internal dialogue while leading a group of children:

Are they going to understand this? Should I rephrase this question? How can I get Tony or Sue to participate?

To the outside observer, a skilled teacher leading and interacting with a group may look like a relaxed, interested individual. Under the surface of the teacher's enthusiastic manner, many decisions are being made. Reciprocal interchange is happening; there's internal dialogue going on. She or he may be watching the clock for time length, watching for both interested and restless behavior, or listening intently for child comments and framing appropriate verbal interaction. With all this going on, many beginning teachers aren't able to truly relax!

Circle time often starts with a few children and others join as they finish chosen pursuits, and/or become attracted to circle activities. Centers differ in philosophy concerning required participation. Staffing may permit other choices.

CIRCLE STARTERS

The following activities are circle-time starters, attention getters, socializers, and wiggle reducers.

CIRCLE TIME
> *I've just come in from outside.*
> *I'm tired as can be.*
> *I'll cross my legs*
> *And fold my hands,*
> *I WILL NOT MOVE.*
> *My head won't move.*
> *My toes are still.*
> *I'll put my hands on my chin,*
> *And when it's quiet, we'll begin!*

WHO'S THAT?

> (Chant or sing to tune of "Ten Little Indians.")

Who's that _____ in the _____
          (boy, girl, lady, man)   (red, blue, etc.)
_____?
(shirt, pants, shoes, etc.)

(Repeat twice.)

Oh, _____ is _____ name, oh.
        (child or adult gives name)   (his/her)

(Teacher supplies name when child is hesitant.)

WIGGLES

I'll wiggle my fingers
And wiggle my toes.
I'll wiggle my arms
And wiggle my nose.
And now that all the wiggle's out,
We'll listen to what circle's about.

CLAPPING START

Turn around and face the wall. Clap, Clap, Clap.
Down upon your knees now fall. Clap, Clap, Clap.
Up again and turn around. Clap, Clap, Clap.
Turn around and then sit down. Clap, Clap, Clap.
Not a sound.

WHERE ARE YOUR _____?

Where are your eyes? Show me eyes that see.
Where are your eyes? Shut them quietly.
Where is your nose? A nose that blows.
Where is your nose? Show me your nose and wiggle
* it so.*
Where is your mouth? Open it wide.
Where is your mouth? With teeth inside.
Smile—Smile—Smile.

I LIKE YOU

(Chant or sing)

I like you.
There's no doubt about it.
I like you.
There's no doubt about it.
I am your good friend.
You like me.
There's no doubt about it.
You like me.

There's no doubt about it.
You are my good friend.
There's my friend (child's name), *and my friend*
(child's name).

(Continue around circle.)

OH HERE WE ARE TOGETHER

(Chant or sing)

Oh here we are together, together, together,
Oh here we are together
At (insert school name) *Preschool*
There's (child's name) *and* (child's name), *and*
*   (names of all children).*
Oh here we are together to have a good day.

WE'RE WAITING

(Circle starter)

We're waiting, we're waiting, we're waiting for
*   (child's name).*

(Repeat until group is formed.)

We're here, because we're here, because we're here,
*   because we're here.*
And my name is _____, and my name is
*   _____.* (Around the circle.)

HELLO

Hello (child's name). *Hello, hello, hello.*
Shake my hand and around we'll go.
Hello (child's name). *Hello, hello, hello.*
Shake my hand and around we'll go.

(Teacher starts; children continue around the circle chanting until all are recognized.)

SECRET

I've got something in my pocket
That belongs across my face.
I keep it very close at hand
In a most convenient place.
I know you couldn't guess it
If you guessed a long, long while.
So I'll take it out and put it on
It's a great big friendly SMILE!

TEN FINGERS

> *I have ten little fingers*
> *And they all belong to me.*
> *I can make them do things.*
> *Would you like to see?*
> *I can shut them up tight*
> *Or open them wide.*
> *I can put them together*
> *Or make them all hide.*
> *I can make them jump high.*
> *I can make them jump low,*
> *I can fold them quietly*
> *And hold them just so.*

EVERYBODY DO THIS

Refrain:
> *Everybody do this, do this, do this.*
> *Everybody do this just like me.*

Actions:
> *Open and close fists*
> *Roll fists around*
> *Touch elbows*
> *Spider fingers*
> *Pat head, rub tummy*
> *Wink*
> *Wave hand good-bye*

(Ask children to create others.)

CIRCLE ACTIVITIES

A circle group keeps its lively enthusiasm and social enjoyment when well planned. The activities that follow involve both language and coordinated physical movement.

Passing Games

Have children arranged in a circle. Pass a small object around the circle. Start by passing it in front of the children, then behind, then overhead, and then under the legs. Directions can be changed on command of the teacher, such as "pass it to your left, pass it to your right," and so on. Ask children for suggestions for other ways to pass the object. Passing a toy microphone can also promote a child's verbal contribution. When a child is done, the microphone is passed to the next child.

TEDDY BEAR CIRCLE PASS

(Have bear in bag behind leader)

> *Love somebody, yes, I do.*
> *Love somebody, yes, I do.*
> *Love somebody, yes, I do.*
> *Love somebody, but I won't tell who.*

(Shake head sideways.)

> *Love somebody, yes, I do.*
> *Love somebody, yes, I do.*
> *Love somebody, yes, I do.*
> *Now I'll show* (him or her) *to you!*
> *Here's a hug—Pass it on.*

(Group continues to chant as each child hugs and hands Teddy to next child. When Teddy returns to leader, last verse is repeated, ending with the following line.)

> *Now back in the bag our hugs are through!*

(Substituted for last line.)

IF YOU'RE HAPPY AND YOU KNOW IT

> *If you're happy and you know it, clap your hands.*
> *If you're happy and you know it, clap your hands.*
> *If you're happy and you know it, then your face*
>   *will surely show it.*
> *If you're happy and you know it, clap your hands.*

(Additional verses.)

> *If you're sad and you know it, wipe your eyes.*
> *If you're mad and you know it, pound your fist.*
> *If you're hungry and you know it, rub your stomach.*
> *If you're silly and you know it, go tee-hee.*
> *If you're cold and you know it, rub your arms.*
> *If you're hot and you know it, wipe your brow.*
> *If you're sleepy and you know it, go to sleep . . .*
>   *snore, snore.*

BALL ROLLING CIRCLE
The ball will roll across our circle.
Touch toes with your neighbors.
Here comes the ball, Susie. "I roll the ball to Susie."

(Teacher says: "Susie roll the ball across the circle and say your friend's name.")

"I roll the ball to _____."

THE CARROT SEED WILL GROW
Carrots grow from carrot seeds,
I'll plant this seed and grow one.
I won't be disappointed if my seed doesn't grow.
What makes seeds grow? I don't know!
So I won't be disappointed if my seed doesn't grow.
My brother said "Na, na. It won't come up. Na, na.
*   It won't come up.*
Na, na. It won't come up. Your carrot won't
*   come up."*

(Repeat above, ending with the following.)

Oh, carrots grow from carrot seeds.
I planted one, it grew. I watered it. I pulled the weeds.
No matter what he said.
Carrots grow from carrot seeds.

Taking Turns and Directing Attention

During circle and conversations and other group activities, the following teacher statements are helpful in emphasizing to children the importance of taking turns:

- "It's Monica's turn now."
- "Barry's turn to talk, and everyone's turn to listen."
- "Listen to Bonnie. Bonnie's lips are moving, and ours are resting."
- "Just one person talks at a time."
- "I am guessing that you really want to say something, Jason, but that you are waiting for your turn."
- "Sierra was telling us a story, so it's her turn. What happened next, Sierra?"
- "Time to give Angel a turn to talk, Aki. Angel, do you live in an apartment house?"

- "Heiko is answering my question now. Wait and you can answer next, Bradford."
- "Raise your hand if you're waiting to tell us about your pet. I see four hands up—September, Ariel, Alexander, and Alwin. You will all have a turn. Alwin, it's your turn now."
- "Wait, Collette, Rio hasn't finished his turn."
- "My turn to talk, Elias. Your turn to listen."

Being a member of a group provides children with two conditions essential for learning: a sense of security and opportunities for social interaction (Dumbro, 1992).

Closing Group Activities

Exciting circles and other group activities sometimes need a quiet, settling close. The following can be used to wind down group activities and prepare excited children for the change to another activity or play.

UP AND DOWN
Up and down,
Up and down,
Clap your hands and turn around.
Up and down,
Up and down,
Clap your hands and sit down.

RAG DOLL
I'm just a limp rag doll.
My arms are limp.
My legs are limp.
My head is limp.
I'm just a limp rag doll.

UP, DOWN, AND REST
Up and down,
Up and down,
Round, round, round,
Up and down.
I stretch, I stretch, I yawn.
I rest and then I start again.
Up and down

(second time—I rest, I rest, I rest is the fifth and ending line.)

Transitions

Disbanding a circle or group at an activity's ending calls for a planned approach. You will need to excuse a few at a time, if the group is of any size. When carpet squares are to be picked up and stacked, or small chairs returned to tables, a reminder is in order: "When you hear your name, pick up your rug square, carry it to the stack."

Transitory statements that relate to the just-completed activity work well: "Crawl like Victor the Boa Constrictor to the block center," or "Let the wind blow you slowly to the water table like it blew in the little tree."

TRANSITION POEM
> *Wiggle both ears.*
> *Touch your nose.*
> *Wiggle your fingers.*
> *Stamp your toes.*
> *Point to your eyes.*
>
> *Your mouth open wide.*
> *Stick out your tongue.*
> *Put it inside.*
> *Trace your lips.*
> *Go "shh!" Don't speak.*
> *Hands on your neck.*
> *Touch both cheeks.*
>
> *Shake your hands.*
> *Now let them sleep.*
> *Bend your knees.*
> *Sit on your feet.*
>
> *Now we finished with this play,*
> *Take your feet and walk away!*

Additional Transitions

A fun way to move children one by one is to recite the rhyme "Jack be nimble, Jack be quick . . . ," substituting the child's name for "Jack": "(Child's name) be nimble, (child's name) be quick, (child's name) jump over the candlestick." (Children clap for the child who jumps over a plastic candleholder and unlit candle.)

Courtesy of Thelma Alaniz

Another way to disband a group is to make a "tickler" from a three-foot long dowel and some yarn. Say to the children, "Close your eyes. When you feel a tickle on your head, it's time to stand and walk carefully through your classmates to the. . . ."

Courtesy of Dianne Ferry

Some statements that are helpful in moving a group of children in an orderly fashion are listed here. Many identify language concepts and serve a dual purpose.

- "Everyone with brown shoes stand up. Now it's time to. . . ."
- "If your favorite sandwich is peanut butter and jelly (ham, cheese, tuna, and so forth) raise your hand. If your hand is up, please tiptoe to the. . . ."
- "Richie is the engine on a slow, slow train. Richie, chug chug slowly to the. . . ." "Darlene is the coal car on a slow, slow train. . . ." (The last child is, naturally, the caboose.)

Adding Multicultural Activities

The inclusion of multicultural and multiethnic aspects to group activities is not a new idea. Songs and finger plays in the native languages of attending children promote acceptance of diversity. Teachers may need parental help in discovering literary material or for translation. Children usually eagerly learn motions and translated words presented with catchy rhythms. Introduce the name of the language when presenting. "This is a song with Russian words. Gregor's mom taught me how to sing it." As with multicultural and multiethnic picture books, stories, and poetry, these activities are not given extra or special status but are everyday, standard activities—ones that many teachers do not wish to neglect. The problem, at times, is finding them when teacher resources abound with "Anglo intense" examples.

Circle-Time Pitfalls

Circle times can fall apart for a number of reasons. An examination of the teacher's goals and planning decisions prior to conducting a circle time may clarify what caused child disinterest or lack of enthusiasm. When circles go poorly, child behavior may be focused away from the circle's theme and action.

Before examining teacher behaviors, other factors should be reviewed, such as the setting, length, and age-level appropriateness of the activity. Then examine whether the children enjoyed, and participated enthusiastically in, the activity and how teacher behavior contributed to this. If the activity was not a success, the activity failed the children rather than vice versa.

A teacher whose goals include child conversation and involvement will not monopolize the activity with a constant up-front presentation. Unfortunately, some beginning teachers seem to possess an overwhelming desire to dispense information, eliminating children's conversation and reactions. When this happens, circle times become passive listening times.

The size of the circle has been discussed in this chapter. Dodge (1988) describes the possible reason(s) teachers attempt large-group circle times:

> Possible Causes: Teachers are more comfortable with their ability to maintain control when the whole group is involved in the same activity. They want to be sure everyone in the group learns the same concepts and skills. Several teachers said that they do most of their teaching at circle time.

Teachers need to understand that large-group instruction at preschool level may cause group disinterest and restlessness by becoming impersonal.

There seems to be a type of adult who is unable to talk to the child, no matter how important or pertinent the child's comments. It's as if a planned step-by-step circle time must be followed. The teacher has become inflexible, a slave to a plan. One-sided conversations turn everyone off but the speaker.

Waiting a long period for a turn during circle time leads to frustration. Children may tune out for this reason. A simple fact that all experienced teachers know is that active, involved children stay focused.

A teacher who constantly asks questions to maintain child attention may defeat his or her purpose. Some teachers do not understand the difference between asking a question with one right answer (to test a child) and asking questions that encourage thinking. Most adults remember from past school experiences how it feels when one missed a question. Unskilled teachers may make children afraid to answer or share their ideas.

Hints for Successful Circle Times

Before you conduct your circle:

- Review your goals for circle times periodically.
- Plan for active child participation and involvement.
- Make proposed circle-time duration appropriate to the group's age.
- Practice language games and activities so you can focus on the children.
- Think about group size and settings (figure 14–2).

FIGURE 14–2   Teachers sometimes lower their voice volume to maintain child focus and attention.

FIGURE 14–3   A finger play is used to focus three-year-olds at small group time.

- Remember it's better to stop before enthusiasm wanes.
- Consider child comfort.
- Identify possible room distractions.
- Keep rules simple, clear, and at a minimum.

During a circle time:

- Focus children at the beginning (figure 14–3).
- State what you expect early, if necessary:
    "Sit where you can see."
    "My turn to talk, your turn to listen."
- Proceed with enthusiasm.
- Try to enjoy and be unhurried.
- Think about including activities that promote child decisions, guessing, voting, creativity, expressing personal preferences, solving problems, making predictions, and child questioning.
- Give children credit for their comments, ideas, and participation.
    "Jason's moving his arms and head."
    "Shawnita told us what she saw in the mirror."
    "Maron thinks our plants need water."
- Stop the rambling child speaker with "It's time for your friends' turn now, Clyde."
- Make eye contact with all children.

- Watch for feedback, and act accordingly.
- Use wind-down activities if the group gets too excited.
- Use wiggle reducers.
- Draw quiet children into participation.
- Reduce waiting times.
- Watch the length of time allowed for the activity.
- Think of an orderly transition to the next activity, which may include the children's taking carpet squares to a storage area.
- Remember that your skill increases with experience.

Educators will always have children, particularly very young preschoolers or culturally diverse preschoolers, who don't readily choose to participate with speech or actions at group times. French (1996) points out that teacher insistence, though well-meaning, is inappropriate:

> The preschool years are a time of rapid language development, and many preschool teachers are appropriately concerned with supporting and fostering this language development. Unfortunately, many teachers translate this concern into an insistence that a child speak up individually in group situations—for example, participating in show-and-tell or responding to questions about a story the teacher has read.

Aides or volunteers attending a circle time need to be alert to child distractions. Moving closer to or between two children may be helpful or quietly suggesting an alternate activity to a disinterested child can aid the teacher leader.

Occasionally one child's silliness or mimicking behavior can lead to circle time disruption as the attention-getting child's behavior challenges the teacher's hold on group focus. Teacher restatement of a circle time rule may be necessary.

Watching Children's Participation Level

As teachers scan faces and observe child vocalization and movement during circle times, obvious differences in children's ability to focus, stay focused, and participate as fully functioning group members are apparent. Many conditions influence each child's ability to concentrate, actively contribute, and follow group activities—age, health, language deficiencies, weather, distractions, home problems, disabilities, and a multitude of other factors may change child behavior at circle on any given day. After a teacher has become familiar with her group and leads a few circle times, she mentally categorizes child behaviors. Often at circle time teachers can tell who is having a bad day. Possible child attending behavior will vary from not focused to completely focused and participating, with other behaviors between these two end points. A child may tune in and out, attend but not participate verbally or with body involvement, or attend and participate sporadically.

As teachers monitor children's group behavior, they become increasingly aware of how teacher behaviors and verbalizations affect children's attending and participation. Ask any practicing teacher about the teacher satisfaction felt at the conclusion of a well-planned and conducted group time where child interest was held and maintained and something of educational quality or value was accomplished. When teachers feel their child group was eager, responsive, and enjoying the group experience and feel that as the teacher they interacted skillfully, it's a memorable teaching moment.

Chants and Choruses

Throughout history, rhythmic chants and choruses have been used in group rituals and ceremonies. The individuals in the group gain a group identity as a result of their participation.

Natural enjoyment of rhythmic word patterns can be seen in a child's involvement in group chants. Child and teacher can also playfully take part in call and response during the preschool day. "I made it, I made it," the child says. "I see it, I see it," the teacher answers, picking up the child's rhythm.

This verbal play is common. Sounds in the community and schoolyard can be brought to the children's attention by teachers who notice them and make comments. Weir and Eggleston (1975) point out that:

Urban sounds are sometimes syncopated and rhythmical, such as the fire siren, people walking on side walks, jack hammers or nailing in nails. These are rhythms that children imitate verbally and that adults can point out to children.

Chants and choruses are mimicked, and sound and word patterns that have regularity and predictability are imitated. Choruses usually involve a back and forth conversation (one individual alternating with another) and involve the rise and fall of accented sounds or syllables.

Children need the teacher's examples and directions, such as, "When it's your turn, I'll point to you," or "Let's say it together," before they can perform the patterns on their own. Chants printed on charts with simple illustrations can enhance chanting and chorus times and tie the oral words to written ones.

Buchoff (1994) believes that chanting promotes successful language experiences regardless of children's background or talent, and helps children learn the importance of clear and expressive pronunciation. Teacher charts developed for chanting can be used over and over and are another way for children to discover the relationship of spoken words and print. Many strong-rhythm chants invite clapping, foot stomping, or a wide variety of other physical movements. The chants that follow are some tried-and-true favorites.

CHANTS

THE GRAND OLD DUKE OF YORK
The grand old Duke of York
He had forty thousand men.
He marched them up the hill.
He marched them down again.
And when you're up, you're up!
And when you're down, you're down.
And when you're half-way-in-between,
You're neither up nor down.

AND IT WAS ME!

I looked in my soup, and who did I see?
Something wonderful . . . and it was me.

Additional verses:
I looked in the mirror, and who did I see?
I looked in the puddle . . .
I looked in a window . . .
I looked in the river . . .
I looked in the pond . . .
I looked at a snapshot . . .
I turned off the television . . .

Ending:
When I'm grown up, I'll still be there.
Right in reflections everywhere.
When I'm grown up, how will it be?
A wonderful world with you and me.

IT'S RAINING IT'S POURING

It's raining, it's pouring.
The old man is snoring.
He went to bed and he bumped his head
And he couldn't get up in the morning.
Rain, rain go away—come again some other day.

MISS MARY MACK

Miss Mary Mack, Mack, Mack
All dressed in black, black, black
With silver buttons, buttons, buttons
All down her back, back, back.

She asked her mother, mother, mother
For fifteen cents, cents, cents
To see the elephants, elephants, elephants
Jump the fence, fence, fence.

They jumped so high, high, high
They touched the sky, sky, sky
And never came back, back, back
Till the fourth of July, ly, ly.

July can't walk, walk, walk
July can't talk, talk, talk
July can't eat, eat, eat
With a knife and fork, fork, fork.

She went upstairs, stairs, stairs
To say her prayers, prayers, prayers
She made her bed, bed, bed
She hit her head, head, head
On a piece of corn bread, bread, bread.

Now she's asleep, sleep, sleep
She's snoring deep, deep, deep
No more to play, play, play
Until Friday, day, day
What can I say, say, say
Except hooray, ray, ray!

PANCAKE

Mix a pancake.
Stir a pancake.
Pop it in the pan.
Fry a pancake.
Toss a pancake.
Catch it if you can.

THE BIG CLOCK

Slowly ticks the big clock

Chorus:
Tick-tock, tick-tock
(Repeat twice.)

But the cuckoo clock ticks double quick

Chorus:
Tick-a-tock-a, tick-a-tock-a
Tick-a-tock-a, tick!

LITTLE BROWN RABBIT

Little brown rabbit went hoppity-hop,

All:
Hoppity-hop, hoppity-hop!

Into a garden without any stop,

All:
Hoppity-hop, hoppity-hop!

He ate for his supper a fresh carrot top,

All:
Hoppity-hop, hoppity-hop!

Then home went the rabbit without any stop,

All:
Hoppity-hop, hoppity-hop!

WHO ATE THE COOKIES IN THE COOKIE JAR

All: *Who ate the cookies in the cookie jar?*

All: (Child's or teacher's name) *ate the cookies in the cookie jar.* (Teacher points to different child for each verse.)

Named person: *Who me?*

All: *Yes you.*

Named person: *Couldn't be.*

All: *Then who?*

Named person: (Child or teacher) *ate the cookies in the cookie jar.*

Newly named person: *Who me?* (and so forth).

Using Accessories

LITTLE THINGS

(to the tune of "Oh My Darling" or chanted)

Little black things, little black things
Crawling up and down my arm.
I am not afraid of them
For they will do no harm.
(Substitute any color for black.)

Materials Needed

The following colors of yarn:

red	green	black	pink
orange	blue	brown	gray
yellow	purple	white	

Instructions

You will need to make a set of eleven colored things for each child. These can be stored easily in zip-lock sandwich bags.

Step 1: For each colored thing, cut five yarn pieces, each measuring eight inches long.

Step 2: Put one yarn piece aside and, keeping the other four together, fold them in half.

Step 3: Using the fifth piece of yarn, tie it around the other four, one inch from the folded ends and knotting it well, to form a "head" and "legs." Fold the knotted ends down to form more legs.

Give each child a bag of "things." Let the children tell you what color to use. While chanting or singing, have the colored thing crawl up and down arms.

Courtesy of MAGIC MOMENTS

FINGER PLAY

Finger play is an enjoyed preschool group (or individual) activity that parents have probably already introduced children to with "peek-a-boo" or "this little piggy went to market." Finger plays use words and actions (usually finger motions) together. Early childhood play frequently goes beyond finger movements and often includes whole body actions.

When learning a finger play, the child usually practices and joins in the finger movements before learning the words. Words can be learned and retained by doing the play over and over again (figure 14–4).

FIGURE 14–4   Actions are sometimes learned before words.

Finger plays are often done with rhymes. Easy-to-remember rhymes give the children pleasure in listening and a chance to feel good about themselves because (1) they quickly become part of a group having fun and doing the same thing, and (2) they experience a feeling of accomplishment when a rhyme has been learned.

Teachers use finger plays to encourage enjoyment of language, to prepare children for sitting, to keep children active and interested while waiting, and as transitions between activities. Finger plays are also used for special purposes, such as quieting a group or getting toys back on the shelves. They can build vocabulary as well as teach facts and can help a child release pent-up energy.

Teachers should practice a finger play and memorize it beforehand to be sure of a clear and smooth presentation. It should be offered enthusiastically, focusing on enjoyment. As with other activities, the teacher can say, "Try it with me." The child who just watches will join in when ready. Watching comes first, one or two hand movements next, and then repetitions, using words and actions together. Each child learns at his or her own rate of speed.

Suggested Finger Plays

Finger plays can be found in many books for early childhood staff members or can be created by the teacher. The following are recommended because of their popularity with both children and teachers.

HICKORY, DICKORY, DOCK
> *Hickory, dickory, dock!*
>> (Rest elbow in the palm of your other hand and swing upraised arm back and forth.)
> *The mouse ran up the clock;*
>> (Creep fingers up the arm to the palm of the other hand.)
> *The clock struck one.*
>> (Clap hands.)
> *The mouse ran down.*
>> (Creep fingers down to elbow.)

> *Hickory, dickory, dock!*
>> (Swing arm as before.)

CHOO! CHOO!
> *Choo-o! Choo-o! Choo! Choo!*
>> (Run finger along arm to shoulder slowly.)
> *This little train goes up the track.*
> *Choo! Choo! Choo! Choo!*
>> (At shoulder turn "train" and head down arm.)
> *But this little train comes quickly back*
> *Choo-choo-choo-choo! Choo-choo-choo-choo!*
>> (Repeat last line.)
>> (Run fingers down arm quickly.)
> *Whoo-o! Whoo-o! Whoo-o!*
>> (Imitate train whistle.)

WHERE IS THUMBKIN?
> *Where is thumbkin, where is thumbkin?*
>> (Hands behind back.)
> *Here I am, here I am.*
>> (One hand out, thumb up. Other hand out, thumb up.)
> *How are you today, sir?*
>> (First thumb bends up and down.)
> *Very well, I thank you.*
>> (Second thumb bends up and down.)
> *Run away, run away.*
>> (First thumb behind back; second thumb behind back.)

> Repeat with:
> *Where is pointer?*
>> (Use first finger.)
> *Where is tall man?*
>> (Use middle finger.)
> *Where is ring man?*
>> (Use ring finger.)
> *Where is pinkie?*
>> (Use little finger.)
> *Where are all the men?*
>> (Use whole hand.)

FAMILY OF RABBITS
> *A family of rabbits lived under a tree,*
>> (Close right hand and hide it under left arm.)

A father, a mother, and babies three.
(Hold up thumb, then fingers in succession.)
Sometimes the bunnies would sleep all day,
(Make fist.)
But when night came, they liked to play.
(Wiggle fingers.)
Out of the hole they'd go creep, creep, creep,
(Move fingers in creeping motion.)
While the birds in the trees were all asleep.
(Rest face on hands, place palms together.)
Then the bunnies would scamper about and run
(Wiggle fingers.)
Uphill, downhill! Oh, what fun!
(Wiggle fingers vigorously.)
But when the mother said, "It's time to rest,"
(Hold up index finger.)
Pop! They would hurry
(Clap hands after "Pop.")
Right back to their nest!
(Hide hand under arm.)

FIREFIGHTERS
Ten little firefighters, sleeping in a row,
Ding, dong goes the bell, down the pole they go.
Jumping on the engine, oh, oh, oh,
Putting out the fire, shhhhhhhhhhhhhhhhhhhh.
And home again they go
Back to sleep again,
All in a row.

THIS IS THE MOUNTAIN
This is the mountain up so high,
(Form a triangle.)
And this is the moon that sails through the sky.
(Make a circle with thumbs and index fingers.)
These are the stars that twinkle so bright.
(Make a small circle with thumb and index, other three fingers moving.)
These are the clouds that pass through the night.
(Make fists.)
This is the window through which I peep,
(Make a square with thumb and index.)
And here am I, fast asleep.
(Close eyes.)

CLAP YOUR HANDS
Clap your hands high,
Clap your hands low,
Pat your head lightly,
And down you go.

I'll touch my hair, my lips, my eyes,
I'll sit up straight, and then I'll rise.
I'll touch my ears, my nose, my chin,
Then quietly, sit down again.

BUTTERFLY
Roly-poly caterpillar
Into a corner crept.
Spun around himself a blanket
Then for a long time slept.
A long time passed (Whisper)
Roly-poly caterpillar wakened by and by.
Found himself with beautiful wings
Changed to a butterfly.

SLEEPY TIME
Open wide your little hands,
Now squeeze them very tight.
Shake them, shake them very loose,
With all your might.
Climb them slowly to the sky.
Drop down like gentle rain.
Go to sleep my little hands,
I'll wake you once again.

A FUNNY ONE
'Round the house
'Round the house
(Put fingers around the face.)
Peep in the window
(Open eyes wide.)
Listen at the door
(Cup hand behind ear.)
Knock at the door
(Knock on head.)
Lift up the latch
(Push up nose.)
And walk in
(Stick out tongue and walk fingers in mouth.)
—I caught you!
(Bite gently down on fingers.)

TWO LITTLE APPLES

Two little apples hanging on a tree,
(Put hand by eyes.)
Two little apples smiling at me.
(Smile.)
I shook that tree as hard as I could.
(Shake tree.)
Down came the apples.
(Make falling motions.)
Mmmm—they were good.
(Rub stomach.)

PEANUT BUTTER AND JELLY

First you take the peanuts and you crunch them
and you crunch them. (Repeat.)
Peanut butter—jelly! Peanut butter—jelly!
Then you take the grapes and you squish them
and you squish them. (Repeat.)
Peanut butter—jelly! Peanut butter—jelly!
Then you take the bread and you spread it and
you spread it. (Repeat.)
Peanut butter—jelly! Peanut butter—jelly!
Then you take the sandwich and you eat it and
you eat it. (Repeat. Then with your mouth
closed hum the refrain as if you had a
mouth full of sandwich.)
Peanut butter—jelly! Peanut butter—jelly!
("Peanut butter" is said in the following fashion:
"Pea" (medium pitch) "nut" (low pitch)
"but" (medium) "ter" (high pitch with hands
above head, fingers shaking to side in
vaudeville-type motion). "Jelly" is said in a
low, throaty voice, accompanied by hands to
opposite side shaking at knee level.)

FIVE LITTLE ASTRONAUTS

Five little astronauts
(Hold up fingers on one hand.)
Ready for outer space.
The first one said, "Let's have a race."
The second one said, "The weather's too rough."
The third one said, "Oh, don't be gruff."
The fourth one said, "I'm ready enough."

The fifth one said, "Let's Blast Off!"
10, 9, 8, 7, 6, 5, 4, 3, 2, 1,
(Start with 10 fingers and pull one down
with each number.)
BLAST OFF!!!
(Clap loudly with "Blast Off!")

BODY-ACTION PLAYS

Encourage children to jump in rhythm to this jump-rope chant while doing what the rhyme says. Use this for working out pent-up energy.

TEDDY BEAR, TEDDY BEAR

Teddy bear, teddy bear, turn around.
Teddy bear, teddy bear, touch the ground.
Teddy bear, teddy bear, show your shoe.
Teddy bear, teddy bear, that will do.
Teddy bear, teddy bear, go upstairs.
(Alternate hands upwards.)
Teddy bear, teddy bear, say your prayers.
Teddy bear, teddy bear, turn off the light.
Teddy bear, teddy bear, say good night.
(Lay down and pretend to snore.)

HEAD, SHOULDERS

Head, shoulders, knees, and toes
(Stand; touch both hands to each part in
order.)
Head, shoulders, knees, and toes.

Head, shoulders, knees, and toes.
That's the way the story goes.
(Clap this line.)
This is my head, this is not.
(Hands on head, then feet.)
These are my shoulders, this is not.
(Hands on shoulders, then knees.)
Here are my knees; watch them wiggle,
(Wiggle knees.)
Touch my armpits and I giggle.
(Hands under armpits with laugh.)

Head shoulders, knees, and toes.
    (Touch in order.)
That's the way the story goes.
    (Clap.)

BEAT ONE HAMMER
My mother told me to tell you
To beat one hammer
    (Pound one fist.)
Like you see me do.
My mother told me to tell you
To beat two hammers
    (Pound two fists.)
Like you see me do.
My mother told me to tell you
To beat three hammers
    (Pound two fists; stamp one foot.)
Like you see me do.
My mother told me to tell you
To beat four hammers
    (Pound two fists; stamp two feet.)
Like you see me do.
My mother told me to tell you
To beat five hammers
    (Add nodding head.)
Like you see me do.
My mother told me to tell you
To beat no hammers
    (Stop!)
Like you see me do.

MY LITTLE THUMBS
My little thumbs keep moving.
My little thumbs keep moving.
My little thumbs keep moving.
    Tra-la tra-la tra-la.
My thumbs and fingers keep moving.
My thumbs and fingers keep moving.
My thumbs and fingers keep moving.
    Tra-la tra-la tra-la.
My thumbs and fingers and hands keep moving.
My thumbs and fingers and hands keep moving.

My thumbs and fingers and hands keep moving.
    Tra-la tra-la tra-la.
My thumbs and fingers and hands and arms keep
    moving.
My thumbs and fingers and hands and arms keep
    moving.
My thumbs and fingers and hands and arms keep
    moving.
    And then I stand right up.
My thumbs and fingers and hands and arms and
    feet keep moving.
My thumbs and fingers and hands and arms and
    feet keep moving.
My thumbs and fingers and hands and arms and
    feet keep moving.
    Tra-la tra-la tra-la.
My thumbs and fingers and hands and arms and
    feet and head keep moving.
My thumbs and fingers and hands and arms and
    feet and head keep moving.
My thumbs and fingers and hands and arms and
    feet and head keep moving.
    Tra-la tra-la tra-la.

Summary

Speaking activities are planned for the young child. Some require simple imitation of words, while others call for the child's creative or expressive response.

Finger plays use words and actions together. They are actively enjoyed by children and build feelings of self-worth. Teachers can memorize finger plays and use them daily.

Circle times instill group spirit and social enjoyment of language. Opening activities capture attention. Chants and choruses add rhythmic word play and often involve physical movement. A smooth transition to other activities takes place when teachers are well prepared.

Teachers evaluate circle times comparing outcomes to goals.

STUDENT ACTIVITIES

1. With a small group of classmates, practice and present a finger play, chant, chorus, or body-action play. Have each student present the activity until it is learned by the others.

2. Make a list of at least five books that are resources for finger plays.

3. Present a finger play, chant, or chorus to a group of young children.

4. List possible reasons that children become disinterested at circle times.

5. Find a finger play that is seasonal (generally used at only one time a year). Bring a copy to class.

6. Create a finger play, chant, or chorus for young children.

7. Observe a circle time and evaluate it. Share it with the class.

8. Tape record or videotape a few of your teacher-led discussions at group time. Analyze your listening skills and whether you dominate conversations. Look at your ability to keep group time lively and child directed. If a child-teacher discussion didn't hold children's interest, determine the reason(s).

9. If you know a song, rhyme, finger play, or movement activity in another language, share it with the class.

10. Create a finger play about making tortillas or using chopsticks. Share with the class.

CHAPTER REVIEW

A. Finish the following:

1. A transitional statement at the end of group time is necessary because

_____.

2. History shows that chants and choruses were used for _____.

3. A successful circle time for young children can be described by the following terms: _____.

B. Why are finger plays so popular with young children?

C. Rearrange and place in the best order or sequence.

1. Child knows words and actions of a finger play.

2. Teacher knows words and actions of a finger play.

3. Teacher practices finger play.

4. Child participates with actions only.

5. Child watches.

6. Teacher presents finger play to children.

7. Teacher evaluates the results of the finger play.

8. Teacher encourages children to join in actions and words.

D. List five signals or attention getters that a teacher could use at the beginning of a circle time.

E. In what ways should an assistant teacher be helpful when another teacher is leading group language activities?

F. Rate the following teacher statements during planned circles.

G = Good Technique   P = Poor Technique

1. "It's my turn to talk."

2. "Stop wiggling, Jimmy."

3. "Everyone's listening, it's time to begin."

4. "When Kate, Tran, and Nancy join us, we'll all be together."

5. "The first one standing can be the first one to leave the circle."

6. "We're finished. Let's go."

7. "Speak up, Gisela. It's time to answer."

8. "Thuy is doing our new finger play the 'right' way."

9. "Watch closely, and make your fingers move just like mine."

10. "Everyone listened to what their friends said and took turns talking today."

RESOURCES

Beckman, Carol, et al. *Channels to Children*, P.O. Box 25834, Colorado Springs, CO 80936. (A wonderful collection of activities based on a theme approach to teaching. Many cross-cultural activities described in last chapter.)

Coglin, Mary Lou. *Chants for Children*. Coglin Publ., Box 301, Manilius, NY 13104. (If you enjoy chanting at circle, this will offer you additional chants to try.)

Crowell, Liz, and Dixie Hibner. *Finger Frolics*. First Teacher Inc., Box 29, Bridgeport, CT 06602.

Dowell, Ruth L. *Move over Mother Goose*. Pollyanna Productions, Mt. Ranier, MD: Gryphon House Inc., 1987.

Ellis, Mary Jackson. *Fingerplay Approach to Dramatization*. Minneapolis: T. S. Denison, 1978.

Finger Plays for Young Children. Scholastic, 2931 East McCarty St., P.O. Box 7502, Jefferson City, MO 65102 (an easel book).

Glazer, Tom. *Eye Winker, Tom Tinker, Chin Chopper: Fifty Musical Finger Plays*, New York: Doubleday, 1973.

Kable, Gratia. *Favorite Finger Plays*, Minneapolis: T. S. Denison, 1979.

Wilmes, Liz, and Dick Wilmes. *Everyday Circle Times*. Mt. Ranier: Gryphon House, 1981. (A collection of ideas for exciting group times.)

CHAPTER 15

Puppetry and
Beginning Drama Experiences

OBJECTIVES

After studying this chapter, you should be able to:

- use puppetry in language arts programming.

- describe young children's puppet play.

- list five teaching techniques that offer young children opportunities for simple dramatization.

Puppets provide countless opportunities for children's speech growth. They match and fulfill many of the preschooler's developmental needs, besides being of high interest. Koons (1986) describes the power of puppet play:

> Imagine a lifeless puppet lying on a table. Suddenly, a child slips his hand into the puppet and it awakens to a life and personality of its own. Magic happens and the world of make-believe begins. Children love to pretend and puppetry allows them to create their own magic.

When used by a child, puppets can be:

- moved and controlled by the child (figure 15–1)
- a challenge involving coordination of speech and movement
- talked to as an accepting companion
- used individually and in group play
- used to create and fantasize
- used to explore another's personality
- a way to release pent-up emotions
- used to relive and imitate experiences
- seen as an adult-like activity
- used to entertain others
- constructed by children

Many of these uses build and develop children's confidence in their own speaking ability.

There are many ways the *teacher* can use puppetry in language development activities. When used by a teacher, puppets can:

- motivate
- gain attention and keep it focused

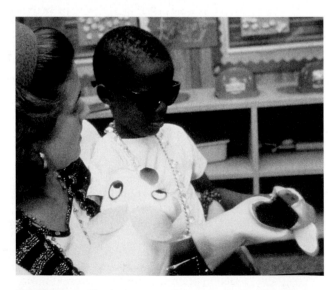

FIGURE 15–1 Exploring puppetry

376

- provide variety in the presentation of ideas and words
- provide a model to imitate
- present stories
- promote child creativity and pretending
- provide a play opportunity that encourages speech and motor-skill coordination
- introduce new information
- promote positive attitudes toward speaking and dramatic activities
- build audience skills
- provide construction activities
- help children express themselves
- build vocabularies
- offer entertaining and enjoyable activities
- provide a wide range of individual personalities through puppets

What can puppets offer both children and their teachers? Hunt and Renfro (1982) believe:

> For the child, the introduction of puppets can create a fresh and creative learning environment. Young children can generally accept the puppet as a non-threatening, sympathetic friend to whom they can entrust their thoughts and feelings without fear of ridicule or reprimand. This friend is privy to the child's inner world and is able also to communicate with the outer world as an intermediary. It is perhaps here that the teacher finds in puppetry its most valuable asset for contributing to the process of education. A skillful teacher can take advantage of special moments of puppet-inspired communication to tune into the child's thinking and to open up new avenues for learning.

Audience Skills

Audience skills are quickly learned, and teachers encourage them through discussion and modeling. Clapping after performances is recommended. Listening and being a quiet audience is verbally appreciated. Teachers and staff need to decide whether a child in the audience can leave during a performance. Most schools adopt this plan of action, and the child is expected to choose a quiet play activity that does not disturb others.

Stimulating Children's Use of Puppets

Teachers can expand children's experiences with puppets in these ways:

- Present puppet plays and skits.
- Find community resources for puppet presentations: puppeteer groups, children's theater groups, high school and elementary classes, and skilled individuals.
- Introduce each puppet periodically and provide new ones when possible.
- Store puppets invitingly.
- Provide props and puppet theaters (figure 15–2).
- Keep puppets in good repair.

A puppet carried in a teacher's pocket can be useful in a variety of teaching situations, as mentioned previously. Children imitate the teacher's use of puppets, and this leads to creative play.

FIGURE 15–2 Young children enjoy watching a puppet performance.

Teacher Puppetry

Children sit, excited and enthralled, at simple skits and dialogues performed by the teacher. Continually amazed by young children's rapt attention and obvious pleasure, most teachers find puppetry a valuable teaching skill.

Prerecording puppet dialogue (or attaching puppet speeches inside the puppet stage) helps beginning teacher puppeteers. With practice, performance skills increase and puppet coordination can then become the main teacher task.

Hunt and Renfro's *Puppetry in Early Childhood Education* (1982) includes many valuable suggestions for increasing teacher puppetry skill, among them developing a puppet voice and personality:

> Discover a voice contrasting to your own. Look at the puppet and see what characteristics its physical features suggest. A deep commanding voice, for example, may be appropriate for a large mouth while sleepy eyes may connote a slow, tired voice. Become fully involved with the character and experiment freely.

> *and*

> A puppet's personality does not develop immediately; rather it evolves over a span of days, weeks, sometimes months.

> . . . it is sometimes easier to pattern a character after a real person than to try to create one that is entirely imaginary. . . . Give the puppet a name.

Naturally, puppet characters in plays or from printed sources already have built-in personalities, but a teacher's daily puppets have no such script and challenge teacher creativity.

Planning and performing simple puppet plays requires time and effort. The plays are selected for suitability and then practiced until the scene-by-scene sequence is firmly in mind. Good preparation helps ensure a smooth performance and adds to children's enjoyment.

Several helpful tips on puppetry follow.

- A dark net peep-hole enables performers to watch audience reactions and helps dialogue pacing.
- Puppets with strong, identifiable personality traits who stay in character are well received. Another way to enhance a puppet's personality is to give it an idiosyncrasy that sets it apart (Hunt and Renfro, 1982).
- Plan your puppet's personality in advance and stick to it. For example, Happy Mabel has the following characteristics: she is always laughing; says "Hot Potatoes!" often; likes to talk about her cat, Christobel; lives on a farm; is an optimist; speaks in a high-pitched voice; lives alone and likes young visitors.
- Use your favorite puppet in at least one activity weekly.

PUPPET ACTIVITIES

Child participation with puppets can be increased when planned puppet activities are performed. The following are a few of the many puppet play activities.

- Invite children to use puppets (with arms) and act out that a puppet is sleepy, hungry, dancing, crying, laughing, whispering, saying "hello" to a friend, climbing a ladder, waving good-bye, and shaking hands. (A large mirror helps children build skill.)
- Ask two volunteers to use puppets and act out a situation in which a mother and child are waking up in the morning. The teacher creates both speaking parts, then prompts two children to continue on their own. Other situations include a telephone conversation, a child requesting money from a parent to buy an ice cream cone, and a puppet inviting another to a party.
- Urge children to answer the teacher's puppet. For example:
  Teacher: "Hi! My name is Mr. Singing Sam. I can sing any song you ask me to sing. Just ask me!"
  or

FIGURE 15–3 A paper-bag puppet interests these two children in the housekeeping area.

Teacher: "I'm the cook. What shall we have for dinner?"

or

Teacher: "My name is Randy Rabbit. Who are you? Where am I?"

- Record simple puppet directions (such as the following) on a cassette tape recorder and have a large mirror available so that the children can see their actions:
  1. Make your puppet touch his nose.
  2. Have your puppet clap.
  3. Kiss your hand, puppet.
  4. Rub your eyes, puppet.
  5. Reach for the stars, puppet.
  6. Hold your stomach.
  7. Scratch your ear.
  8. Bow low.
  9. Hop.

  Set up this activity in an individual, room-divided space (figure 15–3).

- Record simple puppet dramas. After a teacher demonstration, make them available to children on a free-choice basis. Provide a mirror, if possible.

Storage and Theaters

Store puppets in an inviting way, face up, begging for handling; shoe racks, wall pockets, or upright pegs within the child's reach are suggested. An adjacent puppet theater tempts children's use. Old television cabinets (with insides removed and open backs) make durable theaters that the children can climb into. Other theaters can be constructed by the teacher using large packing crates that can be painted and decorated by the children.

Hunt and Renfro (1982) describe what might happen in a puppet corner:

> As soon as a child physically picks up a puppet, he wants to make it talk. By giving it a voice, he also gives it life. In the puppet corner children will experiment without inhibition using different vocal sounds and character voices. No other form of expression, except creative dramatics, offers such a broad range of opportunities for verbal experimentation.

In most centers, rules are set for using puppets. The puppets should stay in certain designated areas and should be handled with care.

Puppet Plays

Familiar and favorite stories make good puppet dramas. Many contain simple, repetitive lines that most of the children know from memory. Children will often stray from familiar dialogues in stories, however, adding their own lines, actions, or settings. Older preschoolers speak through puppets easily; younger children may be more interested in manipulating alone or simple imitating.

When children enlarge or change dialogue or a character's personality, their own individuality directs and creates. Schools can wind up with many versions and interpretations of familiar favorites.

Other Puppetry Tips

- Some children are fearful of puppets. They may even think that a puppet has died when they see the puppet limp on the shelf. With reassurance and additional exposure to teacher puppet use, fear subsides.

- The act of becoming the puppet's persona may be frightening to three-year-olds, i.e., an alligator, a wolf, etc.
- Aggressive puppet play of the "Punch and Judy" type should be redirected. Having puppets punch and hit is common behavior in traditional Punch and Judy shows, and consequently is not presented to young children in school settings. Any modeling of aggressive and violent behavior in puppetry is inappropriate.
- Most public libraries offer puppet shows periodically.
- Parents and volunteers can help construct sturdy classroom puppets.
- Commercial school-supply companies offer well-made, durable puppets and theaters for group use.

PUPPETMAKING

Puppets can be divided into two general categories—those worked with the hands and fingers and those that dangle on strings. Hand puppets are popular in the preschool because they are so versatile and practical. Teacher-made, child-made, as well as commercially manufactured hand puppets are an essential part of most centers.

Moving arms and pliable faces on puppets increase the possibilities for characterization and action. Rubber, plastic, and papier-mâché puppet heads are durable. Cloth faces permit a wider variety of facial expressions.

Papier-Mâché Puppet Heads

Materials

styrofoam egg or ball (a little smaller than the size you want for the completed head), soft enough to have a holder inserted into it
neck tube (made from cardboard—about one-and-a-half inches wide and five inches long, rolled into a circle and taped closed, or plastic hair roller)
bottle (to put the head on while it is being created and to hold it during drying)
instant papier-mâché (from a craft store)
paints (poster-paint variety)
spray-gloss coat (optional)
white glue
(Use instant papier-mâché in well ventilated teacher work areas.)

Construction Procedure

1. Mix instant papier-mâché with water (a little at a time) until it is like clay—moist, but not too wet or dry.
2. Place styrofoam egg on neck tube (or roller) securely. Then place egg (or ball) on bottle so it is steady.
3. Put papier-mâché all over head and half way down neck tube. Coating should be about a half inch thick.
4. Begin making the facial features, starting with the cheeks, eyebrows, and chin. Then add eyes, nose, mouth, and ears.
5. When you are satisfied with the head, allow it to dry at least 24 hours in an airy place.
6. When the head is dry, paint the face with poster paint. When that is dry, coat it with spray gloss finish to seal paint.
7. Glue is useful for adding yarn hair, if desired.

Note that children can make this type of puppet if papier-mâché is eliminated and felt pens are used to define facial features.

Sock Puppets

Materials

old sock, felt, sewing machine

Construction Procedure (see figure 15–4)

1. Use an old wool or other thick sock. Turn it inside out and spread it out with the heel on top.
2. Cut around the edge of the toe (about three inches on each side).

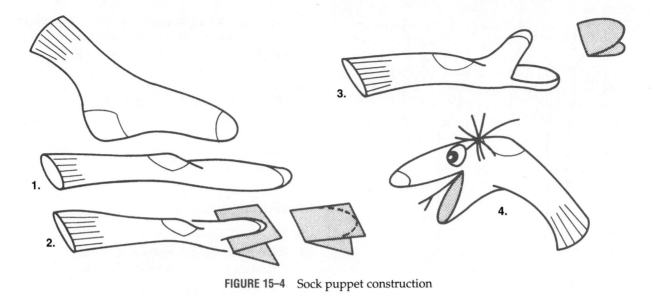

FIGURE 15–4 Sock puppet construction

3. Fold the mouth material (pink felt) inside the open part of the sock and draw the shape. Cut the mouth piece out and sew into position.

4. Turn the sock right side out and sew on the features.

Paper-Bag Puppets

Materials

paper bags, scissors, crayons or marking pens, paste, yarn or paper scraps, and paint (if desired)

Construction Procedure

1. Making paper-bag puppets is quick and easy. Give each child a small paper sack. (No. 6 works well.)

2. Show them how the mouth works and let them color or paste features on the sack.

3. You may wish to have them paste a circle on for the face. Paste it on the flap part of the bag and then cut the circle on the flap portion so the mouth can move again.

FIGURE 15–5 Paper-bag puppet

4. Many children will want to add special features to their paper-bag puppets, for example, a tail or ears (figure 15–5).

Stick Puppets

A stick puppet is a picture or object attached to a stick (figure 15–6). It moves when the puppeteer moves the puppet up and down or from side to side, holding the stick.

FIGURE 15–6   Stick puppets

Materials

paper, glue, scissors, crayons, popsicle sticks (or tongue depressors or cardboard strips)

Construction Procedure

1. Characters and scenery can be drawn by children or preoutlined. Depending on the age of the children, the characters and scenery can then be colored or both colored and cut out.
2. Older children may want to create their own figures.

Pop-Ups

Materials

heavy paper, glue, yarn, stick (tongue depressor or thinner sticks), scissors, plastic, styrofoam or paper cup, felt pens

Construction Procedure

1. Cut circle smaller than cup radius. Decorate face.
2. Slit the cup bottom in the center to allow sticks to move up and down.
3. Glue the face to the stick. Glue on yarn hair.

4. Slip puppet in the cup with stick through cup bottom so that the puppet disappears and can pop up.

Large, Cloth, Hand Puppet

Materials

fabric, sewing machine, felt scraps, yarn, glue, cardboard sheet

Construction Procedure

1. Sew head darts.
2. With right sides together, sew back and front a quarter of an inch from the edge.
3. Pin mouth at quarters. Ease mouth piece and sew.
4. After the mouth is securely in place, glue cardboard to the inside of the mouth (white glue works fine).
5. If arms are desired, slash at side, insert arm, and sew.
6. Decorate as desired (figure 15–7).

Box Puppets

Materials

one small (individual size) box with both ends intact
one piece of white construction paper, 6" × 9"
crayons or poster paints and brush
scissors, sharp knife, glue

Construction Procedure

1. Cut box in half as in view 1, with one wide side uncut. Fold over as in view 2.
2. On construction paper, draw the face of a person or an animal. Color or paint features and cut out face.
3. Add yarn for hair, broomstraws for whiskers, and so on, if desired.
4. Cut face along line of mouth and glue to box as in view 4, so that lips come together as in view 5.

FIGURE 15–7   Large, cloth hand puppets

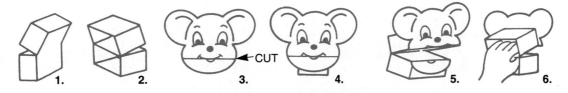

FIGURE 15–8   Box puppet

Jumping Jacks

Materials

stiff paper or oak tag, brads, string, hole punch, dowel, glue, curtain pull (optional)

Construction Procedure (see figure 15–9)

1. Design and cut pattern, making arms and legs long enough to secure behind figure. Cut two body pieces.
2. Glue figure to dowel by inserting between front and back.
3. Brads act as joints. Hole punch and add arms, legs, and string.

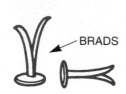
BRADS

Frog and Bird Finger Puppets

Materials

felt fabric, scissors, sewing machine, pattern, elastic ribbon

Construction Procedure

Cut and sew pieces, leaving ends open to insert finger.

Additional Puppet Types

- Wrap-around-finger-band puppet (see figure 15–10).
- Plastic-bottle-head puppet.
- Dustmop-head puppet.
- Favorite-television-character puppet (figure 15–11).
- Garden-glove puppets (different faces can be snapped on or Velcro used) (figure 15–12).
- Suspended toy from stick puppets. (Adding beads to feet give them sound effects.)

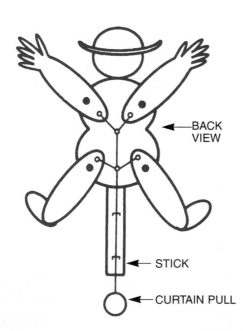

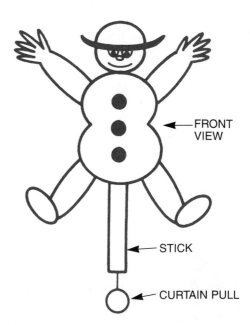

FIGURE 15–9 Jumping jack

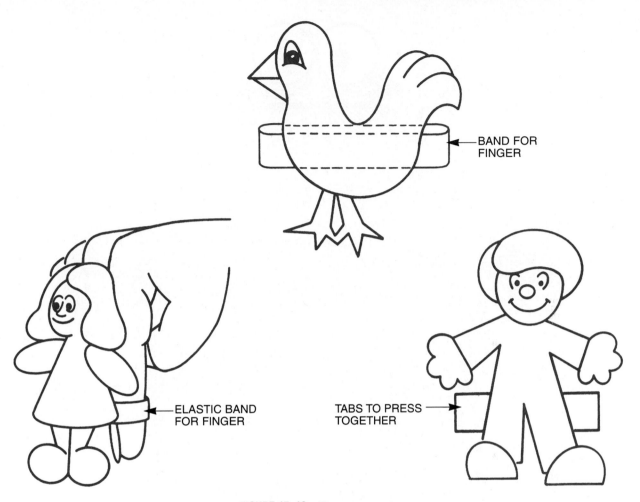

BAND FOR FINGER

ELASTIC BAND FOR FINGER

TABS TO PRESS TOGETHER

FIGURE 15–10 Finger puppets

TEACHER PUPPET PRESENTATIONS

Many simple stories can be shared with children through teacher puppetry. The following story is an example of a tale that lends itself to a puppet presentation. Teachers can create their own stories that appeal to the interests of the children with whom they work. See the end of this chapter for additional puppet patterns.

The Pancake

Narrator:

Once upon a time, an old woman made a pancake. When it was nice and golden brown, it hopped out of the frying pan and began rolling down the road, saying:

Pancake:

Whee! I'm free! Nobody will ever eat me! What a nice day! I'll just roll along till—hey! I wonder what that funny looking round thing is by the river!

FIGURE 15–11   Favorite-television-character puppet

Narrator:

   He didn't know it, but it was a bridge.

Pancake:

   I'll bet I can roll over that thing. Watch this!

I'll just get a head start back here—(backs up) one ... two ... three! (As the pancake starts over the bridge, frog comes up and grabs it.)

Pancake:

   Let me go! Let me go!

FIGURE 15–12   Garden-glove puppets

Frog:

I want to eat you! I love pancakes! (Pancake pulls away and rolls out of sight.)

Frog:

Oh, dear . . . it got away . . . (Frog down. Bridge down. Pancake rolls in.)

Pancake:

That was a close one! I hope I do not meet any other—(Off stage is heard the sound of barking . . .)

Pancake:

What's that sound? I do not think I like it . . . (Dog in, tries to grab pancake.)

Dog:

I want a bite! I love pancakes! (Pancake cries "No! No!" and rolls off.)

Dog:

It got away. Well, better luck next time . . . (Dog out, pancake rolls in.)

Pancake:

Goodness! Everybody seems to love pancakes, but I do not want to be loved that way! (Off stage is heard the sound of "meow!")

Pancake:

Meow? What kind of animal makes that sound? (Cat in, tries to grab pancake, pancake escapes as before.)

Cat:

Meow? meow, no breakfast now! (Cat out, pancake rolls in panting.)

Pancake:

This is dreadful! Everybody I meet wants to eat me! (Bird flies in.)

Bird:

A pancake! Delicious! I'll just peck a few pieces out of it! (Bird starts to peck at pancake, which rolls away crying, "No! No!" Bird follows, then returns alone.)

Bird:

It's too hot to chase it. Besides, it can roll faster than I can fly. (Bird out. Put bridge up again.)

Narrator:

And all day long the pancake rolled until it finally found itself back at the same bridge. (Pancake rolls in.)

Pancake:

(Wearily) Oh, dear . . . here I am again, back at the same bridge . . . I must have been rolling around in circles. And I'm too tired to roll another inch. I must rest. I'll just lie down here next to this round thing over the river . . . (Pancake lies down flat, or leans against the bridge, if possible. Now puppeteer has two free hands to put on frog and dog. But before they come in, we hear their voices.)

Frog's Voice:

(half-whisper) It's mine!

Dog's Voice:

(half-whisper) No, it's mine. I saw it first!

Frog's Voice:

(same) You did not! I saw it first!

Dog's Voice:

(same) Who cares—I'm going to eat it! (Dog and Frog enter and grab the pancake between them.)

Pancake:

Let me go! Let me go! (Frog and dog tussle, drop pancake out of sight, look after it.)

Frog:

You idiot! You dropped it in the water!

Dog:

You're the idiot! You're the one who dropped it!

Narrator:

And as the pancake disappeared beneath the water, they heard it say, (far away voice)

"Nobody will ever catch me . . ." and nobody ever did. (Sloane, 1942)

Teachers find that play situations containing a puppet, animal, or other character that is less knowledgeable and mature than the children themselves promote a feeling of bigness in children. The children are then in the position of taking care of and educating another, which often produces considerable child speech and self-esteem. A well-known commercial language development kit (program) cleverly contains a puppet that has no eyes. Children are urged to help this puppet by describing objects and events.

Simple Drama

Children often playact familiar events and home situations. This allows them to both try out and work out elements of past experiences that they remember for one reason or another. Their play-acting can be an exact imitation or something created by their active imaginations.

Much of children's imaginative play (pretend play) reenacts life situations and leads to creative embellishment. It happens all the time in preschool. Children often only need a jumping off place provided by a room setting, story, or teacher suggestion. Picture what might happen if a teacher says:

"Here comes the parade, let's join it and march."
"A kitten is lost in the play yard, what can we do? Where can we look?"
"The bus just stopped at the gate. Let's go places. Where will we go first? First we need to step up inside and pay our money."
"The astronauts' rocket ship crashed on the moon. Our rocket ship is here. Let's get on and rescue him."
"Let's pretend we're hummingbirds searching for sweet nectar in all the brightly colored flowers."
"My goodness, teddy bear has fallen out of the bed. His leg is hurt. What can we do?"

The teacher's watchfulness and skillfulness will be necessary. Unfortunately, exposure to television violence may seep into play or play may lead to unwise, unsafe actions depending on one's particular play group. The teacher may need to redirect or stop children's actions. But more commonly, the astronaut will be rescued and returned to earth, the kitten will be found, and the bus ride will lead to adventures without difficulties.

In creative drama, the teacher wishes to be a co-participant with children and follow their creative lead. The benefits of creative drama experiences are multiple—social, intellectual, linguistic, and sometimes therapeutic. Creative language use and increased self-esteem are natural outcomes.

Four-year-olds, because of their ability to conceptualize and fantasize, are prime candidates for beginning exposure to this literary form. They pick up both acting skill and audience skill quickly. Three-year-olds enjoy drama presentations and are good audiences. They profit from exposure but can have a difficult time with the acting role. Imitative, pretend play, and pantomime suit their developmental level. Pantomime becomes the foundation on which four-year-olds build their acting skills for created and scripted parts.

Young preschoolers will need teacher prompting and suggestions for acting out (Cooper, 1993). Teachers can ask children how someone might feel or act under certain circumstances. They can also ask children to think about what takes place in their homes, at school, at various times of the day, or in other life settings and situations to determine possible acting scenarios. Positive, appreciative teacher and peer comments concerning convincing or appropriate acting behavior provide additional pointers.

In both drama and pantomime, children can act out all the joy, anger, fear, and surprise of favorite characters. This gives children the opportunity to become someone else for a few minutes and to release their frustration and energy in an acceptable way (Perez, 1986).

After young children become familiar with stories, they thoroughly enjoy reenacting or dramatizing the stories. By using both physical motions and verbal comments, children bring words and actions of the stories to life.

Use of Recordings

Using recordings to stimulate child creative movement and dramatics helps beginning teachers. Many recordings tell children what to do, and teacher and children simply follow along (MacDonald, 1988).

Playacting Tips

Children will act out parts from favorite stories as well as scenes from real life. The teacher sets the stage, keeping some points in mind:

- The children must be familiar with the story in order to know what happens first, next, and last.
- Activities in which the children pretend to perform certain actions, to be certain animals, or to copy the actions of another, help prepare them for simple drama.
- Videotaped plays and films are good motivators.
- A first step is to act without words or while listening to a good story or record.
- The teacher can be the narrator, while the children are the actors.
- Children should be encouraged to volunteer for parts.
- Props and settings can be simple. Ask, "What can be used for a bridge?" or a similar question so children can use their creativity.
- Any of the children's imaginative acts should be accepted, whether or not they are a part of the original story unless they endanger others.
- Individual and group dramatizations should be appreciated and encouraged. Every child who wishes a turn playing the parts should be accommodated.
- No touching guidelines are necessary when vigorous acts are part of dramas.
- With large groups, the teacher can limit acting roles to a manageable number to prevent chaos.
- In child-authored dramas, the teacher may need to clarify the child's intent in story sequences.
- Reenacting stories with different children playing parts is usually done with popular stories.
- Include multicultural stories when possible.

Some classic stories that can be used for playacting (drama) include:

- *Goldilocks and the Three Bears*
- *The Three Little Pigs*
- *The Little Red Hen*
- *Gingerbread Boy*
- *Little Red Ridinghood*
- *Little Miss Muffet*

Fast action and simple story lines are best for the young child. Playacting presents many opportunities for children to develop:

- self-expression
- use of correct speech
- coordination of actions and words
- creative thinking
- self-confidence
- listening skills
- social interaction

Perez (1986) suggests that children should be reminded that when they act they become someone other than who they really are, for a short time. What other people think and feel is often shown by what they do. By observing other people closely, you become more aware of how others do things and show emotion.

As mentioned in Chapter 10, children's own dictated stories are excellent vehicles for dramatization. In child-authored stories, the most popular procedure is for the child-author to choose the role he or she would like to play, and then which classmates will play the rest (Cooper, 1993). Teachers read previously dictated stories before and as children act the roles.

Problem-Solving Drama

Early childhood practitioners may want to try problem-solving dramas with older preschoolers. Imaginary problem-solving situations are suggested by the teacher and are then enacted creatively by children working toward a solution. Children are not given words to say, but character parts are assigned. Sample problems follow:

- A child's shoes are missing, and it's time to go to a party. Characters—mother, grandmother, dog, cat, brother, sister.
- While at the zoo on a preschool field trip, the class learns that a giraffe is loose. The zookeeper asks a group of children to help. Characters—zookeeper, police officer, four children, and their preschool teacher.

Teachers trying this type of creative drama may need to slip in and out of the dramatization serving as a confidant, collaborator, and helpful but not dominating coach.

Drama From Picture Books

Bos (1983), a well-known California workshop leader, tells a funny story about children's love of dramatization. Because picture books are frequently enacted at Bev's center, a child who readily identifies with a particular book character often speaks up saying, "I want to be the rabbit," long before the picture book reading session is finished.

In enacting stories from books or storytelling sources, the teacher may have to read the book or tell the story over a period of time so it is digested and becomes familiar to the children. A discussion of the story can promote children's expression of opinions about enjoyed parts, the feelings of characters, and what might be similar in their own lives. The teacher can then ask "Who's good at crying and can go 'Boo-hoo'?" or "Who can act mad and stomp around the floor?" Most child groups have one or more children ready to volunteer. The teacher can play one of the parts.

Many action- and dialogue-packed picture books, such as the following, lend themselves to child reenactment:

- *The Funny Thing*, by Wanda Gag
- *Rosie's Walk*, by Pat Hutchins
- *The Gingerbread Boy*, by Paul Galdone
- *One Fine Day*, by Nonny Hogrogian

Stories suggested by Perez (1986) include *The Little Rabbit Who Wanted Red Wings*, by Carolyn Bailey, and stories found in *Let's Pretend It Happened to You*, by Bernice Wells Carlson.

Dramatizing Fairy Tales and Folktales

A number of educators, including Howarth (1989), urge teachers to dramatize classic fairy tales and folktales. She suggests:

For two-and-a-half-
and three-year-olds: *The Three Pigs*
The Three Billy Goats Gruff
Goldilocks

For four-year-olds: *Cinderella*
Jack and the Beanstalk
*The Wolf and the Seven
Little Kids*
The Shoemaker and the Elves

Howarth (1989) believes some teachers are reluctant to offer children many of these classic tales because of their inherent violence, and she offers the following to persuade them:

In order to solve life's problems one must not only take risks, one must confront the worst that might happen. Children, like the rest of us, ruminate and worry about these worst things. Fairy tales confront them. This is the chief reason many adults have trouble with fairy tales. They think they can protect children from the hard realities of life. That is the real myth and the children know it.

What a relief it is for a child to find that things she is worried about are taken seriously! Children think a lot about death, separation, and divorce. None of us wants to think about these painful possibilities, yet we must.

Nonfiction books can also be dramatized as Putnam (1991) observes:

. . . dramatize such things as bears hibernating in their dens, dinosaurs moving through swamps, thunderstorms brewing. . . . Invariably, the children appear to be thoroughly absorbed and enjoying themselves, as if at play. They also appear to retain more of the information presented during the reading.

Nonfiction books should not be overlooked by early childhood teachers when looking for dramatization possibilities.

Progressive Skill

Dramatizing a familiar story involves a number of language skills—listening, auditory and visual memory of actions and characters' speech lines, and remembered sequence of events—as well as audience skills. Simple pantomime or imitation requires less maturity. Activities that use actions alone are good as a first step toward building children's play-acting skills. Children have imitated others' actions since infancy, and as always, the joy of being able to do what they see others do brings a feeling of self-confidence. The children's individuality is preserved if differences in ways of acting out a familiar story are valued in preschool settings.

PANTOMIME

Among the all-time favorites for pantomime is the following.

THE BEAR HUNT

We're going on a bear hunt
We're going where?
We're going on a bear hunt.
OK, let's go! I'm not afraid!

Look over there!
What do you see?
A big deep river.
Can't go around it.
Can't go under it.
Have to swim across it.
OK, let's go. I'm not afraid!

What's this tall stuff?
What do you see?
Tall, tall grass.
Can't go around it.
Can't go under it.
Got to go through it.
OK, let's go. I'm not afraid!

Hey, look ahead.
What do you see?
A rickety old bridge.
Can't go around it.
Can't go under it.
Got to go across it.
OK, let's go. I'm not afraid!

Now what's this ahead.
It's a tall, tall tree.
Can't go under it.
Can't go over it.
Have to climb it.
OK, let's go. I'm not afraid!

Do you see what I see?
What a giant mountain!
Can't go around it.
Can't go under it.
Got to climb over it.
OK, let's go. I'm not afraid!

Oh, look at that dark cave.
Let's go inside.
It sure is dark in here.
I think I feel something.
I think it's a nose.
And two furry ears.
HELP! It's a bear!!!!!!!!!!!!!!!
Let's get out of here . . . I'm afraid.

(Pretend to climb back over the mountain and down the tree, run across the bridge, swish through the tall grass, swim the river, open the door, run in, slam the door, collapse in a heap.)

Whew . . . Home at last . . . I was afraid!

Creative Drama Programs

Starting a language program that includes creative drama requires planning. Props and play materials must be supplied for children to explore. When children see simple plays and pantomimes performed by teachers, other children, and adult groups, they are provided with a model and a stimulus. Some drama activity ideas for the older preschool child include:

- Pantomiming action words and phrases: tiptoe, crawl, riding a horse, using a rolling pin.

- Pantomiming words that mean a physical state: cold, hot, itchy.
- Pantomiming feeling words: happy, sad, hurt, holding a favorite teddy bear lovingly, feeling surprise.
- Acting out imaginary life situations: opening a door with a key, climbing in and out of a car, helping to set the table.
- Acting familiar character parts in well-known stories: "She covered her mouth so the clown couldn't see her laugh." "The rabbit dug a big hole and buried the carrot." "He tiptoed to the window, raised the shade, and opened it."
- Saying familiar lines from known stories: "And he huffed and he puffed, and he blew the house down."
- Playing a character in a short story or song that involves both spoken lines and actions.
- Pantomiming actions of a character in a short, familiar story that the teacher reads (or from a teacher-recorded story tape). There are a vast number of commercially recorded stories available at school-supply stores.

Kranyik (1986) suggests the following pantomimes for young children:

- Drink a glass of water. Oh! It turned into hot soup and burned your mouth!
- Eat a bowl of spaghetti.
- Row a boat.
- Pour your milk from the carton to a glass. Drink it.
- Play the piano, trumpet, drums, guitar.
- Try to open a jar that will not open.
- Touch something soft and furry.
- Chew a piece of bubble gum. It gets bigger, bigger, and bigger. Suddenly it breaks.
- You and your mom are in a supermarket. Suddenly, you can't find her, and you feel scared. You look up and down all the aisles trying to find her. There she is. You see her.

Costumes and Props

Imagination and inexpensive, easy-to-make costumes are a great performing incentive. Accessories such as hats can be used in a variety of play and drama situations.

Cutout chartboard or cardboard heads and figures held by the child quickly aid his or her ability to step into character (figure 15–13). (Make sure that chartboard is lightweight and hand holes are comfortable.) Older children may be able to draw their own patterns, or patterns for figures can be found in children's books and can be enlarged with the use of an opaque projector. These props allow children to put their faces into the spaces cut out of the characters' faces and are useful in child dramatization. Some teachers feel these props are physically awkward and prefer, instead, simple costumes.

FIGURE 15–13 Story character boards

ADDITIONAL PUPPETRY IDEAS AND PATTERNS

Paper-Bag Puppets

Construction

Draw a face on the upper part of bag; color. Stuff with cotton or newspaper. Put neck cylinder into head and tie string around neck. (Neck cylinder is made by rolling a piece of tag board and taping together. The roll should fit around the first finger.)

If the puppet needs hair, paste on. Add other distinguishing characteristics. Cut hole in paper or cloth and stick neck cylinder through the hole. Paste, sew, or otherwise fasten. Add hands or paws cut from tag board.

Materials

5" × 8" paper bag
string
crayons or paint
newspapers or cotton
paste
crepe paper or cloth for dress
scissors

Movement

Holding forefinger in neck tube.

Stuffed Cloth Puppet

Construction

Draw head pattern and cut around it on a fold of cloth (white, tan, or pink). Sew around front and back, turn inside out, and stuff with cotton or rags. Insert neck tube and tie. Paint on face. Cut dress and sew to neck tube. Add hands and feet.

Materials

cloth (for head and dress)
scissors
needle and thread
tag board for hands and feet
material for hair (cotton, yarn, and so
   forth)

Stuffed Paper Puppet

Construction

Have the child draw himself or herself or any character the child chooses on a piece of butcher paper. Then trace and cut second figure for the back.

Paper-Bag Puppet Face—Lamb

Basic Puppet Body

FOLD

PLACE THIS PATTERN ON THE FOLD OF A PIECE OF MATERIAL, PIN TO IT, THEN CUT OUT PIECE. CUT ANOTHER—YOU NEED A FRONT AND BACK. WITH RIGHT SIDES TOGETHER, SEW MAKING 1/4" SEAMS ON SIDES. TURN RIGHT SIDE OUT AND PRESS. FOLD TOP OF NECK INSIDE 1/4" AND PLACE AROUND NECK TUBE AND GLUE.

PUPPET HAND— CUT 2 FOR EACH HAND AND SEW OR GLUE TOGETHER. GLUE OR SEW TO SLEEVE.

ACTIVITIES ACTIVITIES ACTIVITIES ACTIVITIES ACTIVITIES ACTIVITIES ACTIVITIES ACTIVITIES

There Was an Old Woman Who Swallowed a Fly

Materials

two large pieces of white poster board
18" × 36" piece of plywood
one skein black rug yarn
one clear plastic drop cloth or ½ yd. clear plastic
½ yd. material (any color or pattern)
marking pens
fishing line (about 18 inches)
two black pipe cleaners
two wiggly eyes
colored feathers
craft glue
woodworking glue
clothespins
thumbtacks and a hammer, or a staple gun

Instructions

Old Woman

Step 1: Enlarge the pattern of the old woman to over twice the pattern size given and trace onto the poster board and onto the plywood.

Step 2: Transfer all of the details onto the poster board old woman. Cut out, including the inner square for the stomach.

Step 3: Use an electric jigsaw and cut out the plywood old woman—including the inner square for the stomach.

Step 4: Using the woodworking glue, spread a thin layer over the entire plywood old woman. Lay the poster board old woman on top and clip with clothespins around the outer and inner edges. Let dry thoroughly before removing the clothespins. If necessary, sand the outer and inner edges to make them smooth.

Step 5: Spread a thin layer of the craft glue on the bottom half of the poster board, up to the neckline.

Step 6: Lay the piece of material wrong side down on top of the glue. Let dry thoroughly.

Step 7: Cut off the excess material from the outer edges and inner stomach.

Step 8: Starting at the outer edges of the hairline, use craft glue to glue the rug yarn onto the poster board. Glue the yarn around and around, filling in the whole area. Glue small pieces of yarn on for the eyes and eyebrows. Let the hair dry thoroughly.

Step 9: Turn the old woman over to the back side.

Step 10: Cut a piece of 18" × 72" clear plastic. Fold the plastic in half widthwise to form two 18" × 36" pieces with a fold at the bottom.

Step 11: Place the plastic on the back of the old woman, with the fold down at the bottom of the stomach hole.

Step 12: Open the plastic, leaving the bottom layer in place on the old woman.

Step 13: Using tacks or a staple gun, attach the bottom layer of plastic around the outer edge of the old woman's body, mouth, and head, making sure the plastic is smooth and tight.

Step 14: Bring the second layer of plastic back up and tack or staple it at the very bottom of the stomach hole. Push the top layer of plastic in from the edge of the bottom piece, forming a loose bag or pocket. Tack the second layer in place up to the neckline in the side with the mouth. *NOTE:* Do not tack the mouth shut! Leave that portion of the plastic open for putting in the animals. Continue tacking at the top of the head and tack the rest of the plastic, continuing to push the plastic in to form a pocket. Trim the excess plastic from around the edges.

Animals

Step 1: Trace each animal onto the poster board. Color each one appropriately and cut out.

Step 2:   Glue two wiggly eyes onto the spider.

Step 3:   Cut each pipe cleaner into fourths and glue four on each side of the spider for legs.

Step 4:   Tie one end of the fishing line to the top of the spider's head. Attach the other end to one of the tacks at the top of the old woman's head (wind the line around the tack or tie a loop).

Step 5:   Place the spider inside the bag so that it extends down into the old woman's stomach. The spider is a permanent part of the old woman and should be left as it is.

Step 6:   Another addition you can make is to add colored feathers to the bird's tail.

Use

Place the old woman against a wall or in front of you. Remove the spider and hold onto it until time to place it back inside the plastic stomach. As you sing or chant place the appropriate animal in the mouth, letting it drop down into the stomach. The spider can be wiggled and jiggled on each verse by holding the fishing line and bouncing it up and down.

from Magic Moments
P.O. Box 53635
San Jose, CA 95135

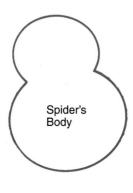

Spider's Body

Summary

Using puppetry for language development is a widely accepted practice in preschools. There are many puppet types to choose from. The ability to coordinate puppet actions and words takes practice and maturity. Teachers find that the more children watch puppets being used, the more they will use them. Puppets that are stored attractively and upright near puppet theaters encourage children's exploration.

There is a wide range of uses for puppets as instructional devices. Puppets are interesting and capture attention as an enjoyable play activity.

Drama is another step on the road to literacy. Simple child dramatizations of favorite stories begin during preschool years. Language programs provide many playacting opportunities. Props, playacting, and pantomime activities motivate this expressive art. Skills are acquired through increased experiences with drama. Planning by the teacher aids children's acquisition of dramatization abilities.

STUDENT ACTIVITIES

1. Make a puppet described in this chapter, or make one of your own choosing.

2. Present a simple puppet play with a few classmates.

3. Collect 10 easy-to-make costume ideas that promote creative drama. Share your ideas with the class.

4. Using a lesson (activity) plan form, describe a simple drama activity for a group of preschoolers.

5. Record a puppet drama and enact the drama with the help of classmates.

6. Construct a puppet theater.

7. Invite a local puppeteer group to share ideas with the class.

8. Bring one simple puppet play script or drama script to class.

9. Create a short puppet play.

10. Find commercial resources for ethnic puppets. Share names of companies and the prices for puppets.

11. Create a puppet from a household item such as a cup or a tube. Share with the class.

12. List community resources that might help young children in your community become more familiar with drama.

13. What nonfiction books dealing with the African-American experience or the Vietnamese-American experience might be appropriate for a preschool dramatization activity? List and discuss with a group of 3 to 4 classmates. Report your findings to the class.

14. Bring 2 books suitable for child dramatization to the next class meeting. Find books not mentioned at this chapter's end.

CHAPTER REVIEW

A. Write a short paragraph describing the reasons puppets are a part of preschool language arts programs.

B. Rate the following teachers using this scale.

+	?	−
definitely promotes puppet interest and use	unable to determine or can't decide	will probably turn children off

1. Mrs. G. (teacher) pulled a small puppet from her smock pocket. Reaching behind Mark, age three, she talked through the puppet. "Mark Allen Graham? Rupert sees what you're doing, and he doesn't like children who break crayons." Mark returns the crayon to the container.

2. Miss R. (teacher) is introducing a small group of children to an activity involving a poem on a chart. "Well, there's Petey, Sam, Scott, Adam, Renee, and Jonathan," Miss R. begins. The puppet in her hand moves and claps, and the puppet's voice is low pitched and deep. "I came to talk to you about rabbits. Does anyone know what rabbits look like? I live in a pocket, you know. I've heard about rabbits, but I've never seen one."

3. Mr. O. (teacher) has a large packing carton in the middle of the classroom. Two children notice the carton and ask, "What's that for?" Mr. O. tells the two children that he noticed the school puppets do not have a puppet theater. "How could we make one from this box?" he asks the children. "You need a window," one child says. "Yes, that's true. I'll draw one. Stand here, please. I'll need the window the right height." The conversation and the project have drawn a larger group of children.

4. Mr. T. (teacher) has noticed a puppet lying on the ground in the playground. He picks it up, examines it, and puts it in his pocket. During circle time, he says, "Orvil (puppet's name) was on the ground in the yard today. Raise your hand if you know where he should be put after we play with him. Olivia, I see your hand. Would you please put Orvil in the place in the classroom that's just for him? Thank you, Olivia. What could happen to Orvil, our puppet, if we left him on the floor or ground?" "He'd get stepped on," Thad offers. "That could happen, Thad," said Mr. T. "Can anyone else think of what might happen to Orvil on the ground outside?" Mr. T. continues. "The ants would crawl on him," Jessica comments.

5. Ms. Y. announces to a group of children, "It's talking time. Everyone is going to talk to Bonzo (the puppet dog) and tell him their names." She reaches behind her and pulls Bonzo from a bag. "Willy, come up and take Bonzo," Ms. Y. directs. "Now, Cleo, you come up here, too. Willy, have Bonzo say, 'Woof, woof, I'm Bonzo.'" Willy fiddles with the puppet and still has not slipped it onto his hand. "We need a barking Bonzo. Who would like to come up, put Bonzo on his hand, and bark?" Ms. Y. asks.

C. Select the best answer for each statement.

1. Because puppets are so appealing, teachers
   a. motivate, model, and plan child activities to enhance the children's experiences.
   b. rarely use puppets in a conversational way, because it interrupts children's play.
   c. feel the large expense involved in supplying them is well worth it.
   d. find child language develops best without teacher modeling.

2. Puppets in preschool centers are used
   a. only by children.
   b. most often to present teacher-planned lessons.
   c. by both teachers and children.
   d. only when children ask for them.

3. Creative playacting (dramatization) is probably more appropriate
   a. for younger preschoolers, aged two to three years.
   b. for older preschoolers.
   c. when children are chosen for familiar characters' parts rather than selected from those children who volunteer for parts.
   d. when teachers help children stick to story particulars rather than promoting new lines or actions.

4. Identifying with a familiar story character through puppet use or playacting may give the child
   a. skills useful in getting along with others.
   b. greater insight into others' viewpoints.
   c. speaking skill.
   d. a chance to use creative imagination.
   e. all of the above.

5. If one is looking for a puppet with an expressive and active movement ability, one should use a
   a. plastic-headed puppet.
   b. papier-mâché-headed puppet with arms.
   c. cloth-headed puppet with arms.
   d. stick puppet.
   e. all the above are equally active and expressive.

6. "Punch and Judy" types of child's play with puppets is
   a. to be expected and needs teacher attention.
   b. a rare occurrence.
   c. best when teacher's performance sticks to the script.
   d. expected and should be ignored.
   e. a good puppetry modeling experience.

RESOURCES

Door puppet playhouse. Fabric Farms, 3590 Riverside Drive, Columbus, OH 43221.
Dress-ups for dramatic play. DRESS-UPS, 652 Glenbrook Road, Stamford, CT 06906.
Felt puppets. Pat's Puppets, 121 W. Simmons, Anaheim, CA 92802.
Puppet patterns. Plaid Enterprises Inc., P.O. Box 7600, Norcross, GA 30091.

BOOKS FOR CREATIVE DRAMATIZATION

Burton, B. (1973). *Buzz, buzz, buzz.* New York: Macmillan.

DePaola, T. (1975). *Strega Nona.* New York: Scholastic Book Services.

Domanska, J. (1969). *The turnip.* New York: Macmillan.

Ets, M. H. (1963). *Gilberto and the wind.* New York: The Viking Press.

Ets, M. H. (1955). *Play with me.* New York: The Viking Press.

Flack, M. (1952). *Ask Mr. Bear.* New York: Macmillan.

Green, N. B. (1975). *The hole in the dike.* New York: Harper & Row.

Hutchins, P. (1969). *The surprise party.* New York: Macmillan.

Hutchins, P. (1986). *The doorbell rang.* New York: Greenwillow Books.

Hutchins, P. (1972). *Goodnight owl.* New York: Macmillan.

Keats, E. J. (1962). *The snowy day.* New York: The Viking Press.

Keats, E. J. (1966). *Jennie's hat.* New York: Harper & Row.

Keats, E. J. (1967). *Peter's chair.* New York: Harper & Row.

Lionni, L. (1969). *Alexander and the wind-up mouse.* New York: Pantheon.

Mayer, M. (1968). *There's a nightmare in my closet.* New York: The Dial Press.

McGovern, A. (1976). *Too much noise.* New York: Scholastic Book Services.

Miller, E. (1964). *Mouskin's golden house.* Englewoods Cliffs, NJ: Prentice-Hall.

Murphy, J. (1980). *Peace at last.* New York: The Dial Press.

Slobodkina, E. (1947). *Caps for sale.* New York: William R. Scott Inc.

Young, M. (1964). *Miss Susy.* New York: Parent's Magazine Press.

WRITING
Print Awareness and Use

CHAPTER 16

Print—
Early Knowledge and Emerging Interest

OBJECTIVES	After studying this chapter, you should be able to:

- discuss the child's development of small hand-muscle control.

- outline the probable sequence of events occurring before a child prints his or her first recognizable alphabet letter.

- describe printscript alphabets.

- using printscript, print both the lowercase and uppercase alphabet.

- describe classroom equipment and settings that promote printscript development.

- plan a print awareness activity.

Two pertinent questions preschool teachers ask themselves concerning print and teaching children to write in printscript are, (1) is it appropriate to offer lessons (activities) that teach print letter recognition and formation at this age? and (2) how is instruction in printscript undertaken? Resolving these questions is made easier by this chapter's discussion.

In the past few years, ideas about the child's development of **writing** (printing) skill has undergone a minor revolution. Today preschool children are seen as writers (Clay, 1991). Older ideas promoted the idea that teaching children to print and read should not be undertaken until children are in kindergarten or first grade. It was felt that at that stage children are mature enough or possess the readiness skills that would make these tasks

much easier. Writing and reading skills were thought to be different from listening and speaking skills. Speech was accomplished without direct or formal teaching over a long period, beginning in infancy. Now, however, educators are revising their thoughts.

Clay (1993) points out that preschool children already know something about the world of print from their environment. She believes this leads children to form primitive hypotheses about letters, words, and messages, both printed and handwritten. It is a widely held view that learning to read and write will be easier for the child who has had rich preschool literacy experiences than for the child who has had little or limited literacy opportunities.

Much of young children's writing is a kind of exploratory play, common in the developmental beginnings of all symbolic media (Dyson, 1993). Print awareness and beginning printing skill and reading awareness and beginning reading skills are

---

Writing — the ability to use print to communicate with others.

now viewed as developing at younger ages, simultaneously with children's growing understandings of a number of other symbol systems. Print awareness describes the child's sensitivity to the presence and use of print in the environment (Cooper, 1993). As Sulzby (1992) points out:

> When given a supportive context . . . young children compose connected written discourse using emergent forms long before they hold conventional ideas about writing.

and

> . . . children's scribbling, drawing-used-as-writing, non-phonetic strings of letters, and invented spellings are now accepted and honored as reflecting underlying understandings about writing.

The clues have been there for some time. Early childhood educators have always had children who asked questions and displayed early attempts and interest in printing, reading, number concepts, and representing life-like objects in drawings. Preschool children can respond to and learn about visual features of print, know some letters, write some words, make up pretend writings such as letters to people, and dictate stories they want written before they have begun to consider how the words they say may be coded into print, and in particular how the sounds of speech are coded in print (Clay, 1993). Through informal daily literacy events and adult-child interactions such as making useful signs, children learn the many purposes and the power of print in their lives and in those of adults (Kantor, Miller, Fernie, 1992). Fields and Lee (1987) point out that adults expect children to talk before they read but may not have noticed that children are interested in writing before they can read.

Alphabet letters appear in four-year-olds' drawings. Young children go through the motions of reading books, and some have a keen interest in numbers and measurement. This supports the idea that children are attempting to make sense out of what they encounter and are expanding their understandings of symbol systems on a number of fronts.

Children do not leap from illiteracy to an understanding that our writing system is alphabetic (Bissex, 1985). They may have hypothesized many conclusions, and may have tried writing with a variety of their own inventions after puzzling over the relationship between print and speech. Elbow (1973) points out writing attempts "naturally" precede reading:

> . . . Very young children can learn to write before they can read. They can write anything they can say, whereas they can read only a fraction of the words they can say. And so writing is easier, quicker, and, in a sense, more "natural" than reading—certainly more easily and naturally learned. Thus writing naturally precedes reading. Writing is the gateway to literacy, not reading. Writing is the realm where children can attain literacy first and best feel on top of it—feel ownership and control over the written word.

As Bissex (1985) observes, "children in a literate society are learning about writing long before they enter school." How? Television, cereal boxes, toothpaste tubes, road signs, and print on buildings. Bissex (1985) adds:

> Before they can write conventionally, they write in their own ways but with the knowledge that writing communicates meanings and words. . . .

Professional practice promotes teachers' supporting, welcoming, and recognizing child efforts and accepting correct and incorrect child conclusions about printing, just as they accepted and supported incorrect or incomplete speech and welcomed it. Earlier practice may have led some teachers to either ignore or defer supportive guidance in printing, the rationale being that this instruction would come later in the child's schooling. Teachers today are encouraged to have faith in children's ability to discover and develop their own writing theories and symbol systems, as they did when they taught themselves to speak. This takes place in a print-rich environment with responsive adults.

Writing awareness and beginning writing attempts make more sense to children who have experienced an integrated language arts instructional approach. The areas of speaking, listening, reading, and writing are interrelated. The child's ability to see how these areas fit together is commonly mentioned in school goals. Adults in classrooms communicate with others on a daily basis both orally and in written form. Written communication offers daily opportunities for teachers to point out print's usefulness. Print's necessity can be discussed and shared.

Increased focus on the literacy of children in the U.S. has provided additional impetus for researching early writing and reading relationships. An increasing number of experts believe children establish early ideas about printing (writing) that serve as a basis for early printing attempts. Caulkins (1979) suggests that children can begin printing the first day they enter kindergarten, and that 90% of all children come to school believing that they can write (figure 16–1). She points out that most children's first drafts concentrate on messages rather than perfection. She advocates children's learning to write in the same way they learned to speak. Generations of children have been asked to learn the letters of the alphabet, sound-symbol correspondences, and a vocabulary of sight words before

FIGURE 16–1   Many children believe they can write.

they learned to write or read. If the same were true of learning to speak, children would be asked to wait until all letter sounds were perfected at age seven or eight before attempting to speak. Throne (1988) suggests that print awareness aids literacy development:

> . . . children . . . begin to understand that reading is getting meaning from print and become aware of the different functions and uses of written language.

Based on the notion that the child constructs from within, piecing together from life experiences the rules of oral language, educators feel that if children are given time and supportive assistance they can crack the writing and reading code by noticing regularities and incongruencies, thus creating their own unique rules. Children would progress at their own speeds, doing what is important to them and doing what they see others do. Jewell and Zintz (1986) have noticed a number of parallels between learning to read and learning to write. Children appear to teach themselves to write in much the same way that they teach themselves to read (figure 16–2). Without formal instruction, they experiment with and explore the various facets of the writing process. They decorate letters and invent their own symbols—sometimes reverting to their own inventions even after they are well into distinguishing and reproducing different, recognizable alphabet letters. Some children expect others to know what they have written, regardless of their coding system.

Natural curiosity leads children to form ideas about print and its use in their lives. Schickedanz (1982) suggests it has often been assumed that children know little or nothing about written language before they receive formal instruction. Evidence indicates, however, that children have extensive knowledge of some aspects of written language. Children who live in an alphabetical, literate environment begin to hypothesize that there are relationships between oral and written language. Written language is invented by children in response to their own social and cultural needs as they interact with the objects of literacy in the society and

FIGURE 16–2   Look at how this child is concentrating.

with the literate members of society (Goodman, 1990).

The concept of writing readiness began with some important figures from the past who influenced the directions that early childhood education has taken (Charlesworth, 1985). It became popular to talk about writing readiness as being that time when an average group of children acquired the capacity, skills, and knowledge to permit the group to accomplish the task. Figure 16–3 compares traditional, readiness, and "natural" instructional approaches. It would be difficult finding a center that doesn't use some elements of each of the three approaches in the instructional program.

Starting from a Different Place

Teachers need to consider all enrolled children ready to learn and progress in language and literacy, with each child starting from a different place (Clay, 1993). Past opportunity and life experiences may have dramatically molded the individual child's

Traditional Approach

- providing play materials and free time
- supplying art materials, paper, writing tools, alphabet toys and games, chalkboard
- reading picture books
- planning program that excludes instruction in naming or forming alphabet letters
- incidental and spontaneous teaching about print

very much the same

Readiness Approach

- providing writing materials and models
- planning program with introduction to tracing, naming alphabet letters, and naming shapes
- reading picture books
- providing a language arts classroom center
- channeling interested children into print and alphabet activities by offering supportive assistance

Natural Approach

- providing writing and reading materials and models
- planning program that emphasizes print in daily life
- promoting dramatic play themes that involve print, such as grocery store, restaurant, newspaper carrier, print shop, and office
- creating a writing center for the classroom
- supplying alphabet toys and models *(very calculated)*
- answering questions and supporting children's efforts
- making connections between reading and writing and speaking
- reading picture books

FIGURE 16–3   Comparison of instructional approaches in printing

literacy behaviors and language competency. Opportunities provided in literacy-rich classrooms with responsive adults will promote child exploration and new understanding and meaning. Teachers hope to expand language competencies that exist in newly enrolled children and introduce children to new activities and opportunities.

Research in Writing Development

In *Literacy Before Schooling* (1982) Ferreiro and Teberosky revolutionized educators' thinking about young children's development of print knowledge and writing. Subsequent research in children's self-constructed knowledge of alphabet forms and printing has resulted, using anthropological, psychological, and other investigative approaches. Ferreiro and Teberosky identified three developmentally ordered levels:

Writing developmental levels

First Level

Children:

- search for criteria to distinguish between drawing and writing. Example: "What's this?" referring to their artwork.
- realize straight and curved lines and dots are present but organized differently in print. Example: Rows and rows of curved figures, lines, and/or dots in art.   *print vs. drawing*
- reach the conclusion that print forms are arbitrary, and ordered in a linear fashion.
- accept the letter shapes in their environment rather than inventing new ones. Example: Rows of one letter appear in linear fashion in art.
- from literacy-rich environments recognize written marks as "substitute objects" during their third year. Example: "What does this say, teacher?" or "This says Mary."

Second Level

Children:

- look for objective differences in printed strings.
- don't realize there is a relationship between sound patterns and print.

example   b a t = bat

Third Level

Children:

- accept that a given string of letters represents their name and look for a rational explanation of this phenomena.

- may create a syllabic hypothesis. *word units*
- may print letter forms as syllables heard in a word. Example: I C (I see).
- may develop knowledge about particular syllables and what letters might represent such a syllable.
- may look for similar letters to write similar pieces of sound.
- begin to understand printing uses alphabet letters that represent sounds; consequently, to understand print one must know the sound patterns of words.

What conclusions of Ferreiro's landmark research may affect language arts program planning and early educators' interaction techniques? Certainly teachers will note attending children's active attempts to understand print. They will realize each child constructs his or her own ideas and revises these understandings as more print is noticed and experienced.

The seemingly strange questions children ask or off-the-wall answers some children give in classroom discussions about print may now be seen as reflecting their inner thoughts at crucial points in their print knowledge.

As teachers view children's artwork, they will see more readily early print forms. Ferreiro's research will also confirm educators' attempts to provide literacy-rich, print-rich classroom environments.

McLane and McNamee (1990) call writing the neglected half of literacy, pointing out the wealth of research on early reading. Some preschoolers demonstrate that they know the names and shapes of alphabet letters. They may also know letters form words and represent sound(s). They might have grasped the idea that spoken words can be written and then read. They may be able to express daily uses of written words. Why would a young child write or pretend to write? It's not an easy motor task. Is it simply imitation? done for adult reaction? done because there's an inner drive to know or become competent? Research has yet to answer these questions. Teachers conjecture reasons with each young child they meet who has beginning printing skills. The reasons aren't as important as teacher reaction and plan to provide additional opportunities to nourish and expand what already exists.

Gill (1992) offers additional steps in the child's development of printing skill:

> As children learn letters of the alphabet, their writing develops from random scribbles, to waves, to letter-like production, to writing actual random letters. Simultaneously, children's pretending-to-read voice and pointing moves from (1) nonunit and nondirectional, to (2) left-to-right, to (3) attention to printed letters, to (4) attention to written word units. As word units are pointed to the initial consonant becomes . . . the beginning of something. Also, simultaneously, children realize the close relationship between the sound made when one says a word and the sound made when saying the name of its initial consonant, and they spell accordingly.

Young Children's Progress

Dyson (1993) believes there is not linear progression in written language development:

> Rather its development is linked in complex ways to the whole of children's symbolic repertoires; its evolution involves shifts of function and symbolic form, social give-and-take, as children explore and gradually control new ways to organize and represent their world and to interact with other people about that world.

At some point, children learn that written marks have meaning. Just as they sought the names of things, they now seek the names of these marks and, later, the meanings of the marks. Because each child is an individual, this may or may not happen during the preschool years. One child may try to make letters or numbers. Another child may have little interest in or knowledge of written forms.

Many children are somewhere between these two examples.

Writing (printscript) is complex. Many subcomponents of the process need to be understood. Development may occur at different rates, with spurts and lags in different knowledge areas. Besides the visual learning of letter features and forms, the ability to manually form shapes, and knowing that writing involves a message, a writer must listen to the sounds of his or her inner speech and find matching letters representing those sounds. Since letter follows letter in printing, the child needs to make continuous intellectual choices and decisions.

Atkins (1984) also discusses events between the ages of three and five:

> . . . children begin to vary their patterns and move from imitation to creation. They produce a mixture of real letters, mock letters, and innovative symbols. They write messages which they expect adults to be able to read. These actions signal several new discoveries which the children are making.
>
> • They are attending to the fine features of writing, noting shapes and specific letters.
> • They are developing an early concept of sign—the realization that symbols stand for something.
> • They are recognizing that there is variation in written language.

Children refine and enlarge these concepts by playing around with writing. They draw, trace, copy, and even invent letter forms of their own.

Print awareness is usually developed in the following sequence:

1. The child notices adults making marks with writing tools.

2. The child notices print in books and on signs. As Chomsky (1971) notes, "When this time comes, a child seems suddenly to notice all the print in the world around him—street signs,

food labels, newspaper headlines, printing on cartons, books, billboards, everything. He tries to read everything, already having a good foundation in translating from pronunciation to print. If help is provided when he asks for it, he makes out wonderfully well. It is a tremendously exciting time for him."

3. The child realizes that certain distinguishable marks make his or her name.

4. The child learns the names of some of the marks—usually the first letter of his or her name. As Jewell and Zintz (1986) point out, while building a sizable store of words recognized on sight, children will begin to make finer and finer distinctions about print by using more and more visual cues. They begin to pay attention to individual letters, particularly the first ones in words.

The usual sequence in the child's imitation of written forms follows.

1. The child's scribbles are more like print than artwork or pure exploration (figure 16–4).

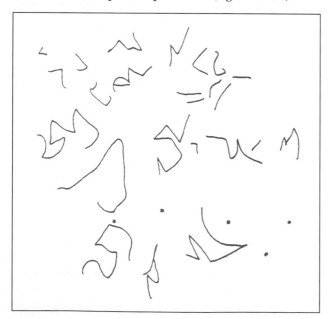

FIGURE 16–4 Scribbles are sometimes print-like. *(From* Integrated Language Arts for Emerging Literacy *by Sawyer and Sawyer, copyright 1993 by Delmar Publishers.)*

2. Linear scribbles are generally horizontal with possible repeated forms. Children's knowledge of linear directionality may have been displayed in play in which they lined up alphabet blocks, cut out letters and pasted them in a row, or put magnetic board letters in left to right rows (figure 16–5).

3. Individual shapes are created, usually closed shapes displaying purposeful lines.

4. Letter-like forms are created.

5. Recognizable alphabet letters are printed and may be mirror images or turned on sides, upside down, or in upright position (figure 16–6).

6. Words or groupings of alphabet letters with spaces between are formed.

7. Invented spelling appears that may include pictured items along with alphabet letters (figure 16–7).

8. Correctly spelled words with spaces separating words are produced.

Atkins (1984) describes early writing as totally egocentric. Self-expression, fun, and play are the real objects, writing is only the medium. It will remain this way, she feels, for most children until near the end of first grade.

FIGURE 16–5 Linear scribbles *(From* Integrated Language Arts for Emerging Literacy *by Sawyer and Sawyer, copyright 1993 by Delmar Publishers.)*

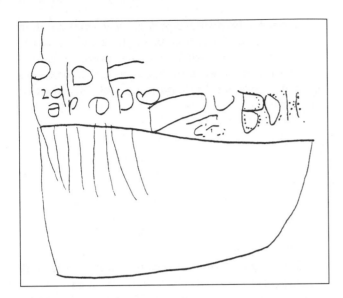

FIGURE 16–6   Recognizable alphabet letters *(From* Integrated Language Arts for Emerging Literacy *by Sawyer and Sawyer, copyright 1993 by Delmar Publishers.)*

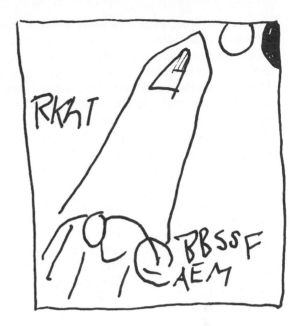

FIGURE 16–7   Child read as "Blast off rocket to the moon."

Invented Spelling (Developmental Spelling)

Invented spelling is something children do naturally. It is a temporary phenomenon that is later replaced with conventional spelling. Teachers, until the mid to late 1980s, gave young children the idea that until they learned to read they needed to write only those words they had memorized or copied. Research has changed educational philosophy and methods. It suggests children's literacy emerges during a span of several years. As young children slowly begin to understand what letters mean and how to string them together, some children will invent spelling. Often the beginning consonant sound of a particular word is printed. A whole sequence might shortly appear and consist of single-letter words.

The invented spelling stage casts teachers in the role of detectives trying to ascertain meanings that the child may perceive as obvious. In their early attempts to write, preschool children invent a system of spelling that follows logical and predictable rules before they learn the conventional forms (King, 1985). Vowels are commonly omitted in invented spellings. Words appear that may look like a foreign language—dg for dog, and jragin for dragon (Vukelich and Golden, 1984).

Identifiable stages in invented spelling are followed by some, not all, children, and are given here for teacher reference:

1. Spelling awareness—alphabet letters represent words. Example: C (See), U (You)

2. Primitive spelling with no relationship between spelling and words. Numbers and letters are differentiated. Example: tsOlf..DO

3. Pre-phonetic spelling initial and final consonants may become correct. Example: KT (cat), CD (candy), RT (write), WF (with)

4. Phonetic spelling—almost a perfect match between the symbols and sounds. Some vowels are used. Some sight words may be correctly spelled. Example: SUM (some), LIK (like), MI (my), ME (me)

5. Correct spelling.

Invented spelling serves as an important stage in the process of deciphering the sound-symbol system of written language (Fields and Lee, 1987). It is felt that at this point phonics becomes important to children. Early on, the child selects letters in his or her inventive spelling that have some relationship to how the word is pronounced. Large items like elephants may be written in huge letters and with more letters than small objects, because the child is operating under the misconception that bigger necessitates more letters (Ferreiro and Teberosky, 1982). A perfectly logical conclusion! The names of letters may represent words (*u* for you) or parts of words. Atkins (1984) defines young writers' invented spelling as using personal logic rather than or in conjunction with standard spelling. Atkins points out that the child's strategy of using a name of a letter has a frustrating side:

> There are only 26 letters in the alphabet but almost twice that many phonemes or sound units. What do children do when they encounter a sound for which there is no ready letter-name match? They use a system of spelling logic based primarily on what they hear but also influenced by subconscious knowledge of the general rules of language usage and of how sounds are formed in the mouth when spoken.

What should an early childhood educator do when he or she encounters invented spelling in a child's work? Faith that children will evolve toward conventional spelling is needed. As Sowers (1982) writes:

> Invented spelling gives young writers early power over words. Professional writers don't worry about correct spelling on their first drafts and neither do inventive spellers.

Moffet and Wagner (1993) note that many primary teachers write out the standard spelling for words below a child's invented-spelling text. By doing so, teachers honor the original but give children experiencing the tension between their spelling inventions and regular standard spellings further information. This enables interested children

to compare. Inventive spellers who realize their spelling differs from text in books and the world around them may experience frustration and confusion. Teachers at this juncture may introduce phoneme spelling by "sounding out" words that they print.

These techniques need to be used carefully with older preschoolers, while considering the child's inventiveness and pride in his or her work. Many preschoolers object to teachers adding any marks on their papers. Graves' (1981) description of early writers notes their fearlessness and egocentricity. Pleased with their own competence, children experiment freely in their new medium.

When a child asks the teacher to write a specific word, the teacher has a chance to help the child with letter sounds (rather than letter names) saying d–o–g as he or she writes it. Time permitting, the teacher can add "It starts with the alphabet letter *d*, like Dan, *D–a–n*."

Parents will need clear explanations concerning why their child's teacher does not correct invented spelling.

Goals of Instruction

Providing experiences that match a child's interests and abilities is the goal of many centers. Most schools plan activities for those children who ask questions or seem ready and then proceed if the child is still interested. Others work with children on an individual basis. Yet others believe in providing a print-rich environment where the child will progress naturally with supportive adults who also model an interest in print, and point out uses of print in daily activities. Fields (1996) urges teachers to plan activities involving authentic writing (printing), defining authentic writing as writing done for "real world" rather than contrived school purposes. An authentic written message often involves a child's need or desire. It is possible to combine these approaches.

As with other language abilities, goals include stimulating further interest and exploration. This should be done in such a way that the child is not confused by instruction that is too advanced or boring.

As stated previously, an important goal concerning print awareness is relating writing to other language arts areas. It is almost impossible to not do so. Teachers are encouraged to consciously mention connections so children will understand how writing fits in the whole of communicating.

A teacher's goal would include the ability to print every lowercase and uppercase alphabet letter in excellent form, offering children the best model possible.

Whole-Language Theory

The whole-language approach suggests reading is a multifaceted process involving more than just learning to read but also learning to read by writing (Engelking, 1989). Early childhood educators adopting whole-language theory give attention to children displaying an interest in printing alphabet letters and invented spelling. The role of teacher in this approach is that of a supportive assistant. Conversations focus on meaning and helping children trying to print something they have in mind. The teacher might pair children with similar interests so child collaboration can take place. Whole-language early childhood classrooms have well-equipped writing centers furnished with abundant child aids.

Older practices are ignored in the whole-language approach. The message "Wait, you're not able or ready to write properly" or "Here, trace or copy these alphabet letters," isn't appropriate. It negates what some preschoolers can do already (Engelking, 1989).

Teachers encourage children to "reason-it-out." Approximations of alphabet letters and words are accepted and given recognition. They preserve and encourage the child's attempts. As more exposure to letter forms takes place and when more precise motor control develops, the child will produce closer approximations to recognizable alphabet letter forms.

Coordination

Children's muscle control follows a timetable of its own. Control of a particular muscle depends on many factors—diet, exercise, inherited ability, and motivation, to name a few. A baby can control his or her neck and arms long before his or her legs. A child's muscle control grows in a head-to-toe fashion. Muscles closer to the center of the body can be controlled long before those of the hands and fingers. Large-muscle control comes before small-muscle control (figure 16–8). Think of a toddler walking; the toddler's legs seem to swing from his or her hips. Just as each child starts walking and develops muscle control at different ages, so too does each child develop fine motor control, which influences his or her ability to control a writing tool.

Schickedanz (1989) discusses problems preschoolers may encounter if they are *required* by "over eager" teachers to print the letters of the alphabet:

FIGURE 16–8 This indoor sand table and its contents offer small motor skill development.

... precise writing is extremely difficult for three- and four-year-olds, who typically grasp writing tools in their fists and guide them with movements started at the shoulder, elbow, or wrist. With the pivot and the writing tool point so far apart, children can't help but write large. ... Furthermore, because preschoolers' spatial skills are limited, it's difficult for them to construct and combine lines in the ways that writing lessons often demand. Four-year-olds who do have advanced fine motor skills that allow them to hold a pencil in a well-controlled finger and thumb grasp still might conceptualize letters in ways that differ from conventional form.

Cognitive Development

Realization that there are written symbols is a first step in writing. The discovery that written language is simply spoken language, ideas, or communication is another step. Mental growth, which allows a child to see similarities and differences in written symbols, comes before the ability to write. The child recognizes that a written mark is a shape made by the placement of lines.

Donoghue (1985) lists seven prerequisite skill areas for handwriting:

- small-muscle development and coordination
- eye-hand coordination
- ability to hold writing tools properly
- ability to form basic strokes (circles and straight lines)
- letter perception
- orientation to printed language, which includes a desire to write and communicate, including the child's enjoyment of writing his or her own name.
- left to right understanding.

The last three skills deal with the child's cognitive development. Schickedanz (1986) points out that learning to write involves much more than just forming alphabet letters:

Learning to write also involves knowing (1) how writing and speech relate, (2) how form and style vary depending on the situation, and (3) how a reader will react to what [is] written. All of these skills depend on sophisticated and complex thinking, much of which may be beyond preschoolers' abilities. Nevertheless, the beginnings of these skills can be found in preschool children.

Play and Writing

Often print, signs, and writing imaginary messages become part of a dramatic play sequence. During play, children may pretend to read and write words, poems, stories, and songs, and may actually make a series of marks on paper. Play encourages children to act as if they are already competent in and able to control the activity under consideration (McLane and McNamee, 1990). Through pretend play they may feel they are already readers and writers; at least a beginning move toward eventual literacy takes place. They observe mom, dad, teachers, and older brothers and sisters using reading and writing in their daily lives. These activities are given status. Early childhood teachers can build on children's early attitudes by modeling, demonstrating, and helping children continue to see the worthwhile aspects of reading and writing.

Drawing Experience

A young child scribbles if given paper and a marking tool. As the child grows, the scribbles are controlled into lines that he or she places where desired (figure 16–9). Gradually, the child begins to draw circles, then a face, later a full figure, and so on. Children draw their own symbols representing what they see around them. Clay (1991) urges teachers to examine one child's drawings over a few weeks time and discover the child is working on a basic plan:

FIGURE 16–9   Children start writing by scribbling and, when older, drawing symbols of the world around them.

His ideas are organized and he produces the same pattern or schema again and again. It seems as if the child has learned a plan of action which produces the pattern or schema. This gives the child enough control over pencil and paper to play with variations, which often leads to new discoveries.

The length of time it takes this process to develop differs with each child.

A profound connection exists between experience and ability in drawing and interest in and ability to write (Balaban, 1980) (figure 16–10). Drawings and paintings not only communicate children's thinking (when they reach the level of drawing that is representative of the environment), but also often display early attempts to create symbols. Some of these symbols may be recognized by adults, but others seem to be unique and represent the world in the child's own way. Children often want to talk about their work and create stories to accompany graphics (Kane, 1982).

Since alphabet letters are more abstract than representative drawing, some educators suggest that drawing precedes writing. Brittain's research (1973) found that children who were making closed forms and recognizable letters in their drawings made closed forms and recognizable letters if they attempted writing. Durkin (1969) identifies a char-

FIGURE 16–10   Crayon use attracts and holds the interest of many preschoolers.

acteristic that was common to almost all children in her research study who read early and continued to hold their lead in reading achievement: The children were described by their parents as "pencil-and-paper kids," whose starting point of curiosity about written language was an interest in scribbling and drawing.

Writing and Exposure to Books

Probably the most common experience that promotes a child's interest in print is hearing and seeing picture books read over and over. Through repeated exposure, the child comes to expect the text to be near or on the same page as the object depicted. Throne (1988) points out that "children begin to understand the conventions of print and how stories work by using familiar and significant texts." Memorized story lines lead to children's questions about print on book pages. Once a word is recognized in print, copying that word onto another paper or manipulating magnetic alphabet letters to form the word is a natural outgrowth. This activity usually leads to parent attention and approval and further attempts. Scribblers, doodlers, drawers, and pencil-and-paper kids are all labels researchers have used to describe children who have an early interest in writing, and much of what they do has been promoted by seeing print in their favorite books.

Children may begin by thinking a reader looks at pictures to know what a book says. Both Clay (1991) and Ferreiro and Teberosky (1982) have tried to discover what young children think about pictures (illustrations) and text and the relationship between the two. Similar conclusions were drawn by both researchers. Ferreiro and Teberosky (1982) describe a sequential change in child behaviors:

- At first the text and the picture are not differentiated.
- Then the children expect the text to be a label for the picture.
- At the third stage the text is expected to provide cues with which to confirm predictions based on the picture.

As they gain more experience with books, they begin to realize that it is the print, not the pictures, that a reader reads (Schickedanz, 1986).

Some important concepts that young children gradually understand concerning print are:

- The print, not the pictures in a book, tells the story.
- There are alphabet letters.
- Words are clusters of letters.
- There are first letters and last letters in words.
- Alphabet letters exist in upper- and lowercase.
- Spaces in printing are there for a reason.
- Punctuation makes words have meaning.

Children may notice left-to-right and top-to-bottom direction of printing and also the left-page-first directional feature.

Berg (1977) concluded that the acquisition of skills in writing and reading and the development of the attitude that books are enjoyable are not simply academic or technical learning. These skills flourish with a warm physical and emotional base with shared enjoyment and intimacy. Most experts believe considerable support exists for the notion that oral language provides a base for learning to write (Dyson, 1987). The importance of emotionally satisfying adult-child interactions in all areas of language arts can't be underestimated.

Planning a Program for Print Awareness and Printing Skill

Program planning is often done on an individual basis. If group instruction is planned, it deals with general background information concerning print use during the school day and print use in the home and community.

A great deal of spontaneous and incidental teaching takes place. Teachers capitalize on children's questions concerning mail, packages, signs, and labels. In most preschool settings, print is a natural part of living, and it has many interesting features that children can discover and notice when teachers focus attention on print.

A discussion is necessary here concerning the practice of asking the child to form alphabet letters and practice letter forms. The dangers in planning an individual or group experience of this nature are multiple. One has to consider whether a child has the physical and mental capacity to be successful and whether the child has an interest in doing the exercise or is simply trying to please adults.

Early writing instruction is not a new idea. Maria Montessori (1967) (a well-known educator and designer of teaching materials) and numerous other teachers have offered instruction in writing (or printing) to preschoolers. Montessori encouraged the child's tracing of letter forms using the first two fingers of the hand as a prewriting exercise. She observed that this type of light touching seemed to help youngsters when writing tools were later given to them. Montessori (1967) designed special alphabet letter cutouts as one of a number of prewriting aids. These cutouts were thought to help exercise and develop small muscles while shapes were learned. Montessori suggests the following:

When ... a child see[s] and touch[es] the letters of the alphabet, three sensations come into play simultaneously: sight, touch, and kinesthetic (muscular) sensation. This is why the image of the graphic symbol is fixed in the mind much more quickly than when it is acquired through sight in ordinary methods.

It should be noted, moreover, that muscular memory is the most tenacious in a small child and is also the readiest; sometimes even he does not recognize a letter when he sees it, but he does when he touches it.

Each center and individual teacher decides whether group printing practice takes place. This text recommends print activity planning that concentrates on awareness of print and its uses in everyday life plus helpful suggestions and encouragement given to individual children who show more than a passing interest. When a child asks for information concerning print or to be shown how to print, he or she is displaying interest and following his or her own curriculum.

Environment and Materials

Children's access to drawing tools—magic markers, chalk, pencils, crayons, brushes—is important so that children can make their own marks (figure 16–11). It is suggested that teachers create a place where children can comfortably use these tools.

Early childhood educators interested in whole-language approaches to instruction may gather ideas from Hayward's (1988) description of a well-managed and functioning whole-language classroom:

... you immediately become aware of ... printed messages about activities for the day, printed examples of child-written (or dictated) work, lots of printed wall charts and big books, printed labels on equipment,

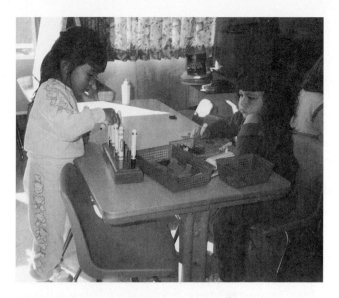

FIGURE 16–11 A clever felt-marker holder that provides quick access and easy return.

shelves, cupboards, to give information about contents and use.

The following early childhood materials help the child use and gain control of small arm and finger muscles in preparation for writing (figure 16–12):

FIGURE 16–12 Scissors in one hand and a writing tool in the other.

- puzzles
- pegboards
- small blocks
- construction toys
- scissors
- eyedroppers

Most schools plan activities in which the child puts together, arranges, or manipulates small pieces. These are sometimes called tabletop activities and are available for play throughout the day. A teacher can encourage the use of tabletop activities by having the pieces arranged invitingly on tables or resting on adjacent shelves.

Early childhood centers create rooms that are full of symbols, letters, and numbers in clear view of the child. Room print should reflect teacher and child interests. Many toys have circles, squares, triangles, alphabet letters, and other common shapes.

Recommended symbol size for preschool playroom display is at least 2 to 2½ inches in height or larger. Teachers can add printing to playrooms in the following ways.

Labeling

artwork

name tags

lockers and storage areas (figure 16–13)

belongings

common objects in the room, such as scissors, paper, crayons, fishbowl, chair, water, door, window, sink, and so on

school areas, such as block, library or reading center, playhouse, art center, science center

place cards for snacks

Display Areas

magazine pictures with captions

current interest displays, for example, "Rocks we found on our walk"

bulletin boards and wall displays with words

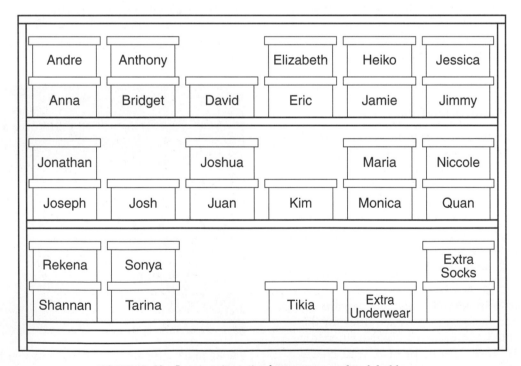

FIGURE 16–13   Large printscript letters are used to label boxes.

wall alphabet guides (Aa Bb . . .)
alphabet charts (figure 16–14)
child's work with explanations, such as "Josh's block tower," or "Penny's clay pancakes"

folding table accordian (figure 16–15)
signs for child activities, such as "store," "hospital," "wet paint," and "Tickets for Sale Here"

INSTRUCTIONS TO MAKE CHART LINER

Cut a piece of Masonite® 12 inches by 36 inches. Make 7 sawcuts 1½" apart, beginning and ending 1½" from either end. Then glue or nail ½" square pieces of wood 12" long to each end.

Note: A teacher-made chart liner is a useful device that helps teachers make evenly spaced guidelines on charts that use lines of print. By placing the chart liner over chart paper, quick guidelines are accomplished by inserting a sharp pencil in sawcut slots.

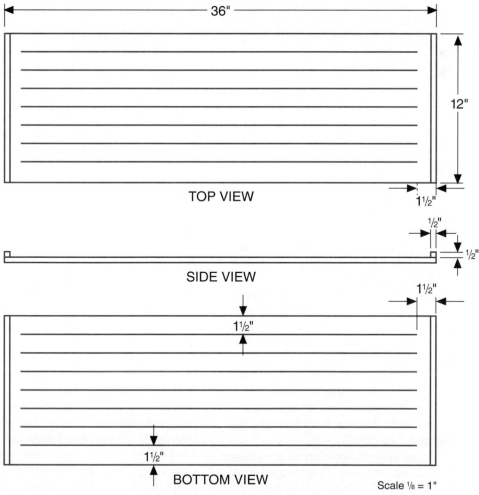

FIGURE 16–14 Making a chart liner

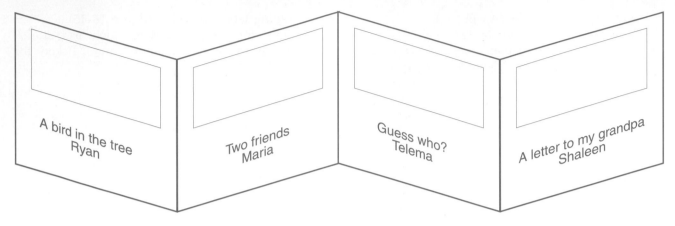

FIGURE 16–15   Folding table accordian

Teacher-Made Materials, Games, and Toys

brightly colored alphabet letters from felt, cardboard, sandpaper, leather, plastic
games with letters, numbers, or symbols
alphabet cards
games with names and words
greeting cards
hats or badges with words

Writing Centers

Writing centers are planned, teacher-stocked areas where printing is promoted. A writing center can be a separate area of a room or it can exist within a language arts center. Child comfort and proper lighting are essential along with minimized distractions. Often dividers or screens are used to reduce outside noise and activity. Supplies and storage areas are provided at children's fingertips so that children can help themselves. Teacher displays or bulletin board areas that motivate printing can be close by. If water-based marking pens are provided, pens with distinct bright colors are preferred (Fields and Lee, 1987).

Through dialogue and exploration at a writing table or center, children are able to construct new ideas concerning print and meaning in a supportive mini-social setting (Rowe, 1989).

There should be a variety of paper and writing tools. Printing stamps and printing ink blocks, a hole punch, and brads are desirable. Old forms, catalogs, calendars, and computer paper may be inviting. Scratch paper (one side already used) or lined paper and crayons placed side-by-side invite use. Most local businesses or offices throw away enough scratch paper to supply a preschool center.

Colored or white chalk has an appeal of its own and can be used on paper, chalkboards, or cement. For variety, use oil pastels, which have bright colors, or soft-lead pencils on paper. Most schools install a child-high chalkboard; table chalkboards are made quickly by using chalkboard paint obtained at hardware or paint stores and scrap wood pieces. Easels, unused wall areas, and backs of furniture can be made into chalkboards.

Primary print typewriters capture interest, and some centers have computers and adult computer advisers. Shape books with blank pages and words to copy and trace appeal to some children, as do large rub-on letters or alphabet letter stickers (these can be made by teachers from press-on labels). Magnetic boards and magnetized letter sets are commonly mentioned as the favorite toy of children interested in alphabet letters and forming words.

Letters, words, and displays are placed for viewing on bulletin boards at children's eye level. Displays in writing centers often motivate and promote print.

First School Alphabets

Parents may have taught their children to print with all capitals. Early childhood centers help introduce the interested child to the letter forms that are used in the first grades of elementary school.

In kindergarten or first grade, printing is done in printscript, sometimes called manuscript printing (figure 16–16) or in a form called D'Nealian print (figure 16–17). Centers should obtain guides from a local elementary school, since letter forms can vary from community to community. As in previous text discussions, manuscript and D'Nealian alphabet forms are provided for teachers in this text so that correct forms can be modeled in classrooms when children happen to notice them and individually when children request specific letter or word graphics.

Teachers need to be familiar with printscript (or any other form used locally). It is easier for a child to learn the right way than to be retrained later. All printing seen by young children in a preschool should be either printscript, using both uppercase (capitals) and lowercase (small letters) or D'Nealian style. Names, bulletin boards, and labels made by teachers should model correct forms. Printscript letters are formed with straight lines, circles, and parts of circles. In figure 16–16, the small arrows and numerals show the direction to follow in forming the letters as well as the sequence of the lines.

The D'Nealian form developed by teacher-principal Donald Neal Thurber, introduced in 1978, has grown in acceptance. Its popularity stems in part from its slant and continuous stroke features, which provide an easy transition to slant and stroke used in cursive writing introduced to children after second grade. Thurber (1988) notes that it takes 58 strokes to print the circle-stick alphabet while only 31 to print D'Nealian. They are arranged in groupings of similarly made patterns. Group I is introduced first to learners, and dots indicate where letter forms start. Teachers and parents are encouraged to use voice inflection to establish rhythm and direction during letter-form introduction and practice

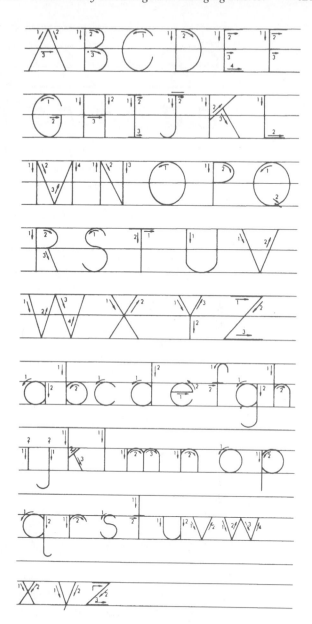

FIGURE 16–16 Printscript alphabet *(Courtesy of the Santa Clara Unified School District, Santa Clara, CA.)*

(figure 16–18). Further information about this alphabet and teaching suggestions can be obtained from Scott, Foresman, Glenview, IL 60025.

Numbers in printed form are called numerals. Children may have used toys with numerals, such

FIGURE 16–17 D'Nealian print *(From D'Nealian® Handwriting by Donald Neal Thurber. Copyright by Scott, Foresman, and Company. Reprinted by permission.)*

Dear Parents:

The following alphabet is how we present the D'Nealian Manuscript Handwriting program.

Letters are presented in a group of similarly made patterns, starting with Group I. When a child can make 3 of any letter with similar size and shape (although it may not be the perfect finished product), *he or she is at his or her skill level for that lesson.* A suggested audio phraseology of how each letter is formed is also included. The teacher uses voice inflection to help establish rhythm and direction control. A great help is having the child write simple 2-, 3-, or 4-letter words as quickly as new letters are presented; for example, a + d gives *dad* and *add.*

Letters start at the dot.

Group 1 — Around-Down Letters

a   Middle start; around down, close up, down, and a monkey tail.

d   Middle start; around down, touch, up high, down, and a monkey tail.

o   Middle start; around, down, and close up.

s   Start below the middle; curve up, around, down, and a snake tail.

c   Start below the middle; curve up, around, down, up, and stop.

g   Middle start; around, down, close up, down under water, and a fishhook.

e   Start between the middle and bottom; curve up, around, touch, down, up, and stop. Or, curved line up, wrap a *c* around it.

q   Middle start; around, down, close up, down under water, and a backwards fishhook.

Group II — Tall Letters

b   Top start; slant down, around up, and a tummy.

k   Top start; slant down, up into a little tummy, and a monkey tail.

f   Start below the top; curve up, around, and slant down. Cross.

l   Top start; slant down, and a monkey tail.

t   Top start; slant down, and a monkey tail. Cross.

h   Top start; slant down, up over the hill, and a monkey tail.

Group III

i   Middle start; slant down and a monkey tail. Add a dot.

m   Middle start; slant down, up over the hill, up over the hill again, and a monkey tail.

r   Middle start; slant down, up, and a roof.

u   Middle start; slant down, around, up, down, and a monkey tail.

w   Middle start; slant down, around, up, and down, around, up again.

y   Middle start; slant down, around, up, slant down under water, and a fishhook.

n   Middle start; slant down, up over the hill, and a monkey tail.

p   Middle start; slant down under water, up, around, and a tummy.

j   Middle start; slant down under water and a fishhook. Add a dot.

v   Middle start; slant down right and slant up right.

x   Middle start; slant down right and a monkey tail. Cross down left.

z   Middle start; over right, slant down left, and over right.

FIGURE 16–18   A letter to parents concerning D'Nealian print

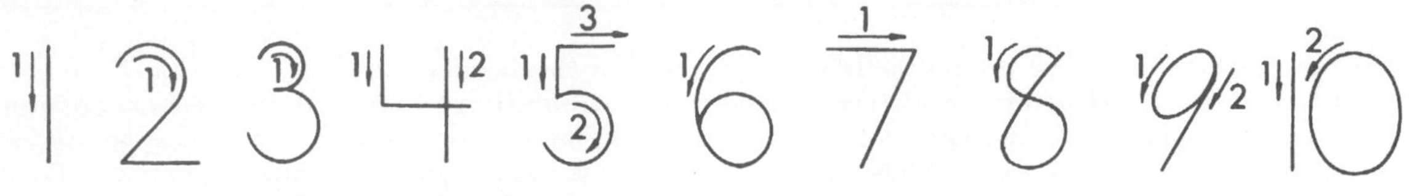

FIGURE 16–19 Printscript numerals *(Courtesy of the Santa Clara Unified School District, Santa Clara, CA.)*

as block sets. Young children will probably hold up fingers to indicate their ages or to tell you they can count. They may start making number symbols before showing an interest in alphabet letters. Numeral forms (figure 16–19) are also available from elementary schools. The numeral forms in one geographic area may also be slightly different from those of another town, city, or state.

Beginning Attempts

In beginning attempts to write, children commonly grasp writing tools tightly and press down hard enough to tear the paper. With time, the mastery of small muscles, children's tense, unschooled muscles relax and forms and shapes start to resemble alphabet forms and recognizable shapes. Deep concentration and effort is observed. All attempts are recognized and appreciated by early childhood teachers as signs of the children's growing interest and ability.

Lewis and Lewis (1964) developed a listing (figure 16–20) that arranges alphabet letters in manuscript print from the most difficult for children to manage and form to the easiest.

Milz (1985) has classified the young child's uses of early writing: (1) establishing ownership or identity; (2) building relationships; (3) remembering or recalling; (4) recording information; and (5) fantasizing or pretending.

Danielson (1992) cites examples from her observation and interaction with four-year-old Justin, in the following:

In establishing *ownership* or *identity*, Justin frequently labeled his work by writing his own name on it. For instance, after listen-

ing to and looking at the book *Feet!* (Parnall, 1988), which features illustrations of many different animals' feet, Justin drew his own feet and wrote his name beside them to denote ownership. He said he needed to put his name on the drawing "so everyone knows they are my feet."

Building relationships includes notes for social interaction through writing. The book *The Jolly Postman* (Ahlberg & Ahlberg, 1986) includes actual letters and envelopes to fairy tale characters. After looking at this book, Justin wanted to write a letter to his mom and wrote I LOVE YOU. This shows his knowledge of letter writing as social interaction and as a means of building and sustaining relationships.

1. q		14. U		27. K		40. F
2. g		15. M		28. W		41. P
3. p		16. S		29. A		42. E
4. y		17. b		30. N		43. X
5. j		18. e		31. C		44. I
6. m		19. r		32. f		45. v
7. k		20. z		33. J		46. i
8. u		21. n		34. w		47. D
9. a		22. s		35. h		48. H
10. G		23. Q		36. T		49. O
11. R		24. B		37. x		50. L
12. d		25. t		38. c		51. o
13. Y		26. Z		39. V		52. l

FIGURE 16–20 Listing of letters from most difficult to form to easiest *(From* Elementary English, *by Lewis and Lewis, 1964.)*

Remembering or recalling is often done in a list-like form with early writers. Justin listed what he wanted for Christmas: BACEBALL UNFOM (baseball uniform) and PUZUL (puzzle).

Recording information took the form of copying verbatim words or titles from the books read. He simply copied the title of the book *The Third Story Cat* (Baker, 1987) from the cover because those words were interesting to him.

Fantasizing or pretending took place when he extended the plots of the stories. *Some of My Best Friends Are Monsters* (Paige, 1988) features the many useful ways monsters could help in real life: "They can help Mom move the refrigerator." Justin added his own idea of how a monster could help in real life: "by fixing the top of a high building."

Justin would be considered "advanced" by most early childhood educators.

Planned Activities—Basic Understandings

Most planned activities in this language arts area, and most unplanned child-adult exchanges during the school day, involve basic understandings. Rules exist in this graphic art as they do in speech. Children form ideas about these rules as they did with oral communication.

Print concerns the use of graphic symbols that represent sounds and sound combinations. Symbols combine and form words and sentences in a prescribed grammatical order. Alphabet letters are spaced and are in uppercase and lowercase form. They are written and read from left to right across a page. Margins exist at beginnings and ends of lines, and lines go from the top to bottom of pages. Punctuation marks end sentences, and indentations separate paragraphs. It is amazing how many rules of printing that interested children discover on their own.

Daily Interactions and Techniques

The techniques listed in this section are purposeful actions and verbalizations used by teachers in printscript instruction. The teacher uses a natural conversational style rather than a formal teaching tone.

Kantor, Miller, and Fernie (1992) make the following teacher suggestions:

- Be aware of the possibilities to use print to support children's social and educational needs in your particular classroom setting.
- Help children make connections between what is being done in the classroom and reading and writing. Connections are best made as literacy is woven in and through the fabric of classroom life, its school culture, and peer culture activities.

Putting the children's names on their work is the most common daily use of printscript. The teacher asks the children whether they want their names on their work. Many young children feel their creations are their very own and may not want a name added. When a paper is lost because it has no name on it, children see the advantage of printing a name on belongings.

All names are printed in the upper left-hand corner of the paper if possible or on the back if child requests (figure 16–21). This is done to train the children to look at this spot as a preparation for reading and writing. Children's comments about their work can be jotted down along the bottom or back of their papers. As Donoghue (1985) points out:

When pupils verbalize satisfactorily, their oral experiences provide meaningful vocabularies for first writing experiences. They enjoy listening to stories as well as composing and sending written messages. They should have many opportunities to dictate stories, poems, reports, plans, ideas and funny and frightening incidents. When writing for the pupils, the teacher is not

FIGURE 16–21   Names are in the upper left-hand corner, but could the letter formation be improved?

Maryellen Donald

FIGURE 16–22   Letters should be large enough for the child to see easily.

only introducing them to writing and reading, but is also helping to bridge a gap between oral and written language.

The teacher can be prepared to do this by having a dark crayon or felt-tip pen in a handy place or pocket. Dictation is written without major teacher editing or suggestions concerning the way it is said. The teacher can tell the child that the teacher will be writing down the child's ideas and then follow the child's word order as closely as possible. Some teachers prefer to print the statement "Chou dictated these words to Mrs. Brownell on May 2, 1998," before or after the child's message. Most teachers would print the child's "mouses went in hole" as "mice went in the hole," which is minor editing. All teacher printing should be in printscript, using both uppercase and lowercase letters and proper punctuation.

When a child asks a teacher to print, the teacher stands behind the child and works over the child's

shoulder (when possible). This way the child sees the letters being formed in the correct position. If the teacher faces the child while printing, the child sees the letters upside down. Some teachers say the letter names as they print them.

Letters or names written for the child should be large enough for the child to distinguish the different forms—over one inch high. This may seem large to an adult (figure 16–22).

Some children will attempt printing and ask questions. Each center should clarify its staff responses to ensure that they are in agreement with the center's language arts program goals and to avoid confusion. The Appendix includes a phonetic guide to English alphabet letter pronunciation.

Some schools encourage teachers to print examples on lined paper if a child says, "Make an *a*" or "Write my name." Others suggest that teachers blend letter sounds as they print words. Many centers expect teachers to respond to the child's request through conversation and by searching for letters on alphabet charts. This encourages the child to make his or her own copy before the teacher automatically prints it.

Teacher techniques often depend on the circumstances of a particular situation and knowledge of the individual child. What works with one child may not work with the next child.

One technique common to all centers is supportive assistance and voiced appreciation of children's efforts. As Fields and Lee (1987) suggest, we can rejoice with a young child over approximations of intent in writing, just as we do with a toddler who makes an imprecise attempt to say a new word.

Children may show their printing attempts to the teacher or point out the names of letters they know. A positive statement to the child is appropriate: "Yes, that is an *a*" or "I can see the *a*, *t*, and *p*" (as the teacher points to each), or "Marie, you did print letters."

With these comments, the teacher encourages and recognizes the child's efforts. Often, the child may have the wrong name or form for a letter. The teacher can react by saying, "It looks like an alphabet letter. Let's go look at our alphabet and see which one."

Atkins (1984) describes supportive assistance in the following way:

> . . . children need . . . adults to provide the tools needed for writing and the time and opportunity to use those tools. They need adults to ensure an atmosphere conducive to exploration and to good feelings about writing. They need adults to accept what is written as worthwhile, and to appreciate the work and effort that goes into learning to write. And, children especially need adults who understand that the errors they make are an important part of the learning process.

The same acceptance and lack of correction on a teacher's part that was suggested with beginning speakers is appropriate for beginning writers. Encourage, welcome, and keep interest in print alive by providing attention. Children have many years ahead to perfect their skill; the most important thing at this early stage is that they are interested in the forms and are supplied with correct models and encouragement.

One technique is to have children who ask for letter forms trace over correct letter models or symbols. This can be done with crayons, felt pens, or other writing tools. To explain the meaning of the word *trace*, the teacher gives the child a demonstration.

When reading charts or books to children, a teacher may move his or her hand across the page beneath words. This is done to emphasize the left to right direction in reading and writing and separations between words. Introducing authors' names periodically helps children realize that they also can create stories, and what they create can be written.

Proponents of Vygotskian theory Bodrova and Leong (1996) suggest the following teacher actions:

- Encourage children to write to communicate even if they scribble. Then write teacher notes about what the child says the writing means or print beneath the work.
- Revisit children's writing and reprocess their ideas. Talk about what they might add.
- Incorporate writing into play. Dramatic play situations might use writing. Acting out stories with peers will also encourage the use of language and writing.

Print in Daily Life

As Fields (1987) has stated, children need to learn what print can do for them in satisfying personal needs. This means something to them; it makes print real. As Throne (1988) notes "children become aware of print by using it for real and meaningful purposes when they dictate and write stories, make signs for the block area, read names on a job chart, write messages, look for EXIT signs, follow recipes, or listen to stories." Children may need teacher assistance in recognizing the usefulness of written messages. Many instances of sending or reading print messages are possible during a school day.

Since print often protects one's safety, there are many opportunities to discuss and point out words that serve this function. Labels and trademarks on classroom items and printed instructions for using certain items offer opportunities for discussing print.

Print activities include dramatic play with themes that involve print and printing labels for many dramatic play props (figure 16–23). Also, Rich (1985) urges preschool teachers to encourage young children to start personal journals in which the children draw, dictate, and write (if able).

PLAY THEMES

Classroom Post Office

Suggested play items:

Stamps (many come with magazine advertisements), old letters, envelopes, boxes to wrap for mailing, scale, canceling stamp, tape, string, play money, mailbag, mailbox with slots, alphabet strips, writing table, felt pens, counter, postal-employee shirts, posters from post office, stamp-collector sheets, wet sponge, teacher-made chart that lists children by street address and zip codes, box with all children's names on printed individual strips, mailboxes for each child.

Taco Stand

Suggested play items:

Counter for customers, posted charts with prices and taco choices, play money, order pads, labeled baskets with colored paper taco items (including cheese, meat, lettuce, salsa, sour cream, avocado, shredded chicken, and onions), customer tables, trays, bell to ring for service, folded cards with numbers, receipt book for ordered tacos, plastic glasses and pitchers, cash register, napkins, tablecloth, plastic flowers in plastic vase, cook's jacket, waiter/waitress aprons, bus-person suit and cleaning supplies, taped ethnic music, plastic utensils, soft pencils or felt pens, line with clothespins to hang orders, paper plates.

A hamburger stand or pizza parlor are other possibilities.

Grocery Shopping

Suggested items:

Shopping-list paper, bookcase, pencils or felt pens, chart with cut magazine pictures or labels from canned goods or vegetables labeled in print by teacher for children to copy if they desire, empty food cartons and cans, plastic food, shopping cart, purse and wallet, play money, brown bags, cash register on box, dress-up clothes for customers and store clerks.

Letter-Writing Classroom Center
(for writing to relatives and friends)

PRINT-AWARENESS ACTIVITIES

Classroom Newspaper

Make a class newspaper. Print children's dictated news or creative language after sharing a local paper with them. Child drawings on ditto master can be duplicated. Add teacher and parent news, poems, captions, drawings, and so forth. Some children may wish to print their own messages. These may range from scribble to recognizable forms and words.

T-Shirt Autograph Day

Each parent is asked to bring an old T-shirt (any size) to school for T-shirt autograph day. Permanent felt markers are used by children under teacher supervision. (Washable markers can also be used, but teachers must iron or put T-shirts in a clothes dryer for five minutes on a hot setting.) T-shirt forms are necessary, and can be made of cardboard. Material must be stretched over form so marks can be added easily. It is a good idea to have children wear plastic paint aprons to protect clothing from permanent markers. Children are free to autograph shirts in any manner they please. A display of T-shirts with writing usually prompts some children to add letters to their own shirts. Most teachers own or can borrow T-shirts with writing.

FIGURE 16–23 Dramatic play themes and activities that promote print awareness and use

Teachers look for functional activities such as:

- Making classroom area rule signs with children. Example: "Return blocks to shelves" and "Park bikes here"
- Making necessary lists of children's names with children. Example: A waiting list
- Making holiday or special occasion cards.
- Making group murals and labeling parts at a later date. Example: Color words or children's ideas (Jane says, "This looks like a cat.")
- Writing what-we-found-out activities. Can be done with many discovery experiences. Example: What floats and what does not?
- Classifying experiences. Example: "Shoes Are Different"—Teacher elicits from the group the kinds of shoes children see others wearing, then lists the names.

Red shoes	Shoes with laces	Sandals
Tony	Becky	Micki
Tonelle	Trent	Nekolla
Star	Tony	Blair
	Ann	

Making classroom news announcements on a large sheet of paper posted at children's eye level is another idea. Examples follow:

- Enrico moved to a new apartment.
- Mrs. Quan is on a trip to Chicago.
- Lia's cat had three kittens.
- Ali is our new friend's name.
- Blue flowers are blooming in the patio.
- Where is our Elmo doll hiding?
- Alonzo is home sick today.

Some preschool classrooms encourage children to write notes by devising mailbox systems or by using stick-on notes on children's lockers. Notes dictated by children can be for parents, school staff, peers, visitors, and so on.

Writing Table or Area

Teachers such as Ballenger (1996) include a writing table or area for children's daily free-choice exploration. Stocked with different paper types, a variety of writing instruments, alphabet letter stencils, letter stamps, and letter model displays, this type of setup makes daily access available and inviting. Ballenger, who works with Haitian preschoolers, found the whole class interested in this type of learning center.

Respecting "I'll Do It My Way!"

Recognizing children need time as well as opportunity, teachers notice individual children involve themselves in classroom literacy events based on their maturity and interest. When a child senses a reason and develops a personal interest in writing or reading, he or she acts on his or her own time table. There seems to exist at this point a desire to proceed his or her own way, retaining ownership for emerging literacy behaviors. The child who examines a classroom alphabet chart and then copies letter forms may choose to share his or her marks with other children and avoid the teacher. Another child the same age may prefer to consult the teacher and show his or her efforts. Other children may ask, "What's this say?" or "What's this called?" In all situations, teachers aim to preserve and promote each child's idea of his or her own competency as a writer or reader.

Left-Handed Children

Left-handedness or right-handedness occurs as the child's nervous system matures. Preschool teachers notice hand preferences when children use writing tools. Some children seem to switch between hands as though hand preference hasn't been established. Most left-handers uses their right hands more often than right-handers use their left hands. Writing surfaces in preschools should accommodate all children. Preschools purchase both right-handed and left-handed scissors.

Teachers should accept hand preference without attempting to change or even point out a natural choice. Seating left-handed children at the ends of tables when possible during activities or making sure left-handers are not crowded against right-handers is a prudent course of action.

PRACTICING AND PROMOTING PRINT AWARENESS

Printscript should come automatically to the teacher. Practice is in order if one cannot easily and correctly print the entire alphabet in both uppercase and lowercase. Before practicing, obtain a local printscript guide from a neighboring elementary school.

To promote interest in printscript or symbols, a teacher can:

- Make labels for familiar objects.
- Make signs that fit in with child's play:
  John and Jerry's Service Station
  Quiet Please
  Don't Walk on the Grass
  Cookies for Sale
- Create wall displays with words.
- Make alphabet charts.
- Make charts with words (figure 16–24).
- Make alphabet and number games.
- Make word games.
- Print stories of children's experiences, as children tell them (figure 16–25).
- Point out words in the environment.
- Point out symbols in the environment.
- Print children's names on artwork.
- Supply scrap paper and a variety of writing tools.
- Make table chalkboards.
- Cut letters in colorful felt, cloth, sandpaper, and tagboard.

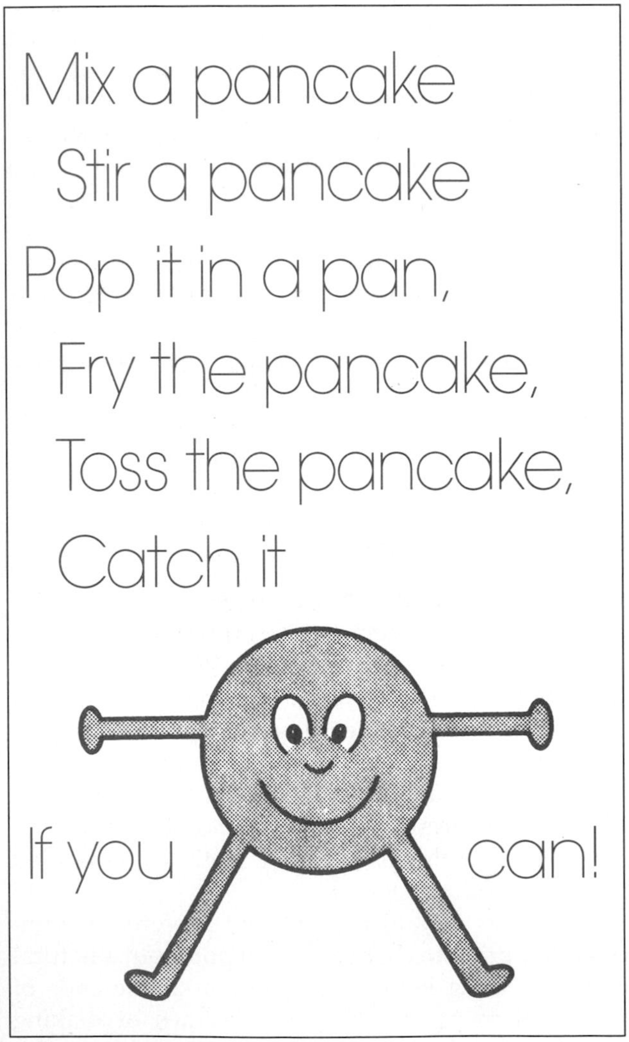

FIGURE 16–24 Poetry chart

The Picnic

We had lunch
in the park.
We sat
on the grass.

FIGURE 16–25 Experience chart

- Help children make their own creative or informative books.
- Make clever name tags.
- Make giant alphabet letters.
- Have children dictate captions for their own photographs.
- Send written messages to children and staff.

Lined Paper

Some children acquire the necessary motor control and can use lined, printed paper (figure 16–26).

Lines can easily be drawn on a chalkboard by the teacher. This provides a large working surface and an opportunity for children to make large-size letters.

FIGURE 16–26 Example of a five-year-old's printing accompanying art. Notice the child's difficulty in placing letter forms on the lines. *(Courtesy of Scott Tracy.)*

Chart Ideas

Printscript can be added to playrooms by posting charts that have been made by the teacher. Charts can be designed to encourage the child's active involvement. Pockets, parts that move, or pieces that can be added or removed add extra interest. Charts made on heavy chart board or cardboard last longer. Clear contact paper can be used to seal the surface. Some ideas for charts include:

- color or number charts
- large clock with movable hands
- chart showing the four seasons
- picture story sequence charts
- calendar
- room task chart ("helpers chart")
- texture chart (for children to feel)
- poetry chart
- recipe chart using step-by-step illustrations
- classification or matching-concepts chart
- birthday charts
- height and weight chart
- alphabet chart
- rebus chart (figure 16–27)

Cromwell (1980) suggests making "key word" charts. Key words can be words inspired by a picture book title, character, etc.; words solicited from children; or words taken from some classroom event or happening. The chosen word is printed by the teacher at the top of a chart. The teacher then asks a small group, "When I say this word, what do you think of?" or "Salt and pepper go together. We see them in shakers sitting on the kitchen table. What goes with (key word)?" or "Tree is the word at the top of our chart. What can we say about the trees in our play yard?" or some such leading question. Children's offered answers are put below the key word on the chart. This activity suits some older four-year-olds, especially those asking "What does this say?" while pointing to text.

Charts of songs or rhymes in the native languages of attending children have been used successfully in many classrooms. Parent volunteer translators are often pleased to help put new or favorite classics into their native tongue. *Uno, Dos, Tres, Inditos*, the Spanish translation of *Ten Little Indians*, has been frequently enjoyed and learned quickly.

Think of all the charts that can include a child's choice, vote, or decision! These charts are limitless. A child can indicate his or her individual selection

FIGURE 16–27   Rebus chart

under the diverse headings by making a mark, printing his or her name, using a rubber stamp and ink pad, or moving his or her printed name to a basket or pasting it onto the chart as shown below.

It's easy to see that placing pictures alongside print makes the task of choosing easier. Simple pictures drawn by the teacher work well. The best charts relate to classroom themes or happenings.

In making a chart, first draw sketches of the way words and pictures could be arranged. With a yardstick, lightly draw on guidelines with a pencil or use a chart liner. Then, printscript words with a felt pen or dark crayon. Magazines, old elementary school workbooks, old children's books, and photographs are good sources for pictures on charts. Brads or paper fasteners can be used for movable parts. Book pockets or heavy envelopes provide a storage place for items to be added later to the chart.

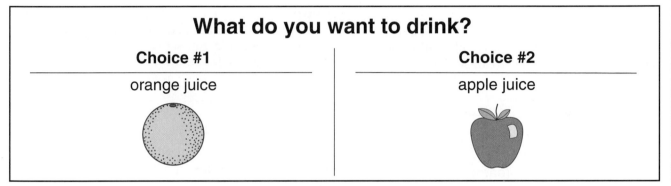

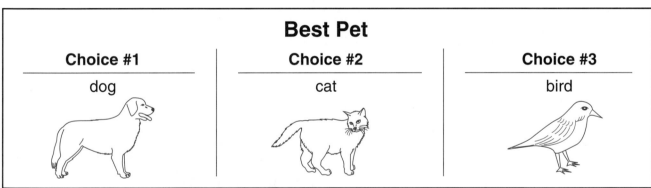

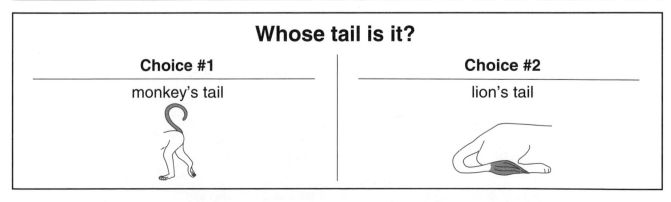

Experience Charts and Stories

The purpose of these charts is to have children recognize that spoken words can be put in written form.

Materials

large paper sheets (newsprint), felt pen or black crayon

Activity

After an interesting activity, such as a field trip, visit by a special speaker, party, celebration, or cooking experience, the teacher can suggest that a story be written about the experience. A large sheet of paper or chart sheet is hung within the children's view, and the children dictate what happened. The teacher prints on the sheet, helping children sort out what happened first, next, and last.

Figures 16–28 and 16–29 show examples of other word and picture charts.

Homemade chart stands can be made by teachers. Commercial chart holders, chart stands, and wing clamps are sold at school supply stores. The alphabet patterns in figure 16–30 are useful for teacher-made games, wall displays, and bulletin boards. Early childhood education students are urged to obtain a full set of lower- and uppercase alphabet letters for future use.

We listen with our (ears) of course.

But surely it is true

That (eyes)

and (lips)

And (hands)

and (feet)

Can help us listen, too.

FIGURE 16–28   Rebus listening chart

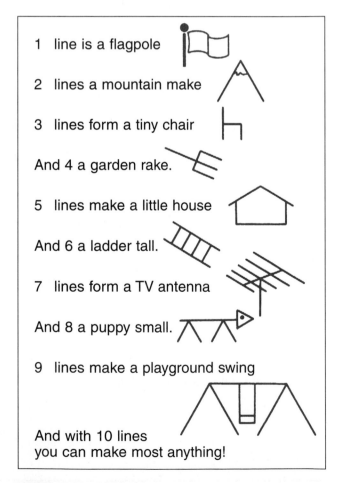

1   line is a flagpole

2   lines a mountain make

3   lines form a tiny chair

And 4 a garden rake.

5   lines make a little house

And 6 a ladder tall.

7   lines form a TV antenna

And 8 a puppy small.

9   lines make a playground swing

And with 10 lines you can make most anything!

FIGURE 16–29   Lines chart

FIGURE 16–30   These letters are about 2 inches high. They are useful patterns for games, wall displays, and bulletin boards. (Not all letters are included.)   *continues*

Chart Books

A number of books called chart or easel books are in print. These giant books are poster size and easily capture children's attention. The print stands out and can't be missed. Creative teachers have produced their own versions with the help of overhead projectors that enlarge smaller artwork. Chart paper or poster board is used. Two commercial big book titles are *Have You Seen Birds?* and *The New Baby Calf*, both published by Scholastic.

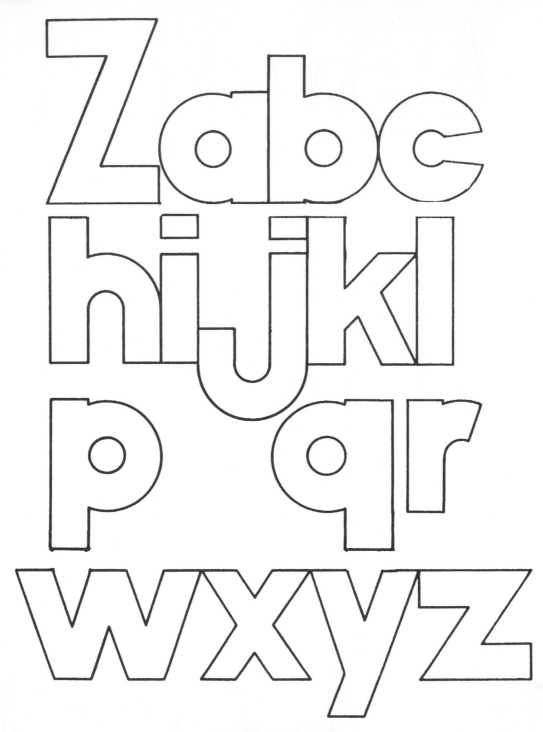

FIGURE 16–30   *continued*

Throne (1988), a kindergarten teacher, points out the benefit of using big books and charts: "... these shared experiences bring the benefits of the bedtime story situation into the classroom because the large, clear print allows the whole class to see the text as we read the story together." Although preschools prefer to use smaller child groups, Throne's comments concerning large, clear print and group sharing appeal to teachers interested in promoting print awareness.

Generating Story Sentences

Story sentence activities are similar to chart activities. A child or a small group of children becomes an author. After a classroom activity or experience, the teacher encourages generating a story (a written sentence). The activity is child centered thereafter, with the teacher printing what the child or group suggests. The teacher can use a hand-wide space between words to emphasize the end of one word and spacing between words, and may talk about letters or letter sounds found at the beginning or end of children's names. It is not unusual for all children in a four-year-old group to recognize all the names of other students in their class. Individual children's ideas and contributions are accepted, appreciated, and recognized by the teacher, and generated sentences are read and reread with the group. Long strips of chart paper or rolled paper can be utilized. Story sentences are posted at children's eye level.

See Appendix for additional teacher-created printscript activities.

Parent Communication

A conversation with or note to the parents of a child who has asked about or started printing can include the following:

- The teacher has noticed the child's interest in printing alphabet letters, numerals, and/or words.

- The teacher is including a printscript and numeral guide for parents who wish to show their children the letter forms at home.
- The early childhood center encourages printing attempts but does not try to teach printscript to every child. Many children are not interested, and others would find it too difficult at their present developmental level.
- A parent can help by having paper and writing tools for the child at home and by noticing and giving attention to the child when he or she comes to the parent with written letters.
- Children who start printing early often write letters and numerals in their paintings. The printing may be backwards, upside down, or sideways; this is to be expected. (Many parents worry unnecessarily when this is noticed.)

Centers plan parent meetings for joint discussion of the appropriateness of printing instruction during preschool years. Directors encounter well-meaning but anxious parents who want their children to learn the alphabet and learn to print. Some parents feel that neglecting this area will place their children at a disadvantage. If the center's position is clear, staff members will be able to give articulate answers concerning the center's programming. Most parents are responsive when teachers explain to them that the primary goal is to enhance their children's self-concept and that it is pointless to teach children the alphabet if the only purpose served is pleasing adults. The assurance teachers give parents that they will provide both basic experiences and opportunities on an individual basis most often satisfies the parents' need to know that the school cares about each child's progress.

Summary

The alphabet and printed words are part of preschool life. A center's goals rarely include teaching all attending children to print, but instead attempt to offer a print-rich environment. For the great majority of preschool children attending child centers, sit-down practice of letter forms is developmentally inappropriate. Some preschool children, on the other hand, will attempt repeatedly to form alphabet letters and practice writing them on their own or with the teacher's supportive guidance. Many children will, however, show beginning interest in the uses of print and print in books.

Numerals are also interesting to young children. These symbols appear daily at school, home, and in the neighborhood. Guides for forming numerals and letters of the alphabet can be obtained from local schools. These guides may vary slightly from city to city.

The ability to print depends on the child's:

- muscle control
- skill in recognizing symbols
- ability to note the placement of lines in a symbol

Printscript is used in preschool, kindergarten, and first grade. Letters are formed with lines and circles in uppercase and lowercase symbols.

Children are ready for printing at different ages. They learn alphabet letters at different rates. Printscript is used for labeling, display, and other activities at early childhood centers.

Equipment and settings for giving children an opportunity to explore printing are available in a childhood center. Materials are arranged within reach. Printing seen on wall displays and charts helps motivate interest.

Printscript is used in a variety of ways. The most common is in planned activities and labeling artwork. A name or sentence should start in the upper left-hand corner and move toward the right.

Teachers need to examine printscript closely and practice so that good models can be supplied. It is also important to encourage children and to recognize their efforts, even if they cannot make correct forms.

Parents should be alerted to children's printing attempts and to the center's policy and practices concerning this language arts skill.

STUDENT ACTIVITIES

1. Observe a morning program for four-year-olds. Cite as many examples as possible of adults' use of written communication and all child exposure to print.

2. Expand the following statement: Practicing alphabet letter formation when a teacher requests it could result in the child's. . . .

3. Without turning back to review the printed alphabet guide given in this unit, print the alphabet in both uppercase and lowercase letters.

4. Obtain a printscript alphabet from the nearest public school. With a red crayon or pen, circle letters that differ (even slightly) from your attempted alphabet. Print all letters you circled on remaining lines using proper form.

5. Observe a preschool program. Notice and list all written forms found in the playroom that are within the children's view. Report the findings to classmates.

6. Find some examples of young children's attempts to make letters and numerals in their drawings. What do you notice about the symbols? Are the lines large, small, slanted, or straight? Are capitals or small letters used? What else do you notice?

7. Take tracing paper to a four-year-old's classroom. Trace examples of child printing (writing) and bring to your next class period. (Talk to your instructor first concerning making school visits and appointments.)

8. Use the following checklist to observe a four-year-old or five-year-old child. Interview the child's teacher for items you were unable to determine. (*Note:* Make sure the teacher knows that this is not a test but an instrument to make you aware of children's emerging abilities.)

Checklist of Print Interest and Understandings

Rate each item as follows. Y = Most of the time
                              S = Sometimes
                              H = Hasn't attempted as yet
                              U = Unable to determine

The child:

_____ Sits through a book reading and enjoys it.

_____ Asks for a book's rereading.

_____ "Reads" parts or lines of a book to another from memory.

_____ Shows an interest in alphabet letters.

_____ Shows an interest in books or environmental print.

_____ Reads children's name tags or signs.

_____ Puts alphabet letters in artwork.

_____ Knows when words are skipped in favorite books.

_____ Plays with marking tools.

_____ Shares written letters or words with others.

_____ Points to print in the work of others.

_____ Wants name and/or labels on work.

_____ Wants to write own name on work.

_____ Knows that print says something.

_____ Produces a row of symbols.

_____ Attempts to copy symbols, letters, or words.

_____ Reads symbols he or she has written.

_____ Invents spellings.

_____ Discusses a use of print.

_____ Knows print can be read.

_____ Wants his or her talk written down.

_____ Recognizes individual alphabet letters.

_____ Recognizes words that start with the same letter.

_____ Can read some environmental signs.

_____ Follows along in chart activities.

_____ Looks at books while alone.

_____ Has an active interest in something else that then gives a low priority to literary activities.

_____ Which statement best describes this child?
   a. Yet to develop an interest in print.
   b. A possible interest is developing.
   c. Has about the same degree of interest as others his or her age.
   d. Has a fairly strong interest.
   e. Has a continual interest that has led to experimentation and printing attempts.
   f. Is very interested in some other area that takes up his or her time and energy.
   g. Prints almost daily and has invented spellings or spells many words correctly.

9. Obtain an order catalog from a preschool supply store or company. Most companies will send the catalogs free of charge. Professional magazines such as _Young Children, Pre-K Today, Instructor, Early Years_, and _Scholastic Teacher_ are good sources for finding supply-catalog addresses. Make a list of any pieces of equipment or supply items that could be used to promote printing.

10. Watch the children's use of crayons or other writing tools. Take notes. Make observations about the following:
    a. Time spent with marking tools.
    b. Manner used (for example, how do the children hold the crayons?).
    c. Do they have good control of both paper and marking tool?

11. Place a pile of paper and two or three felt pens in bright colors on a table. (Pencils are not used often because of safety considerations and the need for sharpening.) Supervise the activity closely—let only two or three children work at a time. Make a waiting list. Then give each interested child a turn. How many of the children tried to make letters? How many said "yes" when you asked them if they wanted you to add their names to their papers?

12. Make chart paper or tag board patterns similar to those in figure 16–30 for the full uppercase and lowercase alphabet. Teacher supply stores and practicing teachers are good resources.

13. Bring an alphabet book to class to share with peers.

14. Use the alphabet book _Letters are Lost_ by L. C. Ernst, 1996, NY: Viking with a group of four year olds. Report happenings to class.

CHAPTER REVIEW

A. Select the correct answer. Most questions have more than one answer.

1. Child-care programs
   a. teach all children to print.
   b. try to teach correct printscript form.
   c. all teach the same printscript form.
   d. help children with printing attempts.

2. Small-muscle control
   a. comes after large-muscle control.
   b. depends on many factors.
   c. is difficult for some preschoolers.
   d. is the only thing involved in learning to print.

3. If drawings have upside-down alphabet letters, teachers should
   a. immediately begin printing lessons.
   b. know that the child may be interested in activities with printed forms.
   c. quickly tell the child that the letters are upside down.
   d. worry about the child's ability to form the letters perfectly.

4. A child's readiness to print may depend on his or her
   a. ability to gather information from his or her senses.
   b. knowledge that letters are formed by placing lines.
   c. home and family.
   d. feelings for the teacher.

B. Place the following in the order in which they occur.

1. a. small-muscle control
   b. large-muscle control
   c. control of fingers

2. a. child makes letters
   b. child makes scribbles
   c. child makes circles

3. a. teacher shows child how to make a *Y*
   b. child knows the name of the letter *Y*
   c. child says, "Teacher, make a *Y* on my paper."

4. a. child tries to write
   b. child sees parent writing
   c. child prints the letter *b*

5. a. child prints letters in artwork
   b. teacher notices and encourages
   c. child knows the names of all the letters in the alphabet

C. Answer the following questions.

1. What are some possible reasons that children ages two to five years may start to print?

2. Give examples of preschool equipment that promotes small-muscle and finger control.

3. What should teachers consider about the printscript form they use?

4. Why are some preschoolers not interested in letters?

5. Muscle control is only part of learning to write. Name other factors that affect readiness for written communication.

6. When a child says, "Is this M?" how should one reply?

7. If a child is not interested in printing, what should be done?

8. If a child says a *b* is an *f*, what might a teacher say?

D. Describe a print-rich classroom.

E. List stages in print awareness that precede invented spelling attempts.

F. Answer the following questions.

1. If a child goes to a teacher to show letters he or she has drawn, how should the teacher react?

2. If two children are arguing over the name of a letter, how should the teacher handle the situation?

3. List three ways a teacher can use printscript during the school day.

G. Print the printscript (or D'Nealian) alphabet in both uppercase and lowercase letters. Also print the numerals 1 through 10.

H. Referring to figure 16–31, list all of the things the teacher might have done to encourage the children's attempts.

FIGURE 16–31

I.   Select the correct answer. All have more than one answer.

1. When a child's first name is to be printed on his or her work, it should be
   a. in the center on top.
   b. in the upper right-hand corner.
   c. in the upper left-hand corner.
   d. done with an uppercase first letter and then lowercase letters.

2. The size of the printscript used with young children
   a. doesn't really matter.
   b. should be large enough to see.
   c. can be of any size.
   d. should be at least two inches high.

3. The teacher who does not know how to form printscript letters can
   a. practice.
   b. use an individual style.
   c. get a copy from an elementary school.
   d. write instead.

J.   Print your full name and address in printscript.

K.   A note to the parents of a child who is interested in learning to print should include what kind of information? State four points that should be included.

L.   Describe your handling of the following situations:

1. Mrs. Mason (parent) insists her child must learn to print because her child's friend has learned.

2. Betsy never wants her name written on her artwork.

3. Chris says, "My *a* is better than Sam's, huh, teacher?"

RESOURCE

Ballenger, C. (1996). Learning the ABCs in a Haitian preschool: A teacher's story. *Language Arts*, 73(5), 317–323.

READING

A Language Art

CHAPTER 17

Reading and Preschoolers

OBJECTIVES	After studying this chapter, you should be able to:
	■ describe reading skills.
	■ list three methods used to teach reading.
	■ discuss the early childhood teacher's role in reading.

At one time, it was thought that there was a magic age when all children became ready for "sit-down" reading instruction. Now it is believed that early childhood teachers at every level must be considered teachers of reading, even if they do not offer formal reading instruction (Saracho and Spodek, 1993). Research and theory suggest that teachers of young children need to be actively engaged in providing experiences that will build children's language and eventually lead children to become readers. These experiences are deemed appropriate if they match the individual child's level of language development and promote new competence in oral and written language.

A wide range of age-appropriate activities involving understanding oral language, awareness of print, intimate experiences with picture books, dramatization, listening, musical activities, and diverse kinds of language arts activities discussed in this text promote emergent literacy and prepare children for the discovery of reading.

Some children who are in early childhood centers and kindergartens can read. Some have picked up the skill on their own; others have spent time with an older brother or sister, parents, or others. Although reading is considered the fourth language art, this chapter does not intend to suggest reading instruc-

tion for groups of young children or even encourage formal instruction for those 1% to 5% of children who can read words during preschool years.

The proportion of students of color projected for the twenty-first century is one-third of the U.S. school population, with many inner-city schools having well over 50% minority populations (Bartoli, 1995). One out of every four children is expected to live in poverty. Learning to read may be an increasing problem for many of these children. Early childhood centers will have to step up efforts to increase child literacy. Walberg (1996) believes elementary schools already have much better prepared students in their kindergartens. He attributes increased child verbalness to preschool attendance along with other factors. Many early childhood centers offer children the opportunity to learn the alphabet and other language skills. Walberg notes preschool ability tests that predominately test vocabulary and verbal items are the best predictors of reading success when formal instruction begins.

Reading

The language arts approach and whole-language approach to reading consider reading as one part of the communication process. The language arts are interrelated—not separate, isolated skills. The teacher is responsible for showing the relationship between the various areas of language arts. In other words, the goal is to help children understand that communication is a whole process in which speaking, listening, written symbols, and the reading of those symbols are closely connected (figure 17–1).

In the past, the logical connection between listening, speaking, written words, and reading was overlooked. The subjects were often taught as separate skills, and the natural connection between each area was not clear to children. In a language arts, whole-language, or natural approach, the connection (the way these areas fit together) is emphasized.

The preschool teacher realizes that certain skills and abilities appear in children before others. Barone (1994) studied the literacy development of a group of four- and five-year-old children exposed prenatally to maternal drug use (figures 17–2 and 17–3). She considered the children's literacy development

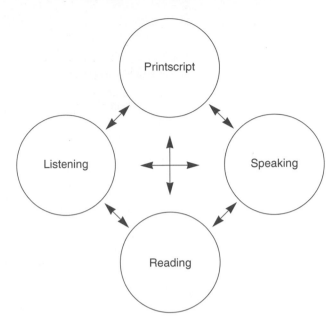

FIGURE 17–1   The four language arts are interrelated and interdependent.

	Name	Book Concepts	Reading	Orthographic Knowledge	Concept/Word
Jose	tight scribble	aware of book organization	retells/oral & book connected	not aware of letters	no/focus on illustration
Jamal	beginning letter/ unable to make letters	aware of book organization	only listens to stories when story-telling strategy used	not aware of letters	no/focus on illustration
Anna	yes	aware of book organization	retells/oral & book connected	aware of letters in name	pointing synchronized to rhythm not to words
Mark	yes	aware of book organization	retells/oral & book connected	aware of letters in name	aware of words/not able to track
Billy	yes	aware of book organization	retells/oral & book connected memorizes predictable text	initial consonants semiphonemic	rudimentary
Jennifer	yes	aware of book organization	retells/oral & book connected	initial consonants semiphonemic	rudimentary

FIGURE 17–2   Four-year-olds literacy summary, "Getting the Idea of Reading and Writing" *(From "The Importance of classroom context: Literacy development of children prenatally exposed to crack cocaine," by D. Barone, 1994,* Research in the Teaching of English, 28(3), *pp. 286–312. Copyright 1994 by the National Council of Teachers of English. Reprinted with permission.)*

	Name	Book Concepts	Reading	Orthographic Knowledge	Concept/Word
"Getting the Idea of Reading and Writing"					
Mario	yes	aware of book organization	retells/prefers book language	initial consonants semiphonemic	track/not pointing to words
Donette	yes	aware of book organization not aware of word	retells/prefers book language	initial consonants semiphonemic	track/not pointing to words
Melisha	initial letter then circles	beginning/end top/bottom sequence of pages	retells/oral & book language	initial consonants semiphonemic	track/not pointing to words
Melina	yes	aware of book organization	retells/oral & book language predictable	initial consonants semiphonemic	rudimentary
"Beginning Readers and Writers"					
Ray	yes	aware of book organization	fluent non-predictable text/word X word	letter-name	full
Curtis	yes	aware of book organization	fluent non-predictable text/word X word	letter-name	full
Josh	yes	aware of book organization	fluent non-predictable text/word X word	letter-name	full

FIGURE 17–3   Five-year-olds literacy summary, "Getting the Idea of Reading and Writing" and "Beginning Readers and Writers" *(From "The Importance of classroom context: Literacy development of children prenatally exposed to crack cocaine," by D. Barone, 1994, Research in the Teaching of English, 28(3), pp. 286–312. Copyright 1994 by the National Council of Teachers of English. Reprinted with permission.)*

as appropriate and similar to unexposed four- and five-year-old children.

Early learning in listening and speaking serve as beginnings for further language and communication. Children's beginning ideas about print, writing, and reading form concurrently, and children may display understanding and skill in all these areas.

Activities with young children can move easily from listening, speaking, seeing, or using printscript to beginning reading attempts: from passive to active participation. It is not uncommon for preschool youngsters to be able to read most of the names of the children in their group after being exposed to the daily use of name tags.

Current Thinking Concerning Early Reading Instruction

Professional literature currently urges preschool teachers to use an integrated approach to language arts. Concerns over national literacy have promoted study and discussion. Most experts recommend a literature-based program for both elementary school and preschool. Ideal classrooms are described as "language rich" or "literacy developing," allowing for a preschool child's discovery of reading. Key ideas presently stress instruction offered in meaningful contexts with children developing strategies to achieve skills they view as useful to them.

Many researchers agree early school experiences play a crucial role in the child's future literacy development (Purcell-Gates, 1995). Goodman and King (1995) point out that children tend to hold implicit language knowledge and learn best by discovering strategies for themselves. They believe teachers should explore effective ways to facilitate language learning by involving children in authentic language uses so that they discover the processes and strategies for themselves. Some preschools have focused on reading mechanics (bits and pieces of the reading process), including practicing individual alphabet letter names, sounds, or phoneme sounds. This is felt to be confusing and unwise.

Sulzby (1992) has given a clear explanation of prior ideas concerning reading readiness and newer emergent literacy theory:

> From a reading readiness perspective, reading meant an accurate reproduction of the printed words on a page of conventionally spelled words. . . . Prior to that, the child was a prereader learning the necessary precursors to real reading.

and

> The precursors of conventional reading and writing are different under the emergent literary perspective. They are emergent behaviors and concepts of reading and writing themselves. Examples are children "reading" from books by looking at the pictures or scribbling letters to grandparents.

Early childhood professionals want to make sure that their programs of activities offer the best in children's literature, not watered-down versions of classics. There is thought to be both older and contemporary literature and language-related activities that have depth, meaning, and linguistic charm that preschoolers should encounter. Meaning and comprehension are aided by discussion and familiarity and can be guided by sensitive teachers who also monitor the appropriateness of what is offered.

Pressure for Formal Reading Instruction in Preschools

John Rosemond (1988) discusses why he believes young children are having reading skills pushed at them in preschool:

> First, it makes parents proud as peacocks to have a three- and four-year-old offspring who can perform the ABCs and other academic trivia.

> Second, a group of preschoolers sitting at a table coloring mimeographed letters and numbers is easier to manage than a group of preschoolers acting like real preschoolers. The issue isn't learning. It's ego and effort, too much of one and not enough of the other.

Research undertaken by Durkin (1966) and subsequent studies by many others cite instances of young children reading before kindergarten. Some parents and educators intrigued by this idea have attempted formal, sit-down instruction with three- and four-year-olds. Cullinan (1977) explains the error of this plan of action:

> . . . a major fallacy in basing programs on early reading studies is that children who learned to read early did not do so from exposure to formal reading instruction. Findings show that children who learned to read early were the ones who were read to, who showed interest in paper and pencil activities, and who were interested in visual distinctions in signs and labels. Their families valued reading as an activity. Someone answered their questions. Children learned messages encoded in writing can be decoded, or read, and that letters represented sounds used in speaking.

In other words, typically children who learned to read while quite young did so by discovering decoding on their own in responsive, literacy-rich family situations.

As Throne (1988) notes, in the last one or two decades, pressures have contributed to the teaching of reading in a more formal, less contextural, less meaningful way. Starting formal academics too early may do more harm than good, Elkind (1988) believes. He points out formal reading instruction in Denmark, where illiteracy rates are very low, is delayed until age seven.

Both Gallagher and Coche (1987) and Piaget and Inheldder (1969) fear that concentrating on early reading-skill instruction may reduce time for play and take away symbolic enrichment time. Play provides the interaction of imagery, imitation, and language, which builds a foundation necessary for learning to read.

All of the pressure preschool teachers feel to begin formal reading instruction grates against the belief system of most early childhood educators (Winn, 1981). Many react to the tragedy of finding an increasing number of children in preschools with purple worksheets to complete before they can play (Manning and Manning, 1983). Researchers have yet to find that early reading instruction is advantageous or better than later instruction. Kelly (1985) voices an opinion and observation that many educators feel is valid:

> Studies show that children who are pushed to read early may not be such avid readers when they're older—which is when it matters—while their classmates who started slower may read often and spontaneously.

Jewell and Zintz (1986) have a position on the teaching of reading that many early childhood professionals endorse:

> There are some four-year-olds interested in mastering print—and they do read. More five-year-olds do, too. Traditionally we have "pushed" reading for six-year-olds, and many have, indeed, learned to read. But there are likely as many seven-year-olds who need to grow into reading more slowly as there are five-year-olds who read early. And a few may not be curious about print until age eight. The school must provide for all children across the range of readiness for reading.

Teacher Awareness of Child Interest and Understanding

Each child will probably hold a totally different view concerning reading (figure 17–4). Possible understandings a preschooler may have include:

- pictures and text have different functions
- print contains the story
- the words the reader says come from the pictures
- stories tend to have some predictable segments and features
- it is possible to write messages
- there are words, and written words are made up of letters
- letters are arranged from left to right
- letters appear in linear fashion to represent the sequence of sounds in spoken words
- spaces delineate word boundaries
- letters come in capitals, in small print, and even in script, but they all have the same significance
- some marks are used to show beginnings and ends of text

The ability to read is present if the child understands and acts appropriately when he or she sees a printed word. In other words, the child must be able to understand the concept that (1) all "things"

FIGURE 17–4 An interest in books can lead to an interest in printed words.

have a name, (2) the name of the thing can be a written word, (3) the two are interchangeable, and (4) the "word symbols" can be read.

Most teachers have had children "read" to them from a favorite, memorized storybook. Generally, a word from the book will not be recognized out of context and read by the child when seen elsewhere. But this behavior, imitative reading, can be an indication of emerging literacy development.

A child may develop the ability to recognize words because of an interest in printing letters. Another child may pick up the sounds of alphabet letters by listening and finding words that start with the same letter. Books and stories can also lead children into early interest and recognition of words (figure 17–5). Some children have the ability to distinguish one word from another word by sight and can easily remember words.

Early readers are children who have a desire to read. They also have had interactions with others who have answered their questions and stimulated their interest. A few children will read between the ages of four and five, but many will not have the capability or interest to read until a later age. Kelly (1985) estimates that only one to three preschoolers out of a hundred can read simple books. A teacher should be aware of each child's capabilities. Fields (1996) reminds teachers that reading pictures is beginning reading. In daily observations and verbal conversations, a child's responses give valuable clues. The wrong answers are as important as the right ones.

The following listing has been identified by Jewell and Zintz (1986) as discernible stages in the child's reading behavior during adult-child reading times:

- listens and looks
- requests repeated readings of favorite books
- corrects adult if a page is skipped
- reads to himself or herself, a doll, or other
- memorizes and reproduces by looking at illustrations (meaning is remembered before exact words)
- supplies words, if adult hesitates, by predicting and/or anticipating events in new books
- identifies specific words

FIGURE 17–5 The child's face reveals her feelings toward the book.

- asks what words say
- repeats phrases and sentences adult reads
- reads most words (adult fills in others)

Unfortunately, few early childhood specialists have been trained to assess reading readiness or teach beginning reading in a manner suited to the developmental level of very young children (Goetz, 1979). Early childhood teachers looking for indicators to identify children who possess "readiness" need to realize that simple recognition of a few sight words is only one area of skill. A more complete listing is outlined by Emery (1975).

The following are Emery's "primary indicators":

- oral vocabulary
- reading curiosity

- auditory discrimination as it relates to clear speech and learning letter sounds
- visual discrimination of letters

Emery's "secondary indicators" include:

- attention
- compliance
- memory as it relates to the general idea of a story
- understanding concepts such as top/bottom, up/down, open/closed, and so forth
- writing in terms of copying straight lines, circles, and so forth
- page turning

Kindergarten teachers facing a wide range of enrolled children's language arts abilities often attempt to assess children's progress in letter identification, phonemic awareness (sound/symbol relationships), sight words, concepts of words, and printing skill. Informal testing is commonplace. Some common informal testing probes and questions follow:

1. Cards with an upper- and lowercase printscript alphabet are displayed one by one.

   "What alphabet letter do you see?"

   "Can you tell me the sound it makes?"

   "Do you know a word that starts with this letter?"

2. The child is given paper and pencil.

   "Please write alphabet letters you know."

   "Tell me about the letters you've written."

3. "Write all the words you know."

   "Can you write your name?"

4. The child is presented a list of common sight words.

   "Do you know any of these words?"

Individualized activities can become an easier task when assessment data has been gathered. Clay (1991) points out what children are doing when they try to read:

> . . . within the directional constraints of the printer's code, language and visual perception responses are purposefully directed

by the reader in some integrated way to the problem of extracting meaning from cues in a text in sequence, so that the reader brings a maximum of understanding to the author's message.

Cambourne (1988) has identified "reading-like" child behaviors, which follow:

1. Recreating text from memory, turning pages randomly.

2. Recreating a text from pictures only. Each picture represents a complete text—no continuity of story line.

3. Same as 1 and 2, with a continuous story line that may or may not match the text in the book.

4. Recreating text from memory, running eyes and/or finger over text but not one-to-one matching of print with meaning.

5. Just turning pages, frontwards and backwards, but obviously engaging with pictures.

6. Sitting next to someone else engaged in behaviors 1 through 5 and sometimes collaborating with or intervening in other's reading-like behavior.

Child Knowledge of Alphabet Letters

In comparing two children, one who knows the alphabet and reads a few words and one who crudely writes his or her own name and makes up barely understandable stories, one may conclude that the first child is bright. However, creativity and logic are important in literacy development, and the second child may be outdistancing the first by progressing at his or her own speed. Literacy at any age is more than merely naming letters or words.

Because of the work of Lomax and McGee (1987) and others, a child's ability to name alphabet letters has been viewed as an indication of the child's ease in learning to read words. Others like Mason (1980) suggest it is other knowledge that is learned along with the ability to name letters that is crucial. Smolkin and Yaden (1992) have attempted to pinpoint the "other information" young children may acquire with repetitive parent-child readings of picture books. They suggest parents who support and guide their child's efforts help children:

> ... gain access to virtually all the ways texts will be used during the many years of schooling that lie ahead: linking text to text, acquiring additional word meanings, relying on prior knowledge to help a text make sense, creating inferences based on information presented by a book, using the structure that a book supplies to supply a reading of that book, and knowing that someone may test the reader on the knowledge being constructed during a reading. In our estimation, these are the ways in which "letter learning" becomes a predictor of reading success in school: this is the "other knowledge" that is crucial to literacy learning.

Children who are permitted and encouraged to discuss book and text features have greater opportunities to assemble a full knowledge of how people use books (Smolkin and Yaden, 1992).

Word Recognition

The typical four-year-old relies on idiosyncratic cues to identify words rather than intuitively making use of letter sounds (Mason, Herman, Au, 1992). For example, when name tags are used with different types of stickers accompanying different child's names, the sticker is usually read (recognized) rather than the print.

A Closer Look at Early Readers

Researchers studying both gifted children and early readers notice that parents overwhelmingly report that they have read to their children from birth on or from the time the children learned to sit up. As Strickland (1982) points out, research shows that early readers who learned to read without systematic instruction had one common experience, despite their different backgrounds. They were all introduced to books between the ages of three and five. A study (Anbar, 1986) of

TYPE OF ACTIVITY	FREQUENCY OF REPORT
Daily readings with pointing at words	6/6
Showing words in magazines	2/6
Teaching names of letters	6/6
Teaching sight vocabulary	5/6
Making rhymes with words	5/6
Playing letter games	6/6
Helping learn sounds of letters	6/6
Helping put words together	6/6
Playing spelling games	6/6
Playing add-a-letter games	1/6
Listening to child read aloud	5/6
Having child read after parent	1/6
Doing alternate reading	2/6
Working on sounding out words	2/6
Providing books on an appropriate level	3/6

FIGURE 17–6 Six parents' reading activities with their children *(From* Early Childhood Research Quarterly 1, *Ablex Publishing Corporation.)*

activities mentioned by the parents of early readers is shown in figure 17–6. Usually, someone reads aloud to those children on a regular basis. Elkind (1988) notes "a Gallup survey of people who have attained eminence makes it very clear that parents of gifted children did not impose their learning priorities upon their young offspring. They followed the child's lead, emphasizing play and a rich, stimulating environment rather than formal instruction."

Studies of the early reader indicate that the child was usually exposed to a wide variety of reading material and enjoyed watching educational television, spending close to equal time in both pursuits (Schnur, Lowrey, and Brazell, 1985). An interest in print characterizes precocious readers, and their parents are described as responsive—noticing child interests and providing help when asked. Lots of child-centered family activities were part of the early reader's family life-style. These children seemed fascinated and obsessed with the alphabet, and parents reported that they answered questions, read to the child, and engaged in play activities with letters and words but had not set out with a systematic plan to teach reading (Salzer, 1985).

Anbar (1986) in completing a study of early readers has identified possible stages in these children's learning process (figure 17–7).

If we could examine parent-child storybook readings closely, simply reading aloud doesn't describe most parent actions accurately. Pointing out book features, relating book happenings to shared family experiences, defining words, turn-taking dialogue, prompting children's identification and naming of illustrations, listening to children's memorized "readings," and other parental interactions are all part of the experience. Educators use the same techniques.

What should happen when a child expects to learn to read the first day of school or kindergarten? Clement and Warncke (1995) suggest:

Stage I	A preliminary period of gaining awareness and general knowledge of books and print (starting any time during the first year)
Stage II	Learning to identify and name the letters and acquiring beginning sight vocabulary (starting around 12–18 months)
Stage III	Learning the sounds of the letters (starting around 20–24 months)
Stage IV	Putting together words (starting around 24–32 months)
Stage V	Active reading from familiar books (starting around 20–30 months)
Stage VI	Sounding out short, unfamiliar words (starting around 32–34 months)
Stage VII	Reading easy, unfamiliar books (around 36 months)
Stage VIII	Reading for enjoyment of content (around 48 months)

FIGURE 17–7 Stages in the learning process of early readers (*From* Early Childhood Research Quarterly 1, *Ablex Publishing Corporation.*)

Because of this expectation teachers may want to "make it happen" even on the first day of school. It does not matter to the child that what she read was simple by adult standards—even if the only thing that the child goes home able to read at the conclusion of the first day of school is the simple sentence that states, "My name is _____." On all following days this simple, close-type reading can be used to enhance the child's perceptions that she can read. A big portion of the battle to improve children's self-esteem and allow the child to believe that she can read and write is won if, indeed, the teacher has the child write and read some every day.

Objectives

Differences exist in the objectives of instruction between (1) educators who believe in readiness activities and (2) educators who advocate natural self-discovery of reading skills. The first group hopes to facilitate learning and enjoyment of reading. The second group foresees the child's experimentation—creating ideas about reading, based on his or her notions of the use of writing and reading, and attempting to crack the code with supportive assistance. Both groups favor a print-rich classroom, and objectives in many programs are based on a consideration of a blending of the two positions. Both groups also agree that experiences with classic and quality literature and dramatic activity help children's emerging literacy.

Programs that choose to include reading readiness among their instructional goals (objectives) plan activities that promote the following skills and attitudes:

- Recognizing incongruities—the ability to see the inappropriateness of a situation or statement, such as "The mouse swallowed the elephant."
- Recognizing context clues—realizing that pictures on the same page give visual clues to the words.

- Acquiring the ability to listen.
- Building vocabulary through first-hand experiences:
  a. recognizing likenesses and differences,
  b. identifying through sight and sound,
  c. rhyming,
  d. increasing memory span,
  e. recalling sequence and content, and
  f. following directions.
- Increasing speech output:
  a. developing attitudes of each child's ability and worth, and
  b. increasing imaginative and creative speech.
- Building critical thinking and problem solving with language:
  a. identifying through clues,
  b. classifying, sorting, and organizing,
  c. developing concepts and recognizing relationships,
  d. anticipating outcomes, and
  e. seeing cause-and-effect relationships.
- Developing self-confidence—attitudes of competence.
- Increasing interest and motivation through enjoyment of and success in language activities.
- Developing left and right awareness.
- Developing positive attitudes toward books and skills in book use:
  a. turning pages, and
  b. storing and handling books with care.

Sequence of Reading Behavior

In the absence of adult intervention that emphasizes another sequence, children generally seem to develop reading and writing abilities as follows:

1. The child develops an awareness of the functions and value of the reading and writing processes prior to becoming interested in acquiring specific knowledge and skills. As Putnam (1994) points out:

   > We know that children learn to read by reading and by following along with the print as they are read to. Children who sit beside a reader and follow the print

   from an early age learn to read quite "naturally." We know that the modeling has a lasting effect; children do what they see others do.

2. The child is likely to give greater attention to words and letters that have some personal significance, such as his or her own name or the names of family, pets, and so forth.

3. The child develops both reading and writing skills simultaneously as complementary aspects of the same communication processes, rather than as separate sets of learning. Neugebauer (1981) urges that "the most important issue is the quantity and quality of experiences the child has with print and with adults who help make print 'work.' It is through such interactions with print that the child acquires the information needed to find out what reading is."

4. The child develops an awareness of words as separate entities (as evidenced when he or she dictates words slowly so that the teacher can keep pace in writing them down) before showing awareness or interest in how specific letters represent sounds.

5. The child becomes familiar with the appearance of many of the letters by visually examining them, playing games with them, and so forth, before trying to master their names, the sounds they represent, or their formation.

6. The child becomes aware of the sound similarities between high-interest words (such as significant names) and makes many comparisons between their component parts before showing any persistence in deciphering unfamiliar words by blending together the sounds of individual letters (Dopyera and Lay-Dopyera, 1992).

As stated earlier in this chapter, the teacher will probably encounter a few preschool children who have already learned how to read simple words and simple books. Another group of children, usually older four-year-olds, seem quite interested in alphabet letters, words, and writing. Teachers should ask questions about the center's goals for each child.

It is important for teachers to be able to help the child's existing reading abilities and actively plan for future reading skill.

Any teacher of young children over the age of three can anticipate working with some children who already have interest in and abilities for reading and writing. As a teacher you should be aware of various methods used to teach reading. This is no less true for the teachers of three-, four-, and five-year-olds than for teachers of six- and seven-year-olds (Dopyera and Lay-Dopyera, 1992).

Reading Methods

Research studies conducted to try to pinpoint the one best method for teaching children to read have concluded that there is no proven best method. The important factors seem to be the teacher's (1) enthusiasm for the method or technique used, and (2) understanding of the method used. The ideal situation for a child learning to read is a one-to-one child-teacher ratio with the reading activity suited to the child's individual capacity, learning style, and individual interests. This is difficult to fulfill in an early childhood learning center due to the number of children per group and the many other duties required of a teacher. Other limitations can include the teacher's amount of training, knowledge of a variety of methods to teach reading, and ability to plan interesting and appropriate activities within a print-rich classroom.

What preschool teachers need to understand is that advocates of many differing methods used to teach reading agree that a rich, strong base in quality children's literature and well-developed oral language and listening skill aid success in whatever reading method is eventually used. Gill (1992) states:

. . . since reading research was first formalized, whether or not a child has been read to from a young age has been one of the strongest predictors of first-grade reading success.

Another factor most reading experts will not dispute is that children need experiences that have focused on the meaning of language. Whichever prereading or reading method is used, it is important for children to recognize that "talk" can be written and that "written talk" can be read.

The Natural Approach

Popular approaches to reading include what has been termed "natural reading." The basic premise of this method centers on the idea that a child can learn to read as he or she learned to talk, that is, with adult attention and help with emerging skills. As Bartoli (1995) explains:

We learn to read in a literate society such as ours the same way we learn to talk, walk, draw, sing: by seeing and hearing reading modeled skillfully for us, by noticing and understanding that this is an interesting and useful thing to do, by being invited to join the process with those who can do it better than we can, by being allowed to try it for ourselves when we desire (occasionally with a little help from our friends), and by being allowed to learn unself-consciously from our own mistakes.

Learning to speak in one's native language is considered a more difficult task than learning to read. In the natural approach, an interest in print (words) leads to invented spelling and reading. Meaning ascends memory and decoding in this method. Huey (1908) anticipated "organic" and natural reading systems by proposing that children learn to read by authoring from their own experiences. He suggested that it was important to expose children to great classic literature as well as child-authored literature (writings) if one wished to promote true literacy.

Educators associated with natural reading include Ashton-Warner (1961), Johnson (1987), and Fields (1987). The well-known work of Allen (1969) has led to a method called the "language-experience approach" and can be thought of as a popular early form of the natural method. Stauffer (1970) points out the specific features of the language-experience approach that he feels make it especially appropriate for young children:

- A base in children's language development and first-hand experiencing.
- Stress on children's interests, experiences, and cognitive and social development.
- Respect for children's need for activity and involvement.
- Requirement for meaningful learning experiences.
- Integration of school and public library resources with classroom reading materials.
- Encouragement of children's creative writing as a meaningful approach to using and practicing reading-writing skills.

Johnson (1987), influenced by the work of Sylvia Ashton-Warner, recommends starting five-year-olds reading through a procedure that elicits children's images. The images are then connected to printed captions. Individual important images merge as meaningful words to be shared with others through sight reading. Slowly, visual discrimination, capitalization, sentence sense, phonetics, and punctuation are accomplished at each child's particular pace.

To many people, the terms *natural* and *organic methods* and *language-experience* and *language arts approaches* are synonymous and describe the same or similar methods of reading instruction. Durkin (1987) points out that teachers should not mistakenly believe "natural" readers (early readers included) developed without help to learn. However, Durkin describes parents of natural readers as spending large amounts of time enjoying their children, reading to them, answering their questions about words or anything else, responding to requests to draw a picture or make a letter, initiating and then responding to questions. Chall (1988) adds that "Some people say you don't have to teach phonics, the kids will get it by themselves. But not every child will get it."

Robisson (1983) recommends the language-experience approach to young children's teachers because this method is a very natural way to build on children's expressive and cognitive activities and because of its flexibility and adaptability. She suggests that new teachers collect a large repertoire of activities from the many writers who have contributed to the development of this method. Allen and Allen's *Language Experience Activities* (1982) is a valuable resource. Since no one reading method is superior, teachers should be able to use features of phonic, linguistic, or sight-word recognition that seem useful at any given time (Robisson, 1983). In other words, combine methods.

The language arts approach to reading instruction introduces children to written words through their own interest in play; their enjoyment of speaking; and by listening to language. Often children's first experience with written words comes from their own speech and actions. A sign that says, "John's Block Tower" or "Free Kittens" may be the child's first exposure to reading. The emphasis is on the fact that words are part of daily living.

The increasing acceptance of the natural or organic methods may in part be due to the bulk of criticism that the other methods have received. These criticisms include:

- An overemphasis on skills (decoding, phonics, letter recognition, and so forth).
- Children's lack of a common background in the reading of literary classics.
- Children's lack of focus on comprehending what's read.
- A questioning of reading circles' oral-reading benefits.
- Poor performance of many children in reading.
- The labeling of slow or immature child readers.
- The number of remedial classes necessary.

The Whole-Language Movement

Much enthusiasm for a reading philosophy and approach called "whole language" is apparent in a growing number of elementary school reading teachers.

Cullinan (1992) discusses terminology and the spread of the whole-language movement:

> . . . whole language means different things to different people. I prefer to focus on

literature-based programs or integrated language arts programs. Whatever we call it, it is a vital grass roots movement that is spreading across the nation and around the world.

She clarifies the movement's three basic beliefs:

> . . . children learn to read by actually reading full texts, not worksheets. Learning in any one area of language helps learning in other areas. Children learn best when language is whole, meaningful and functional. The language of literature becomes the heart of reading and writing programs.

The whole-language approach is very similar to what's termed "natural-language approach" in early childhood books, journals, and professional teacher-training literature. Ferguson (1988) describes whole-language as a philosophy that suggests that children learn language skill by following the natural learning behavior that governs the way they learn to talk. She notes that it is important that writing, listening, reading, and speaking activities grow from a child's experiences and interests. The teacher directs natural curiosity into activities that develop skills.

All sorts of literature (instead of basal readers) are used in whole-language classrooms, including posters, comics, classic literature, quality books, magazines, and newspapers, to mention a few. Poetry, songs, chants, and simple drama activities are among the language activities offered. The whole-language teacher presents opportunities for learning and development by relating activities to a single theme. Spontaneous conversational exchanges are typical and seen as enhancing and extending learning. Teachers using this approach draw attention to connections between speaking, writing, and reading by saying things like "I heard you say boat. This is how you write that. Now let's read it." There are usually no ability-grouped reading circles, and classrooms are described as busy, active, and full of talk.

Goodman (1986) has listed basic beliefs that most early childhood educators attempting whole-language instruction feel are crucial:

- Whole-language learning builds around whole learners learning whole language in whole situations.
- Whole-language learning assumes respect for language, for the learner, and for the teacher.
- The focus is on meaning and not on language itself, in authentic speech and literacy events.
- Learners are encouraged to take risks and invited to use language, in all its varieties, for their own purposes.
- In a whole-language classroom, all the varied functions of oral and written language are appropriate and encouraged (Goodman, 1986).

Since whole language is an emerging philosophy, Baumann (1992) points out "there are no formulas for planning, developing, organizing, and managing whole-language curriculum," consequently, whole-language teachers with similar philosophies may differ in curriculum presented.

Whole-language instruction is not without its critics. Criticism usually centers on the teacher's ability to assess each child's reading progress, lack of instruction in phonics, and a possible "fad" factor (Chall, 1988).

Walmsley and Adams (1993) speak about the challenge apparent in translating whole-language theory into practice:

> Letting go some or all of the traditional teacher's control of the classroom's activities and behaviors does not come easily to teachers, even if they subscribe to a child-centered philosophy. And the consequences of liberating oneself from traditional practice are often not easy to accept. Many of the teachers are finding it hard to adjust to a changed classroom environment, even though few of them have serious doubts about the instructional philosophy they have newly embraced.

Walmsley and Adams predict the whole-language movement will survive but not dominate American public education. Exclusion of phonics instruction by some whole-language teachers and lower reading achievement test scores in some whole-language classrooms have caused additional concern. Coulson (1996) points out that in 1987 California adopted a reading program focused on teaching children to read simply by exposing them to literature. Reading achievement scores fell and California fourth graders tied for last place among states in the 1994 National Assessment of Educational Progress' reading report card.

Resources for early childhood teachers wishing to know more about whole language follow:

Froise, V. (1995). *Whole-language: Practice and theory.* Needham, MA: Allyn.

Raines, S. C., & Canady, R. J. (1990). *Whole language kindergarten.* New York: Teachers College Press.

Sawyer, W. E., & Sawyer, J. C. (1993). *Integrated language arts for emerging literacy.* Albany, NY: Delmar Publishers.

Literature-Based Reading Programs

A literature-based reading curricula has been adopted or recommended in many states. Huck (1992) believes teachers using this approach to reading instruction fall into three groups (or types) depending on how "literature-based" is defined and carried out in their classrooms. The three types Huck identifies may vary somewhat with each teacher.

1. *Literature-based readers.* Basal reading programs that use literature content texts are adopted. In about 80% of these texts, the stories are faithful to the original writing. Books are based upon selections of stories, not whole books. Teachers' guides and workbooks suggest fragmented kinds of word study and fill-in-the-blank exercises.

2. *Basalization of literature.* A literature-based reading program uses real books to study but treats them as basal readers. Teachers buy teachers' guides and milk dry each title with nonrelated activities and worksheets.

3. *Comprehensive literature program.* Literature permeates the curriculum. Teachers read aloud to children; they give children a choice of real books for their own reading; they make use of the fine informational books that we have today to use literature in every area of the curriculum; and they encourage children's response to books through discussion, drama, art, and writing. Their primary goal is to produce children who not only know how to read but also become readers.

Most major publishers are now designing literature-based reading series (Templeton, 1992).

Educators are examining New Zealand's literature-based reading approach, because New Zealand is recognized as the most literate country in the world. The United States, according to a recent study, ranks forty-ninth in literacy among 159 countries of the world (Cutting and Milligan, 1991). New Zealand's instructional approach is very similar to whole-language theory put into practice. The instructional model was instituted after educational research pointed to the success of literature-based models. An influx of culturally diverse children who were not adequately progressing in reading prompted New Zealand's use of new instructional methodology.

Decoding—Phonetic—Reading Approach

Decoding, using a phonetic approach to reading instruction, is based on teaching children the 44 language sounds (*phonemes*), which represent 26 alphabet letters and combinations (*graphemes*). Although phonetic approaches differ widely, most users believe that when children know which sounds are represented by which letters or letter combinations, they can "attack" an unknown word and decode it. Some schools using this approach begin decoding sessions when all sounds have been learned; others expose children to select sounds and offer easily decoded words early. A few phonetic approach systems require teachers to use letter sounds exclusively and later introduce the individual letter names, such as *a, b, c,* and so forth.

Five "word-attack" (or decoding) skills are help-ful in the complicated process of learning to read:

1. *Picture clues*. Using an adjacent picture (visual) to guess at a word near it (usually on the same page).

2. *Configuration clues*. Knowing a word because you remember its outline.

3. *Context clues*. Guessing an unknown word by known words that surround it.

4. *Phonetic clues*. Knowing the sound a symbol represents (See Appendix for English alphabet letter pronunciation guide).

5. *Structural clues*. Seeing similar parts of words and knowing what these symbols say and mean.

Proponents of this method may have the following views that were published by a phonetic-approach (method) advocacy group:

> . . . how can we let [our children] spend six years memorizing words (look-and-say reading system) when they could be decod-ing words and reading in six months or less with intensive phonics and enjoying good literature by second grade? An inten-sive phonics program would not require expensive remedial work or expensive books with words limited to those studied at each grade level. The look-and-say system has almost one out of three failing. (Reading Reform Foundation, 1987)

Cullinan (1992) puts into words the frustration many older reading teachers feel:

> When I started teaching in the 1940s, we were arguing about phonics. Nearly fifty years later, we are still arguing about phonics.

Look-Say Method

Many of the children who do read during preschool years have learned words through a "look-and-say" (whole-word) approach. That is, when they see the written letters of their name or a familiar word,

they can identify the name or word. They have rec-ognized and memorized that group of symbols. It is felt that children who learn words in this fashion have memorized the shape or configuration of the word. They often confuse words that have similar outlines such as Jane for June or saw for sew. They may not know the alphabet names of the letters or the sounds of each letter. This approach was preva-lent in public school reading instruction earlier in this century, and it is still used today. Children who are good at noticing slight differences and who have good memories seem to progress and become successful readers.

Combination or Balanced Approach

Many elementary school districts emphasize that their approach to reading instruction is a combined or balanced approach. This approach offers a rich diet of quality literature and literary experiences plus a sound foundation of phonics.

Factors Influencing Reading Instruction

Bartoli (1995), speaking about reading instruction in public elementary schools, believes children who read successfully more often learn in spite of the system by which they are taught! She expands this position by blaming school district constraints and state tests in the following:

> This is not to blame teachers for children's reading failures, or to deny their incalcula-ble influence on children's motivation and success or to suggest that teachers are not the intelligent, hard-working, dedicated professionals that they are. This is to suggest that, after decades of research, writing, and successful experiments with student-centered teaching and evaluating, most teachers are still constrained by dis-trict and state tests that drive the curricu-lum and reduce the quality of teaching, learning, and evaluating in far too many classrooms.

Teacher and Parent Attitudes

The staff in early childhood centers closely examine the advantages and disadvantages of various methods. Individual plans for individual children are formed, and activities increase children's interest while developing their skills.

Staff members facing "the back-to-academics" push need to be prepared and articulate. If they can discuss the real basics necessary in beginning reading and the benefits of a well-rounded developmental curriculum, which includes physical, social, intellectual, and creative opportunities and plenty of play, they may be able to curb pressure for a more limited academic approach to preschool programs that provide only bits and pieces of reading instruction. The importance of print-rich classrooms and literacy-based curriculum needs to be emphasized.

Most parents understand how critical their children's perception of their own abilities as learners is in determining school success. Parents are aware that early experiences in failing to perform academic tasks beyond children's capacity or developmental level can be detrimental. Most parents listen closely when teachers urge them to analyze the rush in pressuring children to learn to read at age four or five. Many parents want teachers to encourage natural curiosity, promote searching, questioning minds, and prompt a joy in discovery and problem solving. Parents realize that in teaching reading skills teachers must avoid the risk that children will develop a thorough dislike for the activity. Many can relate to the commercial sell and the trend to hurry children in our increasingly technological society. Thinkers as well as socially integrated and creative people will always be our most precious natural resource. Parents need to know that research in the field of education simply does not support the position that reading should be taught as early as possible.

Many parents did not themselves learn to read until age six or seven. They can remember their early feelings about reading instruction and perhaps how this affected their self-esteem as children. Some can describe the importance of play, physical exercise, and access to people who loved books in their early lives. They can remember the pleasure and challenge of reading. Teachers can emphasize their attempts to acquaint children in their programs with a wide variety of quality literary experiences—experiences that would be sacrificed if instruction in skill and reading mechanics were to dominate language arts programming. Offering a well-rounded, developmentally appropriate language arts program that includes integrated speaking and listening activities, an awareness of print, and exposure to reading through books and a variety of other reading activities provides the experiences that will aid children in their eventual quest to learn to read, because they enjoy it and see its value.

Parents who realize that a broad background in quality books and literary experiences is necessary to be considered literate will want this type of language arts program for their children. Most parents also prize their children's comprehension of both oral and written language, which grows in classrooms where discussion flourishes.

Hillerich (1977) has pointed out nine skills and abilities that serve as a foundation for reading. These can be shared with parents who are intent on the school's teaching reading mechanics and isolated skills.

1. Development of an adequate oral language, including both sentence patterns and vocabulary.

2. Awareness of children's ability to use oral context to anticipate a word.

3. Ability to discriminate minor differences between letter forms.

4. Understanding what is meant by "the beginning" of a spoken word.

5. Experience in classifying spoken words according to beginning sounds.

6. Association of consonant letters with the sounds those letters represent at the beginning of a word.

7. Ability to apply the skill of using oral context along with the consonant sound association for the first letter of a printed word in order to read that word.

8. Familiarity with the patterns of the literary language from having been read to.

9. Experience with certain high-frequency words, enabling instant recognition of these printed words.

Speaking about readiness programs and individual differences, Hillerich (1977) states:

> The typical child who has experienced the prereading skills program in or before kindergarten will be ready about the end of kindergarten or beginning of first grade to make use of these skills in actual reading. Of course, there will be some children entering first grade who are well beyond this level and others who have not yet mastered the necessary prereading skills, even though they may have been exposed to them.

READING ACTIVITIES

The following activities deal with the development of the ability to use picture clues and configuration clues, which are both useful to the beginning reader. Note that the following may be developmentally appropriate for only specific groups or individual children.

Picture-Clue Activities

1. Draw several shapes on a piece of paper. Ask the child for a word label for each. Print the word beneath the picture. Ask the child what he or she wants to do with the paper. (Some will want to cut it, color it, or take it home.)

2. Tell the child that you are going to draw objects on the chalkboard and that the child can guess their names. Record the child's guesses next to each object.

Configuration-Clue Activities

1. Use chartboard or newsprint to make a large wall chart called a Name Puzzle. Post it so that the children can see it. Make the configuration outline of each child's and teacher's name.

2. Introduce the activity to interested children by printing your name on a strip of colored construction paper. Outline the name as shown in figure 17–8, and then cut it out. Move to the chart, finding the matching shape. If photos are available, paste these above the shape after pasting the configuration name shape over the matching chart shape.

3. Draw a picture of some simple object (such as a jar, eraser, scissors, classroom toy). Have the child match each drawing with the real object.

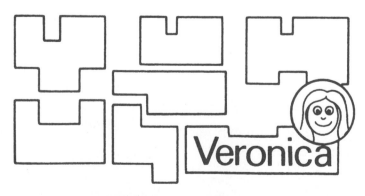

FIGURE 17–8 Name puzzle

4. Trace around objects on the chalkboard. Have the child reach into a bag and feel the object, then guess its name. Write the guess under the chalkboard outline.

Mixed Age Group Activity

Rowley (1992) has shared a clever activity idea called "Reading Buddies." It follows:

> Instilling a love of books and reading has always been a top priority in our preschool program for "at risk" four-year-olds. One of the best and most exciting activities last year involved a class of fifth graders who became "reading buddies" to the preschool children.
>
> Each fifth grade student wrote and illustrated a personalized storybook for a preschool "buddy." The highlight of this endeavor was the fifth graders' visit to our classroom during which they read each storybook and then gave the books to their preschooler partners. I'm sure the older children will long remember the sight of delighted preschoolers clutching their books, then asking for the story to be read again and again.

The Role of Story Times and Book-Reading Experiences

Many teachers who are faced with the responsibility of teaching reading feel that the ease in learning to read is directly related to the amount of time a child has been read to by parents, teachers, and others. Think of the difference in exposure hours between a child who has been read to nightly and one who has not.

Books have a language of their own; conversation is quite different. Books are not just written oral conversation but include descriptions, primarily full sentences, rhythm, dialogue, and much more. Listen to adults as they read books to young children; they adopt special voices and mannerisms and communicate much differently from everyday speech. Through repeated experience, children learn that illustrations usually reflect what a book is saying; this knowledge helps them make educated guesses of both meanings and printed words adjacent to pictures.

Storybook sessions are reading sessions and can greatly affect the child's future with books. Yadin, Smolkin, and Conlon (1989) speak about the foundation for later mastery of reading, which children can acquire from storybook reading:

> . . . storybooks provide a variety of information about the way print communicates meaning and represents the sounds of oral language just as environmental print may influence children's acquisition of print knowledge.

If teachers wish to evaluate how well they are doing in making books important to children in their programs, the following set of questions (Cazden, 1981) will help.

- During free-choice periods, how many children go to the library corner and look at books by themselves?
- How many requests to read during the day do adults get from children?
- How many children listen attentively during story time?
- How many books have been borrowed by parents during the week?
- Which books have become special favorites, as shown by signs of extra wear?

Classroom Resource Books for Children

Classroom reference and word books for children interested in words are a valuable resource. Among the many volumes of this type are:

The Macmillan Picture Wordbook, by Kathleen N. Daly
Macmillan Very First Dictionary, Macmillan Publishers
The Rebus Treasury, compiled by Jean Marzollo, Dial Books

Basal Readers in Elementary Classrooms

About 90% of elementary schools use basal readers to teach reading. Basal readers are packaged in sets or series that are used through as many as seven or eight grade levels. Readers (books) are collections of stories, facts, activities, poems, and assignments of increasing difficulty. As the age level for the reader increases, print becomes smaller, illustrations are less frequent, and book length is longer. Teachers must devote considerable study to the teacher manuals accompanying a series if goals are to be realized. Lesson plans recommend specific activities and procedures, and workbooks are provided to follow and elaborate on readings. Many basal-series packages use a combination of reading approaches, including sight recognition and phonetic decoding.

Durkin (1987) suggests that commercially prepared phonic-instruction workbooks dominate in kindergartens where prereading and reading instruction takes place. Some of this type of instruction has found its way into four-year-olds' classrooms.

Criticism of basal readers abounds. Many worry that the overwhelming use of basal readers in which word usage in early elementary school has been simplified may reduce children's ability to see causal relationships. Bettelheim and Zelan (1981) believe that year after year these texts have become emptier, using fewer words and becoming increasingly repetitious and boring. Additional criticisms include:

- Children's ethnic, geographic, and economic situation and homelife may be extremely different from the experiences depicted in basal books, stories, and illustrations.

- Basal readers are usually the dominant reading materials in the classroom rather than materials of true literary value.

- They may promote learning to read before the child has the necessary understanding (knowledge) to make sense of this prepackaged material.

- They include mind-numbing drills that emphasize letter sounds rather than stories and their meanings.

Honig (1988), a vocal advocate of overhauling basal books, describes them as "bland, boring affairs, stripped of emotion and interest by their emphasis on simple sentence structure and limited vocabulary." Bartoli (1995) believes that despite teacher interest in whole-language or language-experience movements, the reality in the majority of elementary classrooms offering reading instruction is "skill, drill, kill."

Parents' Role in Reading

Parents often want to find ways to help their children succeed in school. Since the ability to read is an important factor in early schooling, parents may seek the advice of the teacher.

Parents need to be aware that reading-like child behavior is not "reading readiness" but rather learning to read, and that centers owe children classrooms in which they are immersed in rich and memorable written language (Doake, 1985). An ample supply of quality picture books, particularly predictable ones, should be available in all early childhood centers.

The importance of home reading needs to be communicated to parents along with parental reading techniques that promote positive child attitudes. Information that helps parents recognize children's reading-like behaviors should be discussed. Parents can be made aware of their opportunity to contribute to their child's reading development.

Doake (1985) describes the teacher's role with parents:

They need to explain why, how, and what they (parents) should be reading to them (children). The characteristics of reading-like behavior can be described and preferably demonstrated to the parent, and its potential made clear. Stress should be placed on parents' inviting their children's participation in shared reading activities by never *demanding* it, encouraging experimentation and approximation, but not requiring accuracy when children attempt to reproduce their favorite stories for themselves.

Many programs keep parents informed of the school's agenda and goals and the children's progress. An early childhood center's staff realizes that parents and teachers working together can reinforce what children learn at home and at school.

The following are suggestions for parents who want to help their children's language and reading-skill development. Many are similar to suggestions for teachers in early childhood centers.

- Show an interest in what children have to say. Respond to children, giving clear, descriptive, full statements.
- Arrange for children to have playmates and to meet and talk to people of all ages.
- Make children feel secure. Encourage and accept their opinions and feelings.
- Develop a pleasant voice and offer the best model of speech possible.
- Encourage children to listen and to explore by feeling, smelling, seeing, and tasting, when possible.
- Enjoy new experiences. Talk about them as they happen. Each community has interesting places to visit with young children—parks, stores, museums, zoos, buses, and trains are only a few suggestions.
- Read to children and tell them stories; stop when they lose interest. Try to develop children's enjoyment of books and knowledge of how to care for them. Provide a quiet place for children to enjoy books on their own (figure 17–9).
- Listen to what children are trying to say rather than how they are saying it.
- Have confidence in children's abilities. Patience and encouragement help language skills grow.
- If parents have questions about their children's language skills, they should consult the children's teachers.

FIGURE 17–9   Look at this preschooler's concentration and focus.

Summary

The fourth area of the language arts is reading. Early childhood centers do not offer formal reading instruction because it is developmentally inappropriate. A few preschoolers do have actual reading skill. The majority of preschoolers, however, are only beginning to form ideas about reading.

The goal of the teacher is to blend the language arts skills—listening, speaking, reading, and print-script—into successful experiences. Because the skills are so closely connected, one activity can flow into another activity in a natural way. This gives young children a clearer picture of communication.

Experiences in classic and contemporary, quality literature and other language arts activities provide a background for reading. Abilities, attitudes (figure 17–10), skills, and understanding grow at an individual rate. There are many methods of teaching language arts; each center decides which course of action or activities are best suited for attending children. Children exposed to a rich offering of language opportunities that includes paying attention to the understanding of written and oral materials are judged to have the best chance of becoming successful and lifelong readers.

A teacher's knowledge of reading skills aids in the identification of beginning readers and helps developmental activity planning. Parents and teachers work together to give children the opportunity to gain reading skill and to keep children's interest alive and personally rewarding.

YES	NO	1. Asks to be read to, or asks for story time.
YES	NO	2. Hurries to be near the reader when story time is announced.
YES	NO	3. Comes willingly when story time is announced.
YES	NO	4. Likes to leaf through picture books.
YES	NO	5. Talks aloud (pretends to read or reads) as books are examined.
YES	NO	6. Looks over shoulder at what another child is "reading."
YES	NO	7. Picks books to "read" with some care (after examining more than one).
YES	NO	8. Has memorized some of the words from some books.
YES	NO	9. Has memorized most of the words in some books.
YES	NO	10. "Reads aloud" to others.
YES	NO	11. Usually enjoys hearing stories read aloud.
YES	NO	12. Borrows books from library.
YES	NO	13. Takes books home to read with no urging by teacher or parents.
YES	NO	14. Laughs aloud or smiles when reading funny material.
YES	NO	15. Asks others to listen as he reads something (of interest to him) aloud.
YES	NO	16. Treats books with care.
YES	NO	17. Asks for help locating book on specific topics.
YES	NO	18. Asks for help locating book about particular characters.
YES	NO	19. Gets "lost" in books and ignores activities in the room.

FIGURE 17–10 Checklist of reading attitudes for young children *(Adapted from* A Primer on Teaching Reading *by George Mason, 1981. F. E. Peacock Publishers Inc.).*

STUDENT ACTIVITIES

1. Invite a kindergarten teacher and a first-grade teacher to discuss their experiences and knowledge about young children and reading.

2. Observe a kindergarten class. List and describe any activities that increase a child's interest in reading or actual reading instruction.

3. Make a chart of printscript words (common words such as dog, cat, and highly advertised words such as those naming commercial beverages or cereals; include children's names). Test these words with a group of four-year-olds in a game-like way. Describe the children's response to your game.

4. Find and borrow the Edward Dolch Basic Reading Word List (Dolch, Edward W. *A Manual for Remedial Reading*. Champaign: Garrard, 1939) from a library. Share it with the group. Note the date it was developed.

5. Create an activity that includes:
   a. speaking and printscript.
   b. listening and printscript.
   c. printscript and reading.

6. In a small group, discuss what you would do and what your limitations would be if you were working with a group of young children and found that two of them were reading a few words.

7. Stage a debate. Divide the class into two groups: one presenting the disadvantages in teaching young children to read before first grade and the other presenting the advantages. Do some research at the library. Have each group discuss its position separately. Debaters from each team need to substantiate arguments by citing experts or written sources. Each team gets one point for each substantiation used during the actual debate.

8. Have volunteers role-play the following situation.

   A parent states to a teacher: "I know you don't believe in teaching Jonathan (her child) the alphabet, but all the other parents are teaching it to their children. Jonathan is going to be behind. The other children will seem bright to their kindergarten teacher, while Jonathan will seem slow."

9. Read the following excerpt and write your reaction(s) in preparation for a class discussion.

   Children begin reading signs and other environmental print (Jell-O and cereal boxes, McDonald's milk cartons, soup cans, toothpaste tubes) on their own when they find it useful or interesting to do so. If you can stand the pressure, take any 3-year-old to the grocery store, and you will quickly see what they are capable of reading (Bartoli, 1995).

CHAPTER REVIEW

A. Discuss the following situations briefly.
   1. A child asks you to listen while he or she reads a favorite book to you.
   2. You have noticed a young child who is able to read all of the printscript in the playroom.
   3. A parent notices his or her child is reading a few words and asks advice as to what to do.

B. How can a teacher include the four language arts in activities?

C. Explain what is meant by:
reading   phonics
readiness   configuration
method   incongruities

D. Select the phrase that best completes each of the following sentences.

1. Between the ages of four and five,
   a. many children learn to read.
   b. a few children learn to read.
   c. children should be given reading instruction.
   d. most children will be ready to read.

2. The language arts are
   a. reading, printscript, and listening.
   b. speaking, reading, and listening.
   c. listening, speaking, writing (print), and reading.
   d. reading readiness, listening, speaking, and alphabet knowledge.

3. Children may begin reading because they
   a. have an interest in alphabet letters.
   b. have an interest in books.
   c. want to see what they say written down.
   d. have an interest in speaking, listening, or writing (printscript).

4. Reading-like behavior
   a. includes a variety of skills, motives, and attitudes.
   b. can be defined as having an interest in reading.
   c. means at a certain age a child will perfect all the skills needed to read.
   d. means that reading should be taught to most preschoolers.

5. Parents and early childhood teachers work together so that
   a. parents will teach their children to read at home.
   b. teachers can teach reading during preschool years.
   c. what children learn at home and school can be reinforced by both parents and teachers.
   d. children's experiences at home and school will be the same.

E. Describe which of the reading instructional methods reviewed in this chapter seems more logical to you and why. Mention the distinguishing features of the method you choose.

F. What factors tend to predict child ease in learning to read?

CHAPTER 18

Developing a Literacy Environment

OBJECTIVES

After studying this chapter, you should be able to:

- explain the need for materials in language-development activities.

- assist teachers in the care, storage, and replacement of materials.

- describe early childhood language games.

This text has emphasized the need to provide children with a wide variety of interesting classroom materials, objects, and furnishings. Such materials are important in keeping programs alive, fascinating, and challenging.

Classroom materials and objects promote language skills in many ways.

- They provide the reality behind words and ideas.
- They provide children with opportunities for sensory exploration that increase children's knowledge of relationships and ability to identify the things around them.
- Materials capture attention, motivate play, and build communication skills.
- Familiar and favorite materials can be enjoyed over and over, with the child deciding how much time to devote to them.
- Many materials isolate one language and perceptual skill so that it can be practiced and accomplished.

In language arts centers, related instructional materials are located in one convenient area. Stocking, supervision, and maintenance of materials, furnishings, and equipment are easily accomplished.

The classroom can be a place to grow, expand, test ideas, and predict outcomes of questions. A prepared environment provides successful experiences for all children in a climate in which ideas and creative learning flourish (Sorenson, 1981).

Neuman and Roskos (1992) state a limited body of knowledge exists regarding how the physical features of a literacy-based classroom enhance learning. A preliminary study examining the impact of literacy-enriched play areas (ones with meaningful print) found preschool children spontaneously used almost twice as much print in their play (Neuman and Roskos, 1990). Consequently, teachers are urged to experiment and creatively design language arts centers and other play centers and monitor the effect of the room and its furnishings on children's language arts.

Language Arts Center

Full of communication-motivating activities, every inch of floor and wall space of a language arts center is used. Small areas are enlarged by building upward with lofts or bunks to solve floor-space problems in crowded centers (figure 18–1). Adding

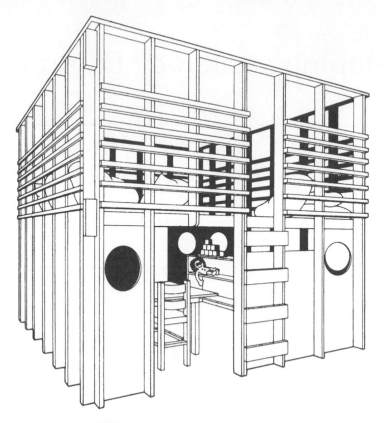

FIGURE 18–1   Solving space problems

areas that children can climb into is another useful space-opening device.

Language centers have three main functions: (1) they provide looking and listening activities for children, (2) they give children an area for hands-on experiences with communication-developing materials, and (3) they provide a place to store materials. The ideal area has comfortable, soft furnishings with ample work space, proper lighting, and screening to block out other areas of active classrooms. Miller (1987) urges teachers to make centers cozy and inviting with pillows, a covered crib mattress, or a bean bag chair or two. He believes the area can become a place of refuge for the child who needs to get away from the bustle of the group and a nice place for the teacher to spend some time with children individually.

Language arts centers should be quiet places that are separated from the more vigorous activities of the average playroom. Suggested furnishings are listed by category.

General-Use Materials
- one or more child-size tables and a few chairs
- shelving
- dividers or screens
- soft cushioned rocker, easy chair, or couch
- soft pillows
- crawl-into hideaways, lined with carpet or fabric (figure 18–2)
- individual work space or study spots
- audio-visuals and electrical outlets
- book racks that display book covers
- chalkboard
- storage cabinets
- flannel board
- pocket chart
- children's file box (figure 18–3)

FIGURE 18–2 A crawl-into area for quiet language activities

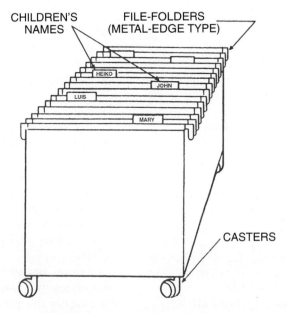

FIGURE 18–3 Children's work file box

FIGURE 18–4 Masking tape Xs indicate seating spots during group times.

- bulletin board
- carpet, rug, or soft floor covering (figure 18–4)
- chart stand or wall-mounted wing clamps
- wastebasket

Writing and Prewriting Materials
- paper (scratch, lined, and typing paper in a variety of sizes)
- table
- file or index cards
- paper-storage shelf
- writing tools (crayons, nontoxic washable felt markers, and soft pencils in handy contact-covered containers)
- primary typewriter
- small, sturdy typewriter table or desk
- word boxes
- picture dictionary
- wall-displayed alphabet guides
- cutouts of colorful alphabet letters
- tabletop chalkboards with chalk
- blank book skeletons
- scissors
- tape
- erasers
- alphabet letter stamps & ink pads
- tracing envelopes, patterns, wipe-off cloth
- large, lined chart paper (or newsprint)
- magnet board with alphabet letters

- hole punch
- yarn

Reading and Prereading Materials
- books (including child-made examples)
- book and audiovisual combinations (read-alongs)
- favorite story-character cutouts
- rebus story charts

Speech Materials
- puppets and puppet theaters
- flannel-board sets
- language games

Audiovisual Equipment
- overhead projector
- record player, headsets, jacks
- story records
- tape recorder, headsets, jacks (figure 18–5)
- language master, recording cards
- picture files
- television screen and VCR
- computer and printer

Adults usually supervise use of audiovisual equipment in a language center, and a number of the simpler machines can be operated by children after a brief training period. Tape recorders and headsets require careful introduction by the teacher.

FIGURE 18–5 Individual listening areas can be created.

Parental Input

Neuman and Roskos (1992) suggest parents be surveyed as to the kinds of literacy activities and situations that occur in their communities. Teachers then could rework play centers to include familiar settings:

> "Travel agency" and "restaurant" play centers may be appropriate to one early childhood environment but not to others where the generic "offices" and "grocery stores" may more likely represent real-world literacy contexts to children.

Farm community classrooms, and city children's classrooms may differ dramatically in literacy-promoting play areas.

Teacher's Role

Teachers are congenial, interested companions for the children: sharing books; helping them with projects; recording their dictation; playing and demonstrating language games; making words, word lists, signs, or charts (figure 18–6); and helping children use the center's equipment.

Hurt no living thing:
Ladybug nor butterfly,
Nor moth with dusty wing,
Nor cricket chirping cheerily
Nor grasshopper so light of leap,
Nor dancing gnat,
Nor beetle fat,
Nor harmless worms that creep.

FIGURE 18–6 Language-center chart

Children direct their own activities. Teachers slip in and out as needed and monitor equipment use. Vigorous or noisy play is diverted to other room areas. Children who have been given clear introductions to a language center's materials, and clear statements concerning expectations in use of the center's furnishings, may need little help. It may be necessary, however, to set rules for the number of children who can use a language center at a given time.

The teacher explains new materials that are to become part of the center's collection. The materials are demonstrated before they are made available to the children.

Posting children's work on the center bulletin board and planning chalkboard activities and printing messages that may catch the children's attention motivate interest in and use of the center. Plants and occasional fresh flowers in vases add a pleasant touch. To help children use equipment, materials, and machines on their own, teachers have become inventive using step-by-step picture charts posted, above or near materials. Color-coded dots make buttons or dials stand out. Some centers control machine use by giving training sessions in which children obtain "licenses." Children without licenses need to have adult companions.

Preschool teachers may be asked to select films and videos for classroom use. Most of these visuals are based on selected children's literature. Gaffney (1988) offers screening suggestions:

> . . . careful consideration of three things; the integrity and level of craft in the film itself: how well the print or print and picture medium was transformed to cinema; and how effectively the film communicates to an audience of children (film stands for both film and video).

Appropriateness and values presented would also be scrutinized.

Another task the teacher may want to undertake is making read-along tape cassettes to accompany a class's favorite books. Ditlow (1988) points out that the popularity of read-alongs cannot be denied, nor can the educational benefits. Children who use read-alongs are learning word recognition as well as some of the more advanced reading skills. For fun and pleasure, the lure of read-alongs makes them one of the best gateways for children into the world of books. Ditlow urges teachers to consider the following when making these classroom aids:

> A narrator's pacing is important. It cannot be too fast, or the child trying to follow along will be lost. If it is too slow, the child will become bored. The inflection and tone of the voice are also vital. The narrator cannot be condescending or patronizing; neither should there be an attempt to "act

out" the story and run the risk of making the story secondary to the performance.

Besides these factors a teacher needs to estimate audience attention span and use a pleasant page-turning signal.

Displays and Bulletin Boards

Interesting eye-level wall and bulletin board displays capture the children's attention and promote discussion. Displaying children's work (with children's permission), names, and themes based on their interests increases their feelings of accomplishment and their sense of pride in their classroom. Displays that involve active child participation are suggested. Many can be designed to change on a daily or weekly basis.

Printscript is used on bulletin boards with objects, pictures, or patterns. Book pockets, picture hooks, ¼-inch elastic attached to clothespins, and sticky bulletin board strips allow pieces to be added and removed.

One bulletin board idea is shown in figure 18–7. The child selects a spot to paste his or her picture

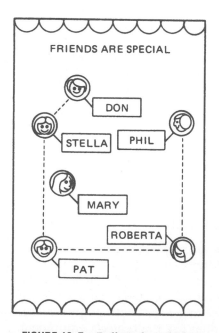

FIGURE 18–7   Bulletin board idea

(photo) and name. A colored line is drawn between the photo and name. Later, colored lines can be drawn connecting friends' pictures.

Chalkboard Activities

One of the most underutilized instructional items in early childhood centers can be the chalkboard. The following chalkboard activities are suggested to help children's language development.

- *Tracing templates and colored chalk*
  Using a sharp tool, cut plastic coffee-can lids into a variety of patterns (figure 18–8). Suspend the patterns on cord (or elastic with clothespins) over the chalkboard.
- *Pattern games*
  Draw figure 18–9 on the chalkboard. Ask the children what shape comes next in the pattern. Then draw figure 18–10 and see whether the children can make a line path from the dog to the doghouse.

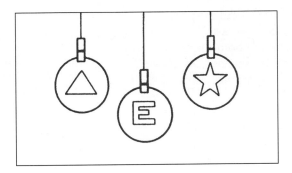

FIGURE 18–8   Coffee-lid chalkboard activity

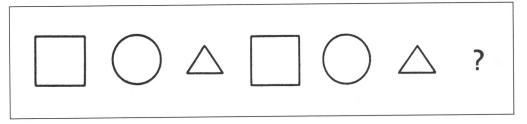

FIGURE 18–9   What comes next in the pattern?

FIGURE 18–10   A left-to-right skill builder

Audiovisual Equipment

Budgets often determine the availability of audiovisual materials in a center. Care of equipment and awareness of operating procedures are important. Special fund-raising projects, rental agreements, borrowing arrangements, or donations have secured audiovisuals for some programs. The machine's instruction manual should be studied for the proper care and maintenance necessary for efficient use.

The following audiovisual equipment enriches a center's language arts program activities.

Camera. Provide photos that are useful in speaking activities, displays, and games.

Slide Projector and Slides. Common home, school, field trip, and community scenes can be discussed, written about (experience stories), or used for storytelling.

Lite-bord™. This is a special display board that uses nontoxic erasable crayons for making colorful drawings and words that glow.

Super 8 Projector and Film Loops. Children enjoy films during group and private showings. Audiotapes can be made for children's or teachers' stories to accompany silent films.

Dukane Projector. Used with or without headsets, this projector provides filmstrip and sound presentations of language arts materials available from commercial suppliers.

Overhead Projectors and Transparencies. Stories with silhouettes or numerous transparency activities can be designed. Small patterns and alphabet letters are enlarged and copied by teachers or children for a variety of uses. MacDonald (1989) suggests drawing or placing images on the screen while storytelling or reading poetry (for example, using a Humpty Dumpty picture sequence while reciting the rhyme).

The overhead projector has been used in beginning reading instruction with "at-risk" children (Heath, 1983). Some, but not all, picture books work well with this instructional technique. If text and illustration appear on the same page, this type of sharing is recommended. Teacher access to overhead transparency-making may be limited; but if available the author strongly recommends this type of alternative storybook reading. Illustrations can be enlarged and enjoyed. Text appears giant-sized.

Opaque Projector. Pages of picture books can be projected on wall areas to offer a new way to read books. Guessing games are also possible. Picture book characters can become life-size companions.

Filmstrip Projector and Filmstrips. Easy operation and low cost make this equipment popular. Teacher-made filmstrips can be created. Newer models have automatic threading and rewind features with both front and rear projection. (Resource: May, J. [1981]. *Films and filmstrips for language arts: An annotated bibliography.* Urbana, IL: NCTE.)

16-mm Film Projectors, Films, and Screens. Many films are made for use with preschool children. Often libraries stock films. Programs attached to public school systems have film catalogs listing available titles. Screens are optional, since blank walls can also be used as projection surfaces.

Language Master. This machine instantly records and plays back. Children can easily operate this equipment. Words and sounds are paired. Prepackaged language development programs can be purchased.

Listening Center Equipment. Headsets accommodating up to eight children at one time adapt to both cassette and record players. Volume control is set on the jack box.

Record Player. Most centers have this piece of equipment. Commercial suppliers of story records are plentiful.

Tape Recorders. This is a popular audiovisual aid that is used frequently in early childhood centers. The tape recorder opens up many activity ideas. Suggestions for language development activities with tape recorders follow:

- Record children's comments about their artwork or project. "Tell me about _____" is a good starter. Put the tape and artwork together in the language center, so that it is available for the children's use.
- Let the children record their comments about a group of plastic cars, human figures, animals, and so on, after they arrange them as they wish.
- Have children discuss photographs or magazine pictures.
- Record a child's comments about a piece of fruit that he or she has selected from a basket of mixed fruit.
- Record a "reporter's" account of a recent field trip.
- Gather a group of common items, such as a mirror, comb, brush, toothbrush. Let the child describe how these items are used.
- Record a child's description of peeling an orange or making a sandwich with common spreads and fillings.
- Record a child's comments about his or her block structures. Take a Polaroid photo and make both tape and photo available in the listening and looking area.

Television Sets and VCRs. These can be purchased as separate units or as combined machines. Children's classic literature is available on cassettes. Local video rental stores and public libraries stock a variety of titles. Limited use and active discussion of what is viewed is recommended.

Discussion or Study Prints. A collection of large posters, photographs, mounted magazine pictures, and life-size book characters can be used in activities. Visuals can increase child verbalization, and serve as creative "jumping off" spots. Displaying too many visuals at the same time is an important consideration, for it may create confusion and cause tune out.

Planning Language Centers and Computer Centers

Once rooms or areas are designated as language centers, staff members classify materials into "looking and listening" or "working with" categories. Display, storage, working space, and looking and listening areas are determined. Activities that require concentration are screened off when possible. Many different arrangements of materials and equipment within a language arts center are possible. Most centers rearrange furnishings until the most functional arrangement is found. For sample arrangements with different functions, refer to figure 18–11.

Many children like to escape noise with a favorite book or puppet. Most centers provide these quiet retreats within a language arts center. School staffs have found creative ways of providing private space. Old footed bathtubs with soft pillows, packing crates and barrels, pillow-lined closets with doors removed, tepees, tents, screened off couch and armchairs have been found workable in some classroom language arts areas.

With fears mentioned earlier in this text concerning the overuse of television and videos, many educators see computer programs as offering a "cartoon world" rather than the real experiences and human interactions upon which real knowledge and literacy depends. Some computer programs designed for preschoolers offer exercises in which small bits of information involving alphabet letters, numerals, and words are paired or matched.

A growing number of computer programs for preschoolers present picture books in colorful and interactive formats. Mercer Mayer's (1994) *Just Grandma and Me* is a prime example. This is one two-and-a-half year old's favorite "puter" program and "do it again" requests follow each presentation as she sits on an adult's lap in front of the computer screen. As the number of quality computer programs increases and more young children are exposed to home computers, early childhood centers with generous budgets or donated resources

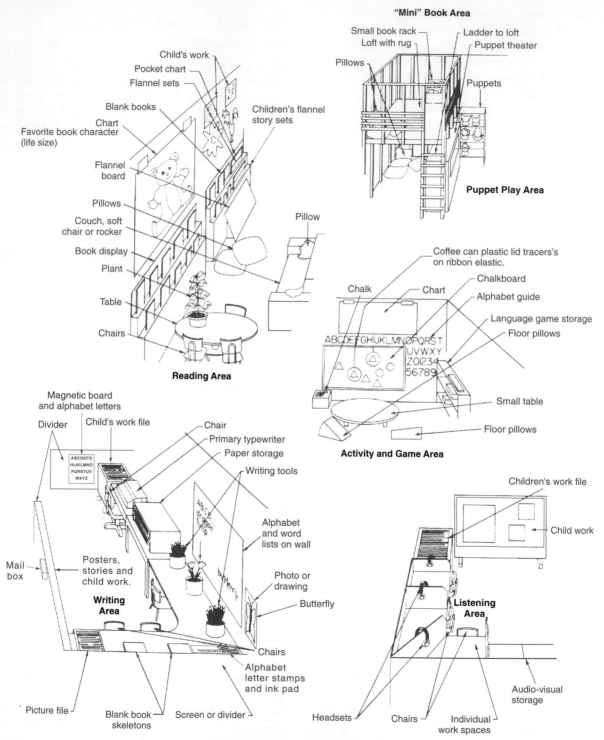

"Mini" Book Area

Small book rack
Loft with rug
Pillows
Ladder to loft
Puppet theater
Puppets

Puppet Play Area

Child's work
Pocket chart
Flannel sets
Blank books
Chart
Favorite book character (life size)
Children's flannel story sets
Flannel board
Pillows
Couch, soft chair or rocker
Book display
Plant
Table
Chairs
Pillow

Reading Area

Coffee can plastic lid tracer's on ribbon elastic.
Chalk
Chart
Chalkboard
Alphabet guide
Language game storage
Floor pillows
ABCDEFGHIJKLMNOPQRST
UVWXY
ZO1234
56789
Small table
Floor pillows

Activity and Game Area

Magnetic board and alphabet letters
Divider
Child's work file
Chair
Primary typewriter
Paper storage
Writing tools

ABCDEFG
HIJKLMNO
PQRSTUV
WXYZ

Mail box
Posters, stories and child work.
Alphabet and word lists on wall
Photo or drawing
Butterfly

Writing Area

Picture file
Blank book skeletons
Screen or divider
Chairs
Alphabet letter stamps and ink pad

Children's work file
Child work

Listening Area

Audio-visual storage
Headsets
Chairs
Individual work spaces

FIGURE 18–11   Language arts center

will make utilizing computers in language arts instruction a higher priority.

The connection between commercial computer programs and important developmental milestones in preschool children's lives (those involving basic ideas about themselves and the world around them) may be weak.

Using the computer as a word processor may be another story. Preschoolers with adult help can come to view the computer as a tool that records important ideas that they want to put in written form.

Summary

When there is a language arts center within an early childhood playroom, language development materials are arranged in one central room location. Children follow their own interests, according to their preferences, which increases the children's interaction with materials and expands language skills.

A language center's material can include a wide range of teacher-made and commercially purchased items. Activities in listening, speaking, writing, and reading (or combinations of these) are side by side, promoting the child's ability to see relationships among them.

Audiovisual materials and equipment are useful language center devices. Costs sometimes limit their availability. Training in the use and care of audiovisual machines is necessary for efficient operation.

STUDENT ACTIVITIES

1. Observe an early childhood program. Describe the use and storage of language development materials.

2. Listen to three story records. Judge and compare the quality of the recordings.

3. Invite an audiovisual company's sales representative to the class to demonstrate the company's product.

4. Develop a price list for five pieces of audiovisual equipment found in this chapter.

5. Interview two early childhood teachers on their use of audiovisuals in their language arts curriculum. Report the findings to the group.

6. Sketch a language arts center to promote dramatizing favorite stories. Label each item and furnishing.

7. Plan and conduct an activity for a group of preschoolers using a tape recorder.

8. Find a school where child computer access is commonplace. Observe and interview staff and children. Report your findings.

9. Borrow audiovisuals appropriate for preschoolers, and evaluate three with classmates. (Try your local library.)

10. Investigate a children's computer (software) program. Report your findings.

CHAPTER REVIEW

A. List the advantages of an early childhood language arts center. What are the disadvantages?

B. List the teacher's duties in a well-functioning classroom language arts center (for example, supervision).

C. Describe or draw a picture of an imaginary language arts center that has a crawl-into bunk or loft area. It should be a place where a child could be alone to enjoy a book.

D. List seven useful machines mentioned in this chapter for classroom language arts centers.

RESOURCE

Mayer, M., & Living Books. (1994). Random House/Broderbund, P.O. Box 6144, Novato, CA 94948-6144, 415-382-7818.

SECTION 8

SETTINGS PROMOTING LITERACY

At Home and School

CHAPTER 19

The Parent-Center Partnership

OBJECTIVES

After studying this chapter, you should be able to:

- describe the parent-teacher partnership that affects language arts programs.

- list types of parent-school communications.

- identify ways in which parents can strengthen a child's language growth.

Although parents and teachers are partners in a child's education, parents are always the child's foremost teachers and models, and the home is the child's first and most influential school (figure 19–1). Parents are usually informed of the school's language and literacy curriculum during enrollment interviews. Most parents are eager to find out how teachers interact with their children on a daily basis to realize their instructional goals. Many educators believe that some parents have a

FIGURE 19–1 A parent and child talking about new concepts.

great need to be told what to do in terms of their children's education and are vulnerable as a result. It is suggested that anxious parents need reassurance and can be encouraged to trust their instincts.

Child literacy at home and school is influenced by three important factors: (1) setting, (2) models, and (3) planned and unplanned events. The setting involves what the home or school provides or makes available, including furnishings, space, materials and supplies, toys, books, and so forth. Access to additional settings outside the home is also considered (figure 19–2). Time allowed or spent in community settings can increase or decrease literacy. Family economics may determine the opportunities and materials that are available, and family ingenuity may overcome a lack of monetary resources. As Mavrogenes (1990) points out, most things that parents can do to encourage reading and writing involve time, attention, and sensitivity rather than money. All parents can be instrumental in fostering literacy. The usefulness of speaking, writing, and reading can be emphasized in any home. Children's literature may be borrowed from public libraries and other sources in almost all communities.

FIGURE 19–2 A trip to a fire station might include trying on a helmet and boots. *(Courtesy of Scott C. Tracy)*

Cooper (1993) points out the difference between home and primary school language learning:

> ... school learning is not the same as out-of-school learning. School learning is programmed, timed, and encapsulated, whereas out-of-school learning usually arises out of a meaningful and present context.

Although preschools are not as programmed as elementary schools and much of the learning in preschools goes hand-in-hand with first-hand exploration, parents still have a big edge over group programs in offering intimate, individualized adult-child learning situations.

Adults and older children in a family who model reading and writing can instill attitudes that these pursuits are worthwhile. Children will learn the speech they hear; children learn best by example.

Family interactions during activities involve both the quality and quantity of communication. The supportive assistance given at home, the atmosphere of the home, parent-child conversations, and joint ventures can greatly affect the child's literacy development.

King (1985) describes parental actions and conversations that successfully promote language:

> Successful parents listen to *what* children say and respond to them. They interpret the child's language attempts and reply with related action accompanied by words and sentences. Learning is greater where children are supported by caring adults who share their world with them and enter into the children's worlds of play and talk, tuning in to their feelings and experiences. The essential element is the intimacy between child and adult who share a common environment which fosters the understanding of meanings intended.

Researchers trying to identify differences in parent interactions that produce fast or slow language developing children noted the following as contributing factors to foster child development in language:

1. Parent's speech was related to what the child was intending to do (Cross, 1978).
2. Parent responses expanded and extended the child's ideas, which made increasing demands on the child to produce language (Cross, 1978).
3. Parent had an accepting and non-directive style (Nelson, 1973).

McKenzie (1985) notes children who found their efforts and attempts at language received and valued developed the confidence to continue. Children's learning flourishes when they are allowed some degree of control over their own actions and when they interact with adults who are receptive, less concerned with rightness and wrongness, and more likely to respond in ways that stretch thinking.

Parent Guidelines for Literacy and Language Development

The techniques or actions recommended to help children's language and literacy development apply to both teachers and parents. Parents have different and more varied opportunities to use these techniques. The following guidelines have been gathered from a variety of sources dealing primarily with parent-child relations and some have been mentioned previously in this text.

Hints for Promotion of Literacy

- Spend some time with each child every day. At school, the teacher has many children to attend to and may not give a child individual attention (Mavrogenes, 1990).
- Have children match buttons, beans, blocks, or toys by colors, shapes, sizes; this kind of categorizing is an important thinking skill.
- Sort groceries by categories (canned goods, vegetables, fruits, etc.) (Mavrogenes, 1990).
- Keep in mind that children's early experiences with print, writing tools, alphabet letters, and books can be puzzling. When children ask questions, they should readily be given assistance and answers, while they are focused. Parents are interrupted frequently, and children's questions may seem endless, but parents get used to slipping quickly in and out of children's play. This type of on-the-move teaching is natural and different from sit-down structured teaching to which the child tunes out as interest wanes.
- Offer what is just a little beyond what the child already knows in a supportive, enthusiastic, discovery setting. Interactions between parents and children should be shared and enjoyable.
- Turning conversations into commands aimed at teaching language arts turns children away.
- Arrange things so that children have many opportunities to see operations from beginning to end. For example, make butter from whipping cream or applesauce from picked apples. Make cloth from yarn (knitted, crocheted). Make peanut butter. Grow pumpkins, and make pumpkin pie or pumpkin bread, as well as jack-o'-lanterns. Children often are not aware of the origins of the things we take for granted (Hutinger, 1978).
- Encourage each success or honest effort with a smile of approval or loving words.
- Be available as a resource person. When children ask questions that you can't answer, don't hesitate to seek help from others.
- Help children to feel secure and successful. Your interactions can build feelings of self-worth if children's ideas and opinions are valued, or feelings of worthlessness if their ideas and opinions are negated or ignored.

Stimulating Speaking Abilities

- Talk to children lovingly, taking care to speak naturally and clearly. Listen when children want to tell you something; don't nag or interrupt children when they are speaking (but do make an effort to correct speech errors casually, that is, without drawing attention to the error). Read stories, poems, jingles, and riddles to children; don't regard incorrect speech as "cute" or encourage baby talk (but don't expect perfect speech from the preschooler, either). Encourage play with puppets, bendable family dolls, dress-up clothes, play stores, doctor kits, and play telephones, letting the children act out various events and practice the language patterns we use in our daily lives. Encourage children to tell you stories (Rogers, 1986).
- Increase your attempts to build vocabulary by including new and descriptive words in your vocabulary.
- Give attention; listen for intent rather than correctness. Show children that what they say is important. Communicate with children at

their eye level, when possible. Expand and tactfully extend children's comments; talk on the children's chosen subjects.

- Use your best speech model—standard English, if it comes naturally. If you speak a language other than English, provide a good model of that language.
- Become a skilled questioner by asking questions that promote thinking, predicting, and a number of possible answers based on the children's viewpoints.
- Encourage children to talk about whatever they are making, but don't keep asking them, "What is it?" (Hutinger, 1978).
- Talk frequently; give objects names; describe the things you do; speak distinctly and be specific; use full sentences; encourage children to ask questions; and include children in mealtime conversations.

The following are suggestions from Mavrogenes (1990):

- Talk about what children are interested in and patiently answer their questions.
- Encourage children to develop their interests and talk about them.
- Do things together and talk about them: shopping, zoo, museums, movies, concerts, worship services, television, library, sports, and hobbies.
- Allow children to take the lead and direct the talk.
- Listen to your children so that you learn about them and show that you're interested in them.
- Provide young children with a play telephone and teach them how to use it.
- Ask children to describe objects they see.
- Talk with children to describe objects they see in a picture. Then hide the picture and see how many objects they can recall.
- Sing to and with children.
- Make games of spontaneous rhyming.
- Make up chants to do chores by.

Building Print Awareness and Skill

- Provide literature and a language-rich setting in the home.
- Write down the things children tell you about their pictures. Make books of each child's work and photographs, and talk about the books (Hutinger, 1978).
- Read family letters and mail to children along with circulars, junk mail, restaurant menus, wrappers and packaging, signs, labels, building identifications, catalogs, brand names, and calendars.
- Provide scrap paper and writing tools, and reserve an area in the home as a writing center for children's use.
- Make or buy alphabet letter toys or word books.
- Ask teachers for copies of the alphabet your children will use in kindergarten.
- Encourage scribbling and doodling.
- Write messages to children or make signs for their play, such as "Mark's boat."
- Talk about what you are writing and its use to you.
- Read signs when driving or walking, especially safety signs.
- Point out print on home equipment and products.
- Encourage interest in paper and crayon activities by showing children their names in print. Give attention to their attempts to copy their names or write them from memory.

The following are suggestions from Mavrogenes (1990):

- For pretend play provide bank forms, memo pads, doctors' prescription pads, school forms, store order pads, and ordering pads used in restaurants. This kind of play stretches children's imaginations and broadens their experiences.
- Help children in writing letters to grandparents, sick friends, book authors, or famous people.
- Put little notes in children's lunch boxes or backpacks. These can be picture notes or simple messages like "Hi, I love you."

- Make "books" for children's writing and drawing. Fold several sheets of paper together or staple sheets together.

- Model writing for children; write private notes, grocery lists, and recipes with children. These things show how useful writing is.

- Praise children's attempts to invent their own spelling; these show that they are learning the relationship between print and speech. "Correct" spelling will follow later.

- Don't criticize neatness, spelling, or grammar; it is important that children learn that writing is communication and fun.

Cooper (1993) describes the many ways parents can introduce young children to print in the environment:

> . . . their own names, street signs, stop signs, business signs, price tags, and so on. Young children at home also observe parents actively engaged in meaningful writing activities, such as composing a grocery list, looking up a telephone number, or sending a get-well card.

Providing Experiences Outside the Home

- Take trips to interesting places: bowling alley, shoe-repair shop, bakery, zoo, farm, airport, different kinds of stores, and train and bus trips. When you get back, make drawings related to the trip. Talk about it. Recreate it in creative dramatics. Effective trips can be quite simple but need careful planning. Visit community events such as 4-H fairs, craft shows, antique-auto shows, new-car shows, farm-equipment displays (Hutinger, 1978).

- Having children accompany you to the store, bank, post office, zoo, or park can turn the trip into an educational excursion. A home has many advantages that a school cannot duplicate (Rogers, 1986).

Promoting Listening

- Try teaching children to listen and identify sounds, such as the whine of car tires, bird calls, insect noises, and sounds of different kinds of doors closing in the house. Records, television, and storybooks also stimulate interest in listening (Rogers, 1986).

- Be a good listener—pause before answering, and wait patiently for children to formulate answers or speech.

Promoting an Interest in Reading

- Reading is dependent on facility with oral language. Children who talk easily, handle words skillfully, ask questions, and look for answers usually become good readers. Parents have an easy job compared with teachers who have groups of children to help. Parents should talk to their infants, chant nursery rhymes, and sing old folk songs and lullabies. This is the beginning of conversation, which is basic to reading (Larrick, 1980).

- Stop reading to a child who has lost concentration. Search for enthralling books.

- Read to children every day. Be sure to read quality stories that are written for the appropriate age level. Ask librarians for help (Hutinger, 1978). See figure 19–3 for a listing of books with an element of predictability. Finding predictable picture books that include repetitive features enhances the child's feelings of being part of the telling. Competency increases when the child knows what comes next after a few readings. An appealing book selected by a parent can be read with enthusiasm and animation.

- Get children actively involved, participating in reading by chanting lines, pointing, speaking in different voices for each character, or whatever is natural and logical for the book's text or format.

AUTHOR	TITLE	PUBLISHER
Arno, E.	*The Gingerbread Man*	Crowell
Bang, M.	*Ten, Nine, Eight*	Greenwillow
Baum, A. & J.	*One Bright Monday Morning*	Random House
Berenstain, J. & S.	*Bears in the Night*	Random House
Bonne, R., & Mill, A.	*I Know an Old Lady*	Rand McNally
Brandenberg, F.	*I Once Knew a Man*	Macmillan
Brown, M.	*One, Two, Three*	Little, Brown
Brown, M.	*The Three Billy Goats Gruff*	Harcourt
Brown, M. W.	*Goodnight Moon*	Harper and Row
Burmingham, J.	*Mr. Grumpy's Outing*	Holt
Cameron, P.	*"I Can't," Said the Ant*	Coward, McCann and Geoghegan
Charlip, R.	*What Good Luck! What Bad Luck!*	Scholastic
Charlip, R., & Supree, B.	*Mother Mother I Feel Sick Send for the Doctor Quick Quick Quick*	Random House
Chwast, S.	*The House That Jack Built*	Random House
Cowley, J.	*Mouse*	Shortland Publications
DeRegniers, B.	*Willy O'Dwyer Jumped in the Fire*	Atheneum
Emberly, B. & E.	*On Wide River to Cross*	Prentice-Hall
Flack, M.	*Ask Mr. Bear*	Macmillan
Galdone, P.	*The Three Billy Goats Gruff*	Seabury
Graham, J.	*I Love You, Mouse*	Harcourt
Hazen, B.	*The Me I See*	Abingdon
Hoban, T.	*Just Look*	Greenwillow
Hogrogian, N.	*One Fine Day*	Macmillan
Hutchins, P.	*The Surprise Party*	Collier
	Rosie's Walk	Macmillan
Isadora, R.	*Max*	Collier
Kellogg, S.	*Won't Somebody Play With Me?*	Dial
Kraus, R.	*Bears*	Scholastic
Langstaff, J.	*Oh, A-Hunting We Will Go*	Atheneum
	Soldier, Soldier, Won't You Marry Me?	Doubleday
Leodhas, S. N.	*All in the Morning Early*	Holt
Martin, B. Jr.	*Brown Bear, Brown Bear, What Do You See?*	Holt
	A Ghost Story	Holt
	The Haunted House	Holt
	Tatty Mae and Catty Mae	Holt
	Ten Little Squirrels	Holt
	Welcome Home, Henry	Holt
	When It Rains . . . It Rains	Holt

FIGURE 19–3 Predictable books *continues*

AUTHOR	TITLE	PUBLISHER
Mayer, M.	*What Do You Do With a Kangaroo?*	Macmillan
Merriam, E.	*Do You Want To See Something?*	Scholastic
Sendak, M.	*Chicken Soup with Rice*	Scholastic
Shaw, C. B.	*It Looked Like Spilt Milk*	Harper
Shulevitz, U.	*One Monday Morning*	Scribner's
Slobodkina, E.	*Caps for Sale*	Scholastic
Spier, P.	*The Fox Went Out on a Chilly Night*	Doubleday
Stevenson, J.	*"Could Be Worse!"*	Puffin
Stover, J.	*If Everybody Did*	McKay
Thomas, P.	*"Stand Back," Said the Elephant, "I'm Going to Sneeze"*	Lothrop, Lee and Shephard
Viorst, J.	*Alexander and the Terrible, Horrible, No Good, Very Bad Day*	Atheneum
Zolotow, C.	*If It Weren't for You*	Harper

FIGURE 19–3 *continued*

- Give reading status and importance; read recipes and directions (figure 19–4).
- A child's age will determine, in part, what he or she will find interesting in a book. The preschooler is interested in rhyming words, repetitions, characters the child's own age, bright colors, and fun things to feel. The more a child is exposed to pleasurable reading activities, the greater will be his or her interest in reading. Read aloud and provide books for browsing and a special place to keep the collection. Enjoy reading and encourage children to read a wide variety of materials. Go to the library. Arrange a time to read with children. You may read your own materials separately or read the same story together. Provide reading-related activities. Encourage children to write stories. Try storytelling without a book (Ransbury, 1986).
- Children will become readers only if their emotions are engaged and their imaginations are stretched and stirred by what they find on the printed page. The truly literate are not those who know how to read, but those who read fluently, responsively, critically, and because they want to (Sloan, 1985).

- It is wise to select from among the best books for even the youngest children. The best are well-designed with uncluttered pages, interesting print, and colorful pictures that stimulate young imaginations. If children are introduced to excellence from the beginning, they will gradually develop a taste for the finest (Sloan, 1985).
- Parents often think that children learn about reading in school. The truth of the matter is that many children already know a lot about reading when they enter kindergarten, because parents have been teaching their children about reading since they were born. Methods that parents use to teach differ from those used by school teachers. Parents help children every day—when they take them to the grocery store or point out street signs. Experience with print gives a broad and meaningful introduction to reading. Reading really cannot be learned very well if it is first taught only with lessons on isolated letters and sounds. If reading is to make sense to children, they must see how it is used in life (Schickedanz, 1983) (figure 19–5).
- When children select books, show a genuine interest; don't criticize children's selection.

AUTHOR	TITLE	PUBLISHER
Asche, F.	*Sand Cake*	Parents Magazine Press
Asche, F.	*Good Lemonade*	Franklin Watts
Brandenberg, F.	*Fresh Cider and Pie*	Macmillan
Brown, M.	*Stone Soup*	Charles Scribner's Sons
Carle, E.	*Pancakes, Pancakes*	Alfred A. Knopf
Carle, E.	*The Very Hungry Caterpillar*	Philomel
Dalgliesh, A.	*The Thanksgiving Story*	Charles Scribner's Sons
dePaola, T.	*Pancakes for Breakfast*	Harcourt Brace Jovanovich
deRegniers, B. S.	*May I Bring a Friend?*	Atheneum
Galdone, P.	*The Gingerbread Boy*	Houghton Mifflin
Galdone, P.	*The Little Red Hen*	Houghton Mifflin
Hoban, R.	*Bread and Jam for Frances*	Scholastic
Lasker, J.	*Lentil Soup*	Albert Whitman
Mandry, K.	*How to Make Elephant Bread*	Pantheon
Marshall, J.	*Yummers*	Houghton Mifflin
Mayer, M.	*Frog Goes to Dinner*	Dial
McCloskey, R.	*One Morning in Maine*	Viking
McCloskey, R.	*Blueberries for Sal*	Viking
Patz, N.	*Pumpernickel Tickle and Mean Green Cheese*	Franklin Watts
Politi, L.	*Three Stalks of Corn*	Charles Scribner's Sons
Seidler, R.	*Panda Cake*	Scholastic
Sendak, M.	*Chicken Soup with Rice*	Harper and Row
Seuss, Dr.	*Green Eggs and Ham*	Random House
Yaffe, A.	*The Magic Meatballs*	Dial

FIGURE 19–4 Books that encourage reading recipes and homecooking experiences

- When children ask for the pronunciation of words, tell them the words; don't analyze the words or sound them out.
- Discuss authors and illustrations at times.
- Enjoy humor or fun in books. Relate book happenings to the children's real-life experiences.
- Parents have a much better chance to help children form good attitudes about books than do teachers, because of the close, personal relationship between parent and child. Intimate discussions and warm, relaxed, unpressured readings are typical in home experiences.

Parents also can best match the books to their children's interests.
- Subscribe to children's magazines or borrow copies from libraries.
- Warm up questions set the stage and help children anticipate what will happen (Glazer, 1981).
- Point as you read. For very young children point to things in pictures as you talk about them. Pointing helps focus attention, thus lengthening the time children will sit still for a story. It also develops visual literacy, the idea that pictures have meaning (Glazer, 1981).

How Reading to Your Children Helps Them

1. They understand the similarities and differences between spoken and written language and learn that marks on paper have meaning.

2. They learn some of the components of a story (character, plot, complication, resolution, setting, etc.).

3. They learn the parts of a book (cover, title page, illustrations, print).

4. They learn how words can create imaginative worlds and how to use their own imaginations.

5. They learn how to pay attention to words, understand questions, and give answers.

6. They learn the meaning of words and expand their knowledge about the world.

7. They practice the skills they are learning at school or in centers.

8. They learn how to listen and how to treat books.

9. Your relationship with your children improves as you do something fun together.

10. Most important, your children will come to like books and reading and will learn that reading is *fun*.

FIGURE 19–5 *(Reprinted by permission of the publisher, The National Association for the Education of Young Children.)*

- Try asking what the child expects the book to be about from looking at the cover (Glazer, 1981).
- Look for ways to involve the child during readings (Glazer, 1981).
- Stop and let the child supply words.
- Talk about words (unusual ones) the child may not understand.

Mavrogenes (1990) gives parents the following pointers:

- Let children see you reading so that you provide a model for them to follow.
- Provide books, magazines, newspapers, and a comfortable special reading area.
- Take children to the neighborhood library to get library cards, choose books, and listen to stories or watch films; remember that children can get their own library cards as soon as they can sign their names.
- Read road signs, store signs, package labels; find license plates from different states.
- Book projects: Make puppets, draw maps, build homes with blocks, read other books by the same author or illustrator, look up unknown or special words, draw pictures, make bookmarks, act out characters.
- As the child tells you a story, write it down so he or she can see it in print. Read and savor it together.
- Give children their own bookcases, perhaps a cardboard carton covered with contact paper.
- Give books as birthday and holiday presents so that books become special and pleasurable.
- Have children draw pictures; make up a booklet of the pictures.
- Show children pictures and ask what might happen next after the action shown; such prediction is an important reading skill.

Strickland (1990) has pinpointed specific parental reading behaviors that promote positive effects:

Research on home storybook readings has further identified a number of specific interactive behaviors that support the positive effects of read-aloud activities. Those behaviors include questioning, scaffolding (modeling dialogue and responses), praising, offering information, directing discussion, sharing personal reactions, and relating concepts to life experiences. Although many parents engage their children in such interactive behaviors rather naturally, teachers need to share these facts with parents and encourage them to read to their children daily.

The value of parents instilling a love of reading (being read to) can't be underestimated. As Huck (1992) points out:

. . . research has been substantiating what literate families have done naturally and intuitively. They have been sharing books with children for their delight and enjoyment—not to teach them to read. Yet their children have become avid readers and writers.

Parents need to know group readings in classrooms have many child-literacy advantages. In parent at-home readings, the child is free to interrupt the story with unlimited comments and questions. As the child makes references to past experience, the parent will fully understand comments that connect to shared family occasions and happenings. Each child's comments show the child is trying to derive meaning from the story and incorporate what the story has offered into his or her view of life.

Parents bent on teaching their preschoolers to actually read should heed Clay's (1991) advice:

> Yet a loud warning must be sounded to over-eager parents! It is folly to kill curiosity and interest with over-instruction. Resist the temptation to tell the child what to attend to. Follow the child's line of interest and support what he or she is trying to figure out.

Many preschool children learn to read letters and words. This is different from getting meaning from a line of text in a book.

Parents who may wish to rate themselves using figure 19–6 may discover they are already promoting child language and literacy in a number of ways.

Parent Storytelling

The magic of parental storytelling not only improves child listening but also broadens child interests and opens new worlds of discovery (Fredericks, 1989). Following are tips from professional storytellers:

1. Select a story that will interest both you and the children. Your enthusiasm for a story is important in helping the children enjoy the story, too.

2. Practice the story several times before you share it with the children. Learn all you can about the characters, settings, and events within the story.

3. Decide how to animate the story. Practice some hand gestures, facial expressions, or body movements that will spice up the story for the children.

4. Practice different accents, voice inflections (angry, sad, joyous), and loud and soft speech patterns to help make characters come alive as well as add drama to your presentation.

5. Create some simple puppets from common household objects such as wooden picnic spoons, paper plates, or lunch bags. Draw individual character features on each item and use them during your story.

6. Promote your storytelling time. Make an announcement about an upcoming story or design a simple "advertisement" for a story and post it in advance.

7. Design a simple prop for the children to use during the telling of a story: a paper boat for a sea story, a magnifying glass or camera for a mystery story, or a paper flower for a springtime story.

8. Have the children suggest new props, gestures, or voice qualities that would be appropriate for retelling of the story at a later date.

9. After telling a story, talk about it with the children. Ask them to tell you the most enjoyable or memorable parts.

Being a good storyteller takes a little practice, but the time invested can make a world of difference in helping children appreciate good literature.

Use the following ratings: O = often, S = sometimes, I = infrequently, D = doesn't apply.

Parent attempts to:

_____   1. Initiate family discussions at mealtimes.

_____   2. Give full attention to child's comments.

_____   3. Add descriptive or new words in conversation.

_____   4. Take child to library.

_____   5. Take time at post office to discuss letters and postage.

_____   6. Discuss children's books.

_____   7. Read to child daily.

_____   8. Point out print around the house.

_____   9. Accept child's opinions.

_____ 10. Use dictionary with child.

_____ 11. Talk on the child's chosen subject.

_____ 12. Ask questions that promote child's descriptions or predictions.

_____ 13. Listen patiently.

_____ 14. Discuss TV programs.

_____ 15. Plan community outings.

_____ 16. Invite interesting people to home and promote interactions with child.

_____ 17. Correct child's speech casually with little attention to errors.

_____ 18. Encourage child hobbies.

_____ 19. Answer questions readily.

_____ 20. Discuss care and storage of books.

_____ 21. Play word games or rhyme words playfully.

_____ 22. Talk about how print is used in daily life.

_____ 23. Find books on subjects of interest to child.

_____ 24. Consult with child's teacher.

_____ 25. Give attention and notice accomplishments.

_____ 26. Take dictation from child.

_____ 27. Try not to interrupt child's speech frequently.

_____ 28. Initiate family reading times and family discussions of classics.

_____ 29. Establish a book center in the home.

_____ 30. Create child writing or art center in the home.

_____ 31. Give books as gifts.

_____ 32. Provide different writing tools and scrap paper.

_____ 33. Provide alphabet toys in the home.

FIGURE 19–6 Parent self-rating

Home Reading Centers

Home reading centers are a lot like school reading areas. A comfortable, warm, private, well-lighted place free of distraction works best. Adjacent shelving and a chair for parent comfort is important to book-sharing times. Window seats and room dividers make cozy corners. Parents can get creative in selecting and furnishing reading centers.

Family book collections build children's attitudes concerning books as personal possessions and give books status. Families model appropriate storage and care in home reading centers.

Library Services

Parents are sometimes unaware of children's library services. Children's librarians are great sources of information and often offer children a wide-ranging program of literary events and activities. They are good at finding books that match a particular child's interest. Teachers who are in touch with a preschool child's emerging interests can alert parents.

Building home book collections can be a real problem for some parents. Economics and library availability may thwart parent desires. Gottschall (1995) reports many parents living in the inner city in unsafe neighborhoods leave their homes only to get food and take children to school.

Home Visits

In trying to understand attending children, especially "silent ones" or culturally diverse ones, a home visit may help to plan for children's individual needs. Kiefer (1985) reminds teachers:

> In many cultures the family unit represents a powerful force in the child's life. A visit to the child's home (when welcomed by parents) can reveal not only patterns of language use which may not be apparent in a school situation but also help to establish a feeling of trust and cooperation between parents and teacher.

Villarruel, Imig, and Kostelnik (1995) caution home visitors to watch their nonverbal communications:

> However, nonverbal behavior means different things to various cultures. The significance of eye contact, facial expressions, proximity, touching, body language, and gestures varies considerably.

Teachers may be perceived as government officials who cannot be trusted by some immigrant groups.

As Villarruel, Imig, and Kostelnik point out, miscommunication is a common phenomenon among individuals from the same cultural background. When individuals from different language and cultural backgrounds interact, the likelihood of misunderstandings increases substantially.

Parents Who Speak Other-Than-English Languages

Centers have become increasingly sensitive to other-than-English-speaking parents who are often eager to promote their child's literacy.

Projects such as Family Initiative for English Literacy (FIEL), which serves families in the El Paso, Texas area, have designed unique parent-child literacy classes (Quintero and Velarde, 1990).

In projects such as this, parents become skilled and responsive oral language interactors who together with their child discover practical uses for print in social and community settings. Reading books aloud in both languages is encouraged. Educators model book-reading technique.

Family literacy programs attempt to break the cycle of intergenerational illiteracy by providing services to both parent and child. Programs vary from community to community as each program tries to meet the needs of participants. Participants are often parents who lack basic literacy skills and may need to acquire positive self-concepts to encourage their children's school success. Family literacy programs and adult literacy programs can be located through County Offices of Education or state agencies. Edwards, Fear, and Gallego (1995) advise preschool practitioners not to suggest that limited English-speaking parents speak English at home.

Directors and administrators can receive information and a multitude of resources concerning exemplary family literacy programs from:

National Center for Family Literacy
Waterfront Plaza, Suite 200
325 W. Main St.
Louisville, KY 40202-4251

Division of Adult Education and Literacy
    Clearinghouse
U.S. Department of Education
400 Maryland Ave. S.W.
Washington, DC 20202-7240

Early childhood centers can often locate family literacy programs and identify resources by contacting their state Director of Adult Education.

A growing number of communities are instituting publicly funded family literacy programs. Many of these programs are designed to provide:

- child care
- transportation
- introduction to literacy-building home activities
- access to community services
- involvement in children's school activities
- bilingual support and promote pride in language and culture
- increased parental self-esteem.

Parent Education Projects

Minnesota initiated parent training programs during the late 1970s and Missouri is credited as the first state in the U.S. to mandate all school districts provide parent education and support services (Winter and Rouse, 1990). The Parents as Teachers (PAT) project was initiated in 1981 with 350 families. It has been replicated under different names in over fifty sites nationwide. Starting at a child's birth, the project helps parents understand their child's individual development and promotes emergent literacy. Personalized home visits, group meetings, ongoing monitoring, and periodic screening, referral, and guidance services have effectively worked toward the project's goal of having children reach age 3 without undetected developmental delay or handicapping conditions. Among the literacy building activities considered "particularly powerful" in the PAT methodology is in-home parent storybook reading. Reading-aloud activities seemed to influence family social-interactional quality as well as child literacy. Further information about the project is available by contacting Parents as Teachers National Center, Marillac Hall, University of Missouri, 8001 Natural Bridge Road, St. Louis, MO 63121.

Television Viewing and Young Children's Language Development

Parents often ask teachers about the value of television, videos, and their children's viewing habits. A review of research generally supports the idea that children's television viewing casts children as "watchers" rather than active participants in language exchanges with others. The effect of viewing on particular children differs. After children become readers, studies show reading development is adversely affected when viewing is excessive.

Television programs that stress educational or informative material don't seem to have harmful potential. Again, the amount of viewing time is critical. Since research offers so many conflicting views, teachers can't give definitive answers to parents. Educators can express their concern that heavy television and video viewing rob a child of a literacy-rich home environment, one that is necessary for the child's optimum growth. Real first-hand experiences, exposure to books, and conversations with interested and responsive family members stack the odds in the favor of emerging literacy and can't be replaced by television or videos. Some young children watch an average of four hours of television a day or 28 hours a week (Levin and Carlsson-Paige, 1994). In low-income families, they spend an estimated 50% more time watching television (Miedzian, 1991).

What's excessive viewing? Research suggests over 10 hours of viewing weekly (U.S. Department of Education, 1991). Young Americans, on average, now spend more hours in front of the set than at any other activity except sleeping (Healy, 1990).

Extensive television viewing contributes to reduced language competency (DeGaetano, 1993). An increasing number of alarmed educators and researchers warn excessive, unsupervised television and video viewing by young children promotes negative effects including:

- aggressive and violent behavior (Anderson and Collins, 1988)
- decreased imagination, cooperation, and success in relationships (Singer, 1980)
- vulnerability to stimulus addiction so child needs overstimulation to feel satisfied (DeGaetano, 1993)
- immunity to vicarious emotional stresses resulting in inability to produce socially acceptable emotional responses (DeGaetano, 1993)
- poor reading comprehension, unable to persevere to an outcome (DeGaetano, 1993)
- listening problems (Healy, 1990)
- pronunciation difficulty (Healy, 1990)
- unable to make mental pictures (visual imagery) (Healy, 1990)
- unable to remember or decipher meaning from what's viewed or heard because of the passive aspect of television viewing (Healy, 1990)
- hindered development of metalinguistic awareness (Examples: Child's understanding that letters make up words, written words are linked together into meaningful sentences, a word is made from printed marks, one reads from left to right in English, and terms such as author, title, illustration, etc.) (Healy, 1990).
- decreased verbal interactions with family
- decreased opportunities to experience life and exercise verbal problem solving.

Educators are beginning to believe children's excessive television viewing, and societal attitudes concerning reading and intellectual pursuits, are our nation's greatest threat to literacy and the development of our children's thinking abilities.

Healy's (1990) advice to parents concerning television viewing follows:

- Place firm limits on television and video use, and encourage children to plan ahead for favorite shows.
- Participate with children whenever possible.
- Talk with children about television content, methods of audience manipulation, point of view, etc.
- If you want children to become readers, show them how to turn off the tube and pick up a book.
- Remember, what is pleasantly relaxing to your brain may not be good for theirs.
- Give substitute caregivers strict guidelines regarding television and video use.

School success and *Sesame Street* may not be compatible Healy (1990) warns parents. Preschoolers seduced by visual flash and gimmicks may habituate to the "easy pleasure of viewing" and find school and reading demanding. Learning and entertainment don't often walk hand-in-hand in the real world. Teachers don't sell knowledge; children and adults work for it.

Most educators suggest that parents limit and guide children's viewing. Screening programs and videocassettes is a wise move because of varying quality and values presented. Conversational follow-up after watching programs together gives parents their best opportunity for promoting language development. As Honig (1983) points out, children learn best from educational television shows if adults who watch television with them explain difficult words and ideas and build on the concepts that were introduced. Parents can talk about what has happened, what could have happened, and what may happen.

Teachers alert parents to consider how to use television in positive ways. Recognized benefits of some children's programs include relaxation and entertainment, exposure to new experiences and ideas, vocabulary enlargement, introduction to classic children's literature, and educational information. Criscuolo (1982) suggests that parents should:

- Limit … the amount of television a child watches, leaving time for reading and other more active pursuits.
- Serve as an example by limiting the amount of television parents watch and scheduling times when the set is switched off and the entire family reads something.
- Ask children to describe favorite TV characters, using a variety of different words that stimulate the use of a rich vocabulary. This makes parents aware of the types of qualities children admire.
- Encourage children to watch programs like *Sesame Street*.

Stedman (1996) advises families and students to reorder their priorities, with reading books and doing schoolwork taking precedence over MTV, video games, and aimless Internet surfing. Other suggestions include:

- Finding local PBS (public broadcasting) listings of appropriate programs.
- Purchasing or borrowing follow-up materials, such as *Sesame Street Magazine*, puppets, toys, and books.

Home-School Communication

Schools differ widely both in the amounts of written home-school communication and time spent talking or meeting with parents. Most preschool teachers desire more time and more conversations and additional written communication with parents. This suits some parents who seem to be seeking supportive assistance in child rearing. Each parent group and center is unique, and consequently tremendous differences exist in the degree to which preschools and parents work together. Most centers try to provide some type of parent assistance. Parents who receive help and support feel more open to contribute to the school's activities (Wardle, 1987).

Parent-school contacts usually take place in at least four ways:

1. daily conversations
2. written communications
3. planned parent meetings, workshops, and social events
4. individual conferences

On the Fly

Teachers have a good chance to share children's interests and favorite school activities with the parent at the end of the day, when parents arrive to take their children home from the center: books, play objects, and child-created or constructed work can be mentioned. Children spend time with and talk about what excites them; the observant teacher is aware of attending children's at-school play and work. Parents are usually interested in what their children have shared about their homes and out-of-school activities.

Bulletin Boards

Many schools use "parent" bulletin boards as a communicative device. Schools receive more announcements of literary happenings in their communities than do parents. Language-developing local events and activities can be advertised to parents. Short magazine and newspaper articles of interest can be posted at eye-catching levels.

Planned Meetings

Planned meetings include individual and group gatherings.

Conferences

Parents need to know how the school plans for their children's individual interests and growth. When children have interests in alphabet letters, dramatizing, or special-topic books, parents and teachers can discuss related school and home activities.

Goal Identification Meetings

Meetings with parents and staff identify language arts planning areas and parents' wishes and concerns. A center's language arts goals reflect the ideas of both parents and staff. Parents, as well as teachers, value the development of young children's listening, speaking, writing, and reading skills. Teachers contribute ideas and play an integral role in the home-school partnership.

Method-and-Material Review Meetings

A meeting can be planned to take a closer look at the preschool's planned language program, materials, and language arts center. Parents get a first-hand look and an opportunity to explore. Teachers conduct sample activities and demonstrate material and equipment use. Parents may ask questions about their children's use of or interest in a center's planned opportunities.

Parent-Teacher Study Meetings

Some possible themes of study meetings include (1) the effects of television viewing on children's language development, (2) bilingualism, or (3) free and inexpensive home toys that promote language. The center's staff, parents, outside experts, or films can present ideas to be studied and discussed. This type of meeting helps inform all who are present. Differing views clarify everyone's thinking.

It's a good idea to analyze what's really important to communicate to parents concerning children's language arts development. The following items are the author's high-priority topics:

1. So many parents show concern over their children's articulation and vocabulary. Clay (1991) discusses how children's speech errors may unnerve and worry parents:

   > Parents may be disconcerted to find that a child's language, which at three was apparently error-free and highly grammatical, becomes full of errors a year later. But research has shown that this often indicates progress. At each successive stage the child masters a limited range of simple structures. When he tries more complicated structures to deal with his more complicated thinking, his attempts again become hypotheses which are again tested by whether he is understood or not.

   It is helpful to assure parents that the school's staff monitors fluency and to share typical child speech characteristics. Such discussions often relax parents and dispel their fears. Hints concerning simple modeling of correct forms are well-received by most parents.

2. Sharing information on school interaction techniques that the staff uses to increase children's speech by listening, following children's leads, and expanding interest in daily conversation is very important.

3. Parents need to know how influential they are in modeling an interest in and positive attitudes toward reading, writing, and speaking. Their ability to listen closely to ideas rather than judging correctness of grammar or ideas should be discussed.

4. Another topic to discuss with parents is the warm, unpressured social environments that promote conversations about pleasurable happenings.

5. Reading picture books and sharing stories with the family at home will stimulate children's desire for more. Discussing quality books and "advertising" books to children can perhaps combat a television dominance in the home.

6. The child's home access to creative materials, such as drawing and marking tools, is important.

7. Parents have many questions about early reading and writing of alphabet letters. Both reading and writing acquisition is aided by a widely enriching home and preschool curriculum that preserves children's feelings of competence by offering that which is slightly above their level and related closely to their present interests.

School Lending Libraries

Increasingly centers are aware of the benefits of school lending libraries. Though extra time and effort is involved in this provision to parents, centers are sensitive to the plight of parents who are economically distressed and pressed for time. Lending libraries should give parents book reading tips and pointers in parental reading technique as well as calm possible parent fears that a borrowed book might get lost or defaced. Workshops and written book reading aids can include what to do when a(n):

- child wants a book read over and over.
- older child or relative reads to a preschooler.
- parent finds his or her child writing in a borrowed book.
- child asks questions often.
- child wants to retell a story.
- book does not interest a child.
- child wants to sleep with a book.
- child is rough or tears pages.
- child wants to use a book as a building block or to sit on, and so on.
- child notices some feature in a book that the reader does not see.
- child relates a book's story line to past experience.
- child wants to read a book to an adult.
- child always becomes sleepy when reading books.
- child notices that a page has been skipped or a word misread.

Parents may feel inadequate when assessing a book's quality and appreciate both a school's family library selections and its convenience. Some schools interview or question parents concerning their child's favorite reading topics and make every effort to probe family book choices and needs. Multicultural sensitivity is an important interview consideration.

Rules and procedures for check-out and return are prepared in print for parents. Staff time, center budget, and staff availability are key factors in deciding whether a family lending library is a viable activity. Brock and Dodd (1994) believe a family lending library is one way teachers can collaborate with parents to share specific knowledge about reading, as well as the joys of reading, which may enable children to grow and blossom into lifelong readers.

Working With Hard-to-Reach Parents

Centers incorporate family dinners and provide child care to increase parental attendance at home-

school meetings. Every effort is made to make the center staff and facility as non-intimidating as possible and to convince every parent they can contribute to child literacy.

Mavrogenes (1990) believes educators should be aware they may need to tell some parents what to do and provide leadership. She hopes many teachers have acquired training in parent-teacher relations and are armed with strategies to reach parents successfully. Outstanding parent support programs often have coordinators whose job it is to offer parental education and additional services.

Live demonstrations, specific instructions concerning parent teaching techniques, and use of materials in the home describe most supportive assistance programs. Stressing the practical purposes of reading and writing in the home, and the interrelatedness of listening, speaking, reading, and writing is the preferred course of action.

Daily Contacts

Greeting both parents and children as they arrive starts a warm, comfortable atmosphere, encourages talking, and sets the tone for conversation. Short, personal comments build parent-school partnership feelings, and help children enter the school discussing the morning's happenings. Children are offered choices of possible activities through certain statements such as "We've put red playdough on the table by the door for you," or "The matching game you told me you liked yesterday is waiting for you on the shelf near the bird cage."

Parent mailboxes can hold daily teacher messages. Important milestones, such as the child's first interest in or attempt at printing alphabet letters or his or her name, or first created stories, should be shared. A short note from the teacher about a child's special events is appreciated by most parents. A note about special daily happenings such as "I think Toni would like to tell you about the worm she found in the garden," or "Saul has been asking many questions about airplanes," keeps parents aware of their children's expanding interests.

Written Communication

Often centers prepare informal letters or newsletters that describe school happenings or daily themes. Figures 19–7 and 19–8 are two examples of this type of teacher-parent communication.

A written communication may concern the following:

- Local library addresses or a description of services or programs such as story hours or puppet shows.
- Local children's theater or drama productions.
- Children's book stores.
- Film presentations of interest to the young child.
- Special community events.
- Adult programs, workshops, meetings, and so forth, that include topics concerned with the development of children's language arts.
- Requests for "junk" materials useful in language arts games or activities.

Monthly Newsletters

If a school is trying to help parents expand their children's experiences, newsletters can suggest family outings and excursions to local community events and low-cost and free entertainment. Dates, times, costs, telephone numbers, and simple maps can be included. Wardle (1987) describes newsletter production as a team project:

> A newsletter is a team project. The size of your staff will determine the number of people available to work on it. One person should be responsible to pull it together while other staff members work on specific pages. Children can illustrate pages after they've been typed—drawing in margins only!

> Completed newsletters can be handed out to parents at pick-up or drop-off time. Try to keep the newsletter upbeat and fun with jokes, quotes, and anecdotes scattered throughout the pages.

SMALL, SMALLER, SMALLEST

Dear Parents,

We are studying the size of things, and will have many discussions this week comparing two or more objects or people. In similar discussions at home, emphasize the endings of size words (*-er*, *-est*).

Following are some activities you may wish to try where size can be discussed. Note the words *big*, *bigger*, and *biggest* or *tall*, *taller*, *tallest*, or others could also be appropriately used.

1. Sort bottle caps, canned food cans, spoons, crackers (round or square, but don't mix; stick to one shape).
2. Discuss your pet's size in relation to a neighbor's pet.
3. Take a large piece of paper and cut into square pieces. Discuss small, smaller, smallest.
4. Look for round rocks or pebbles and compare sizes. Ask the child to line them up from small to smallest.
5. Play games involving finding objects smaller than your shoe, finger, a coin, and so on, or smaller than a ball but larger than a marble.

You'll find many opportunities to compare size in your neighborhood or on walks, or in the course of daily living.

Sincerely,

Your partner in your child's education

Your child's preschool teacher

FIGURE 19–7 Sample of informal letter to parents to strengthen school learning

Dear Parents:

This week we've talked about many means of transportation—of how we use animals and machines to take us from one place to another.

We built things, painted things, and learned songs and heard stories about different vehicles such as bikes, cars, trucks, buses, boats, trains, airplanes, horses and wagons, etc., and even took a bus ride.

Here are some suggested home activities to reinforce school learning:

- Talk about places you go together in your car.
- Save large cardboard boxes—line them up, and pretend they're railroad cars.
- Save old magazines. Let your child find "Vehicles that move things from place to place." They may want to find, cut, and paste pictures.
- Take a walk, and find all the moving vehicles you can.
- Sing a train song, "I've Been Working on the Railroad," or any other.
- Plan a ride on or in a vehicle that's new to the child.

As you enjoy life together you may want to point out and talk about transportation.

Sincerely,

P.S. Here's a rebus poem to share.

 Sam wanted to go to the zoo.

The family wanted to go there too.

The [car] was out of gas.

And the [bus] didn't go past

their [house], so what could they do?

How could they get to the zoo?

FIGURE 19–8   A partnership letter

Parent Resources

Centers sometimes provide informational articles, magazines, and books that may be borrowed for short periods or available at the school's office. Photocopied magazine articles in manila folders that have been advertised on the school's parent bulletin board are a good resource for busy parents.

Descriptions of home activities aiding children's language development can be either created by the teacher or commercially prepared. Information on children's books and reading can be obtained from:

American Library Association, 50 E. Huron St., Chicago, IL 60611.

Association for Library Service to Children. (1981). *Let's read together: Books for family enjoyment* (4th ed.). Chicago: American Library Association.

Butler, D. (1985). *Babies need books*. New York: Atheneum.

Children's Book Council Inc., 67 Irving Place, New York, NY 10003.

Copperman, P. (1986). *Taking books to heart*. Menlo Park, CA: Addison-Wesley.

Cullinan, B. E. (1992). *Read to me: Raising kids who love to read*. New York: Scholastic.

International Reading Association, 800 Barksdale Road, P.O. Box 8139, Newark, DE 19714.

Trelease, J. (1995). *The read-aloud handbook*. New York: Penguin Books.

Parents as Program Volunteers

The role of parents, relatives, neighbors, and community has changed. Most early childhood educators realize home and school literacy learning are intimately intertwined. Parents and community volunteers and resources are seen as vital parts of language arts instruction. The teacher's goal is to involve and invite parents and community figures and resource people to participate in a relationship that urges them to become active participants in children's language learning and literacy. Parents can help teachers plan relevant topics and they are well aware of children's past and present experiences with language and print in their neighborhoods and communities. Most parent groups include willing volunteers who donate their time, talents, skills, and abilities or share hobby collections with the children (figure 19–9). The following are some of the ways parents can contribute:

- Celebrating "book week."
- Explaining occupations. Encourage parents to be guest speakers, discussing their occupations. Ask them to bring in items used in their occupations and to wear the clothing associated with their jobs.
- Demonstrating special skills and hobbies. From yoga to weaving, parents' simple demonstrations interest children.

FIGURE 19–9 Parent volunteers are a welcomed resource.

- Providing cooking demonstrations. Cooking demonstrations by parents can add to children's language knowledge.
- Organizing field trips. Parents may volunteer their time or suggest places to go.
- Organizing fund-raisers.

In addition to volunteering their time, parents can be good resources for providing materials. Many parents often work in businesses where useful language arts materials are discarded, such as scrap paper, cardboard, and so forth. The parent is usually more than willing to obtain these previously discarded materials, especially if they are unable to volunteer their time to the center.

Many parent volunteers enjoy making language-developing games and visuals. Parent creativity and ability can astonish teachers. Art, photography, sewing, and carpentry talents lend themselves to creating and constructing many classroom materials. Repairing a school's books, flannel-board sets, and puppet collections can be an ongoing task. Directing the efforts of volunteers and preparing for them takes time but saves much more time in the long run. Most schools survey parents for unique skills, hobbies, and abilities by sending home questionnaires. Even the busiest parents seem to find time to share their expertise as visiting guest speakers. Through the joint efforts of home and school, centers are able to provide a wider range of language-developing experiences for attending children.

Summary

Schools differ in both the amount and types of interactions between families and the center. School personnel need to clarify priorities that they wish to communicate to parents concerning children's language development. By teachers and parents working together, children's learning experiences can be reinforced and expanded.

Contact with parents takes place in a variety of ways, both planned and unplanned, including daily conversations, written notes and letters, and scheduled conferences. Centers are interested in promoting the reading of quality books in the home and alerting parents to community opportunities. Parent volunteers can aid goal realization in the language arts by sharing their talents, hobbies, labor, time, and energy. Together, home and school can work toward children's language growth and competence.

STUDENT ACTIVITIES

1. Photocopy the following, and cut the sections into cards. Rate each card before joining a group of classmates to discuss ratings.

Rating Scale

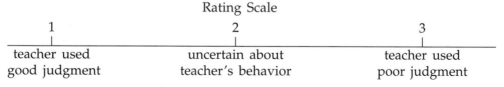

1	2	3
teacher used good judgment	uncertain about teacher's behavior	teacher used poor judgment

A field trip is in progress. Mrs. Winkler, a parent, is acting as a volunteer supervisor. A teacher overhears Mrs. Winkler tell her group to be quiet and listen to her explanation of what is happening at the shoe factory. The teacher tactfully suggests to Mrs. Winkler that the children may wish to ask questions.	During a study meeting, two parents are having a heated discussion concerning television's value. A teacher offers her views. Her views happen to support one side of the argument.
Mr. Sousa is a violinist. He is also Tami's father. Tami's teacher sends a special note to Mr. Sousa, inviting him to share his talents with the class. The note mentions that he will be allowed to play the violin for a five-minute period.	Mr. Thomas, a teacher, knows about a book sale at a local children's book store. He includes the item in the school's newsletter to parents.

Sending written messages to parents is not personal, Ms. Garcia (a teacher) feels. She telephones parents in the evening with news of milestones their children have accomplished in the school's language arts program.	Parent bulletin-board posting is part of Miss Alexian's duties. She feels parents rarely read posted materials. At a staff meeting, she asks others for helpful ideas for displays that would grab parents' attention.
Mr. Washington, a teacher, greets the children by waving from across the room or saying "Hi, Mark, I'm glad you're here."	"Oh, that's not the right way to ask a child about his or her artwork," Mrs. Yesmin, a teacher, says to Patsy's father.
"You're her teacher. Why ask me what she does at home? It's what goes on at school I'm interested in!" says Mrs. McVey, Pam's mother. "Knowing how Pam spends her time at home helps me plan school activities," explains Mrs. Lerner, Pam's teacher.	"Do you read to your child?" Miss Hernandez asks Mike's mother. "Of course, didn't you think I did?" the child's mother answers.
"There's an article on the parent bulletin board about children's use of slang words that you might want to look over, Mrs. Chung," says Mr. Benjamin (a teacher) to one of the parents.	During a parent-teacher meeting, Mrs. Texciera says, "Jill's work is always so messy." Miss Flint, the teacher, answers, "With time, it will improve. She's working with small puzzles and painting. This will give her more practice and control."
"Oh, don't worry about Jon watching television, Mr. Dunne."	"There isn't one good video for preschoolers, Mr. Perez!"

2. With a group of classmates list ideas for parents to obtain inexpensive quality books for home libraries and book corners.

3. Plan a parent newsletter for a local preschool center with helpful information concerning children's language development.

4. Invite a school's director to discuss parent involvement in a school's language arts goals.

5. Identify three books that might help parents understand children's language development or that might provide home activity ideas. Cite the title, author, and copyright date.

6. Find three magazine articles that might be useful in a discussion concerning home television viewing.

7. Interview a few parents of preschoolers. Ask, "What three communication skills do you feel are important for your child's success in elementary school (which he or she will attend after preschool)?"

8. Discuss the following statement with a classmate: "Many parents are so busy and tired after work that parent meetings are just an added burden."

9. Visit a family literacy program and interview its director. Report findings to class.

CHAPTER REVIEW

A. In a short paragraph, describe parent involvement in an early childhood center's language arts program.

B. List the teacher's duties and responsibilities in school-home communications.

C. What is the meaning of the following statement? "Early childhood centers reinforce home learnings just as homes can reinforce center learnings."

Appendix

Suggested Musical Records and Tapes (Chapter 2)

The following are available from Educational Activities, P.O. Box 87, Baldwin, NY 11510, 516-223-4666; and from Kimbo Educational, P.O. Box 477, Long Branch, NJ 07740, 732-229-4949.

Tonja Evetts Weimer

Fingerplays and Action Chants (1986)
Vol. 1—Animals
Vol. 2—Family and Friends
Pittsburgh, PA: Pearce-Evetts Productions

Kathy Poelker

Look at My World
Amazing Musical Moments (1985)
Wheeling, IL: Look At Me Productions

Raffi

Singable Songs (1976)
More Singable Songs (1979)
Baby Beluga (1989)
Corner Grocery Store (1982)
Rise and Shine (1982)
Raffi's Christmas Album (1983)
One Light, One Sun (1985)
Ontario, Canada: Troubadour Records

Hap Palmer

Sea Gulls (1978)
Walter the Waltzing Worm (1982)
Freeport, NY: Educational Activities

Greg and Steve

We All Live Together, Vols. 1–4 (1975–1980)
On the Move With Greg and Steve (1983)
Holidays and Special Days (1989)
Los Angeles, CA: Youngheart Records

Carol Hammett and Elaine Bueffel

It's Toddler Time (1982)
Toddlers on Parade (1985)
Longbranch, NJ: Kimbo Educational

Mary Louise Reilly and Lynn Freeman Olson

It's Time for Music (1985)
Sherman Oaks, CA: Alfred Publishing Co.

Georgiana Liccione Stewart

Bean Bag Activities (1977)
Get a Good Start (1980)
Preschool Playtime Band (1987)
Longbranch, NJ: Kimbo Educational

Rosemary Hallum and Henry "Buzz" Glass

Fingerplays and Footplays (1987)
Freeport, NY: Educational Activities

Sharon, Lois, and Bram

Mainly Mother Goose (1984)
Toronto, Ontario, Canada: Elephant Records

Fred Koch

Did You Feed My Cow? (1989)
Lake Bluff, IL: Red Rover Records

(From Wolf, J. (January 1992). Creating music with young children. *Young Children, 47*(2). Washington, DC: NAEYC, 56–61.)

Developmental Checklist (Chapter 6)

	PRESENT	DATE OBSERVED
Two-Year-Olds		
Receptive:		
Understands most commonly used nouns and verbs		
Responds to 2-part command		
Enjoys simple story books		
Points to common objects when they are named		
Understands functions of objects, e.g., cup/drink		
Expressive:		
Verbalizes own actions		
Uses 2- to 3-word phrases		
Asks *what* and *where* questions		
Makes negative statements		
Labels action in pictures		
Approx. 50-word vocabulary		
Answers questions		
Speech sounds:		
Substitutes some consonant sounds, e.g., *w* for *r*, *d* for *th*		
Articulates all vowels with few deviations		
Three-Year-Olds		
Receptive:		
Understands size and time concepts		
Enjoys being read to		
Understands *if*, *then*, and *because* concepts		
Carries out 2–4 related directions		
Responds to *or* questions		
Expressive:		
Gives full name		
Knows sex and state *girl* or *boy*		
Uses 3- to 4-word phrases		
Uses -s on nouns to indicate plurals		

continues

Developmental Checklist *(continued)*

	PRESENT	DATE OBSERVED
Three-Year-Olds *(continued)*		
Expressive:		
Uses -ed on verbs to indicate past tense		
Repeats simple songs, finger plays, etc.		
Speech is 70%–80% intelligible		
Vocabulary of over 500 words		
Four-Year-Olds		
Receptive:		
Follows 3 unrelated commands		
Understands sequencing		
Understands comparatives: big, bigger, biggest		
Expressive:		
Has mastery of inflection (can change volume and rate)		
Uses 5+ word sentences		
Uses adjectives, adverbs, conjunctions in complex sentences		
Speech about 90%–95% intelligible		
Speech sounds:		
s, sh, r, ch		
Five-Year-Olds		
Receptive:		
Demonstrates preacademic skills such as following directions and listening		
Expressive:		
Few differences between children's use of language and adults'		
Can take turns in conversation		
May have some difficulty with non-verb agreement and irregular past tenses		
Communicates well with family, friends, and strangers		
Speech sounds:		
Can correctly articulate most simple consonants and many digraphs		

(Adapted from Developmental Checklist *by ESP Inc., 1983.)*

Reggio Emilia Reading List (Chapter 6)

Edwards, C. (1993). Partner, nurturer and guide: The roles of the Reggio teacher in action. In C. Edwards, L. Gandini, & G. Forman (Eds.), *The hundred languages of children: The Reggio Emilia approach to early childhood education.* Norwood, NJ: Ablex.

Hendrick, J. (Ed.). *First steps toward teaching the Reggio way.* Upper Saddle River, NJ: Prentice-Hall, Inc.

Gandini, L. (1993). Fundamentals of the Reggio Emilia approach to early childhood education. *Young Children, 49*(1), 4–8.

Additional Stories (Chapter 10)

THE LITTLE ELF WHO LISTENS

—Author Unknown

Do you know what an elf is? No one ever saw an elf, but we can pretend it is a little boy about the size of a squirrel. This elf I'm going to tell you about lived at the edge of a big woods.

He played with chattering chipmunks, with bushy-tailed squirrels, and with hopping rabbits. They were his best friends.

Now, this little elf had something very special. His fairy godmother had given him *three pairs* of listening ears! That would be *six* ears, wouldn't it?

There was a *big* pair of ears, a *middle-sized* pair of ears, and a *tiny* pair of ears.

When the little elf wore his *big* ears, he could hear the faintest (smallest) sounds in the woods—leaves falling from the trees, the wind whispering to the flowers, the water rippling over stones in the little stream. He could hear the dogs barking far, far away. The little elf always told his friends, the squirrels, the chipmunks, and the rabbits, about the dogs, so they could run and hide. They were very thankful.

The little elf wore his *tiny* ears when the storms came and the wind blew loud and fierce, and when the thunder roared and crashed. The little animals, who had only one pair of ears apiece, were frightened by the loud noises, but their friend, the elf, told them that the wind and the thunder were important. After them would come the rain, and the rain was needed to help the food to grow.

Most of the time the little elf wore his *middle-sized* ears. He liked them best of all. He listened to all the middle-sized sounds with them, not the very loud and not the very soft sounds.

One morning some children came to the woods to pick flowers. "What shall we do with our pretty flowers?" a little girl asked.

A boy called Billy said, "Let's take them to school." "Let's!" the little girl agreed. "We can show them to the other children."

The little elf listened, and he wished that he could go to school. He wanted to see and hear what the children did at school.

He told his friends, the squirrels, the chipmunks, and the rabbits, about it, but they said, "No, an elf can't go to school. School is just for children."

The little elf decided he would go to school anyway. So the next morning he crept out of his warm bed of leaves under the toadstool and skippety-skipped down the road toward the school.

Soon he came to a big building. Girls and boys were playing out on the playground. There was a red, white, and blue flag flying high on a pole, so the little elf knew this was really the school.

Just then a bell rang, and the children all went inside. The little elf quietly slipped inside too.

You were the girls and boys playing outside. You are the children that the little elf followed.

Which pair of ears do you think he will have to use?

—His *big* ears because you talk too low, as if you were afraid of your own voice?

—His *tiny* ears because you talk so loud that you sound like a thunderstorm?

—Or his *middle-sized* ears because you are talking just right—loud enough so everyone in the room can hear, but not so loud that you seem to be shouting? Remember, the little elf likes his *middle-sized* ears best!

Suggestion: It's a good idea to show tiny, middle-sized, and big ears drawn on the chalkboard or on paper or on the flannel board.

(A follow-up to this story could be sorting objects into three groups by size.)

LITTLE DUCK

(A good group-participation story. Children imitate the actions with teacher [Scott, 1968].)

Run	=	Slap thighs quickly
Walk	=	Slap thighs slowly
Big Steps	=	Thump fists on chest
Swim	=	Rub palms of hands together rapidly
Bang	=	Clap hands once

Little Duck was scolded for eating too many bugs, so he said to his mother, "I am going to run away. Then I can eat anything I like."

So Little Duck left the barnyard and his own dear mother who loved him. He walked down the road on his little flat feet. (Action)

Little Duck met a cow who was munching hay.

"Have some," offered the cow.

Hay was much too rough for Little Duck to eat because he had no teeth to chew it. He thanked the cow for her thoughtfulness and walked on. (Action) Suddenly, he heard a big BANG. (Clap) Little Duck trembled with fright.

"Oh, oh, that must be a hunter with a gun," he cried.

Little Duck ran away from there fast. (Action) Then Little Duck heard some BIG LOUD steps coming toward him. (Action) He hid in some bushes until the big steps went by.

"Why, that was only a HORSE," said Little Duck happily.

Little Duck met a dog with a bone.

"Have some," said the dog.

"No, thank you," said Little Duck as he walked on. (Action)

Little Duck came to a pond. He jumped into the water and swam across the pond. (Action) He climbed out of the water and walked on. (Action)

Suddenly Little Duck heard a fierce sound, "Grrrrrrowl, Rrrrrrruff."

Right in front of Little Duck sat a fox!

"Yum, yum," said the fox, smacking his lips. "Duck for dinner!"

"Oh, oh!" cried Little Duck as he began to run. (Action)

He ran and ran faster and faster. (Action) He came to the pond and swam across. (Action) The fox was right behind him.

Suddenly there was a loud BANG. (Action) When the fox heard the big noise, he turned and ran away. (Action)

Little Duck felt safer now, but he kept right on running. (Action)

He passed the horse—and the cow—and the dog with a bone. Soon he was back in the barnyard with his own dear mother who loved him.

He said:

"I'm a little duck as you can see,
And this barnyard is the best place for me."

Little Duck knew that being scolded was for his own good, and he never ate too many bugs again. He never ran away again, either.

Peck, P. C. (1968). Special permission granted by Weekly Reader Corporation.

I'M GOING TO CATCH A LION FOR THE ZOO

—Author Unknown, Traditional

I'll get up in the morning (yawn and stretch)
I'll put on my clothes (go through motions)
I'll take a long piece of rope down from the wall (reach up)
I'll carry it over my shoulder (push up arm to shoulder)
Open the door (pretend to turn door handle)
And close the door (clasp hands)
I'm going on a lion hunt, and I'm not afraid (slap hands on knees)
Whoops—comin' to a hill (climbing with hands)
Now I'm crossing a bridge (pound closed fists on chest)
And I'm crossing a river (motion as though swimming)
Now I'm going through tall grass (rub hands together)
Whoops—I'm walking in mud (poke air-filled cheeks)
I'm going on a lion hunt, and I'm not afraid (slap hands on knees)
Comin' to a lion territory—want to catch a lion
With green stripes and pink polka dots
Have to go tippy-toe (finger tips on knees)
I'm climbing up a tree (climb up and look all around)
No lion!
Going in a dark cave (cup hands around eyes and look around)
Oh, a lion!
(The trip back home is exactly the same, only in reverse and faster. The cave is first and slam the door is last.)
Home at last. I'm not going on any more lion hunts. I've found a lion, and I'm afraid.
(This story is full of child participation and action. It takes teacher practice, but is well worth the effort.)

Note: This is a variation of "Bear Hunt."

HOW SAMMY SNAKE GETS A NEW SKIN

Pauline C. Peck (1968)

"My skin is too small,"
  said Sammy Snake.
"I need a new skin."
  Sammy met Toby Turtle.
"I need a new skin,"
  said Sammy.
"Where can I get one?"
"I don't know," said Toby,
"I never need a new skin."
  Sammy met Katy Caterpillar.
"I need a new skin,"
  said Sammy.
"Where can I get one?"
"I know," said Katy.
    "Spin a cocoon, the way I do."
"I can't do that," said Sammy.
  And he slid away.
  Sammy met Grampa Snake.
"I need a new skin,"
  said Sammy.
"Where can I get one?"
"I know," said Grampa.
"You just wiggle and wiggle."
Sammy wiggled and wiggled.
He wiggled his old skin right off!
And do you know what?
Underneath his old skin
there was a shiny new skin
that was JUST RIGHT!

Scott, L. B. (1968). *Learning time with language experiences for young children.* New York: McGraw-Hill.

HALLOWEEN HOUSE (A Cut and Tell Story)

—Author Unknown

(For this story, a large sheet of orange construction paper and a pair of scissors are needed.)

Hugo, the bear, and his friend, Bitsy, the mouse, wanted to give a Halloween party for all of the forest animals, but they didn't have a house, just a small den and a hole in the ground.

They thought about the fun they'd all have wearing scary costumes and telling ghost stories. Hugo wanted to make honey cookies, and Bitsy knew how to make a delicious mouse candy from maple sugar and pine nuts.

But, alas, they had no house.

One day while walking through the forest together, Hugo found a large piece of orange paper. Running as fast as he could, carrying the paper in one hand and Bitsy in the other, Hugo went straight to his den.

"Watch this," he said, putting Bitsy down. Hugo folded the paper and cut a round house shape with a big door.

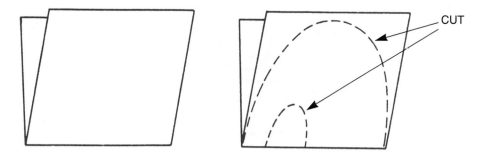

"You need a window," said Bitsy. So, Hugo cut a window.

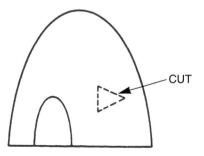

"But, I need a small door, too," Bitsy said. Hugo cut a small door.

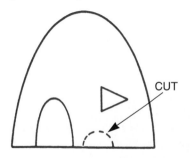

"Now we can invite all our friends to a Halloween party, whoopee!" said Hugo.
"Wait a minute. Just wait a minute," said Bitsy. "We need a jack-o-lantern!"
"We already have one!" Hugo said.
(Unfold the house.)

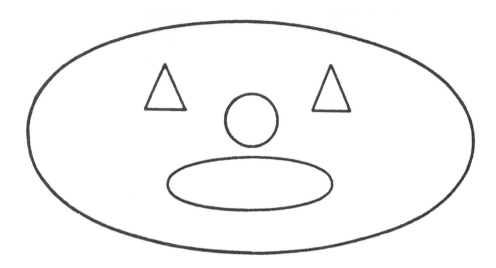

THE CROOKED-MOUTH FAMILY

—Author Unknown

There are many versions of this action story. This one, however, appeals to young children and never fails to bring laughter and requests to have it repeated. Before beginning the story, quietly light a candle—preferably a dripless one.

Once there was a family called The Crooked-Mouth Family.
The father had a mouth like this.
    (Twist mouth to the right.)
The mother had a mouth like this.
    (Twist mouth to the left.)
The Big Brother had a mouth like this.
    (Bring lower lip over upper lip.)
The Big Sister had a mouth like this.
    (Bring upper lip over lower lip.)
But the Baby Sister had a pretty mouth just like yours.
    (Smile naturally.)

(Repeat mouth positions as each character speaks.)

One night they forgot to blow the candle out when they went upstairs to bed.

The father said, "I'd better go downstairs and blow that candle out."

(With mouth still twisted to the right, blow at the flame being careful not to blow it out.)

"What's the matter with this candle? It won't go out."

(Repeat blowing several times.)

"I guess I'd better call Mother. Mother! Please come down and blow the candle out."

Mother said, "Why can't you blow the candle out? Anybody can blow a candle out. You just go like this."

(She blows at the flame, mouth still twisted to the left.)

"I can't blow it out either. We'd better call Big Brother."

(Change to father's mouth.)

"Brother! Please come down and blow the candle out."

Big Brother said, "That's easy. All you have to do is blow hard."

(With lower lip over upper, hold the candle low and blow.)

Father said, "See. You can't blow it out either. We'll have to call Big Sister. Sister! Please come down and blow the candle out!"

Big Sister said, "I can blow it out. Watch me."

(With upper lip over lower, candle held high, blow several times.)

Father said, "That's a funny candle. I told you I couldn't blow it out."

Mother said, "I couldn't blow it out, either."

Big Brother said, "Neither could I."

Big Sister said, "I tried and tried, and I couldn't blow it out."

Father said, "I guess we'll have to call Baby Sister. Baby! Please come down and blow the candle out."

Baby Sister came downstairs, rubbing her eyes because she had been asleep. She asked, "What's the matter?"

Father said, "I can't blow the candle out."

Mother said, "I can't blow it out either."

Big Brother said, "Neither can I."

Big Sister said, "I can't either."

Baby Sister said, "Anybody can blow a candle out. That's easy." And she did.

THE BIG-MOUTHED FROG

Courtesy of Katherine Blanton

A small big-mouthed frog decided to leave home and see the world. The first creature the frog met went "Quack, quack." "Hi, I'm a big-mouthed frog, and I eat bugs. Who are you and what do you eat?" "I'm a duck, and I eat seeds and grain," said the duck. "So long Mr. Duck, I'm off to discover the world!" "Meow, meow." "Hi, I'm a big-mouthed frog! I eat bugs. Who are you and what do you eat?" "Silly child, I'm a cat, and cream is what I prefer—purr purr," said Ms. Cat. "Goodbye Ms. Cat. I'm off to discover the world and all that's in it!" "Bow wow. Bow wow." "Hi there, I'm a big-mouthed frog, and I eat bugs. Who are you, and what do you eat?" "I'm Bowser the Beagle and I chew on bones." "You're a bowser?" "Nope, I'm a dog!" "See you later, I'm off to discover the world and all that's in it." "Moo, moo." "Hi up there," yelled the big-mouthed frog. "I'm a big-mouthed frog, I eat bugs. Who are you, and what do you eat?" "I'm a cow, and I eat grass—watch out, move aside, I might step on you." "Goodbye cow I'm off to see the world." "Hiss Hiss." "Hi there I'm a big-mouthed frog and I eat bugs. Who are you, and what do you eat?" "I'm a SNAKE, AND I EAT BIG-MOUTHED FROGS!!!!" "Ooooo oooo you don't say," said the frog. (This last line is said with the mouth compressed in a small circle!)

FOOLISH FRED

—Traditional

"Fred, Fred, we are so very poor! You will have to go to work," mother said. "Yes, mother, I will see if the farmer will give me a job," Fred said.

"Be sure to put your pay in your pocket," said Fred's mother.

The next day Fred worked cleaning the barn for the farmer. "Thank you for your work, Fred," said the farmer. "I have no money, but here is some milk for your day's work." "Thank you," said Fred. I will do just as mother told me, and put my pay in my pocket Fred thought. He poured the milk into his pant's pocket, and walked home.

"Where is your pay?" said his mother.

"I put it in my pocket just as you said, but now it's not there!" "Foolish Fred! You should have carried it in your hands carefully," said his mother. "OK. I'll do that next time."

The next day Fred got a job with the baker at the bakery. He frosted all the cakes, and put colored sprinkles on the cookies. "I have no money," said the baker at the end of the day, "but take this cat as pay; he's a very good cat for catching mice." "Thank you," said Fred.

Fred carried the cat in his hands just as his mother said, but the cat went "Psssssst! Psssssst!" and scratched his hands. "Ouch, ouch," Fred said as he dropped the cat.

"Where is your pay?" his mother said. "It was a big cat, and it bit me and ran away," Fred told his mother. "You should have tied it with a string and pulled it home," said mother. "Yes, that's a good idea. I'll do that next time," answered Fred.

The next day Fred worked for the butcher. "Here Fred, I have no money, but here is some very good meat for your pay," said the butcher. "My mother will like that," said Fred. "Thank you."

Fred tied the meat with a string and pulled it all the way home.

"Foolish Fred, we can't eat this meat. It's too dirty!" his mother said. "You should have carried it on your back!" "I will next time, mother," he said.

The next day, Fred got a job with a man who was an animal doctor. He fed and gave water to all the animals the doctor was taking care of. At the end of the day the animal doctor said, "I have no money but take this donkey." "Thank you," Fred replied, putting the donkey that was almost as big as Fred on his back. Slowly, Fred walked home with the great weight on his back weaving and staggering on the street.

"Ha . . . ha, you look so funny. They will like you in my circus. Will you come and work for me and travel with the circus?" said the man. "Can my mother come, too?" asked Fred. "Oh, yes" said the circus man. "You can bring her on the donkey's back." "Thank you! Please stay here. I will be right back," said Fred as he walked off with the donkey still on his back. The man sat down to wait and laughed again as Fred walked toward home.

"Ah, here they come, and look—there's Fred's mother on the donkey and the donkey is on Fred's back." He held his sides laughing at the sight. Foolish Fred.

Now Foolish Fred and his mother live happily with the circus, and they are not poor.

Flannel Board Activity Sets (Chapter 12)

Note: Author suggests enlarging some set pieces in this section. Many copying machines have enlargement features, or an overhead projector can be used.

APPLE AND WORM

Pieces: apple, worm

Action: Move the worm to fit the following positional words:

in	on	front	side	bottom	behind
out	off	back	top	under	

THE HARE AND THE TORTOISE

(Adapted from Aesop)

Pieces: rabbit   dog   rabbit running   finish line flag
          turtle   hen   rabbit sleeping   tree

One day the rabbit was talking to some of the other animals. "I am the fastest runner in the forest," he said. "I can beat anyone! Do you want to race?"

"Not I," said the dog.

"Not I," said the hen.

"I will race with you," said the turtle.

"That's a good joke," said the rabbit. "I could dance around you all the way and still win."

"Still bragging about how fast you are," answered the turtle. "Come on, let's race. Do you see that flag over there? That will be the finish line. Hen, would you stand by the flag so that you can tell who wins the race?"

"Dog, will you say the starting words—get on your mark, get ready, get set, go!"

"Stand there," said the dog. "Get on your mark, get ready, get set, go!"

The rabbit ran very fast. He looked over his shoulder and saw how slowly the turtle was running on his short little legs. Just then he saw a shady spot under a tree. He thought to himself—that turtle is so slow I have time to rest here under this tree. So he sat down on the cool grass, and before he knew it, he was fast asleep.

While he slept, the turtle was running. (Clump, Clump—Clump, Clump) He was not running very fast, but he kept on running. (Clump, Clump—Clump, Clump) Pretty soon the turtle came to the tree where the rabbit was sleeping. He went past and kept on running. (Clump, Clump—Clump, Clump)

The turtle was almost to the finish line. The hen saw the turtle coming and said, "Turtle, keep on running. You've almost won the race."

When the hen spoke, the rabbit awoke. He looked down by the finish line and saw the turtle was almost there. As fast as he could, the rabbit started running again. Just then he heard the hen say, "The turtle is the winner!"

"But I'm the fastest," said the rabbit.

"Not this time," said the hen. "Sometimes slow and steady wins the race."

Put on turtle, dog, hen, rabbit at left edge of board.

Add finish line flag on right edge of board. Move hen by flag.

Put on running rabbit. Remove standing rabbit.

Add sleeping rabbit while removing running rabbit.

Change sleeping rabbit to running rabbit.

FIVE YELLOW DUCKLINGS

(A flannel-board poem)

Pieces: five yellow ducklings   1 mother duck   1 pond (large enough for five ducklings)

Special permission granted by *Adventures in Felt* © 1972.

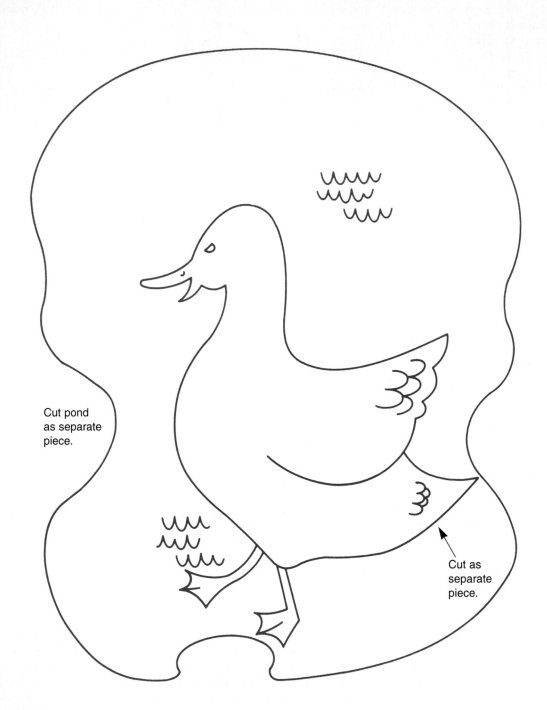

Cut pond
as separate
piece.

Cut as
separate
piece.

Five yellow ducklings went swimming one day,	*Place pond, mother duck, and five ducklings on flannel board.*
Across the pond and far away.	
Old mother duck said, "Quack, Quack, Quack,"	
Four yellow ducklings came swimming back.	*Remove one duckling.*
Four yellow ducklings went swimming one day,	
Across the pond and far away.	
Old mother duck said, "Quack, Quack, Quack,"	
Three yellow ducklings came swimming back.	*Remove one duckling.*
Three yellow ducklings went swimming one day,	
Across the pond and far away.	
Old mother duck said, "Quack, Quack, Quack,"	
Two yellow ducklings came swimming back.	*Remove one duckling.*
Two yellow ducklings went swimming one day,	
Across the pond and far away.	
Old mother duck said, "Quack, Quack, Quack,"	
One little duckling came swimming back.	*Remove one duckling.*
One yellow duckling went swimming one day,	
Across the pond and far away.	
Old mother duck said, "Quack, Quack, Quack,"	
No little ducklings came swimming back.	*Remove last duckling.*
Old mother duck said, "Quack, Quack, Quack," (very loudly)	
Five yellow ducklings came swimming back.	*Add five ducklings.*

Suggestions:
  Have children listen and participate when mother duck says "Quack, Quack, Quack." The last "Quack, Quack, Quack" should be louder than the first five. This is a good poem for children to dramatize. Outline a pond area with chalk, tape, or use an old blue blanket. Decide which child (duckling) will not return in the order of the poem. Teacher reads poem as five ducklings swim across pond. Teacher can demonstrate how ducklings waddle, and how hands can be used for ducks' beak. This poem leads well into discussions about loud and soft or "inside and outside" voices.

THE BIG, BIG TURNIP

(Traditional)

Pieces: farmer   turnip   daughter   cat
              farmer's wife   large piece of ground   dog   mouse

Cut line →

Cut line

A farmer once planted a turnip seed. And it grew, and it grew, and it grew. The farmer saw it was time to pull the turnip out of the ground. So he took hold of it and began to pull.

He pulled, and he pulled, and he pulled, and he pulled. But the turnip wouldn't come up.

So the farmer called to his wife who was getting dinner.

Fe, fi, fo, fum.

I pulled the turnip,

But it wouldn't come up.

And the wife came running, and she took hold of the farmer, and they pulled, and they pulled, and they pulled, and they pulled. But the turnip wouldn't come up.

So the wife called to the daughter who was feeding the chickens nearby.

Fe, fi, fo, fum.

We pulled the turnip,

But it wouldn't come up.

And the daughter came running. The daughter took hold of the wife. The wife took hold of the farmer. The farmer took hold of the turnip. And they pulled, and they pulled, and they pulled, and they pulled. But the turnip wouldn't come up.

So the daughter called to the dog who was chewing a bone.

Fe, fi, fo, fum.

We pulled the turnip,

But it wouldn't come up.

And the dog came running. The dog took hold of the daughter. The daughter took hold of the wife. The wife took hold of the farmer. And the farmer took hold of the turnip. And they pulled, and they pulled, and they pulled. But the turnip wouldn't come up.

The dog called to the cat who was chasing her tail.

Fe, fi, fo, fum.

We pulled the turnip,

But it wouldn't come up.

And the cat came running. The cat took hold of the dog. The dog took hold of the daughter. The daughter took hold of the wife. The wife took hold of the farmer. The farmer took hold of the turnip. And they pulled, and they pulled, and they pulled. But the turnip wouldn't come up.

So the cat called the mouse who was nibbling spinach nearby.

Fe, fi, fo, fum.

We pulled the turnip,

But it wouldn't come up.

And the mouse came running.

"That little mouse can't help," said the dog. "He's too little."

"Phooey," squeaked the mouse. "I could pull that turnip up myself, but since you have all been pulling, I'll let you help too."

Place farmer on board. Cover turnip so that only top is showing with ground piece, and place on board.

Move farmer next to turnip with hands on turnip top. Place wife behind farmer.

Place daughter behind farmer's wife.

Place dog behind daughter.

Place cat behind dog.

So the mouse took hold of the cat. The cat took hold of the dog. The dog took hold of the daughter. The daughter took hold of the wife. The wife took hold of the farmer. The farmer took hold of the turnip. And they pulled, and they pulled, and they pulled. And up came the turnip.

Place mouse behind cat.

And the mouse squeaked, "I told you so!"

Remove ground.

THE LITTLE RED HEN

Pieces:
cottage	sticks	fox
little red hen	fire	sack
mouse	pot	two large rocks
rooster	table	

It was morning. In the cottage where the little red hen and the rooster and the mouse lived, little red hen was happily setting the table for breakfast.

Place cottage, table, and hen on board.
Add rooster.
Add mouse.

"Who will get some sticks for the fire?" said little red hen.

"I won't," grumbled the rooster.

"I won't," squeaked the mouse.

"Then I'll do it myself," said the little red hen, and off she went to gather them.

Remove hen.

When she returned with the sticks and had started the fire, she asked, "Who will get water from the spring to fill the pot?"

Replace with hen and sticks. Place fire over sticks.

"I won't," grumbled the rooster.

"I won't," squeaked the mouse.

"Then I'll do it myself," she said and ran off to fill the pot.

Place pot over fire.

"Who will cook the breakfast?" said the hen.

"I won't," grumbled the rooster.

"I won't," squeaked the mouse.

"Then I'll do it myself," said the hen, and she did.

When breakfast was ready, the hen, the mouse, and the rooster ate together but the rooster spilled the milk, and the mouse scattered crumbs on the floor.

Remove hen. Return hen.
Move hen, mouse, and rooster near table.

"Who will clear the table?" said the hen.

"I won't," grumbled the rooster.

"I won't," squeaked the mouse.

"Then I'll do it myself," said the hen. So she cleared everything and swept the floor.

The lazy rooster and mouse by this time had moved closer to the fire, and had fallen fast asleep.

Move rooster and mouse near the fire.

"Knock, knock, knock," the noise at the door awakened them.

"Who's that?" said the rooster. "Oh it might be the mail carrier with a letter for me," so the mouse went to the door and opened it without looking out the window first to see who was there.

It was a fox. "Help," said the mouse, but the fast old fox, quick as a wink, caught not only the mouse, but also the rooster and the little red hen. Quickly he popped them all into his sack and headed off toward home, thinking about the fine dinner he was bringing to his family.

Place fox and sack on board. Hide rooster, mouse, and hen behind sack.
Remove cottage.

The bag was heavy, and home was a long way, so the fox decided to put it down and rest.

Put fox in horizontal position.

"Snore, Snore, Snore," went the fox.

Little red hen said to the rooster and mouse, "Now we have a chance to escape. I have a pair of scissors and a needle and thread in my apron pocket. I've cut a hole in the bag. Hurry and jump out, find a rock, the biggest one you can carry, and bring it back quickly. "Snore, Snore, Snore," went the fox. Soon the mouse and the rooster returned with large rocks. They pushed them into the sack, and the hen sewed the hole up. Off they ran to their home. They closed the door and locked it, and they bolted the windows. They were safe now.

Remove hen, rooster and mouse from sack.
Add rocks.
Move rocks behind sack.

The fox didn't know he'd been fooled until he got home and opened his sack.

Remove fox and sack with rocks.

The mouse and the rooster were so happy to be home that they didn't grumble and fight anymore; they even helped to cook the dinner with smiles on their faces.

Place cottage, hen, rooster, and mouse beside it on board.

Cut line

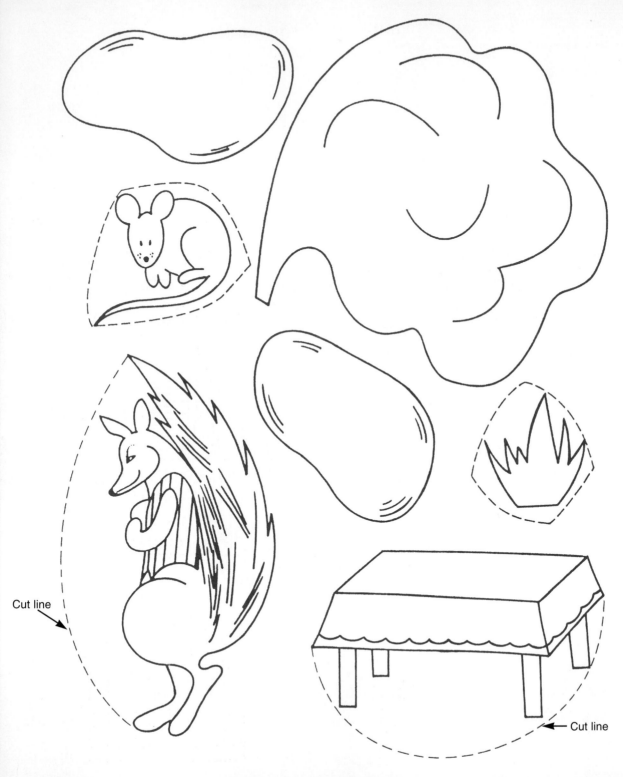

Cut line

Cut line

HUSH, LITTLE BABY

(Flannel-board song)

Pieces: mother   billy goat
         sleeping baby   cart
         crying baby   bull
         mocking bird   dog
         ring   horse
         looking glass

Courtesy of *Adventures in Felt* © Copyright 1972.

Hush, little baby, don't say a word, Mama's going to buy you a mockingbird.	*Place mother and crying baby on her lap.*
If that mockingbird won't sing, Mama's going to buy you a diamond ring.	*Add ring.*
If that diamond ring turns to brass, Mama's going to buy you a looking glass.	*Add looking glass.*
If that looking glass gets broke, Mama's going to buy you a billy goat.	*Add billy goat.*
If that billy goat won't pull, Mama's going to buy you a cart and bull.	*Add cart and bull.*
If that cart and bull turn over, Mama's going to buy you a dog named Rover.	*Add dog.*
If that dog named Rover won't bark, Mama's going to buy you a horse and cart.	*Add horse and move cart from bull.*
If that horse and cart break down, YOU'LL be the sweetest little baby in town.	
Lullaby, baby sweet of mine, you'll be asleep by half past nine.	*Replace crying baby with sleeping baby.*

Cut line

Printscript Activities (Chapter 16)

Teacher-Created Activities

These were based on (1) a particular group of enrolled children; (2) an individual child's interest; or (3) a classroom's unit or theme study. Some suit younger preschoolers, others were enjoyed by older preschoolers who had developed considerable interest in print and print form. Activities suggested represent a variety of skill levels, and don't appear in a simple to complex order.

Clay-on Patterns

These patterns can be used to enhance small, manipulative-muscle use and tracing skills.

Materials:
    clay and contact-covered cardboard sheets with patterns (figure A–1).

Activity:
    Child rolls and forms clay over the cardboard patterns.

Commercial Names and Trademarks

Some children delight in reading their favorite brand names. Many trademarks and product logos have appeared on television, in magazines, in fast-food restaurants, or on products seen in the home. It's surprising how familiar children are with this type of print.

Materials:
    scissors, cardboard, contact paper (optional). Use commercial print cut from ads, or packaging of home products. Mount on stiff paper or cardboard. Get as close to the color and original letter type as possible. Collect pictures of the product, toy food, drink, cereal, etc. the print represents. Mount on cardboard or stiff paper. Cover with clear contact paper.

Activity:
    Child pairs print with picture. Child may want to "read" print labels to adult or another child.

Connecting Dots

The dot patterns for this activity can be made quickly by the teacher on paper or chalkboard and used as a free-play choice. The purpose of this activity is to enhance small-muscle use and children's skills in forming and recognizing symbols.

FIGURE A–1 Patterns

Materials:
paper and writing tools (or chalkboard and chalk)

Activity:
Dots are connected to form symbols (figure A–2).

Sorting Symbols

This activity enhances small-muscle use and the children's skills discriminating symbol differences.

Materials:
paper, writing tool, scissors, paste

Activity:
After the teacher cuts the symbols in squares from sheets, the children are asked to mix them all together and then find the ones that are the same to paste onto another sheet of paper.

Variation:
The teacher can make a cardboard set of symbols that can be sorted by children as a table game (figure A–3).

Alphabet Song

The rhyming song is an easy and fun way for children to recognize letter names.

Materials:
a long printscript alphabet line (figure A–4).

Song:
ABCDEFG
HIJKLMNOP
QRSTU and V
WX and Y and Z.
Now I've said my ABCs,
Tell me what you think of me.

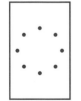  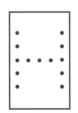 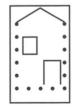

FIGURE A–2   Connecting-dots activity

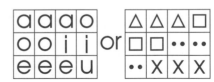

FIGURE A–3   Symbol cards for sorting game

| Aa | Bb | Cc | Dd | Ee | Ff | Gg | Hh | Ii | Jj |

FIGURE A–4   Printscript alphabet line

Activity:

Children sing the song while one child or the teacher touches the corresponding letter on the alphabet line. The teacher can ask the group to sing slowly or quickly, in a whisper or a loud voice, or in a high or low voice.

Gift Wrap

Children are given the opportunity to creatively wrap gifts while learning the usefulness of print.

Materials:

empty boxes, wrapping paper, scissors, decorative stickers, thin-line markers, list that includes the names of all in the class (including teachers), stamps, masking tape, card strips or paper strips preprinted with "To" and "From," small inexpensive gift items or clay child-made objects

Activity:

Children wrap the gifts in boxes with wrapping paper and dictate messages or try to write names on paper or card strips.

Secret Words

This activity promotes visual discrimination and children's recognition of symbols.

Materials:

white crayon, white paper, water colors, and brush

Activity:

The teacher uses white crayon to write a symbol or word on white paper. The crayon should be thickly applied. The teacher demonstrates how the symbol appears when water color is painted over the whole paper. The children can guess the shape names.

Sticker Pictures

The children are shown the relationship between objects and words.

Materials:

stickers, paper strips, felt markers

Activity:

The teacher has each child choose a sticker for his or her paper strip. The child names the sticker, and if the child desires, the teacher writes the name of the sticker on back of strip. The children can then decorate the sticker strips.

Label Fun

The children recognize the print word forms for classroom objects.

Materials:

press-on labels (large size), felt marker

Activity:
Each child is given 5 to 10 labels and told to choose 10 items on the child's body or in the room on which he or she will stick word labels. Child is told to stick labels on something that has not been labeled by another. Teacher prints child's dictated word(s).

Alphabet Walk

This is another group activity to promote children's recognition of alphabet letters.

Materials:
large newsprint art paper, felt marker or dark crayon, masking tape

Activity:
The teacher makes giant letters on art paper, one letter per sheet. The children are told that the teacher is going to place giant letters around the room, and the children are going to choose a child to stand by a letter and wait to be told how the chosen child should move to get to the next one. Have four children choose four friends to walk to the letter A, which teacher points out to them. Teacher selects another child to think of a way, besides walking, that the four children can move to the second letter. The teacher can give suggestions like crawling, hopping, tiptoeing, walking like an elephant, and so forth. Children clap for first four, and another four are selected and directed to walk to another letter.

Find Your Shoe

This group activity shows the usefulness of print.

Materials:
press-on labels, marking pen

Activity:
The children are asked to take off their shoes and put them in front of them. The teacher asks what will happen to the shoes if everyone puts the shoes in one pile and the teacher mixes up the pile. The teacher introduces the idea that shoes would be easier to find if the children's names were added to each shoe by putting a press-on label on the inner sole. Labels preprinted with the child's name are given to each child. The child puts the labels on his or her shoes. The shoes go in a pile, which the teacher mixes. Each child describes his or her shoes to a friend and asks the friend to find the shoes. Two or three friends look in the pile for the shoes at a time. The rest chant "Shoes, shoes come in red, white, and blues . . . Shoes, shoes we will count to 10 and then back to your place and sit again." (Slowly) "1, 2, 3, 4 . . . ."

Alphabet Potato Prints

The children recognize letter names.

Materials:
potatoes, sharp knife (for teacher's use), thick paint, paper, flat containers

Activity:
The teacher cuts potato halves into letters or symbols. Some letters need to be reversed for printing. Prints are made by children.

Alphabet Macaroni Prints

This activity promotes shape discrimination and small-muscle activity.

Materials:
   alphabet soup macaroni (sand, rice, or salt can also be used), glue and brushes, paper, felt pen

Activity:
   Each child traces his or her name or a shape by painting over lines with thinned white glue. The macaroni is then spooned over the glue. When the glue is dry, shake the loose macaroni into a container. The end result will be raised, textured letters (figure A–5). The teacher should demonstrate this process.

ABC "Paste-on" Group Wall Poster

Small-muscle use and symbol recognition are enhanced.

Materials:
   alphabet letters or words cut or torn from magazines or newspapers, large-size poster paper or chart paper

Activity:
   A montage effect is created by having children paste letters where they choose on a piece of paper. During a period of one week, the children can return to the work and paste on more letters. At a group time, children are asked to point to three letters or words (or phrases) that they wish the teacher to read.

Alphabet Eaters

Large-muscle use and visual discrimination are enhanced.

Materials:
   cards with printscript alphabet letters (small enough to be slipped into animal's mouth), sturdy boxes on which animal heads and alphabet strips are glued (holes are cut in the opposite sides of boxes so children can reach in for cards)

Activity:
   A child selects a card and "feeds" it to the animal that has a similar alphabet letter on the strip under its mouth (figure A–6).

Footprint Alphabet Walk

This activity promotes large-muscle use and symbol recognition.

FIGURE A–5   Alphabet macaroni pictures

FIGURE A–6 Alphabet "eaters" and cards

Materials:
  large cardboard (or cloth) on which 26 footprints have been traced, cardboard footprint cutouts each with a printscript alphabet letter (three sets can be made—lowercase, uppercase, and numerals, if desired), covered with clear contact paper or made from plasticlike material.

Activity:
  Children place cutout footprints over footprint of the correct letter (figure A–7).

Tracers

Tracers can be used over and over again. Waxy crayons or felt markers wipe off with a soft cloth. They can be used to help children recognize and discriminate among symbols and enhance small-muscle coordination.

Materials:
  acetate or clear vinyl sheets, cardboard, scissors, strapping or masking tape, paper, felt pen

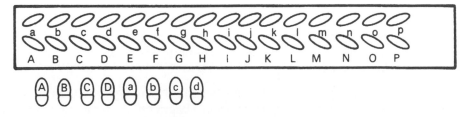

FIGURE A–7 Footprint alphabet walk

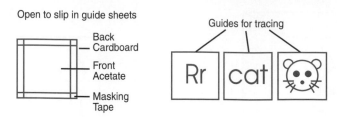

FIGURE A–8 Tracers

Construction:

Attach acetate to cardboard, leaving one side open to form a pocket. Make letter or word guide sheets. Simple pictures can also be used (figure A–8).

Activity:

A child or the teacher selects a sheet and slips it into the tracer pocket. A wax crayon or marker is used by the child to trace the guide sheet. A soft cloth erases the crayon or marker.

Alphabet Bingo

This activity promotes letter recognition and discrimination.

Materials:

cardboard, felt pen, scissors, pencil, ruler, paper, old pack of playing cards, glue, clear contact paper

Construction:

Cardboard is cut to make four or more 8½" × 11" sheets (any similar size is also suitable). Each sheet is divided into 9 or 12 sections. An alphabet letter is added to each section. Make sure each sheet has a different combination of letters. Cover the sheets with clear contact paper. Turning to the pack of old playing cards, glue paper to the front side of each playing card. Add letters of the alphabet. Covering the cards with clear contact paper will make the cards more durable. For markers, cut paper into small pieces; bottle caps or poker chips may also be used.

Activity:

The teacher passes out the sheets to the children. Holding up a playing card (with a letter on it), the teacher asks whether any child has that letter on his or her sheet. If so, the child should cover the letter with a marker. The game is over when every child who wishes completes his or her sheet. At that time, all markers are removed and a new game begins. Many four-year-olds are able to play this game without teacher help after playing it a few times.

Popcorn Names

This activity promotes small-muscle use and symbol recognition.

Materials:

alphabet letters (drawn by the teacher on 8½" × 11" sheets), liquid white glue with brush or stick applicator, (which can be colored by the teacher by shaking popcorn in a bag with dry tempera paint) (Note: Use a well ventilated area when working with dry tempera paint.)

FIGURE A–9 Popcorn names

Activity:
Children paste the popcorn on lines forming letters (figure A–9).

Variation:
Colored fish tank rocks, fresh peas, pebbles, seeds, or salt can also be used.

Drawing Activities

Words on Drawings

In this labeling activity, children select words that can be added to their drawings.

Materials:
felt pen or crayons

Activity:
The teacher asks each child individually whether words can be added to his or her painting, drawing, or illustration. Make sure the child realizes that the teacher is going to write on the drawing. It is a good idea to show the child what has been done to another child's picture beforehand. Most children will want words added, but some will not. It is best to limit this activity to the children who are making symbols of faces, figures, houses, and so forth, in their work. Younger children might not be able to decide what to have written on their work when asked, "Would you like me to put a word name on something you've drawn in your picture?"

Rebus Stories

Teachers can use drawings or photographs to encourage child participation during storytelling time. At a crucial point in the story, the teacher pauses and holds up a picture, and the children guess the next word in the story. Teachers can name the picture and resume the story if the children haven't guessed the word. Any guess that is a close approximation is accepted; for example, "It is a truck, Josh, a fire truck." The rebus story in figure A–10 is an example of teacher authorship. Many additional teacher-created rebus stories are possible.

DUCK AND BEAR TAKE A TRIP

This is and this is his friend .

 cried one day and said "Let's take a vacation!" had not

learned to fly.   "I get tired walking." said .   "Let's ask

wise old how we can take a trip when a  won't walk

and a can't fly."   Wise old said, "That's not a problem.

Both of you can ride your  to the airport.   Buy a ticket

FIGURE A–10   This rebus story, created by a teacher, uses computer-generated graphics.   *continues*

and watch the  . On an

can sit down and doesn't have to know how to fly.

When the  lands, rent a  .

In a  can sit and can sit too."

"Thank you, wise old ." "You're very welcome,  ."

"Now take along a  so you can write me a postcard," said .

FIGURE A–10 *continued*

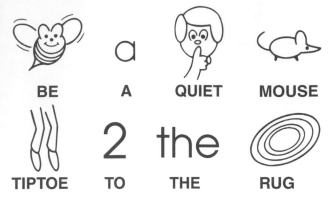
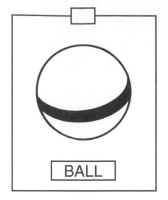
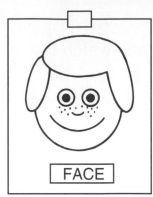

FIGURE A–11 This rebus story, created by a teacher, uses computer-generated graphics.

FIGURE A–12 Labeling pictures

- *Guessing rebus messages (for older preschoolers)*
  The sets of pictures in figure A–11 are put up on the wall. The teacher asks the children to find the message by guessing the word for each picture. The teacher writes the correct words underneath the pictures.
- *Labeling pictures*
  Tape pictures like the ones in figure A–12 on a display board using masking tape. Write identifying names dictated by children underneath each picture.
- *Daily helper identification*
  Make a chart with the children's names printed next to a picture of their jobs for the day (figure A–13).

Chalk Talk

This activity motivates children's interest in letter forms.

Materials:
  chalk, chalkboard, chalkboard eraser

Activity:
  Teacher presents the rhyme and drawings on the chalkboard (figure A–14). When the activity ends, ask whether anyone would like a turn at the chalkboard. A "line fence" on the chalkboard between children helps each to know his or her drawing area.

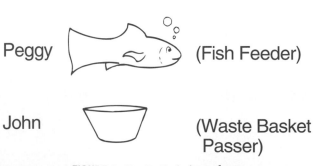

FIGURE A–13 Daily helper chart

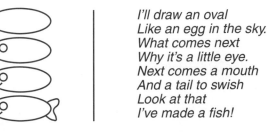

DRAW A FISH

*I'll draw an oval
Like an egg in the sky.
What comes next
Why it's a little eye.
Next comes a mouth
And a tail to swish
Look at that
I've made a fish!*

FIGURE A–14 Chalk talk

Alphabet Pronunciation Guide (Chapter 16)

Symbols	*Sounds as in the Words*	*Symbols*	*Sounds as in the Words*
a	fat, apple, asks	m	him, me, custom
ā	ate, name	n	sun, not, even
b	rib, big	o	ox, on, not
c	traffic, cat, certain	ō	go, open, home
d	lid, end, feed	p	sip, pat
e	end, wet, pen	r	ran, rip, very
ē	me, Elaine, eat	s	kiss, so, last, sugar
f	if, leaf, full	t	hit, top
g	rag, go, gem	u	up, rug, custom
h	hat, how, high	ū	useful, unite
i	it, individual, pin	v	give, have, very
i	piece, niece	w	we, win, watch
ī	ice, while	x	box
j	jump, jeep	y	yea, you
k	lick, kiss, milk	ȳ	my, cry
l	will, late, little	z	zoo, fuzz

Vowel Digraph Sounds

ai . . . . snail		ey . . . . key	
ay . . . . say		ey . . . . they	
ea . . . . lead		oa . . . . float	
ea . . . . tea		oe . . . . hoe	
ee . . . . sheep		ow . . . . grow	
ei . . . . receive		ou . . . . though	
ie . . . . believe			

Vowel Diphthongs

oa . . . . foal	ue . . . . sue
oi . . . . toil	ew . . . . new
ou . . . . though	
oy . . . . soy	

Checklist for the Development of Reading Behaviors (Chapter 17)

1 YEAR

_____ Handles books without necessarily verbalizing.

_____ Crumples, tears, and chews books.

_____ Ignores print.

15 MONTHS

_____ Turns book pages in random order.

_____ Verbalizes while pointing to pictures in books.

_____ Points to pictures of known objects when objects are named.

_____ Pats pictures of things liked.

_____ Points to round things (circles, balls, the letter *o*).

18 MONTHS

_____ Orients pictures to line of vision.

_____ Asks for pictured objects and animals to be named.

_____ Demonstrates pictured action.

_____ Tells a "story" related to pictures on pages.

_____ Answers questions about story that has been read aloud several times.

_____ Shows concern for book's condition.

_____ Guesses outcomes when hearing new story.

2 YEARS

_____ Has a favorite book.

_____ Pretends to read (holds book and talks).

_____ Turns pages right-to-left.

_____ Asks for stories to be read aloud.

_____ Remains attentive as story is read.

_____ Remembers names of picture book characters.

_____ Recalls plots of stories read aloud.

_____ Asks what the printed words say.

30 MONTHS

_____ Can turn to the front of a book when asked.

_____ Can turn to the back of a book when asked.

_____ Can point to the top of a page when asked.

_____ Can point to the bottom of a page when asked.

_____ Pretends to pick up objects pictured on pages.

_____ Enjoys looking through picture books.

_____ Likes hearing and repeating nursery rhymes.

_____ Completes oral sentence by saying the last word omitted by an adult (while looking at a picture book illustration).

_____ Talks to book characters (slaps, kisses, and so forth).

_____ Reacts emotionally to story content.

_____ Repeats sentence verbatim.

_____ Asks for a book about a particular topic to be read aloud.

_____ Rejects changed oral version of a familiar story.

_____ Tells purpose of coloring book.

_____ Can tell what common adjectives are not (wet is not dry).

_____ Notices capital letters in color.

3 YEARS

_____ Remains attentive as story is read aloud, even when pictures are not visible.

_____ Can choose two pictures as being the same when given three to choose from.

_____ Can relate activities in the order in which they occurred.

_____ Can name some of the capital letters in own name.

_____ Asks to see pictures when listening to someone read aloud.

4 YEARS

_____ Can rearrange a set of pictures in an order appropriate for a story.

_____ Can name six or more capital letters.

_____ Points to printed area of page as the place to look when you read.

_____ Chooses a set of letters when given letters and numbers and asked to point to a word.

_____ Copies letters, reversing only a few.

_____ Can retell the plot of a short story after hearing it only once.

5 YEARS

_____ Can spell three or more words orally.

_____ Asks what letter sequences spell.

_____ Recognizes letters comprising own name.

_____ Recognizes words from signs, food containers, and television commercials.

_____ Can select and order letters to form own name.

_____ Can point to capital (or "big") letters on a page of print.

_____ Copies letters from books on separate paper.

_____ Tells story appropriate to newspaper comic strip.

Glossary

Accommodation — the process by which new experiences or events change existing ideas or thought patterns.

Acuity — how well or clearly one uses senses; the degree of perceptual sharpness.

Affective sphere — the affectionate feelings (or lack of them) shaped through experience with others.

Articulation — the adjustments and movements of the muscles of the mouth and jaw involved in producing clear oral communication.

Assimilation — the process that allows new experiences to merge with previously stored mental structures.

Attachment — a two-way process formed through mutual gratification of needs and reciprocal communication influenced by the infant's growing cognitive abilities. Sometimes referred to as bonding.

Auditory — relating to or experienced through hearing.

Black English — a language usually spoken in some economically depressed black homes. A dialect of nonstandard English having its own rules and patterns.

Classify — the act of systematically grouping things according to identifiable common characteristics; for example, size.

Communication — the giving (sending) and receiving of information, signals, or messages.

Concept — a commonly recognized element (or elements) that identifies groups or classes, usually has a given name.

Conceptual tempo — a term associated with Jerome Kagan's theory of different individual pacing in perceptual exploration of objects.

Convergent thinking — moving toward a single, acceptable, conventional solution to a problem.

Cooing — an early stage during the prelinguistic period in which vowel sounds are repeated, particularly the u-u-u sound.

Culture — all the activities and achievements of a society that individuals within that society pass from one generation to the next.

Curriculum — an overall plan for the content of instruction to be offered in a program.

Deaf — children whose hearing is so impaired that they are unable to process auditory linguistic information, with or without amplification.

Dialect — a variety of spoken language unique to a geographical area or social group. Variations in dialect may include phonological or sound variations, syntactical variations, and lexical or vocabulary variations.

Divergent thinking — differing lines of thinking and possible searching for a new idea(s).

Dramatic play — acting out experiences or creating drama episodes during play.

Ebonics — a nonstandard form of English, a dialect often called Black English that is characterized by not conjugating the verb "to be" and by dropping some final consonants from words.

Echolalia — a characteristic of the babbling period. The child repeats (echoes) the same sounds over and over.

Emergent literacy — young children's language arts concepts, behaviors, and skills which precede and can develop into reading, conventional writing, and a body of literacy knowledge.

Equilibrium — a balance attained with consistent care and satisfaction of needs that leads to a sense of security and lessens anxiety.

Expansion — a teaching technique that includes the adult's (teacher's) modeling of word(s) or grammar, filling in missing words in children's utterances, or suggesting ideas for child exploration.

Explanatory talk — a type of conversation characterized by a speaker's attempt to create connections between objects, events, concepts, or conclusions in order to promote understanding in the listener.

Expressive jargon — a term describing a child's first attempts at combining words into narration that results in a mimic of adult speech.

Gaze coupling — infant-mother extended eye contacts.

Grammar — the word order and knowledge of "marker" word meanings necessary to send communications to (and receive them from) another in the same language.

Hearing disorders — characterized by an inability to hear sounds clearly. May range from hearing speech sounds faintly or in a distorted way, to profound deafness.

Holophrases — the expression of a whole idea in a single word. They are characteristic of the child's language from about 12–18 months.

Impulsive — quick to answer or react to either a simple or complex situation or problem.

Inflections — the grammatical "markers" such as plurals. Also, a change in pitch or loudness of the voice.

Inner speech — mentioned in Vygotsky's theory as private speech that becomes internalized and is useful in organizing ideas.

Joint attention — child's awareness that he or she must gain and hold another's focus during communicational exchanges to get his or her message understood.

Language — the means by which a person communicates ideas or feelings to another in such a way that the meaning is mutually understood.

Listening — recognizing and interpreting sounds and oral symbols.

Literacy — involves complex cognitive interactions between readers and their texts and between background knowledge and new information. It involves both skill and knowledge and varies by task and setting. Different types of literacy are described—prose, document, quantitative, academic, workplace, and functional.

Moderation level — an individual preferred state of arousal between bored and excited when learning and pleasure peak.

Modifier — a word that gives a special characteristic to a noun (for example, a *large* ball).

Morpheme — the smallest unit in a language that by itself has a recognizable meaning.

Morphology — the study of the units of meaning in a language.

Neuroscience — study and research concerned with brain growth and development.

Otitis media — inflammation and/or infection of the middle ear.

Overregularization — the tendency on the part of children to make the language regular, such as using past tenses like -ed on verb endings.

Perception — mental awareness of objects and other data gathered through the five senses.

Phonation — exhaled air passes the larynx's vibrating folds and produces "voice."

Phoneme — one of the smallest units of speech that distinguishes one utterance from another.

Phonetic — pertaining to representing the sounds of speech with a set of distinct symbols, each denoting a single sound.

Phonology — the sound system of a language and how it is represented with an alphabetic code.

Pragmatics — the study of how language is used effectively in a social context; varying speech patterns depending on social circumstances and the context of situations.

Prosodic speech — the child's use of voice modulation and word stress to give special emphasis and meaning.

Reflective — taking time to weigh aspects or alternatives in a given situation.

Regularization — a child's speech behavior that indicates the formation and internalization of a language rule (regularity).

Resonation — amplification of laryngeal sounds using cavities of the mouth, nose, sinuses, and pharynx.

Responsive mothers — mothers who are alert and timely in responding to and giving attention to infant needs and communications.

Rhythm — uniform or patterned recurrence of a beat, accent, or melody in speech.

Scaffolding — a teaching technique helpful in promoting languages, understanding, and child solutions. It includes teacher-responsive conversation, open-ended questioning, and facilitation of children's initiatives.

Selective mutism — a behavior that describes child silence or lack of speech in select surroundings and/or with certain individuals.

Semantics — the study of meanings, of how the sounds of language are related to the real world and our own experiences.

Sensory-motor development — the control and use of sense organs and the body's muscle structure.

Speech and language disorders — communication disorders that affect the way people talk and understand and range from simple sound substitutions to not being able to use speech and language at all.

Standard English — substantially uniform formal and informal speech and writing of educated people that is widely recognized as acceptable wherever English is spoken and understood.

Subculture — an ethnic, regional, economic, or social group exhibiting characteristic patterns of behavior sufficient to distinguish it from others within an embracing culture or society.

Symbol — something standing for or suggesting (such as pictures, models, word symbols, and so forth).

Synapse — the gap-like structure over which the axon of one neuron beams a signal to the dendrites of another forming a connection in the human brain. Concerns memory and learning.

Syntax — the arrangement of words as elements in a sentence to show their relationship.

Telegraphic speech — a characteristic of early child sentences in which everything but the crucial word(s) is omitted, as if for a telegram.

Transmission teaching — a teaching style based on the belief that child learning takes place through teacher verbalization, explanation, and the sharing of books.

Whole language — a philosophy and reading-instruction approach integrating oral and written language. Advocates believe that when children are given literature-abundant and print-rich environments they will follow their natural curiosity and learn to read as they learned to speak. A thematic focus is used. Teachers seize opportunities to connect and interrelate language arts areas.

Writing — the ability to use print to communicate with others.

References

Acredolo, L., & Goodwyn, S. (March/April 1992). In A. P. Matheny, Communicating by gesture, *Twins*, *8*(5), 44–45.

Acredolo, L. P., & Goodwyn, S. W. (1986). Symbolic gesturing in language development. *Human Development*, *28*, 53–58.

Ahlberg, J., & Ahlberg, A. (1986). *The jolly postman*. Boston, MA: Little, Brown.

Ainsworth, M. D. S., & Bell, S. M. (1972). Mother-infant interaction and development of competence. *ERIC Document*, ED 065 180.

Allen, R. V. (1969). *Language experiences in early childhood*. Chicago, IL: Encyclopedia Britannica.

Allen, R. V., & Allen, C. (1968). *Language experience in reading*. Chicago, IL: Encyclopedia Britannica.

Allen, R. V., & Allen, C. (1982). *Language experience activities*. Boston, MA: Houghton Mifflin.

Allen, V. G. (1992). Teaching bilingual and ESL children. In J. Flood et al. (Eds.), *Handbook of Research on Teaching the English Language Arts*. New York: Macmillan Publishing Company, 356–364.

Almy, M. (1975). *The early childhood educator at work*. New York: McGraw-Hill.

Anbar, A. (1984). Natural reading acquisition of preschool children. Doctoral dissertation. State University of New York at Buffalo.

Anbar, A. (March 1986). Reading acquisition of preschool children without systematic instruction. *Early Childhood Research Quarterly*, *1.1*, 69–83.

Anderson, D., & Collins, P. (April 1988). *The impact on children's education: Television's influence on cognitive development*. Office of Educational Research and Improvement. U.S. Department of Education.

Anderson, R. (October 1988). Putting reading research into practice. Interview with C. H. Goddard. *Instructor*, 31–37.

Anderson, R. C., Hiebert, E. H., Scott, J. A., & Wilkinson, I. A. (Eds.). (1985). *Becoming a nation of readers: The report of the national commission on reading*. Washington, DC: National Institute of Education.

Andress, B. (November 1991). From research to practice: Preschool children and their movement responses to music. *Young Children*, *47*(1). Washington, DC: National Association for the Education of Young Children, 22–27.

Angelou, M. (1969). *I know why the caged bird sings*. New York: Random House.

Applebee, A. N. (1978). *The child's concept of story*. Chicago, IL: The University of Chicago Press.

Applebee, A. N. (1992). Background for reform. In Langer, J. A. (Ed.). *Literature Instruction*. Urbana, IL: National Council of Teachers of English.

Applebee, A. N. (1992). Environments for language teaching and learning: Contemporary issue and future directions. In Flood, J. et al. (Eds.). *Handbook of Research on Teaching the English Language Arts*. New York: Macmillan, 549–556.

Applebee, A. N. (1992). The background for reform. In Langer, J. A. (Ed.). *Literature Instruction*. Urbana, IL: National Council of Teachers of English.

Arbuthnot, M. H. (1953). *The Arbuthnot anthology*. Glenview, IL: Scott, Foresman.

Arbuthnot, M. H., & Root, S. L. Jr. (1968). *Time for poetry*. Glenview, IL: Scott, Foresman.

Arenas, S. (July–August 1978). Bilingual/bicultural programs for preschool children. *Children Today*, 37–45.

Ashton-Warner, S. (1961). *Teacher*. New York: Bantam.

Atkins, C. (November 1984). Writing: Doing something constructive. *Young Children*, *40.6*, 31–36.

Atwerger, B., Edelsky, C., & Flores, B. (November 1987). Whole language: What's new? *Reading Teacher*, *40.2*.

Bader, B. (1976). *American picturebooks from Noah's Ark to the beast within*. New York: Macmillan.

Baker, A., & Greene, E. (1987). *Story telling: Art and technique* (2nd ed.). New York: R. R. Bowker.

Baker, L. (1987). *The third story cat*. Boston, MA: Little, Brown.

Balaban, N. (April/May 1980). What do young children teach themselves? *Childhood Education*, *33.2*, 56–61.

Ballenger, C. (September 1996). Learning the ABC's in the Haitian preschool: A teacher's story. *Language Arts*, *73*(5), 317–323.

Barnes, D. (1976). *From communication to curriculum*. Harmondsworth, England: Penguin Books.

Baron, N. (December 1989). Pigeon-birds and rhyming words: The role of parents in language learning. *Digest Monograph*, Language in Education Series. Report EDO-FL-89-08, ERIC/CLL.

Barone, D. (October 1994). Importance of classroom context: Literacy development of children prenatally exposed to crack/cocaine—Year two. *Research in the teaching of English, 28*(3), 286–312.

Barrio-Garcia, C. (December 1986). The silent handicap. *American Baby, 47*(12), 32–41.

Barrs, M., Ellis, S., Tester, H., & Thomas, A. (1989). *The primary language record*. Portsmouth, NH: Heinemann.

Bartoli, J. S. (1990). On defining learning and disability: Exploring the ecology. *Journal of Learning Disabilities, 23*, 628–631.

Bartoli, J. S. (1995). *Unequal opportunity: Learning to read in the U.S.A.* New York: Teachers College Press.

Batchelder, M. (1979). *The puppet theatre handbook*. New York: Harper and Row.

Bateson M. (1979). The Epigenesis of conversational interaction. *Before Speech*. Bullowa, M. (Ed.). London: Cambridge University Press.

Baumann, J. F. (1992). Organizing and managing a whole language classroom. *Reading Research and Instruction, 31*(3), 1–14.

Bayless, K., & Ramsey, M. (1978). *Music: A way of life for the young child*. St. Louis, MO: C. V. Mosby Company.

Beals, D. E. (1993). Explanatory talk in low-income families' mealtime conversations. *Applied Psycholinguistics, 14*, 489–513.

Beck, M. (1982). *Kidspeak*. New York: New American Library.

Bee, H. (1981). *The developing child*. New York: Harper & Row.

Beers, C. S., & Beers, J. W. (November 1980). Early identification of learning disabilities: Facts and fallacies. *Elementary School Journal, 36.4*, 30–36.

Bellugi, U. (1977). Learning the language. *Readings in Psychology Today*. Schell, R. (Ed.). New York: Random House.

Benard, B. (November 1993). Fostering resiliency in kids. *ASCD Educational Leadership, 51*(3), 44–48.

Bender, J. (January 1971). Have you ever thought of a prop box? *Young Children, 28.3*, 47–53.

Berg, L. (1977). *Reading and loving*. Henley and Boston: Routledge and Kegan.

Berk, L. E., & Winsler, A. (1995). *Scaffolding children's learning*. Washington, DC: National Association for the Education of Young Children.

Bernal, E. M. (1978). The identification of gifted Chicano children. *Educational Planning for the Gifted*. Baldwin, A. Y., Gear, G. H., & Lucito, L. J. (Eds.). Reston, VA: Council For Exceptional Children.

Bernstein, B. (1962). Social class, linguistic codes and grammatical elements. *Language and Speech, 5*, 31–46.

Bernstein, B. (1972). A critique of concept compensatory education. *Functions of Language in the Classroom*. Cazden, C. B., Humes, D., & John, V. P. (Eds.). New York: Teachers College Press.

Bernstein, J. E. (1977). *Books to help children cope with separation and loss*. New York: R. R. Bowker.

Bettelheim, B. (1976). *The uses of enchantment*. New York: Alfred A. Knopf.

Bettelheim, B., & Zelan, K. (1981). *On learning to read*. New York: Alfred A. Knopf.

Biber, B., Shapiro, E., & Wickens, D. (1977). *Promoting cognitive growth: A developmental-interaction point of view*. Washington, DC: National Association for the Education of Young Children.

Bishop, R. S. (1990). Walk tall in the world: African American literature for today's children. *Journal of Negro Education, 59*(4), 556–565.

Bishop, R. S. (1992). Multicultural literature for children: Making informed choices. In Harris, V. J. (Ed.). *Teaching Multicultural Literature in Grades K–8*. Norwood, MA: Christopher-Gordon, 37–54.

Bissex, G. L. (1985). Watching young writers. In Jaggar, A., & Smith-Burke, M. T. (Eds.). *Observing the Language Learner*. Newark, DE: IRA and Urbana, IL: NCTE (co-publishers), 99–115.

Bloodstein, O. (1975). *A handbook on stuttering*. Chicago: National Easter Seal Society of Crippled Children and Adults.

Bloom, L. (1970). *Language development: Form and function in emerging grammars*. Cambridge, MA: MIT Press.

Bloom, L. (1973). *One word at a time*. The Hague: Mouton.

Blum, I., Koskinen, P. S., Tennant, N., Parker, E. M., Straub, M., & Curry, C. (1995). *Using audiotaped books to extend classroom literacy instruction into the homes of second-language learners*. (Reading Research Report No. 29). Athens, GA: NRRC, Universities of Georgia and Maryland College Park.

Bodrova, E., & Leong, D. (1996). *Tools of the Mind*. Englewood Cliffs, NJ: Prentice-Hall, Inc.

Bornstein, M. (Dec. 1991–Jan. 1992). In Goodman, S. Presumed innocents, *Modern Maturity, 34*(6), American Association for Retired Persons, 24–28.

Bos, B. (1983). *Creativity*. San Jose City College Workshop.

Bos, B. (January 1988). Working the magic. *Pre-K Today, 2.6*. New York: Scholastic, 21–23.

Boutte, G., Van Scoy, I., & Hendley, S. (November 1996). Multicultural and nonsexist prop boxes. *Young Children, 52*(1), 34–39.

Braine, M. D. S. (1973). The ontogeny of English phrase structures: The first phase. *Studies of Child Language Development*. Ferguson, C. A., & Slobin, D. I. (Eds.). New York: Holt, Rinehart, and Winston.

Brause, R. S., & Mayher, J. S. (1991). Our students. In Flood, J. et al. (Eds.). *Handbook of Research on Teaching the English Language Arts*. New York: Macmillan Publishing Company, 259–272.

Brazelton, T. B. (1979). Evidence of communication in neonatal behavioral assessment. *Before Speech*. Bullowa, M. (Ed.). London: Cambridge UP.

Brazelton, T. B. (1983). In Restak, R. M. Newborn knowledge. *Human Development*, Annual Editions 83/84. Guilford, CT: The Dushkin Publishing Group Inc., 83–85.

Brazelton, T. B., & Als, H. (1979). Four early stages in the development of mother-infant interaction. *Psychoanalytic Study of the Child, 34*, 349–370.

Bredekamp, S. (1987). *Position statement on standardized testing of young children 3 through 8 years of age*. Washington, DC: NAEYC.

Bredekamp, S. (May 1988). Interview with Susan Landers. Early testing: Does it help or hurt? *The APA Monitor, 19.5*, 17–19.

Bredekamp, S., & Copple, C. (Eds.). (1997). *Developmentally appropriate practice in early childhood programs*. Washington, DC: National Association for the Education of Young Children.

Breneman, L. N., & Breneman, B. (1983). *Once upon a time*. Chicago, IL: Nelson-Hall.

Briggs, K. (May 1988). Perspective from an independent publisher. *CBC Features, 41.3*, 2–3.

Brimer, M. A. (1969). Sex difference in listening comprehension. *Journal of Research and Development in Education, 9*, 19–25.

Brittain, W. L. (March 1973). Analysis of artistic behavior in young children. *Final Report, ERIC, ED 128 091*. Ithaca, NY: Cornell University.

Brock, D. R., & Dodd, E. L. (March 1994). A family lending library: Promoting early childhood literacy development. *Young Children, 49*(3), 16–21.

Broman, B. (1978). *The early years*. Chicago, IL: Rand McNally College Publishing.

Brophy, J. (1991). Teacher influences on student achievement. *American Psychologist, 41*, 1069–1077.

Brophy, J. E. (1977). *Child development and socialization*. Chicago, IL: Science Research Associates.

Brown, M. (1947). *Stone soup*. New York: Charles Scribner's Sons.

Brown, M. W. (1959). *Nibble, nibble*. Menlo Park, CA: Addison-Wesley.

Brown, R. (1973). *A first language*. London: Allen and Unwin.

Bruner, J. S., (1966). *Toward a theory of instruction*. Cambridge, MA: Harvard University Press.

Buchoff, R. (May 1994). Joyful voices: Facilitating language growth through rhythmic responses to chants. *Young Children, 49*(4), 26–30.

Buchwald, J. (1984). Medical clues from babies' cries. *Discover, 5.9*, 49–51.

Buckleitner, W., & Olsen, K. (August 1989). Kids at the keyboard. *Exchange, 68*, 38–41.

Burchfield, D. (November 1996). Teaching all children: Four developmentally appropriate curricular and instructional strategies in primary-grade classrooms. *Young Children, 52*(1), 4–10.

Busy Bee Children's Center. (1989). Teacher observation. Santa Clara.

Cai, M., & Bishop, R. S. (1994). Multicultural literature for children: Towards clarification of the concept. In *Need for story* (pp. 11–27). Urbana, IL: National Council of Teachers of English.

Cambourne, B. (1988). *The whole story: Natural learning and the acquisition of literacy in the classroom*. New York: Ashton Scholastic.

Caplan, T., & Caplan, F. (1983). *The early childhood years*. New York: G. P. Putnam's Sons.

Carew, J. V. (1980). Experience and the development of intelligence in young children at home and in day care. *Monographs of the Society for Research in Child Development, 45.187*, 56–78.

Carter, M., & Jones, E. (September/October 1995). Documenting teacher talk: An exercise in modeling. *Child Care Information Exchange, 105*, 82–83.

Caulkins, L. M. (1979). Speech given at Columbia University.

Cawlfield, M. E. (May 1992). Velcro time: The language connection. *Young Children, 47*(4). Washington, DC: National Association for the Education of Young Children, 26–30.

Cazden, C. (1979). Peekaboo as an instructional model. *Papers and Reports on Child Language Development, 17*, 1–19.

Cazden, C. (1981). *Language in early childhood education*. Washington, DC: NAEYC.

Cazden, C. B. (1972). *Child language and education*. New York: Holt, Rinehart, and Winston.

Cazden, C. B. (1981). Language development and the preschool environment. *Language in Early Childhood Education*. Cazden, C. B. (Ed.). Washington, DC: NAEYC.

Chall, J. (October 1988). Climbing out of the fourth grade slump. Interview with Mary Harbaugh. *Instructor, 97.9*, 51–58.

Chambers, D. W. (1970). *Story telling and creative drama*. Dubuque, IA: Brown.

Charlesworth, R. (Spring 1985). Readiness—Should we make them ready or let them bloom? *Day Care and Early Education, 11.4*, 53–58.

The Children's Television Resource and Education Center. (1989). *TV Monitor, 4*(1).

Chomsky, C. (August/September 1971). Write now, read later. *Childhood Education, 47.2*, 42–47.

Chomsky, N. (1968). *Language and mind*. New York: Harcourt, Brace, and World.

Choosing a child's book. (1986). New York: Children's Book Council.

Chou, H. V., & Pullinan, C. A. (1980). Teacher questioning: A verification and an extension. *Journal of Reading Behavior, 12*, 69–72.

Chukovsky, K. (1963). *From two to five*. Berkeley, CA: University of California.

Chung, U. K. (1994). The effect of audio, a single picture, multiple pictures, or video on second language listening comprehension. *Dissertation Abstracts International, 55*, 892.

Church, E. B. (August 1987). You are special. *Pre-K Today, 1.6*, 21–22.

Clark, E. (1978). Awareness of language. In Sinclair, A. et al. (Eds.). *The Child's Conception of Language*. New York: Springer-Verlag, 17–43.

Clark-Stewart, K. A. (1973). Interactions between mothers and their young children: Characteristics and consequences. *Monographs of the Society for Research in Child Development, 38*, 6–7.

Clay, M. (1991). *Becoming literate: The construction of inner control*. Portsmouth, NH: Heinemann Educational Books.

Clay, M. (1991). Child development. In Flood, J. et al. (Eds.). *Handbook of Research on Teaching the English Language Arts*. New York: Macmillan, 40–45.

Clay, M. (1993). *An observational survey of early literacy achievement*. Auckland, New Zealand: Heinemann.

Clement, J. (March 1981). Promoting preschool bilingualism. *KEYS to Early Childhood Education, 2.3*, 43–51.

Clements, N. E., & Warncke, E. W. (March 1994). Helping literacy emerge at school for less-advantaged children. *Young Children, 49*(3), 22–26.

Cochran-Smith, M. (1984). *The making of a reader*. Norwood, NJ: Ablex.

Coffman, S. (December 1986). In Barrio-Garcia, C. The silent handicap. *American Baby, 47*(12), 32–41.

Cole, M. L., & Cole, J. T. (1989). *Effective intervention with the language impaired child*, (2nd ed.). Rockville, MD: Aspen Publishers Inc.

Commission of Reading. (1985). *Becoming a nation of readers*. Washington, DC: National Institute of Education.

Condon & Sanders. (1983). In Restak, R. M. Newborn knowledge. *Human Development*, Annual Editions 83/84. Guilford, CT: The Dushkin Publishing Group Inc.

Conklin, N. F., & Lourie, M. A. (1983). *A host of tongues*. New York: The Free Press.

Cooper, P. (1993). *When stories come to school*. New York: Teachers & Writers Collaborative.

Copperman, P. (1982). *Taking books to heart*. Menlo Park, CA: Addison Wesley.

Cose, E. (1997). *Color-blind*. New York: HarperCollins.

Costa, A. (1990). Personal communication, June 1988. In Healy, J. M. *Endangered Minds: Why Children Don't Think and What We Can Do About It*. New York: Simon & Schuster.

Costa, A. L. (1991). The search for intelligent life. In *Developing Minds: A Resource Book for Teaching Thinking*. Alexandria, VA: Association for Supervision and Curriculum Development.

Coulson, A. J. (October 1996). Schooling and literacy over time: The rising cost of stagnation and decline. *Research in the Teaching of English, 30*(3), 311–327.

Covey, S. R. (1989). *The seven habits of highly effective people*. New York: Simon & Schuster.

Cox, V. E. L. (1981). The literature curriculum. In Lamme, L. *Learning to Love Literature*. Urbana, IL: NCTE, 1–12.

Crago, M. (1992). Ethnography and language socialization: A cross-cultural perspective. *Topics in Language Disorders, 12*, 28–39.

Criscuolo, N. P. (1982). *You can use television to stimulate your child's reading habits*. Newark, DE: International Reading Association, 5–6.

Cromwell, E. (1980). *Early reading through experience*. Washington, DC: Acropolis Books Limited.

Cross, T. G. (1978). Mother's speech and its association with rate of linguistic development in young children. In Waterson, N., & Snow, C. E. (Eds.). *The Development of Communication*. Chichester, England: Wiley.

Cullinan, B. (1977). Books in the life of the young child. In Cullinan, B., & Carmichael, C. (Eds.). *Literature and Young Children*. NTCE: Urbana, IL, 1–16.

Cullinan, B. E. (1977). *Literature and young children*. Cullinan, B. E. & Carmichael, C. W. (Eds.). Urbana, IL: NCTE, 1–16.

Cullinan, B. E. (October 1992). Whole language and children's literature. *Language Arts, 69*(6), 426–430.

Cullinan, B. E. (September 1994). In L. R. Putnam, Reading instruction: What do we know now that we didn't thirty years ago? *Language Arts, 71*(5), 362–366.

Cummins, J. (1979). Linguistic interdependence and the educational development of bilingual children. *Review of Educational Research, 49*, 222–251.

Cummins, J. (1984). Minority students and learning difficulties: Issues in assessment and placement. In Lebrun, Y. & Paradis, M. (Eds.). *Early Bilingualism and Child Development*. Amsterdam: Swets Publishing Service.

Cummins, J. (1986). Empowering minority students: A framework for intervention. *Harvard Educational Review, 56*, 372–390.

Curran, L. (1994). *Language arts & cooperative learning*. San Clemente, CA: Kogan Cooperative.

Curry, N. E., & Johnson, C. N. (1990). *Beyond self-esteem: Developing a genuine sense of human value*. National Association for the Education of Young Children: Washington, DC.

Cutting, B., & Milligan, J. L. (1991). Learning to read in New Zealand. In C. Kamii, M. Manning, & G. Manning (Eds.), *Early literacy: A constructivist foundation for whole language* (pp. 83–90).

Daniel, J. (March 1995). NAEYC's contractual commitment to children. *Young Children, 50*(3), 2.

Danielson, K. E. (April 1992). Learning about early writing from response to literature. *Language Arts, 69*, 274–280.

Danoff, J., Breitbart, V., & Barr, E. (1976). *Open for children*. New York: McGraw-Hill.

Davidson, J. (February 1988). Computers for preschoolers? *Pre-K Today, 2.5*, 32–41.

Davidson, J. (1989). *Computers in early childhood education*. Albany, NY: Delmar Publishers Inc.

de Villiers, P. A., & de Villiers, J. G. (1979). *Early language*. Cambridge, MA: Harvard UP.

DeGaetano, G. (1993). *Television and the lives of our children*. Redmond, WA: Train of Thought Publishing.

Delaney, Sister St. John. (January 1988). A home reading corner. *Pre-K Today, 2.4*, 34.

DeLawter, J. (1992). Teaching literature: From clerk to explorer. In Langer, J. A. (Ed.). *Literature Instruction*. Urbana, IL: NCTE, 101–130.

Deman, G. (1988). *When you've made it your own . . . teaching poetry to young people*. Portsmouth, NH: Heinemann.

DeVries, R., & Kohlberg, L. (1987). *Constructivist early education: Overview and comparison with other programs*. Washington, DC: National Association for the Education of Young Children.

Diaz, R. M., & Lowe, J. R. (1987). The private speech of young children at risk: A test of three deficit hypotheses. *Early Childhood Research Quarterly, 2.2*, 27–33.

Dickinson, D. K., & Snow, C. E. (March 1987). Interrelationships among prereading and oral language in kindergarteners from two social classes. *Early Childhood Research Quarterly, 2.1*, 1–25.

Ditlow, T. (May–December 1988). Making a book into a successful cassette. *CBC Features, 41.3*, 4–6.

Doake, D. B. (1980). Report on the shared book experience approach to learning to read. Unpublished paper. School of Education. Acadia University.

Doake, D. B. (1985). Reading-like behavior: Its role in learning to read. In Jaggar, A., & Smith-Burke, M. T. (Eds.). *Observing the Language Learner*. Newark, DE: IRA and Urbana, IL: NCTE (co-publishers), 82–98.

Dodge, D. (May 1988). When your program is off track. *Child Care Information Exchange, 61*, 42–48.

Donoghue, M. R. (1985). *The child and the English language arts*. Dubuque, IA: Brown.

Dopyera, J., & Lay-Dopyera, M. (1992). *Becoming a teacher of young children*. New York: McGraw.

Douglass, R. (March 1959). Basic feeling and speech defects. *Exceptional Children, 35.4*, 18–23.

Dumbro, A. (1992). The group process. In A. Mitchell & J. David (Eds.), *Explorations with young children* (pp. 77–88). Mt. Rainier, MD: Gryphon House.

Dumbro, A. (1992). Literacy in early childhood. In A. Mitchell & J. David (Eds.), *Explorations with young children* (pp. 161–176). Mt. Rainier, MD: Gryphon House.

Dumtschin, J. U. (March 1988). Recognizing language development and delay in early childhood. *Young Children, 43.3*, 16–24.

Durkin, D. (1966). *Children who read early*. New York: Teachers College Press.

Durkin, D. (1980). *Strategies for identifying words*. New York: Allyn and Bacon.

Durkin, D. (1983). *Teaching them to read*. New York: Allyn and Bacon.

Durkin, D. (September 1987). A class-observation study of reading instruction in kindergarten. *Early Childhood Research Quarterly, 2.3*, 275–300.

Duthie, C., & Zimet, E. K. (1992). Poetry is like direction for your imagination. *The Reading Teacher, 46*(1).

Dyson, A. H. (January 1990). Symbol makers, symbol weavers: How children link play, pictures, and print. *Young Children, 45*(2), 50–57.

Dyson, A. H. (October 1987). Oral language: The rooting system for learning to write. *Language Arts, 58.3*, 86–92.

Dyson, A. H. (1993). From prop to mediator: The changing role of written language in children's symbolic repertoires. In B. Spodek & O. N. Saracho (Eds.), *Language and literacy in early childhood education* (Vol. 4, pp. 21–41). New York: Teachers College Press.

Education Product Report, 68. (1975). EPIE Exchange Institute, 77.

Edwards, P. (1996). Creating sharing time conversations: Parents and teachers work together. *Language Arts, 73*(5), 344–349.

Edwards, P., Fear, K., & Gallego, M. (1995). Role of parents in responding to issues of linguistic and cultural diversity. In E. Garcia, & B. McLaughlin (Eds.), *Meeting the challenge of linguistic and cultural diversity in early childhood education*. New York: Teachers College Press.

Egan, K. (1988). *Primary understanding: Education in early childhood*. London: Routledge.

Elardo, R., Bradley, R., & Caldwell, B. M. (1977). A longitudinal study of the relation of infants' home environments to language development at age three. *Child Development, 48*, 595–603.

Elbow, P. (1973). *Writing without teachers*. London: Oxford University Press.

Elkind, D. (1971). Cognition in infancy and early childhood. *Human Development and Cognitive Process*. Eliot, J. (Ed.). New York: Holt, Rinehart, and Winston.

Elkind, D. (January 1988). Educating the very young: A call for clear thinking. *NEA Today, 6.6*, 37–39.

Elleman, B. (1995). Handling stereotypes. *Book Links, 4*(5), 4.

Emde, R. (1989). Toward a psychoanalytic theory of affect: The organizational model and its propositions. In Greenspan, S. I., & Pollack, G. H. (Eds.). *The Course of Life*, 1. Infancy, International University Press: Madison, CT, 165–192.

Emery, R. L. (1975). *Reading fundamentals for preschoolers and primary children*. Columbus, OH: Charles E. Merrill.

Engelking, K. (May 1989). The reading/writing connection. Unpublished Master's thesis. Boise State University.

Epstein, A., Schweinhart, L., & McAdoo, L. (1996). *Models of early childhood education*. Ipsilanti, MI: High/Scope Press.

Erikson, E. (1950). *Childhood and society*. New York: W. W. Norton.

Eveloff, H. H. (1977). Some cognitive and affective aspects of early language development. *Child Development Contemporary Perspectives*. Cohen, S., & Comiskey, T. (Eds.). Itasca: F. E. Peacock, 140–155.

Eyler, F. (May 18, 1987). In Kunerth, J. Born communicators. *Orlando Sentinel, 3L*.

Farr, M. (1992). Dialects, culture, and teaching the English language arts. In Flood, J. et al. (Eds.). *Handbook of Research on Teaching the English Language Arts*. New York: Macmillan, 365–369.

Fein, G. (December 1981). Pretend play: New perspectives. *Child Development, 30.6*, 81–93.

Ferguson, P. (May 1988). Whole language: A global approach to learning. *Instructor, 97.9*, 23–28.

Ferguson, P., & Young, T. (December 1996). Literature talk: Dialogue improvisation and patterned conversations with second language learners. *Language Arts, 73*(8), 597–600.

Ferreiro, E. (1985). Literacy development: A psychogenetic perspective. In Olson, D., Torrance, N., & Hildegard, A. (Eds.). *Literacy, Language, and Learning: The Nature and Consequences of Reading and Writing*. New York: Cambridge University Press, 217–228.

Ferreiro, E., & Teberosky, A. (1982). *Literacy before schooling*. Exeter, NH: Heinemann.

Fields, M. (1987). NAEYC developmentally appropriate guidelines and beginning reading instruction. Conference presentation. NAEYC. Chicago.

Fields, M. (November 1996). *Authentic reading and writing activities for beginners*. Presentation made at the annual conference of the National Association for the Education of Young Children, Dallas, TX.

Fields, M. V. (1987). Conference presentation. NAEYC Conference. Chicago.

Fields, M. V., & Lee, D. (1987). *Let's begin reading right*. Columbus, OH: Charles E. Merrill.

Finn, P. (May 1980). Developing critical television viewing skills. *Educational Forum, 44.2*, 41–48.

Fischer, K. (1986). In Friedrich, O. What do babies know? *Human Development 85/86*. Guilford, CT: The Dushkin Publishing Group Inc.

Fisher, M. (1975). *Who's who in children's books*. New York: Holt, Rinehart, and Winston.

Flores, M. I. (July 1980). Helping children learn a second language. *KEYS to Early Childhood Education, 1.6*, 17–27.

Fogel, A. (March/April 1992). In Matheny, A. P. Communication by gesture. *Twins, 8*(5), 44–45.

Fraiberg, S. (1987). *Selected writings of Selma Fraiberg*. Athens, OH: Ohio State UP.

Fredericks, A. D. (October/November 1989). The magic of storytelling. *Reading Today, 7*(2), 13.

Freedman, D. G. (1964). Smiling of blind infants. *Journal of Child Psychology and Psychiatry, 5.174*, 86–92.

Freedman, D. G. (1979). *Human sociobiology*. New York: The Free Press.

Freeman, R. S. (1967). *Children's picture books*. New York: Century House.

French, L. (January 1996). "I told you all about it, so don't tell me you don't know:" Two-year-olds and learning through language. *Young Children, 51*(2), 17–20.

Friedrich, O. (1986). What do babies know? *Human Development 85/86*. Guilford, CT: The Dushkin Publishing Group Inc.

Fujiki, M., & Brinton, B. (1984). *Language, speech, and hearing services in schools, 15.2*, 98–109.

Gaffney, M. (May–December 1988). A film on its own: Looking at media based on literature. *CBC Features, 41.3*, 8–10.

Gage, D., & Cooksey, K. (December 1991–January 1992). Tell me a story. *Modern Maturity, AARP, 34*(6), 72–74.

Galda, L. (October 1989). Children and poetry. *The Reading Teacher, 43*(1), 66–71.

Galda, L., Cullinan, B., & Strickland, D. (1993). *Language, literacy, and the child.* Orlando, FL: Harcourt Brace.

Gall, M. D. (1984). Synthesis of research on teachers' questioning. *Educational Leadership, 42*, 40–47.

Gallagher, J. M., & Coche, J. (September 1987). Hothousing: The clinical and education concerns over pressuring young children. *Early Childhood Research Quarterly, 2.3*, 203–210.

Gandini, L. (1993). Fundamentals of the Reggio Emilia approach to early childhood education. *Young Children, 49*(1), 4–8.

Gandini, L. (1997). In J. Hendrick (Ed.), *First steps toward teaching the Reggio way.* Upper Saddle River, NJ: Prentice-Hall.

Garcia, E. (1991). Effective instruction for language minority students: The teacher. *Journal of Education, 173*(2), 130–141.

Garcia, E., & McLaughlin, B. (Eds.). (1995). *Meeting the challenge of linguistic and cultural diversity in early childhood education.* New York: Teachers College Press.

Garcia-Barrio, C. (August 1986). Listen to the music! *American Baby, 48*(8), 46, 67–69.

Gardner, H. (1993). *Multiple intelligences.* New York: Basic Books.

Gardner, H. (1996). *Frames of mind: The theory of multiple intelligences.* New York: Basic Books.

Garvey, C. (1977). *Play.* Cambridge, MA: Harvard UP.

Garvey, C. (1984). *Children's talk.* Cambridge, MA: Harvard UP.

Geller, L. G. (1985). *Word play and language learning for children.* Urbana, IL: NCTE.

Genesee, F., & Nicoladis, E. (1995). Language development in bilingual preschool children. In E. Garcia & B. McLaughlin (Eds.), *Meeting the challenge of linguistic and cultural diversity in early childhood education.* New York: Teachers College Press.

Genishi, C. (1985). Observing communicative performance in young children. In Jaggar, A., & Smith-Burke, M. T. (Eds.). *Observing the Language Learner.* IRA and NCTE (co-publishers), 131–142.

Gertel-Rutman, S. (January 1988). Arranging the library center. *Pre-K Today, 2.6.* New York: Scholastic, 23–24.

Gibson, E. J. (1969). *Principles of perceptual learning and development.* New York: Appleton-Century-Crofts.

Gill, J. T. (October 1992). Development of word knowledge as it relates to reading, spelling, and instruction. *Language Arts, 69*(6), 444–453.

Ginott, H. (1972). *Teacher and child.* New York: Macmillan.

Glazer, J. I. (1981). Reading aloud with young children. In Lamme, L. (Ed.). *Learning to Love Literature.* Urbana, IL NCTE, 37–46.

Glazer, J. I. (1986). *Literature for young children.* Columbus, OH: Charles E. Merrill.

Glazer, S., & Burke, E. (1994). *An integrated approach to early literacy: Literature to language.* Needham Heights, MA: Allyn & Bacon.

Gleason, J. B. (1981). An experimental approach to improving children's communicative ability. *Language in Early Childhood Education.* Cazden, C. B. (Ed.). Washington, DC: NAEYC.

Gleason, J. B. (May 18, 1987). In Kunerth, J. Born communicators. *Orlando Sentinel, 3L.*

Goetz, E. M. (July 1979). Early reading. *Young Children, 34.6*, 94–99.

Golden, J. M., Meiners, A., & Lewis, S. (January 1992). The growth of story meaning. *Language Arts, 69*, 22–27.

Gonzalez-Mena, J. (1976). English as a second language for preschool children. *Young Children, 32*(1), 16–21.

Goodman, K. (1986). *What's whole in whole language.* Portsmouth, NH: Heinemann Educational Publishers.

Goodman, K. S. (September 1992). Whole language is today's agenda in education. *Language Arts, 69*, 354–362.

Goodman, Y. (1986a). Children coming to know literacy. In Teale, W., & Sulzby, E. (Eds.). *Emergent Literacy.* Norwood, NJ: Ablex, 1–14.

Goodman, Y. (1986b). *Emergent literacy: Writing and reading.* Norwood, NJ: Ablex.

Goodman, Y. (1990). *How children construct literacy.* Newark, DE: International Reading Association.

Goodman, Y., & King, M. (January 1995). In Focus on research for the 21st century: A diversity of perspectives among researchers. *Language Arts, 72*(1), 56–60.

Goodman, Y. (1985). Kidwatching: Observing children in the classroom. In Jaggar, A., & Smith-Burke, M. T. (Eds.). *Observing the Language Learner.* Newark, DE: IRA and Urbana, IL: NCTE (co-publishers).

Goodman, Y. (1990). *How children construct literacy.* Newark, DE: IRA.

Gordon, A. (1984). *A touch of wonder.* Old Tappan, NJ: Revell.

Gordon, E. (August 1986). In Garcia-Barrio, C. Listen to the music! *American Baby, 48*(8), 46, 67–69.

Gottesman, A. (October 27, 1993). Method lets students invent spellings. *The Idaho Statesman, A–1.*

Gottschall, S. M. (May 1995). Hug-a-book: A program to nurture a young child's love of books and reading. *Young Children, 50*(4), 29–35.

Gowen, J. W. (March 1995). The early development of symbolic play. *Young Children, 50*(3), 75–84.

Grant, R. (1995). Meeting the needs of young second language learners. In E. Garcia, & B. McLaughlin (Eds.), *Meeting the challenge of linguistic and cultural diversity in early childhood education.* New York: Teachers College Press.

Graves, D. H. (1981). Patterns of child control of the writing process. In Walshe, R. D. (Ed.). *Donald Graves in Australia.* Exeter, NH: Heinemann.

Greenberg, H. M., Dr. (1969). *Teaching with feeling.* New York: Pegasus.

Greenspan, S. I. (1997). *The growth of the mind and the endangered origins of intelligence.* Reading, MA: Addison-Wesley.

Greenspan, S. I., & Greenspan, N. T. (1985). *First feelings: Milestone in the emotional development of the child.* New York: Viking.

Greenspan, S. I., & Meisels, S. (June 1994). Toward a new vision for the developmental assessment of infants and young children. *Zero to three: Bulletin of the National Center for Clinical Infant Programs, 14*(6), 1–8.

Grey, K. (May 1996). In S. Lapinski, Signs of intelligence, *Child, 11*(4), 46–51.

Griffing, P. (January 1983). Encouraging dramatic play in early childhood. *Young Children, 38.2*, 45–51.

Hakuta, K. (1986). *The mirror of language.* New York: Basic Books.

Hale, E. (January 12, 1997). Flap over Ebonics clarifies the problem, but not the solution. *The Idaho Statesman*, p. A12.

Hall, E. (1982). *Child psychology today*. New York: Random House.

Hall, M. A. (1970). *Teaching reading as a language experience*. Columbus, OH: Merrill.

Halliday, M. (1973). *Explorations in the functions of language*. London: Edward Arnold.

Halliday, M. A. K. (1973). The functional basics of language. In Bernstein, B. (Ed.). *Class, codes, and control, 2, Applied Studies Toward a Sociology of Language*. Boston, MA: Routledge and Kegan.

Halliday, M. A. K. (1975). *Learning how to mean: Explorations in development of language*. London: Edward Arnold.

Halliday, M. A. K. (1979). One child's protolanguage. *Before Speech*. Bullowa, M. (Ed.). London: Cambridge UP, 171–190.

Hanley, K. S. (July 1995). Board books. *Book Links*, 4(6), 43–47.

Hansen, V. J. (January 1991). The language arts interact. *Handbook of Research in Language Arts*, 805–819.

Harker, J. O., & Green, J. L. (1985). When you get the right answer to the wrong question: Observing and understanding communication in classrooms. In Jaggar, A., & Smith-Burke, M. T. (Eds.). *Observing the Language Learner*. Newark, DE: IRA and Urbana, IL: NCTE, 221–231.

Harris, J. (1990). *Early language development*. London: Routledge.

Harris, V. J. (January 1991). Multicultured curriculum: African American children's literature. *Young Children*, 40(2). Washington, DC: NAEYC, 37–44.

Harris, V. J. (1993). From the margin to the center of the curricula: Multicultural children's literature. In B. Spodek, & O. Saracho (Eds.), *Language and literacy in early childhood education* (pp. 123–140). New York: Teachers College Press.

Harvey, S., Mcauliffe, S., Benson, L., Cameron, W., Kempton, S., Lusche, P., Miller, D., Schroeder, K., & Weaver, J. (December 1996). Teacher-researchers study the process of synthesizing in six primary classrooms. *Language Arts*, 73(8), 564–574.

Hastings, S., & Ruthenberg, D. (1975). *How to produce puppet plays*. New York: Harper and Row.

Hayward, R. A. (May 1988). Inside the whole language classroom. *Instructor*, 97.9, 15–19.

Healy, J. M. (1987). *Your child's growing mind*. New York: Doubleday.

Healy, J. M. (1990). *Endangered minds*. New York: Simon & Schuster.

Healy, M. K., & Barr, M. (1992). Language across the curriculum. In Flood, J. et al. (Ed.). *Handbook of Research on Teaching English Language Arts*. New York: Macmillan, 820–826.

Heath, S. B. (1983). *Ways with words: Language, life, and work in communities and classrooms*. Cambridge, MA: Cambridge University Press.

Hendrick, J. (Ed.). (1997). *First steps toward teaching the Reggio way*. Upper Saddle River, NJ: Prentice-Hall, Inc.

Hillerich, R. L. (February 1976). Toward an assessable definition of literacy. *The English Journal*, 65, 29–31.

Hillerich, R. L. (1977). *Reading fundamentals for preschool and primary children*. Columbus, OH: Charles E. Merrill.

Hirsch, E. D., Jr. (January 1988). Cultural literacy: Let's get specific. *Today*, 6.6, 37–39.

Hoban, R. (1972). *Egg thoughts and other Frances songs*. New York: Harper and Row.

Hoggart, R. (1970). *Speaking to each other, 2*. London: Chatto and Windus.

Holdaway, D. (1979). *The foundations of literacy*. New York: Ashton Scholastic.

Holdaway, D. (1986). The structure of natural learning as a basis for literacy instruction. In M. Sampson (Ed.), *The pursuit of literacy: Early reading and writing*. Dubuque, IA: Kendall/Hunt Publisher.

Holdaway, D. (1991). Shared book experience: Teaching reading using favorite books. In C. Kamii, M. Manning, & G. Manning (Eds.), *Early literacy: A constructivist foundation for whole language* (pp. 91–110). Washington, DC: National Education Association of the United States.

Holmes, D. L., & Morrison, F. J. (1979). *The child*. Monterey, CA: Brooks-Cole.

Honig, A. S. (November 1981). What are the needs of infants? *Young Children*, 36.5, 38–41.

Honig, A. S. (May 1988). Humor development in children. *Young Children*, 43.4, 60–73.

Honig, A. S. (July 1995). Singing with infants and toddlers. *Young Children*, 50(5), 71–78.

Honig, W. (October 14, 1988). In Watson, A. Dick and Jane Meet the Classics. *San Jose Mercury News*, 4L.

Horrworth, G. L. (1966). Listening: A facet of oral language. *Elementary English*, 43, 856–864, 868.

Hostetler, A. J. (July 1988). Why baby cries: Data may shush skeptics. *The APA Monitor*, 19.7, 27–32.

Hough, R. A., Nurss, J. R., & Goodson, M. S. (1984). Children in day care: An observational study. *Child Study Journal*, 14.1, 33–41.

Hough, R. A., Nurss, J. R., & Wood, D. (November 1987). Tell me a story. *Young Children*, 43.1, 71–75.

How does your child grow and learn? (1982). A Guide for Parents of Young Children. Jefferson City, MO: Missouri Department of Elementary Education and Secondary Education.

Howarth, M. (November 1989). Rediscovering the power of fairy tales. *Young Children*, 45(1), 58–59.

Hoy, J., & Somer, I. (Eds.). (1974). *The language experience*. New York: Dell.

Huck, C. (1976). *Children's literature in the elementary school*. New York: Holt, Rinehart, and Winston.

Huck, C. S. (November 1992). Literacy and literature. *Language Arts*, 69(7), 520–526.

Huey, E. B. (1908). *The psychology and pedagogy of reading*. New York: Macmillan.

Huey, F. (November 1965). Learning potential of the young child. *Educational Leadership*, 40.6.

Hunt, J. M. (1961). *Intelligence and experience*. New York: The Ronald Press.

Hunt, T., & Renfro, N. (1982). *Puppetry in early childhood education*. Austin, TX: Renfro Studios.

Hutinger, P. L. (Spring 1978). Language development: It's much more than a kit. *Day Care and Early Education*, 5.2, 44–47.

Hymes, D. (1971). Competence and performance in linguistic theory. *Language Acquisition: Models and Methods*. Huxley, R., & Ingram, E. (Eds.). New York: Academic Press.

Identifying and serving recent immigrant children who are gifted. (1992). *ERIC Digest E520*. Reston, VA: Council For Exceptional Children.

Itzkoff, S. (1986). *How we learn to read*. New York: Paideia Publishers.

Jacobson, A. L. (July 1978). Infant day care: Toward a more human environment. *Young Children, 33.5*, 31–36.

Jacobson, R. (1968). *Child language*. The Hague: Monton.

Jaffe, N. (1992). Music in early childhood. In A. Mitchell, & J. David (Eds.), *Explorations with young children* (pp. 215–228). Mt. Rainier, MD: Gryphon House.

Jaggar, A. (1980). Allowing for language differences. In Pinnell, G. S. (Ed.). *Discovering Language with Children*. Urbana, IL: NCTE, 25–28.

Jaggar, A. M. (1985). On observing the language learner: Introduction and overview. In Jaggar, A., & Smith-Burke, M. T. (Eds.). *Observing the Language Learner*. Newark, DE: IRA and Urbana, IL: NCTE (co-publishers).

Jalongo, M. (January 1996). Teaching young children to become better listeners. *Young Children, 51*(2), 21–26.

Jaronczyk, F. (November 1984). The art of story time. *First Teacher, 5.11*, 18–24.

Jenkins, E. C. (1973). Multi-ethnic literature: Promise and problems. *Elementary English, 31.6*, 17–26.

Jespersen, O. (1945). *Mankind, nation, and individual from a linguistic point of view*. Bloomington, IN: Indiana UP.

Jewell, M. G., & Zintz, M. V. (1986). *Learning to read naturally*. Dubuque, IA: Kendall/Hunt.

Johnson, K. (1987). *Doing words*. Boston, MA: Houghton Mifflin.

Jones, E. (November 1995). Children need rich language experiences. *Child Care Information Exchange, 106*, 62.

Jones, E., & Villarino, G. (January 1994). What goes up on the classroom walls—and why? *Young Children, 49*(2), 38–39.

Jones, P. S. (1990). *In the land where the mountains are gone*. Unpublished master's thesis, Wright State University. Dayton, OH.

Judy, S. (1980). *The ABCs of literacy*. Oxford: Oxford UP.

Junker, K. S. (1979). Communication starts with selective attention. *Before Speech*. Bullowa, M. (Ed.). London: Cambridge UP, 307–320.

Kagan, J. (1971). *Change and continuity*. New York: John Wiley & Sons.

Kagan, J. (April 1988). Affect and cognition. *The APA Monitor, 19.4*, 17–26.

Kamii, C., Manning, M., & Manning, G. (Eds.). (1991). *Early literacy: A constructivist foundation for whole language* (pp. 9–16). Washington, DC: National Education Association of the United States.

Kane, F. (May/June 1982). Thinking, drawing—Writing, reading. *Childhood Education, 33.5*, 292–297.

Kantor, R., Miller, S. M., & Fernie, D. E. (1992). Diverse paths to literacy in a preschool classroom: A sociocultural perspective. *Reading Research Quarterly, 27*(3), 185–201.

Katz, B. (1983). *Bedtime Bear's book of bedtime poems*. New York: Random House.

Katz, L. (November 1993). In Scott, W. Teaching young children. *ASCD Update, 35*(9), 1–8.

Katz, L., & Chard, S. (1989). *Engaging children's minds: The project approach*. Norwood, NJ: Ablex Publishers.

Kay, J. (April 12, 1996). Therapy helps stutterers speak out. *The Idaho Statesman*, 2D.

Kaye, K. (1979). Thickening thin data: The maternal role in developing communication and language. *Before Speech*. Bullowa, M. (Ed.). London: Cambridge UP, 191–206.

Kelly, M. (September 4, 1985). At 4, reading shouldn't be an issue. *San Jose Mercury News*, 16E.

Kiefer, B. Z. (1985). Cultures together in the classroom: "What you Sayin'?" In Jaggar, A., & Smith-Burke, M. T. (Eds.). *Observing the Language Learner*. Newark, DE: IRA and Urbana, IL: NCTE (co-publishers), 159–172.

King, M. L. (1985). Language and language learning for child watchers. In Jaggar, A., & Smith-Burke, M. T. (Eds.). *Observing the Language Learner*, Newark, DE: IRA and Urbana, IL: NCTE (co-publishers), 19–38.

Kitano, M. (May 1982). Young gifted children: Strategies for preschool teachers. *Young Children, 37.4*, 29–31.

Klaus, M. H., & Klaus, P. H. (1985). *The amazing newborn*. Menlo Park, CA: Addison Wesley.

Kohl, H. (1982). *Basic skills*. Boston, MA: Little, Brown.

Koons, K. (May 1986). Puppet plays. *First Teacher, 7.5*, 56–64.

Kozol, J. (1985). *Illiterate America*. New York: Anchor Press/Doubleday.

Kranyik, M. A. (May 1986). Acting without words. *First Teacher, 7.5*, 65–71.

Krashen, D., & Biber, D. (1988). *On course*. Sacramento, CA: Association for Bilingual Education.

Kratochwill, T. R. (1981). *Selective mutism*. Hillsdale, NJ: Lawrence Erlbaum Associates, Publishers.

Kucenski, D. (1977). Implication and empirical study of a sequential musical sensory learning program on the infant learner. *Dissertation Abstracts International, 38*, 4646A. Doctoral dissertation, Northwestern University.

Labov, W. (1985). *Study report*. Washington, DC: National Science Foundation.

Lair, J. (1985). *I ain't much baby but I'm all I got*. New York: Fawcett.

Lambert, W. (July 1986). In Wells, S. Bilingualism: The accent is on youth. *U.S. News and World Report, 101.8*, 89–92.

Lamme, L. L. (1981). *Learning to love literature*. Urbana, IL: NCTE.

Landers, S. (May 1988). Early testing: Does it help or hurt? *The APA Monitor, 19.5*, 37–40.

Landreth, C. (1972). *Preschool learning and teaching*. New York: Harper and Row.

Langer, J. A. (1992). Rethinking literature instruction. In Langer, J. A. (Ed.). *Literature Instruction*. Urbana, IL: NCTE, 35–53.

Langer, J. A., & Applebee, A. N. (1986). Reading and writing instruction: Toward a theory of teaching and learning. In Rothkopt, E. Z. (Ed.). *Review in Education, 13*, 171–194.

Lapinski, S. (May 1996). Signs of intelligence. *Child, 11*(4), 46–51.

Larrick, N. (September 11, 1965). The all-white world of children's books. *Saturday Review*, 63–65.

Larrick, N. (1975). *A parent's guide to children's reading*. New York: Bantam Books.

Larrick, N. (Fall 1980). Parents and teachers—Partners in children's reading. An interview. *Education Update #7*.

Lear, E. (1946). *The complete nonsense book*. New York: Dodd Mead.

Lee, L. L. (1970). The relevance of general semantics to development of sentence structure in children's language. *Communication: General Semantics Perspectives*. Thayer, L. (Ed.). New York: Spartan Books.

Leland, J., & Joseph, N. (January 13, 1977). Hooked on Ebonics, *Newsweek*, 78–79.

Lenneberg, E. H. (1971). The natural history of language. *Human Development and Cognitive Processes*. Eloit, J. (Ed.). Toronto: Holt, Rinehart, and Winston.

Lentz, K. A., & Burris, N. A. (January/February 1985). How to make your own books. *Childhood Education, 37.5. Journal of ACEI*, 199–202.

Leone, A. H. (May 1986). Story telling. *First Teacher, 7.5*, 41–46.

Lerner, J. (1976). *Children with learning disabilities*. Boston: Houghton Mifflin.

Lesser, G. (1974). *Children and television*. New York: Random House.

Lester, B. (1983). There's more to crying than meets the ear. *Child Care Newsletter, 2.2*. Johnson and Johnson Co., 4–8.

Levin, D., & Carlsson-Paige, N. (July 1994). Developmentally appropriate television: Putting children first. *Young Children, 49*(5), 38–44.

Levitt, A. G., & Uttman, J. A. (February 1992). From babbling towards the sound systems of English and French: A longitudinal two-case study. *Journal of Child Language, 19*(1). Cambridge University Press, 19–26.

Lewis, C. (1976). *Writing for children*. New York: Bank Street College.

Lewis, E. R., & Lewis, H. P. (December 1964). Which manuscript letters are hard for first graders? *Elementary English*.

Lewis, M., & Rosenblum, L. A. (1974). *The effect of the infant on its caregiver*. New York: John Wiley & Sons.

Lieven, E. V., Pine, J. M., & Barnes, H. D. (June 1992). In Individual difference in early development: Redefining the referential-expressive distinction. *Journal of Child Language, 19*(2). Cambridge University Press, 306.

Lindfors, J. W. (1985). Oral language learning. In Jaggar, A., & Smith-Burke, M. T. (Eds.). *Observing the Young Language Learner*. IRA & NCTE (co-publishers), 41–56.

Lindgren, M. (Ed.). (1991). *The multicolored mirror: Cultural substance in literature for children and young adults*. Fort Atkinson, WI: Highsmith Press.

Lindsay, V. (1920). *Collected poems*. New York: Macmillan.

Linn, M. C. (1987). American educational research association meeting presentation. Chicago, IL.

List, H. (January 1984). Kids can write the day they start school. *Early Years, 15.3*, 40–51.

Lomax, R. G., & McGee, L. M. (1987). Interrelationships among young children's concepts about print and reading: Toward a model of word reading acquisition. *Reading Research Quarterly, 22*, 177–196.

Loughlin, C., & Martin, M. (1987). *Supporting literacy*. New York: Teachers College Press.

MacDonald, M. B. (1992). Valuing diversity. In A. Mitchell, & J. David, (Eds.), *Explorations with young children* (pp. 103–120). Mt. Rainier, MD: Gryphon House.

MacDonald, M. F. (January 1989). Don't overlook your overhead? *Instructor, 98.5*, 88–92.

MacDonald, M. R. (1988). *Booksharing: 101 programs to use with preschoolers*. Hamden, CT: Library Professional Publications.

Machado, J., & Meyer, H. C. (1993). Early childhood student teaching. Albany, NY: Delmar Publishers Inc.

Maclean, M., Bryant, P., & Bradley, L. (1987). Rhymes, nursery rhymes, and reading in early childhood. *Merrill-Palmer Quarterly, 33*(3), 255–282.

Mallan, K. (1994). "Do it again, Dwayne": Finding out about children as storytellers. In A. Trousdale, C. Woestehoff, & M. Schwartz (Eds.), *Give a listen* (pp. 13–18). Urbana, IL: National Council of Teachers of English.

Manning, M., & Manning, G. (1983). The schools' assault on childhood. In McKee, J. (Ed.). *Early Childhood Education 83/84*. Guilford, CT: Dushkin Publishing Group.

Manson, B. (1983). *Fairy poems for the very young*. New York: Doubleday.

Marantz, K., & Marantz, S. (1993). *Multicultural picture books: Art for understanding others*. Worthington, OH: Linworth Publishing Inc.

Marten, M. (1978). Listening review. *Classroom-Relevant Research in the Language Arts*. Washington, DC: Association for Supervision and Curriculum Development, 48–60.

Martinez, M., & Roser, N. (1985). Read it again: The value of repeated readings during storytime. *The Reading Teacher, 38*, 782–786.

Martinez, N., & Johnson, M. (September 22, 1987). Read aloud to give kids the picture. San Jose, CA: *San Jose Mercury News, 4L*.

Martinez, M. G., & Roser, N. L. (1992). Children's response to literature. In Flood, J. et al. (Eds.). *Handbook of Research on Teaching the English Language Arts*. New York: Macmillan, 643–654.

Masataka, N. (June 1992). Pitch characteristics of Japanese maternal speech to infants. *Journal of Child Language, 19*(2). Cambridge University Press, 213.

Mason, J. M. (1980). When do children begin to read: An exploration of four- year-old children's letter and word reading competencies. *Reading Research Quarterly, 15*, 203–227.

Mason, J. M., Herman, P. A., & Au, K. H. (1992). Children's developing knowledge of word. In Flood, J. et al. (Eds.). *Handbook of Research on Teaching English Language Arts*. New York: Macmillan, 721–730.

Matheny, A. P. (March/April 1992). Communicating by gesture. *Twins, 8*(5), 44–45.

Mattick, I. (1981). The teacher's role in helping young children develop language competence. *Language in Early Childhood Education*. Cazden, C. B. (Ed.). Washington, DC: NAEYC.

Mavrogenes, N. A. (May 1990). Helping parents help their children become literate. *Young Children, 45*(4), 4–9.

Mayer, M., & Living Books. (1994). *Just grandma and me*. [CD-ROM]. Novato, CA: Random House/Broderbund.

McCord, S. (1995). *The storybook journey: Pathways to literacy through story and play*. Columbus, OH: Merrill.

McDonald, D. T., & Simons, G. M. (1989). *Musical growth and development*. New York: Schirmer Books.

McKenzie, M. G. (1985). Classroom contexts for language and literacy. In Jaggar, A., & Smith-Burke, M. T. (Eds.). *Observing the Language Learner*. Newark, DE: IRA and Urbana, IL: NCTE (co-publishers), 233–249.

McLane, J. B., & McNamee, G. D. (1990). *Early literacy*. Cambridge, MA: Harvard University Press.

Meers, H. J. (1976). *Helping our children talk*. New York: Longman Group.

Menyuk, P. (1991). Linguistics and teaching the language arts. In Flood, J. et al. (Eds.). *Handbook of Research on Teaching the English Language Arts*. New York: Macmillan Publishing Company, 24–29.

Miedzian, M. (1991). *Boys will be boys: Breaking the link between masculinity and violence*. New York: Doubleday.

Miller, J. (November 1990). Three-year-olds in their reading corner. *Young Children, 46*(1), 51–54.

Miller, K. (August/September 1987). Room arrangement. *Pre-K Today, 2.1*, 28–33.

Milne, A. A. (1961). *When we were very young*. New York: Dutton.

Milz, V. (1985). First graders' uses for writing. In Jaggar, A., & Smith-Burke, M. T. (Eds.). *Observing the Language Learner*. Newark, DE: IRA and Urbana, IL: NCTE (co-publishers), 173–189.

Minuchin, P. (September 1987). Schools, families, and the development of young children. *Early Childhood Research Quarterly, 2.3*, 245–254.

Mitchell, A., & David, J. (Eds.). (1992). *Explorations with young children*. Mt. Rainier, MD: Gryphon House.

Moffett, J., & Wagner, B. J. (January 1993). What works is play. *Language Arts, 70*(2), 32–36.

Monaghan, A. C. (1971). *Children's contacts: Some preliminary findings*. Unpublished term paper. Harvard Graduate School of Education.

Montessori, M. (1965). *The discovery of the child*. New York: Ballantine Books.

Montessori, M. (1967). *The absorbent mind*. New York: Holt, Rinehart, and Winston.

Montessori, M. (1967). *The discovery of the child*. New York: Ballantine Books.

Moon, J. (October 1996). *Focus on the year 2000, CACEI*. Keynote address given at the Fall Study Conference at California State University-Hayward, Walnut Creek, CA.

Moore, R. (1991). *Awakening the hidden storyteller*. New York: Random House.

Morrow, L. M. (1988). Young children's responses to one-to-one story readings in school settings. *Reading Research Quarterly, 23*, 89–107.

Moss, B. (February 1995). Using children's nonfiction tradebooks as read-alouds. *Language Arts, 72*(2), 122–126.

Muir, P. (1954). *English children's books, 1600–1900*. London: B. T. Batsford Limited.

Myhre, S. M. (July 1993). Enhancing your dramatic-play area through the use of prop boxes. *Young Children, 48*(5), 6–11.

Nash, J. M. (February 3, 1997). Fertile minds. *Time, 149*(5), 48–56.

National Association for the Education of Young Children. (November 1990). Position statement on school readiness. *Young Children, 46*(1), 21–23. Washington, DC: Author.

National Association for the Education of Young Children. (November 1995). Position statement: Quality, compensation, and affordability. *Young Children, 51*(1), 39–41.

National Association for the Education of Young Children. (January 1996). Position statement: Responding to linguistic and cultural diversity—Recommendations for effective early childhood education. *Young Children, 51*(2), 4–12.

National Association for Hearing and Speech Action (NAHSA). Rockville, MD.
   (1983). About stuttering
   (1983). Answers, questions about language
   (1985). About articulation problems
   (1985). Otitis media and language development
   (1985). Recognizing communication disorders
   (1985). Speech and language disorders and the speech-language pathologist

National catalog of story telling resources, NAPPS (National Society for Preservation and Protection of Story Telling), National Story Telling Resource Center, P.O. Box 112, Jonesborough, TN 37659.

Nelson, K. (1973). *Structure and strategy in learning to talk*. Monographs of the Society for Research in Child Development, 38.

Nelson, K. (1985). *Making sense: The acquisition of shared meaning*. New York: Academic Press.

Nelson, M. A. (1972). *Children's literature*. New York: Holt, Rinehart, and Winston Inc.

Neuman, S. B., & Roskos, K. (1990). Influence of literacy enriched play settings on preschoolers' engagement with written language. In McCormick, S., & Zutell, J. (Eds.). *Literacy Theory and Research: Analyses from Multiple Paradigms*. National Reading Conference: Chicago, 179–187.

Neuman, S. B., & Roskos, K. (November 3, 1992). Literacy objects as cultural tools: Effects on children's literacy behaviors in play. *Reading Research Quarterly, 27*, 203–225.

Neuman, S. B., & Roskos, K. A. (1993). *Language and literacy learning in the early years: An integrated approach*. New York: Holt, Rinehart & Winston, Inc.

News for parents. (September 1980). Newark, DE: International Reading Association, 2–5.

Newson, J. (1979). The growth of shared understandings between infant and caregiver. *Before Speech*. Bullowa, M. (Ed.). London: Cambridge UP, 207–222.

Nichols, R. (1984). Factors in listening comprehension. Speech Monographs, 15, 154–163.

Nicolopoulou, A., Scales, B., & Weintraub, J. (1994). Gender differences and symbolic imagination in stories of four-year-olds. In A. H. Dyson & C. Genishi (Eds.), *The need for story* (pp. 102–123). New York: National Council of Teachers of English.

Nino, A., & Bruner, J. (1978). The achievement and antecedents of labeling. *Journal of Child Language, 5*, 1–15.

Noori, K. (March 1996). Writing my own script: Pathways to teaching. *Young Children, 51*(3), 17–19.

Norton, D. E. (1983). *Through the eyes of a child*. Columbus, OH: Charles E. Merrill.

Nunnelly, J. C. (November 1990). Beyond turkeys, Santa, snowmen, and hearts: How to plan innovative curriculum themes. *Young Children, 46*(1), 24–29.

O'Rourke, S. (1990). Personal communication, September 1988. In Healy, J. M. *Endangered Minds: Why Children Don't Think and What We Can Do About It*. New York: Simon & Schuster.

Oken-Wright, P. (January 1988). Show-and-tell grows up. *Young Children, 43.2,* 52–63.

Ornstein, R., & Sobel, D. (1987). *The healing brain.* New York: Simon & Schuster.

Osborn, J. D., & Osborn, D. K. (1983). *Cognition in early childhood.* Athens, GA: Education Associates.

Paige, R. (1988). *Some of my best friends are monsters.* New York: Bradbury.

Paley, V. (1981). *Wally's stories.* Cambridge, MA: Harvard University Press.

Pappas, C. C. (October 1991). Fostering full access to literacy by including information books. *Language Arts, 68,* 449–462.

Parents As Teachers. (1986). *Parents as teachers program planning and implementation guide.* Jefferson City, MO: Missouri Department of Elementary and Secondary Education.

Parnall, P. (1988). *Feet!* New York: Macmillan.

Peck, J. (1989). Using storytelling to promote language and literacy development. *The Reading Teacher, 43*(2), 138–141.

Pellegrini, A. D. (1980). The relationship between kindergartners' play and achievement in prereading, language, and writing. *Psychology in the Schools, 17,* 530–535.

Pellegrini, A., & Galda, D. (1982). Effects of thematic-fantasy play training on the development of children's story comprehension. *American Educational Research Journal, 19.3,* 101–116.

Pellowski, A. (1977). *The world of story telling.* New York: R. R. Bowker.

Perez, J. (May 1986). Don't perform share? *First Teacher, 7.5,* 50–55.

Pflaum, S. W. (1986). *The development of language and literacy in young children.* Columbus, OH: Charles E. Merrill Publishing Company.

Pflaum, S. W. (1986). *The development of language and reading.* Columbus, OH: Charles E. Merrill Publishing Company.

Phillips, C. B. (January 1988). Nurturing diversity for today's children and tomorrow's leaders. *Young Children, 43.2,* 42–47.

Phillips, S. (1972). Participant structures and communicative competence: Warm Springs children in community and classroom. In Cazden, C., John, V., & Hymes, D. (Eds.). *Functions of Language in the Classroom.* New York: Teachers College Press, 370–394.

Piaget, J. (1952). *The language and thought of the child.* London: Routledge and Kegan Paul.

Piaget, J., & Inheldder, B. (1969). *The psychology of the child.* New York: Basic Books.

Pica, R. (1995). *Movement, music, and the young child.* Albany, NY: Delmar Publishers Inc.

Pick, A. (August 1986). In Garcia-Barrio, C. Listen to the music! *American Baby, 48*(8), 46, 67–69.

Pines, M. (November 1983). Can a rock walk? *Psychology Today, 39.11,* 46–50, 52, 54.

Pinnell, G., & Jaggar, A. M. (1992). Oral language: Speaking and listening in the classroom. In Flood, J. et al. (Eds.). *Handbook of Research in Teaching English Language Arts.* New York: Macmillan, 691–720.

Poltarnees, W. (1972). *All mirrors are magic mirrors.* New York: The Green Tiger Press.

Powell, R. E. (September 1992). Goals for language arts program: Toward a democratic vision. *Language Arts, 69,* 342–343.

Premack D. (1985). Gavagai! or the future history of the animal language controversy. *Cognition, 19,* 207–296.

Purcell-Gates, V. (January 1995). Focus on research for the 21st century: A diversity of perspectives among researchers. *Language Arts, 72*(1), 56–60.

Pushaw, D. R. (1976). *Teach your child to talk.* New York: Dantree Press.

Putnam, L. (October 1991). Dramatizing nonfiction with emerging readers. *Language Arts, 68*(6), 463–469.

Putnam, L. R. (September 1994). Reading instruction: What do we know that we didn't know thirty years ago? *Language Arts, 71*(5), 362–366.

Quintero, E., & Velarde, M. C. (May 1990). Intergenerational literacy: A developmental bilingual approach. *Young Children, 45*(4), 10–15.

Raines, S., & Isbell, R. (1994). *Stories: Children's literature in early education.* Albany, NY: Delmar Publishers.

Rainey, E. W. (1978). *Language development for the young child.* Atlanta, GA: Humanics Press.

Ransbury, M. K. (1986). *You can encourage your child to read.* Newark, DE: International Reading Association.

Reading Reform Foundation. (August 17, 1987). *San Jose Mercury News, 16E.*

Reimer, K. M. (January 1992). Multiethnic literature: Holding fast to dreams. *Language Arts, 69,* 14–21.

Renzulli, J. (October 1986). Interview quote in Alvino, J. Guiding your gifted child. *American Baby, 48*(10), 54, 57–58.

Reznick, J. S. (December 10, 1996). In M. Elias, Talking doesn't indicate tot's progress study finds. *The Idaho Statesman,* p. D2.

Reyes, L. O. (1987). *Demographics of Puerto Rican/Latino students in New York and the U.S.* Unpublished manuscript: Aspira of NY Inc.

Rhodes, L. K. (February 1981). I can read! Predictable books as resources for reading and writing instruction. *Reading Teacher, 34,* 511–518.

Rich, D. (October 1988). Activities to strengthen reading at home. Part 2. *Instructor, 98.2,* 89–96.

Rich, S. J. (November 1985). The writing suitcase. *Young Children, 40.5,* 31–36.

Rivers, K. (November 24, 1996). Once upon a time [Florida supplement]. *Orlando Sentinel.*

Robertshaw, S. (1994). Find your funny bone? *Mature Outlook, 11*(5), 68.

Robisson, H. F. (1983). *Exploring teaching in early childhood education.* Boston, MA: Allyn and Bacon.

Rogers, N. (1986). *Your home is your child's first school.* Newark, DE: International Reading Association.

Rosemond, J. (April 10, 1988). The ABCs can wait until school starts. *San Jose Mercury News, 3L.*

Rosemond, J. (September 1988). Taming the TV monster. *Better Homes and Gardens, 66.9,* 26.

Rosenblatt, L. M. (1938). *Literature as exploration* (4th ed.). Boston, MA: Modern Language Association.

Roser, N. L., Hoffman, J. V., Labbo, L. D., & Forest, C. (January 1992). Language charts: A record of story time talk. *Language Arts, 69,* 44–51.

Roskos, K. A., & Neuman, S. B. (January 1994). Of scribbles, schemas, and storybooks: Using literacy albums to document young children's literacy growth. *Young Children, 49*(2), 78–85.

Rowe, D. W. (1989). Author/audience interaction in the preschool: The role of social interaction in literacy lessons. *Journal of Reading Behavior, 21*(4), 311–349.

Rowley, R. (January 1992). Caregivers' corner: Reading buddies. *Young Children, 47*(2). Washington, DC: NAEYC, 55.

Rubin, R. R., & Fisher, J. J. (1982). *Your preschooler.* New York: Macmillan.

Salzer, R. T. (1985). Early readers. Conference presentation, NAEYC Conference, New Orleans, LA.

Salzer, R. T. (May 1984). Early reading and giftedness—Some observations and questions. *Gifted Child Quarterly, 25.3,* 112–121.

Saville-Troike, M. (1978). *A guide to culture in the classroom.* Rosslyn, VA: National Clearinghouse for Bilingual Education.

Saville-Troike, M. (1980). Discovering what children know about language. In Pinnell, G. S. (Ed.). *Discovering Language With Children.* Urbana, IL: NCTE, 109–112.

Sawyer, D. (1969). *The way of the storyteller.* New York: Viking.

Schickedanz, J. (August/September 1989). What about preschoolers and academics? *Reading Today, 7*(1). Newark, DE: IRA, 24.

Schickedanz, J. A. (1982). The acquisition of written language in young children. In Spodek, B. (Ed.). *Handbook of Research in Early Childhood Education.* New York: The Free Press.

Schickedanz, J. A. (1983). *Helping children learn about reading.* Washington, DC: NAEYC.

Schickedanz, J. A. (1986). *More than the ABCs: The early stages of reading and writing.* Washington, DC: National Association for the Education of Young Children.

Schickedanz, J. A. (1993). Designing the early childhood classroom environment to facilitate literacy development. In B. Spodek, & O. Saracho (Eds.), *Language and literacy in early childhood education* (pp. 141–145). New York: Teachers College Press.

Schimmel, N. (1978). *Just enough to make a story.* Berkeley, CA: Sister's Choice Press.

Schnur, J., Lowrey, M. A., & Brazell, W. (1985). *A profile of the precocious reader.* Hattiesburg, MI: University of Southern Mississippi, College of Education and Psychology.

Schomberg, J. (May, 1993). Messages of peace. *Book Links, 3*(1), 9–11.

Schram, P. (October/November 1993). As quoted in "Tell me a tale." *Mature Outlook Newsletter,* 7.

Schwartz, S. (February 1980). The young gifted child. *Early Years, 11.5,* 55–62.

Scott, L. B. (1968). *Learning time with language experiences for young children.* New York: McGraw-Hill.

Sebesta, S. L., & Iverson, W. J. (1975). *Literature for Thursday's child.* San Francisco, CA: Science Research Association Inc.

Segal, M. (October 1987). Should superheroes be expelled from preschool? *Pre-K Today, 1.8,* 37–45.

Self, F. (January 1987). *Choosing for children under three. CBC Features.* New York: The Children's Book Council Inc., *41.4,* 2–3.

Shapiro, E., & Mitchell, A. (1992). Principles of the Bank Street approach. In A. Mitchell & J. David (Eds.), *Explorations with young children.* Mt. Rainier, MD: Gryphon House.

Shedlock, M. (1951). *The art of story telling.* New York: Appleton.

Sheldon, A. (January 1990). Kings are royaler than queens: Language and socialization. *Young Children.* Washington, DC: NAEYC, 4–9.

Sherwin, A. (Spring, 1987). Your baby at 12 months. *The Beginning Years, 11*(7), 27–30.

Sigel, I. E. (1982). The relationship between distancing strategies and the child's cognitive behavior. In L. M. Laosa & I. E. Sigel (Eds.), *Families—Research and practice: Vol. 1. Families as learning environments for children* (pp. 47–86). New York: Plenum.

Singer, D. G., & Revenson, T. A. (1979). *A Piaget primer: How a child thinks.* New York: Internation.

Singer, J. (1980). The power and limitations of television: A cognitive-affective analysis. In Tannenbaum, P. (Ed.). *The Entertainment Functions of Television.* Hillsdale, NJ: Lawrence Erlbaum Associates.

Sivulich, S. S. (1977). Strategies for presenting literature. In Cullinan, B. E., & Carmichael, C. W. (Eds.). *Literature and Young Children.* Urbana, IL: NCTE, 120–129.

Skarpness, L. R., & Carson, D. K. (December 1987). Correlates of kindergarten adjustment: Temperament and communicative competence. *Early Childhood Research Quarterly, 2.4,* 215–229.

Skutnabb-Kangas, T., & Toukomaa, P. (1976). *Teaching migrant children's mother tongue and learning host country in the context of the socio-cultural situation of the migrant family.* Helsinki: Finnish National Commission for UNESCO.

Sloan, G. D. (1985). *Good books make reading fun for your child.* Newark, DE: International Reading Association.

Sloane, G. L. (1942). *Fun with folk tales.* New York: Dutton.

Slobin, D. I. (1971). *Psycholinguistics.* Glenview, IL: Scott, Foresman.

Smilansky, S., & Shefatya, L. (1990). *Facilitating play: A medium for promoting cognitive, socio-emotional, and academic development in young children.* Gaithersburg, MD: Psychosocial and Educational Publications.

Smith, C., & Foat, C. (1982). *Once upon a mind.* North Central Regional Extension Publication, Kansas State University.

Smith-Burke, M. T. (1985). Reading and talking: Learning through interaction. In Jaggar, A., & Smith-Burke, M. T. (Eds.). *Observing the Language Learner.* Newark, DE: IRA and Urbana, IL: NCTE (co-publishers), 199–211.

Smolkin, L. B., & Yaden, D. B. Jr. (October 1992). O is for mouse: First encounters with the alphabet book. *Language Arts, 69*(6), 432–441.

Snow, C., De Blauw, A., & Van Roosmalen, G. (1979). Talking and playing with babies. *Before Speech.* Bullowa, M. (Ed.) London: Cambridge UP, 269–288.

Snow, C., & Tabors, P. (1993). Language skills that relate to literacy development. In B. Spodek & O. N. Saracho (Eds.), *Language and literacy in early childhood education* (Vol. 4, pp. 1–20). New York: Teachers College Press.

Snow, C. E. (1991). The theoretical basis for relationships between language and literacy development. *Journal of Research in Childhood Education, 6,* 5–10.

Soderman, A. K. (March 1984). Schooling all 4-year olds: An idea full of romance, fraught with pitfalls. *Education Week,* 14.

Sorenson, M. (1981). Setting the stage. In Lamme, L. L. (Ed.). *Learning to Love Literature.* Urbana, IL: NCTE, 13–27.

Soto, L. D. (January 1991). Understanding bilingual/bicultural young children. *Young Children, 40*(2), 30–36.

Sowers, S. (1982). In Walshe, R. D. (Ed.). *Children want to write.* Exeter, NH: Heinemann Books.

Spelke, E. (1986). In Friedrich, O. What do babies know? *Human Development 85/86.* Guilford, CT: The Dushkin Publishing Group Inc.

Spencer, M. (1987). *How texts teach what readers learn.* Victoria, British Columbia: Abel Press.

Spieker, S. (September 13, 1987). Study links tots' smiles. *San Jose Mercury News, 8B.*

Spitzer, D. R. (1977). *Concept formation and learning in early childhood.* Columbus, OH: Charles E. Merrill.

Spodek, B., & Saracho, O. N. (1993). *Language and literacy in early childhood education* (Vol. 4). New York: Teachers College Press.

Stanchfield, J. (September 1994). In L. R. Putnam, Reading instruction: What do we know now that we didn't know thirty years ago? *Language Arts, 71*(5), 326–366.

Stauffer, R. C. (1970). *The language experience approach to the teaching of reading.* New York: Harper and Row.

Stedman, L. C. (October 1996). An assessment of literacy trends, past and present. *Research in the Teaching of English, 30*(3), 238–302.

Stenning, K., & Mitchell, L. (1985). Learning how to tell a good story: The development of content and language in children's telling of one tale. *Discourse Processes, 8,* 261–279.

Stevens, J. H. Jr. (November 1981). Everyday experiences and intellectual development. *Research in Review, Young Children, 36.1,* 41–53.

Stewig, J. W. (1977). Encouraging language growth. In Cullinan, B. E., & Carmichael, C. W. (Eds.). *Literature and Young Children.* Urbana, IL: NCTE, 17–38.

Stewig, J. W. (1982). *Teaching language arts in early childhood.* New York: Holt, Rinehart, and Winston.

Strickland, D. (December 4, 1982). In The last word on the first "R." *New York Daily News, 13F.*

Strickland, D. (September 1994). Educating African American learners at risk. *Language Arts, 71*(5), 328–335.

Strickland, D. S. (1977). Promoting language and concept development. In Cullinan, B. E., & Carmichael, C. W. (Eds.). *Literature and Young Children.* Urbana, IL: NCTE, 39–58.

Strickland, D. S. (March 1990). Family literacy: Sharing good books. *Young Children, 43*(7). Washington, DC: NAEYC, 518–519.

Strickland, D. S., & Feeney, J. T. (1992). Development in the elementary school years. In Flood, J. et al. (Eds.). *Handbook of Research on Teaching the English Language Arts.* New York: Macmillan.

Strickland, D. S., & Morrow, L. M. (January 1989). Interactive experience with storybook reading. *The Reading Teacher, 58*(2), 322–323.

Strickland, D. S., & Morrow, L. M. (January 1990). Sharing big books. *The Reading Teacher,* 342–344.

Sulzby, E. (1992). The development of the young child and the emergence of literacy. In Flood, J. et al. (Eds.). *Handbook of Research on Teaching the English Language Arts.* New York: Macmillan, 273–285.

Sulzby, E. (April 1992). Research directions: Transitions from emergent to conventional writing. *Language Arts, 69,* 290–297.

Tarrow, N. B., & Lundsteen, S. W. (1981). *Activities and resources for guiding young children's learning.* New York: McGraw-Hill.

Taylor, J. K. (October 1993). Learning through movement. Conference presentation, SRAEYC. Twin Falls, ID.

Teele, D., Klein, J., & Rosner, B. (1989). Epidemiology of otitis media during the first seven years of life in children in greater Boston: A prospective cohort study. *Journal of Infectious Diseases, 160,* 83–94.

Templeton, S. (October 1992). New Trends in an historical perspective: Old story, new resolution—Sound and meaning in spelling. *Language Arts, 69*(6), 454–463.

Throne, J. (September 1988). Becoming a kindergarten of readers. *Young Children, 43.6,* 10–16.

Thurber, D. (1988). *Teaching handwriting.* Glenview, IL: Scott, Foresman.

Tizard, B. et al. (1972). Environmental effects on language development: A study of young children in long-stay residential nurseries. *Child Development, 43.4,* 337–358.

Tooze, R. (1959). *Story telling.* Englewood Cliffs, NJ: Prentice-Hall.

Torrey, J. W. (1979). Reading that comes naturally: The early reader. In Waller, G. W., & MacKinnon, G. E. (Eds.). *Reading Research: Advances in Theory and Practice.* New York: Academic Press.

Tough, J. (1973). *Focus on meaning: Talking to some purpose with young children.* London: George Allen and Unwin.

Tough, J. (1976). *Listening to children talking.* London: Schools Council Publications.

Tough, J. (1977). *Talking and learning: A guide to fostering communication skills in nursery and infant schools.* London: Ward Lock.

Trelease, J. (1982). *The read-aloud handbook.* New York: Penguin Books.

Trelease, J. (March 1986). Why reading aloud makes learning fun. *U.S. News and World Report, 17,* 35–36.

Tronick, E. (May 18, 1987). In Kunerth, J. Born communicators. *Orlando Sentinel, 3L.*

Trousdale, A. M. (February 1990). Interactive storytelling: Scaffolding children's early narratives. *Language Arts, 69*(2), 164–173.

Tunnell, M. O. (December 1994). The double-edged sword: Fantasy and censorship. *Language Arts, 71*(6), 606–611.

U.S. Department of Education. (1991). *Help your child become a good reader.* Washington, DC: Author.

U.S. Department of Education, National Center for Educational Statistics. (1993). National Household Education Survey. Washington, DC: Author.

Urzua, C. (1980). Doing what comes naturally: Recent research in second language acquisition. In Pinnell, S. E. (Ed.). *Discovering Language with Children.* Urbana, IL: NCTE, 33–38.

Vardell, S. M. (September 1994). Nonfiction for young children. *Young Children, 49*(6), 40–41.

Villarruel, F., Imig, D., & Kostelnik, M. (1995). Diverse families. In E. Garcia & B. McLaughlin (Eds.), *Meeting the challenge of linguistic and cultural diversity in early childhood education.* New York: Teachers College Press.

Vold, E. B. (1992). Multicultural education in early childhood classrooms. *NEA Early Childhood Education Series*. Washington, DC: NEA Professional Library.

Vukelich, C., & Golden, J. (January 1984). Early writing: Development and teaching strategies. *Young Children, 39.5*, 37–45.

Vygotsky, L. S. (1978). *Mind and society: The development of higher psychological process*. Cambridge, MA: Harvard University Press.

Vygotsky, L. S. (1980). *Mind in society*. Cambridge, MA: Harvard University Press.

Vygotsky, L. (1986). *Thought and language*. Cambridge, MA: MIT Press.

Vygotsky, L. S. (1987). Thinking and speech. In R. W. Rieber & A. S. Carton (Eds.), *The collected works of L. S. Vygotsky* (N. Minick, Trans.). New York: Plenum.

Wagner, B. J. (1992). Imaginative expression. In Flood, J. et al. (Eds.). *Handbook of Research on Teaching the English Language Arts*. New York: Macmillan, 787–804.

Walberg, H. J. (October 1996). U.S. schools teach reading least productively. *Research in the teaching of English, 30*(3), 328–343.

Walmsley, S., & Adams, E. L. (April 1993). Realities of "Whole Language." *Language Arts, 70*(4), 272–280.

Wardle, F. (November–December 1987). Getting parents involved! *Pre-K Today, 2.3*, 71–75.

Waring-Chaffee, M. B. (September 1994). "RDRNT . . . HRIKM" (Ready or not, Here I come!"): Investigations in children's emergence as readers and writers. *Young Children, 49*(6), 52–55.

Washington, J., & Craig, H. K. (June 1995). In brief *The Council Chronicle*, National Council of Teachers of English, 4(6), 5.

Watson, C. (1978). *Catch me and kiss me and say it again*. New York: Philomel Books.

Weir, M. E., & Eggleston, P. (November/December 1975). Teacher's first words. *Day Care and Early Education, 13.5*, 71–82.

Weiser, M. G. (1982). *Group care and education of infants and toddlers*. St. Louis, MO: C. V. Mosby.

Weiss, C. E., & Lillywhite, H. S. (1981). *Communicative disorders*. St. Louis, MO: C. V. Mosby.

Weissman, J. (1979). Sound story. *Hello Sound*. Mt. Rainier, MD: Gryphon House.

Weitzman, E. (1992). *Learning language and loving it*. Toronto, Canada: A Hanen Centre Publication.

Wells, G. (1981). *Learning through interaction: The study of language development*. Cambridge, MA: Cambridge University Press.

Wells, G. (1985). *Language, learning, and education*. Berkshire, England: Windsor, NFER-NELSON.

Wells, G. (1986). The meaning makers. Portsmouth, NH: Heinemann.

Werner, E. E., & Smith, R. S. (1982). *Vulnerable, but invincible*. New York: McGraw-Hill.

Weymouth, F. W. (1963). Visual acuity of children. *Vision of Children, A Symposium*. Hirsch, M. J., & Wick, R. E. (Eds.). Philadelphia.

White, B. (1973). *The first three years of life*. Englewood Cliffs, NJ: Prentice-Hall.

White, B. L. (1986). A person is emerging. *Parents As Teachers Program Planning and Implementation Guide*. Jefferson City, MO: Missouri Department of Elementary and Secondary Education.

White, B. L. (1986). The learning experience. *Parents As Teachers Program Planning and Implementation Guide*. Jefferson City, MO: Missouri Department of Elementary and Secondary Education.

White, B. L. (1987). *The first three years of life*. Englewood Cliffs, NJ: Prentice-Hall.

Wiltz, N. W., & Fein, C. G. (March 1996). Evolution of a narrative curriculum: The contributions of Vivian Gussin Paley. *Young Children, 51*(3), 61–68.

Winn, M. (1981). *Children without childhood*. New York: Pantheon.

Winter, M., & Rouse, J. (February 1990). Fostering intergenerational literacy: The Missouri parents as teachers program. *The Reading Teacher, 43*(6), 382–386.

Wolf, J. (January 1992). Creating music with young children. *Young Children, 47*(2). Washington, DC: NAEYC, 56–61.

Wolf, J. (May 1994). Singing with children is a cinch. *Young Children, 49*(4), 20–25.

Wong-Fillmore, L. (1976). *The second time around: Cognitive and social strategies in second language acquisition*. Unpublished doctoral dissertation. Stanford, CA.

Wong-Fillmore, L. (1982). Instructional language as linguistic input: Second language learning in classrooms. In Wilkinson, L. C. (Ed.). *Communicating in the Classroom*. New York: Academic Press, 283–296.

Wong-Fillmore, L. (1985). Second language learning in children: A proposed model. *Conference Proceedings, ERIC Document 273149*. Arlington, VA.

Wong-Fillmore, L. (1986). Research currents: Equity and excellence. *Language Arts, 63*, 474–481.

Yaden, D. Jr., Smolkin, L. B., & Conlon, A. (1989). Preschoolers' questions about pictures, print, convention, and story text. *Reading Research Quarterly, 24*(2), 188–214.

Yawkey, T. D., Yawkey, M., Askov, E., Cartwright, C., Du Puis, M., & Fairchild, S. (1981). *Language arts and the young child*. Itasca, IL: F. E. Peacock.

Yokota, J. (March 1993). Issues in selecting multicultural children's literature. *Language Arts, 70*.

Zill, N., Collins, M., West, J., & Hauskin, E. G. (November 1995). Approaching kindergarten: A look at preschoolers in the United States. *Young Children, 51*(1), 35–38.

Index

Note: Entries in **bold type** reference titles. Page numbers in **bold type** reference non-text material.